INDUSTRIAL MAN

Under the Editorship of

ALFRED L. SEELYE

HARPER & BROTHERS

NEW YORK

INDUSTRIAL MAN *Businessmen and Business Organizations*

EDITED BY

W. LLOYD WARNER

University Professor of Behavioral Sciences
Michigan State University

NORMAN H. MARTIN

Professor of Business Administration
Michigan State University

To the memory of Edmund E. Day

Library of Congress catalog card number: 58-7023

CONTENTS

Contents

Contents

Contents

CHARTS

TABLES

Tables

Chapter 1

BUSINESSMEN AND BUSINESS LIFE

UNDERSTANDING BUSINESSMEN: PROBLEMS AND DILEMMAS

Although American business leaders are some of the most influential and highly respected men of our time they are threatened constantly by powerful attacks often coming from other respected leaders of this country. The great industrial organizations they control and the capitalistic economy in which they operate have, as everyone knows, contributed greatly to our collective wealth and to our spiritual and material well-being. Our standard of living is the envy of the world. Moreover, billions of dollars and entire fortunes from great corporations and their owners have been given to the advancement of learning, the support of the arts, the strengthening of the church, and to civic improvement. The names of Rockefeller, Carnegie, Rosenwald, Ford, Hill, Guggenheim, and others in the popular mind symbolize industrial enterprise, corporate wealth, and technological advance; more importantly, they stand for medical progress and scientific research, for art museums, great libraries, schools, liberal colleges, and for the support of the scholars, artists, and others whose creative works make many of these institutions of our advanced civilization possible. Yet important theologians, philosophers, scholars, and other intellectuals whose work benefits from the freely given wealth of the men of the great corporations as well as millions of ordinary men fear and condemn them.

Most of these cultural leaders are men of integrity and not egocentric ingrates. The common men who follow them are good citizens. The question arises, what do they fear? Why do they attack? And, one must add, why is there such ready defense and impassioned advocacy of the leaders and their organizations? What is the nature of big business, of its leaders and this capitalistic society which prompts such hostility, grudging admiration, or deep respect?

To answer these questions and provide sound evidence for judging the many issues involved and the positions taken we must ask more fundamental questions. What kind of men are business executives? What are their private worlds? What do psychological investigations tell us about them? What are their social origins?

What is the nature of their roles in industry and the world around them? What are the great industrial corporate hierarchies like as systems? How do these systems operate? How well and in what way do they function for themselves and the economy and the society? What are the meanings and significances of industrial conflict and coöperation?

In brief, what do we know about businessmen and business life in America?

Who and what big business leaders are has been the object of some of the best research and some of the most acute economic, social, and psychological analyses of this generation. Why the business executive acts and thinks the way he does is a continuing subject of philosophical, moral, and theological inquiry. The interest and knowledge range through such important aspects of executive life as decision-making, the social structure of the great hierarchies of business enterprise, the changing relations of owners and managers and those of managers and workers, and the meanings of industrial conflict and coöperation. The psychological and personal factors that operate for success and failure in the careers of business leaders and the social characteristics and origins of men who advance to business leadership are only a few of the subjects about which the many disciplines have produced enormous quantities of valuable evidence. But here is the rub. It is not that too little is known, but rather that too much is available on many, many aspects of business life and business leaders for ready comprehension. The evidence is from the most diverse disciplines and literatures, much of it insufficiently assembled, sifted, and competently organized to give the interested reader time and opportunity to cover what is known.

This book has undertaken to resolve this problem. We first intended writing the entire book, stating in our own words what we had learned from research and the writings of others, but further consideration led us to compose the present volume, and to try what we believe is a better and more effective way to communicate what is known about business leaders. A brief summary of the work done to prepare this book and a quick inspection of its contents will indicate what it is about. A fourth of it is written by us; this includes the present chapter, the introductory statements to all chapters, and a number of selections. The rest of the book is composed of selections from the writings of some of the foremost authorities. They range from social theorists such as Radcliffe-Brown and Mayo to contemporary writers who have investigated the practical problems of modern management (see biographical notes).

This first chapter supplies some of the theoretical foundations and assumptions on which the others rest. Although the book is more a "reader" than our own writing, we have tried to make it something more than what is ordinarily meant by a reader, for we have attempted to weave diverse selections into a comprehensive composition about businessmen.

With the growing and changing complexity of the modern corporate enterprise, it has been inevitable that considerable effort on the part of both scholars and practitioners be directed toward gaining insights into its character, its relationship to other facets of American society, and into the direction of its change.

Within the academic world this effort has been the concern not only of schools of business but increasingly of the social sciences as well. The behavioral sciences have contributed major insights into the influence of social factors upon the workings of the organization and upon the motivations of workers. Small group theory, representing one of the more recent advances, has built strong foundations for both the description and explanation of work groups; communication theory has related its findings to the management process. No longer is it necessary to depend completely upon intuition in the selection and placement of individuals in various positions. In the field of psychology, the assessment of personality has developed from both a theoretical and a practical point of view; both clinical psychology and psychiatry have marked out the province of mental hygiene with relatively well-defined landmarks.

Nor has this advance been limited to the efforts of students in academic institutions. In the beginning, industry made its contribution primarily by coöperating in research efforts initiated by academicians. Gradually, however, business has taken on more and more responsibility for initiating systematic investigation into the many facets of industrial life. Research departments in many large corporations have been set up to deal with problems of personnel, organization, marketing, and public relations as well as the more conventional technical fields. Unfortunately, however, not too many of their findings have been published for the benefit of other investigators.

The search for answers has proceeded on both a theoretical and a practical level. For many the most basic concern was to develop systematic knowledge; for others the overriding interest was to find more immediate solutions to the many problems confronting them. In many instances the gulf between these two divergent positions has created impatience and antagonism with the result that the two schools of thought have failed to communicate with one another.

With the advent of growing self-consciousness and insight, there

4

has been a tendency to adhere strongly to a particular stream of thought or philosophy. Cults and fads in management have dominated the scene for a time only to fade and be replaced by others. During the 1920's the doctrine of scientific management was religiously followed. In time, however, the narrowness of this point of view was broadened by the thinking of others. Mary Parker Follett, Urwick, Gulick, Mooney, Barnard, and others contributed fresh insights into the process of management. Within the past decade or two, the human-relations approach has received increased attention and, still more recently, criticism and revision. The search continues; the answers are still to be found.

Several areas of investigation appear to be strongly indicated.

Knowledge of management functions has focused most strongly upon the lower and middle executive levels to the exclusion of the top management group. Higher-level executives have seemed content to have researchers look no higher than the heads of their foremen. Description and explanation of the corporate management level—the policy-making committees, the presidential and vice-presidential positions and activities, the boards of directors and their relationships to their organization and to others—are vitally needed.

Of equal necessity is research into the dynamics of organization change. Here principles of growth and development must be ascertained. It has been observed, for example, that quite frequently a line of policy in a given organization will gradually or even abruptly shift. In many instances it is difficult to determine exactly who initiated the action chain or orientation bringing about reversal. Relatively little systematic insight exists in relation to the influence of such a change upon the organization and even less in terms of its impact upon its members and upon the surrounding community.

Nor is it clear how industrial enterprise is influenced by the community. Preliminary observations would seem to indicate that such variables as social stratification, size, ethnic composition, geographic region, and so forth are directly related to the speed and intensity of change in organizations. To what extent and in what manner are still unknown.

From the standpoint of industrial man, possibly more is known, but many unexplored areas remain. It is important that we know more of the context of growth. What kinds of environments are most conducive to the development of the full potential of the individual? What is the nature of this process? What happens to his personality when he falters or fails—when his career line is interrupted? Recently considerable work has been done in relation to creativity and the determination of conditions conducive to it. Nevertheless much remains.

Finally, inquiry must turn to the ultimate in all considerations—the realm of ethics and morality. While the problem of equating the dictates of practical business life and the ethical and moral imperatives is comparatively time-worn, it is only in relatively recent years that systematic thinking has directed its attention toward the economic world and entrepreneurial behavior. When seen in terms of the current period of rapid and traumatic change, the need to find stability looms large and vital. Of equal importance is the necessity to relate the internal workings of industrial and business organizations to the democratic ideals of the American free enterprise system.

We shall begin our inquiry into what the business leader is by viewing him as an individual and a person. We shall turn to the functions of the businessman in the industrial hierarchy, examine the conditions and nature of his decisions, ask ourselves how he makes them and how effectively or not they are communicated to, and acted on, by others. Throughout this part of our inquiry we will concentrate on the jobs of management and on the motivations that underlie business activity.

Having learned something about the goals and tasks of managers, we shall examine their immediate business worlds, the small and large kingdoms they direct and govern, all this to learn what businessmen are, why they act as they do, and in what ways they define their roles. We shall follow this with evidence about the different types of business structures, with examination of the so-called vertical and horizontal organizations. We shall call on the social anthropologists and sociologists to help us with the concept of the division of labor for understanding managerial hierarchies and employee morale. Conflicting opinions about "human relations" in industry, "benevolent autocracies," and the plea for the hard-boiled economics of the market place to dominate the decisions of managers are presented.

Theories about the nature of conflict and coöperation will lay the foundations for discussions about labor-management relations. Social theory about the life of man and his organizations will permeate the discussions about industry in the American society and the life and place of managers in the community.

Evidence and theories about occupational mobility and the career experience of America's business elite will introduce a closer inspection of the person and the role of businessmen; case histories to illustrate our points about personality and its effect on business careers are given. With this background of evidence from the several sciences and scholarly disciplines, in the last chapters we shall present some of the prevailing ideologies about businessmen and some of the principal issues and dilemmas of industrial man. Thus we shall return to the area of controversy whence we started, but this time equipped with more valid and reliable evidence.

AMERICAN CAPITALISM: THE STRUCTURE OF BUSINESS ENTERPRISE

The capitalistic economy in which American business executives develop their careers may be viewed as a vast interconnected set of relations composed of constituent parts, the whole composing a recognizable system within the total society. The several parts are (1) the structural *form* of the economic life as a system of interrelated enterprises and statuses (of which executive positions are but one type) that orders the economic activities of those in the system; (2) the technology that instrumentalizes the economy and adapts it and the whole society to the resources of the natural environment; and (3) the economic beliefs and values (including conscious and unconscious feelings as well as rational principles) that guide, direct, and motivate individual efforts and group demands. All these are necessary vital elements of the entirety, and all contribute significantly to what each executive is and must be to survive and prosper in our competitive economy.

All the parts of this capitalistic order are emergent and changing, each within itself, each with the other, each within the whole economy and the larger American society. As the technology becomes more scientific and rational, the forms of corporate organization expand and reorder the relations of men; concomitantly, values and beliefs about how managers and workers should act, what capitalistic enterprise should be, and what its obligations and rights ought to be also undergo change. The face of America has been altered and our way of life revolutionized by the machine and the ways of scientific technology, yet the machine and its scientific rationale could not be what they are without the molding influence of the powerful values and beliefs of American culture. Within this entire system the executive, owner or manager, occupies an important place. What his place is, how the managerial role functions in business life, and what the man himself is as a person and individual will be objects of our present inquiry.

Our economic system performs a number of necessary functions for the larger American social system. Through the ever-increasing application of technical and scientific knowledge and the skillful use of tools and machines, our economic system produces more abundantly and efficiently for the material wants and needs of our huge population. Through morally ordering the relations among the different statuses such as managers and workers or buyers and sellers, it provides the rights and duties, the obligations and privileges for those who work and for those who exchange goods and services in the American social system. An economy without morals is an economy without order, one that is incapable of establishing the solid foundations necessary for the increasing rationality of business and the successful use of scientific principles in technological advancement. Moreover, the whole economic system must be animated by values and beliefs which permeate the individual lives of everyone, values and beliefs which are the motivating forces and purposes driving men to economic action. The values and beliefs are not merely those of an abstract bloodless Economic Man but of the total animal and the whole moral as

8

well as economic being. Such values and beliefs and their economic products supply the positive and negative sanctions, the rewards and punishments that encourage approved behavior and discourage infractions of the rules of the game. Promotions, pay and profits, increasing or decreasing prestige, the acquisition or loss of power, expanding or contracting feelings of well-being all sanction and largely control the lives of business executives.

In this kind of economic system the material and nonmaterial "objects" of production, the tangible and intangible goods, are both *objects* of utility and *symbols* of value; as such they belong to both the symbolic and technical worlds of American life. As objects they are the material goods of utility; as symbols they often are signs of power, prestige, and position. Both are important to those who manage. The great desk in the large quiet office high in the executive tower is an object of economic utility, but to the man who sits behind it and for those who come from down below to stand before it the great solid object becomes a symbol of far more important meanings than its dollar value as an economic object.

THE AUTONOMOUS EXECUTIVE IN THE EMERGENT ECONOMIC ORDER

There are certain basic processes operating in the moving equilibrium of this emergent economy and society. At times the social equilibrium approximates a balance and at others moves towards an imbalance in the whole society or in one of its parts. At all times the whole American economic and social system flows in the general direction of increasing diversity and greater differentiation and heterogeneity of the several parts. Social, technical, and religious experimentations are integral parts of this emergent process. At the level of the technology new scientific knowledge and specialized skills and tools are invented, rationalized, and integrated into the basic older forms of technological adaptation. The assembly line, after trial and error and constant rethinking by all levels of management and labor, replaces the separate machine and the skilled craftsman; automation replaces the assembly line.

9

Meanwhile the social organization and institutional life of the American social order constantly change. Old forms are modified or disappear as new forms come into being. The social organization being the moral order where the rules and principles of human conduct are expressed in men's actions, thoughts, and values holds men firmly to the deep and sometimes darkly hidden roots of tradition and the past. Yet it too changes and initiates change. The family of today is not the family of yesterday: the chain store, the super market, federal power over corporate structure, and the increasingly unified national rather than local community are new "moral" forms that bring order into the lives of contemporary Americans. The business leader rising to ascendancy experiences all these changes. He and his family move from Chicago to Atlanta, and from there to Los Angeles and back to Boston as he rises in the corporate hierarchy and America is increasingly held more tightly within the bonds of its newly developing social structure. Meanwhile he, his wife, and children feel the traditional age-old pull of parents to their children.

At the level of signs and symbols, the new media of communication and the modified older ones—radio, TV, and print—exert a generalizing influence that helps pull Americans closer together. Yet increasingly specialized knowledge, new ways of thinking about the world and man, produce variations in thought and action which may be of crucial significance for an industry or the competitive survival of a corporation. These have their own little private worlds of esoterica, scientific or not, which must be sufficiently translated into common discourse to be used by industry and society. Very often it is the business leader who must be responsible for the decisions which make these bodies of knowledge available to the world of commerce and the common life of the nation.

Despite the movement of our emergent society towards increasing diversity of knowledge, counter tendencies contribute their significant and important share to our development as a nation. Increasing heterogeneity, specialization, and diversity with all their experimental new forms constantly are under the pressure of the conservative counter tendencies of homogeneity which reorder the "new" and merge them into the simpler forms of the old; there is a constant salutary reduction of the possible variety of new forms of behavior. Thus the moving equilibirum of the American economy flows towards new and expanded forms but always under the conservative restraints that reduce some of the new forms of organization, ways of thinking, new technologies into the more homogeneous, older forms.

At the level of the manager and executive such an emergent capitalistic society means that the constantly increasing social and economic heterogeneity and the vast structural changes of American life must produce in each individual manager a personality that is adapted to, and is a coherent part of, the larger emerging society. If the individual does not develop such a personality he is less likely to reach executive position and, should he attain it, is more likely to fail there. For he must make decisions which allow and encourage his company to compete successfully in an economy and society where the demands of the indefinite future and of the unyielding past create dilemmas and issues that can be dealt with only by one personally sensitive to the changing meanings of our life.

At the higher reaches of the corporate hierarchies, individual autonomy is officially sanctioned and publicly praised. More precisely, such executive autonomy means that decision-making comes from within the person, not from without. Generally in America this is felt to be a necessary and commendable part of the mature individual's activities. Buck-pass as much as he will in the end, the executive must believe he is capable of choosing what must or must not be done; he must believe he can solve his own problems and be willing to suffer or enjoy the consequences.

As used here "individual autonomy" means both moral and intellectual autonomy, the freedom and the strength to think and act. Ideally the individual executive applies the moral and intellectual rules, as an individual, to himself and others. As our economy becomes more extended and more varied, the areas of decision-making for each manager necessarily become more complex and demanding. Moreover, as our status system becomes increasingly flexible and open, ambitious individuals move from

11

status to status and from place to place. Those who do, and they are in the majority at all levels of the economy, are faced with major personal and status problems rarely dealt with by their ancestors. When an executive moves from one community to another and from position to position he must constantly redefine who he is and what he must do largely on his own. He must have the internal resources to do this or he faces failure and defeat.

Yet executives who lean on group and traditional authority are present in large numbers and often are highly successful men. Such men, if they are intelligent, sometimes gain the great benefit of group knowledge and with it they can reduce risk and the dangers of disaster. If their advisors are wise and able and the pressures immediately around them adjust them to reality, their sense of timing, of yielding adaptively to the flow of events within a corporation, an industry, or perhaps the country, may help them make better decisions than the more independently minded. The autonomous man may act so much from within that his response to the needs of the outside world are not adaptive. In fact, such extreme types are unlikely to succeed in the competitive world of the executive.

THE ROLE AND OPERATIONAL WORLD OF THE EXECUTIVE

The executive operates in dual worlds—the world of the physical, the predictable, and the known on the one hand, and the realm of the social-political, the relatively unknown and unpredictable, on the other. In order to function successfully, he must be able to perform with skill in both.

The first of these worlds, the physical, consists of a number of varied activities. It involves the determination of plant layout, product mix, production process, and system of maintenance. From the standpoint of sales, decisions as to systems of distribution, discount rates, warehousing, shipping, and servicing constitute a major part of this world. Pricing, buying, costing, financing, and promoting, while frequently entailing a high degree of uncertainty and risk, still involve physical events, the behavior of which can be predicted with fair accuracy. Here is the objective universe of executive behavior.

Interwoven with this aspect of the executive life is another and different world. In order to carry out his various responsibilities, the executive is involved with people; not only does he have to work with them, but he has to use them as means to reach organizational goals. Individuals are not, however, merely passive objects being acted upon; rather, they act in terms of their own interests and conception of the situation. They are not isolated entities but join together to form coalitions. Here is the world of inner politics, of maneuver, and of withholding information and action. Clique membership and sponsor-protégé relationships become necessary not only to get things done but also as requisites for furthering one's career line. Decisions are not made purely on the basis of the so-called "law of the situation" but also in terms of estimates of how one's superiors, associates, and subordinates will react. In this frequently shifting and ephemeral set of relationships, it is sometimes difficult to make sound decisions that will maximize the success both of the organization and of oneself.

It is difficult to set forth any universal generalizations with regard to the role of the executive, for it will vary with the size and type of organization, functional position, and level. The role of an executive in a steel company will, for example, differ considerably from that of his counterpart in, say, a retailing organization or an advertising agency. The position of Number 1 in an organization calls for a set of capacities different from those of a Number 2 or a Number 3; the role of an executive in a young and growing organization is frequently not similar to that found in an older and more stabilized one. These differences exist, but certain generalizations may be stated with a fair amount of assurance.

Probably the key dimension in the role of the executive is that of a decision-maker. By "decision-making" here is meant the taking of action or policy having organizational impact, action that is comparatively irreversible and in the form of commitment. Consequences of such decisions are frequently difficult to estimate; many are unanticipated, especially when there is a high degree of uncertainty and risk. The role is one calling for a great deal of firmness and conviction with respect to goals and for a high degree of insight into the means available to accomplish them.

A second and highly significant aspect of the executive role might be called the coördinating function. The task here is that of securing a meshing of multiple and differing activities and processes. This involves the relating of the general to the specific and, conversely, of the specific to the general. It is concerned with the ordering of resources, jobs, and people in time. It entails taking initiative, directing, and follow-up; it requires the construction and maintenance of an effective communication system and pattern of information, that is to say, of an efficient team operation.

Another phase of the role revolves more specifically around the position of the executive as a symbol of authority. The administrator here must be able to establish and maintain effective social distance between himself and his superiors, associates, and subordinates. He must exercise influences and power; he has to be able to take objective and sometimes ruthless action toward people in the light of the welfare of the organization. He is a symbol. He is a judge. He is an arbitrator.

The executive must also fulfill the position of leader. In this sense, the administrator must be capable of anticipating and filling the needs of his organization—stability of communication, solidarity, resolution of problems, support, and confidence. The post is one calling for a high degree of sensitivity to the social and psychological climate of the organization.

Still another phase of the role complex centers in what might be called the moral or ethical function of the executive. To a considerable extent, the manager sets the standards of behavior for the organization. In this respect he serves as a behavioral model for his subordinates. At the same time, however, he must closely conform to the standards of his colleagues, the organization, and the larger society. He therefore both sets and conforms to moral and ethical standards.

Finally, we may consider the executive as a creator of order. In a sense this function is a result of the effectiveness with which he discharges the other aspects of his role. It does, however, deserve to be mentioned separately. The events making up the life of any organization can become quite chaotic and disturbing. The responsibility of the administrator is to find ways of reducing chaos and achieving order.

Each of these areas constitutes a vital part of what we have called the role of the executive. Each is exceedingly complex, and we have in this section only briefly described the essence of each phase. The popular conception of an executive is that of a man behind a massive desk devoid of papers, flanked on one side by a battery of telephones and on the other by secretaries and assistants. Harassed by a continuous stream of questions and opinions, he must make rapid-fire decisions, dash from one conference to another, handle a multitude of appointments, and still maintain an appearance of poise. For the most part, he appears to carry the organization along on the impetus of his own energy.

To a certain extent, this is an accurate picture and for many of the executives running America's business and industry, the scene is identical—one of a high incidence of stress and pressure. However, the picture lacks depth. It does not give the viewer a full appreciation of the work of the executive, its variation, its interest, and its ramifications. What are the activities that an executive engages in to carry out the functions which he must fulfill? We shall take each of the major functions outlined and describe characteristic activity surrounding it.

In his role as decision-maker, the administrator must make consistent choices—consistent in the sense that the action fits in with previous and other future commitments; consistent in the sense that they are coördinate with actions taken and to be taken by others within the organization. This means that not only does the executive have to develop and maintain a good intelligence system whereby he can get information about what is going on around him, but also that he must devote some of his time to assessing what he learns. He must deliberate. In many instances, and this is especially true at higher levels of management, he must rely upon members of his staff to get information for him and to convey it to him with a minimum of filtering and a maximum of accuracy. What is required here is a high degree of skill in communication

15

with people, a sensitivity to their actions and reactions, and a sense of contrast and differentiation. The executive must establish his own networks of communication—upward, downward, and sideward. This he does through his own actions, by a process of asking and not asking and of receiving and not receiving information so that others over a period of time come to know what they should tell him and what they should not.

The decision is, in addition, more often than not influenced by previous commitments and the the anticipated reactions of others. Faced with the necessity to function as part of the team, the executive "buffers" propose action up and down the line. In most organizations, "inner" divisions develop—informal cliques through which the administrator can try out ideas, clear away impediments, and gain support. Thus, many a so-called decision is, in reality, a slowly forged chain of events culminating in a satisfactory line of action rather than proceeding through a single individual making up his mind.

Making sound decisions is, moreover, more than a matter of choosing the best alternative. Equally important is the timing of action. It is here that knowledge of the emerging organizational picture is most crucial. In order to determine "when," the executive must be able to see and know the developing design of events so that he can fit the particular action he has decided upon to them. Timing is a matter, in the final analysis, of being "in phase" with surrounding events. Again, a sound and far-reaching system of intelligence is mandatory.

The second function we listed was that of achieving coördination. In the final analysis coördination is a matter of providing members of the executive team with the best communication system, the best pattern of information, and the best set of decision rules, given the probability of events and the cost of maintaining such a system. Therefore, the executive is engaged in selectively giving information to colleagues, to subordinates, and to superiors. He must make policy where necessary, fix rules, follow up, clarify, review, and approve. He must hold conferences and be involved in conferences—sometimes to the extent that a great deal of his time is taken up in rounds of meetings. He must determine the most efficient division of labor from the standpoint both of his total organizational unit and of his key associates and subordinates. This means that he has to determine his most efficient organizational arrangement; that in the process of creating his own team he has to determine what activities he will keep himself and what ones he will delegate to others. Usually this involves different behavior toward the various members of his staff. Some require a maximum of structuring and follow-up; others need relatively little. Much depends upon the accuracy of this appraisal.

Turning next to the third aspect of the role complex of the executive—his position as authority figure, as judge, and as arbitrator—it may be said that this is one of the most difficult and exacting of tasks. Here we are involved in the problem of discipline.

The rudiments of discipline lie within the differential exercise of rewards and punishments. Although the administrator endeavors ultimately to place the source of discipline within the individual himself, it frequently is necessary for him to exert his authority and dispense reward or punishment depending upon the situation and the individuals involved. In order to do this, he must achieve a position of authority and objectivity. This means that he must not get overinvolved with individuals who are under him; it means that he must maintain the right amount of social distance between himself and his superiors. He must maintain the position of impartiality.

When questions are referred to him for decision and when problems arise, they usually are the result of divergence of opinion. He has to determine not only whether he should get involved in the dispute but also, once he is involved, how the question should be decided or resolved. Quite frequently, in such situations, considerable hostility is generated. The executive has to learn how to deal with emotion.

In his role as leader, the executive must fulfill the position of a symbol—a symbol of solidarity, of direction, and of power. This means that he must carefully pick the particular roles that are called for by the situation and the times. It means that he must carefully plan for and rehearse his actions so that they fit the role in question. In this sense, the executive must be an actor.

The leader must also, as we have indicated, be capable of anticipating and fulfilling the needs of his organization. Here again a good and adequate system of intelligence is essential, for he must be able to piece together the fragments of information relative to the system of events making up the organizational life. From the composite picture he forms, he then must be able to pick out clues as to what is required to make the organization an efficiently functioning unit. The activity involved here is clearly in the category of an art form. The executive must display energy where energy is called for; he must initiate where no one else knows when or how to move; he must be decisive where others are vacillating. The role is one calling for conviction and certainty.

We turn lastly to the executive as a creator of morality. If we define morality as the standards of right behavior held by the group, then the executive is the individual who must represent and crystalize the fundamentals of this code. By his actions he not only conforms to the pattern but reinforces it and by so doing sets standards for others to emulate. In so doing, he must be perceptive of the actions of others and sensitive to their reactions to himself and to their colleagues and subordinates.

From these perceptions, he must then determine what standards of right behavior should be formalized into rules so that they govern the entire organization. Once these rules are set, they must then be promulgated in such a manner that they can be enforced and blend with the policy and rule system of the organization.

THE BUSINESSMAN, THE WORKER, AND THE LARGER SOCIETY

For the most part the world of the executive and that of the worker are far apart—worlds bridged by the foreman and the union. Yet the worker exercises considerable influence on the thinking of the businessman both by communication through his foreman and through the pressures exerted by his union. Problems of morale, of productivity, of absenteeism and turnover, of recruitment and of wages play such a strong role in the affairs of the executive that he turns them over, in all but very small companies, to a specialized personnel department. Nevertheless, they continue to occupy his attention.

From the standpoint of the businessman, concerned fundamentally with organization survival, the worker is a doer of work, somebody who must be hired, trained, and motivated to do the best job of which he is capable. In addition, he must be directed and told what to do. He must keep his superiors informed of things that he does and problems that he runs into. In its simplest form, this is the conception that average businessmen have of their workers.

The worker, however, tends to resist this particular conception. He has his own aspirations and his own ideals and feelings. He makes these known in a variety of ways—through direct communication upward, through so-called "soldiering" on the job, through his group leader, and through both active and passive resistance to the directions of his superior. With the advent of unions, an agency came into existence whereby the workers joined ranks and began to exert power and influence as an organized entity.

At first management fought the unions. Management organized their own company units, blacklisted union leaders, and employed strikebreakers. In many instances, they refused to talk with the unions. The history of union-management strife was long and bitter. Gradually, however, management came to the realization that the union was a permanent part of the industrial scene and that some sort of coöperative arrangement was essential. Today unions constitute one of the most powerful organizations in American society.

It became, then, a major task on the part of management to establish stable and productive relationships with the union. This, in the great majority of cases, has been accomplished and institutionalized so that the interests, sometimes diverse and sometimes almost congruent, of worker, manager, and owner are worked out through peaceful and constructive means.

Over and beyond the area of union-management relations, businessmen have become increasingly aware of the necessity to motivate the worker to come up to his full capacity. In the competitive struggle for survival they found that in many instances the "good" worker makes the difference.

19

In the initial stages this awareness took the form of "scientific management." Each detail of the worker's job was broken down into its component parts and the best methods to accomplish the tasks were worked out. Time and motion studies became part of the order of the day; incentive systems were instituted. Feeling that the worker lacked the capacity to do this for himself, management did it for him.

The worker, however, appeared to lack a feeling of identity with the organization. With his work fragmented and routinized, he was not always highly motivated. Research pointed out what everyone knew, that he was a social being with his own needs and that his work group and its values were highly influential in determining his conduct. With these new insights, management readjusted its perspective. The "human-relations" approach came into being. Foremen were trained to understand human behavior and to take this understanding into account when dealing with workers; decision-making was decentralized as far as possible and every attempt was made to acquaint the worker with the affairs of the company. In some instances, organizations went so far as to institute what has been referred to as "bottoms-up" management.

Probably every organization has adjusted differently to the problem of bridging the gap between itself and its work force. In some instances, remarkable success has been achieved; in others the gulf is still wide. New approaches have arisen and have been applied; others undoubtedly will appear. In the final analysis, however, the solution turns upon the sincerity and foresight of businessmen and workers—not upon techniques.

The businessman cannot, however, be understood solely from the standpoint of his organizational involvement. The larger context of his activities must be set forth if we are to gain a full appreciation of business life.

As the primary representative of his organization, the executive is directly and influentially involved in his community. We refer to customer relationships, to the system of distribution through wholesalers and retailers, to wage policies, and to involvement in community affairs and government. The responsibilities of business to the social community have only recently come to be regarded as having any real significance—of being of any import over and beyond marketing and selling concerns. The modern-day business enterprise, however, has come to realize its importance, not only for its personnel directly concerned with public relations, but also for its executive group as a whole. As the administrator moves up within the hierarchy of management he must take on more and more responsibilities for community relationships.

From the standpoint of the executive himself, not only does he move within the world of his organization, but he also is a member of his community. Both he and his family must move socially; they possess certain rank and they must live up to the expectations consistent with position. The businessman must have and use the necessary symbols of status; he must live in the right neighborhood, have the right kind of house, and associate with accepted members of his social group. If his income changes, or if he is promoted within the hierarchy of his company, he must make the necessary changes socially. Climbing the organization ladder means climbing the social ladder as well. Failure to do so sooner or later works negatively against organization success.

The two systems tend to be mutually reinforcing; the two worlds —the social and the occupational—are complementary. The executive relates with a certain group of associates while he is on the job and with a similar group of individuals when he is at home. Behavior patterns, codes of conduct, ideals and symbols tend to be common to both worlds so that communication and social relations become easy and proceed with a minimum of conflict and uncertainty. Only when the executive moves up to a higher occupational stratum, is he involved in a conflict situation. Then he must "shift gears" in both worlds.

Chapter 2

THE PERSONALITIES

OF MANAGERS

INTRODUCTION

Business leaders are born to, and come from, the common stream of American culture. They are not a separate, remote ruling class with sons trained for a leadership which forms them into beings whose inner worlds are alien and different. Yet it is clear that certain kinds of personalities make successful leaders and other kinds seem to doom men to failure. These personalities, which hinder or help them achieve and rise to power and position, are formed in the ordinary cultural matrices in which all of our personalities come into being. Yet research evidence indicates that particular milieus, and experiences within them, have peculiarities that are identifiable and significant in the careers of successful men. The personalities of executives are products of their past and present learning experiences within a cultural context—they result from unique experiences but of a commonplace type through which most of us travel during maturation. It is important to ask a number of questions about successful and unsuccessful business executives.

What are their personalities like? Are they different from other men? Do they share common psychological characteristics among themselves? Can we isolate particular kinds of personality characteristics which make for success or failure in business life? Do their social and psychological experiences in childhood and later life appear to be similar or are they very different? In brief, what is the private world of the businessman? And what is the significance of personality in business achievement?

The role of the parent, particularly of the mother and, more generally, of the family, functions more potently than all others in the formative experiences which early mold the person and predispose the executive towards his ultimate career. Moreover, the role of the recognized and unrecognized sponsor in adolescence and early maturity is also a powerful factor. Yet were the personality of the executive different he might not successfully relate himself to the very important person who so often beneficently operates in the lives of mobile business leaders.

The selections in this chapter introduce us to several summary statements about the personalities, qualities, and characteristics of successful men. These are followed by case histories, some of them analyzed and generalized into larger understandings about personality, concluding with the theoretical problem of the individual and personality in a complex society such as America. This chapter will present the career lines of business leaders, emphasizing the person, the basic elements of character formation, as well as the significant events in the long-time career from first jobs to positions of power.

The brief introduction to a chapter by the editors tells its essential significance. The titles and their descriptions give the place and meaning of each part of the chapter for this book.

The name of the author of each selection is placed before the beginning of his contribution. Brief biographical information is supplied in the Notes on the Authors (pp. 551–557). Because of space economies most of the articles are not reprinted here in their original form but have been cut with footnotes reduced to a minimum. The bibliography should be used for references to the entire article or book as well as for other important publications.

THE PSYCHODYNAMICS OF THE EXECUTIVE ROLE

William E. Henry

The personality characteristics of big business leaders, such as the ability "to leave home" emotionally, the nature of the mobility drive, and the acceptance and use of authority, are examined and their significance for success indicated.

Modern business executives have in common many personality characteristics, which are a reflection partly of the socially stereotyped conception of the businessman and partly of some underlying similarities of personality structure. The successful executive represents a crystallization of many of the attitudes and values generally accepted by middle-class American society. Acquisitiveness and achievement, self-directedness and independent thought, are in this group counterbalanced by uncertainty, constant activity, the continual fear of losing ground, and the inability to be introspectively casual.

The business executive is a central figure in the economic and social life of the United States. His direction of business enterprise and his participation in informal social groupings give him a significant place in community life. In both its economic and its social aspects the role of the business executive is sociologically a highly visible one. It has clearly definable limits and characteristics known to the general public. These characteristics indicate the function of the business executive in the social structure, define the behavior expected of the individual executive, and serve as a guide to the selection of the novice.

Social pressure plus the constant demands of the business organization of which he is a part direct the behavior of the executive into the mold appropriate to the defined role. "Success" is the name applied to the whole-hearted adoption of the role. The in-

Note: See Notes on the Authors, page 553, and item 112 in the bibliography for the full reference to this selection.

dividual behaves in the manner dictated by the society, and society rewards the individual with "success" if his behavior conforms to the role. It would punish him with "failure" should he deviate from it.

Participation in this role, however, is not a thing apart from the personality of the individual. It is not a game that the person is playing; it is the way of behaving and thinking that he knows best, that he finds rewarding, and in which he believes. Thus the role as socially defined has its counterpart in the personality structure. To some extent, too, the personality structure is reshaped to be in harmony with the social role. The extent to which such reshaping of the adult personality is possible, however, seems limited. An initial selection process occurs which reduces the amount of time involved in teaching the appropriate behavior. Persons whose personality structure is most readily adaptable to this particular role tend to be selected, whereas those whose personality is not already partially akin are rejected.

This [section] describes the personality communalities of a group of successful business executives. The research upon which it is based explored the general importance of personality structure in the selection of executive personnel. Many aptitude tests have been employed in industry to decrease the risk involved in the hiring of untried personnel and to assist in their placement. These tests have been far less effective in the selection of high-level executive personnel than in the selection of clerical and other non-administrating persons. Many business executives have found that persons of unquestioned high intelligence often turn out to be ineffective when placed in positions of increased responsibility. The reasons for their failure lie in their social relationships. No really effective means has yet been found to clarify and predict this area of executive functioning. It is to this problem that our research[1] is directed.

[1] The research undertaken will be described in its entirety in a subsequent report. In summary it involved the study of over one hundred business executives in various types of business houses. The techniques employed were the Thematic Apperception Test, a short undirected interview, and a projective analysis of a number of traditional personality tests. The validity of our analyses, which were done "blind," rested upon the coincidence of identical conclusions from separately analyzed instruments, upon surveys of past job per-

From the research it became clear that the "successful"[2] business executives studied had many personality characteristics in common. (It was equally clear that an absence of these characteristics was coincident with "failure" within the organization.) This personality constellation might be thought of as the minimal requirement of "success" within our present business system and as the psychodynamic motivation of persons in this occupation. Individual uniqueness in personality was clearly present; but, despite these unique aspects, all executives had in common this personality pattern.

ACHIEVEMENT DESIRES

Successful executives show high drive and achievement desire. They conceive of themselves as hard-working and achieving persons who must accomplish in order to be happy. The areas in which they do their work are clearly different, but each feels this

---

formance, and upon the anecdotal summary of present job behavior by the executive's superiors and associates. The writer wishes to express his thanks to these executives; to Dr. Burleigh Gardner, of Social Research, Inc., under whose auspices the study was made; and to Carson McGuire, Robert F. Peck, Norman Martin, and Harriet Bruce Moore, of the University of Chicago, for their assistance in the collection and analysis of data and the clarification of conclusions.

[2] Success and failure as here used refer to the combined societal and business definitions. All our "successful" executives have a history of continuous promotion, are thought to be still "promotable" within the organization, are now in positions of major administrative responsibility, and are earning salaries within the upper ranges of current business salaries. Men in lower supervisory positions; men who are considered "failures" in executive positions; and men in clerical and laboring jobs show clear deviations from this pattern. This suggests, of course, that this pattern is specific for the successful business executive and that it serves to differentiate him from other groupings in industry.

The majority of these executives come from distributive (rather than manufacturing) businesses of moderately loose organizational structure in which cooperation and team work are valued and in which relative independence of action is stressed within the framework of a clearly defined overall company policy. In organizations in which far greater rigidity of structure is present or in which outstanding independence of action is required, it is possible that there will be significant variations from the personality pattern presented here. We are currently extending our data in these directions.

drive for accomplishment. This should be distinguished from a type of pseudo-achievement drive in which the glory of the end product alone is stressed. The person with this latter type of drive, seldom found in the successful executives, looks to the future in terms of the glory it will provide him and of the projects that he will have completed—as opposed to the achievement drive of the successful executive, which looks more toward the sheer accomplishment of the work itself. The successful business leader gets much satisfaction from doing rather than from merely contemplating the completed product. To some extent this is the difference between the dreamer and the doer. It is not that the successful executives do not have an over-all goal in mind or that they do not derive satisfaction from the contemplation of future ease or that they do not gain pleasure from prestige. Far more real to them, however, is the continual stimulation that derives from the pleasure of immediate accomplishment.

MOBILITY DRIVE

All successful executives have strong mobility drives. They feel the necessity of moving continually upward and of accumulating the rewards of increased accomplishment. For some the sense of successful mobility comes through the achievement of competence on the job. These men struggle for increased responsibility and derive a strong feeling of satisfaction from the completion of a task. Finished work and newly gained competence provide them with their sense of continued mobility.

A second group relies more upon the social prestige of increased status in their home communities or within the organizational hierarchy. Competence in work is of value and at times crucial. But the satisfactions of the second group come fom the social reputation, not from the personal feeling that necessary work has been well done. Both types of mobility drive are highly motivating. The zeal and energy put into the job is equal in both instances. The distinction appears in the kinds of work which the men find interesting. For the first group the primary factor is the nature of the work itself—is it challenging, is it necessary, is it interesting? For the second group the crucial factor is its relation to their goals of status mobility—is it a step in the direction of increased prestige, is it appropriate to their present position, what would other people think of them if they did it?

THE IDEA OF AUTHORITY

The successful executive posits authority as a controlling but helpful relationship to superiors. He looks to his superiors as persons of more advanced training and experience, whom he can consult on special problems and who issue to him certain guiding directives. He does not see the authorities in his environment as destructive or prohibiting forces.

Those executives who view authority as a prohibiting and destructive force have difficulty relating themselves to superiors and resent their authority over them. They are either unable to work smoothly with superiors or indirectly and unconsciously do things to obstruct the work of their bosses or to assert their independence unnecessarily.

It is of interest that to these men the dominant crystallization of attitudes about authority is toward superiors and toward subordinates, rather than toward self. This implies that most crucial in their concept of authority is the view of being a part of a wider and more final authority system. In contrast, a few executives of the "self-made," driving-type characteristic of the past of business enterprise maintain a specific concept of authority with regard to self. They are the men who almost always forge their own frontiers, who are unable to operate within anyone else's framework, and to whom co-operation and team work are foreign concepts. To these men the ultimate authority is in themselves, and their image does not include the surrounding area of shared or delegated power.

ORGANIZATION AND ITS IMPLICATIONS

While executives who are successful vary considerably in their intelligence-test ratings, all of them have a high degree of ability to organize unstructured situations and to see the implications of their organization. This implies that they have the ability to take several seemingly isolated events or facts and to see relationships that exist between them. Further, they are interested in looking into the future and are concerned with predicting the outcome of their decisions and actions.

This ability to organize often results in a forced organization, however. Even though some situations arise with which they feel unfamiliar and are unable to cope, they still force an organization upon it. Thus they bring it into the sphere of familiarity. This tendency operates partially as a mold, as a pattern into which new or unfamiliar experiences are fit. This means, of course, that there is a strong tendency to rely upon techniques that they know will work and to resist situations which do not readily fit this mold.

DECISIVENESS

Decisiveness is a further trait of this group. This does not imply the popular idea of the executive making quick and final decisions in rapid-fire succession, although this seems to be true of some of the executives. More crucial, however, is an ability to come to a decision among several alternative courses of action—whether it be done on the spot or after detailed consideration. Very seldom does this ability fail. While less competent and well-organized individuals may become flustered and operate inefficiently in certain spots, most of these men force their way to a conclusion. Nothing is too difficult for them to tackle and at least try to solve. When poorly directed and not modified by proper judgment, this attitude may be more a handicap than a help. That is to say, this trait remains in operation and results in a decision-making action regardless of the reasonableness of the decision or its reality in terms of related facts. The loss of this trait (usually found only in cases in which some more profound personality change has also occurred) is one of the most disastrous for the executive: his superiors become apprehensive about him. This suggests an interesting relationship to the total executive constellation. The role demands conviction and certainty. Whenever a junior executive loses this quality of decisiveness, he seems to pass out of the socially defined role. The weakening of other aspects of the ideal executive constellation can be readily reintegrated into the total constellation. The questioning of the individual's certainty and decisiveness, however, results in a weakening of the entire constellation and tends to be punished by superiors.

STRONG SELF-STRUCTURE

One way of differentiating between people is in the relative strength or weakness of their notions of self-identity, their self-structure. Some persons lack definiteness and are easily influenced by outside pressures. Some, such as these executives, are firm and well-defined in their sense of self-identity. They know what they are and what they want and have well-developed techniques for getting what they want. The things they want and the techniques for getting them are, of course, quite different for each individual, but this strength and firmness is a common and necessary characteristic. It is, of course, true that too great a sense of self-identity leads to rigidity and inflexibility; and, while some of these executives could genuinely be accused of this, in general they maintain considerable flexibility and adaptability within the framework of their desires and within the often rather narrow possibilities of their own business organization.

ACTIVITY AND AGGRESSION

The executive is essentially an active, striving, aggressive person. His underlying motivations are active and aggressive—not necessarily is he aggressive and hostile overtly in his dealings with other people. This activity and aggressiveness are always well channeled into work or struggles for status and prestige—which implies a constant need to keep moving, to do something, to be active. This does not mean that they are always in bodily movement and moving physically from place to place (though this is often true) but rather that they are mentally and emotionally alert and active. This constant motivator unfortunately cannot be shut off. It may be part of the reason why so many executives find themselves unable to take vacations at leisure or to stop worrying about already solved problems.

APPREHENSION AND THE FEAR OF FAILURE

If one is continually active and always trying to solve problems and arrive at decisions, any inability to do so successfully may well result in feelings of frustration. This seems to be true of the executives. In spite of their firmness of character and their drive to activity, they also harbor a rather pervasive feeling that they may not really succeed and be able to do the things they want to do. It is not implied that this sense of frustration comes only from their immediate business experience. It seems far more likely to be a feeling of long standing within them and to be only accentuated and reinforced by their present business experience.

This sense of the perpetually unattained is an integral part of this constellation and is part of its dilemma. It means that there is always some place to go, but no defined point at which to stop. The executive is "self-propelled" and needs to keep moving always and to see another goal ever ahead, which also suggests that cessation of mobility and of struggling for new achievements will be accompanied by an inversion of this constant energy. The person whose mobility is blocked, either by his own limitations, or those of the social system, finds this energy diverted into other channels. Psychosomatic symptoms, the enlargement of interpersonal dissatisfactions, and the development of rationalized compulsive and/or paranoid-like defenses may reflect the redirection of this potent energy demand.

STRONG REALITY ORIENTATION

Successful executives are strongly oriented to immediate realities and their implications. They are directly interested in the practical, the immediate, and the direct. This is, of course, generally good for the immediate business situation, though the executive with an overdeveloped sense of reality may cease to be a man of vision; for a man of vision must get above reality to plan and even dream about future possibilities. In addition, a too strong sense of reality, when the realities are not in tune with ambitions, may well lead to a conviction that reality is frustrating and unpleasant. This happens to many executives who find progress and promotion too slow for their drives. The result is often a restlessness rather than an activity, a fidgetiness rather than a well-channeled aggression, and a lack of ease that may well disrupt many of their usual interpersonal relations.

THE NATURE OF THEIR INTERPERSONAL RELATIONS

In general the mobile and successful executive looks to his superiors with a feeling of personal attachment and tends to identify himself with them. His superior represents for him a symbol of his own achievement and desires, and he tends to identify himself with these traits in those who have achieved more. He is very responsive to his superiors—the nature of this responsiveness, of course, depends on his other feelings, his idea of authority, and the extent to which he feels frustrated.

On the other hand, he looks to his subordinates in a detached and impersonal way, seeing them as "doers of work" rather than as people. He treats them impersonally, with no real feeling of being akin to them or of having deep interest in them as persons. It is as though he viewed his subordinates as representatives of things he has left behind, both factually and emotionally. Still uncertain of his next forward step, he cannot afford to become personally identified or emotionally involved with the past. The only direction of his emotional energy that is real to him is upward and toward the symbols of that upward interest, his superiors.

This does not mean that he is cold and that he treats all subordinates casually. In fact he tends to be generally sympathetic with many of them. This element of sympathy with subordinates is most apparent when the subordinate shows personality traits that are most like those of the superior. Thus the superior is able to take pride in certain successful young persons without at the same time feeling an equal interest in all subordinates.

THE ATTITUDE TOWARD HIS OWN PARENTS

In a sense the successful executive is a "man who has left home." He feels and acts as though he were on his own, as though his emotional ties and obligations to his parents were severed. It seems to be most crucial that he has not retained resentment of his parents, but has rather simply broken their emotional hold on him and been left psychologically free to make his own decisions. We have found those who have not broken this tie to be either too dependent upon their superiors in the work situation or to be resentful of their supervision (depending, of course, upon whether they are still bound to their parents or are still actively fighting against them).

In general we find the relationship to the mother to have been the most clearly broken tie. The tie to the father remains positive in the sense that he views the father as a helpful but not restraining figure. Those men who still feel a strong emotional tie to the mother have systematically had difficulty in the business situation. This residual emotional tie seems contradictory to the necessary attitude of activity, progress, and channeled aggression. The tie to the father, however, must remain positive—as the emotional counterpart of the admired and more successful male figure. Without this image, struggle for success seems difficult.

THE NATURE OF DEPENDENCY FEELINGS AND CONCENTRATION UPON SELF

A special problem in differentiating the type of general successful executive is the nature of his dependency feelings. It was pointed out above that the dependency upon the mother-image must be eliminated. For those executives who work within the framework of a large organization in which co-operation and group-and-company loyalty are necessities, there must remain feelings of dependency upon the father-image and a need to operate within an established framework. This does not mean that the activity-aggression need cannot operate or that the individual is not decisive and self-directional. It means only that he is so within the framework of an already established set of over-all goals. For most executives this over-all framework provides a needed guidance and allows them to concentrate upon their achievement and work demands with only minimal concern for the policy-making of the entire organization. For those executives who prefer complete independence and who are unable to work within a framework established by somebody else, the element of narcissim is much higher and their feelings of loyalty are only to themselves rather than to a father-image or its impersonal counterpart in company policy. These feelings differentiate the executives who can co-operate with others and who can promote the over-all policy of a company from those who must be the whole show themselves. Clearly there are situations in which the person highly concentrated upon self and with little feeling of dependency loyalty is of great value. But he should be distinguished in advance and be placed in only situations in which these traits are useful.

The successful executive represents a crystallization of many of the attitudes and values generally accepted by middle-class American society. The value of accumulation and achievement, of self-directedness and independent thought and their rewards in prestige and status and property, are found in this group. But they also pay the price of holding these values and of profiting from them. Uncertainty, constant activity, the continual fear of losing ground, the inability to be introspectively leisurely, the ever present fear of failure, and the artificial limitations put upon their emotionalized interpersonal relations—these are some of the costs of this role.

THE PERSONALITY OF A SUCCESSFUL MAN

W. Lloyd Warner and James C. Abegglen

The psychological factors which contribute to the success
of a big business leader are examined in full detail.

Mobility may be seen as a continual process of departing-arriving-departing, . . . The mobile man is that person who is able successfully to initiate and sustain this complex, interwoven series of changes. He must learn, rapidly and thoroughly, the new behaviors in each new situation. He must be able to tolerate uprooting himself and to make use of, or create, the opportunities to move to a new position. He must be able to leave his past behind as he moves into each new present.

Like most of the mobile men interviewed, Donald Hayes gave few details concerning the kind of life he lived as a boy. That it was not an easy or affluent one is clear enough. His father was a

Note: See Notes on the Authors, pages 557 and 551, and item 243 in the bibliography for the full reference to this selection.

machinist and the family lived in Cleveland. "My father used to like to drink, and spent little time at home. I can't remember my father ever doing anything for us. Yes, my mother had to work. She took in washing, and we were still delivering it until after we were married. Mother was always even-tempered, hard-working. She made a good home with what she had to do with. She was always serious but she was a good mother. She had to make all our clothes and there were five boys to take care of."

Asked further for childhood memories, Hayes said: "It was just hard work! Period. It was hard work on my wife's side too. That's why we appreciate the dollar today.". . . .

Hayes was born the son of an occasionally employed laborer, primarily supported by his mother's work as a laundress. He does not suggest that he was acutely deprived as a child, but, rather, that the family lived in constant financial difficulty.

We have a picture of a mobile man, a man from a poor and difficult background, who has worked his way through a variety of situations and locations to arrive at some eminence as a business and community leader. We find him at fifty-five years of age on a kind of plateau, with a new home, relatively new business position, solid community position, and able to review his career and life with some satisfaction.

Against this outline of the basic events in the social mobility of Donald Hayes it is now possible to ask what kind of person he is. What set off all this movement? What is a man like who accomplishes all this? How does he approach the world and how does he feel about other people? The interview with him provides a good deal of information, and the analysis of the Thematic Apperception Test[3] material provides more.

---

[3] The Thematic Apperception Test was invented by Professor Henry Murray, of Harvard University (see *Explorations in Personality*, Oxford University Press, 1938). It provides evidence and understanding about the organization of the psychic life of the individual, probing beneath the conscious level to the deeper emotional structure of the personality. Such people as Harriet Moore, of Social Research, Inc., of Chicago, and Professor William Henry, of the University of Chicago, have adapted it for the practical purposes of business administration. Many business firms now use this instrument for the evaluation and selection of personnel.

. . . From the TAT:

Hayes is a bright man, of above average intelligence, without any great brilliance or creativity. He is not a highly imaginative person, but rather works within the facts and situation at hand. He is direct in his approach to problems, and does not get involved in either details of situations or in side-issues. He organizes his thinking well, and is mark-edly crisp and decisive, making up his mind quickly and following his line of thought through to a solid and definite conclusion. He does not look for problems in his approach to situations, but takes them as he finds them. Further, he does not appear much aware of an audience as he works. Rather, he works for the personal satisfactions it brings him—because he must, in other words, because he is that kind of person. He is not at all a show-off and is notably realistic and accurate in his judgments.

That Hayes, too, felt his father inadequate is clear. While he describes his mother as even-tempered, hard-working, and a good homemaker, he says of his father: "He was very hot-tempered. He was hard on all his boys as long as he was able to swing a stick. . . . As for childhood worries, I worried about my father's condi-tion, and that he might hurt my mother." Of his mother and father he said, "My mother was very good at getting along with people. Maybe I learned a little of that from her. About the only thing I can remember my father saying is, 'Go to work.' "

This picture of the parents and Hayes' feelings about them is amplified through the TAT.

Hayes portrays his home as an emotionally and physically impover-ished place, and the people in it as being in conflict with each other. His description of the mother is of a stern, rigid, moral person. She ap-pears to him to be a person who tries to control him and to be repressive rather than giving him the independence he demands. He appears to be concerned over the fact that he found it necessary to reject the advice, rules, and guidance his mother pressed on him, but he feels a deep need to be a self-directing person and moved gently but firmly away from her control.

At the same time, it is clear that he felt his mother cared for him and was aware of her interest and concern over him. He portrays his mother as attempting to negotiate and smooth over differences between his father and himself, and it is his mother who wants him to remain in the home in the face of the indifference and outright rejection of him by his father.

The directness with which some of these underlying feelings were expressed and the sharpness with which they are felt by Hayes are indicated by this explicit response to a TAT picture showing a young man and an older woman alone in a room, the woman with her back turned to the man.

This young fellow, I think, has had a spat or fight with his father. His father's told him to get out and the mother's tried to act as a peacemaker and she's failed. She wanted the boy to stay and I think he's going to leave anyway. The mother doesn't want to see him go. [What was the fight about?] Money. The boy got in some kind of trouble and he tried to get his father to bail him out, and his father said no.

. . . From this background Hayes emerged an independent and solitary figure. Again from the TAT we find that:

He is first of all a man who must set his own goals and tasks. He sees himself as an independent person, although on the whole he does not introspect about himself or his behavior. His relations with authority, sharply affected by his basic experience with his father, will be cautious and reserved. He waits upon proof that he can trust others, and is most reluctant to put himself in a position of dependence on others. Doubtless this is a result of his family experiences of unreliability.

The intensity and sharp focus of drive in this man have left little interest, time, or energy for anything outside his career. He first of all does not find it easy to get along with other men. His attitude toward them, perhaps basically a result of his relations with his father, seems mixed. The TAT analysis states:

Hayes' relations with other men are marked by two definite and seemingly incompatible reactions. He is not himself an outgoing hail-fellow type, but waits to be approached generally. He is, however, very positive in his feeling toward other men. He likes to feel that they are interested in him, and he gets great satisfaction from being with them. However, and this counter-current runs strong, Hayes does not really trust other men, for he believes that if he places reliance on them, they will or at least are likely to let him down. He will therefore by choice make some effort to work with other men in a solid and cooperative manner. He does not really feel competitive toward them and is quite willing to share his work where possible. At the same time he does not believe basically that this cooperative arrangement will work out, for he sees other men as unreliable. Therefore he believes he must fall back on his own resources and make his own way unaided.

Like all of these mobile men, Hayes is married—like most, he married when he was rather young. Like his other relationships, his marriage is another measure of the kind of relations with people and approach to life that he has developed. The TAT analysis says this:

In a total picture of limited and cautious relations with others and of controlled emotions, Hayes' relations with women are undoubtedly most limited. He could by no means be called a sensual man. Sexuality appears to play little part in his behavior directly. He portrays relations with women as essentially distracting and frivolous. Although there is no indication that he feels himself to be sexually inadequate, and such a problem would be inconsistent with his generally high level of self-confidence, he does portray women as sexual aggressors and himself as determined not to get involved with them as sexual objects. He appears to divorce his home and wife from sexuality and rather portrays his relations in the home as comfortable, and essentially asexual.

Some confirmation of Hayes' attitude toward his home as a protected haven is provided in the interview where he remarks of his wife's social activity: "Mrs. Hayes doesn't have time for afternoon bridge parties or cocktail parties; we don't go to night clubs. Certain things creep into a man's life that way, and you begin to worry about what each other is doing. You can't work that way. It usually ends in a broken home. I don't think you can burn the candle at both ends. We'll build another house; that will keep us busy." Again we find the concentration and the need for independence which is seen as a minimum involvement with other people.

It is clear that this man was both willing and able to initiate and sustain the process of departure, arrival, and departure necessary to social mobility. Departure, emotionally and physically, from the home is a task assigned all men in our culture. Not all accomplish this task, but maturity as we see it depends among other matters on the ability to break the ties to the parents to a degree sufficient to enable the maturing child to function as a social entity separate from his family of birth. It is incumbent on the adult male in our society to establish his own home, and, in full social development, to establish his own family, and raise his children.

CASE HISTORIES OF TWO "UNSUCCESSFUL" MEN

W. Lloyd Warner and James C. Abegglen

> The personality characteristics that operated in the private worlds of two men that helped them advance to leadership, yet did not allow them ultimate success, are discussed.

The history and career of Jeffrey Collins is on the whole similar to that of most mobile men. His father was not a successful man. The elder Mr. Collins owned a farm in Ohio but lost it and moved to a small town where the grandfather owned a second-hand store. After some years of working as a clerk in the store, Mr. Collins tried farming again, but again failed after two years, and once more went back to the job in the store. During this period, when Jeffrey Collins was eleven, he began to work at odd jobs and delivered papers to help support the family. There followed a succession of after-school and summertime jobs until high school graduation when he went to work in a factory on the assembly line.

A period in the army during the First World War seemed to provide the critical break in Collins' career, for he left home to enlist and during his period of service managed to obtain a commission by studying intensively for the examinations for officer training and successfully passing them. "After my experience in the army, I realized the opportunities were not in my home town, and I sort of swore an oath to myself never to go back." He took a job as office boy in a manufacturing plant elsewhere, and worked in a variety of jobs in this and another firm for the next thirteen years.

Note: See Notes on the Authors, pages 557 and 551, and item 243 in the bibliography for the full reference to this selection.

A chance meeting, through an introduction by older friends, brought Mr. Collins to the attention of an older man who was in the process of setting up an insurance company. Offered a job, Collins accepted, and moved to Cincinnati to work for this new firm. He traveled for a time, worked in the office for a time, and within six years was promoted to vice president of what had become a leading firm in its field.

Many other moves and changes went with this rapid career advancement of Jeffrey Collins, of course. From the small Ohio town he had moved through a number of residences to an expensive suburb of Cincinnati. He owned a twelve-room home there, and became active in community affairs. He worked as a fund-raiser, and then on the board of the local Red Cross, and he and his wife joined the Plank and Tap, a high-status club with limited membership. Mrs. Collins busied herself in community affairs as well, becoming president for a time of the suburban Women's Club.

This is in brief outline a history of movement, change, and achievement similar to most of the mobile elite. At the same time, this career must have contained the elements that set it off from the majority of the mobile elite, for at the present time Jeffrey Collins may serve as an example of the mobile man who is finally defeated.

About two years ago Collins' business position was taken away from him. He kept the title, and presumably the salary, but found a major part of his responsibility and authority removed. At the time of the interview, the Collinses no longer had the house in the suburb, but were living in a five-room apartment in the city, in an old but respectable apartment neighborhood. The Collinses have dropped their club membership because the group was "too crowded," and Mr. Collins indicated that his community activities had terminated during the past several years. In addition, Mrs. Collins has dropped her club activities because "I don't like women's clubs."

No doubt as a result of some or all of these changes, Mr. Collins greeted the interviewer by saying, "Do you feel you have such a man as you are looking for in me?" That is, he had come to doubt his own success, although the measure of it was in both his position and his prestige as compared with his past. . . .

Altogether the success and prestige Jeffrey Collins acquired at such cost to himself and with enormous labor and tenacity appear to be melting away. His social memberships, as well as those of his wife, the home he acquired, and even the job position he attained, all are dwindling. This is not the case of a worn-out old man, at least in years, for Collins is only fifty-four years old. But the steady upward curve of his career, maintained over a period of more than thirty years, suddenly dipped and seems to be directed steadily downward.

Collins is a rather sad figure now. He is somewhat bitter over his present status—"I think there should have been more recognition of those who helped get the company on its feet." Something of the inevitable loneliness of such a man who has been mobile and left people behind, and now is himself left, comes through. "We don't know people much around here yet." And, "We don't have *close* friends, but it's awfully good to run into old friends when you're out of town and take up where you left off! You could almost say my friends are in steps." Fatigue finds expression as Collins describes an ideal vacation—"one where I can get far away from competition."

Two elements in this remark are important: first, the reference to an inability or failure to move from the company or to travel; and, second, the uncertainty about his abilities and goals implied in the reference to lack of education. The central fact in the lives of these men is movement, and, as we saw in the case of Donald Hayes, this means detaching oneself from people and places in a continual sequence and driving on for ever new or renewed goals. The whole process of mobility requires a subtle balance between this drive for independence, withdrawal, and departure, and the opposing and necessary need to attach to others, and be respected and honored by them. A succesfuly mobile man like Donald Hayes is able to maintain this balance—to work with people and be attractive to them, yet leave them behind without guilt or regret.

The difference between Jeffrey Collins and those mobile men whose mobility drive continues is illustrated by his relations with other men. We have noticed that most of the men established themselves in a protégé relationship with an older man who provided a model for them and also rewarded them during their training period. It is a requisite of this protégé system that the model be left behind, without a continuing attachment. The man who served as a model for Collins, the president of his firm, was a person he could not leave. When he remarks that "I think I should have left after getting the experience . . ." he is doubtless correct. For to adopt a new role as a senior man, and to realize the training fully, it would be necessary for him to leave this relationship behind and use the experience, with all its ramifications, in a new situation.

Collins required a subordinate and protected relationship. Moreover, he was not able to sustain the constant departures that continued mobility required. As a result, he remained in a situation that finally defeated him.

Closely related to this factor in Collins' career is the other element of his remark, his regret over his lack of formal training. Repeatedly in the interview he points up the difference between himself and others in the firm in education, and his wife remarked, "The Phi Beta Kappa keys and fraternity pins give him a large-sized inferiority complex." Underlying this expression of lack of self-confidence for Jeffrey Collins is the fact that, while he rejected the life and status and behavior of his parents, he was not able to set clearly for himself, as an independent person, the goals of his life.

The dual elements of dependence on others and reluctance to set personal goals are both commented on in the TAT analysis. Of course, the strength of these tendencies in Jeffrey Collins should not be overestimated. Like all of the mobile men studied he is intelligent, decisive, and direct. Far more than most persons he is independent and self-directing. He was able to leave the home and for a long time sustain the drive that originally caused him to be a hard-working, self-directing business man. However, two essential elements in occupational mobility—the energy and will to sustain the continual departures mobility prescribes, and the self-direction and independence—must be present in large degree and vitally maintained throughout the career. When the opposite trends to affiliate with other people and become close and dependent on them find too great expression, the chances for failure in the mobility process are greatly increased and result in men like Jeffrey Collins.

The history of this man illustrates that the process of social mobility is enormously demanding of the energies of able men. When the personality dynamics of the individual are not adjusted to these demands, he becomes enervated and, in middle years, becomes fatigued and dull. The whole process of his career turns back on itself to leave an empty and regretful individual, lonely and withdrawn.

A third group in the mobile elite is perhaps the most dramatic and striking in history and personality, for the need to be mobile and to be detached from people and places occurs here in an extreme form. This group too is self-defeating, but in a different way from Jeffrey Collins. All of these men have been occupationally mobile, to an extreme degree. All have come a long way to their present business and economic positions. But as the case of Donald Hayes suggested, and Jeffrey Collins further indicated, this process of mobility has many of the components of self-destruction in it.

In order to achieve solid position at high levels of our society it is necessary not only to be mobile in job and income, but to re-express this new status in terms of manner of living and social relationships acceptable to ever higher social strata. To arrive at the final and stable high status these men aspire to, they and their families must be accepted into, and become part of, the community of highly placed, prestigeful, and powerful members of their society. As we have seen, all of these mobile men, as a necessary part of the equipment that makes it possible for them to be mobile and leave people behind without fear or regret, have difficulty in easily relating themselves to others over a period of time. They have difficulty in accepting and imposing the kinds of reciprocal obligations that close friendship and intimate social contacts imply. They typically are isolated men; in only the exceptional case, not so far considered, do they achieve in all respects the kind of status and prestige they aspire to.

This characteristic, the need to remain uninvolved with and detached from others, finds its extreme expression in men like Walter Evans. The history and personality of this man provide a picture of the genesis and outcomes of the mobility sequence when carried very nearly to its limits, within the overall compass of successful movement.

All of the dissociation from the past, both social and spatial, characteristic of the mobile man, is markedly present in Evans' history. "Mother was left an orphan when she was small and was raised by some neighbors. My father was left an orphan too, and was raised by a brother and his wife." As to spatial movement, frequent changes in location are among his earliest memories. "We moved thirteen times in fifteen years always to a new home Dad had just built. He would sell it at a profit and move on. But it was hard on the furniture, and it was hard on Mother. The only reason Dad quit was that she just couldn't take it any more."

Evans' father was a pipe-fitter by trade and the family was brought up in South Bend, Indiana. As with the other mobile men, the mother is the primary source of the training necessary for later mobility aspirations. "Dad's always been a hard worker. He likes to work, and has a lot of ability, but he just lost his confidence due to an accident. Besides, it was awfully hard for Dad to change. Maybe he was more stubborn than I am. I have changed and have been able to adjust myself to the trend of the times and Dad wasn't able to do that. Perhaps the main reason Dad quit work in the tire company we had was because Mother made him clean up before he came home. She always had great ideas. The grocery and food business she considered degrading. I can't figure out where she got those notions. I had to take piano lessons from the best teacher around." Again, like most of these men he says, "I'm more like my mother."

Walter Evans doesn't express his feelings about his father quite so openly as some of these men, but they can be read between the lines of his remarks. "After Dad had his accident, he slipped fast. The last thirty years he's just made a living. Yes, actually I've done very much better than Dad did. There were years during the twenties when he applied for job after job, and he'd be passed along, but before he was they'd always find out where I was and what I was doing. Naturally they were more interested in a younger man, and I had a reputation by then. It got so I hated to see him go see anybody who knew both of us."

Evans is now executive vice president of a nation-wide chain of restaurants. He hasn't stopped moving. "I won't stay here long at the present level. I should be president of the company in about two years. I'll test them out on it and if I don't think I'll get it I'll start to look around. I feel I could run any business better than it's being run now. I wouldn't hesitate to take over the presidency of General Motors tomorrow." He has no qualms about moving. "If I felt a move was the best thing, we moved. Sometimes Mrs. Evans didn't know about it until the day before the move but she never objected."

Evans is another of these mobile men, self-confident, hard-driving, from a background typical of his kind. He's come a long way and, like Donald Hayes but unlike Jeffrey Collins, he's still moving. But in one respect he is different, for in all his relations with others he is quite evidently unpleasant, overbearing, and aggressive. Evans talked about his fellow executives—"I lie awake nights thinking of ways in which the firm can get ahead over night. It's easy as falling off a log—they're stupid guys, the ones I work with and the leaders of competitive companies." Asked if any of the men he works with are close friends, he said, "Who has any good friends? Maybe one or two but if I left the present company I'd find new ones and the old ones would be forgotten. So would I. Oh, sure, I have plenty of friends. I could call any bank president in St. Louis and you'd have dinner with him because of my friendship with him. But it doesn't mean anything. I learned a long time ago not to form close attachments. It's easier to fire the guy when you are moved ahead of him. I think that's very important. Yet I'm friendly. I make a point of never hurting anyone unnecessarily but rather try to make any place better for my having been there." Evans later gave an interesting example of his kind of friendship: "This guy got me a job with this company. He knew me and knew what I can do." Asked if he sees this man now, Evans replied, "Yes, maybe once a year. When he's in trouble he calls. But he's not with the company any more; he didn't seem to fit into the business. He's a promoter actually. He does a terrific job as long as he can get somebody else to do the work. That's why I didn't follow him except when he fit into *my* picture."

The approach of this man to his home life and his wife's role in his career is summed up by him—"I've read the magazine articles that say a man should marry the girl with more of everything than he has, that through her contacts with other wives he can get ahead. I've proved that this is not necessarily true and should write an article of my own to show how. Instead of marrying up, I married down. My wife had less of everything, money and contacts even, than I had. I've kept my home life completely separated from business always. My wife has never met the business associates' wives and never will if I can help it."

. . . The braggadocio in his remarks and the fact that he felt compelled to portray himself in this way to a stranger, the vehemence, and reiteration cause wonder. A partial answer can be gathered from the report of the TAT analyst:

The underlying characteristic of Evans' approach to the world is his drive to be free of all kinds of restrictions, personal or moral. For example, in his dealings with other people, particularly with women, his first impulse is to lash out, to find their weak spots and use this knowledge to assert his own dominance. At the same time he is very aware of appearances and sensitive to the way in which his behavior is seen and judged by others. As a result, in order to keep up appearances and avoid the punishment that might result from this behavior, he tries to hold himself in and keep from exceeding the bounds of propriety in his behavior toward others.

Evans is not simply an amoral man. [Although he so describes himself, for in the interview he says, "I'd rather read a biography of Dillinger than a light novel. Maybe you don't think much of Dillinger but he was successful in what he attempted."] However, he is made uncomfortable by moral restrictions and feels deeply that mortality serves to defeat its possesor. For example, he says of one character, "She's too steeped in her ideals of what's right and wrong. They are too deeply beaten into her. It would keep her from ever being noticed." We may take this to be an expression of his own feelings toward the moral code he has been trained in by his parents, and his conscious reaction from that code.

As with his morality, so with Evans' reaction to other people. He is a man who must, to accomplish his goals, feel that he is free of other persons. He requires a specific goal, and will work most effectively when he feels he can concentrate absolutely all his attention, thought, and efforts on that goal. Rules and people, morals and affections, are constricting and dangerous. They are both tempting and weakening, and serve to prevent the independence and freedom from his situation that Evans requires.

In the TAT analysis the following attitudes are revealed:

Evans has no difficulty in maintaining his feelings of superiority and distance from women, including the mother. Sexuality is intriguing, amusing, and necessary, but he does not get so involved as to develop a close attachment to any woman as a result of sexual needs. Rather he will treat women either as sexual objects—and therefore easily dealt with and disposed of—or as social objects, to be used in establishing the kind of social milieu he feels necessary to his career.

In his relations with men, however, Evans has a good deal more difficulty maintaining the high degree of freedom and independence and dominance he needs to be comfortable. His approach to other men is hesitant, and he feels uncertain of himself in relation to them. He mistrusts other men, feels they are thinking ahead of him, and using him rather than his being in a dominant position. This causes him considerable dis-ease and in defense he seeks to establish his own individuality distinct from them. Specifically in terms of his father, Evans does not see his father as really part of the family and avoids contact with him in a family situation. In a man-to-man relationship he seems to feel that his father is potentially stronger than he, definitely not a helpful person, but rather a person who is amused and gratified by the difficulties his son gets into. This mistrust of the father is reflected in his attitude toward other males, and gives rise in behavior to the cold and calculating interaction with other men that Evans displays.

Evans is not the tough, independent, and ruthless person he appears to be. He is a man who is afraid of being placed in a position of dependence or weakness toward others; to avoid this, he tries to deny his basically strong morality and becomes immoral. In his relations with other people he becomes hostile and distant, in fear of the weakness that he feels close relations with people will bring.

This type of man is not common in the mobile group. . . .

In terms of social mobility, however, the important fact to keep in mind is that this type of man is placed in a dilemma by his mobility. The set of feelings and attitudes toward others that Walter Evans displays represents in somewhat extreme form the "departure" aspect of the typically mobile man. These attitudes facilitate his personal adjustment to this difficult mobility process; but, at the same time, they make it impossible for him to achieve a high level of social status in both the occupational and social hierarchies. The very qualities that make for rapid movement, ready departure, and easy accommodation to ceaseless and drastic change make it impossible for these men, when higher occupational positions are attained, to build for themselves and their families the social relations that solid status in their communities requires. Even to move to the highest occupational levels they find themselves caught in the system of their own making. Evans realizes this dimly. His wife is isolated from him, his position, and its social correlates. She remains the naïve, poorly educated, socially withdrawn person he married down to, as he puts it. Her present role is of his making, for it is the way he must have his wife. Yet—"My wife just plain don't know what I've done. She'd be more interested in me being a $60-a-week grocery store clerk and be home. It would be a wonderful deal if she could work well with the other wives. My getting the presidency would be easy then."

One central characteristic of business leaders is their enormous concentration on their careers. All of these mobile men show up in the interviews to be devoting almost all of their energies to the forwarding of their business careers, the company they are with, and their position in the company. This fact becomes apparent in men like Jeffrey Collins who, when put in a limited business position, have little or nothing else to do, no non-business interests or activities to turn to, and who do not seem to be able to refocus their energies. This group of men seem to be listless and apathetic, defeated men.

This driving concentration on the career is necessary to mobility. The task of moving through the business hierarchy is a hard, demanding one, and requires the intense focusing of great interests and energies and skills. We have seen that this is a characteristic of these men, the ability to focus their energies in this fashion on the tasks they set themselves. Without this capacity they would not have moved as they have.

At the same time, this is the narrowest definition of their task, for they are moving through the total social system—whether or not they realize it. They cannot and do not move alone. In order to reach the goals they set themselves, they must be able to define what they are doing and want to do in broader terms than the immediate job. Again, a basic dilemma and contradiction appear, for this necessary entire concentration on business makes it impossible for them to develop the broader interests and activities necessary to participate with the kinds of people they encounter as they move up in the business hierarchy. . . .

Even though most of these men are not as vehement in isolating their wives as Walter Evans, they share many basic attitudes. First, the wife must accept and work toward the goals set by the mobile man. She above all must learn to tolerate and even encourage the long hours, many business trips, and frequent moves dictated by the nature of her husband's career needs. She must provide him a base of operations, but a base that is not demanding and that will provide continual support, or, failing that, at least in no way interfere with the problems that he is concerned with.

The wife must not be demanding of her husband, either of his time or of his interest. Manifest by the kind of job concentration these men reveal, even their sexual activity is limited. This tremendous concentration of energy no doubt has its source, to a great extent, in sexual energy. No deflection is tolerated. Repeatedly in the psychological analyses they see sexual relations as limiting, frivolous, and unreal.

No doubt these two elements, the capacity to leave, arrive, and leave again, and the unconscious faith in the malleability of their world, are a substratum of attitudes. Along with these common characteristics the mobile men are alike in other important respects. They share a high level of energy, an ability to expend enormous effort on achieving a desired end. This factor is closely related to the capacity for complete concentration. To them the career and its immediate environs are all that matter. They can focus their entire selves on their job, to the exclusion of all other matters, daydreams, family, social life, or any extra interests that might intrude. Coupled with, and partly a result of, their belief in the efficacy of hard work to gain reward, this provides them a powerful advantage over less energetic competitors.

Many other psychological factors are shared by the men of the mobile elite. They are not brilliant men, usually, but they do have an intelligence level substantially above average. More interesting is their utter realism. Their judgments are quick, tough, and accurate. They do not become distracted. They do not mistake some minor issue for the main problem as it concerns them, nor do they wander away from this main problem. They see people accurately with no sentimentality. This is not a meanness but a kind of cold hard vision, always directed by the overriding need to work problems through to solutions, to work situations through to a rewarding conclusion.

All of these characteristics are important to the mobility process they are engaged in. These men are quick to pick up cues. They can move into new situations successfully without letting themselves get involved prematurely. They can approach people easily, but always with an inner reservation that leaves them free to move out and on when they need to.

All of these psychological characteristics, however, are effective only if set in the context of the basic ability to depart and arrive and depart that mobility demands. The emotional approach of these men to other people is essential to their successful exploration of their other capacities to advance their mobility. This emotional approach is also the basic cause of the price they pay for mobility—isolation, fatigue, and the inability to make their final arrival in a high-status community position.

PROMOTABLE EXECUTIVES

C. Wilson Randle

The qualities and characteristics of 3000 executives are examined to determine which are significant for the prediction of success when executives are promoted.

Every executive is composed of a mix of qualities or characteristics—complex and never quite duplicated in any other executive.

Note: See Notes on the Authors, page 556, and item 184 in the bibliography for the full reference to this selection.

Some are associated with work performance, some are mental, and some are personal.

In individuals, certain of these characteristics are outstanding, the majority are average, and a number are weak. The promotability of an executive is determined by *what* qualities are outstanding and *what* qualities are weak. Moreover, the presence or lack of promotability seems to rest more on outstanding and weak qualities than on those of average strength. The former make a man rise above the ranks or let him be pulled down, whereas the latter are not distinguishing though they may be necessary to the total makeup of the executive.

In the research study at hand, it has been found that there are certain characteristics—eight in number—which generally identify the promotable executive wherever he may be found. These may be called "universals."

In addition, certain other characteristics—variable in number—tend to discriminate between promotable and nonpromotable executives at given management levels or in specific functional areas of the business. Thus, top management promotability is distinguished by certain unique qualities, in contrast with lower management levels; and the financial executive has standards of promotability not common to sales or engineering.

In short, the distinguishing characteristics of promotable executives consist not only of "universals" but also of discriminating qualities attached to particular management levels or particular functional areas. Therefore, to identify a man for promotability, two kinds of yardsticks are employed: (1) He must meet the criteria for promotability found in all executives. (2) He should also meet the criteria which discriminate at the management level and in the functional area in question.

The research results presented in this article set forth these various yardsticks.

For the present study of 3,000 executives, complete detailed appraisals of each person were available.[4] Approximately half of the appraisals were based on identical evaluation methods, and so could be subjected to detailed statistical analysis.

[4] From the files of Booz, Allen and Hamilton.

All management levels above foremen and all functional areas of the business are covered in the sample. There are 25 companies —all of them successful—varying in size from $10 million to over $1 billion in annual sales. While most are manufacturing firms, there are also two each in finance, utilities, service, and mining and extraction.

The study is based on actual qualities of actual executives. The sample is large enough to provide statistically significant numbers of executives in various management levels and functional areas. This is a study in depth, then, based on a sample which can be validly analyzed by respective parts. It is believed that most of the difficulties of former studies have thus been overcome.

The accumulation, evaluation, and analysis of the data to determine the distinguishing characteristics of promotable executives involved a series of six major steps:

1. *Classification of executives*—On the basis of the appraisals, all executives were divided into three groups: (a) *promotable*—those who could now or within a reasonable time be advanced to a higher management job; (b) *satisfactory*—now successfully carrying out the duties of the position but not promotable; (c) *inadequate*—now "over their heads," not successfully measuring up to requirements.

2. *Identification of executive characteristics*—Appraisals were analyzed to determine the characteristics possessed by the executives in the sample.

3. *Analysis of total executive group*—Promotable, satisfactory, and inadequate executives were studied to determine the presence and degree of each characteristic among the executives so rated, i.e., the percentage of cases where it appeared as an (a) outstanding, (b) average, or (c) weak quality.

4. *Analysis of management level groups*—Executives were next divided into three organizational levels—top, middle, and lower. For each level, promotable, satisfactory, and inadequate executives were again studied to see what characteristics they possessed in what degree.

5. *Analysis of functional area groups*—Executives were next divided into four functional area groups—sales, manufacturing, engineering and research, finance and accounting. Again an analysis was made to see what characteristics promotable, satisfactory, and inadequate executives possessed in what degree.

6. *Tabulation of promotable characteristics*—Based upon the fore-going analysis and correlations, tables were constructed showing what characteristics appeared to determine promotability (a) for executives in general, (b) for executives classified by organizational level, and (c) for executives classified by functional area.

MEN AND MEASURES

The first two steps listed above—the classification of promotable executives and the identification of their distinguishing qualities—rest squarely on the results of a series of individual appraisals.

Appraisal results were achieved through a four-part program so organized and integrated as to provide an accumulation of evidence behind the findings:

(1) Each executive's background and experience were analyzed in detail. This covered age; education; professional, social, and civic activities; work experience; health; and family relationships. Such an analysis indicated what areas of competency the executive possessed (both actual and potential), his past progress and recognition record, his leadership record, and his adjustments.

(2) A thorough appraisal of each executive was made by five of his business associates who were best qualified for the task. This was done on an independent, noncollaborative basis, and covered job performance, human relations skills, mental attributes, and personal characteristics.

(3) A battery of written tests was given each executive, covering mental ability, interests, and personality characteristics. Tests were kept to a supporting rather than a primary role. They were employed as a diagnostic tool to indicate what areas needed further exploration, as an aid in explaining other findings, and as further confirming evidence of executive characteristics.

(4) Each executive was given a thorough interview lasting from one and one-half to three hours. This interview was conducted only after a complete review of all other appraisal results. It was employed to clear up areas of question, to verify other appraisal findings, and to gain first-hand impressions of the executive such as were not available from the other techniques.

Each of these four parts yielded certain appraisal findings. Those having a persuasive accumulation of evidence were considered

53

confirmed. Others were discarded. The confirmed evaluation results became the basis for the appraisal summaries. Each such
summary included a statement of the outstanding, average, and
weak characteristics of the executive; the positions he seemed best
qualified to fill; his potential for future advancement; and his development needs.

Thus the appraisal summary both identified executive characteristics and indicated whether, on the basis of all appraisal findings,
the executive was promotable, satisfactory, or inadequate. To
arrive at this latter determination, the executive was measured
both against the requirements of his current position and against
positions for which he appeared eligible.

Appraisal judgments derived in this manner have stood up well
over a period of time. In many instances, we have gone back to the
same companies to evaluate the same group of executives—from
two to eight years after the initial appraisal. This subsequent experience has shown that "promotable" and "inadequate" ratings
are quite accurate—thus confirming the crucial distinction between
these two groups. This proven distinction supports the predictive-
ness of the findings reported here. The "satisfactory" executive
group has been less stable, but this is not inconsistent. Rather, it
would be expected that men not clearly marked for promotion or
failure might turn out either way.

PROMOTION PROPORTIONS. The appraisal results based on
identical evaluation methods—specifically 1,427 cases—were used
exclusively for preparing the statistical tables in order to assure
the greatest possible validity. The balance of the total sample of
3,000, which involved some variance in the appraisal approach to
meet conditions present in the various companies, served to provide background, confirmation, and interpretative information.

The 1,427 executives were rated as follows in the appraisal
summaries:

	Number	Per cent
Promotable	498	35%
Satisfactory	770	54
Inadequate	159	11
Total	1,427	100%

Analysis of the appraisal information disclosed more than 100 identifiable characteristics possessed by the 1,427 executives in the sample. But only 30 were of sufficient occurrence to be regarded as prevailing or "common denominator" characteristics. Chart 1 lists and briefly defines these qualities.

It will be seen at once that some of these characteristics are broader in scope than others. This is particularly true for the first four—position performance, intellectual ability, human relations skill, and personal characteristics. These are composite or general qualities basically made up of a number of characteristics, many of which also appear individually on the list. Other qualities differ in degree or scope. Few are mutually exclusive; many overlap.

All of this is by way of saying that the 30 common-denominator characteristics follow the expected pattern of human qualities. They cannot be neatly packaged and compartmentalized because they do not occur in individuals in this fashion. At the same time, through usage many of the terms employed here have acquired a definite meaning in people's minds. They tend to be better understood, and hence to be more practicable, than terms which might be constructed for the purposes of this study.

Thus characteristics have been identified and defined as they were found to exist. As long as certain of them add up to a promotable executive, it is immaterial that individually they are not clear-cut. It is the whole man who is being appraised for advancement; it is the whole man who must carry out the responsibilities of the new position.

DISTINGUISHING QUALITIES. The next step was to determine just which of these 30 qualities seemed best to indicate promotability. To be accepted as such, a quality had to be significantly present in executives who had been judged promotable and significantly absent in those who had been judged inadequate. To be on the safe side, the threshold of acceptability was raised to more than double that required for statistical significance.

. . . Promotability in all executive categories is distinguished by the eight qualities of position performance, drive, intellectual ability, leadership, administrative ability, initiative, motivation, and creativeness. In addition, promotability is distingushed for the

CHART 1.   EXECUTIVE CHARACTERISTICS

1. *Position performance*—How well the executive carries out the duties of his present job.
2. *Intellectual ability*—Ability to solve problems, to adapt to new situations, to analyze and make judgments.
3. *Human relations skill*—Ability to motivate people and get them to work together.
4. *Personal characteristics*—The total of temperament or personality characteristics bearing on executive functioning.
5. *Technical knowledge* — The knowledge of functional skills needed to carry out position requirements.
6. *Breadth of knowledge* — Range of interests. Use of information and concepts from other related fields of knowledge.
7. *Planning* — Looking ahead. Developing programs and work schedules.
8. *Administration* — Organizing own work and that of others. Delegation, follow-up, control of position activities.
9. *Accomplishment* — Effective use of time. Amount of work produced.
10. *Quality*—Accuracy and thoroughness. High standards.
11. *Dependability*—Meets schedules and deadlines. Adheres to instructions and policy.

12. *Acuteness* — Mentally alert. Understands instructions, explanations, unusual situations and circumstances quickly.
13. *Capacity*—Mental depth and breadth; reservoir of mental ability.
14. *Flexibility* — Adaptable. Adjusts rapidly to changing conditions. Copes with the unexpected.
15. *Analysis and judgment* — Critical observer. Breaks problem into components, weighs and relates; arrives at sound conclusions.
16. *Creativeness*—Original ideas. An inquiring mind. Fresh approaches to problems.
17. *Verbal facility* — Articulate. Communicative — generally understood by persons at all levels.
18. *Socialness* — Makes friends easily. Works "comfortably" with others. Has sincere interest in people.
19. *Acceptance* — Gains confidence of others; earns respect.
20. *Sensitivity*—Has a "feel" for people; recognizes their problems. Quick to pick up "the way the wind is blowing." Is considerate of others.
21. *Leadership*—Receives loyalty and cooperation from others. Manages and motivates others to full effectiveness.

CHART 1. (*Continued*)

22. *Developing others* — Develops competent successors and replacements.
23. *Motivation* — Has well-planned goals. Willingly assumes greater responsibilities. Realistically ambitious.
24. *Attitude*—Enthusiastic, constructive, optimistic, loyal. Good orientation to company, position, and associates.
25. *Vision*—Has foresight; sees new opportunities. Appreciates, but not bound by, tradition or custom.

26. *Self-control* — Calm and poised under pressure.
27. *Initiative* — Self-starting. Prompt to take hold of a problem. Sees and acts on new opportunities.
28. *Drive*—Works with energy. Not easily discouraged. Basic urge to get things done.
29. *Self-confidence* — Assured bearing. Inner security. Self-reliant. Takes new developments in stride.
30. *Objectivity* — Has an open mind. Keeps emotional or personal interests from influencing decisions.

composite executive by six specially applicable qualities (which do not always discriminate in the various subgroups): acceptance, socialness, analysis and judgment, planning, flexibility, and accomplishment.

In Table 1, the percentage presence of the various distinguishing characteristics is shown for promotable and inadequate executives in this all-inclusive or composite group. The double rule in the middle of the table simply separates the discriminating from the nondiscriminating items, while within each of these two divisions the single rule separates the generalized items (applicable to all executives) from the specialized items (applicable to this category only). The same practice is followed in the subsequent tables for the subgroupings.

INTERPRETATION OF FIGURES. The meaning of the table is easily interpreted. For example, the table shows that while position performance is present as an outstanding quality in 50% of all executives rated as promotable, it is present as an outstanding quality in only 5% of executives rated as inadequate. Conversely, only 1% of promotable men were weak in this respect, while 33% of inade-

TABLE 1. Distinguishing Characteristics of the Composite Executive

| Characteristic | Percentage Presence | | | |
| | As an Outstanding Quality | | As a Weak Quality | |
	Promotable Executives	Inadequate Executives	Promotable Executives	Inadequate Executives
Discriminating				
For all categories				
Position performance	50%	5%	1%	33%
Drive	47	14	9	32
Intellectual ability	44	8	3	30
Leadership	41	6	15	56
Administration	40	6	9	48
Initiative	38	7	5	35
Motivation	34	8	3	23
Creativeness	30	6	5	36
For this category only				
Acceptance	54%	20%	8%	30%
Socialness	53	23	7	35
Analysis and judgment	52	14	6	36
Planning	34	10	8	37
Flexibility	30	7	5	29
Accomplishment	27	7	3	29
Nondiscriminating				
For all categories				
Dependability	27%	16%	1%	7%
Self-control	25	10	12	21
Verbal facility	21	9	1	11
Self-confidence	14	5	4	13
Sensitivity	13	4	8	11
Objectivity	6	3	3	12
For this category only				
Attitude	48%	30%	3%	20%
Quality	28	8	4	9
Vision	10	3	2	18

quate executives were rated weak on position performance. In other words, a man displaying a high degree of position performance is much more likely to be promotable.

This, of course, is an obvious fact. However, as Justice Holmes once remarked, "Emphasis on the obvious is often more important than elucidation of the obscure." The fact that position performance is a strong indication of promotability certainly commends the current practice of promoting the good performer. At the same time, it does not support the position often taken that this is the sole criterion. Seven other characteristics are likewise important.

As for the nondiscriminating qualities, it can be seen, for example, that attitude is present as an outstanding quality in 48% of promotable executives. This standing alone would seem to commend it as a distinguishing attribute. But the inadequate executive is found to possess an outstanding attitude in 30% of the cases studied. The difference between the two $(48\% - 30\% = 18\%)$ does not meet the statistical significance threshold. Hence attitude is regarded as a nondiscriminating quality. Or take a look at self-control—it is weak in 12% of promotable executives and in 21% of inadequate executives. The difference of only 9% is not significant.

It should be again emphasized that both a good attitude and self-control are very necessary executive qualities. But all executives tend to possess them—so they are not helpful in trying to determine promotability.

It should also be noted that in the case of the composite executive, and even more so in regard to the special categories to follow, candidates for promotion should be looked at in terms of *all* the items listed, above and below the double rule. They need a minimum of every quality that shows up as outstanding for promotable executives in the particular category. In every instance there is a certain complex of qualities which people who succeed as executives must have. But it is only the discriminating items which, when present in a candidate to a significant extent, denote the fact that he is more likely to succeed in the new position than other candidates who have significantly less of the same qualities.

MANAGEMENT LEVELS

Generally, the discriminators tend to become more valid and useful as we approach the "local environment" of the executive. Thus, looking at the executive by management levels proves more valuable than regarding him as a composite individual.

Table 2. Distinguishing Characteristics by Management Levels

Characteristic	Top Level		Middle Level		Lower Level	
	Promotable Executives	Inadequate Executives	Promotable Executives	Inadequate Executives	Promotable Executives	Inadequate Executives
For all categories						
Discriminating						
Position performance	64%	11%	47%	6%	39%	2%
Drive	55	22	42	17	50	5
Intellectual ability	58	27	42	6	34	0
Leadership	46	5	40	8	36	5
Administration	55	11	39	6	31	3
Initiative	46	14	33	4	42	7
Motivation	88	14	32	10	30	3
Creativeness	34	8	25	8	34	3
For this category only						
Dependability	63	24	—	—	—	—
Planning	46	19	29	6	31	9
Accomplishment	39	1	—	—	—	—
Quality	40	11	—	—	—	—
Flexibility	—	—	31	6	32	7
Analysis and judgment	—	—	51	12	42	3
Acceptance	—	—	54	15	—	—
Capacity	—	—	—	—	53	5

Percentage Presence as an Outstanding Quality

TABLE 2. Distinguishing Characteristics by Management Levels (Continued)

| | Percentage Presence as an Outstanding Quality | | | | | |
| | Top Level | | Middle Level | | Lower Level | |
Characteristic	Promotable Executives	Inadequate Executives	Promotable Executives	Inadequate Executives	Promotable Executives	Inadequate Executives
	Nondiscriminating					
For all categories						
Dependability	—	—	25%	6%	23%	20%
Self-control	32%	11%	23	4	23	17
Verbal facility	31	27	17	8	14	1
Self-confidence	26	11	11	8	9	1
Sensitivity	32	11	11	2	2	0
Objectivity	16	5	3	4	2	0
For this category only						
Vision	21	8	9	4	4	0
Breadth of knowledge	39	19	33	17	30	15
Quality	—	—	22	6	30	10
Accomplishment	—	—	27	6	16	2

For the 1,427 cases studied, the division according to levels is:

Executive Level	Number	Per cent
Top—presidents, vice presidents, treasurers, secretaries, controllers, etc.	355	25%
Middle—division heads, plant superintendents, chief accountants, chief engineers, etc.	680	48
Lower—department heads, staff assistants, technical assistants, etc.	392	27
Total	1,427	100%

The distinguishing characteristics of executives in various levels are shown in Table 2.

It will be observed that some of these distinguishing qualities run with even strength through all management levels. Drive, initiative, and creativeness are examples. Other qualities tend to vary directly with the management level involved, being especially discriminating at the top. This pattern can be observed in position performance, intellectual ability, leadership, administration, motivation, and planning.

AT THE TOP. Several of the findings concerning the top level call for comment. Of particular significance is motivation, which shows up as an outstanding quality in 88% of promotable executives while appearing in only 14% of inadequate executives. Of the various qualities found at the top, this seems to carry the strongest power of delineation. Perhaps the reason is that the chief executive must have well-planned goals toward which he strives. He must set the course and serve as an example for all others in the management structure.

The absence of flexibility and analysis and judgment from the list of characteristics which discriminate at the top is particularly striking. This does not mean these qualities were not conspicuous at this level, but rather, again, that they occur too uniformly at the top to set promotable executives apart from those who are not promotable.

The top level, finally, is distinguished by three special qualities that fail to discriminate for other levels. These are quality, accomplishment, and dependability. The last of these is distinguishing for no other group into which executives are classified in this study. This is a single exception, and presumably it illustrates the unique need for an outstanding degree of dependability at the top.

MIDDLE AND LOWER. For both the middle and lower levels, flexibility and analysis and judgment are discriminating. The middle level has one distinguishing quality unique to itself—acceptance. The lower level in a similar manner is distinguished by capacity—a quality apparently so unusual at this level that it becomes discriminating.

The forward thinking executive is constantly on the lookout for assistance in making his manpower decisions more accurate. He is alert to standards that can improve the handling of his most important asset—his executive resources. The standards presented here do not approach perfection, for this goal is impossible when dealing with a subject as complex and intangible as executive characteristics. Yet they do provide additional knowledge in an area where there is great need for more reliable information. They provide central tendencies. Used judiciously, they can be of real benefit to the executive seeking help in a most difficult yet critical task.

. . . The thesis [is] advanced [here] that certain qualities indicate promotability in all executives. Other qualities are useful for distinguishing promotable executives at given management levels or in specified functional areas. Still others, in terms of identifying promotability, are sterile. From these various qualities or standards come several aids to improve executive appraisal and selection. . . .

BUREAUCRATIC STRUCTURE AND PERSONALITY

Robert K. Merton

Organizations tend to select and mold individuals to fit need and circumstance. A foremost sociologist considers the possible interaction of highly formalized structures (bureaucracy) and personality.

A formal, rationally organized social structure involves clearly defined patterns of activity in which, ideally, every series of actions

Note: See Notes on the Authors, page 555, and item 156 in the bibliography for the full reference to this selection.

is functionally related to the purposes of the organization.[5] In such an organization there is integrated a series of offices, of hierarchized statuses, in which inhere a number of obligations and privileges closely defined by limited and specific rules. Each of these offices contains an area of imputed competence and responsibility. Authority, the power of control which derives from an acknowledged status, inheres in the office and not in the particular person who performs the official role. Official action ordinarily occurs within the framework of preexisting rules of the organization. The system of prescribed relations between the various offices involves a considerable degree of formality and clearly defined social distance between the occupants of these positions. Formality is manifested by means of a more or less complicated social ritual which symbolizes and supports the "pecking order" of the various offices. Such formality, which is integrated with the distribution of authority within the system, serves to minimize friction by largely restricting (official) contact to modes which are previously defined by the rules of the organization. Ready calculability of others' behavior and a stable set of mutual expectations is thus built up. Moreover, formality facilitates the interaction of the occupants of offices despite their (possibly hostile) private attitudes toward one another. In this way, the subordinate is protected from the arbitrary action of his superior, since the actions of both are constrained by a mutually recognized set of rules. Specific procedural devices foster objectivity and restrain the "quick passage of impulse into action." [6]

The ideal type of such formal organization is bureaucracy and, in many respects, the classical analysis of bureaucracy is that by Max Weber.[7] As Weber indicates, bureaucracy involves a clear-

[5] For a development of the concept of "rational organization," see Karl Mannheim, *Mensch und Gesellschaft im Zeitalter des Umbaus* (Leiden: A. W. Sythoff, 1935), esp. pp. 28 ff.

[6] H. D. Lasswell, *Politics* (New York: McGraw-Hill, 1936), pp. 120–21.

[7] Max Weber, *Wirtschaft und Gesellschaft* (Tubingen: J. C. B. Mohr, 1922), pt. III, chap. 6, pp. 650–678. For a brief summary of Weber's discussion, see Talcott Parsons, *The Structure of Social Action* (New York: McGraw-Hill, 1937), esp. pp. 506 ff. For a description, which is not a caricature, of the bureaucrat as a personality type, see C. Rabany, "Les types sociaux: le fonctionnaire," *Revue generale d' administration*, LXXXVIII (1907), 5–28.

cut division of integrated activities which are regarded as duties inherent in the office. A system of differentiated controls and sanctions is stated in the regulations. The assignment of roles occurs on the basis of technical qualifications which are ascertained through formalized, impersonal procedures (e.g. examinations). Within the structure of hierarchically arranged authority, the activities of "trained and salaried experts" are governed by general, abstract, clearly defined rules which preclude the necessity for the issuance of specific instructions for each specific case. The generality of the rules requires the constant use of *categorization,* whereby individual problems and cases are classified on the basis of designated criteria and are treated accordingly. The pure type of bureaucratic official is appointed, either by a superior or through the exercise of impersonal competition; he is not elected. A measure of flexibility in the bureaucracy is attained by electing higher functionaries who presumably express the will of the electorate (e.g. a body of citizens or a board of directors). The election of higher officials is designed to affect the purposes of the organization, but the technical procedures for attaining these ends are carried out by a continuous bureaucratic personnel.[8]

The bulk of bureaucratic offices involve the expectation of lifelong tenure, in the absence of disturbing factors which may decrease the size of the organization. Bureaucracy maximizes vocational security.[9] The function of security of tenure, pensions, incremental salaries and regularized procedures for promotion is to ensure the devoted performance of official duties, without regard for extraneous pressures.[10] The chief merit of bureaucracy is its technical efficiency, with a premium placed on precision, speed, expert control, continuity, discretion, and optimal returns on input.

[8] Karl Mannheim, *Ideology and Utopia* (New York: Harcourt, Brace, 1936), pp. 18 n., 105 ff. See also Ramsay Muir, *Peers and Bureaucrats* (London: Constable, 1910), pp. 12–13.

[9] E. G. Cahen-Salvador suggests that the personnel of bureaucracies is largely constituted of those who value security above all else. See his "La situation matérielle et morale des fonctionnaires," *Revue politique et parlementaire* (1926), p. 319.

[10] H. J. Laski, "Bureaucracy," *Encyclopedia of the Social Sciences.* This article is written primarily from the standpoint of the political scientist rather than that of the sociologist.

The structure is one which approaches the complete elimination of personalized relationships and nonrational considerations (hostility, anxiety, affectual involvements, etc.).

Bureaucratization is accompanied by the centralization of means of production, as in modern capitalistic enterprise, or as in the case of the post-feudal army, complete separation from the means of destruction. Even the bureaucratically organized scientific laboratory is characterized by the separation of the scientist from his technical equipment.

Bureaucracy is administration which almost completely avoids public discussion of its techniques, although there may occur public discussion of its policies.[11] This "bureaucratic secrecy" is held to be necessary in order to keep valuable information from economic competitors or from foreign and potentially hostile political groups.

In these bold outlines, the positive attainments and functions of bureaucratic organization are emphasized and the internal stresses and strains of such structures are almost wholly neglected. The community at large, however, evidently emphasizes the imperfections of bureaucracy, as is suggested by the fact that the "horrid hybrid," bureaucrat, has become an epithet, a *Schimpfwort*. The transition to a study of the negative aspects of bureaucracy is afforded by the applications of Veblen's concept of "trained incapacity," Dewey's notion of "occupational psychosis" or Warnotte's view of "professional deformation." Trained incapacity refers to that state of affairs in which one's abilities function as inadequacies or blind spots. Actions based upon training and skills which have been successfully applied in the past may result in inappropriate responses *under changed conditions*. An inadequate flexibility in the application of skills will, in a changing milieu, result in more or less serious maladjustments.[12] Thus, to adopt a barnyard illustration used in this connection by Burke, chickens may be readily conditioned to interpret the sound of a bell as a signal for food. The

---

[11] Weber, *op. cit.*, p. 671.

[12] For a stimulating discussion and application of these concepts, see Kenneth Burke, *Permanence and Change* (New York: New Republic, 1935), pp. 50 ff.; Daniel Warnotte, "Bureaucratie et Fonctionnarisme," *Revue de l'Institut de Sociologie*, XVII (1937), 245.

same bell may now be used to summon the "trained chickens" to their doom as they are assembled to suffer decapitation. In general, one adopts measures in keeping with his past training and, under new conditions which are not recognized as *significantly* different, the very soundness of this training may lead to the adoption of the wrong procedures. Again, in Burke's almost echolalic phrase, "people may be unfitted by being fit in an unfit fitness"; their training may become an incapacity.

Dewey's concept of occupational psychosis rests upon much the same observations. As a result of their day to day routines, people develop special preferences, antipathies, discriminations and emphases.[13] (The term psychosis is used by Dewey to denote a "pronounced character of the mind.") These psychoses develop through demands put upon the individual by the particular organization of his occupational role.

The concepts of both Veblen and Dewey refer to a fundamental ambivalence. Any action can be considered in terms of what it attains or what it fails to attain. "A way of seeing is also a way of not seeing—a focus upon object A involves a neglect of object B."[14] In his discussion, Weber is almost exclusively concerned with what the bureaucratic structure attains: precision, reliability, efficiency. This same structure may be examined from another perspective provided by the ambivalence. What are the limitations of the organization designed to attain these goals?

For reasons which we have already noted, the bureaucratic structure exerts a constant pressure upon the official to be "methodical, prudent, disciplined." If the bureaucracy is to operate successfully, it must attain a high degree of reliability of behavior, an unusual degree of conformity with prescribed patterns of action. Hence, the fundamental importance of discipline which may be as highly developed in a religious or economic bureaucracy as in the army. Discipline can be effective only if the ideal patterns are buttressed by strong sentiments which entail devotion to one's duties, a keen sense of the limitation of one's authority and competence, and methodical performance of routine activities. The efficacy of social

[13] *Ibid.*, pp. 58–59.
[14] *Ibid.*, p. 70.

structure depends ultimately upon infusing group participants with appropriate attitudes and sentiments. As we shall see, there are definite arrangements in the bureaucracy for inculcating and reinforcing these sentiments.

At the moment, it suffices to observe that in order to ensure discipline (the necessary reliability of response), these sentiments are often more intense than is technically necessary. There is a margin of safety, so to speak, in the pressure exerted by these sentiments upon the bureaucrat to conform to his patterned obligations, in much the same sense that added allowances (precautionary overestimations) are made by the engineer in designing the supports for a bridge. But this very emphasis leads to a transference of the sentiments from the *aims* of the organization onto the particular details of behavior required by the rules. Adherence to the rules, originally conceived as a means, becomes transformed into an end-in-itself; there occurs the familiar process of *displacement of goals* whereby "an instrumental value becomes a terminal value."[15] Discipline, readily interpreted as conformance with regulations, whatever the situation, is seen not as a measure designed for specific purposes but becomes an immediate value in the life-organization of the bureaucrat. This emphasis, resulting from the

---

[15] This process has often been observed in various connections. Wundt's *heterogony of ends* is a case in point; Max Weber's *Paradoxie der Folgen* is another. See also, MacIver's observations on the transformation of civilization into culture and Lasswell's remark that "the human animal distinguishes himself by his infinite capacity for making ends of his means." See R. K. Merton, "The Unanticipated Consequences of Purposive Social Action," *American Sociological Review,* I (1936), 894–904. In terms of the psychological mechanisms involved, this process has been analyzed most fully by Gordon W. Allport, in his discussion of what he calls "the functional autonomy of motives." Allport amends the earlier formulations of Woodworth, Tolman, and William Stern, and arrives at a statement of the process from the standpoint of individual motivation. He does not consider those phases of the social structure which conduce toward the "transformation of motives." The formulation adopted in this paper is thus complementary to Allport's analysis; the one stressing the psychological mechanisms involved, the other considering the constraints of the social structure. The convergence of psychology and sociology toward the central concept suggests that it may well constitute one of the conceptual bridges between the two disciplines. See Gordon W. Allport, *Personality* (New York: Henry Holt & Co., 1937), chap. 7.

displacement of the original goals, develops into rigidities and an inability to adjust readily. Formalism, even ritualism, ensues with an unchallenged insistence upon punctilious adherence to formalized procedures.[16] This may be exaggerated to the point where primary concern with conformity to the rules interferes with the achievement of the purposes of the organization, in which case we have the familiar phenomenon of the technicism or red tape of the official. An extreme product of this process of displacement of goals is the bureaucratic virtuoso, who never forgets a single rule binding his action and hence is unable to assist many of his clients.[17] A case in point, where strict recognition of the limits of authority and literal adherence to rules produced this result, is the pathetic plight of Bernt Balchen, Admiral Byrd's pilot in the flight over the South Pole.

> According to a ruling of the department of labor Bernt Balchen . . . cannot receive his citizenship papers. Balchen, a native of Norway, declared his intention in 1927. It is held that he has failed to meet the condition of five years' continuous residence in the United States. The Byrd antarctic voyage took him out of the country, although he was on a ship carrying the American flag, was an invaluable member of an American expedition, and in a region to which there is an American claim because of the exploration and occupation of it by Americans, this region being Little America.
>
> The bureau of naturalization explains that it cannot proceed on the assumption that Little America is American soil. That would be *trespass on international questions* where it has no sanction. So far as the bureau is concerned, Balchen was out of the country and *technically* has not complied with the law of naturalization.[18]

Such inadequacies in orientation which involve trained incapacity clearly derive from structural sources. The process may be

[16] See E. C. Hughes, "Institutional Office and the Person," *American Journal of Sociology*, XLIII (1937), 404–413; R. K. Merton, "Social Structure and Anomie," *American Sociological Review*, III (1938), 672–682; E. T. Hiller, "Social Structure in Relation to the Person," *Social Forces*, XVI (1937), 34–44.

[17] Mannheim, *Ideology and Utopia*, p. 106.

[18] Quoted from the *Chicago Tribune* (June 24, 1931, p. 10) by Thurman Arnold, *The Symbols of Government* (New Haven: Yale University Press, 1935), pp. 201–2. (My italics.)

briefly recapitulated. (1) An effective bureaucracy demands reliability of response and strict devotion to regulations. (2) Such devotion to the rules leads to their transformation into absolutes; they
are no longer conceived as relative to a given set of purposes.
(3) This interferes with ready adaptation under special conditions
not clearly envisaged by those who drew up the general rules.
(4) Thus, the very elements which conduce toward efficiency in
general produce inefficiency in specific instances. Full realization of
the inadequacy is seldom attained by members of the group who
have not divorced themselves from the "meanings" which the rules
have for them. These rules in time become symbolic in cast, rather
than strictly utilitarian.

Thus far, we have treated the ingrained sentiments making for
rigorous discipline simply as data, as given. However, definite
features of the bureaucratic structure may be seen to conduce to
these sentiments. The bureaucrat's official life is planned for him in
terms of a graded career, through the organizational devices of
promotion by seniority, pensions, incremental salaries, *etc.,* all of
which are designed to provide incentives for disciplined action and
conformity to the official regulations.[19] The official is tacitly expected to and largely does adapt his thoughts, feelings, and actions
to the prospect of this career. But *these very devices* which increase
the probability of conformance also lead to an over-concern with
strict adherence to regulations which induces timidity, conservatism, and technicism. Displacement of sentiments from goals onto
means is fostered by the tremendous symbolic significance of the
means (rules).

Another feature of the bureaucratic structure tends to produce
much the same result. Functionaries have the sense of a common
destiny for all those who work together. They share the same interests, especially since there is relatively little competition insofar
as promotion is in terms of seniority. In-group aggression is thus
minimized and this arrangement is therefore conceived to be positively functional for the bureaucracy. However, the esprit de corps

[19] Mannheim, *Mensch und Gesellschaft,* pp. 32–33, stresses the importance
of the "Lebensplan" and the "Amtskarriere." See the comments by Hughes,
op. cit., 413.

and informal social organization which typically develops in such situations often leads the personnel to defend their entrenched interests rather than to assist their clientele and elected higher officials. As President Lowell reports, if the bureaucrats believe that their status is not adequately recognized by an incoming elected official, detailed information will be withheld from him, leading him to errors for which he is held responsible. Or, if he seeks to dominate fully, and thus violates the sentiment of self-integrity of the bureaucrats, he may have documents brought to him in such numbers that he cannot manage to sign them all, let alone read them.[20] This illustrates the defensive informal organization which tends to arise whenever there is an apparent threat to the integrity of the group.[21]

It would be much too facile and partly erroneous to attribute such resistance by bureaucrats simply to vested interests. Vested interests oppose any new order which either eliminates or at least makes uncertain their differential advantage deriving from the current arrangements. This is undoubtedly involved in part in bureaucratic resistance to change but another process is perhaps more significant. As we have seen, bureaucratic officials affectively identify themselves with their way of life. They have a pride of craft which leads them to resist change in established routines; at least, those changes which are felt to be imposed by coworkers. This nonlogical pride of craft is a familiar pattern found even, to judge from Sutherland's *Professional Thief,* among pickpockets who, despite the risk, delight in mastering the prestige-bearing feat of "beating a left breech" (picking the left front trousers pocket).

In a stimulating paper, Hughes has applied the concepts of "secular" and "sacred" to various types of divisions of labor; "the sacredness" of caste and *Stände* prerogatives contrasts sharply with the increasing secularism of occupational differentiation in our mo-

---

[20] A. L. Lowell, *The Government of England* (New York, 1908), I, 189 ff.

[21] For an instructive description of the development of such a defensive organization in a group of workers, see F. J. Roethlisberger and W. J. Dickson, *Management and the Worker* (Boston: Harvard School of Business Administration, 1934).

bile society.[22] However, as our discussion suggests, there may ensue, in particular vocations and in particular types of organization, the *process of sanctification* (viewed as the counterpart of the process of secularization). This is to say that through sentiment-formation, emotional dependence upon bureaucratic symbols and status, and affective involvement in spheres of competence and authority, there develop prerogatives involving attitudes of moral legitimacy which are established as values in their own right, and are no longer viewed as merely technical means for expediting administration. One may note a tendency for certain bureaucratic norms, originally introduced for technical reasons, to become rigidified and sacred, although, as Durkheim would say, they are *laïque en apparence.*[23] Durkheim has touched on this general process in his description of the attitudes and values which persist in the organic solidarity of a highly differentiated society.

Another feature of the bureaucratic structure, the stress on depersonalization of relationships, also plays its part in the bureaucrat's trained incapacity. The personality pattern of the bureaucrat is nucleated about this norm of impersonality. Both this and the categorizing tendency, which develops from the dominant role of general, abstract rules, tend to produce conflict in the bureaucrat's contacts with the public or clientele. Since functionaries minimize personal relations and resort to categorization, the peculiarities of individual cases are often ignored. But the client who, quite understandably, is convinced of the "special features" of *his* own problem often objects to such categorical treatment. Stereotyped behavior is

[22] E. C. Hughes, "Personality Types and the Division of Labor," *American Journal of Sociology,* XXXIII (1928), 754–768. Much the same distinction is drawn by Leopold von Wiese and Howard Becker, *Systematic Sociology* (New York: John Wiley & Sons, 1932), pp. 222–25 *et passim.*

[23] Hughes recognizes one phrase of this process of sanctification when he writes that professional training "carries with it as a by-product assimilation of the candidate to a set of professional attitudes and controls, *a professional conscience and solidarity. The profession claims and aims to become a moral unit.*" Hughes, *op. cit.,* p. 762 (italics inserted). In this same connection, Sumner's concept of *pathos,* as the halo of sentiment which protects a social value from criticism, is particularly relevant, inasmuch as it affords a clue to the mechanisms involved in the process of sanctification. See his *Folkways* (Boston: Ginn & Co., 1906), pp. 180–181.

72

not adapted to the exigencies of individual problems. The impersonal treatment of affairs which are at times of great personal significance to the client gives rise to the charge of "arrogance" and "haughtiness" of the bureaucrat. Thus, at the Greenwich Employment Exchange, the unemployed worker who is securing his insurance payment resents what he deems to be "the impersonality and, at times, the apparent abruptness and even harshness of his treatment by the clerks. . . . Some men complain of the superior attitude which the clerks have."[24]

Still another source of conflict with the public derives from the bureaucratic structure. The bureaucrat, in part irrespective of his position with*in* the hierarchy, acts as a representative of the power and prestige of the entire structure. In his official role he is vested with definite authority. This often leads to an actually or apparently domineering attitude, which may only be exaggerated by a discrepancy between his position within the hierarchy and his position with reference to the public.[25] Protest and recourse to other officials on the part of the client are often ineffective or largely precluded by the previously mentioned esprit de corps which joins the officials

[24] " 'They treat you like a lump of dirt they do. I see a navvy reach across the counter and shake one of them by the collar the other day. The rest of us felt like cheering. Of course he lost his benefit over it. . . . But the clerk deserved it for his sassy way.' " (E. W. Bakke, *The Unemployed Man,* New York: Dutton, 1934, pp. 79–80). Note that the domineering attitude was *imputed* by the unemployed client who is in a state of tension due to his loss of status and self-esteem in a society where the ideology is still current that an "able man" can always find a job. That the imputation of arrogance stems largely from the client's state of mind is seen from Bakke's own observation that "the clerks were rushed, and had no time for pleasantries, but there was little sign of harshness or a superiority feeling in their treatment of the men. . . ."

[25] In this connection, note the relevance of Koffka's comments on certain features of the pecking-order of birds. "If one compares the behavior of the bird at the top of the pecking list, the despot, with that of one very far down, the second or third from the last, then one finds the latter much more cruel to the few others over whom he lords it than the former in his treatment of all members. As soon as one removes from the group all members above the penultimate, his behavior becomes milder and may even become very friendly. . . . It is not difficult to find analogies to this in human societies, and therefore one side of such behavior must be primarily the effects of the social groupings, and not of individual characteristics." K. Koffka, *Principles of Gestalt Psychology* (New York: Harcourt, Brace, 1935), pp. 668–9.

into a more or less solidary in-group. This source of conflict *may* be minimized in private enterprise since the client can register an effective protest by transferring his trade to another organization within the competitive system. But with the monopolistic nature of the public organization, no such alternative is possible. Moreover, in this case, tension is increased because of a discrepancy between ideology and fact: the governmental personnel are held to be "servants of the people," but in fact they are usually superordinate, and release of tension can seldom be afforded by turning to other agencies for the necessary service.[26] This tension is in part attributable to the confusion of status of bureaucrat and client; the client may consider himself socially superior to the official who is at the moment dominant.[27]

Thus, with respect to the relations between officials and clientele, one structural source of conflict is the pressure for formal and impersonal treatment when individual, personalized consideration is desired by the client. The conflict may be viewed, then, as deriving from the introduction of inappropriate attitudes and relationships. Conflict with*in* the bureaucratic structure arises from the converse situation, namely, when personalized relationships are substituted for the structurally required impersonal relationships. This type of conflict may be characterized as follows.

The bureaucracy, as we have seen, is organized as a secondary, formal group. The normal responses involved in this organized network of social expectations are supported by affective attitudes of members of the group. Since the group is oriented toward secondary norms of impersonality, any failure to conform to these norms will arouse antagonism from those who have identified them-

[26] At this point the political machine often becomes functionally significant. As Steffens and others have shown, highly personalized relations and the abrogation of formal rules (red tape) by the machine often satisfy the needs of individual "clients" more fully than the formalized mechanism of government bureaucracy.

[27] As one of the unemployed men remarked about the clerks at the Greenwich Employment Exchange: " 'And the bloody blokes wouldn't have their jobs if it wasn't for us men out of a job either. That's what gets me about their holding their noses up.' " Bakke, *op. cit.,* p. 80.

selves with the legitimacy of these rules. Hence, the substitution of personal for impersonal treatment within the structure is met with widespread disapproval and is characterized by such epithets as graft, favoritism, nepotism, apple-polishing, etc. These epithets are clearly manifestations of injured sentiments.[28] The function of such "automatic resentment" can be clearly seen in terms of the requirements of bureaucratic structure.

Bureaucracy is a secondary group structure designed to carry on certain activities which cannot be satisfactorily performed on the basis of primary group criteria.[29] Hence behavior which runs counter to these formalized norms becomes the object of emotionalized disapproval. This constitutes a functionally significant defense set up against tendencies which jeopardize the performance of socially necessary activities. To be sure, these reactions are not rationally determined practices explicitly designed for the fulfilment of this function. Rather, viewed in terms of the individual's interpretation of the situation, such resentment is simply an immediate response opposing the "dishonesty" of those who violate the rules of the game. However, this subjective frame of reference notwithstanding, these reactions serve the latent function of maintaining the essential structural elements of bureaucracy by reaffirming the necessity for formalized, secondary relations and by helping to prevent the disintegration of the bureaucratic structure which would occur should these be supplanted by personalized relations. This type of conflict may be generically described as the intrusion of primary group attitudes when secondary group atti-

---

[28] The diagnostic significance of such linguistic indices as epithets has scarcely been explored by the sociologist. Sumner properly observes that epithets produce "summary criticisms" and definitions of social situations. Dollard also notes that "epithets frequently define the central issues in a society," and Sapir has rightly emphasized the importance of context of situations in appraising the significance of epithets. Of equal relevance is Linton's observation that "in case histories the way in which the community felt about a particular episode is, if anything, more important to our study than the actual behavior. . . ." A sociological study of "vocabularies of encomium and opprobrium" should lead to valuable findings.

[29] *Cf.* Ellsworth Faris, *The Nature of Human Nature* (New York: McGraw-Hill, 1937), pp. 41 ff.

tudes are institutionally demanded, just as the bureaucrat-client conflict often derives from interaction on impersonal terms when personal treatment is individually demanded.[30]

The trend toward increasing bureaucratization in Western society, which Weber had long since foreseen, is not the sole reason for sociologists to turn their attention to this field. Empirical studies of the interaction of bureaucracy and personality should especially increase our understanding of social structure. A large number of specific questions invite our attention. To what extent are particular personality types selected and modified by the various bureaucracies (private enterprise, public service, the quasi-legal political machine, religious orders)? Inasmuch as ascendancy and submission are held to be traits of personality, despite their variability in different stimulus-situations, do bureaucracies select personalities of particularly submissive or ascendant tendencies? And since various studies have shown that these traits can be modified, does participation in bureaucratic office tend to increase ascendant tendencies? Do various systems of recruitment (e.g. patronage, open competition involving specialized knowledge or "general mental capacity," practical experience) select different personality types? Does promotion through seniority lessen competitive anxieties and enhance administrative efficiency? A detailed examination of mechanisms for imbuing the bureaucratic codes with affect would be instructive both sociologically and psychologically. Does the general anonymity of civil service decisions tend to restrict the area of prestige-symbols to a narrowly defined inner circle? Is there a tendency for differential association to be especially marked among bureaucrats?

The range of theoretically significant and practically important questions would seem to be limited only by the accessibility of the

---

[30] Community disapproval of many forms of behavior may be analyzed in terms of one or the other of these patterns of substitution of culturally inappropriate types of relationship. Thus, prostitution constitutes a type-case where coitus, a form of intimacy which is institutionally defined as symbolic of the most "sacred" primary group relationship, is placed within a contractual context, symbolized by the exchange of that most impersonal of all symbols, money. See Kingsley Davis. "The Sociology of Prostitution," *American Sociological Review,* II (1937), 744–55.

concrete data. Studies of religious, educational, military, economic, and political bureaucracies dealing with the interdependence of social organization and personality formation should constitute an avenue for fruitful research. On that avenue, the functional analysis of concrete structures may yet build a Solomon's House for sociologists.

Chapter 3

THE CAREER LINE:

OCCUPATIONAL AND

SOCIAL MOBILITY

INTRODUCTION

The individual careers of all men in Western industrial societies closely reflect and express the kind of society in which they occur. If the economic order is free and open or high position restricted to the few and advancement slow, biographies and personal experiences reveal these social differences. More often than not the careers of executives can be viewed as occupational movement into positions vacated by those who have moved up.

Study of occupational succession with its various rules and phases of entrance, occupancy, and exit is necessary to understand and interpret the individual careers of business executives. However, personality plays its positive and negative part in determining the career of the executive even though the career lines necessarily follow rather closely the accepted paths of achievement and advancement. An individual's social characteristics as well as personal qualities are evaluated by his peers and superiors and are themselves of enormous importance in his success or failure. Is he a bright man, can he relate effectively to those around him, and can he make good decisions easily?

A whole melange of social factors are also operative and of the highest importance in the development of his career. Is he from the wrong side of the tracks? If so, what is the effect? Does he have highly placed relatives in the firm and does he have an Ivy League education? Did he marry well and did this accelerate or impede his movement to higher position?

In brief, what kind of people get to the top? What are their *social* characteristics? And what is the effect of the different kinds of industrial organizations on men with different backgrounds and their advancement? What happens to the freewheeling enterpriser and the tycoon of legend or the precisely and properly trained business school graduate in a bureaucracy? Finally, what are the patterns of mobility in the infinite variety of situations that make up the continuing life of business enterprise?

The several selections in this chapter cover a wide area of knowledge about the careers of executives. Inquiries and answers are given about occupational succession, the observed patterns of executive mobility, the social and economic characteristics of American big businessmen, as well as the business elite in business bureaucracies. In the last selection we see John P. Marquand's banker hero, Charles Gray, at the moment when he moves into high executive position. We learn from Charles and his wife what it is like and how it feels when it happens.

OCCUPATIONAL SUCCESSION

W. Lloyd Warner and James C. Abegglen

The rules of occupational succession cannot be properly understood in purely economic terms. The factors of family, of father and son, and the relations of generations are involved.

. . . *Occupational succession* [is that] ordered process by which individuals succeed each other in occupations. The study of occupational succession, therefore, consists of examining the circulation and movement of personnel through positions, and of de-

Note: See Notes on the Authors, pages 557 and 551, and item 244 in the bibliography for the full reference to this selection.

termining the regularities and uniformities which have to do with entering, holding, and leaving a given status. In the present discussion we are concerned with a *type* of status, the big business owner and manager, and with but one kind of elite, the business and owning class. More particularly, this investigation of occupational succession is concerned with how this society orders and determines which men, through the changing generations of individuals, shall occupy certain occupational statuses.

To found our investigation soundly, it is necessary to relate occupational theory, particularly that of occupational succession, to theory of family structure, for the two are interdependent. Men are born to fathers who are at given occupational levels, they grow to maturity, learn and follow a particular profession in life, marry, sire sons who are reared to maturity and work at their own trades or professions. We shall extend our view back to the preceding generation so that the fathers of the present business elite are also related to their fathers; thus we shall be examining three generations. At the level of fact and evidence we shall be examining a particular man, and at times his paternal grandfather and his father, and their occupations.

Meanwhile we will expand our evidence by studying occupational succession throughout all industries and all regions of the United States. Broad as well as limited generalizations are thus possible and can be scientifically formed about occupational succession and the activities of the ambitious. We can thus place a particular man or a particular occupation into a more general category, such as a generation or region; we can see the individual in his appropriate universe and compare his occupational level with that of other individuals; or we can move to more abstract levels and relate any of the facts about a particular man to the whole occupational structure of the United States. This, of course, is always in terms of the limitations set up by the research, the study of occupational succession and the American business elite.

What has just been said needs more theoretical and technical treatment. The kinship dimension does not change through life: the position of fathers and sons or of wives' fathers and their daughters remains structurally the same. Although their behavior through the years changes, their positions are fixed by a biological base socially recognized in the kinship structure. No matter how great the occupational or social distance may become, they always remain a birth cycle[1] apart. A birth cycle is a unit of *time* between one's own birth and one's procreation of another individual. Consequently the movement or lack of movement among occupations can be measured timewise by use of the birth cycle. The type of occupational status of each son will be the same as, or different from, his father's. Each man marries a woman who is the daughter of a man of either the same or different status.

If there is no difference between the positions of the son and father, and they hold occupations at the same level, there has been no movement and no occupational distance separates them. If there has been movement, the distance and its direction (up, down, or across) can be identified and measured. The men who moved from the working class of their fathers to the business elite, and thus in one birth cycle moved upward through several loosely defined occupational strata, were mobile at a far more rapid rate than those who rose to the business elite from the white-collar class of their fathers after the fathers had risen from the laboring group. The distance covered was the same, the direction taken the same, but the time involved was cut in half and the velocity accordingly doubled.

Since the occupational movement of fathers and sons can be identified and measured, it is possible to measure the amount of movement from different occupational distances into the elite. This is accomplished by equating all business leaders as sons (in the family universe) of one generation and their fathers as the generation "above" in occupational succession. This being operationally feasible, the amount of movement from each occupational level into the elite can be measured, as well as the time it took in terms of one or two generations (or of the years within a lifetime).

---

[1] Kingsley Davis and W. Lloyd Warner, "Structural Analysis of Kinship," *American Anthropologist*, XXXIX, 2 (April–June, 1937), 291–313.

Equally important, the immobility of occupational succession in the business elite can be determined.

At further levels of generalization we will be able to speak of the characteristics of the top occupational status and of kinds of movement out of it and into it from the rest of the occupational universe.

Children are born to the social and economic position of their parents; it is therefore possible, by ascertaining the parents' status, to learn whether men of the elite are all from families of similar positions or from families of different positions. Since a family's socioeconomic position is largely dependent on the father's occupational place in the economic order, it is possible to examine the life careers of the men of the elite and to trace their present status back through their occupational history to the time when they were children and still dependent on, and identified with, the status of their fathers and their families.[2]

The biological level, composed of parents and children, more particularly fathers and sons, provides a consistent unit of measurement for the occupational nearness and distance, closure and access, existing between two or more generations. When this unit of measurement is combined with a time unit such as the age of the business leader when he achieved a position in the elite, the velocity of movement as well as the direction and amount may be determined and the degree of occupational *dispersal* measured. The occupational *dispersal* of three generations of fathers and sons may be confined to one occupational level, to two, or spread from the top to the bottom. The velocity may be spoken of as measurable by one, two, or three generations of time for any occupational movement. The *direction* of movement of fathers and sons may be *all* upward, or up and down. But all of it will always be seen from the position of those who belong *now* to the present business elite. We will see their lives and the generations out of which they come from the perspective of their present position. Consequently our

---

[2] The problem involved is occupational mobility and, more generally, occupational succession. However, when occupational mobility takes place usually social mobility takes place too; consequently we have sometimes referred to this as social mobility, following general practice. The reader, however, can determine by context when we are referring quite specifically to one or the other. . . .

study is limited. It does not try to examine the careers of the men who are presently at other levels. It does not present, for example, the social backgrounds or careers of white-collar men or workers who have or have not tried to advance themselves to the business elite. Nor can it say whether all the sons of professional men would or would not welcome the opportunity to acquire the prestige, the honor, and the power of status in the elite.

Another way by which the relation of the occupations of one generation to those of the succeeding ones may be examined is to learn the occupation of the wife's father. The fathers of the wives of the present elite (and the mothers of the sons of the elite) provided the occupational origins of the women who greatly influenced the occupational careers of the men studied. A study of the women these men marry also helps determine whether the men (1) move into the elite by marriage and possibly acquire their high position without earning it; (2) achieve elite position and then marry a woman at their newly acquired rank; or (3) marry either at their level of origin, or someone along the route to high position. Hence the study of the occupational succession of males to the elite must also be a research on the women who marry them. Some women from the lower occupational origins marry men born to the elite, others marry men of low origins, and some women of the elite marry men of their own occupational class.

Occupation, marriage, and descent are inextricably interwoven into *one* status-giving system since all members of the family are classified as similar or the same for basic purposes of social identification. Should the sons and daughters inherit their family's occupational rank, should the rules of marriage require that they mate with those of the same occupational level, and should these occupational orders be ranked, the combination of endogamy and occupational inheritance would conform to one type of caste system. There would be no movement from one level to another. Such a system would be closed. No occupational status would be open to those above or below it. There would be no vertical *status* movement.

At the other pole would be a system in which there were no formal or informal rules, beliefs, or values separating those who wish to marry or preventing men at any level and occupation from moving to any other. There is no such system existing in the world. Our own system of marriage and occupational succession falls between these two extremes.

From these considerations, we can distinguish (and validate empirically) several types and varieties of elite in the American business world. Each type may be re-divided, according to scientific purpose, into subcategories based upon kind of industry, region, ethnic group, education, and other such factors.

From the point of view of personnel at the elite level, there are two major types: the birth elite and the mobile elite. The birth elite is divided into two major types: recent, of one generation; and old, of two or more generations. The mobile elite includes those men who achieved the position by movement into it from positions outside it, usually but not always from occupations lower than the present one. Men coming to the elite from the laboring, white-collar, and small business classes rise of course to this higher level; most men coming from the farming classes also rise to the status.

But some men, possibly a minority, from the professional classes move laterally, not vertically, into the business elite. This is so because sons of men in high-ranking professions and government positions and sons of a small percentage of farmers are by the judgments of our culture ranked equally with those of the business elite. The son or daughter of a banker or of the president of a great business enterprise, when marrying the daughter or son of a prominent lawyer or government official or high military officer, does not necessarily marry beneath him; *socially* he may be marrying above himself.

Since marriage may be important in the rise of the mobile man, several subtypes of *mobile* elite in terms of marriage need to be distinguished. They are (1) those who rose from the lowest level to the top of the business world and who (a) married women of their own level, (b) married women from levels between their own and the top, or (c) married women after they arrived (or when they achieved top status); (2) men from the white-collar, (3) small business, and (4) farming classes who climbed to the elite and who married women below them, at their own, at an intervening, or at the elite level; (5) men from the professional group (including, among others, government officers, military men, doctors, and lawyers) and a few farmers who moved *across* and into (or up to) the business elite and married women at the top or at some lower level.

Those statuses which are impossible, or almost so, for those outside to enter we shall call closed. Those not so limited we shall call open and free. The status of a person may be fixed in one position. When an individual can move he is comparatively free—that is, his position is not fixed.

The movement up we shall call *achieved status* or *achieved occupation*.[3] Occupational succession of the business elite means either continuance of sons at their fathers' positions in the elite or a movement of men from outside into such positions. The continuation in the same position may be accompanied by marriage to someone at the same level (endogamy) or to someone outside it.[4] If the latter, it may be to one equivalent to, or below, the elite.

PATTERNS OF MOBILITY WITHIN INDUSTRIAL ORGANIZATIONS

Norman H. Martin and Anselm L. Strauss

All advancement to higher goals is not necessarily up. The route to vertical mobility may be across—horizontal. The problem for the individual executive is to be able to assess the meaning of a given pattern of movement for his success.

[3] Ralph Linton, *The Study of Man* (New York: D. Appleton-Century Co., 1936).

[4] The term "same", which we have frequently used, needs further scrutiny, for it has two meanings in this context. It may mean that a son inherits or acquires the identical position in the same firm so that, for example, when his father retires from that position, the son becomes president and owner of the A.B.C. Shoe Manufacturing Company. It also can mean that the son acquires the same *kind* (category) of position as the father. He may become a business executive in another large firm and thus achieve a similar position in the same ranked category.

Note: See Notes on the Authors, pages 555 and 556, and item 152 in the bibliography for the full reference to this selection.

The organizational structure of an industrial enterprise has dual and interrelated functions. From the standpoint of management, it provides for an orderly hierarchy of responsibility and authority— a division of work rationally planned to meet the objectives of efficient operation. Vertical and horizontal movement of personnel through the various positions making up the organization is executed so as to make certain that competent men get in the right places at the right time. From the standpoint of the individual member, on the other hand, organization provides a stable set of expectations as to how they, as well as others, should act. Of equal importance, it provides a number of channels through which mobile individuals can move to realize personal objectives.[5]

This paper centers specifically upon the mobility aspects of industrial organization—upon the patterned movements of personnel within companies. It aims at developing a frame of reference for the interpretation and understanding of the phenomena of mobility within organizations.[6]

THE DEVELOPMENT OF CAREER LINES

Over time, the paths of movement of personnel through the system of positions making up a company's organization structure tend to become more or less stabilized. Patterns of vertical and horizontal movement evolve, to form various types of career lines which terminate at various levels of the management hierarchy. These career lines, which are somewhat analogous to the trunks and branches of trees, provide escalators for mobile individuals.

[5] This point of view has received considerable attention (see Chester I. Barnard, *The Functions of the Executive* [Cambridge: Harvard University Press, 1947]).

[6] A considerable literature on occupational mobility has developed within recent years. Perhaps the most comprehensive general work on this subject is W. Lloyd Warner and James C. Abegglen, *Occupational Mobility in American Business and Industry* (Minneapolis: University of Minnesota Press, 1955). Two other works may be cited: Oswald Hall, "The Informal Organization of Medical Practice in an American City: Case Study of a Profession" (unpublished Ph.D. dissertation, Department of Sociology, University of Chicago, 1944), and Howard S. Becker, "Role and Career Problems of the Chicago Public School Teacher" (unpublished Ph.D. dissertation, Department of Sociology, University of Chicago, 1952).

The majority of these lines are minor and terminate at lower executive levels; others move beyond these positions and branch off into middle management; a few major lines lead to the top. A typical career line consists of a series of vertical and horizontal movements from position to position, i.e., vertical movement from section leader to department head within a given division; horizontal movements from department head to department head in different divisions; following this, vertical movement to division head; and so on. Ideally, horizontal mobility—the movement of an individual laterally along a given level of management—gives that person breadth of experience. Vertical mobility, of course, is movement of an individual up or down in the management hierarchy and consists of shifts from one level of responsibility to another.

Within the total complex of positions, certain ones operate as critical junctures or testing points. The performance of the individual at these crucial points determines the type of career line along which he will move—whether he moves on along a line to intermediate or higher management, horizontally to other line or staff jobs, or terminates his career at the level involved.

Typically, these turning points are quasi-training positions. For example, in the production division of one large company, the positions of assistant division manager and plant superintendent serve this function. Management can directly observe the individual being considered for higher management. They can determine his capacity to handle complex human relationships, to assume the initiative in unstructured situations, to handle responsibility, and to be adept at long-range decision-making—all of which are characteristic situations confronting higher management. If his performance is judged to be satisfactory, he moves into a line of progression leading to higher management; if it is somewhat less than satisfactory, he may be moved horizontally for further testing and training, or he may be moved into the next highest position, to remain there for the duration of his career.

At any given level in the executive hierarchy alternative channels of potential movement are present. In some instances these channels are multiple; the individual may move in any one of several directions—vertically or horizontally. In other instances the alternatives are more restricted and may even be closed. They are dead ends. This frequently happens in highly specialized types of jobs. In the case of those positions which function as critical turning points, numerous alternative paths of movement exist. This is necessary so that management can protect itself in cases where they have mistakenly judged the competence of an individual.

In order to make certain that competent and trained individuals move into the right places at the right time, more or less exact and differential training is provided at the various positions. At certain levels this takes the form of highly technical training in specific functions and areas; at others it is oriented toward the development of breadth of experience. This locus is related to a number of variables: the technological requirements of the industry, the type of organization, and the mobility structure.

For example, in one organization with a complex technology and division of labor, the pattern of movement of mobile personnel through lower levels of management is primarily vertical. Little horizontal movement occurs. Training is highly specialized. A primary concern of the management is to make certain that its first-line supervision is technically specialized. Interdepartmental coordination consequently becomes a primary function and the responsibility of middle management.

In contrast, another organization with a relatively simple technology has developed a mobility pattern in which a high degree of horizontal mobility exists at the lower executive levels. The aim of training here is to achieve a variety of experience in first-level supervision and, by so doing, to localize responsibility for coordination well down in the management hierarchy. Its organization structure is relatively flat. In both instances, therefore, a relationship holds between mobility structure, technology, organization philosophy, and type of training. It becomes a major problem in management to achieve the right blending of these components.

The speed at which individuals move along specific career lines tends to follow fairly identifiable timetables. Acceptable age ranges are identifiable for the various strata. While these age ranges are not usually defined explicitly, they nonetheless exist in terms of some of the criteria used by management in determining who moves and who does not. A given individual being considered for advancement may, for example, be passed over because he is "too old" or, less frequently, "too young." If an individual does not move out of a given position and into another by a certain age, there will be a high probability that he will never move farther. He will, in a sense, have his mobility terminated at that level.

The existence of these career timetables enables individuals to assess their mobility prospects and even to predict their chances of advancement to higher levels. A person who does not progress in accordance with these age timetables may know, therefore, that his potential for higher levels of management has been judged unfavorably.

In general, individuals who ultimately reach higher levels in the management hierarchy tend to move rapidly along specific career lines leading to the top. Warner and Abegglen in their studies of occupational mobility in American business and industry note: "Within fifteen years of becoming self-supporting, more than half of the men studied were major executives and a quarter were minor executives."[7]

In order to facilitate the progression of men into higher executive levels and still achieve requisite competence, a skipping of levels may frequently be observed. An individual moves in an orderly manner from one position to the next and from level to level up to a point. He then moves around a given layer of management to a higher position in the hierarchy. In this manner relatively young men assume top-management responsibilities.

Horizontal and vertical movements, therefore, mesh and mutually support each other. On the one hand, horizontal movement may be thought of as being in the service of the vertical in the sense that a company is concerned with training and educating people and testing potential executives. They are also finding terminal places for mediocrity and taking care of those who were misjudged or who faded out. Gaps created by unforeseen circumstances must be filled by trained individuals with a minimum of delay, trouble spots taken care of by shifting versatile men along the line. On the other hand, although perhaps in a more minor sense, we may con-

[7] Warner and Abegglen, *op. cit.*, pp. 116–117.

ceptualize the vertical system as being in the service of the horizontal. It is essential that the executive positions in all the various divisions of a company be staffed by competent and trained personnel. Major and minor career lines exist. These lines siphon off executives into the various levels and divisions. Thus there must be more or less permanent works managers and division superintendents; likewise there must be general foremen and plant superintendents. These people come from off the major vertical ladder—either on their way up or on their way off; others move directly into these positions via subsidiary and more minor career lines. From the standpoint of the student of organization, all these interlocking horizontal and vertical movements add up to an organized system.

At this point it may be well to cite a concrete illustration of some of the already made points. Our example is a large, multi-plant industry engaged in the production of automobile parts. Movement of personnel through the lower levels of the management hierarchy is almost exclusively vertical. Little or no horizontal mobility exists at these lower levels. When it does occur, it tends to be limited to movement within one plant and between departments and is an indicator of unsatisfactory performance.[8] The position of general foreman (the top position at foremen levels) is the initial juncture or crossroad for mobile personnel. Individuals whose performance is highly satisfactory move on into superintendencies or may even jump beyond into higher positions. Those judged to be less competent may be shifted horizontally or may stay where they are.

Considerable horizontal movement of personnel occurs at the middle-management levels. Indeed here, in contrast to lower levels, failure to move horizontally is an indicator of only mediocre performance. This horizontal mobility occurs not only within the various departments and divisions of a single plant but also between plants. It brings about breadth of experience and also en-

---

[8] The situation is analogous to that frequently encountered in officer candidate schools during World War II. A candidate about whom there was some doubt as to capacity was given a series of trials in various positions. Horizontal mobility was an indicator of possible failure.

ables management to judge the potential of the men and to decide whether they should be moved into branch lines terminating in middle management or into career channels leading to top executive positions. This level is therefore a second critical juncture. At the higher executive levels the pattern of movement again tends to be primarily vertical.

Identifiable timetables of progression exist. Individuals must have moved through the foreman ranks and be ready for middle management at latest by the time they are around thirty-five years of age. Otherwise they tend to remain in lower-management positions. Between the ages of thirty and forty, they perform at middle-management levels and are seasoned, as it were, by a variety of experience. Upward movement out of this level must generally occur before the individual reaches forty or, at a maximum, forty-five.

In the company being discussed the main career line to the top centers in the largest of the plants. Most top executives have received the bulk of their training here. From the standpoint of the mobile individual it becomes imperative that sooner or later he get into the career lines of that plant. The characteristics of this career line, therefore, are quite specific: movement up is relatively rapid and clearly defined; youthful age limits circumscribe times by which movement must be made; horizontal mobility at certain crucial junctures is well planned to insure adequate training and testing; the final sequence of positions centers within the largest of the several plants.

In addition to this main career line, branch-off lines lead to middle-management positions. Movements along these lines are not so rapid as that characterizing those who move higher. At some point or other along the career line a faltering or a stumbling occurred, with the result that extra horizontal mobility was necessary. Sometimes these men were held at a given position well beyond the critical age range; at other times they were blocked by competitors who were more powerfully sponsored. On the other hand, some of these career lines are purely local. Movement is confined to one of the smaller plants.

THE MOBILITY STRUCTURE FROM THE STANDPOINT OF THE INDIVIDUAL

From the standpoint of the mobile individual—the person ambitious to move ahead and up—the established patterns of movement in an organization present avenues of advancement. The perceptive individual can, for the most part, determine the channels through which he must move in order to realize his personal ambitions. Cues by which he can assess his own position and his potential for future advancement exist in a variety of forms.

One fundamental cue is the pattern of advancement already established—the complex of vertical and horizontal movements leading to specific levels of management. This, coupled with the timetables setting the ages at which movement must take place, enables him to judge his own progress. Given a stable organization, he can frequently do this with considerable accuracy.

Other cues are more subtle. At times it is difficult to determine whether a movement is a promotion or a demotion. This is especially true when we realize that too much horizontal mobility may actually act as a demotion unless it is coupled with ultimate vertical movement. The individual is growing older, and his mobility potential thereby becomes more limited because of the existence of timetables of advancement. In some industries this is so clearly realized that young executives refuse to accept more than one or two horizontal movements.

A similar comment is applicable to movements into staff positions. These positions are frequently filled by individuals who have not "made the grade" in the line. Such personnel, however, are mixed with others who are definitely competent and are there for clear reasons of function. It requires considerable discernment on the part of the mobile individual to determine the category into which he falls.

From the standpoint of pure tactics, the mobile individual would do well to become attached to a sponsor—an individual in a superior position who can pull him along. Over and beyond this, he must also acquire the ways of behavior acceptable to higher management. This means that he must, in a sense, secede from the ways of thinking and behavior of the management level in which he holds membership and adopt, instead, the norms and orientation of the level to which he aspires. A sort of "anticipatory socialization" must occur; the values of the higher group are taken as a fundamental frame of reference by the mobile person. This process, however, is not without its difficulties. Merton brilliantly characterizes the difficulty as follows:

What the individual experiences as estrangement from a group of which he is a member tends to be experienced by his associates as repudiation of the group, and this ordinarily evokes a hostile response. As social relations between the individual and the rest of the group deteriorate, the norms of the group become less binding for him. For since he is progressively seceding from the group and being penalized by it, he is the less likely to experience rewards for adherence to the group's norms. Once initiated, this process seems to move toward a cumulative detachment from the group, in terms of attitudes and values as well as in terms of social relations. And to the degree that he orients himself toward out-group values, perhaps affirming them verbally and expressing them in action, he only widens the gap and reinforces the hostility between himself and his in-group associates. Through the interplay of dissociation and progressive alienation from the group values, he may become doubly motivated to orient himself toward the values of another group and to affiliate himself with it. There then remains the distinct question of the objective possibility of affiliating himself with his reference group. If the possibility is negligible or absent, then the alienated individual becomes socially rootless. But if the social system realistically allows for such change in group affiliations, then the individual estranged from the one group has all the more motivation to belong to the other.[9]

SPONSORSHIP

Progression of individuals along given career lines is not only a result of technical competence and of being available and trained at the right time. A major influence determining who moves and

---

[9] Robert K. Merton and Alice S. Kitt, "Reference Group Theory and Social Mobility," in *Class, Status, and Power: A Reader in Social Stratification,* ed. Reinhard Bendix and Seymour M. Lipset (Glencoe: Free Press, 1953), pp. 409–10.

how far is the action of a sponsor. In many instances, and especially at higher levels, this is almost a necessary condition for mobility.

The relationship of sponsor and protégé tends to be a reciprocal one of mutual benefit and occurs for a variety of reasons: the protégé may complement his superior by being strong in an area of activity where his sponsor is weak; he may serve in a role as detail man, adviser, or confidant. Regardless of reasons, when the sponsor rises, the protégé moves with him. From the standpoint of the protégé, therefore, he benefits by being pulled up in the hierarchy.

A given sponsor may have a cluster of protégés surrounding him. Ties of loyalty as well as need compel him to push for advancing "his men" as he moves up. As a result, top-management echelons of many companies are made up of interlocking cliques—certain powerful sponsors and their adherents. The mobility patterns in any organization are, therefore, to a considerable extent influenced by the phenomenon of sponsorship.[10]

Such arrangements are not without merit. From the standpoint of efficiency, it is possible for work to get done in an easy manner. Many smoothly working teams of executives evolve. Solidarity is high; common values and styles of action make for consistent behavior. On the negative side, however, the play of "internal politics" can create conflicts and anxiety. Executives who are not members of the cliques may be short-circuited and even undermined. Organizational efficiency may suffer. Serious problems develop when protégés lose their sponsors either because they are dropped or because the sponsor himself loses power because of shifts within the organization. The organization is then faced with the problem of working with individuals who no longer have a place within the scheme of things.

The existence of systems of sponsorship and resultant problems have been well documented in the histories of large companies.

[10] Two excellent articles may be pointed out: Everett C. Hughes, "Queries concerning Industry and Society Growing Out of Study of Ethnic Relations in Industry," and Orvis Collins, "Ethnic Behavior in Industry: Sponsorship and Rejection in a New England Factory," in *Human Relations in Administration,* ed. Robert Dubin (New York: Prentice-Hall, Inc., 1951), pp. 240–49.

The history of the Ford Motor Company—and this is by no means an isolated example—clearly spells out processes of sponsorship and the results of powerful sponsors leaving the company. Harry Bennett, one of the recent powers in that organization, makes the succinct comment, "Well, Edsel and I had this much in common: When he went, he left a lot of 'orphans' in the plant; and when I left, so did I."[11]

To cite another example: The vice-president in charge of sales of a large industrial concern resigned his position for personal reasons. During the course of his career, he had sponsored several individuals into positions as department sales managers. While these managers were competent enough and remained in their positions, it soon became apparent that the new vice-president was not going to move them higher into zone and district positions. Their techniques of operation did not fit into his philosophy and strategies. Other individuals were promoted around them. Their reactions varied: one became passive and did only the minimum work required; another began to build a little empire of his own, communicating with associates and higher management only when required; others became hostile and aggressive. In brief, they became problems for management.

It would appear that the organizational structure of any concern is a result of the interplay of several factors. Ideally, such a structure should be the result of rational planning and should be developed in accordance with an over-all theory of management and policy. Actually, however, other factors, e.g., individual personalities, play a decisive role. Executives become concerned with developing their own positions and extending their power; positions are created; power struggles evolve. While this is not a universal phenomenon, it is of sufficient generality to be reckoned with. It comes directly to the fore in the activities of sponsors. Here the power structure is superimposed upon the rationally conceived organization. Career lines are frequently affected, causing changes which have an impact both upon management objectives of achieving an orderly and effective system of executive development and

[11] Harry Bennett, *We Never Called Him Henry* (New York: Gold Medal Books, Fawcett Publications, Inc., 1951), p. 166.

upon the mobility aspirations of conscientious and ambitious personnel.[12]

CONSEQUENCES OF FAILURE

The meshing of horizontal and vertical movements of personnel is not always perfect. Individuals are moved into positions prematurely, sponsors drop protégés, and miscalculations are made. Problems are therefore created which must be dealt with. Incompetent individuals have to be moved into positions where they cannot do serious damage but where their experience can still be used; frustrated mobility drives must be diverted into harmless channels. In any organization such malfunctioning and changes are inevitable.

The correction most obviously takes the form of firing, but more subtle means are frequently used, such as open or concealed demotion and arrest of further promotion, which common parlance refers to as "kicking a man upstairs," "shunting him to another department," and "banishment to the sticks." Indeed, unless an organization is willing openly to remove personnel from important positions by outright firing or demotion, it must resort to less blunt tactics.[13] These techniques are well worth studying, for they are related to organizational functioning in determinable and important ways. Why a man is demoted or blocked, how, when, and what are his responses, may be fateful, or at least significant, both for the person and for the organization.

Unless the incompetent individual is fired, he frequently is not told bluntly or directly that he is being removed from a position because of failure in meeting company requirements. The typical procedure is simply that the man receives his orders from an appropriate superior, usually without much choice of alternative, and

[12] It is not intended that a moral judgment of good or bad be made here. Our intention is simply to point out the existence of power structures in many concerns and to indicate their impact, an impact that should be taken into account by management.

[13] The recent *Fortune* magazine article on "How To Fire an Executive" (October, 1954), by Perrin Stryker, suggests that expulsion of top personnel is neither a simple matter nor necessarily the method of demotion most practiced.

must shift to the new position within a matter of days. He may know or guess that he has failed, but there are hedges for his hurt ego in so far as he is shunted or promoted rather than openly fired or demoted.

Such removals from positions have been termed "cooling out" by one sociologist, Erving Goffman,[14] who has borrowed the term from the con man's vocabulary. There it refers to the psychological disturbance which arises when the "mark's" ego is hurt after he discovers that he has been "taken" by the con man; therefore, the latter usually provides a mechanism whereby the victim will be cooled out; otherwise he will go to the police or create other embarassing disturbances. Like the con man, any organization, Goffman suggests, must protect itself against the consequences of demoting its members by seeking to minimize humiliation and loss of self-esteem.

There are numerous organizational methods for cooling out, but any given organization cannot make casual selection among them. These methods flow both from the organizational structure and from accepted ways of behavior. If horizontal movement, for example, is used, then a flexible organization structure must exist. Otherwise there would be no place to shunt these men. Assigning them to staff positions requires the practice of a staff philosophy of management. Movement per se, indeed, must be a part of the accepted ways of behavior.

Thus in one concern studied—an organization with a broad and flexible system of positions—horizontal shunting, either within branches or between branches, is combined with honorific or terminal promotions. Occasionally, and especially at the upper ranks, a relatively functionless post is created to slide a man into. Staff positions, therefore, frequently function as receptacles for incompetency. These methods of removing men are closely linked with the nature of the vertical and horizontal mobility routes in the company.

Among other methods for cooling out, we might mention the following: use of seniority to slow up promotions, destruction of

[14] Erving Goffman, "On Cooling the Mark Out: Some Aspects of Adaptation & Failure," *Psychiatry*, XV (1952), 451–63.

mobility drives, forcing of resignation, open demotion, bribing the failure out of the organization, progressive down-grading by merging departments, continual and rapid transfer from one branch to another, and continual bypassing. In some instances an organization has occasion to cool out men temporarily, often with the tacit or overt understanding that the move is not permanent. Sometimes this happens when a man is promoted too rapidly to be competent at handling his post. He is then shunted to another department or division at the same rank. If he fails again, he is given a terminal promotion.

RESPONSES TO BEING COOLED OUT

There are both short- and long-range responses to the cooling-out process. The former are probably less important, both for the men themselves and for the company. Some men, as we have pointed out, temporarily withdraw, become hostile, apathetic, and morose. Overt hostility seems to be more characteristic of men at lower levels; higher up, there appears to be an attempt at covering up, carrying on, and putting a good public face on the matter. The long-range responses are more serious. We have already pointed out some of these in our illustration of the effects of sponsors dropping protégés. At lower levels, supervisors may become antimanagement in orientation. They may strongly identify downward, turning, as it were, to face-to-face relationships with employees for their chief work satisfactions. At higher levels executives may become increasingly intractable and develop a tough, hard-boiled quality and an individualistic philosophy which makes them treasure autonomy. They may come to look upon their departments or divisions as private bailiwicks and develop possessive attitudes toward them. Along with this goes a rationale or myth of indispensability. Superiors find them unduly centered upon their own departments and complain that communication between themselves and these department heads is poor. They tend not to delegate authority properly, gathering control into their own hands. This means that they provide inadequate training for rising subordinates.

Such long-range effects of personal failure within the organization call forth answering responses from the organization. We might visualize this as a series of gestures taking place over a lengthy period of time. The company makes judgments upon men, cools out those who fail in specific ways, is met with answering responses from the men, and in turn must respond to their responses. The company has to set some of its internal policy, therefore, to take into account such untoward and unforeseen eventualities as the intractableness of executives who have been cooled out.

There are several approaches which companies use in responding to such situations. Training programs and seminars frequently are useful in broadening the perspectives of these men. Attempts are made to build up their self-esteem by broadening their responsibilities and giving them special assignments. In still other instances companies respond by formalizing channels of communication—by forcing such executives to make periodic reports. Frequent horizontal shifting tends to break down departmental thinking and possessiveness and to nip in the bud any potential colleagueship of these executives stemming from their similar predicaments. From the standpoint of organization structure, it may even be necessary to create staff positions to house those who have been kicked upstairs.

Thus the organizational strategies for handling partial or complete failures of personnel are many and add up to a complex system of policy acts. Such a system for handling failure is integral to getting men allocated, jobs done, and administrative leaders, high and low, picked, trained, and developed.

A stable organization and a systematic meshing of methods of cooling out thus go hand in hand. A system of mutually supporting methods wherein those methods do not run excessively afoul of one another cannot exist when the organization is undergoing great policy changes or has just terminated a major power struggle. Major organizational changes eventuate not merely in the supplanting of old demotional procedures by new ones but in the piling-up of old. The picture is further complicated because in large organizations shifts of power go on continually with different degrees of speed and intensity in the several component divisions. These may be expected to affect, directly or indirectly, the cooling-out procedures of each.

IMPLICATIONS

It is believed that the ideas set forth in the preceding sections provide a substantially correct picture of certain significant aspects of the mobility structure found within industrial organizations. The main outline of these ideas should serve to provide a basis for further investigation into this highly relevant facet of industrial management.

We have pointed out several important elements of mobility structures and have emphasized the necessity to view this structure within the context of the over-all organization and its history. In venturing this interpretation, we have pointed to some of the significant problems which must be faced as a result of the malfunctioning of the mobility process.

Further research and ultimate refinement and expansion of these ideas are, of course, necessary. Different types of mobility patterns are certain to be found, for it may be predicted that varying types of companies will evolve differing sequences of movements through the management hierarchy. Comparative studies of occupational mobility in different industrial concerns, both simple and complex, are surely in order to add to our understanding both of organizations and of careers within them.

The systematic procedures for cooling out can also be viewed from the social-psychological or career perspective. To ask what happens to a man as he moves through these successive positions is equivalent to asking what effects his occupation has upon him both sequentially and in the long run. It is no easy matter to pin down the steps in the psychology of his change. Psychologists usually are content with characterizing the personalities of executives either without saying much about how the person got that way or speculating fairly generally about the social context within which personality is affected. The impact of occupational position upon personality can be studied more pointedly by tying the psychologist's kind of research into organizational and career investigation. It is just here that further studies of the effects of demotion and the arresting of promotion should prove most valuable. The fateful periods in a man's life are frequently associated with personal and public recognition of failure. In so far as the type of failure and the handling of it are not unique but are common and related to organizational structure, there is the possibility of determining and studying the crucial turning points in personality development within occupational worlds.

THE SOCIAL ORIGINS AND ACQUIRED CHARACTERISTICS OF BUSINESS LEADERS

W. Lloyd Warner and James C. Abegglen

Is this society more open to competition by all or more rigid and less free? The social origins and characteristics of the 8300 big businessmen here presented tell the answers and give us knowledge about the present condition of executive life.

. . . Who are the business leaders of contemporary America? What are their occupational origins? Who were their fathers and their paternal grandfathers? By comparing the proportions of business leaders of the different occupational backgrounds with the proportions of such occupations in the total American society, we were able to determine which occupations were overrepresented and underrepresented among the leaders studied. Business executives or owners of large businesses produced about eight times (7.75) more than the proportions of these occupations in the general population would lead one to expect. Three other categories were also overrepresented in terms of their proportions in the general population: the sons of owners of small businesses ranked second with 3.60, the sons of professional men third (3.50), and the sons of foremen (1.33) ranked slightly above expectancy.

Four of the eight general occupational categories were under-

Note: See Notes on the Authors, pages 557 and 551, and item 244 in the bibliography for the full reference to this selection.

represented. The sons of white-collar men (clerks and salesmen) were slightly underrepresented (0.80). These were followed by the sons of skilled laborers (0.63). The ratio of mobility into the business elite for the sons of farm tenants and owners is 0.45, which is superior in ranking only to two other categories, the semi-skilled and unskilled laborers (0.16) and farm laborers (0.00).

Perhaps an easier way to report these results is to say that for every 10 men who might have been expected to be business leaders on the basis of their occupational backgrounds and the proportion of such men in the general occupational population, there were approximately 80 sons of business leaders, 40 sons of small businessmen, about 40 sons of professional men, and slightly over 10 sons of foremen. For every 10 that might have been expected from the category clerks and salesmen, there were only 8, for skilled laborers only 6, for farm tenants and owners between 4 and 5. Fewer than 2 out of the expected 10 turn up for the semiskilled or unskilled and almost none for farm laborers.

Although these great disparities among the several categories of occupational origins of the 1952 business leaders show clearly that many factors were operative to determine similarities and differences, a comparison of the findings of 1928 (Taussig and Joslyn) and today yields differences which not only speak in a limited way for themselves but indicate that more general interpretation would be significant. In 1928, the ratio for laborer backgrounds was 0.25 compared with 0.32 for 1952; the ratio of white-collar men improved from 0.71 in 1928 to 0.80 in 1952. The farmers changed little in these years (0.32 to 0.33). On the other hand, both the professional and business categories dropped, the former from 4.33 to 3.50 and the latter from 9.67 to 4.73. . . . Clearly, there has been not only an increase in the proportion of the men who come from the lower ranks, but an accompanying decrease in the proportion of sons of highly placed men, particularly of businessmen. Certainly occupational succession (within the limits of this study) is more fluid, and more vertical mobility has been taking place.

. . . Most of the men of the business elite were born in the big cities. When the proportions of the business leaders born in the several sizes of community are compared with the proportions for the total population, it is found that relatively few are from small-town or rural backgrounds. When the occupation of father, the region of birth, and the size of birthplace are considered jointly, the very small part played by the small-town and rural South in business leadership is sharply revealed.

When the findings of this research are reviewed in terms of general thinking regarding occupational mobility, it appears that the role of immigration in mobility has been misinterpreted. While it is quite true that immigrants do not often achieve the highest status positions in American business, their disadvantage is less than might be assumed, for 5 per cent of the business elite were foreign-born, while about 10 per cent of the U.S. population were born abroad. Further, and more significant, the sons of foreign-born men of lower status are successfully mobile in a higher proportion than the sons of native-born men of lower status.

This general finding is consistent with the role territorial mobility has been found to play in occupational mobility. The relationship between these two forms of social movement is an intimate one: those men who are mobile through social space are also mobile through geographic space. It may be concluded from this that the act of movement, spatially, establishes many of the preconditions for social and occupational mobility. The territorially mobile man is disengaged from the web of relations that determines his social position, and the son of an immigrant is that man least engaged with his cultural past. The physical mobility of Americans is a precondition to the changes in social position that have been found to take place increasingly in American business.

The previous questions and answers have dealt with the kinds of persons who have high-status business positions, the proportions of individuals who are mobile or are the sons of those in the elite, and their geographic origins. It is essential for an understanding of these social facts to examine some of the factors that influence them. In the formulation of this research the following questions were asked with respect to education and mobility:

How important is education, both the amount and kind, in successful mobility? . . .

Most of the business leaders were college men, well over half being college graduates. Seventy-six per cent of the men studied had gone to college, 57 per cent had graduated, 19 per cent had not. However, one-fifth of the whole group (19 per cent) had not only graduated but had gone on to advanced graduate study. Comparatively, the American businessman tends to be a highly educated man: whereas 76 out of every 100 of the business elite had gone to college, only 13 of every 100 adult males (30 years and over) in the general population had some college training; 57 of every 100 business leaders had graduated, as compared with 7 out of every 100 in the general population.

More than half of the adult males in the general population had not attended high school, compared with only 4 out of 100 leaders. Nine per cent of the leaders had some high school but did not graduate and 11 per cent graduated but did not go on to college, compared with 16 per cent in each of these two categories in the general population.

But what kinds of men received a higher education? Were they sons of the elite or men from the wrong side of the tracks? Who were the men who did not go on to college? Nine out of every 10 sons of professional men and business leaders had been to college and 7 of the 10 had graduated.

Over half of the sons of semiskilled or unskilled laborers had been to college (52 per cent) and 36 per cent had graduated. Seven out of every 10 sons of fathers of the white-collar level had been to college and 5 out of 10 had graduated. In general, men originating from all levels went to college, but those from higher levels attended and graduated from college in higher proportions. Another moderately accurate measurement of the effect of occupational rank on education is obtained from a comparison of the percentages of men of diverse origins who did not graduate from high school. Whereas only 3 per cent of the sons of professional men and 3 per cent of those of business leaders quit school before graduating from high school, one-third of the sons of unskilled and semiskilled laborers and one-fourth of the sons of skilled laborers failed to go on. The other levels fell between the two extremes.

Despite the fact that men from higher levels receive more education than those from lower levels, at all levels of occupational background college graduates make up the largest single educational group.

Business leaders of 1952 are better educated than the leaders of 1928. For example, whereas in 1952 only 4 out of every 100 leaders had less than a high school education, 27 did in the earlier group; and only 32 per cent were college graduates in 1928, compared with 57 per cent in 1952. In 1952, the proportion of college graduates from each occupational category, including skilled and unskilled laborers, was greater than the proportion of college graduates in the entire sample for 1928. Furthermore, a large number of these men, both those with and those without college training, prepare themselves for careers by taking commercial training—in colleges or universities, by correspondence courses, or in business colleges. One-fourth of the leaders had taken correspondence courses or gone to business college and one-third had some kind of commercial training in a college or university.

Education is now one of the principal avenues to business leadership. The mobile men use it in greatly increased numbers in their drive to places of leadership and power. Clearly education helps many from all levels to reach the top, yet financial and other restrictions on access to higher education is also an important factor in the maintenance of occupational inheritance by the elite.

In terms of the effect on the individual's hopes and beliefs, the factors in getting to the top include also the amount of time he must work to achieve this goal. This study asked a number of questions related to this problem. Some of them were as follows:

How long did it take for top executives to reach their present positions from the time of their entry into the business world?

What were the differences in length of time required for the sons of business leaders and for those whose fathers occupied lower economic ranks?

What is the relation between achievement time and the separate factors of education, financial aid, and influential connections? For example, to what extent, if any, does a man improve his chances of *early* success by obtaining a college degree?

The average business leader in our study has almost reached his fifty-fourth birthday (53.7 years). He entered business a few months after reaching his majority (21.4 years). It took him almost 24 years to reach his present business position. Occupational origin has an effect on the age of entering business: sons of laborers become self-supporting earlier (before reaching 19) than those of any other occupational category. The sons of professional men and businessmen do not enter business until they are nearly 22.

The length of time before reaching a top business position was shortest for the sons of major executives (20.6 years) and longest for the sons of laborers (26 years). The sons of farmers took about a year less than those of laborers (25.1 years). On the whole, territorial mobility, while an integral part of the mobility process, seems to be related to retardation of the career, although some men would probably not have advanced so far if they had not been territorially mobile in their careers. Men who have moved about a lot tend to achieve business leadership later than those who stay closer to home.

These successful men tended to move from one firm to another; only a fourth of those we studied remained with a single firm. These changes occurred before as well as after they had attained high position. Usually, the men from lower levels who were mobile moved from firm to firm more often than those from higher ranks. Furthermore, men of college education moved less often.

The percentage of sons in the same enterprises as their fathers varies with both the size and type of enterprise—the larger the firm the smaller the proportion of men with fathers in the same firm. The principal industries in which fathers and sons are found in the same enterprises are real estate, wood and coal products, personal services, and security and commodity brokers. Throughout the larger enterprises there has been a decided decrease in the proportion of men in the same firm as the father. The stronghold of inherited position today in America is in the smaller enterprises; the larger enterprises are more open to competition for men rising from lower occupational levels.

Only a very small percentage of the business leaders received financial aid—some 6 per cent. Of those who did, the sons of big businessmen far outranked all others: 17 per cent compared with 6 per cent of the sons of professional men, 3 per cent of small businessmen, and less than 1 per cent (0.6) of the sons of laborers. There has been a decided decrease in such help since 1928. At that time, 13 per cent of the leaders had been assisted financially, as compared with 6 per cent in 1952.

The research questions and answers until now have been directed to the relations of fathers and sons and the family of birth, emphasizing the effect of social and economic place on the careers of American business leaders. We turn now to another social factor. The marriages of Americans influence, and are influenced by, the patterns of their careers. Do such men marry above or below their levels of origin? Do men of lower rank marry women of similar status or do they marry above themselves? Do the sons of big businessmen marry the daughters of men of the same high position or do they often marry the ambitious daughters of fathers from the lower occupational ranks? The answers to these questions are important in their own right, but their social implications for rank and social mobility are still more important, for if men born to high rank marry women of similar origin the effect is to decrease the fluidity of the society and to increase closure; on the other hand, frequent marriage above or below the level of origin reduces the effect of status and emphasizes the values of freedom of choice, individuality, and flexibility of status. These statements become even more significant when two or more generations, which do or do not emphasize hereditary status at marriage, are involved.

Approximately half of the wives of the business leaders studied (51 per cent) were the daughters of business or professional men, and about a sixth were from the laboring class. Men born to high station married women from similar backgrounds in greater proportion than did any other class; but in general the men studied married women from their own occupational level more than any other group of women. The men whose fathers were white-collar workers married out of their occupational origins more than any others did; men with laboring, farmer, and big business backgrounds were more likely than others to marry within their occupational origins. In general, both endogamic and exogamic factors seem to be operating in the choice of mates. Flexibility, individual choice, freedom to go beyond the confines of the occupational level—all are exhibited in the kinds of marriages made by the business leaders.

When the effect of the paternal grandfather's generation on the marriages of the elite is examined there appears to be a definite relation between choice of mate and status of the grandfather. If he was of high status it is more likely that his grandson (the business leader) will marry a highly placed woman than if he was of lower status, this being true even if the father of the leader was a big businessman. Furthermore, the lower the status of the grandfather the greater the likelihood the grandson will not marry a highborn woman.

The effect of a college education is to increase the likelihood of marriage at higher levels. Both inherited status and education influence the selection of the mates of business leaders.

The question arises, what effect did in- and out-marriage have on the careers of these men? The sons of the elite who married the daughters of laborers took 23 years to achieve their positions at the executive level; those who married at their own level took 2 years longer (25 years). The laborer who "marries the boss's daughter" takes almost exactly the same amount of time for achievement as the one who marries someone from his own level of origin (25.9 years for the first, 26.1 for the latter). The general effect of marriage on the career is quite similar for all categories; there is only a limited range of difference in time for the careers of men who marry above or below their occupational origins. The status of the wife generally does not have a direct effect on accelerating the career of the business leader.

In the broadest sense, this research indicates that at the levels studied here American society is not becoming more castelike; the recruitment of business leaders from the bottom is taking place now and seems to be increasing. Mobility to the top is not decreasing; in fact, for the last quarter century it has been slowly increasing. In spite of the pessimistic predictions about an immobilized society, this evidence shows that our society, although much like what it has been in past generations, is more flexible than it was; more men and their families are in social motion; pessimism about decreased flexibility and mobility is not warranted.

Despite these facts, the operation of rank and the effects of high birth are strongly evidenced in the selection of the American business elite. Men born to the top are more likely to succeed and have more advantages than those born further down. There is not full freedom of competition; the system is still sufficiently status-bound to work to the considerable advantage of men born to higher position. Fathers at the elite levels still find it possible to endow their sons with greater opportunity than those further down enjoy. Nevertheless, they do so now in decreased numbers. The sons of men from the wrong side of the tracks are finding their way increasingly to the places of power and prestige. The values of competitive and open status are felt more today than yesterday and those of inherited position and fixed position, while still powerful, are less potent now than they were a generation ago.

THE BUSINESS ELITE IN BUSINESS BUREAUCRACIES[15]

William Miller

The big executive of early free enterprise in America yielded much of his freedom of choice in action to the bureaucracies that were erected to reduce risk, increase yield, and exercise power. The careers of some of our greatest business leaders at the beginning of this century were part of this development.

By 1902, when the Morgan spokesman, George F. Baer, made his prideful remark about how "God, in his infinite wisdom," had

[15] . . . . A full discussion of the method used in selecting the business leaders of 1901–1910 and a list of the men and their companies appear in William Miller, "American Historians and the Business Elite," *Journal of Economic History,* vol. IX, no. 2 (November 1949), the first essay in the series. The others are, "The Recruitment of the Business Elite," *Quarterly Journal of Economics,* vol. LXIV, no. 2 (May 1950), and "American Law-

Note: See Notes on the Authors, page 555, and item 162 in the bibliography for the full reference to this selection.

"given control of the property interests of the country" to "the Christian men" who then managed them,[16] many of these Christians had already learned that what God might give, men might take away. Among them, indeed, was Baer himself whose career as Morgan's "confidential legal advisor,"[17] though it had brought him to the head of numerous great enterprises, resembled a new type in American business life. Louis D. Brandeis said in the 1890's, "I would rather have clients than be somebody's lawyer," and to a considerable degree he satisfied his preference.[18] Baer's career, as was especially plain during the coal strike which was the occasion of his Calvinistic utterance, was more like that of a trained professional no longer free to have clients or to reject them, but tied to the service of a single business interest that could move him about like an ordinary employee.

Even more representative of this type of "captive" professional —for these men engaged in fewer independent ventures than Baer—were such company lawyers as Vanderbilt's Chauncey M. Depew, Huntington's Charles H. Tweed, Harriman's Robert S. Lovett, each at some time president or board chairman of one or more of his sponsor's firms and always on call to the great man himself. Properly classified here too are the counterparts of company lawyers in the "law factory" of a Paul D. Cravath, George W.

---

yers in Business and Politics," *Yale Law Journal,* vol. LX, no. 1 (January 1951).

Originally 190 business leaders were selected for the research on which this study is based. For five, however, career information was unavailable, so that 185 are studied here. Each of these men was either president or board chairman in the decade 1901–1910 of at least one of the largest American corporations in the following fields (the number in parenthesis is the number from each field): Manufacturing and Mining (61); Railroads (57); Public Utilities (30); Finance—Commercial Banking (19) and Life Insurance (9); or was a partner in one of the five leading unincorporated investment banking houses (9). The extent of the influence of these men in the business community generally is suggested by the following statistics: the 174 men whose directorships are known held 2720 such offices; a few held more than 100 each; the average was about 16.

[16] *Dictionary of American Biography,* essay on Baer.
[17] As he described himself in *Who's Who in America.*
[18] Alpheus T. Mason, *Brandeis* (New York: The Viking Press, 1946), p. 86.

Wickersham, or William N. Cromwell, which by the end of the nineteenth century had become "virtually an annex to some group of financial promoters, manipulators, or industrialists."[19] Of Cravath, his associate Robert T. Swaine tells this story:

> Early one morning when he had not yet arrived at the office, [Otto] Kahn [of Kuhn, Loeb] wanted to see him in a great hurry. One of the younger associates sought to locate Cravath by telephone, but in vain; going downstairs at 52 William Street to tell Kahn of the futility of his efforts, he met Cravath coming in the door and rushed up with: "I've been looking all over for you; Mr. Kahn wants to see you at once." Cravath broke into a broad smile: "You make me feel just like my father did when he used to say to me: 'Paul, come to the woodshed.' "[20]

This new ubiquitousness of lawyers at big businessmen's elbows, not to say under their thumbs, reflects an epochal change in the structure of American big business enterprises and in their relation to their employees and to society at large. First among the railroads, but by the turn of the century in many other lines as well, the characteristic big business firm had become a big bureaucracy. Functions at each level of operation, supervision, and policy making had become more or less strict and specific, channels of authority and communication had been set up, and hierarchies of ascent had become articulated. Lifetime, salaried careers thus had become attainable, leading all the way to the top, albeit, as Max Weber has pointed out, "the bureaucratic official" is always "appointed by a superior authority"[21]—a higher functionary, a college of cardinals, a board of directors, the "organization" itself.

In such bureaucracies, ideally, as Weber said, "control" is exercised "on the basis of knowledge"; the "development of bureaucracy . . . tends to eliminate . . . the occupation of offices on

---

[19] Adolf A. Berle, Jr., "Modern Legal Profession," in *Encyclopedia of the Social Sciences,* IX, 341. See also John R. Dos Passos, *The American Lawyer* (New York: Banks Law Publishing Co., 1907); Robert T. Swaine, *The Cravath Firm,* 3 vols. (New York: Privately printed, 1946, 1948); and J. Willard Hurst, The Growth of American Law (Boston: Little, Brown and Co., 1950), chap. xiii.

[20] Swaine, *Cravath Firm,* II, 127.

[21] H. H. Gerth and C. Wright Mills (trans. and eds.) *From Max Weber* (New York: Oxford University Press, 1946), p. 200.

an honorary basis or as an avocation by virtue of wealth."[22] The upshot, however, is not "democratization" but rather the rise of a new elite: "The most decisive thing here . . . is the leveling of the governed in opposition to the ruling and bureaucratically articulated group, which in turn may occupy a quite autocratic position."[23] This new elite, in Weber's terms, may "increase its power by the knowledge growing out of experience in the service."[24] To become even more firmly seated it may enlist expert technicians not the least useful of whom were those qualified to serve as intermediaries with the leveled populace. Knowledgeable lawyers, expert in their own fields, also fitted this second role. Trained in advocacy and persuasion as well as in the law, they were among the first professional lobbyists and public relations men as well as the first formally certified business experts. Their new importance by the turn of the century reflects the growth of bureaucratic managements typically in need of help in navigating legal and political labyrinths and in conciliating public groups often made hostile by the results.[25]

[22] Talcott Parsons (trans. and ed.) *Max Weber: The Theory of Social and Economic Organization* (New York: Oxford University Press, 1947), pp. 339, 340. This, of course, need not mean that those with wealth could not also acquire the requisite knowledge.

[23] Gerth and Mills, *From Max Weber*, p. 226 (italics Weber's). On the extent to which big business in most recent times takes this "leveling of the governed" for granted, see "Is Anybody Listening?" *Fortune*, September 1950.

[24] Parsons, *Max Weber*, p. 339. Weber also says in this connection: "Every bureaucracy seeks to increase the superiority of the professionally informed by keeping their knowledge and intentions secret. Bureaucratic administration always tends to be an administration of 'secret sessions': in so far as it can, it hides its knowledge and action from criticism." (Gerth and Mills, *From Max Weber*, p. 233.)

[25] The persistence of "anti-trust" agitation as a political topic in the United States is one index of the need to conciliate the public. At the time of the passage of the Sherman Act in 1890, conservative Republican Senator Orville Platt said: "The conduct of the senate . . . has not been in the line of honest preparation of a bill to prohibit and punish trusts . . . the whole effort has been to get some bill headed: 'A Bill to Punish Trusts' with which to go to the country." It was this Act of which Mr. Dooley said at the time of the formation of the United States Steel Corporation in 1901: "What looks like a stone-wall to a layman is a triumphal arch to a corporation lawyer." On the Interstate Commerce Act of 1887, Senator Nelson W. Aldrich said: The

That men risen to power as bureaucrats or as their professional adjuncts had not wholly superseded independent entrepreneurs in the key positions in the American economy by 1900 is indicated by the histories of some of the leaders who were still at the head of great business enterprises. Of 185 men so placed in the decade 1901–1910,[26] 14 per cent either started the firms through the development of which, by expansion or more commonly by merger, they had attained their peak positions,[27] or bought these firms or high places in them with resources accumulated in independent ventures. Hugh J. Chisholm of the International Paper Company, Anthony N. Brady of the Brooklyn Rapid Transit Company, and Frederick Ayer of American Woolen, were such men. So, too, though each ultimately paid for his independence by being squeezed out of his own firm, were John C. Osgood, one of the organizers of the Colorado Fuel and Iron Company; Frederick A. Heinze, founder of the United Copper Company; and George Westinghouse, founder of the Electric and Manufacturing Company which still bears his name.

Twenty-seven per cent of these 185 business leaders, moreover, and certainly not the least able ones, may be said to have inherited their high positions. This suggests that while kinship ties may have become more honored in the breach in the transfer of business power, and inherited wealth and tradition less convincing than "self-help" and bureaucratic "rationality" as legitimations of such power, dynasties still could be established and maintained.[28] Most

---

act was "a delusion and a sham . . . an empty menace to great interests, made to answer the clamor of the ignorant and the unreasoning." (Quoted from Thomas C. Cochran and William Miller, *The Age of Enterprise*, New York: The Macmillan Co., 1942, pp. 171–172.) On more recent times see J. K. Galbraith, "Monopoly and Concentration of Economic Power," in Howard S. Ellis, ed., *A Survey of Contemporary Economics* (Philadelphia: The Blakiston Co., 1948), pp. 115–124.

[26] See footnote, pp. 109–110 above.

[27] Here and elsewhere, "peak" or "listed" position, company, or industry refers to the presidency, chairmanship, or partnership which, as indicated in the footnote on pp. 109–110, made men eligible for this study.

[28] On the importance of businessmen's dynastic aspirations, see Joseph A. Schumpeter, *Capitalism, Socialism and Democracy* (New York: Harper & Brothers, 1942), pp. 156 ff.

of the men in this group had taken over their father's, father-in-law's, or uncle's firms. Others had used their continuing connection with such firms or funds available through them to gain key positions in major outside companies. In the latter class, typically, are sons, sons-in-law, and nephews of great merchants or private bankers—James Stillman and August Belmont in New York, Gordon Abbott in Boston, Henry A. Blair and Henry G. Foreman in Chicago. Among the more direct heirs, besides bankers like J. P. Morgan, Henry Lee Higginson, or Frank E. Peabody, are Daniel Guggenheim in copper, Henry O. Havemeyer in sugar, Morgan G. Bulkeley in life insurance, Cornelius K. G. Billings in Chicago utilities. Even railroad presidents George Jay Gould and Louis W. Hill may be included here, each having reached the top of his father's highly bureaucratized company by a route so direct as to leave him virtually unaware of the articulated channels through which henceforth he was expected to work.

All the rest of these 185 leaders, however, except for the 12 per cent who were lawyers,[29] climbed the bureaucratic ladder, not infrequently, of course, after their family status, education, and other social endowments helped them get the proper start. These bureaucrats make up 47 per cent of the whole group. Typical is Charles S. Mellen, who at the age of eighteen began as a clerk in the cashier's office of the Northern New Hampshire Railroad. From here he "rose in his profession," as his biographer puts it, "through successive positions on the Central Vermont" and other roads.[30] After a novitiate of almost a quarter of a century, during which he never forsook railroading, he became second vice-president of the New York, New Haven and Hartford. In 1897, Mellen was made president of the Northern Pacific, only to be moved

[29] Since all the men studied were selected because of their *business* positions, the group of lawyers includes only those who actually were president or board chairman of business corporations in 1901–1910. No regular members of "law factories" are included. Thus the group is not representative in size or composition of the whole class of business or corporation lawyers. Since this is so and since even most of the lawyers included here had professional rather than distinctly business careers, little more will be said of them. A study of professional careers in the business community is reserved for another occasion.

[30] *Dictionary of American Biography,* essay on Mellen.

114

seven years later back to the New Haven also as president. After a stormy decade, he was ousted in 1913.

Scarcely any of these bureaucrats ever satisfied the urge, if indeed they ever had it,[31] to launch a company of their own, "to plunge into and toss upon the waves of human affairs," as Carnegie said, "without a life-preserver in the shape of a salary."[32] More than 80 per cent of them never headed an enterprise—never were sole owner, partner, president, or chairman—before attaining the eminent office that makes them of interest here. That is not to say that their ascent, once auspiciously under way, was unfaltering or automatic. Nor does it compromise the designation of their careers as bureaucratic to point out that many of them, like many lawyers, became the favorites—with all the hazards of that predicament—of men of more elevated rank.[33]

Jesse T. Welborn, for example, had "advanced through regular stages"[34] in the Colorado Fuel and Iron Company from book-

[31] Eight of these men who themselves never started a business were part of a large panel of outstanding men in all fields who in 1902 were asked if they would advise "a young man of experience and ability, at a fair salary, to go into business for himself." One of the eight gave no answer. The remaining seven said "yes" even if it was "upon borrowed capital." (Nathaniel C. Fowler, Jr., *The Boy: How to Help Him Succeed,* Boston: Oakwood Publishing Co., 1902, pp. 167 ff.)

[32] Andrew Carnegie, *The Empire of Business* (New York: Doubleday, Page & Co., 1902), p. 190.

[33] It may be true, as Robert K. Merton says in summarizing Weber's theory that "bureaucracy maximizes vocational security." (Robert K. Merton, *Social Theory and Social Structure,* Glencoe, Ill.: The Free Press, 1949, p. 152.) But in business at least this is relatively certain only in comparison to the "vocational security" of the ordinary worker. It has yet to be shown that the bureaucrat, even on the highest levels, is more secure than the great "captain of industry," for example, either in his hold on his status or in the psychological attributes of it. Even while the bureaucrat may be supposed, in Weber's terms, to be "set for a 'career' . . . in which *tenure for life* is presupposed," Weber notes that "this is not recognized as the official's right to the possession of the office." (Gerth and Mills, *From Max Weber,* pp. 202, 203. Italics Weber's.) I am aware that this complicates the ideal bureaucratic picture with "patrimonial" factors; but it seems that in business at least the hierarchical nature of ascent may not be altogether divorced from the patrimonial aspects of tenure. Indeed, it may well be that the higher a bureaucrat goes the more dependent is his tenure on patrimonial factors.

[34] Will C. Ferril (ed.), *Sketches of Colorado* (Denver: Western Press Bureau Co., 1911), p. 179.

keeper to vice-president in charge of sales and traffic, when in 1907 the Rockefellers, who a few years earlier had acquired the company, made him president. James T. Harahan had risen "through successive stages"[35] in railroading from clerk on the Boston and Providence to second vice-president of the Illinois Central, when Harriman in 1906 ousted president Stuyvesant Fish of the latter road and put Harahan in his place. Mellen himself, who soon after becoming president of the New Haven was regarded as "The Railroad Lord of New England,"[36] once said of his experiences there, "I suppose that there is more or less prejudice against me because I wear the Morgan collar, but I am proud of it." After Morgan's death in 1913, Mellen said: "I took orders from J. P. Morgan, Sr. I did as I was told. . . . So far as I was concerned, the handwriting was on the wall the moment the old man breathed his last."[37]

The distribution by career types of the 185 business leaders of the decade 1901–1910 is summarized in the accompanying table.

TABLE 3.   American Business Leaders by
Type of Career

Type of Career	Number	Per Cent
Professional (lawyers only)	23	12
Independent entrepreneur	25	14
Family	51	27
Bureaucratic	86	47
Total cases	185	100

That this early in the twentieth century almost half of the leaders in American business were men who had been salaried office-holders virtually their entire business lives is remarkable enough. Such men, predominant in railroads, were also most numerous in nearly every major business field, while independent entrepreneurs were fewest in every field but one.

The whole group, nevertheless, remains representative of what

[35] *Independent,* 61:1491 (December 20, 1906).

[36] *World Today,* 13:829 (August, 1907).

[37] Clarence W. Barron, *More They Told Barron* (New York: Harper & Brothers, 1931), pp. 153, 168.

appears to have been a transition period not simply in the form of the typical big business career but in the environment that made new careers possible and in the sanctions that eventually made them preferred. Earlier, so great a proportion of American business leaders could not have been subordinates, of however high rank, for so long a term; the rarity before the last quarter of the nineteenth century of companies in which hierarchical careers could be followed makes this certain. Today, on the other hand, the number of great hierarchical organizations and the scope of their activities make it almost as certain that the proportion of bureaucrats among business leaders has become far larger than ever before, and that the proportion of great independent entrepreneurs has fallen.

That the latter trend was well under way before the turn of the century is suggested not only by the small representation of independent entrepreneurs among the men studied but also by the distribution of these men by period of birth. Considerably more than half of those born before 1840 were to become bureaucrats and this proportion remained more or less unchanged for those born later. The percentage of independent entrepreneurs, however, dropped from 26 to 8, even though such entrepreneurs tended to attain their peak offices at a relatively early age.

How much further this percentage has dropped, how indeed it has tended to disappear, is suggested by a study of presidents of big corporations today. Of 159 such presidents, only four—a scant 2.5 per cent—"started out as self-employed. Just one of these four was able to boost his company to national significance and remain president—the other three men shortly sought employment with established concerns."[38]

"Starting your own company," says the report of this recent study, "is one way to be president," but "the evidence shows that engineers and lawyers have a much better chance to become president of a successful firm." So great, indeed, is the current demand for such professionals that young men now study law or engineering often with no idea of independent practice and many forego

[38] "More Facts About Presidents," in *The Corporate Director* (November 1950). Virtually all of these presidents were of firms large enough to be listed on the New York Stock Exchange.

practice altogether and start immediately in administrative posts. In the middle of the nineteenth century, however, such opportunities were rare and in any case grasping them would have been frowned upon.

In that era, when the older leaders in the present study started work, young men, whether professionally trained or not, who had no prospect of inheriting a business and yet who at the age of twenty-five or thirty still clung to wage or salary jobs, merited as little regard in the business community as spinsters of the same age did at home. Roles of a sort, of course, were prescribed for both spinsters and employees, but for the latter at least these were likely still to be such as cramp the spirit and cloud over the blue sky of aspiration. Many businessmen, on the other hand, still took pride in being able to point to rising enterprises started by youths they had trained, and to such youths being in business for oneself still appeared to be worth much immediate risk and effort. As Carnegie put it, "there is no great fortune to come from salary, however high, and the business man pursues fortune."[39]

As the end of the nineteenth century approached, however, many able young men had begun to leave their jobs not only to start their own firms—a venture that would appear quixotic today —but more and more to transfer to competing bureaucracies—a step that already aroused resentment. Thus, as early as 1877, J. N. A. Griswold, chairman of the board of the Burlington railroad, wrote to his vice-president, C. E. Perkins, about the loss of William B. Strong to the Santa Fe, of which Strong later became president:

> This want of candor, to call it by no worse name, leads me to think it just as well that he should go. To me it seems inexpedient to hold men in our employ who are as restless as Mr. Strong seems to be, who without looking far into the future, lets himself out to the highest bidder— irrespective of his well assured position with us in which he stood directly in the line of promotion.[40]

[39] Carnegie, *Empire of Business,* p. 190.
[40] The Burlington Archives, Newberry Library, Chicago, Ill. I am indebted for this to Professor Thomas C. Cochran, who has permitted me to see the material he has collected for his forthcoming book on the railroad executive in the nineteenth century.

Acts like Strong's eventually forced the heads of older firms to face up to the fact that the defection of promising young men was weakening their own growing organizations and to the need to devise new incentives if they were to keep such men. This was as true in family enterprises which had been able for a time to hold onto competent young relatives—before such practices fell from grace and were branded as nepotic—as in other companies. Andrew Carnegie's perspicacity in recognizing this problem and his originality in dealing with it unquestionably were among his greatest business assets.[41] The princely nature of the incentives he offered to the "young geniuses" of his early executive teams—men contemporary on the whole with the younger ones studied here—is probably the measure of what was first needed to retain the loyalty of ambitious men to organizations not of their own making. The example of most such men, in turn, is probably what was next needed to provide stature for salaried executive positions generally.

That the old individualist sanctions died hard, even so, is suggested by the careers of such erstwhile Carnegie "geniuses" as Charles M. Schwab and William E. Corey. Each had been promoted step by step in the Carnegie company to an eminence just below that of the founder himself. Each next advanced to the presidency of the august United States Steel Corporation. There each held his position until ultimately frustrated by hierarchical protocol and probably by the demands of respectability made even by this most imposing business bureaucracy lest it offend the stock-buying public. It was the private antics of Schwab and Corey that prompted the remark attributed to Morgan: "The trouble with the United States Steel Corporation is to find a president of ability who does not need all his time to spend his salary properly."[42] Thus

---

[41] See the discussion in Herbert N. Casson, *The Romance of Steel* (New York: A. S. Barnes & Co., 1907), pp. 145 ff.

[42] Barron, *More They Told Barron*, p. 218. The rumors about Schwab's heavy gambling are said to have speeded his departure from the Steel Corporation (Barron, p. 86). He was succeeded by Corey, one of whose "closest friends" is reported to have told *World's Work*, 6:4027 (June 10, 1903), that "Corey's life is tempered to his business duties, simple, regular, such a life as others of the men who are doing great things persist in leading. Nor is

119

each was forced out and considerably later in life than would seem to have been usual two or three decades earlier proceeded to acquire (with others, of course) a great new steel company of his own.

Schwab and Corey were offering themselves, so it seems now, as hostages to their image of a freer past. Others among these younger transitional men also struck out independently, one at least to give lessons to ambitious bureaucrats of the future. He was George W. Perkins, who had climbed the ladder in the New York Life Insurance Company and in 1901 was rewarded with a partnership in the House of Morgan itself. Nine years later he resigned the more freely to write and speak of the conflict within men he had known who had been nurtured on the precepts of self-dependence and self-help only to become ensnared, as they saw it, in the new bureaucratic processes of conference, consultation, and compromise.

Many of their contemporaries, nevertheless, appear to have become better adjusted to the emergent conditions than did Schwab, Corey, or Perkins. One reason for this may be that bureaucratic business careers were already becoming honorific. As early as 1908, William C. Brown, who that year became president of the New York Central Railroad, was widely acclaimed as "the man who stayed on his job"[43]—a slogan which, had it been fol-

---

there any danger of his 'going up in the air.' " Casson also wrote of Corey in 1907: "He has few interests, if any, outside of his office. Not only is he president of the biggest corporation in this world—he is part of the mechanism itself . . . He has sunk himself, his personal likes and dislikes, in the socialized steel business." (*Romance of Steel,* p. 160). Yet that very year Corey had left his wife for the musical comedy singer Mabelle Gilman, and was eventually involved in a sensational divorce.

Allan Nevins notes that Rockefeller's partner, Henry H. Rogers, "would have liked to head the Standard himself [when Rockefeller stepped down], though he knew that his gambling propensities, diversity of interests, and unhappy public reputation made any thought of his selection preposterous." (Nevins, *John D. Rockefeller,* 2 vols., New York: Charles Scribner's Sons, 1940, p. 437.)

[43] *Harper's Weekly,* 52:11 (June 20, 1908). For the era in which career men were hardly likely to get to the top even in railroading, see Edward C. Kirkland, *Men, Cities, and Transportation,* 2 vols. (Cambridge: Harvard University Press, 1948), II, 452–454.

lowed a few decades earlier even in the railroad industry, probably would not have won Brown or anyone else much eminence or much fame. A little later, Edwin Hawley, credited by contemporaries with being "the country's leading railroad man since the death of Harriman," said that "a young man who jumps from one pursuit to another can never become proficient—that is, highly so —in any field of endeavor."[44] His advice, and that of others of his time as different and as differently situated as Henry Lee Higginson and Louis D. Brandeis, was to select a field and remain in it so as to become "expert" or "professional." In the Commencement Day address at Brown University in 1912, since reprinted as *Business—A Profession,* Brandeis said:

The once meager list of the learned professions is being constantly enlarged. Engineering in its many branches already takes rank beside law, medicine and theology. Forestry and scientific agriculture are securing places of honor. The new professions of manufacturing, of merchandising, of transportation and of finance must soon gain recognition. The establishment of business schools in our universities is a manifestation of the modern conception of business.[45]

Though increasingly honorific, bureaucratic business careers have continued since the time of Schwab and Corey to involve able young men in conflicts between their personal aspirations and the health of their firms. This is partly due to the persistence of the self-help ideology which shames men with slogans such as "always a yes man, never a boss"; and partly to the separation of ownership and management which Weber presented as an ideal of bureaucratic organization but which, given American traditions, has only heightened the war between the self-help ideology and the realities of bureaucratic life.[46]

[44] *St. Louis Post Dispatch,* February 1, 1912.
[45] Louis D. Brandeis, *Business—A Profession* (Boston: Small, Maynard & Co., 1914), p. 1. For Higginson's views, see Samuel A. Eliot, *Biographical History of Massachusetts* (Boston: Massachusetts Biography Society, 1911–1918), vol. IX (no pagination).
[46] See Parson, *Max Weber,* p. 331. For an illuminating account of the nature of this "war" in a man who eventually became president of the New Jersey Bell Telephone Company and one of the most enlightening writers on

Largely for these reasons the old difficulty of maintaining the allegiance of able executives has had to be constantly fought. Even as late as 1947, *Nation's Business,* the organ of the United States Chamber of Commerce, featured an article on this theme. To the uncertain though highly placed and highly paid hero of the piece who one day asked himself, "Am I a failure? Where did I make the wrong turn? Did I sacrifice my independence for security? Wouldn't I have done better if I had gone into business for myself?" this article replied: "You're happy with your work and richer than you know."[47] Such pronouncements have served less as balm to disenchanted bureaucrats than as symptoms of their ambivalent position. A striking instance of how this ambivalence might disrupt an organization was the split, early in 1950, between Charles Luckman and Lever Brothers, the American company of Unilever, Ltd., of which Luckman was president. "On the record," said *Business Week* at the time, "shifts in Lever personnel since Luckman took over have been broad and frequent. This is apparently what caused Unilever to lay down its ultimatum for a wider management base. . . . To nail down strategic executive posts and prevent turnover, Unilever had a plan for a wider participation in authority and earnings. Luckman wouldn't buy it, and that was the end."[48]

The persistence, nevertheless, with which most American firms have attacked this problem and the means they have employed— liberal executive bonus plans, broader participation of administrators in ownership, and especially noncontributory pensions for management—have added to the seriousness of another and I think even more fateful source of trouble. That is not so much the problem of bridging the conflict of loyalties in able bureaucrats as of disencumbering the bureaucracy itself of incompetents, often risen to key positions, who have proved altogether too loyal. I say more fateful, for this newer problem, especially, mirrors a charac-

---

bureaucracy in business, see Chester I. Barnard, "Collectivism and Individualism in Industrial Management," an address delivered in 1934 at the Fourth Annual Economic Conference for Engineers at the Stevens Institute of Technology Engineering camp, and printed by the Institute.

[47] *Nation's Business* (October 1947), pp. 40 ff.

[48] *Business Week* (January 28, 1950), p. 21.

teristically closed economy in which huge enterprises are astride the major avenues of opportunity. Top management in such enterprises often appears unable to avoid promoting faithful or friendly men who themselves have no way to go but up. Such men, in turn, even when endowed with exceptional talent for bureaucratic ascent, often prove to be cliquish and otherwise irresponsible as top executives. In emergencies they and their cabals may pull their firms down, and with them in most recent times the whole rigid system.[49]

The problem of what to do with such men, who nowadays are sometimes raised to board chairman, may already be noted in the transition period around the turn of the century when such chairmanships first were becoming fashionable. Then as now it had become apparent that for many men—for independent entrepreneurs drawn into the bureaucratic vortex as well as for true-blue bureaucrats themselves—the greater their business success, the greater their personal insecurity; the higher their ascent, the nearer their approach to failure. How often this paradoxical history marked the careers principally of former independent entrepreneurs is evident from the series of cases in Arthur S. Dewing's *Corporate Promotions and Reorganizations,* written at the end of this epoch.[50] How general it was up and down the line of the emergent bureaucratic organizations is equally evident from Frederick W. Taylor's classic *Principles of Scientific Management,* issued at about the same time.[51]

[49] See Chester I. Barnard, *The Functions of the Executive* (Cambridge: Harvard University Press, 1938), pp. 224–225 and chap. xvii, esp. pp. 272–278; Talcott Parsons, "The Professions and Social Structure," in Talcott Parsons, *Essays in Sociological Theory Pure and Applied* (Glencoe, Ill.: The Free Press, 1949), p. 198; and Schumpeter, *Capitalism, Socialism and Democracy, passim.*

[50] Cambridge: Harvard University Press, 1914; see especially chap. xxi, pp. 558–560. See also Frederick W. Taylor, "Shop Management," first published in 1903 and reprinted with other works of Taylor's in *Scientific Management* (New York: Harper & Brothers, 1947). See pp. 17, 18.

[51] New York: Harper & Brothers, 1911. See especially chap. ii where the prevailing system of "initiative and incentive" is contrasted with Taylor's "scientific management." In the former, in the vernacular of our own time, management did not manage, but left the initiative and planning of production to the worker.

This situation heightens interest in the general question not only of the structure of big business careers in this transition period but also of the means by which such careers were attained—by the most able big businessmen as well as by others who also rose to the top.

For some of the men studied here, an answer to this question is comparatively easily arrived at, though it may itself raise other more difficult questions. Henry H. Rogers, for example, one of the older and most independent of these men, was perhaps more richly endowed than many of his contemporaries with what Peter Cooper once called the "knack for contriving."[52] (Why this was so is one of those more difficult points.) His innovations in oil refining and pipe-line transportation probably gave the early impetus to his ascent. Yet Rogers, by his own description, was also "a gambler" often out to "have a little fun" and "always for fighting." "Once when Rogers had A. C. Burrage [a copper magnate] at the foot of the table with four other guests, one of the guests said to Mr. Rogers: 'How can you tolerate that Mr. Burrage opposite to you at the table?' Rogers said: 'I am enjoying it immensely. I was thinking all the time how he would look after I plucked him.' " "Almost the whole story of his gas interests," says one of Rogers' biographers, "was one of warfare, as was his connection with copper." John D. Rockefeller once said that "in working with so many partners," among them Rogers, "the conservative ones are apt to be in the majority, and this is no doubt a desirable thing when the mere momentum of a large concern is certain to carry it forward."[53] But that was hardly Rogers' view; he abhorred partners and involved the Standard Oil Company in the copper business and other speculations against the wishes of Rockefeller himself.[54] One of Rogers'

[52] Edward C. Mack, *Peter Cooper* (New York: Duell, Sloan and Pearce, 1949), p. 109.

[53] These quotations are from John T. Flynn, *God's Gold* (New York: Harcourt, Brace & Co., 1932), p. 336; Matthew Josephson, *The Robber Barons* (New York: Harcourt, Brace & Co., 1934), p. 338; Barron, *More They Told Barron*, p. 77; *Dictionary of American Biography*, essay on Rogers; John D. Rockefeller, *Random Reminiscences of Men and Events* (New York: Doubleday, Page & Co., 1909), p. 6.

[54] Cf. note 42, above. Of Archbold, who succeeded Rockefeller when Rogers wanted that role for himself, Nevins writes, "Never as cautious as

last enterprises—which probably speeded his death—was the construction, virtually with no outside financial assistance, of the 443-mile, $40,000,000 Virginia Railway tying the rich coal fields of West Virginia to the port of Norfolk.[55]

Equally simple in its way, though different enough to be instructive, is the story of another of these men, Conrad H. Matthiessen, in his own view like Rogers a self-made man. In 1897, at the age of 32—precocious, surely, by this time—Matthiessen became the first president of the "glucose trust," just organized as the Glucose Sugar Refining Company. The following year he was reported to have received the then extraordinary annual salary of $75,000, three times that of the president of the United States.

My success, as you call it [Matthiessen told reporters], is due to hard work and that alone. . . . I started at the bottom. [Then he said], My father was president of the old Chicago Sugar Refining Company [the keystone of the new "trust"] and when I came West [from Yale] he put me in as a workman at $1.50 a day. . . . I was gradually promoted and in 1890 [just four years out of college] the management of the company was given to me.[56]

Even where other types of careers may be as clearly outlined as those of Rogers (independent) and Matthiessen (family-made), reasons for the successive steps in them may often be more difficult to expose. This is especially true of careers which were largely hierarchical.

In owner-manager and family firms, the individual and the enterprise almost always must rise and fall together. The ups and

---

Rockefeller, he had learned from him that in a multitude of councillors there is wisdom; he believed in a large executive committee, and insisted that it hold daily meetings to present a variety of points of view . . . He reserved his judgment until the end, and usually based it upon a consensus of opinion." (Nevins, *Rockefeller*, II, 433.)

[55] *Dictionary of American Biography*, essay on Rogers; Nevins, *Rockefeller*, II, 436. On Rogers generally, see Barron, *More They Told Barron*, pp. 76, 89.

[56] *New York World* (March 27, 1898); and from an unidentified newsclip in the *New York Times* "morgue" but obviously from the same period and probably based on the same interview as that reported in the *World*. For the large holdings of the Matthiessen family, see Dewing, *Corporate Promotions*, chap. iv.

downs of both, in turn, are largely ascribable to their adaptability —itself often a matter of the personality of the controlling entrepreneur—in meeting objective economic changes such as those affecting the market for commodities or capital, the techniques of production, the size and quality of the labor force, and so forth. Moreover, the competition among such firms and hence among the individuals whose fates are so closely tied to them is largely for advantage in regard to these objective factors. The course of bureaucratic firms and the competition, where it exists, among them, are also affected by changes in their relation to these factors. But the fate of *individual bureaucrats* and hence the competition for preferment within the bureaucracy—the firm in Kenneth Burke's terms, becoming less the "agency" and more the "scene" of the drama[57]—appear to involve in addition a host of other variables.

Among bureaucrats, for example, an individual's success, as defined by his progress up the ladder, may conceivably have been won despite a concomitant decline in his firm's position, or, indeed, because of it, such a decline sometimes causing a shuffle in management that results in extraordinarily rapid advancement for whole teams of executives. The careers of many railroad men, risen to the presidency of their firms in this transitional period while the firms were clearly on the way to receivership, are striking examples of this.

. . . An individual bureaucrat's failure—failure meaning that ascent ceased below the ladder's top—may have occurred while his hierarchical firm, even largely through his efforts, was itself riding a wave of prosperity and unprecedented growth. Take the career of Theodore N. Vail, who, after making a notable record in government service, joined the Bell Telephone system in 1878. From the start Vail "was doing the creative thinking for the group" that controlled the American Bell Telephone Company (then the parent firm) "and really carried on the functions of president." But even in 1887, when the latter office became vacant, he "was

[57] Kenneth Burke, *The Grammar of Motives* (New York: Prentice-Hall, Inc., 1945). This entire work is given to an elaboration of the interrelations of Burke's "pentad"—act, scene, agent, agency, purpose.

given neither the title nor the prestige of the position. Members of the Boston aristocracy monopolized the honors. Furthermore, the Bostonians brought in a good many of their friends to the various departments . . . friends who were not always in sympathy with the far-seeing ideas of Vail, nor were they attracted by his gruff and blunt forthrightness." Snubbed by these men, Vail quit the firm in 1887, not to return until 1907 when a group of New York bankers supplanted the Bostonians in control and invited him to be the titular head of the American Telephone and Telegraph Company, which had become the parent corporation.[58]

Vail's unsuccessful competition with "members of the Boston aristocracy" is an early illustration of Chester I. Barnard's dictum that "where in a general society a low status is assigned, e.g. on race, nationality, sex, age, education, ownership of property, or family, it is difficult in general to acquire high status in formal organizations in that society." The careers of many other bureaucrats studied here illustrate Barnard's corollary that "where there is high social status it tends to facilitate attainment of high organization status, though less so in democratic than in aristocratic societies."[59]

In either case, it follows that bureaucratic careers must often be explained not only in terms of the firm's success in exploiting traditional market and similar external factors, but also of the bureaucrat's own success in exploiting personal factors derived largely from his personal or family status. As Barnard puts it:

Perhaps often and certainly occasionally men cannot be promoted or selected, or even must be relieved, because they cannot function, because they "do not fit," where there is no question of formal competence. This question of "fitness" involved such matters as education, experience, age, sex, personal distinctions, prestige, race, nationality, faith, politics, sectional antecedents; and such very specific personal traits as manners, speech, personal appearance, etc.[60]

[58] See N. R. Danielian, *A. T. & T.* (New York: The Vanguard Press, 1939), pp. 45, 70–71.
[59] Chester I. Barnard, *Organization and Management* (Cambridge: Harvard University Press, 1949), p. 330.
[60] Barnard, *Functions of the Executive,* p. 224.

"Old Corneel" Vanderbilt, late in life, once admonished a photographer: "Here, don't rub out the wrinkles and paint me up that way. I ain't particularly pretty as I know of, but I'm dammed if I'll travel in disguise."[61] As early as 1902, however, young aspirants for business success were already advised: "Be manly, and look it. Appear the gentleman, and be the gentleman. What's the good of unknown good? Negotiable intrinsic value must have the appearance of intrinsic worth."[62]

In white-collar work, especially in the whole range of the executive hierarchy, there are few if any adequate standards of efficiency, few if any accurate measurements of performance. One consequence of this at high levels, as Peter F. Drucker says in his study of General Motors, is that "a false sentimentality" is permitted to operate, "which evaluates executives according to the lip-service they pay to humanitarian principles rather than according to their achievements," especially when the principles are those of a forceful superior like Alfred P. Sloan, Jr.[63] Concerning the lower levels, the Standard Oil Company of New Jersey said late in 1949: "We are still in the dark on how to pre-select potential leaders. . . . There is no complete agreement on the exact criteria for discriminating the good from the bad."[64]

In ascent through white-collar channels, therefore, much more than through others, the display and manipulation of personal factors is likely to be most important. "Ability" is likely to be judged, as in the cited instance of Edward T. Jeffery, by the capacity to be congenial with colleagues, compatible with superiors. Barnard writes of this situation: " 'Learning the ropes' in most organizations is chiefly learning who's who, what's what, why's why of its informal society." Yet this process, he adds, often results in "excessive compatibility . . . 'single track minds' and excessively

[61] Wheaton J. Lane, *Commodore Vanderbilt* (New York: Alfred A. Knopf, Inc., 1942), p. 330.
[62] Fowler, *The Boy,* pp. 101–102.
[63] Peter F. Drucker, *Concept of the Corporation* (New York: John Day Co., 1946), p. 65. See also Drucker, *The New Society* (New York: Harper & Brothers, 1950), pp. 222 ff.
[64] *Business Week* (December 10, 1949), p. 34.

crystallized attitudes and in the destruction of personal responsibility."[65]

Perhaps it was a view of this crippling effect of bureaucratic life and a determination to escape it that impelled Henry H. Rogers and Henry M. Flagler, individualists caught for a time in the Standard Oil Company in this transition period, to undertake their own great private enterprises—Rogers with his $40 million railroad already described; Flagler with his $30 to $40 million development of Florida.[66]

But even such Paul Bunyanesque ventures were unavailable to salaried bureaucrats and their professional retainers to whom, as Mellen said, "the fortune generally comes when it is too late for us to enjoy it."[67] Nor was the spirit likely to move them, even had they the required capital. For early in this century, as the press and politics of the time made abundantly clear, the condition was already growing which *Fortune* in 1950 described in its full development:

The businessman used to get satisfaction out of being the man on the hill, the patron of the arts, the payer of the church mortgage—and did not everyone agree that it was right and proper that he be entrusted with the destiny of the country? Now, satirized in countless novels, politically a prophet without honor, he is stripped of the former dignities and of much of the old feeling of moral contribution.[68]

The question of what alternative modes of self-expression, then, conscious or darkly shrouded even from themselves, such "stripped" men of business have employed in the bureaucracies that utterly absorbed them must be answered more fully before the policies of these bureaucracies in the past fifty years toward the different segments of the community at large can be fully understood.

[65] Barnard, *Functions of the Executive*, pp. 121, 225.

[66] Sidney W. Martin, *Florida's Flagler* (Athens: University of Georgia Press, 1949), is largely devoted to this. See also Nevins, *Rockefeller,* II, p. 435.

[67] Letter of Mellen's in files of James T. White and Co., November 23, 1912.

[68] "Is Anybody Listening?," *Fortune* (September, 1950), 178.

THE BIG BUSINESS EXECUTIVE

Mabel Newcomer

Little study has been made of the total business experience and training of individuals who reach the top executive positions or of how this is changing. Analysis of three generations of presidents and board chairmen of the largest railroad, public utility, and industrial corporations in America gives needed insight into this process.

We recently started to give a lot of attention to the hiring of office boys. We have suddenly waked up to the fact that office boys have a way of growing up to be contenders for the presidency.

—A Corporation President[69]

The executives of 1900 were working in a period when "big business" was developing very rapidly. . . . Half of the business concerns included in this study had been in existence ten years or less. This meant that a large number of the executives were the first to head their companies. They had no accepted procedures to follow, no trained staff to carry on the business, and no predecessors to advise them. Whatever the advantages or disadvantages of such a situation, it demands different skills and presumably offers greater risks than the administration of a well-established and successful going concern.

Among the 1900 group of executives, two out of five were the first presidents or board chairmen of their companies. Among the industrials this was true for three out of five. For the 1925 executives, only one in eight was a "first" top executive, and among the 1950 group these were only one in twenty-five.

[69] The quotation at the head of this chapter is taken from J. Elliott Janney, "Company Presidents Look at Their Successors," *Harvard Business Review,* XXXII, No. 5 (September–October, 1954), 49.

Note: See Notes on the Authors, p. 555, and item 171 in the bibliography for the full reference to this selection.

LENGTH OF SERVICE WITH COMPANY BEFORE
ATTAINING PRESIDENCY

In view of the youth of the companies themselves, there was little opportunity for the 1900 group of executives to have gained experience from long periods of service with their corporations. More than half of this group of executives had never worked for the corporations they headed except as many of them were themselves the organizers of the enterprise. This is in sharp contrast to the situation today. Only 23 per cent of the 1950 executives came from outside the corporation, and less than 20 per cent of the more recent appointees of this group came from outside. The great ma-

TABLE 4. Length of Employment with Corporation Before Becoming President or Board Chairman[a]

Years of Employment	Number of Executives			Percentage of Executives		
	1900	1925	1950	1900	1925	1950
None	186	102	201	59.2	30.9	22.9
1–10	69	90	151	22.0	27.3	17.2
11–20	30	59	163	9.6	17.9	18.6
21–30	16	46	199	5.1	13.9	22.7
Over 30	13	33	162	4.1	10.0	18.5
Total	314	330	876	100.0	100.0	100.0
No information	2	—	6			

[a] The median length of employment was "none" for the 1900 executives, 7.5 years for the 1925 executives, and 16 years for the 1950 executives.

jority of the 1950 group had some previous service with their corporations, and the service for most of them was fairly long. Three-fifths of them had been with the company more than 10 years when they became chief executive. This is shown in Table 4. The median years of service before reaching the top was 16 years, and for the more recent appointees of this group 19 years. One executive reached the top position only after 52 years of service with his company.

The average length of service for the 1950 group before the presidency is shortest for the public utility executives and longest for the industrial executives. However, promotion is slowest in the railroads. The average length of service is shorter for the railroads than for the industrials because the railroads select their top officials from outside the company more frequently than the industrials. The median length of service prior to the presidency, in the 1950 group, for those coming up within the company is 20 years for the public utilities, 21 years for the industrials, and 25 years for the railroads. The median for the three groups is 21 years, and for the recent appointees 23 years.

Not only have the majority of executives of the 1950 group had long service with their companies before reaching the top; a large proportion of them have had their entire business experience with their own companies. The proportion with no outside business experience is shown in Table 5. The increase in the numbers with no

TABLE 5. Percentage of Executives with Business Experience Limited to Their Own Company

	1900	1925	1950
Factors in obtaining office			
Founders	1.1	3.8	8.0
Inheritors	94.1	93.5	77.2
Executives who worked up	7.3	15.8	29.0
Type of business			
Railroad	4.8	7.2	20.9
Public utility	5.3	9.6	11.3
Industrial	8.6	27.1	30.6
All executives	6.8	20.0	22.1

outside experience between the 1900 and 1925 groups is largely to be explained by the increased length of life of the corporations. The smaller increase in the proportion whose business experience is limited to their own company among the 1950 executives as compared with those of 1925 is due primarily to the decline in inheritance. It is to be expected that those who inherit the family business will normally start with the family company. It is true that the proportion of inheritors with no outside experience has declined over the period studied, but it was still 77 per cent in the 1950 group. At the same time, among those reaching the top by long service the number who have had no outside experience, although much smaller than among the inheriting group, increased from 16 to 29 per cent between 1925 and 1950. These data are given in Table 5. This increase in the proportion of those working up within the corporation who have had no experience with another business concern can be explained only on the assumption that long service with the company is increasingly recognized as a qualification for leadership. There has been no increase in the average length of life of the corporations themselves in this period that can account for this.

The proportion of officers with no outside experience is highest among the industrial corporations, largely because of the greater amount of inheritance in this group. However, the small percentage of public utility officials with no outside experience, as compared with the railroad officials, is not to be explained in this way, since the number of inheritors is very small in both these groups.[70]

The average number of years of service is longest for the heirs and for those who work up within the corporation. These two groups normally spend most of their working lives with the same corporation. The heirs, on the average, have 21 years of service to their credit before reaching the top. Several waited more than 40 years for promotion, and one waited 50 years. A vice presidency may come early, but there are often more sons than presidencies and chairmanships, and the father may himself remain in office until he is eighty or more.

Those who work up without benefit of family wait a little longer —25 years on the average instead of 21. Eleven of this group served more than 45 years before reaching the presidency. One attained it, as noted earlier, only after 52 years of service. The corporation itself discourages shifting from one company to another. Most of the private pension systems and stock options available to junior executives lose all or most of their value when the individual leaves the company. At the same time the lengthening period of service within the company has created some uneasiness on the part of the authorities on executive qualifications.

In most of the discussions of the kind of experience that is desirable for a top executive a broad experience is emphasized. To illustrate, McMurry says: "The kind of person who has the pa-

[70] See Table 5.

tience and submissiveness to be content for the major portion of his career to remain as second or third man in an organization is not inherently an entrepreneur."[71] And further: "A man habituated for years to thinking almost exclusively, for example, in terms of sales or production will experience great difficulty, in spite of his honest efforts to the contrary, in reorienting his thinking to see the whole operation in balanced perspective. Almost inevitably he will find himself seeing the organization's problems primarily from the perspective of his old specialty."[72] And J. B. Sheridan:

We are raising a lot of thoroughly drilled "yes ma'ms" in the big corporations, who have no minds of their own; no opinions. As soon as the old individualists die, and there are not so many of them left, I think the corporations will have a lot of trouble in getting good executives. After a man has served 20 or 30 years in one of these monstrous corporations he is not liable to have much mind of his own.[73]

In practice, however, there appears to be little effort to seek outside talent. Rather, the corporations are attempting to achieve the necessary perspective and breadth by sending some of their best executives to university training programs for executives.

PRINCIPAL FACTORS IN OBTAINING EXECUTIVE OFFICE

Any attempt to trace the way in which office was obtained must take into account first such factors as family influence, financial control, and individual initiative and effort. Second, it is important to trace the channels through which the individual has risen within the corporation, both the departments and the specific offices.

The principal factors that have been responsible for the attainment of a top executive position have been classified as (1) work in organizing a corporation, (2) inheritance, (3) investment, (4) success in another company, (5) working up within a company, and (6) all other factors. It is obvious that more than one

---

[71] R. N. McMurry, "Man-Hunt for Top Executives," *Harvard Business Review,* XXXII, No. 1 (January–February, 1954), 59.

[72] *Ibid.,* pp. 58–59.

[73] Director of Missouri Committee on Public Utility Information in a letter quoted in Carl D. Thompson, *Confessions of the Power Trust* (New York: Dutton, 1932), pp. 14–15.

of these factors may operate in individual cases and this makes any classification somewhat arbitrary even when the information concerning the individual is fairly complete. The resulting grouping of individuals has all the limitations of a value judgment based on inadequate data, but it is believed that even with these limitations it throws some light on the relative importance of the various factors in the different periods under consideration.

When an individual organizes his own enterprise and heads it, the way he came into office is clear. When he is a member of a group launching a new enterprise, he may be chosen because he has provided most of the capital, or because he is adjudged the ablest administrator. Ordinarily the individual who became president after participating in the organization of a corporation has been classified in the first group regardless of the specific contribution he may have made to it. All who were preceded in office by relatives have been classified as inheritors, although many have worked up within the company in a very real sense and have had to demonstrate administrative ability as well as put in long years of apprenticeship before reaching the top.

The category of "investment" has been reserved for those who neither participated in the organization of the company nor were preceded in office by other members of the family. They have made substantial investments in the corporation after it was organized and are presumably the largest single investors in the company if not the owners of a majority of the shares of stock. Or they are the representatives of the owners. Those who were chosen for "success in another company" are men who had demonstrated administrative ability in high office in other companies and had no close connection with the company that selected them. Most were presidents of similar but smaller companies. Some were vice presidents of other similar companies, and some came from quite different kinds of business. Most had no experience with the company itself, but if an individual was brought into the company at the vice president level and promoted to president within a year or two, it has been assumed that he was brought in with prompt promotion in mind, and he has been included in this group.

"Working up within the company" is applied to all with no rela-

tives in high office before them and who have several years of service (usually five or more), some promotion within the company,
and no important investment. Most of those included in the "all
other" group were officials of subsidiaries at the time of consolidation, with neither special merit or large investment clearly demonstrated. A few of this group have had other kinds of connections
with the company they headed—as suppliers, as customers, or as
agents for special and temporary activities. Presumably the members of this group were chosen largely on merit, but there was not
the same degree of competition that appears to prevail for the

TABLE 6. Principal Factors in Obtaining Executive Office

Principal Factor	Number of Executives			Percentage of Executives		
	1900	1925	1950	1900	1925	1950
Working in organizing corporation	92	52	50	29.5	16.3	6.0
Inheritance	17	45	114	5.5	14.1	13.8
Investment	60	46	58	19.5	14.4	7.0
Success in another company	42	38	151	13.6	11.9	18.2
Working up within company	55	120	421	17.9	37.4	50.8
Other	43	19	35	14.0	6.0	4.2
Total	309	320	829	100.0	100.0	100.0
No information	7	10	53			

group chosen from unrelated companies. They fall somewhere between those who have worked up within the company and those
who have demonstrated success in another company.

The proportions falling in these different categories are given in
Table 6. This shows clearly the decline in the number of organizers
and investors and the great increase in the number promoted from
within. There has been some decrease in the proportion of those
inheriting office in recent years—a substantial decrease if allowance is made for the growing opportunity for inheritance.[74] And

[74] See discussion above, pp. 83–84 [not reprinted here; see complete edition of *The Big Business Executive*].

there has been some increase in the proportion chosen for success in another company. In short, two-thirds of the 1950 executives appear to have been selected for personal achievement either within their own company or in another company, as compared with less than one-third in the 1900 group. They are administrators rather than innovators and risk takers.

The proportion chosen for success in other companies, while increasing, is still small in view of the emphasis placed by authorities on the qualifications for business leadership, on the desirability of breadth of experience and the importance of having had actual responsibility for making important decisions. This implies that suc-

TABLE 7. Principal Factors in Obtaining Executive Office for 1950 Officials, by Type of Business

Principal Factors	Number of Executives			Percentage of Executives		
	Rail-road	Public Utility	Indus-trial	Rail-road	Public Utility	Indus-trial
Work in organizing corporation	—	9	41	—	5.7	7.1
Inheritance	4	6	104	4.4	3.8	18.0
Investment	14	10	34	15.5	6.3	5.9
Success in another company	27	42	82	29.7	26.4	14.2
Working up within company	46	82	293	50.5	51.6	50.6
Other	—	10	25	—	6.3	4.2
Total	91	159	579	100.0	100.0	100.0
No information	2	23	28			

cessful executives in other business concerns are likely to be better qualified for the job than second-ranking executives within the corporation. In spite of this, nearly three times as many executives were chosen from officials who had worked up within the company as were chosen from outside. Some of these, of course, had had a good deal of independence as the chief executives of subsidiaries, but most were merely vice presidents in charge of some specialized department of the corporation.

Tables 7 and 8 show the principal factors in obtaining executive

TABLE 8. Principal Factors in Obtaining Executive Office for 1950 Officials, by Size of Corporation
(Assets in millions of dollars)

Principal Factors	Number of Officials				Percentage of Officials			
	Assets 100 or Less	Assets 101–200	Assets 201–500	Assets over 500	Assets 100 or Less	Assets 101–200	Assets 201–500	Assets over 500
Work in organizing corporation	17	20	10	3	6.6	8.4	5.1	2.1
Inheritance	41	42	22	9	16.0	17.5	11.1	6.6
Investment	18	17	18	5	7.0	7.0	9.1	3.7
Success in another company	55	48	30	18	21.5	20.1	15.1	13.2
Working up within company	115	105	104	97	44.9	43.9	52.5	71.3
Other	10	7	14	4	3.9	2.9	7.1	2.9
Total	256	239	198	136	100.0	100.0	100.0	100.0
No information	19	18	13	3				

office for the railroads, public utilities, and industrials separately for 1950, and for all corporations for 1950 broken down by size of corporation. The most striking differences among the three types of corporation are the comparatively small proportion of industrial executives taken from outside concerns and the larger proportion of inheritors in this group. Investors are most frequently found among the railroad executives. All three groups are obtaining approximately half of their chief executives from within.

TABLE 9.   Outstanding Voting Stock Owned by Executives in Their Own Corporations, 1952, by Size of Corporation[a]
(Assets in millions of dollars)

Percentage of Stock Held	All Corporations	Percentage of Executives			
		Assets 100 or Less	Assets 100–200	Assets 201–500	Assets Over 500
None	2.1	3.7	0.9	2.6	0.7
Less than 0.1	48.8	26.6	43.8	56.3	82.7
0.1–1.0	32.0	41.6	36.3	30.2	12.0
1.1–5.0	11.0	19.6	11.4	5.7	3.8
5.1–10.0	3.0	3.3	5.4	1.6	0.8
10.1–25.0	2.0	3.3	1.8	2.1	—
25.1–50.0	0.8	1.9	0.4	0.5	—
Over 50.0	0.3	—	—	1.0	—
	100.0	100.0	100.0	100.0	100.0
Number of cases	765	214	226	192	133
No information[b]	117	61	31	19	6

a Compiled from data in notices of annual stockholders' meetings.
b These include very recent appointees and executives of corporations in which stock is closely held.

Analyzing the factors by size of corporation, the most important difference is the increase in the proportion of executives who have worked up within the company as the size of the corporation increases, with a correspondingly smaller proportion of executives from all other sources. Whether this is due primarily to the fact that the large corporations have more administrative talent to select from or to other factors is not clear. It is not wholly the result of the larger number of investors and inheritors in the smaller companies, since the proportion chosen for success in other companies also declines in the larger corporations.

Taking the executives as a whole, the proportion that apparently

139

obtained office through investment has declined. Exact data on the stockholdings of the chief executives are not available for the two earlier periods, but the number of shares held is, of course, regularly reported today in the notices of stockholders' meetings for all corporations with widely distributed stock ownership. And these data are given for the 1950 group of executives in Tables 9 and 10.

The proportion of voting stock held by the executives, as

TABLE 10. Proportion of Outstanding Voting Stock Owned by Executives in Their Own Corporation, 1952, by Type of Business and Length of Service[a]

Percentage of Stock Held	Type of Business			Length of Service of Appointees	
	Railroad	Public Utility	Industrial	Over 10 Years	10 Years or Less
None	5.7	3.4	1.1	1.2	2.8
Less than 0.1	70.1	69.4	39.9	33.3	61.1
0.1–1.0	16.1	21.8	37.6	38.5	27.0
1.1–5.0	6.9	3.4	13.8	16.8	6.6
5.1–10.0	1.2	0.7	4.0	4.8	1.6
10.1–25.0	—	0.7	2.3	3.7	0.5
25.1–50.0	—	—	1.1	1.4	0.2
Over 50.0	—	0.7	0.2	0.3	0.2
	100.0	100.0	100.0	100.0	100.0
Number of cases	87	147	531	336	429
No information[b]	6	35	76	52	65

[a] Compiled from data in notices of annual stockholders' meetings.
[b] These include very recent appointees and executives of corporations in which stock is closely held.

shown in these tables, understates somewhat the number of large holdings since these appear in disproportionate numbers in the corporations in which stock is held by a small group of individuals, and holdings for these are not usually reported in notices of stockholders' meetings. However, the tables record the holdings of 87 per cent of the executives, and some of the missing individuals are new appointees in corporations for which stocks are widely scattered. Consequently, when allowance is made for this bias in the record, it is still clear that the great majority of the officials hold less than 1 per cent of the voting stock. They did not in the first place obtain their positions through their own legal control, and the authority with which the office endows them is dependent on the continuing approval of directors and stockholders. This also means that they are for the most part dependent on their salaries rather than on their dividends for their incomes, although dividends on 1 per cent of the stock of a billion-dollar corporation can mount up to substantial sums.

Further analysis of the data in Table 9 shows that stockholdings are lowest in the largest corporations. In corporations with assets in excess of half a billion dollars, only 5 per cent of the executives own as much as 1 per cent of the stock of their corporations, whereas more than one-fourth of the executives in the smallest corporations own more than 1 per cent of the stock. Comparison of the different kinds of business reveals the fact that executive stock ownership is higher among the industrial executives than among the railroad and public utility executives. And comparison of the earlier and later appointees shows a substantial decline in ownership in the latter group. This is partly because they tend to increase stockholdings over the years, stimulated by stock-participation plans and also, doubtless, assisted by their own growing income. It is also a reflection of the decline in the number who have achieved office by inheritance or investment and of the increase in the number who have worked up within the corporation. Even in the earlier group of appointees, however, only about 10 per cent own as much as 5 per cent of the stock of their corporations.

CORPORATE POSITIONS HELD PRIOR TO CHIEF EXECUTIVE OFFICE

The principal channels through which those that have worked up within the company eventually reached the top are given in Table 11 for 1925 and 1950. The group of 1900 executives who rose within the company is too small to make such a classification meaningful for them and consequently has not been included here. Some of these executives have had a widely varied experience within the company in the course of their service, but this has usually come at the beginning, when they had not yet found their proper niche, or at the end, after they had been chosen to succeed the president and were being trained by him for the succession.

Most of the executives have clearly specialized in some division of the company through most of their service, and even as vice presidents are commonly labeled as specializing in sales, production, finance, or whatever department they head. In fact, it is common practice for each important department to be headed by a vice president. The group classified as "general" in Table 11 includes such officers as the assistant to the president and others not attached to any of the special divisions listed.

The earlier training of the officials is closely related to the of-

TABLE 11. Departments Within Corporations Through Which Executives Reached Top Position[a]

	1925			1950		
	Railroads and Public			Railroads and Public		
Departments	Utilities	Industrials	Total	Utilities	Industrials	Total
Operations and production	28	23	51	70	105	175
Finance	5	7	12	15	57	72
Sales and advertising	—	11	11	3	55	58
Legal	9	13	22	16	32	48
Receivers	—	—	—	4	2	6
Personnel	—	—	—	—	1	1
General and other	6	10	16	7	16	23
Total	48	64	112	115	268	383
No information	4	4	8	13	25	38

Header spanning: "Number of Executives" spans all data columns.

[a] This includes only those executives who worked up within the corporation which they finally headed and does not include experience with other business concerns.

fices they hold. The engineers have for the most part been engaged in operations or production, and the lawyers have served as general counsel or in the legal department. But the original specialty is less closely related to the particular office held as they rise to the top. The nonprofessional college graduates are more likely than the professional group to have engaged in sales and advertising or in finance, although most of the small group with graduate degrees in business administration are in these departments. And those without college degrees are found in disproportionate numbers in finance. Most of the noncollege group started as clerks, bookkeepers, and office boys. Very few started as manual laborers. The engineers appear to have more manual labor to their credit than those who did not get beyond the secondary schools.

There is little evidence to support the statement frequently made that the sales managers are more likely to succeed than the production managers. Although there are many outstanding executives in the 1950 group who have come up through sales, there are also some conspicuous failures among those who advanced from

TABLE 12. Frequency of Vice-Presidential Office among Executives and Average Length of Service as Vice President

	1900	1925	1950
Per cent of total who served as vice president	17.2	35.2	58.2
Per cent of those promoted from within corporation who served as vice president	42.2	50.9	75.6
Median years of vice-presidential service	4	6	7

sales managers—and this was a period in which conspicuous failures were rare. Moreover, the growth of the professionally trained group—whose members are rarely found in sales departments—at the expense of the nonprofessional salaried administrator appears to contradict the belief that the sales managers are most likely to reach the top.[75] It cannot be assumed, on the other hand, that because the largest group has come up through operations and production this is the surest road to the top, since there is probably a larger group of officials to draw on in the operations and production divisions than in the other branches. Executives selected from the sales and financial divisions increased in numbers more rapidly than those selected from the operations and legal divisions between 1925 and 1950. Whether this reflects a growing preference for this training or merely a larger group of officials to select from is not known.

There is good reason to believe that those close to the head of-

[75] Only one in five of the sales group had any professional training, compared with nearly half of the operations and production group.

143

fice are more likely to be noticed and advanced than those more remote from headquarters. But vice presidents are usually chosen to represent each important division of the company, and in the end the president is usually selected from among the vice presidents. Of the 882 presidents and board chairmen in the 1950 group, 513 had previously been vice presidents of their companies. This is a much higher proportion than is found among the 1925 group, one-third of whom had served as vice presidents, or among the 1900 group, only one-sixth of whom had served as vice presidents. The difference is due in part to the greater number of the more recent executives chosen from within the company, and in part to the growing custom of giving vice-presidential rank to the important officials, such as the secretary, comptroller, treasurer, and general manager. The older corporations had no such galaxy of officers to select from. The officer finally chosen is often the executive vice president. In fact it is often assumed that the executive vice president when given this position has already been selected for the presidency. The data on vice presidents advanced to the chief executive offices are given in Table 12.

INFLUENCE OF CHIEF EXECUTIVES IN SELECTION OF SUCCESSORS

The foregoing data give some indication of the kind of training the executives have had and of the influences that appear to have operated in the final selection. The selection is made, however, by individuals who necessarily take into account a larger variety of factors than can be measured and who probably could not themselves state with any degree of conviction just why they have found one man rather than another best qualified for the job. Technically, the selection is made by the board of directors, but unless there is active board opposition to the outgoing executive, his recommendation for a successor will ordinarily be sought and approved. Often the chief executive selects his successor years in advance and trains him for the job. Assistants to the presidents often succeed them in office; but whether they were selected for succession before they became the presidents' assistants or whether their success as assistants was what placed them in the line of succession is not always clear, though instances of both can be found.[76] Some executives never squarely face the problem of replacement until the time arrives. This is not surprising in view of the fact that the executives themselves are usually expected to take the initiative, and they are not all prepared either to give up control or to take any steps toward that end.

When a chief executive officer dies while in office without having selected a successor, the board necessarily takes the initiative. A few other instances have been found where the initiative was taken by the board—or, in case of financial difficulties, the bankers—but without apparent opposition from the retiring officer. No instance has been found, although doubtless they occur, of the board going against the expressed wishes of the retiring officer.

Even when the recommendation comes from the executive officer, however, it is not necessarily a one-man decision. The recommendation may well be preceded by consultation with other officers, and particularly with directors. Even without formal consultation, the attitude of others in the organization must often influence the president's choice. But there is every indication that the final selection is usually made from a rather limited circle. Small corporations with a dearth of administrative talent sometimes make an extensive search for a new executive officer, even hiring experts to do the job for them. But the big corporations,

[76] Specific instances of a president selecting his successor are as follows: Deupree of Procter and Gamble was selected for the presidency by W. C. Procter (*Fortune*, XLV, No. 5 [May, 1952], 134); Colbert of Chrysler was "hand-picked" by his predecessor Keller, now chairman, and trained for the job over a period of twenty years. Keller himself had been selected by Chrysler (*Fortune*, XLIX, No. 4 [April, 1954], 220). Gaugler of American Cyanamid was selected by his predecessor, Bell (*Fortune*, XLV, No. 6 [June, 1952], 124). And Cordiner of General Electric was the choice of C. E. Wilson, his predecessor, and worked with Wilson for some years before he became president (*Fortune*, XLV, No. 5 [May, 1952], 154). These were chosen from within the company. Colley of Atlantic Refining chose Supplee as his successor on the basis of his administration record in a milk company. He was brought to Atlantic Refining as a vice president several years in advance of promotion (*Fortune*, XLVIII, No. 2 [August, 1953], 128). Porter of National Distillers chose Bierwirth, a banker, as his successor (*Fortune*, XLVIII, No. 4 [October, 1953], 148). And Ferry, chairman of Packard, took Nance from General Electric to head Packard (*Fortune*, XLVI, No. 5 [November, 1952], 118).

145

with a large group of administrators of their own to draw on, tend to select from within. This is clear from the proportion of chief executives who were promoted from within, which increases, as shown in Table 8, as the size of the corporation increases.

AGE OF ATTAINING CHIEF EXECUTIVE OFFICE

The average age of reaching the presidency or board chairmanship has increased. The difference is not as great as the growing length of service with the company might lead one to expect, since

TABLE 13. Age Distribution of Corporation Executives, First Year of Office

Age	Number of Executives			Percentage of Executives		
	1900	1925	1950	1900	1925	1950
21–30	19	10	21	6.1	3.0	2.4
31–40	55	45	80	17.5	13.7	9.1
41–50	114	139	300	36.3	42.3	34.1
51–60	93	100	352	29.6	30.4	40.0
61–70	27	34	108	8.6	10.3	12.3
71–80	5	1	17	1.6	0.3	1.9
81 and over	1	—	1	0.3	—	0.1
Total	314	329	879	100.0	100.0	100.0
No information	2	1	3			

this is compensated for in part by a decreased period of service in other business concerns. Nevertheless, the median age of attaining the top position has advanced from 48 for the 1900 executives to 52 for the 1950 executives. And when a comparison is made between the earlier appointees of the 1900 group and the later appointees of the 1950 group, the median age of appointment is found to have increased from 46 to 55. Moreover, the average length of service in the top position has increased so that the average age of the incumbents as of 1900 and 1950 respectively advanced from 53 to 61. These comparisons are given in Tables 13 and 14.

Table 15 also shows the differences in the age of attaining the top position as among the railroads, public utilities, and industrials as well as among corporations of different sizes. The railroad exec-

TABLE 14. Range of Executives' Ages, First Year of Office and Year of Record

Range	Age in First Year of Office			Age in Year of Record[a]		
	1900	1925	1950	1900	1925	1950
Youngest	21	24	23	26	31	33
First quartile	41	43	45	45	53	57
Median	48	49	52	53	58	61
Third quartile	54	55	57	60	64	67
Oldest	84	73	82	83	91	93

[a] These are computed from the ages of those actually in office in the year specified. The number of cases is: 1900, 192; 1925, 313; 1950, 686.

utives tend to attain the top office a little later than the public utility and industrial executives, and the heads of the largest corporations reach the top a little later than the heads of the smaller corporations.

The age of attaining the top position varies considerably with the way in which the office was attained. This is apparent in Table 16. The youngest groups are those who organize their own business concerns and those who inherit office. In 1900 the inheritors were much the youngest group, but in 1950 the organizers were the youngest. And at the other end of the scale, the oldest group (except in 1925) is the group that worked up within the company.

TABLE 15. Median Age of Appointments to Office

	1900	1925	1950
All executives	48	49	52
Railroad	50	51	55
Public utility	46½	45½	52
Industrial	47	48	51
Smallest group	46	46	51
Largest group	50½	50	53
Earlier appointees	46	46	47
Later appointees	49	50	55

147

One of the qualifications usually advanced for choosing a top administrator is that he should still be in his prime, and also young enough to have a reasonable term of office before retiring, in order to establish and carry out his policies. There is some agreement that a reasonable term is ten years or more.[77] Using ten years as a test, and sixty-five as a reasonable age of retirement, any candidate for promotion to a top executive post would be disqualified on the basis of age if he had passed his fifty-fifth birthday. That no such test is in fact generally applied is apparent from the above data. Half of the later appointees of the 1950 group had passed their fifty-fifth birthday at the time of promotion. This was also true of the railroad executives, early and recent appointees alike.

TABLE 16.   Median Age of Attaining Presidency in Relation to Way in Which Office Was Attained

Principal Factor in Obtaining Office	1900	1925	1950
Work in organizing company	45	$45\frac{1}{2}$	43
Inheritance	38	45	45
Investment	48	$51\frac{1}{2}$	51
Success in another company	49	48	52
Working up within company	51	50	54
Other	49	51	49
Entire group	48	49	52

And for all executives of the 1950 group, 315, or 36 per cent,[78] had passed their fifty-fifth birthday when they were promoted, 57 had passed their sixty-fifth birthday, 21 had passed their seventieth birthday, and 3 had passed their eightieth birthday.

Most, but not all, of those past 70 when they obtained the top position were either large investors or held a chairmanship that did not carry with it the title of chief executive officer. But the same cannot be said for the group appointed in their sixties and late

[77] See, e.g., M. E. Dimock and H. K. Hyde, "Executive Appointment in Private and Public Bureaucracies," in R. K. Merton and others, *Reader in Bureaucracy* (Glencoe: Free Press, 1952), p. 324.
[78] When those younger men who went out of office before the end of ten years are added to this group, the proportion in office for not more than ten years before age 65 is well over half.

fifties. Comparatively few of these were on a semiretired basis. The great majority of those appointed after fifty-five have been chief executive officer, often president and chairman combined, who obtained the position, apparently, on merit or as a reward for long service. And the number of chief executive officers who relinquish this office at sixty-five, even when they shift from the presidency to the chairmanship, is comparatively small.

The data on age distribution do not bear out the belief frequently expressed that big business executives suffer from overwork and worry and die at a comparatively early age from heart failure or ulcers.[79] It is possible that this applied to the vice presidents, but in view of the relatively advanced age at which the final promotion is likely to occur, it seems probable that those who live long enough to reach the top are a comparatively hardy group. A comparison of the age distribution in 1950 of chief executives between sixty and seventy with the age distribution of the total white male population in their sixties in that year shows that the decline in the number of executives between sixty-five and sixty-nine as compared with the number between sixty and sixty-four was approximately the same as the decline in the total male population between these two age groups. Yet the total male population includes all those living, whether active or retired, whereas the executive group includes only those still in active service. It is true that the group of executives between sixty-five and sixty-nine includes some new appointees, but it is also true that retirements exceeded new appointments in this age group.

TERMS OF OFFICE AND TOTAL YEARS OF SERVICE

The terms of office as president, chairman of the board, or both are given in Table 17 so far as these are available. A small number of 1925 executives and most of the 1950 executives are still in office.

The 1900 executives were operating in a period of almost revo-

---

[79] See, e.g., the statement by B. C. Forbes, that the "trend is towards younger men" because "the pace is much more strenuous" than earlier, and "more die at a comparatively early age" (*America's Fifty Foremost Business Leaders,* New York: B. C. Forbes, 1948, p. viii).

lutionary change, with financial control shifting from group to group, new and larger combinations swallowing earlier large combinations, and numerous highly speculative ventures being launched only to fail completely at an early date. Consequently, terms of office were abnormally brief. The 1925 group, operating in a more settled period and directing older and better established businesses, had much longer tenure of office on the average. For the 1950 group, insofar as comparisons can be made, the median

TABLE 17.   Terms of Office of Corporation Executives[a]
(Percentage distribution)

Number of Years	Entire Group		Selected Group[b]		
	1900	1925	1900	1925	1950
Less than 10	49.7	15.2	75.4	37.6	46.8
10–19	26.0	36.7	17.7	46.1	25.9
20–29	16.8	29.4	5.4	14.5	18.2
30–39	4.4	12.1	0.8	0.9	5.7
40 and over	3.2	6.7	0.8	0.8	3.4
	100.0	100.0	100.0	100.0	100.0
Number of cases	316	330[c]	130	117	263
Median years of office	10	19	3	12	11

   [a] Includes terms as either president or chairman or the two combined. In a few instances where a term was interrupted by some other activity, such as public office, the total years of service as chief executive have been used to determine length of service, deducting years in other activities.
   [b] Since the majority of the 1950 group are still in office, only those whose service had terminated prior to January 1, 1955, can be used for this comparison. In order to make the data comparable with earlier periods, only those whose service had terminated prior to January 1, 1905, and January 1, 1930, are included. This tends to include a disproportionately large number of those with short terms of office, but the trends should be indicated by this comparison.
   [c] All the 1925 group has been included, although 15 are still in office. The terms of office of these have been taken as of January 1, 1955. All have been in office 30 years or more. Some, however, who have not yet reached the 40-year mark may do so before the end of their term, thus increasing this group at the expense of the 30–49-year group.

term of office has declined below that of 1925. The reasons for this appear to be, first, that these officials attained office at a somewhat more advanced age, and second, that retirement plans are beginning to apply to the top officials as well as the other employees. Some corporations, notably Standard Oil of New Jersey, retire chief executives as well as other employees at sixty-five, but that this policy is not yet widespread, as applied to presidents and board chairmen, is clearly indicated by the fact that the average

150

age of retirement is above sixty-five. The average term of office is not markedly different for the different types of business. Consequently, the data have not been broken down by business categories.

The data in Table 17 make it clear that a large proportion of executives do not have the minimum span of office generally regarded as desirable in order to carry through their policies, even though large numbers are allowed to continue in office long after sixty-five. If, in the future, the average age of attaining office should continue to increase as it has in the past, and at the same time an increasing proportion of corporations should retire their top officials at sixty-five, the number getting as much as ten years in office to develop their programs will become a small minority. This raises questions as to how the desired continuity is to be achieved. It is possible that policy determination will become increasingly a group activity, so that frequent changes in the top executives will matter less. Or the trends may be reversed, either through more rapid promotion or the abandonment of early retirement programs.

Comparative figures for total periods of service with the companies these executives eventually headed are given in Table 18. The median years of service for the 1900 group was 15 and for the 1925 group 32. Comparing only those of the 1925 and 1950 executives who had completed their service by January 1, 1930, and January 1, 1955, respectively, the medians were 22 years for the earlier group and 35 years for the later.

A considerable number of executives in each of the three groups have given 60 years or more of service to their companies. The longest service record found in any period among those who have completed their service is that of W. J. Jenks, who started as telegraph operator for the Norfolk and Western Railway in 1886 and rose to the presidency at the age of sixty-six after 50 years of service. At seventy-six he became chairman of the board, and he retired in 1954 at the age of eighty-four, a total service of 68 years. Among those still in office, A. V. Davis, now chairman of the board of Alcoa, has been with his company 66 years. S. H. Kress has been in the retail business continuously for 67 years, although his chain stores are only 58 years old. And George L. Hartford, chairman of the board of the Great Atlantic and Pacific, began as a full-time worker in his father's store in 1880. This gives him 74 years in the same business. Longer working lives have been found. C. W. Nash, for instance, who began work at seven[80] had 77 years of work to his credit when he retired shortly before his death in 1948; but his working life covered a great variety of businesses.

It seems probable that in the future the average years of service will increase very little and may even decline. Although the tendency to select the executive from those with long service within the company is, if anything, gaining, this factor will probably be largely offset by the growing requirement of university degrees, which de-

TABLE 18.   Total Years of Service with Corporation
(Percentage distribution)

| Number of Years | Entire Group | | Selected Group[a] | | |
	1900	1925	1900	1925	1950
Less than 10	38.7	5.5	62.7	14.7	10.6
10–19	24.3	17.9	18.6	30.2	12.9
20–29	14.1	20.1	10.1	22.4	14.1
30–39	12.1	22.2	3.9	12.1	22.7
40 and over	10.8	34.4	4.7	20.6	39.6
	100.0	100.0	100.0	100.0	100.0
Number of cases	313	321	129	116	255

a Those whose services ended before January 1, 1905, 1930, and 1950 respectively.

lay the age of beginning work, and by the increasing—although not yet widely accepted—tendency to enforce retirement for top officials as well as for others. The maximum working life between graduation from college and sixty-five is about 45 years. But among the 1950 executives more than one in twenty has already exceeded this span with his company, and the great majority are still serving.

TERMINATION OF OFFICE

The age of termination of office, like the length of tenure, is available for the entire group only for 1900. However, the record is

[80] See above, p. 88 [not reprinted here; see complete edition of *The Big Business Executive*].

nearly enough complete for the 1925 group to make comparisons possible, and the same kind of comparison for the three periods can be made for age of termination of office as for the term of office. The median age of termination of office for all executives was fifty-nine for 1900 officials and seventy for the 1925 group. The median age of termination of office for that part of each· of the three groups that was out of office before 1905, 1930, and 1955 respectively, was fifty-three, sixty-three, and sixty-seven. If there is the same spread between the 1925 and 1950 groups when the 1950 officials finally retire, the median age of retirement for this group will be well over seventy. The median ages of termination of office for different kinds of business and for different sizes

TABLE 19. Median Age of Termination of Office

| | Entire Group | | Selected Group[a] | | |
	1900	1925	1900	1925	1950
All corporations	59	70	53	63	67
Railroads	61	69	57	64	66½
Public utilities	58	70	55	57½	68
Industrials	61	70	52	63	66
Largest companies	60	69	57	64	66
Smallest companies	60	70	54	62	65

[a] Those whose service ended before January 1, 1905, 1930, and 1955 respectively.

of corporations are given in Table 19. The variations for most of these are not marked.

The record of reasons for termination of office is necessarily incomplete. The great majority of the 1950 group of executives are still in office, and even for the 1925 group fifteen still held office as of the end of 1954. All the executives included in the 1950 group were actually in office in 1900, but were not included in the 1900 sample because their businesses at that time were still small.

Since all but a very small number of the 1925 group are now out of office, a comparison between the complete 1900 list and that for 1925 is possible. This is given in Table 20. For 1950 the only comparison that can be made is of the group whose office had terminated by January 1, 1955. These have been compared with the same groups for the two earlier periods, i.e., those out of office by January 1, 1905 and 1930 respectively, in Table 21.

The causes of termination of office are not always clear. Only when individuals die while in office is the reason for termination of office beyond question. For the other groups, the reasons for quitting are likely to be complex and not always frankly stated. The group classified here under retirement are those aged sixty-five and over who appear to have left voluntarily, or because of company retirement policies, and who have not gone into another busi-

TABLE 20. Reasons for Termination of Office

	Number of Executives		Percentage of Executives	
	1900	1925	1900	1925
Death	99	157	31.6	51.0
Retirement[a]	58	108	18.5	35.1
Resignation[b]	37	13	11.8	4.2
Other office in company[c]	9	9	2.9	2.9
Change in control[d]	70	16	22.4	5.2
Failure[e]	40	5	12.8	1.6
Total	313	308	100.0	100.0
No information	3	22		

[a] Includes only those who did not go into some other business.
[b] Includes those leaving voluntarily, usually for better position.
[c] Vice chairman of board, chairman of finance committee, vice president, etc.
[d] Includes both those who sold control and those who were appointees of a group which sold out or lost control.
[e] Includes both failures of the company, and failure of the individual to meet the approval of the directors. Failure of the company is responsible for 4.5 per cent in 1900 and 1.0 per cent in 1925.

ness. Voluntary resignations include mostly younger men who have left for other, more attractive, activities. Those who have taken lesser offices in their own companies are usually older men accepting a less demanding position, mostly part-time and advisory. A few, however, have accepted a clear demotion in their own companies. Change in control is sometimes the result of the officer himself selling his holdings in the company, although more often he is the appointee of some other financial interest which has lost control or voluntarily sold out. Failures include both failure of the company, and failure of the officer in question to meet the directors' approval. The actual number of these is probably larger than the figures in Tables 20 and 21 indicate, since financial difficulties often result in change in control or in consolidation with more successful concerns rather than in winding up the business. And where the individual himself is unsuccessful, he may appear on the public record as retiring or resigning voluntarily to take another position. It is exceptional for an open split to occur.

The comparatively small proportion of the 1900 executives, as compared with the later groups, who retired or died in office reflects the revolutionary changes in business organization and control that were taking place in this period. Under the more settled condi-

TABLE 21. Reasons for Termination of Office of a
Selected Group of Executives[a]
(Percentage distribution)

	1900	1925	1950
Death	19.2	38.4	28.7
Retirement	10.8	39.2	46.9
Change in control	36.2	8.0	4.6
Failure	17.7[b]	.9[b]	6.1[b]
Voluntary resignation	14.6	12.5	8.0
Other offices	1.6	.9	5.7
	100.0	100.0	100.0

[a] Those whose services ended before January 1, 1905, 1930, and 1955 respectively.
[b] Failure of the company alone accounts for 6.2 per cent in 1900, none in 1925, and 2.0 per cent in 1950.

tions of the nineteen-twenties the great majority of officers either retired or died in office. The relative proportions of those dying and retiring shift somewhat for the 1950 group, nearly half of those out of office to date having retired. This change is to be expected, as a combined result of the increase in automatic retirement practices and the increase in average length of life. Death and retirement combined account for about the same proportion of cases in each of the two later periods.

There has been some recurrence in the past year or so in fights for control of even the very large companies, and recurrence, also, in combinations. The shifts in control in the New York Central, the New York, New Haven and Hartford, and the Central of Georgia railways are instances of the first, and the combinations among the second-rank automobile companies are instances of the second. Other cases, including several not yet settled, could be cited. But they do not bulk large enough to have much influence on the proportions of those out of office for these reasons.

MR. AND MRS. CHARLES GRAY LEARN CHARLES IS A SUCCESS

John P. Marquand

> Charles and Nancy Gray arrive at the boss's house for dinner. It's a command performance of "Point of No Return." Does Charley or his principal competitor get the job? The scene feels and reads like some of the personal accounts told to the editors of this book by big business executives.

It was good business to learn unobtrusively all one could about one's superiors and through his years at the Stuyvesant Bank Charles had collected a considerable amount of information about Mr. Anthony Burton and his background. He had picked this up gradually, a little here and there from occasional remarks that Mr. Burton had made when there was general conversation, and more from Arthur Slade. In the course of time, Charles had been able to sift fact from gossip and to make his own evaluations, until now, if necessary, he could have written from memory a biographical character sketch of Tony Burton, and he could have filled in any gaps from his own firsthand observations of Tony Burton's habits. He knew that Tony Burton was both typical and exceptional—a rich man's son with inherited ability and with ambition that had somehow not been dulled by his having always been presented with what he had wanted. Though Charles knew that he

Note: See Notes on the Authors, page 555, and item 146 in the bibliography for the full reference to this selection.

would always observe Tony Burton from a distance, it was fascinating to speculate upon his drives and problems.

His life and Tony Burton's were actually two complete and separate circles, touching at just one point, and they were circles that would never coincide. Though they each could make certain ideas comprehensive to the other, the very words they used had different meanings for each of them. Security, work, worry, future, position, and society, capital and government, all had diverging meanings. Charles could understand the Burton meanings and could interpret them efficiently and accurately, but only in an objective, not in an emotional way, in the same manner he might have interpreted the meanings of a Russian commissar or a Chinese mandarin. He could admire aspects of Tony Burton, he could even like him, but they could only understand each other theoretically.

When Tony Burton said, for instance, as he was recently fond of saying, that the neighborhood where he lived on Roger's Point was running down, it was not what Charles would have meant if he had made the statement. Tony Burton did not mean that any place on Roger's Point was growing shabby or that crude parvenus had pushed in on Roger's Point. He only meant that several places during the war had changed hands rather suddenly—nothing along the shore, of course, but in back. He did not mean that the new owners of these places were financially unstable or made noises when they ate their food. He only meant that one of the owners was the president of an advertising agency and that another controlled the stock of a depilatory preparation. Though these people were agreeable and wanted to do better, their having been allowed to buy into Roger's Point indicated that the general morale was running low. It would not have happened, for instance, when Mr. Burton, Senior, was alive. That was all he meant.

Tony Burton's father, Sanford Burton, had bought all of Roger's Point in 1886, when there were no houses there, and he had built the Burton house in 1888. He had already formed the brokerage firm of Burton and Fall, and the Point had been a profitable real estate investment. It had not been difficult to sell off parts of it around the turn of the century to the proper sort of person. Simpkins, a director of U.S. Steel, had bought the cove, and the Marshalls, the Erie Railroad Marshalls, had bought the place next, and the Crawfords, the Appellate Justice Crawfords, were there also. Charles could remember most of the owner's names. It was good business to know them as many of them had accounts at the Stuyvesant Bank. In fact Charles knew the names as well as did the watchman at the beginning of the private road.

"I'm going to Mr. Anthony Burton's," he said, and he could even employ the proper tone, intellectually, "Mr. Burton is expecting me for dinner."

"You needn't have told him all the family history," Nancy said. "Why didn't you tell him you're forty-three years old and show him our wedding certificate?" She was telling him indirectly that she was feeling better, that she was all right now.

It was impossible to forget Tony Burton's house once you had been inside it. In summer or winter the air in the hall was balmy like the evening and fragrant with the scent of hothouse flowers. It was a huge oak-paneled hall, with a double staircase and a gallery and a Romanesque fireplace. For a second he and Nancy stood in the shaded light of the hall almost indecisively. There was an especial feeling of timidity when one went there, a furtive sense of not belonging. Yet in another way he was perfectly at ease for at those semiannual dinners Tony Burton had always made them feel most welcome. Besides, each summer there was always that all-day party for everyone at the bank, with three-legged races and potato races and pingpong and bridge for the wives. Mrs. Burton, too, always made the bank wives feel comfortable. The bright light from the open parlor door shone across the dusky hall and Tony Burton was already in the oblong of light, a white carnation in the lapel of his dinner coat, holding out both hands, one for Nancy and one for him.

"Home is the sailor, home from sea," Tony Burton said, "and the hunter home from the hill. I wish you wouldn't always surprise me, Nancy my dear. Why are you more beautiful every time I see you, or do I just forget?"

"It might be that you just forget, mightn't it?" Nancy asked.

Tony Burton laughed. He had a delightful laugh.

158

"We've really got to do something about seeing each other more often," he said. "It's been too long, much too long. Why don't you come to work some morning instead of Charley? I'm getting pretty sick of seeing Charles around." He laughed again and slapped Charles on the back and they walked behind Nancy into the drawing room.

Charles knew all about Tony Burton's drawing room, too, both from Tony Burton and from Arthur Slade. Mrs. Burton and the girls, before the girls had been married, had made Tony Burton do it entirely over. The enormous Persian carpet had come from the Anderson Gallery and so had the two Waterford chandeliers. Charles remembered them very well because Tony Burton had sent him to the auction to bid them in on one of the first occasions that Tony had ever paid any attention to him, and this did not seem so long ago. He also remembered the huge canvas of a mass of square-rigged ships—the British fleet at anchor. Mrs. Burton was always buying new things for the living room and besides Tony always loved boats. The cup he had won in one of the Bermuda races was standing on the concert grand piano. You could roll up the carpet and clear out all the furniture. It had been a great place for dancing before the girls had married.

"Althea," Tony Burton said, "I told you Nancy Gray would be wearing a long dress."

"Oh, my dear," Mrs. Burton said, "I should have called you up. Tony's getting so absent-minded lately. He spoke of it as supper. There should be set rules for short and long. Now just the other evening at the Drexels' the same thing happened to me. I thought it was dinner and it was supper. But the men thought this up. We didn't, did we?"

"Charles should have told me," Nancy said. "Why didn't you tell me it was supper, Charley?"

"It's always some man's fault, isn't it, Charley?" Tony Burton said.

"That's one of the truest things you ever said, sweetheart," Mrs. Burton said. "Everything that happens to a woman is always some man's fault."

"Jeffreys can bring us almost anything," Tony Burton said, "from sherry and a biscuit to Scotch on the rocks, but Charley and I will stick to dry Martinis, won't we, Charley? What will you have, Nancy my dear?"

"A Martini," Nancy said, "and if I don't like it I can blame it on the men."

"But not on Tony," Mrs. Burton said. "Blame it on Jeffreys. Tony mixes terrible Martinis. Don't you think so, Mr. Gray, or have you ever tried one of his Martinis?"

It was characteristic of that relationship and perfectly suitable that Mrs. Burton should call him Mr. Gray. It meant that he was a business friend of Tony Burton's, or associate might have been a better word, who had come to supper on business with his little wife. She knew how to put Tony's business friends and associates at their ease, but there were certain limits and certain degrees of rank. They were not on a first-name basis yet and he was just as glad of it. It would have embarrassed him acutely, it would have seemed like a breach of etiquette, if he were to call Mrs. Burton Althea. He knew his place and they could meet on common ground by his calling Mr. Burton Tony and by Mrs. Burton's referring to Nancy as "my dear."

Tony Burton looked at him in a fixed, cool way that made Charles think that perhaps he had said too much. It was necessary not to forget just who he was and what he was. It was necessary to assume a convivial attitude and yet not too convivial, to be familiar and yet not overfamiliar.

"Sometimes you have a cryptic quality, Charley," Tony Burton said. "I never seem to know lately whether you're laughing at me or not. Sometimes you're an enigma."

"Well," Charles answered, "sometimes you're an enigma to me."

When he heard Tony Burton laugh he knew that he had been familiar but not too familiar.

"Oh, Jeffreys," Tony Burton said. "How about another one, Charley?"

"No, thanks," Charles said.

"Definitely not?"

"Definitely," Charles said. "You might start talking about books and authors again and I want to understand everything you say tonight."

Charles himself could not gather what this was leading up to, but as he watched Tony Burton he could see that Tony's face was set in the expression he always wore when he was about to say a few graceful words before a group of people.

"Perhaps I'm being cryptic now," he said, "but all I'm saying is that I wish we might all be friends. I really hope we can be, in spite of anything that may happen in the future, and the future isn't as clear as it used to be. That's all I'm trying to say. And now if you girls will excuse us, I'm going to take Charley into the library. Charley and I want to have a little talk tonight but we'll be back as soon as we can."

Mrs. Burton stood up and as Charles rose he felt a slight wave of nausea. He could only put one interpretation on that hope for friendship. He guessed the final answer to their little talk already. He felt the back of his chair biting into the palm of his hand but he still had to say the right thing.

"Why, of course," he said, "we'll always be friends, Tony." He said it automatically but he knew that they never had been and they never would be friends. They might wish it but it would never work for either of them, no matter what might happen.

Charles was no longer thinking clearly as he walked with Tony Burton from the dining room. What he desired most was to behave in such a way that no one would have the satisfaction of seeing how deeply he was hurt. That desire was partly discipline and partly human instinct for concealment. His own reaction was what shocked him most because he had believed that he was prepared for bad news and that he would not consider bad news as complete a disaster as was indicated by the sinking feeling in the pit of his stomach. Yet after that first moment the shock was giving way to relief. He suddenly felt free and a weight was lifted from him. There was no reason for him to try any longer, not the slightest reason. He did not know what he would say or do in that final interview but there was nothing more that he could expect from Tony Burton. He would never have to be obsequious and careful again. He would never have to go through anything like that dinner. If Tony wished that they could still be friends, this meant at least that Tony liked him personally, but that was inconsequential. There was no room for personal likes in a corporation.

"It's over," he said to himself as he walked across the hall. "Thank God, it's over." It was the first time he had felt really free since the moment he had met Jessica at the firemen's muster.

Tony Burton's room had always reminded him of a corner of a men's club. It was filled with the mementos of the travels of Tony Burton, gathered on that trip to Bagdad and on two world cruises. There was a gilded Chinese Buddha on the mantel above the arched fireplace, and a Chinese ancestral portrait and other things, but Charles was no longer obliged to be interested in them. He seated himself in a comfortable armchair without waiting to see if it was Mr. Burton's chair or not. He no longer had to bother.

Tony Burton was still standing and again he wore the look he customarily assumed when he prepared to say a few graceful yet pointed words.

"Close the door, please, Jeffreys, when you go out," Tony Burton said.

It was like a meeting in the bank directors' room when someone who came in with papers was told to close the door when he left. Charles leaned back comfortably in his chair. It was up to Tony Burton and he did not have to try. He was thinking of other talks in other libraries, the Judge's library at Gow Street and that hypocritical library of Mr. Lovell's and his own library at Sycamore Park. Thank God, it was all over, but he still had a detached, academic sort of curiosity. He was waiting to see how Tony would handle the situation. Tony was sometimes slow and fumbling with decisions but when he made up his mind he carried them through cleanly.

"This friendship in business—" Tony Burton said. "It's always bothered me. They shouldn't be mixed together." He must still have been thinking of that speech in the dining room.

"They don't mix together," Charles said. "Don't try to make them, Tony." It was the first time he had ever spoken to Tony Burton exactly as an equal and it was a great relief. He flicked off the ash of his cigar and picked up his brandy glass and waited.

162

"And yet they must mix," Tony Burton said. "None of us can help it, Charley. If you see somebody every day, if you have any human instincts at all, you get interested in him. You're bound to like him, or things about him. I like everybody at the bank. They're like members of my family. Now take Blakesley. What do you think of Blakesley, Charley?"

It was not a fair question and there was no reason to give a fair answer and besides it did not matter what he thought of Roger Blakesley.

"What do you want me to think?" he asked, and he was glad to see that Tony did not like the answer.

"It isn't what I want." Tony Burton gave his head an exasperated shake. "You and I are alone here, and you don't have to be so damned careful. There's no necessity for it any more. I want your opinion of him. Do you like him or don't you?"

"All right," Charles said, "as long as it doesn't matter any more, Tony. He's conscientious, energetic, and well-trained, but I don't like him much. Why should I?"

"I rather like him," Tony Burton said. "He's been on my conscience lately. He's been so damned anxious, so damned much on his toes. He's always in there trying."

"I don't know what else you could expect," Charles said, and he was almost amused, now that there was nothing to gain or lose. "I've been trying pretty hard myself."

"Of course I'm out of touch with things, being where I am," he [Burton] said, "but I've been getting an idea lately . . . and maybe I'm entirely wrong. I wish you'd tell me, Charley. You're more in touch with the office than I am and you're in a position to know Blakesley. . . . It seems to me that he has some idea that we're considering him for Arthur Slade's place. Do you know anything about this, Charley?"

"My God," Charles said. "My God"; and he had a hysterical desire to laugh and then he found that he was laughing. "What did you think that Roger was considering?"

"I didn't give it much thought until about ten days ago," Tony Burton said. "I'm glad if it amuses you. It doesn't amuse me. When anyone gets ideas like that it's a problem what to do with him

163

later. You never thought that any of us were considering Blakesley seriously, did you? He was useful while you were away but he is not the right material. Of course, there had to be a decent interval after Arthur died but it never occurred to me that you'd have any doubts about it. Your name's coming up before the directors on Monday. Now what do you think we'd better do about Blakesley?"

Suddenly Charles felt dull and very tired.

"You'd better tell him something, Tony," he said, "instead of teasing him to death."

They were on a different basis already, now that he was a vice-president. Automatically, his thoughts were running along new lines, well-trained, mechanically perfect thoughts, estimating a new situation. There would be no trouble with the directors. There were only five vice-presidents at the Stuyvesant, all of the others older than he, most of them close to the retirement age, like Tony Burton himself. . . . Nancy would understand. Nancy had more ambition for him than he had for himself. Nancy would be very proud. They would sell the house at Sycamore Park and get a larger place. They would resign from the Oak Knoll Club. And then there was the sailboat. It had its compensations but it was not what he had dreamed.

"A week from Saturday there'll be a little dinner. It's customary," Tony Burton said. "You'd better be ready to make a few remarks."

"All right," Charles said, "if it's customary."

"And now we'd better go back and see what the girls are doing, unless you have something else on your mind."

"Oh, no, Tony," he answered, "I don't think there's anything else."

Nancy and Mrs. Burton were sitting together on a sofa in the living room and he thought they both looked relieved to see the men come back.

"Well," Mrs. Burton said, "I hope you two have settled the affairs of the world. You look as though you have, and poor Mr. Gray looks tired."

He saw Nancy look at him and Nancy looked tired too. He

164

wanted very much to tell her the news but it would have sounded blatant. Then Tony Burton must have noticed that there was a sense of strain.

"I don't see why you keep on calling Charley Mr. Gray," he said, "when Charley's in the family—or at least he will be on Monday," and then he must have felt that he should explain the situation further because he turned to Nancy. "I don't suppose this comes as any great surprise. Why should it? It's hardly talking out of school. Charley's name is going before the directors on Monday, but I've spoken to them already. There won't be any trouble."

If it meant more to Nancy than it did to him, it made everything all the better, and he was very much impressed at the way she took it. She looked as though she had known all the time that he would be the new vice-president, that nothing else could possibly have happened. She was fitting into her new position more than adequately.

"I can't say I'm surprised," she said, "but it's nice to know definitely . . . Tony."

A minute before she would never have dreamed of calling him Tony, but it sounded very well.

"As long as we're all in the family," Tony Burton went on, "I was just telling Charley that I've been worried about Blakesley lately. Do you suppose he really may have thought that he was being considered?"

"Now that you mention it," Nancy said, "I think perhaps he did —a little."

Chapter 4

THE GOALS AND TASKS
OF MANAGEMENT

INTRODUCTION

Men who occupy the managerial positions of our industrial and business organizations do so for a variety of reasons. The owner of a small business may be pursuing the goal of immediate and short-range profit; another is primarily interested in forming a monument to himself; still another is in search of power. Within the ranks of the large corporation the same diverse pattern of motivation may be found. Some are motivated by the drive for security and the need to fulfill the expectations of their peers; some are "organization men"; others seem to be searching for prestige. Business decisions, therefore, are not always based purely upon an economic model in the sense of maximizing profit. Diverse forces drive executives toward different aims. Consequently, their decisions cannot always be predicted with any degree of certainty, nor can the underlying rationale always be understood in the same terms.

Not only will the goals of management vary with the motivational patterns of men who make up the managerial ranks, but they will also depend to a considerable extent upon the particular situation of the business or industry at the time. Thus, a firm which is in a good strategic position with reference to the price structure and the market will behave differently from a firm in a poor position and struggling to gain its share. Newly established firms will have different problems and different goals from those of old and securely established organizations. Differences in business situations and perspectives influence the goals and tasks of management.

Fundamentally, the job of a manager is to manage the business in such a way that it will survive and grow. This requires dealing with men, development of a team, allocation of resources, securing of sources of supply and systems of distribution, and determining the best system of production and the most profitable product mix. These are some of the things that constitute the jobs of management.

So much for the general picture. What of the motivational patterns and responsibilities of the other levels of management—the middle and lower ranks? Research indicates that they all possess a common identification with the organization, but at the higher levels the goals of the executive are translated directly into organizational objectives whereas at the middle and lower levels the goals are set by technical conditions. Here it is necessary for the administrator to fit his own personal goals to those of the organization. The possibility of frustration tends, therefore, to be much greater.

The task of management at the intermediate and lower levels lies almost completely within the field of managing men and materials. The lower levels oversee the direct operations of the firm—production, selling, buying, and distributing. Here is the concrete job of managing work and workers. At the intermediate level, the scope of the task broadens but in essence it remains the same. It therefore becomes the job of top management to find ways to build into these jobs more of a feeling of participating in managing the business—of having some voice in directing the affairs of the organization.

Undoubtedly, this area of business enterprise is one characterized by great variety and sometimes vagueness. In many instances, the manager is not really aware of his goals and the goals of the organization. Policies outlining major objectives are not clearly set forth; organizing philosophies are absent. In many instances, the individual manager literally follows intuition with the result that organizational success is more by chance than by plan. It is imperative, therefore, that management think through its own goals and the plans for achieving them. Strategies must develop—strategies consistent not only with the objectives of the organization and its situation but also with one another.

167

THE MOTIVATIONS OF BUSINESSMEN

George Katona

The motivational forces shaping business enterprise are many and varied. They are related to the internal and external conditions in which the organization operates. While profit is, without question, the primary objective of businessmen, it is by no means the only one nor is it always maximized. Strivings for security, power, and prestige frequently play important and sometimes opposing roles.

. . . We must first consider the objectives which firms seek to attain through their decisions and actions. Regarding both business motivations and decisions, we can rely on a variety of observations and case studies, and can also make use of psychological concepts and findings. But empirical investigations that would provide quantitative information about the frequency of various kinds of motives, or of various kinds of decisions, under different conditions, are almost entirely lacking. The discussion . . . will therefore deal primarily with principles on a hypothetical level rather than present tested generalizations.

PROFIT MOTIVE AND PROFIT MAXIMIZATION

WHAT ARE PROFITS? The concept "profit" must be clarified first. Profits are not objectively given data. After they have been determined for a given period and especially after they have been reported and published, they may assume the role of facts in the minds of people outside the business firm and even of those who determined them. But determining how much profit was made in a given period is not an operation of simple fact-finding or arithmetic. It involves subjective considerations and is influenced by the attitudes and motives of the business owners or managers.

The simple definition of profits as the difference between what a

Note: See Notes on the Authors, page 553, and item 119 in the bibliography for the full reference to this selection.

commodity costs the seller and what he sells it for does not cover all that enters into the determination of profits, except in certain simple situations that are not typical in business life. Let's say John Jones, a bookkeeper, collects stamps as a hobby. One Saturday afternoon, while he is making the rounds of the stamp dealers to see what he can buy to add to his collection, a dealer offers him $3 for a stamp he once bought for $2. Because John has seen another stamp he would rather own, he accepts the offer, figuring that it has netted him a $1 profit. For John Jones the determination of costs is simple. He does not consider the value of his own time in effecting the transaction, or overhead, or taxes, or the need for maintaining reserves.

When we apply our definition of profit to business life, however, we meet with some difficulties. The price for which goods are sold is easily enough determined, and it is a relatively objective procedure to determine the total amount of sales for a year. But what is the cost of a commodity? What are the costs of producing a Chevrolet car and what are the total annual expenses of the Chevrolet Company?

In determining their costs, businessmen are guided by accounting practices and conventions which are not rigid and unchangeable and which leave them much latitude. Of course, there are costs that are objectively measured—wages and salaries and the cost of raw materials, for instance. But costs also depend on depreciation rates, on valuation of inventories, on allocation of overhead, advertising, sales, and developmental expenses. Multiproduct firms, dealing in several products, are the rule and not the exception, which means that the cost and profit of a specific product depend on the allocation of joint costs. How to apply the accounting principles, when to deviate from them, whether to transfer some "profits" to special reserve funds or to draw on such funds—all this depends on subjective considerations, on the businessman's frame of reference and expectations.

To be sure, the businessman's latitude is severely limited. Habits are powerful constraining forces. Businessmen habitually determine the excess of their net assets at the end of a year over their

net assets at the beginning of the year and make their valuations of
their assets in a conventional way. Also, naturally, the facts themselves present upper and lower limits to valuations. And yet, habits
can be given up and new decisions can be made. Often, with regard
to cost allocation, developmental expenses, and reserves, decisions
must be made. In other words, the exact amount of profits shown
depends on business decisions.

All this is, of course, well known insofar as the general principles
are concerned. With respect to the different considerations that
enter into the process of cost and profit determination under different conditions, our knowledge is limited. Empirical studies concerning the dynamics of those processes are needed. But what we
have said about the subjective character of profits may suffice as an
introduction to the problem with which we are concerned. The
analysis of profit motives, to which we now turn, will proceed in
stages, although the different aspects of the problem are interrelated. The first question to be taken up refers to the "subject" of the
profit motive, the person, group, or institution seeking profits. The
second concerns the time period within which profits are considered. The kind of profits considered and the means by which
profits are achieved will then be discussed and will lead to a study
of pecuniary motives that are not directly or not primarily profit
motives.

PROFITS FOR WHOM? If a man is engaged in a business of
his own, if he uses exclusively his own funds and has no employees,
the problem as to the subject of the profit motive may not arise. It
may be said that he strives to make profits for himself and for nobody else. The problem is somewhat more complicated in the case
of a large business enterprise in which the owner, the major partner,
or the holder of the majority stock is also the principal manager.
Still, the two cases are similar. But how about the large corporations, which at present account for the bulk of American production and distribution? As a rule, the "owners," that is, the holders
of common stock, are widely scattered, and there is no individual
holder or group of holders who control a substantial share of the
capital. Business funds are supplied not only by those who purchase common or preferred stock but also by those who invest in

bonds, and by banks as well as by suppliers and customers. Neither the stockholders nor the lenders are, as a rule, the managers of the corporation, nor do they have a substantial direct influence on the management's decisions. The ownership interest of the management itself is usually very small. Yet the management is self-perpetuating and frequently supervises itself by controlling the selection of members of the board of directors or by relegating that board to an advisory position. Although there are marked differences in this situation among American corporations, there can be no doubt that complete separation of ownership and management functions is a widespread situation. Therefore, we must ask: For whom do business executives strive to make profits?

The legalistic answer to this question is: The owners hire the manager to make profits for them, the owners. In sharp contrast to this assertion, one may quote recent statements of a number of corporation executives to the effect that they have responsibilities toward their stockholders, employees, and customers, and strive to strike a balance among these three groups of interests. Psychological studies of group membership, of belonging to, and identifying oneself with, groups, lead to a view which appears to be different from both statements.

If all motives were ego-centered, one might argue that the managers strive to maximize their own salaries or remuneration. The objective of getting the highest possible profit for oneself from the corporation's activities, that is, the objective of "milking" the company one directs, may prevail in one or the other exceptional instance, but it is contrary to the institutional patterns prevailing in our economy.

Furthermore, this objective is contrary to psychological principles of group belonging. We are not only part of our family, or of groups consisting of our neighbors or business associates, but the we with which we identify ourselves may also comprise our business enterprise. Although exact investigations are not available, it is probable that as a rule business managers identify themselves with the businesses they manage. Identification with the business in which one is employed may exist even in low-level employees or may occasionally be missing in high-level employees. But usually

171

the corporation or business enterprise has psychological reality for at least the executives. It is perceived by them as acting, as having objectives of its own, and as persisting beyond their association with it. The psychological reality of the firm appears to be especially pronounced in the minds of executives when management responsibilities are divided among several persons, as is frequent with many of the large corporations that are not managed by an autocratic president and his subordinates.

It follows that the corporation manager, as a rule, does not think separately of the interests of the owners, the employees, and the customers. On the contrary, he may think of the interests of his corporation without regard to the special interests of owners, employees, or customers. He thinks and acts as if it were his corporation, even if he has no ownership share in it. Improvement in the situation of the business enterprise brings him genuine satisfaction, and deterioration in its situation causes genuine worry, without regard to whether the improvement or deterioration affects his own position.

But . . . group belonging varies from time to time. At a given moment, during a conference with a customer, for instance, a business executive may identify himself with his firm, and a few minutes later he may think and act as a family member to whom social relations with this customer may be important. Ego-centered motives of business executives may then be in conflict with business motives. But it seems—although no definite statement can be made about this—that usually they are not. Institutional practices may have contributed to this situation. It has been found, for instance, that moderate increases or decreases in corporation profits rarely have a direct effect on the executives' remuneration or on the assurance with which they hold their positions. The personal motivation of the executives—to satisfy their ego, to have power, security, and larger and larger income—may be and often is satisfied through identification with their firms. Rivalry between executives of the same firm exists. But usually it seems to take the form of striving for a larger share for one's own department. The production vice-president wants larger funds for engineering developments, the sales vice-president wants larger advertising budgets, and so on, because they think that this is in the best interest of the firm. Ego-centered motives may be responsible for the executive's thinking but they do not detract from his identification with the firm.

It appears, then, that the current widespread split between ownership and management functions does not provide valid arguments against the role assigned to the profit motive in our economy. As a rule, a salaried executive will strive for profits for his firm. This conclusion may be somewhat restricted through the extension of group belonging beyond the limits of the business enterprise. As we have said before, people are members of several groups at the same time and identify themselves with several groups. Although a business executive may have the strongest identification with his own enterprise, he may at the same time be a member of larger groups. The entire trade or business he is engaged in—say, steel, automobile, or cigarette manufacturing—may constitute such a group, and the executive of one company may endeavor to establish a satisfactory market for steel, automobiles, or cigarettes, instead of devoting himself exclusively to his company's affairs. Identification with one's country may result in patriotic motivation which, like identification with one's trade, may represent a restrictive influence on the identification with one's business. We shall take up the problems posed by these larger "wholes" when we discuss the question of the kind of profits for which businessmen strive.

PROFITS—WHEN? The profits for which businessmen and business executives strive are, of course, future profits. The conception of maximizing future profits is a difficult one even in pure theory, as exemplified by such a typical formulation as: "The entrepreneur maximizes the present value of his prospective net receipts." In setting up mathematical models, economists have devised several approaches to the question of what businessmen should do. Sometimes, in the models, past profit rates are substituted for expected profits; sometimes future profits are discounted so that a dollar's worth of next year's profits has a higher current value than a dollar's worth of profits to be made two years hence; and sometimes large uncertain future profits are equated with smaller but certain profits. Are any of these procedures justified in the sense that they correspond with what businessmen actually have in mind? This question leads us to the study of businessmen's time perspective and their profit expectations.

Survey findings appear to indicate that businessmen as a rule have some profit expectations. They concern either specific transactions or the total profits of the firm. In contemplating and discussing large deals—be they accepting orders, purchasing goods, or making investments—expected profits are referred to, as revealed by company records as well as interviews with businessmen. Advance budgeting, a common accounting practice, tends to make the profit expectations definite. But often enough the figures written down are considered as illustrations only, or different contingencies are represented by several sets of figures. Similarly, businessmen, if induced to do so for the purpose of presenting their arguments to their bankers, directors, or colleagues, or to answer opinion questionnaires, may estimate that the next year's sales of their firm should be 12 per cent higher, and the next year's profits 8 per cent higher, than the preceding year's. What is meant, in most cases, is the expectation of an upturn, somewhat larger in sales than in profits, of an order of magnitude approximately indicated by the figures.

We showed above that the determination of profits depends upon subjective considerations. It is rather generally agreed that businessmen have even greater latitude in estimating expected profits than in calculating past profits. Definite opinions about future profits—as expressed in such statements as, "The firm will make $50,-000 in this transaction" or "Next year's profits will be 8 per cent higher than last year's"—are no doubt held with lesser certainty than opinions as to current profits. But the direction of a change in profits, or whether a future transaction will be profitable or unprofitable, is often thought to be known with great assurance. The general knowledge that the future is uncertain, or the experience that one has been wrong in the past, is frequently disregarded. Businessmen in their business planning, just like consumers in other kinds of decisions, are found to have definite expectations of the type of "I expect an upward (or downward) trend" or "This would work out well (or badly)," which they hold with great confidence.

On the other hand, it cannot be said of businessmen—any more than of people in other walks of life—that they have definite expectations all the time concerning all matters of interest to them. Such expectations arise only when the future matters: when the time perspective extends far enough and when there is need for genuine decisions rather than going on with habitual patterns of business action.

There is ample evidence for contradicting the statement that every business action is based on definite expectations. Take, for instance, a retailer who reorders some merchandise. He may do so following customary practices (rules of thumb). He places an order when his stocks are depleted—and in large firms a relatively low-level employee may do so when a predetermined point of inventory depletion has been reached—without giving any thought to probable future sales or profits. But reordering may also be the result of a genuine decision. It may then be done even though stocks are still plentiful. Because of new developments and anticipations the retailer may decide on a policy of increasing his stock of given merchandise. He may expect sales and profits in some lines of goods to increase, or shortages to develop, and such expectations may shape his decision and action.

. . . When, under what circumstances, do definite expectations arise? Only when strong motivational forces create a problem situation and call for genuine decisions. . . . What is the origin of expectations? This question is, of course, closely related to the first.

Profit expectations may be based on one's own past business experience. If circumstances are expected to be similar in the future to what they were in the past, future profits may be gauged according to past profits. But profit expectations may also be based on considerations other than one's own business experience. Among the variety of factors that may play a role, the general economic outlook appears to loom largest. In numerous surveys, businessmen have usually been found to have opinions about the trend of business fluctuations, opinions sometimes independent of their own business experiences. They have opinions about whether the economy is prosperous or a depression prevails, and whether the general business trend points upward, downward, or is uncertain in its direction.

Empirical investigations of business attitudes have not progressed far enough, and it is, therefore, not possible to list all the factors that may shape profit expectations and to assign frequency values to them. But it is probable that, in addition to the general economic outlook, new technological developments in one's own firm or in a competitor's firm, as well as assured or alleged knowledge about competitors' plans and intentions, play a role in reorganizing a businessman's frame of reference. In view of the multitude of such influences, it is not permissible for the scholar to identify expected profits with past profits without special studies or to argue that as a rule expected profits are based on past profits.

One further problem must be mentioned because it may be of special importance in business life. Suppose developments occur that call for new considerations and decisions. Psychologically, the stimuli and motivational forces press toward a reorganization of the field. But the reorganization is not achieved. Definite expectations do not emerge. In simple terms: The businessman cannot make up his mind about what will happen and what he should do. Among consumers, under such conditions of uncertainty, we encountered two frequent types of reactions: taking no action or continuing with the habitual pattern of behavior. It is possible that this happens in business life, too. Postponing a decision is the easiest and simplest way out. It is, however, also possible that even under conditions of great subjective uncertainty business decisions must be made. How and in what direction—these are questions for future research. Some recent theoretical considerations suggest answers—such as equating large uncertain profits with small, more certain profits—but no evidence is known to the author supporting this or any other view.

What, then, can we conclude about the profit motive? Since, at least in instances when they matter, future profits have psychological reality, it is possible for businessmen to be motivated by them and to work and act to attain them. But expected profits are rarely exact quantitative data. Businessmen can often distinguish between more or less satisfactory avenues of action, but they can hardly ever know what decision will result in maximum future profits. It would appear, therefore, that studying the amounts of profits businessmen expect is not among the most urgent tasks of research. Empirical studies might better turn toward determining the length of the prevailing time perspective and the certainty or uncertainty of profit expectations under different circumstances. The answer to the question, "Profits—When?" will vary greatly, and it may be useful to investigate the relation of the answers to such variables as business structure, business cycles, and business attitudes.

WHAT KIND OF PROFITS? The term "maximum profits" must be qualified further. The instances in which the term has a clear, unequivocal meaning are rarely typical of business life. Suppose I want to sell my house and have three offers for it. The meaning, then, of maximization is clear: I will accept the highest of the three offers. But complicating factors may enter even into such a simple case. Given certain expectations, I may decide not to accept any of the offers but to close up or rent the house and wait for a higher future offer. In business transactions there is usually even greater question as to the best way of making the most profit. There are usually many more alternatives than in the case of wanting to sell a house, and it is, as a rule, not possible for a businessman to weigh rationally all possible alternatives and to decide which will yield the highest profits.

Does, then, profit maximization mean striving toward the highest *known* profit? Methods to increase profits may be known and may, nevertheless, be shunned. The typical American businessman is not a fly-by-night trader who charges what the traffic can bear. This statement means, first, that profits are not sought by any and all means. Certain ways of making profits are excluded by law: businessmen in general do not attempt to maximize their profits if doing so involves the risk of going to jail. Other means of maximizing profits are excluded by conventions. There are, in most trades, certain things that are just not done. To offend customers, suppliers, competitors, employees, or public opinion in general is usually considered bad business even if it should lead to higher profits. This means that maximization is restricted by the extension both of the ego and of the time perspective. Insofar as businessmen consider the future of their businesses or as they identify themselves with their markets or their customers, they would not produce or sell shoddy goods in order to achieve higher profits.

That the term "maximization" must include such considerations as maintenance of the firm's good will or the reputation of its brand name is not the only qualification we have to consider. Unusually high profits may, in the opinion of some businessmen, lead to the introduction of new taxes or of government regulation and control. They may lead to wage demands on the part of the employees. Or they may lead to the entry of new firms into the business field. Therefore, it may be that less than what is known to be the maximum possible profit is sought. How do these questions add up? If businessmen strive for profits but not for maximum profits, what is their clear aim? It may be that they seek to attain "satisfactory" profits. Satisfactory profit is a psychological concept. It is meaningful only if there exist habitual standards that make it recognizable to businessmen. Empirical studies currently available are not sufficient to enable us to give a final answer in this respect. But it appears probable that, at least in many cases, striving for satisfactory profits has real meaning and represents a force motivating business.

Standards exist according to which current and expected profits are being evaluated. Within our institutional setup, the preceding year's profits represent the most important standard. Corporations generally publish their profits in comparison with those made the year before. Our newspapers contain daily a large number of reports of the type "The XYZ Corporation in the last quarter (or the last year) made $3.10 per common share, as against $2.78 a year ago." Similarly, in internal balance sheets and in budget calculations, profits are usually compared with those made the year before. It may happen, of course, that the standard is set not by the last year's profits but by the average profits or by the highest profits achieved in several preceding years, or by some rates of return on sales or capital. Whatever is the case, one meaning of the term "satisfactory profit" evolves clearly: It should not be lower than the preceding year's profit, or should not be lower than whatever is considered the standard profit. Striving toward satisfactory profits means, first of all, attempting to avoid a reduction in profits. Not to make less money than last year, or than whatever is considered "normal," appears to be one of the strongest motivational forces of businessmen.

What else do satisfactory profits mean? How much more do businessmen desire to make than they made the year before, or than they think is their normal profit? It is not possible to give a definite answer to this question, but it appears that regular, gradual, small advances in the profit rate are usually preferred to large upward jumps. Because of adverse effects upon public opinion, legislation, customers, and labor, unusually high profits are not generally desired or sought.

The standard which gives meaning to the term "satisfactory profit" may be found in other firms' profit development instead of in that of one's own business enterprise. Not doing worse than one's competitors may replace the aim of not doing worse than the preceding year. Doing slightly better than one's competitors may take the place of doing somewhat better than the year before. In times of a general business decline, the term "satisfactory profits" may have a different meaning than in terms of a business upswing. During a depression, profit reductions may be expected and considered satisfactory, provided they are smaller than the profit reductions shown by competitors.

Some preliminary investigations seem to show that not only satisfactory overall profits but also satisfactory profits in different lines of one's business may act as motivational forces. Businessmen appear to be highly conscious of the "margin" (rate of gross profit) on each of their usually numerous products and often look for high-margin items to add to their lines. There is some evidence that manufacturers and wholesalers, as well as retailers, sometimes introduce new articles because their margin appears high. Insofar as this observation can be confirmed, the profit motive appears to be a force contributing to changes in established business practices and to diversification and expansion of business firms.

Thus there are numerous tasks for future empirical studies on the role and function of profit motives. First of all, however, information is needed about the profit standards businessmen have in mind and about any other standards they may use in measuring their success or failure. In this connection, certain preliminary investigations make it probable that pecuniary motives exist that are not directly profit motives. It has been found that interest in business volume often transcends interest in business profits.

When in recent studies top executives of large corporations were asked about their own and their competitors' profits during preceding quarters and years, it was found that they frequently did not have the answers at their fingertips. When, however, they were asked about their own and their competitors' volume of business, and especially about their own and their competitors' share in the total market, exact answers were quickly forthcoming. Such findings are, of course, not conclusive, and it cannot be proved at present that the view to be set forth is correct. But it is possible that some businessmen gauge their success primarily in terms of their relative volume rather than in terms of their profits. Our newspapers and trade journals regularly publish the share of General Motors, Ford, Chrysler, and other automobile manufacturers in the automobile market; of Lucky Strike, Chesterfield, Camel, and other cigarette brands in the cigarette market. Businessmen in general know their own and their leading competitors' share in the trade, know of orders received by their competitors, and direct their business rivalry primarily toward increasing their share in the market.

Striving for volume, attempting to increase one's share in the market, may serve the purpose of securing profits in the long run. In a formal sense—in theoretical methods—of course, the aim "maximum volume" will rarely be exactly the same as the aim "maximum profit." We are, however, concerned only with the direction of the motivational forces, and it appears that the two drives usually reinforce each other rather than conflict with each other. But it may also happen that increase in volume or the growth of one's firm is desired irrespective of its contribution to future profits. This would imply that striving toward larger volume may become an objective in itself. It may then be related to the social desires of businessmen. This is the problem which we shall take up next when we raise the question about the role and place of pecuniary motives within the framework of business motivation.

THE MOTIVATIONAL PATTERNS

We know that the psychological field usually contains diverse forces driving us toward different aims. Some of them may conflict and some may reinforce each other. If it were true that business-men are single-minded, governed by nothing but the profit motive, then we would have to assume that human beings change when they enter their business offices. That one single motive becomes paramount, and the motivational pattern is ruled by one objective alone, may occasionally happen in family life, in the sphere of scientific research, or in business. But this cannot be assumed to be generally true under all circumstances. The investigation of motivational patterns in business must begin with an enumeration of the variety of factors which have been found to enter into these patterns, and must then proceed to the question of whether under certain conditions some of the motives become prevalent while others fade away.

In listing the factors that may play a role in business motivation, we may refer first to the biological needs that drive men to secure subsistence. Another basic motivational force is relief of anxiety which, in the case of business activities, may lead to striving for security. One possible way of achieving subsistence as well as security, in our institutional setup, is through making money. We engage in business in order to make money, which we desire, need, and plan to use for the sake of other more basic or more immediate satisfactions. In certain circumstances, the means may become ends, and we may strive for profits for the sake of the profits themselves. More generally, however, the desire for security implies striving for continuous, regular income rather than short-period maximum profits. The anxiety-security mechanism may be much stronger in the negative than in the positive sense. Avoidance of bankruptcy, avoidance of business losses, and avoidance of a decline in profits may on this level of motivation be stronger drives than those directed toward increasing profits.

Next we must take social needs into account. The phenomenon

of group membership makes the desire to occupy an esteemed, a high, or even an outstanding position in one's group understandable. We strive for approbation by those belonging to our group. We desire prestige among our business associates, neighbors, and fellow citizens; our ambitions are linked with the esteem and opinion of others regarding our position and progress.

The urge for prestige may develop into a desire to influence other members of our group, to control or dominate them—in short, into a striving for power. There are indications that the prevailing institutional setup has greatly enhanced the desire for power among American businessmen. This desire is closely connected with the striving for profits and the striving for regular and secure profits. A business firm which rules and dominates its market is usually more profitable and has less to fear from sudden adverse developments than a firm which is in a weak position vis-à-vis its suppliers, competitors, and customers. The relative size of a firm in its trade, as well as the absolute size of the firm's physical assets and capital funds, is related to the firm's power position. Outstanding and acknowledged quality of a product or the service of a firm, or the popularity of its brand name, is a further means that makes for supremacy of the firm over its competitors and customers. Striving for control of the market may become the motivational factor of the highest visibility, because it is interlocked with several other motivational forces.

With respect to striving for power, ego-centered motivations of business executives often coincide with their business or group motivations. A president of a weak firm may be a dictator in his own office but must assume a subordinate role in negotiating with suppliers and customers. The head or executive of a powerful firm may, however, exercise power all around and thus satisfy personal as well as business drives.

The feeling of achievement is, however, not necessarily accomplished through the reaction of other people. Inherent satisfactions may be derived from a job well done without the approbation or even awareness of others. Professional pride may be derived from business activities even if they do not contribute to prestige of power. There are values and satisfactions in self-realization, and there is dissatisfaction in tasks not completed, in failure, in not getting ahead with a task. Desire for progress or for growth may be the joint result of subsistence needs, of social needs, and of the urge toward self-realization. Because of our identification with the business enterprise which we own or manage, or in which we are employed, these forces again may be centered in the business firm instead of in our own advancement. Self-realization may be achieved through the progress or growth of the business enterprise of which we are a part.

We said before that the going concern is commonly viewed as a living entity of itself. Self-realization of a business concern represents, then, a topic worth further study. A corporation is not conceived by its executives simply as an organization making money, or making automobiles. It has to carry out its functions, complete the tasks taken up, and expand to justify itself. It has been recently pointed out that here may be found one of the most important explanations of the fact that our large corporations are continuously expanding in diverse fields that are often foreign to their original activity. Small investments may be made, for instance, in order to study the use of by-products or waste products. When some progress has been achieved, the task once begun is pushed toward completion. There is a drive, perhaps even a compulsion, to follow through after one has begun. Or materials purchased from other firms are studied, then manufactured experimentally in a pilot plant, and ultimately manufactured on a large scale. Or the technical know-how in the firm's laboratories drives toward self-realization and, ultimately—to give one example—General Motors becomes the leading producer of Diesel locomotives.

The structure that results from the interplay of the diverse motivational forces must be assumed to vary greatly under different conditions. When, under what conditions, will one or the other motive play a leading role? Empirical studies have not progressed far enough to permit a definite answer to this question. Nevertheless, we may contrast two extreme business situations and try to describe the differences in the motivational patterns that would prevail under the two different sets of conditions. We shall take up first the business enterprise that is in a precarious situation; for instance, a new firm with insufficient capital struggling to stay in business, or any business firm under adverse conditions or in the midst of a severe depression. Then, disregarding intermediate situations, we shall discuss the motivational forces that may influence a well-established firm operating under prosperous conditions.

The first major difference between the psychological fields in which business firms operate under the two situations is probably in their time perspective. In the first case, what will happen years from now hardly enters into consideration. Long-range transactions that would bring large profits after many years, investments that would pay only after some time, are ruled out. The immediate problems are pressing. The main aim is survival. The means to this end may be sought and found in quick profits, even though they may be lower than possible future profits. Or, they may be found in transactions that contribute to liquidity and solvency. To reduce debts or to build up liquid funds may become the strongest business motive. Under these conditions, not only will the pecuniary motives be of short range, but they will also prevail in preference to non-pecuniary motives. Satisfaction of social needs, self-realization, or the urge for growth will play minor roles.

In the case of a well-established business firm operating under prosperous conditions, the time perspective will usually extend into the relatively distant future. Transactions that may not bring any profit for a number of years and long-range investments may be contemplated. Whether or not they will be made will depend on the businessman's expectations. The nature of the profit expectations, their degree of certainty, and all the factors shaping those expectations will greatly contribute to decision formation.

Not only the time period considered but also the scope of the motivational forces will be extended under prosperous conditions. The company's volume and its share in the market will become important considerations. The good will of the firm or the reputation of the firm's brand name may be given greater weight than the size of liquid assets and profits. Reputation among customers and among suppliers may be assigned large pecuniary value. Beyond the desire to maintain a strong market for his goods, the businessman's interest may extend to the entire country. Maintenance of full employment and avoidance of depression may become goals that influence specific business decisions.

The so-called nonpecuniary motives may loom large in the case of well-established businesses operating under prosperous conditions. Improving the living and social standards of the firm's employees or even of the town in which the factory is located may be viewed as being in the interest of the firm itself. Employee relations and productivity of the employees may be thought to be improved by such indirect means as building recreational facilities or hospitals, or by slum clearance. Desire for prestige will be interwoven with more specific business motives.

All this adds up to a weakening of the motivational forces directed toward high immediate profits. Furthermore, under these conditions businessmen will be aware of dangers inherent in large profits and will study the vulnerability of a condition which may be viewed by others as representing excessive profits.

We have discussed two extreme situations. Naturally, intermediate conditions prevail very often, that is, conditions which the businessmen consider neither precarious nor highly prosperous. Not much is known about the motivational patterns prevailing under intermediate conditions, but it is probable that both the length of the time perspective and the role played by social needs increase as we go farther from the first and approach the second extreme situation. Furthermore, striving for increased profits may be more prevalent in a situation that is relatively close to precarious conditions, and striving to avoid reduction in profits more prevalent in a situation that is relatively close to prosperous conditions.

Two paradoxical conclusions emerge. It appears, first, that the worse the situation, the more powerful is the urge toward high or maximum immediate profits, and the less powerful the nonpecuniary motives. Second, it appears that the desire to avoid a decrease in profits may be stronger than the desire to increase profits.

Differences in business situations other than those between precarious and prosperous conditions should be studied with regard to their influence on the structure of motivational patterns. It is possible, for instance, that prevalent motivational patterns may differ as between new and old industries or relatively competitive and relatively monopolistic fields of business. It has been argued that businessmen in new industries (for instance, in the airplane industry or electronics) are characterized by a much greater degree of venturesomeness than businessmen in old industries (for instance, in the railroad or coal-mining industry). Or it is possible that in business fields in which there are no established leaders and into which entry is easy (as examples, women's dress manufacture or the laundry or the baking industries may be mentioned) a much greater degree of uncertainty and a shorter time perspective prevail than in such fields as the aluminum or the automobile industry, where a few established firms are believed to occupy a secure position.

These considerations point toward important tasks for future research. First, the facts themselves must be established and, second, careful studies must be undertaken to shed light on the causes of the differences in motivational patterns—provided such differences are found to prevail. The two tasks are closely connected, because it is possible that the age of an industry or its degree of competitiveness as such does not make for differences in business motives. It may be that, without regard to the business structure, there are periods in each industry in which business leaders, so to speak, relax and are interested only in preserving what they have; and other periods in which striving to expand and to gain advantages over competitors are most significant. (In the "old" railroad industry, for instance, the introduction of lightweight, air-conditioned trains and Diesel engines may have constituted expansion.)

Those who assume that the motives of executives in old and new industries differ sometimes explain the differences by the traits of the executives themselves. Men of inherently conservative character are thought to seek employment and advancement in old industries, while men of imagination, endowed with an enterprising spirit, strive to promote new industries. Yet another type of causation, namely, the shaping of personalities by the atmosphere and conditions prevailing in the industry in which one works and with which one identifies oneself, appears possible and even more probable. On the other hand, there may be instances in which a business executive relinquishes his position and enters a different field of business because his own motivational pattern is not in accord with that of the business in which he has worked.

Information is needed, furthermore, about the motives of executives of large as against small business firms. It may be argued, and it has been said, that large firms with large staffs tend to be bureaucratic; not only the day-to-day work but also the decision formation is routinized, that is, follows established rules. Therefore, for large firms, it is difficult, if not impossible, to deviate from habitual business procedures that are directed toward preserving the *status quo* instead of toward gaining new advantages. Small firms, on the other hand, are described as flexible; they may change their decisions frequently and even embark on adventures.

On the other hand, however, small firms are usually in a more precarious position than large firms. Therefore, possibly only large firms can make the really long-range plans that are needed for new ventures. Furthermore, small firms usually require outside financing for expansion, while large firms often have substantial liquid reserves or can use profits for such purposes. Strings are commonly attached to borrowing money, and the consent of the lenders to any but conservative procedures is rarely obtainable. In these respects, again, the facts themselves are disputed and require study. The question is whether the size of their business is a factor shaping or even determining the outlook, the ambition, and the motives of businessmen.

The prevailing structure of the motivational patterns in the American economy has been changing in the past and will no doubt change in the future. Capitalism as we know it now differs from nineteenth-century capitalism and probably from future capitalism. What has been described, for instance, as the probable differences in the motivations of prosperous and weak business firms may not have existed a few decades ago and may not be true a few decades hence. The frame of reference of a business community may vary greatly from time to time and from country to country. There are some indications, but hardly any reliable data, that in the nineteenth century in the United States the appreciation of, and the striving toward, higher profits was more pronounced than now, and certain motivational forces played a role at that time which we have omitted from consideration. We have not referred, in describing the present situation, to businessmen's pleasure in risk taking or even in gambling. Nor have we given any consideration to the possibility that some people may consider business as an adventure or as a way to get rich quickly, or that some may seek the thrill of playing with other people's money.

The given description of the current situation applies to a period in which many businessmen assume a somewhat apologetic viewpoint. Instead of being proud of profits made, they see a need to justify them and, in some cases and in a certain sense, to excuse them. It is, of course, possible that this represents nothing but tactics, that is, an attempt to influence wage negotiations, tax legislation, or other public policies. It is also possible that it represents a superficial rationalization or is completely insincere. Still, in all probability, the point of view, if repeated over and over again, changes the psychological field both of those who pronounce it and those who hear it. The motives and actions of businessmen who proclaim publicly and proudly their objective of making large profits may differ greatly from those of businessmen who are apologetic about their profits.

Much further empirical research is needed with respect to the characterization of currently prevailing motivational patterns, their relation to business structure, and their origin. Such research is possible because business motives, like other intervening variables, can be analyzed by observing business behavior under different conditions as well as by recording the explanations businessmen themselves give of the reasons for their behavior.

THE TASKS OF MANAGEMENT

Peter F. Drucker

The first and primary function of the management of a business enterprise is economic. It can be judged only by

Note: See Notes on the Authors, page 552, and item 68 in the bibliography for the full reference to this selection.

the economic results: consumer goods and services desired by the consumer at a price he is willing to pay. The first job of management is, therefore, managing a business; the second is managing managers; and the third, managing workers and work.

Despite its crucial importance, its high visibility, and its spectacular rise, management is the least known and the least understood of our basic institutions. Even the people in a business often do not know what their management does and what it is supposed to be doing, how it acts and why, whether it does a good job or not. Indeed, the typical picture of what goes on in the "front office" or on "the fourteenth floor" in the minds of otherwise sane, well-informed and intelligent employees (including, often, people themselves in responsible managerial and specialist positions) bears striking resemblance to the medieval geographer's picture of Africa as the stamping ground of the one-eyed ogre, the two-headed pygmy, the immortal phoenix and the elusive unicorn. What then is management: What does it do?

There are two popular answers. One is that management is the people at the top—the term "management" being little more than euphemism for "the boss." The other one defines a manager as someone who directs the work of others and who, as a slogan puts it, "does his work by getting other people to do theirs."

But these are at best merely efforts to tell us who belongs in management (as we shall see, they don't even tell us that). They do not attempt to tell us what management is and what it does. These questions can only be answered by analyzing management's function. For management is an organ; and organs can be described and defined only through their function.

Management is the specific organ of the business enterprise. Whenever we talk of a business enterprise, say, the United States Steel Company or the British Coal Board, as deciding to build a new plant, laying off workers or treating its customers fairly, we actually talk of a management decision, a management action, a management behavior. The enterprise can decide, act and behave only as its managers do—by itself the enterprise has no effective existence. And conversely any business enterprise, no matter what

its legal structure, must have a management to be alive and functioning. (In this respect, there is no difference between private
enterprise, the nationalized industries of Great Britain, such old-
established government monopolies as a Post Office, and the "min-
istries" and "trusts" of Communist Russia.)

That management is the specific organ of the business enterprise
is so obvious that it tends to be taken for granted. But it sets management apart from all other governing organs of all other institutions. The Government, the Army or the Church—in fact, any
major institution—has to have an organ which, in some of its function, is not unlike the management of the business enterprise. But
management as such is the management of a *business* enterprise.
And the reason for the existence of a business enterprise is that it
supplies economic goods and services. To be sure, the business
enterprise must discharge its economic responsibility so as to
strengthen society, and in accordance with society's political and
ethical beliefs. But these are (to use the logician's term) accidental
conditions limiting, modifying, encouraging or retarding the economic activities of the business enterprise. The essence of business
enterprise, the vital principle that determines its nature, is economic
performance.

THE FIRST FUNCTION: ECONOMIC PERFORMANCE

Management must always, in every decision and action, put economic performance first. It can only justify its existence and its authority by the economic results it produces. There may be great
non-economic results: the happiness of the members of the enterprise, the contribution to the welfare or culture of the community,
etc. Yet management has failed if it fails to produce economic results. It has failed if it does not supply goods and services desired by
the consumer at a price the consumer is willing to pay. It has failed
if it does not improve or at least maintain the wealth-producing
capacity of the economic resources entrusted to it.

In this management is unique. A General Staff will ask itself
quite legitimately whether its basic military decisions are compatible with the economic structure and welfare of the country. But

it would be greatly remiss in its duty were it to start its military deliberations with the needs of the economy. The economic consequences of military decisions are a secondary, a limiting factor in these decisions, not their starting point or their rationale. A General Staff, being the specific organ of a military organization, must, by necessity, put military security first. To act differently would be a betrayal of its responsibility and dangerous malpractice. Similarly, management, while always taking into consideration the impact of its decisions on society, both within and without the enterprise, must always put economic performance first.

The first definition of management is therefore that it is an economic organ, indeed the specifically economic organ of an industrial society. Every act, every decision, every deliberation of management has as its first dimension an economic dimension.

MANAGEMENT'S FIRST JOB IS MANAGING A BUSINESS

This apparently obvious statement leads to conclusions that are far from being obvious or generally accepted. It implies both severe limitations on the scope of management and manager, and a major responsibility for creative action.

It means in the first place that the skills, the competence, the experience of management cannot, as such, be transferred and applied to the organization and running of other institutions. In particular a man's success in management carries by itself no promise —let alone a guarantee—of his being successful in government. A career in management is, by itself, not a preparation for major political office—or for leadership in the Armed Forces, the Church or a university. The skills, the competence and the experience that are common and therefore transferable are analytical and administrative—extremely important, but secondary to the attainment of the primary objectives of the various non-business institutions. Whether Franklin D. Roosevelt was a great President or a national disaster has been argued hotly in this country for twenty years. But the patent fact that he was an extremely poor administrator seldom enters the discussion; even his staunchest enemies would consider it irrelevant. What is at issue are his basic political

decisions. And no one would claim that these should be determined by the supply of goods and services desired by the consumer
at the price the consumer is willing to pay, or by the maintenance
or improvement of wealth-producing resources. What to the manager must be the main focus is to the politician, of necessity, only
one factor among many.

A second negative conclusion is that management can never be
an exact science. True, the work of a manager can be systematically
analyzed and classified; there are, in other words, distinct professional features and a scientific aspect to management. Nor is managing a business just a matter of hunch or native ability; its
elements and requirements can be analyzed, can be organized
systematically, can be learned by anyone with normal human endowment. . . . [The] proposition that the days of the "intuitive"
managers are numbered [must be kept in mind]. [It is assumed]
that the manager can improve his performance in all areas of
management, including the managing of a business, through the
systematic study of principles, the acquisition of organized knowledge and the systematic analysis of his own performance in all
areas of his work and job and on all levels of management. Indeed,
nothing else can contribute so much to his skill, his effectiveness
and his performance. And underlying this theme is the conviction
that the impact of the manager on modern society and its citizens
is so great as to require of him the self-discipline and the high
standards of public service of a true professional.

And yet the ultimate test of management is business performance. Achievement rather than knowledge remains, of necessity,
both proof and aim. Management, in other words, is a practice,
rather than a science or a profession, though containing elements of
both. No greater damage could be done to our economy or to our
society than to attempt to "professionalize" management by "li-
censing" managers, for instance, or by limiting access to management to people with a special academic degree.

On the contrary, it is the test of good management that it enables
the successful business performer to do his work—whether he be
otherwise a good manager or a poor one. And any serious attempt
to make management "scientific" or a "profession" is bound to

lead to the attempt to eliminate those "disturbing nuisances," the unpredictabilities of business life—its risks, its ups and downs, its "wasteful competition," the "irrational choices" of the consumer—and, in the process, the economy's freedom and its ability to grow. It is not entirely accident that some of the early pioneers of "Scientific Management" ended up by demanding complete cartelization of the economy (Henry Gantt was the prime example); that the one direct outgrowth of American "Scientific Management" abroad, the German "Rationalization" movement of the twenties, attempted to make the world safe for professional management by cartelizing it; and that in our own country men who were steeped in "scientific management" played a big part in "Technocracy" and in the attempted nation-wide super-cartel of the National Recovery Act in the first year of Roosevelt's New Deal.

The scope and extent of management's authority and responsibility are severely limited. It is true that in order to discharge its business responsibility management must exercise substantial social and governing authority within the enterprise—authority over citizens in their capacity as members of the enterprise. It is also a fact that because of the importance of the business enterprise, management inevitably becomes one of the leading groups in industrial society. Since management's responsibility is always founded in economic performance, however, it has no authority except as is necessary to discharge its economic responsibility. To assert authority for management over the citizen and his affairs beyond that growing out of management's responsibility for business performance is usurpation of authority. Furthermore management can only be one leading group among several; in its own self-interest it can never and must never be *the* leading group. It has partial rather than comprehensive social responsibility—hence partial rather than comprehensive social authority. Should management claim to be *the* leading group—or even to be the most powerful of leading groups—it will be either rebuffed and, in the process, be shorn of most of the authority it can claim legitimately, or it will help into power a dictatorship that will deprive management as well as all other groups in a free society of their authority and standing.

But while the fact that management is an organ of the business enterprise limits scope and potential, it also embodies a major responsibility for creative action. For management has to *manage*. And managing is not just passive, adaptive behavior; it means taking action to make the desired results come to pass.

The early economist conceived of the businessman and his behavior as purely passive: success in business meant rapid and intelligent adaptation to events occurring outside, in an economy shaped by impersonal, objective forces that were neither controlled by the businessman nor influenced by his reaction to them. We may call this the concept of the "trader." Even if he was not considered a parasite, his contributions were seen as purely mechanical: the shifting of resources to more productive use. Today's economist sees the businessman as choosing rationally between alternatives of action. This is no longer a mechanical concept; obviously what choice the businessman makes has a real impact on the economy. But still, the economist's "businessman"—the picture that underlies the prevailing economic "theory of the firm" and the theorem of the "maximization of profits"—reacts to economic developments. He is still passive, still adaptive—though with a choice between various ways to adapt. Basically this is a concept of the "investor" or the "financier" rather than of the manager.

Of course, it is always important to adapt to economic changes rapidly, intelligently, and rationally. But managing goes way beyond passive reaction and adaptation. It implies responsibility for attemping to shape the economic environment, for planning, initiating and carrying through changes in that economic environment, for constantly pushing back the limitations of economic circumstances on the enterprise's freedom of action. What is possible— the economist's "economic conditions"—is therefore only one pole in managing a business. What is desirable in the interest of the enterprise is the other. And while man can never really "master" his environment, while he is always held within a tight vise of possibilities, it is management's specific job to make what is desirable first possible and then actual. Management is not just a creature of the economy; it is a creator as well. And only to the extent to which it masters the economic circumstances, and alters them by conscious, directed action, does it really manage. To manage a business means, therefore, to *manage by objectives.* . . .

MANAGING MANAGERS

To obtain economic performance there must be an enterprise. Management's second function is therefore to make a productive enterprise out of human and material resources. Concretely this is the function of managing managers.

The enterprise, by definition, must be capable of producing more or better than all the resources that comprise it. It must be a genuine whole: greater than—or at least different from—the sum of its parts, with its output larger than the sum of all inputs.

The enterprise cannot therefore be a mechanical assemblage of resources. To make an enterprise out of resources it is not enough to put them together in logical order and then to throw the switch of capital as the nineteenth-century economists firmly believed (and as many of their successors among academic economists still believe). What is needed is a transmutation of the resources. And this cannot come from an inanimate resource such as capital. It requires management.

But it is also clear that the "resources" capable of enlargement can only be human resources. All other resources stand under the laws of mechanics. They can be better utilized or worse utilized, but they can never have an output greater than the sum of the inputs. On the contrary, the problem in putting non-human resources together is always to keep to a minimum the inevitable output-shrinkage through friction, etc. Man, alone of all the resources available to man, can grow and develop. Only what a great medieval political writer (Sir John Fortescue) called the "intencio populi," the directed, focused, united effort of free human beings, can produce a real whole. Indeed, to make the whole that is greater than the sum of its parts has since Plato's days been the definition of the "Good Society."

When we speak of growth and development we imply that the human being himself determines what he contributes. Yet, we habitually define the rank-and-file worker—as distinguished from the manager—as a man who does as he is directed, without responsibility or share in the decisions concerning his work or that of others. This indicates that we consider the rank-and-file worker in the same light as other material resources, and as far as his contribution to the enterprise is concerned as standing under the laws of mechanics. This is a serious misunderstanding. The misunderstanding, however, is not in the definition of rank-and-file *work,* but rather in the failure to see that many rank-and-file *jobs* are in effect managerial, or would be more productive if made so. It does not, in other words, affect the argument that it is managing managers that makes an enterprise.

That this is true is shown in the terms we use to describe the various activities needed to build a functioning and productive enterprise. We speak of "organization"—the formal structure of the enterprise. But what we mean is the organization of managers and of their functions; neither brick and mortar nor rank-and-file workers have any place in the organization structure. We speak of "leadership" and of the "spirit" of a company. But leadership is given by managers and effective primarily within management; and the spirit is made by the spirit within the management group. We talk of "objectives" for the company, and of its performance. But the objectives are goals for management people; the performance is management performance. And if an enterprise fails to perform, we rightly hire not different workers but a new president.

Managers are also the costliest resource of the enterprise. In the big companies one hears again and again that a good engineer or accountant with ten or twelve years of working experience represents a direct investment of $50,000 over and above the contribution he has made so far to the company's success. The figure is, of course, pure guess—though the margin of error may well be no greater than that in the accountant's meticulous and detailed calculation of the investment in, and profitability of, a piece of machinery or a plant. But even if the actual figure were only a fraction, it would be high enough to make certain that the investment in managers, though, of course, never shown on the books, outweighs the investment in every other resource in practically all businesses. To utilize this investment as fully as possible is therefore a major requirement of managing a business.

196

To manage managers is therefore to make resources productive by making an enterprise out of them. And management is so complex and multi-faceted a thing, even in very small business, that managing managers is inevitably not only a vital but a complex job.

MANAGING WORKER AND WORK

The final function of management is to manage workers and work. Work has to be performed; and the resource to perform it with is workers—ranging from totally unskilled to artists, from wheelbarrow pushers to executive vice-presidents. This implies organization of the work so as to make it most suitable for human beings, and organization of people so as to make them work most productively and effectively. It implies consideration of the human being as a resource—that is, as something having peculiar physiological properties, abilities and limitations that require the same amount of engineering attention as the properties of any other resource, e.g., copper. It implies also consideration of the human resource as human beings having, unlike any other resource, personality, citizenship, control over whether they work, how much and how well, and thus requiring motivation, participation, satisfactions, incentives and rewards, leadership, status and function. And it is management, and management alone, that can satisfy these requirements. For they must be satisfied through work and job and within the enterprise; and management is the activating organ of the enterprise.

There is one more major factor in every management problem, every decision, every action—not properly speaking, a fourth function of management, but an additional dimension: time. Management always has to consider both the present and the long-range future. A management problem is not solved if immediate profits are purchased by endangering the long-range profitability, perhaps even the survival, of the company. A management decision is irresponsible if it risks disaster this year for the sake of a grandiose future. The all too common case of the management that produces great economic results as long as it runs the company but leaves behind nothing but a burned-out and rapidly sinking hulk is an example of irresponsible managerial action through failure to balance present and future. The immediate "economic results" are actually fictitious and are achieved by paying out capital. In every case where present and future are not both satisfied, where their requirements are not harmonized or at least balanced, capital, that is, wealth-producing resources, is endangered, damaged or destroyed.

The time dimension is inherent in management because management is concerned with decisions for action. And action is always aimed at results in the future. Anybody whose responsibility it is to act—rather than just to know—operates into the future. But there are two reasons why the time dimension is of particular importance in management's job, and of particular difficulty. In the first place, it is the essence of economic and technological progress that the time-span for the fruition and proving out of a decision is steadily lengthening. Edison, fifty years ago, needed two years or so between the start of laboratory work on an idea and the start of pilot-plant operations. Today it may well take Edison's successors fifteen years. A half century ago a new plant was expected to pay for itself in two or three years; today, with capital investment per worker ten times that of 1900, the pay-off period in the same industry is ten or twelve years. The human organization, such as a sales force or a management group, may take even longer to build and to pay for itself.

The second peculiar characteristic of the time dimension is that management—almost alone—has to live always in both present and future. A military leader, too, knows both times. But rarely does he have to live in both at the same time. During peace he knows no "present"; all the present is a preparation for the future of war. During war he knows only the most short-lived "future"; he is concerned with winning the war at hand to the practical exclusion of everything else. But management must keep the enterprise successful and profitable in the present—or else there will be no enterprise left to enjoy the future. It must simultaneously make the enterprise capable of growing and prospering, or at least of surviving in the future—otherwise it has fallen down on its responsibility of keeping resources productive and unimpaired, has destroyed capital. (The only parallel to this time-squeeze is the dilemma of

198

the politician between the responsibility for the common good and the need to be re-elected as a prerequisite to making his contribution to the common good. But the cynical politician can argue that promises to the voters and performance once in office need not resemble each other too closely. The manager's action on present results, however, directly determines future results, his action on future results—research expenditures, for instance, or plant investment—profoundly influences visible present results.)

THE INTEGRATED NATURE OF MANAGEMENT

The three jobs of management: managing a business, managing managers and managing worker and work, can be analyzed separately, studied separately, appraised separately. In each a present and a future dimension can be distinguished. But in its daily work management cannot separate them. Nor can it separate decisions on present from decisions on future. Any management decision always affects all three jobs and must take all three into account. And the most vital decisions on the future are often made as decisions on the present—on present research budgets or on the handling of a grievance, on promoting this man and letting that one go, on maintenance standards or on customer service.

It cannot even be said that one job predominates or requires the greater skill or competence. True, business performance comes first—it is the aim of the enterprise and the reason for its existence. But if there is no functioning enterprise, there will be no business performance, no matter how good management may be in managing the business. The same holds true if worker and work are mismanaged. Economic performance that is being achieved by mismanaging managers is illusory and actually destructive of capital. Economic performance that is being achieved by mismanaging work and worker is equally an illusion. It will not only raise costs to the point where the enterprise ceases to be competitive; it will, by creating class hatred and class warfare, end by making it impossible for the enterprise to operate at all.

Managing a business has primacy because the enterprise is an economic institution; but managing managers and managing workers and work have primacy precisely because society is not an economic institution and is therefore vitally interested in these two areas of management in which basic social beliefs and aims are being realized.

. . . We must, however, never allow ourselves to forget that in actual practice managers always discharge . . . three jobs in every one action. We must not allow ourselves to forget that it is actually the specific situation of the manager to have not one but three jobs at the same time, discharged by and through the same people, exercised in and through the same decision. Indeed, we can only answer our question: "What is management and what does it do?" by saying that it is a multi-purpose organ that manages a business *and* manages managers *and* manages worker and work. If one of these were omitted, we would not have management any more—and we also would not have a business enterprise or an industrial society.

THE DETERMINATION OF POLICY

Richard M. Cyert, Herbert A. Simon, and Donald B. Trow [1]

The notion of a businessman as a rational individual systematically choosing from among alternatives is not complete. Alternatives, problems, and consequences are not usually "given" but must be sought. "The decision-maker is usually concerned with finding a *satisfactory* alternative—one that will attain a specified goal and at the same time satisfy a number of auxilliary conditions."

Decision-making—choosing one course of action rather than another, finding an appropriate solution to a new problem posed by a changing world—is commonly asserted to be the heart of ex-

[1] . . . This is a preliminary report on research carried out under a grant from the Ford Foundation for studies in organization and decision-making. The authors are grateful to the Foundation for its support, to the executives of the company that opened its doors to them, and to colleagues and graduate students who have assisted at various stages of data collection and analysis.

Note: See Notes on the Authors, pages 552, 556, and 557, and item 58 in the bibliography for the full reference to this selection.

ecutive activity in business. If this is so, a realistic description and theory of the decision-making process are of central importance to business administration and organization theory. Moreover, it is extremely doubtful whether the only considerable body of decision-making theory that has been available in the past—that provided by economics—does in fact provide a realistic account of decision-making in large organizations operating in a complex world.

In economics and statistics the rational choice process is described somewhat as follows:

1. An individual is confronted with a number of different, specified alternative courses of action.

2. To each of these alternatives is attached a set of consequences that will ensue if that alternative is chosen.

3. The individual has a system of preferences or "utilities" that permit him to rank all sets of consequences according to preference and to chose that alternative that has the preferred consequences. In the case of business decisions the criterion for ranking is generally assumed to be profit.

If we try to use this framework to describe how real human beings go about making choices in a real world, we soon recognize that we need to incorporate in our description of the choice process several elements that are missing from the economic model:

1. The alternatives are not usually "given" but must be sought, and hence it is necessary to include the search for alternatives as an important part of the process.

2. The information as to what consequences are attached to which alternatives is seldom a "given," but, instead, the search for consequences is another important segment of the decision-making task.

3. The comparisons among alternatives are not usually made in terms of simple, single criterion like profit. One reason is that there are often important consequences that are so intangible as to make an evaluation in terms of profit difficult or impossible. In place of searching for the "best" alternative, the decision-maker is usually concerned with finding a *satisfactory* alternative—one that will attain a specified goal and at the same time satisfy a number of auxiliary conditions.

201

4. Often, in the real world, the problem itself is not a "given," but, instead, searching for significant problems to which organizational attention should be turned becomes an important organizational task.

Decisions in organizations vary widely with respect to the extent to which the decision-making process is *programmed*. At one extreme we have repetitive, well-defined problems (e.g., quality control or production lot-size problems) involving tangible considerations, to which the economic models that call for finding the best among a set of pre-established alternatives can be applied rather literally. In contrast to these highly programmed and usually rather detailed decisions are problems of a non-repetitive sort, often involving basic long-range questions about the whole strategy of the firm or some part of it, arising initially in a highly unstructured form and requiring a great deal of the kinds of search processes listed above. In this whole continuum, from great specificity and repetition to extreme vagueness and uniqueness, we will call decisions that lie toward the former extreme *programmed,* and those lying toward the latter end *non-programmed.* This simple dichotomy is just a shorthand for the range of possibilities we have indicated.

It is our aim in the present paper to illustrate the distinctions we have introduced between the traditional theory of decision, which appears applicable only to highly programmed decision problems, and a revised theory, which will have to take account of the search processes and other information processes that are so prominent in and characteristic of non-programmed decision-making. We shall do this by recounting the stages through which an actual problem proceeded in an actual company and then commenting upon the significance of various items in this narrative for future decision-making theory.

The decision was captured and recorded by securing the company's permission to have a member of the research team present as an observer in the company's offices on substantially a full-time basis during the most active phases of the decision process. The observer spent most of his time with the executive who had been assigned the principal responsibility for handling this particular problem. In addition, he had full access to the files for information about events that preceded his period of observation and also interviewed all the participants who were involved to a major degree in the decision.

THE ELECTRONIC DATA-PROCESSING DECISION

The decision process to be described here concerns the feasibility of using electronic data-processing equipment in a medium size corporation that engages both in manufacturing and in selling through its own widely scattered outlets. In July, 1952, the company's controller assigned to Ronald Middleton, an assistant who was handling several special studies in the accounting department, the task of keeping abreast of electronic developments. The controller, and other accounting executives, thought that some of the current developments in electronic equipment might have application to the company's accounting processes. He gave Middleton the task of investigation, because the latter had a good background for understanding the technical aspects of computers.

Middleton used three procedures to obtain information: letters to persons in established computer firms, discussions with computer salesmen, and discussions with persons in other companies that were experimenting with the use of electronic equipment in accounting. He also read the current journal literature about computer developments. He informed the controller about these matters principally through memorandums that described the current status of equipment and some of the procedures that would be necessary for an applications study in the company. Memorandums were written in November, 1952, October, 1953, and January, 1954. In them, in addition to summarizing developments, he recommended that two computer companies be asked to propose possible installations in the company and that the company begin to adapt its accounting procedures to future electronic processing.

In the spring of 1954 a computer company representative took the initiative to propose and make a brief equipment application study. In August he submitted a report to the company recommending an installation, but this was not acted upon—doubt as to the adequacy of the computer company's experience and knowledge in application being a major factor in the decision. A similar approach was made by another computer company in September, 1954, but terminated at an early stage without positive action. These experiences convinced Middleton and other executives, including the controller, that outside help was needed to develop and evaluate possible applications of electronic equipment.

Middleton drew up a list of potential consultants and, by checking outside sources and using his own information, selected Alpha as the most suitable. After preliminary meetings in October and November, 1954, between representatives of Alpha and the company accounting executives, Alpha was asked to develop a plan for a study of the application of electronic data-processing to sales accounting. Additional meetings between Alpha and company personnel were held in February, 1955, and the proposal for the study was submitted to the controller in March.

Although the proposal seemed competent and the price reasonable, it was felt that proposals should be obtained from another consulting firm as a double check. The controller agreed to this and himself selected Beta from Middleton's list. Subsequently representatives of Beta met with Middleton and other department executives. Middleton, in a memorandum to the controller, listed criteria for choosing between the two consultants. On the assumption that the written report from Beta was similar to the oral proposal made, the comparison indicated several advantages for Beta over Alpha.

After the written report was received, on May 2, the company's management committee authorized a consulting agreement with Beta, and work began in July, 1955. The controller established a committee, headed by Middleton, to work on the project. Middleton was to devote full time to the assignment; the other two committee members, one from sales accounting and one from auditing, were to devote one-third time.

The consulting firm assigned two staff members, Drs. Able and Baker, to the study. Their initial meetings with Middleton served the purpose of outlining a general approach to the problem and planning the first few steps. Twenty-three information-gathering studies were defined, which Middleton agreed to carry out, and it was also decided that the consultants would spend some time in field observation of the actual activities that the computer might replace.

During July, Middleton devoted most of his time to the twenty-three studies on volume of transactions and information flow, obtaining data from the sales department and from the field staffs of the other two committee members. Simultaneously, steps were taken to secure the co-operation of the field personnel who would be visited by the consultants early in August.

On July 22 Middleton submitted a progress report to the controller, describing the data-gathering studies, estimating completion dates, and summarizing the program's objectives. On July 25 the consultants met with Middleton and discussed a method of approach to the design of the data-processing system. The field trip took place early in August. The consultants obtained from field personnel information as to how accounting tasks were actually handled and as to the use actually made of information generated by the existing system.

On August 8 Middleton submitted another progress report, giving the status of the data-gathering studies and recording some ideas originating in the field trip for possible changes in the existing information-processing system. On August 10 he arranged with the assistant controller to obtain clerical assistance on the data-gathering studies, so that the consultants would not be held up by lack of this information, and on August 17 this work was completed.

On the following day the consultants met with the company committee to review the results of the twenty-three studies. They then listed the outputs, files, and inputs required by any sales accounting system the company might adopt and drew a diagram showing the flow of the accounting information. The group also met with the assistant controller and with the controller. The latter took the opportunity to emphasize his basic decentralization philosophy.

Upon returning from his vacation early in September, Middleton discussed the flow diagram in greater detail with Able and Baker, and revisions were made on the basis of information Middleton supplied about the present accounting system. Baker pointed out that all the alternative systems available to the company could be defined by the location of seven principal functions and records. Further analysis reduced this number to three: stock records, pricing of orders, and accounts receivable. The possible combinations of locations of these gave eighteen basic alternative systems, of which eight that were obviously undesirable were eliminated. Middleton was to make a cost analysis of the existing system and the most decentralized of the proposed systems, while the consultants were to begin costing the most centralized system.

Middleton reviewed these tentative decisions with the other members of the company committee, and the group divided up the work of costing. Middleton also reported to the controller on the conference, and the latter expressed his attitudes about the location of the various functions and the resulting implications for the development of executive responsibility.

During the next week, in addition to working on his current assignments, Middleton gave an equipment salesman a preliminary overview of the probable requirements of a new system. Next, there was a two-day meeting of the consultants and the company's committee to discuss the form and implications of a centralized electronic system. The consultants presented a method of organizing the records for electronic processing and together with the committee calculated the requirements which this organization and company's volume of transactions would impose on a computer. The group then discussed several problems raised by the system, including the auditing problems, and then met with the assistant controller to review the areas they had discussed.

On the following day, Middleton summarized progress to date for the controller, emphasizing particularly the work that had been done on the centralized system. The controller expressed satisfaction with several new procedures that would be made possible by an electronic computer. During the next several days the committee members continued to gather the information necessary to determine the cost of the present system. Middleton also checked with the assistant controller on the proposed solutions for certain problems that the consultants had indicated could not be handled readily by a computer and relayed his reactions to the consultants.

A week later the consultants returned for another series of meetings. They discussed changes that might be necessary in current practices to make centralized electronic processing possible and the way in which they would compare the centralized and decentralized proposals. The comparison presented some difficulties, since the data provided by the two systems would not be identical. A general form for a preliminary report was cleared with the assistant controller, and a date was set for its submission. The processing, outputs, and costs for the two alternatives would be described, so that additional information required for a final report could be determined.

During the next week Middleton continued collecting cost data. He phoned to the consultants to provide them with important new figures and to inform them of the controller's favorable reaction to certain proposed changes in the system that had implications for the company's policies.

On October 17 Baker met with Middleton to review the content of the accounting reports that would be produced by the centralized system, to discuss plans for the preliminary report, and to discuss the relative advantages and disadvantages of the centralized and decentralized systems. On the next day, Middleton checked on their decisions relative to the report with the controller and assistant controller and raised the possibility of an outside expert being retained by the company to review the final report submitted by Beta. During the last days of this week, Middleton attended the national meeting of a management society, where he obtained information about the availability of computers and computer personnel and the existence of other installations comparable to that contemplated for the company.

Work continued on the planning and costing of the two systems —Middleton worked primarily on the decentralized plan, and the consultants on the centralized. On October 27 the two consultants met with Middleton and they informed each other of the status of their work. Baker discussed methods for evaluating system reliability. Plans for the preliminary report were discussed with the company committee and the assistant controller. Since the controller strongly favored decentralization of authority, the question was raised of the compatibility of this with electronic processing in general and with the centralized system in particular. The groups concluded, however, that centralization of purely clerical data-processing operations was compatible with decentralization of responsibility and authority.

After several meetings between the committee and the consultants to iron out details, the preliminary report was presented to the company committee, the controller, and the assistant controller on November 3. The report was devoted primarily to the centralized system. The following points were made in the oral presentation: (1) that both the centralized and decentralized proposals would yield substantial and roughly equivalent savings but that the centralized system would provide more and better accounting data; (2) that the alternatives had been costed conservatively; (3) that the centralized system involved centralization of paper work, not of management; (4) that not all problems raised by the centralized system had been worked out in detail but that these did not appear insurmountable; (5) that the centralized system would facilitate improved inventory control; and (6) that its installation would require nine to twelve months at a specified cost. At this meeting the group decided that in the final report only the two systems already considered would be costed, that the final report would be submitted on December 1, and that investigation of other accounting applications of the system would be postponed.

In informal conversations after the meeting the controller told Middleton he had the impression that the consultants strongly favored the centralized system and that he believed the cost considerations were relatively minor compared with the impact the system would have on executives' operating philosophies. The assistant controller told Middleton he thought the preliminary report did not adequately support the conclusions. The committee then reviewed with the assistant controller the reasons for analyzing in detail only the two extreme systems: the others either produced less information or were more costly.

The next day the committee met with the controller and assistant controller to determine what additional information should be requested for the final report. The controller outlined certain questions of practicability that the final report should answer and expressed the view that the report should contain a section summarizing the specific changes that the system would bring about at various levels of the organization. He thought the comparison between systems in the preliminary report had emphasized equivalence of savings, without detailing other less tangible benefits of the centralized system.

Middleton reported these discussions to the consultants and with them developed flow charts and organization charts for inclusion in the final report, settled on some intermediate deadlines, and worked up an outline of the report. Within the company he discussed with the controller and assistant controller the personnel and organizational requirements for installation of an electronic system and for operation after installation. Discussion focused on the general character and organizational location of the eventual electronic-data-processing group, its relation to the sales accounting division, and long-term relations with manufacturing accounting and with a possible operations research group.

On November 14 the controller, on recommendation of Middleton, attended a conference on automation for company senior executives. There he expressed the view that three to five years would be required for full installation of a centralized electronic system but that the fear of obsolescence of equipment should not deter the company in making the investment. He also concluded that a computer installation would not reverse his long-range program for decentralizing information and responsibility.

Middleton, his suggestion being accepted, made tentative arrangements with an independent expert and with two large computer companies for the review of the consultants' report. Middleton presented to the controller and assistant controller a memorandum he had prepared at the latter's request, establishing a new comparison of the centralized and a modified decentralized system. The modification made the two systems more nearly comparable in data-processing capacity, hence clarified the cost comparison, which was now in favor of the centralized system. Consideration of the possibility of starting with a partially electronic decentralized system as a step toward a completely electronic system led to the decision that this procedure had no special advantages. The controller reported that conversations with the sales manager and the president had secured agreement with the concept of removal of stock record-keeping from field locations—an aspect of the plan to which it had been assumed there would be sales department opposition. The group discussed several other specific topics and reaffirmed that the final report should discuss more fully the relative advantages and disadvantages of centralized and decentralized systems.

Toward the end of November there was further consultation on the report, and final arrangements for its review were made with the two equipment companies and the independent expert. Each equipment company was expected to determine the method for setting up the proposed system on its computer and to check the consultants' estimates of computer capacity. During this week the controller informed the company's management committee that the report from the consultants would be submitted shortly and would recommend a rather radical change to electronic data-processing.

The final report, which recommended installation of the centralized system, was submitted on December 1. The report consisted of a summary of recommendations, general description of the centralized system, a discussion of the installation program, and six appendixes: (1) statistics on volume of transactions (the twenty-three studies); (2) costs of the present system; (3) the requirements of a fully centralized system; (4) changes in allocation of functions required by the system; (5) an outline of the alternative decentralized system; and (6) a description of the existing system in verbal and flow-chart form. When the report was received and reviewed initially, the company's committee members and the consultants made some further computations on installation costs.

At a meeting the following Monday the assistant controller proposed an action program: send copies of the report to equipment companies, send copies to the sales department, and await the report of the independent expert. The controller decided that the second and third steps should be taken before giving the report to the machine companies, and the assistant controller indicated to Middleton some points requiring further clarification and elaboration.

By January 7 Middleton had prepared an outline for a presentation of the report to the sales department. This was revised on the basis of a meeting with the other interested accounting executives. A final outline was agreed upon after two more revisions and three more meetings. The report was presented on January 28 to the president and to six of the top executives of the sales department. The presentation discussed large-scale computers briefly, described with flow charts the proposed system, emphasized the completeness and accuracy of the information produced, discussed costs and savings, and mentioned the current trend in other companies toward electronic data-processing.

At Middleton's recommendation the same presentation was made subsequently to top members of the accounting department and still later to a group from the manufacturing department. At the same time the preliminary report of the independent expert was received, agreeing that the electronic installation seemed justifiable and stating that there might not be any cost savings but that it would make possible numerous other profitable applications of the computer. The consultants' report was then distributed to the computer companies, and Middleton began more detailed planning of the installation.

Middleton, the assistant controller, and the controller now met with the independent expert, who reported his conclusions: the feasibility study was excellent, the estimates of processing time were probably optimistic, the installation program should provide for an early test run, and the two principal available computers were highly competitive. Independent confirmation had been obtained on the last two points from another outside source. Middleton now proposed that the company proceed with its planning while awaiting the final written report from the independent expert and the proposals of the equipment companies. The assistant controller preferred to wait until these reports were actually in hand.

During the next week the equipment companies proceeded with their analysis, meeting several times with Middleton. Baker sent a memorandum on his estimates of processing time to meet the criticism of the independent expert. Middleton prepared two charts, one proposing a schedule and the staffing requirements for the installation phase, the other proposing organizational arrangements for the computer center. Middleton and the assistant controller presented these to the controller at the beginning of February, discussion centering responsibility for accuracy of input information.

Middleton and the assistant controller also had a meeting with sales executives who reported that on the basis of their own internal departmental discussions of the consultants' report they were in general agreement with the program. Middleton and one of the other committee members then spent two days inspecting computer installations in two other companies.

In the middle of February the two equipment companies presented their reports, each bringing a team of three or four men to present their recommendations orally. The two recommendations were substantially alike (except for the brand of the machine recommended!), but one report emphasized the availability of its personnel to give help during the installation planning stage.

Discussions were held in the accounting department and with consultant Baker about these reports and the next steps to be taken. The question was debated whether a commitment should be made to one equipment company or whether a small group should continue planning the system in detail, postponing the equipment decision until fall. Most of the group preferred the former alternative.

On February 15 the controller, in conference with the assistant controller and Middleton, dictated a letter to the company's president summarizing the conclusions and recommendations of the study and requesting that the accounting department be authorized to proceed with the electronics program.

On the following day the controller read the letter to the management committee. The letter reviewed briefly the history of the project and summarized the conclusions contained in the consultants' report: that there was ample justification for an electronic-data-processing installation; that the installation would warrant use of the largest computers; and that it would produce savings, many intangible benefits, and excess computer capacity for other applications. The letter quoted the consultants' estimate of the cost of the installation and their recommendation that the company proceed

212

at once to make such a conversion and to acquire the necessary equipment. It then cited the various cross-checks that had been made of the consultants' report and concluded with a repetition of the conclusions of the report—but estimating more conservatively the operating and installation costs—and a request for favorable management committee action. Supplementary information presented included a comparison of consultant and equipment company cost estimates and a list of present and proposed computer installations in other companies. After a few questions and brief discussion, the management committee voted favorably on the recommendation, and the controller informed Middleton of the decision when the meeting ended.

THE ANATOMY OF THE DECISION

From this narrative, or more specifically from the actual data on which the narrative is based, one can list chronologically the various activities of which the decision process is composed. If we wish to describe a program for making a decision of this kind, each of these activities might be taken as one of the steps of the program. If the rules that determined when action would switch from one program step to another were specified, and if the program steps were described in enough detail, it would be possible to replicate the decision process.

The program steps taken together define in retrospect, then, a program for an originally unprogrammed decision. The program would be an inefficient one because it would contain all the false starts and blind alleys of the original process, and some of these could presumably be avoided if the process were repeated. However, describing the process that took place in terms of such a program is a useful way of organizing the data for purposes of analysis.

In order to make very specific what is meant here by a "program," Chart II has been prepared to show the broad outlines of the actual program for the first stages of the decision process (through the first seven paragraphs of the narrative).

SUBPROGRAMS. The various program steps of the decision process fall into several subprograms, some of which have been indicated in Chart II. These subprograms are ways of organizing

CHART II. PROGRAM STEPS FROM INCEPTION OF THE PROBLEM TO SELECTION OF A CONSULTANT

Keeping-up program (paragraphs 1 and 2 of narrative):
    Search for and correspond with experts;
    Discuss with salesmen and with equipment users;
    Search for and read journals;
Procurement program (paragraph 3):
    Discuss applications study with salesmen who propose it;
    Choice: accept or reject proposed study;
    (If accepted) transfer control to salesmen;
    Choice: accept or reject applications proposal;
    (If rejected) switch to consultant program;
Consultant program (paragraphs 4 through 7):
    Search for consultants;
    Choice: best consultant of several;
    Transfer control to chosen consultant;
    Choice: accept or reject proposal;
    (If accepted): begin double-check routine;
    Request expenditure of funds;
    (If authorized) transfer control to consultants;
    And so on.

the activities *post factum,* and in Chart II the organizing principle is the method of approach taken by the company to the total problem. It remains a question as to whether this organizing principle will be useful in all cases. As in the present example, these subprograms may sometimes be false starts, but these must be regarded as parts of the total program, for they may contribute information for later use, and their outcomes determine the switching of activity to new subprograms.

In this particular case the reasons for switching from one subprogram to another were either the proved inadequacy of the first one or a redefinition of the problem. Other reasons for switching can be imagined, and a complete theory of the decision process will have to specify the conditions under which the switch from one line of attack to another will occur.

COMMON PROCESSES. In the whole decision-making program there are certain steps or "routines" that recur within several of the subprograms; they represent the basic activities of which the whole decision process is composed. For purposes of discussion we have classified these common processes in two categories: the first comprises processes relating to the communication requirements of the organization; the second comprises processes relating directly to the solution of the decisional problem.

COMMUNICATION PROCESSES. Organizational decision-making requires a variety of communication activities that are absent when a decision is made in a single human head. If we had written out the program steps in greater detail, many more instances of contacts among different members of the organization would be recorded than are now explicit in the narrative. The contacts may be oral or written. Oral contacts are used for such purposes as giving orders, transmitting information, obtaining approval or criticism of proposed action; written communications generally take the form of memorandums having the purpose of transmitting information or proposing action.

The information-transmitting function is crucial to organizational decision-making, for it almost always involves acts of selection or "filtering" by the information source. In the present instance, which is rather typical in this respect, the consultants and subordinate executives are principal information sources; and the controller and other top executives must depend upon them for most of their technical information. Hence, the subordinate acts as an information filter and in this way secures a large influence over the decisions the superior can and does reach.

The influence of the information source over communications is partly controlled by checking processes—for example, retaining an independent expert to check consultants—which give the recipient an independent information source. This reduces, but by no means eliminates, filtering. The great differences in the amounts and kinds of information available to the various participants in the decision process described here emphasize the significance of filtering. It will be important to determine the relationship of the characteristics of the information to the resultant information change and to explore the effects of personal relations between people on the filtering process and hence upon the transmission of information.

PROBLEM-SOLVING PROCESSES. Alongside the organizational communication processes, we find in the narrative a number of important processes directed toward the decision problem itself. One of the most prominent of these is the search for alternative courses of action. The first activities recounted in the narrative—writing letters, reading journals, and so on—were attempts to discover possible action alternatives. At subsequent points in the process searches were conducted to obtain lists of qualified consultants and experts. In addition to these, there were numerous searches—most of them only implicit in the condensed narrative—to find action alternatives that would overcome specific difficulties that emerged as detail was added to the broader alternatives.

The data support strongly the assertion made in the introduction that searches for alternative courses of action constitute a significant part of non-programmed decision-making—a part that is neglected by the classical theory of rational choice. In the present case the only alternatives that became available to the company without the expenditure of time and effort were the systems proposals made early in the process by representatives of two equipment companies, and these were both rejected. An important reason for the prominent role of search in the decision process is that the "problem" to be solved was in fact a whole series of "nested" problems, each alternative solution to a problem at one level leading to a new set of problems at the next level. In addition, the process of solving the substantive problems created many procedural problems for the organization: allocating time and work, planning agendas and report presentations, and so on.

Examination of the narrative shows that there is a rich variety of search processes. Many questions remain to be answered as to what determines the particular character of the search at a particular stage in the decision process: the possible differences between searches for procedural alternatives on the one hand, and for substantive alternatives, on the other; the factors that determine how many alternatives will be sought before a choice is made; the conditions under which an alternative that has tentatively been chosen will be subjected to further check; the general types of search strategies.

The neglect of the search for alternatives in the classical theory of decision would be inconsequential if the search were so extensive that most of the alternatives available "in principle" were generally discovered and considered. In that case the search process would have no influence upon the alternative finally selected for action. The narrative suggests that this is very far from the truth—that, in fact, the search for alternatives terminates when a satisfactory solution has been discovered even though the field of possibilities has not been exhausted. Hence, we have reason to suppose that changes in the search process or its outcome will actually have major effects on the final decision.

A second class of common processes encompasses information-gathering and similar activity aimed at determining the consequences of each of several alternatives. In many decisions, certainly in the one we observed, these activities account for the largest share of man-hours, and it is through them that subproblems are discovered. The narrative suggests that there is an inverse relation between the cost or difficulty of this investigational task and the number of alternative courses of action that are examined carefully. Further work will be needed to determine if this relation holds up in a broader range of situations. The record also raises numerous questions about the *kinds* of consequences that are examined most closely or at all and about the conditions under which selection of criteria for choice is prior to, or subsequent to, the examination of consequences.

Another set of common processes are those concerned with the choices among alternatives. Such processes appear at many points in the narrative: the selection of a particular consulting firm from a list, the choice between centralized and decentralized electronic-data-processing systems, as well as numerous more detailed choices. These are the processes most closely allied to the classical theory of choice, but even here it is notable that traditional kinds of "maximizing" procedures appear only rarely.

In some situations the choice is between competing alternatives, but in many others it is one of acceptance or rejection of a single course of action—really a choice between doing *something* at this time and doing nothing. The first such occasion was the decision by the controller to assign Middleton to the task of watching developments in electronics, a decision that initiated the whole sequence of later choices. In decisions of this type the consequences of the single alternative are judged against some kind of explicit or implicit "level of aspiration"—perhaps expressed in terms of an amount of improvement over the existing situation—while in the multiple-alternative situations, the consequences of the several alternatives are compared with each other. This observation raises a host of new questions relating to the circumstances under which the decision will be formulated in terms of the one or the other of these frameworks and the personal and organizational factors that determine the aspiration levels that will be applied in the one-alternative case.

Another observation derivable from our data—though it is not obvious from the condensed narrative given here—is that comparability and non-comparability of the criteria of choice affects the decision processes in significant ways. For one thing, the criteria are not the same from one choice to another: one choice may be made on the basis of relative costs and savings, while the next may be based entirely on non-monetary criteria. Further, few, if any, of the choices were based on a single criterion. Middleton and the others recognized and struggled with this problem of comparing consequences that were sometimes measured in different, and incomparable, units, and even more often involved completely intangible considerations. The narrative raises, but does not answer, the question of how choices are made in the face of these incommensurabilities and the degree to which tangible considerations are overemphasized or underemphasized as compared with intangibles as a result.

CONCLUSION

We do not wish to try to transform one swallow into a summer by generalizing too far from a single example of a decision process. We have tried to illustrate, however, using a large relatively nonprogrammed decision in a business firm, some of the processes that are involved in business decision-making and to indicate the sort of theory of the choice mechanism that is needed to accommodate these processes. Our illustration suggests that search processes and information-gathering processes constitute significant parts of decision-making and must be incorporated in a theory of decision if it is to be adequate. While the framework employed here—and particularly the analysis of a decision in terms of a hierarchical structure of *programs*—is far from a complete or finished theory, it appears to provide a useful technique of analysis for researchers interested in the theory of decision as well as for business executives who may wish to review the decision-making procedures of their own companies.

MANAGERIAL STRATEGIES

David G. Moore

In order to function successfully in situations of uncertainty and risk, it is necessary for managers to find the right strategies for dealing with the socioeconomic system within which they operate. These strategies serve as a basis for action and reflect a more or less rational evaluation of the elements of the environment.

While the socio-economic environment in which a business operates is limited and somewhat predictable, there are also many unpredictable elements arising from chance factors, extraneous influences, incomplete knowledge, and the sheer complexity of the situation. These elements of unpredictability create on the one hand opportunity and on the other insecurity. They provide an opportunity for the single-minded, purposeful businessman to establish an advantageous set of relations with various other elements of the socio-economic environment. He can, if he is imaginative and insightful, envision a business situation and combination of circumstances not perceived by others. He can, if he is energetic and decisive, seize upon a situation before others grasp it. He can, if he is lucky, stumble upon a set of favorable conditions. He can, if he is persuasive, change the perception of others regarding a particular business situation. He can manipulate and take advantage of the "aberrant" behavior of others caused by factors "ex-

Note: See Notes on the Authors, page 555, and item 166 in the bibliography for the full reference to this selection.

traneous" to expected socio-economic roles. He can in a variety of ways utilize the unpredictable elements of the socio-economic environment to achieve his own business ends.

At the same time, the element of unpredictability in the socio-economic environment creates a degree of insecurity or at least vague uneasiness. The businessman can "lose his shirt" if he does not take proper action, if he perceives incorrectly, if he guesses wrong. Thus, he finds himself attracted by opportunity and pushed by insecurity to seek the right "system" or *modus operandi* for dealing with the socio-economic complex. He is confronted in a way with the social psychological problem of acting purposefully in an open-ended, relatively unpredictable situation. Under these circumstances, he feels compelled, if he behaves consciously at all, to structure the situation in one way or another and to develop a design for action. He develops a *strategy* on which he can base action.

A strategy may reflect a more or less rational evaluation of the elements of the socio-economic environment. In some cases, it may evolve from a systematic analysis of the "facts" and logical deductions from these. In other cases, it may be founded on stereotyped notions of the socio-economic behavior of people, folklore, individual emotions and sentiments, imitation of the successful actions of others, slavish following of economic "style" trends, the advice of professionals, and pure guesses. At its most rational, the development of a business strategy is based on probabilities. Indeed, the whole pattern of business activity would change if all the facts of human behavior were generally understood and predictable. The challenge and dynamics of business lie in the unpredictable areas of the socio-economic environment and in the eternal quest for a new "angle."

The strategies of a particular business tend to evolve and develop with the growth and extension of the business activity. The evolution of strategies is more or less synonymous with business growth although obvious lags can develop as the business becomes an organized activity with concomitant problems of communication and coordination. The evolution of strategies in a particular business proceeds in more or less well-defined stages. The first stage is the creation of the business activity itself. Businesses come into existence in a variety of ways. However, the process is largely the same. Someone or some small group of individuals possesses, develops, or stumbles on potential assets or resources which, when combined with certain other assets, provide the conditions favorable to the development of a business. A potential asset can be almost anything—money, real estate, talent, skill, class position, personality, an invention, or what have you. The act of combining is the crucial element of a creative strategy; a single asset is valuable only in combination. The strategy in this initial stage, then, is that of envisioning an advantageous combination. Such a combination might be something as mundane and unoriginal as putting Aunt Mabel's bequest and Junior's interest in tinkering with other people's automobiles together with an empty lot on a busy corner and opening a gas station. Or it may be as imaginative and unique as combining, in the manner of Henry Ford, mechanical ingenuity, a buggy, a gasoline engine, and new ideas of mass production to create an automobile industry.

The creative strategy of business is frequently undeveloped and unbalanced in its initial form. It tends to emphasize the special interests, talents, possessions, behavior, and general orientation of the founding father. If the business is to survive in a competitive world, the original strategy usually must be consolidated. Consolidation involves the development of additional strategies for dealing with all of the elements of the socio-economic environment which support the business activity. If the first stage of a business requires a Promoter or Activity Generator, the next stage requires a Businessman or Consolidator. This is the stage when the business develops "sound business practices."

As the business grows and problems of adjustment increase, a new stage is reached—that of organization. The excess work and new functions must be done through people and/or machines. At first, the organization may develop in a more or less haphazard fashion; an employee or machine is introduced to handle a specific activity or function. However, at some point in the growth of the business, a strategy of organization emerges. The notions of efficient organization emerge. Thus, the organization itself as a rationalization of means to ends becomes a strategic device for insuring

221

an advantageous position in the socio-economic environment. This is the stage of the Manager or the Administrator.

The organization creates new problems of adjustment. Various jobs and positions in the organization are introduced with which people identify and around which they organize their interests, attitudes, ambitions, and social life in general. These new elements must be reckoned with in managing the organization and dealing with the external problems of the business. A job is more than a piece of a broader strategy for achieving efficient organization or meeting an external problem. It is also a man or a group of men whose lives, ambitions, and identities may be intricately bound up with these activities and for whom a specific job or a specific strategy is a means to personal ends. The organization creates a whole new class of interrelated socio-economic groups or roles which must be considered in planning the over-all business strategy of the company.

From the standpoint of employees, the problem of adjustment is to a considerable extent one of adjusting to the demands of the job and the system of interaction created by the organizational strategy of management. Adjustment is often difficult partly because work, no matter how you "slice" it, is still work and partly because the organizational strategies of many companies are conceived in mechanical rather than human terms. This introduces problems of motivation, coordination, communication, and control which are the key problems of the administrator and which are ordinarily dealt with through a hierarchy of authority.

A well-nigh universal characteristic of business is that everyone has a boss; everyone except the chairman of the board is outranked by somebody else. A formal status system is introduced which has important implications regarding the human relations which develop in the organization.

Of significance, also, is the informal status system which arises outside the established hierarchy. This system involves a definition of the social importance of jobs and functions in terms of value judgments which may be brought into the organization from the outside community or may be internal to the organization itself. Internal values seem to be based largely on the ranking of the strategies of the business. Certain strategies stand out as crucial. These must be accomplished and fulfilled first. Other strategies are of secondary importance. The relative dominance or subordination of strategies depends on a variety of factors—tradition, significance to the survival of the organization, chance factors, emotions and sentiments, etc. However, the ultimate decision rests with top management which is faced with the crucial question of reconciling the many strategies which characterize the highly developed business organization. If the various strategies are not reconciled in some way and remain discordant and conflicting, this lack of harmony is likely to be reflected throughout the organization in the form of conflicting lines of authority, conflicting policies and controls, conflicting functions, and ultimately conflicting employees at the different levels. Efforts at reconciliation may range all the way from no reconciliation at all through inconsistent reconciliation which is characteristic of most companies, to an elaborate and well-integrated philosophy of business and management. In a sense, this question of ordering and integrating strategies constitutes a new phase of strategic development. Indeed, a strategy for reconciling strategies is needed; and we reach, if you please, the stage of Plato's Philosopher-King. The issue does become almost a political, ethical, and philosophic consideration with notions of decentralization of authority, multiple management, balanced responsibilities, creative integration, industrial democracy, and even a philosophic acceptance of conflict as "right" and "good" in itself.

Organization introduces still other aspects of social behavior. For one thing, as it persists through time, it develops a history, legends, heroic figures, sanctions, and all the other paraphernalia of social organization. It takes on institutional qualities and becomes something greater and more enduring than its members who come and go. It develops a "life" and "existence" of its own which is personified (even in a legal way!) and which has in a sense a character, personality, or kind of social as well as economic role. Under these circumstances, decisions and behavior are governed to a considerable extent by the appropriateness of the action in terms of the character of the organization and whether it is right for this kind of institution.

While it is interesting and revealing to classify the strategies of a company in terms of its stages of development, strategies can also be grouped in terms of the various elements of the socio-economic environment towards which they are directed. Since we are ana-lyzing . . . an already well-established business organization, it is more useful for us to classify strategies in these terms.

Certain strategies have to do with the way the organization fits into the chain of economic and technological events which mold and process the materials of the earth and distribute the products of these efforts to the customer. A business or industrial organiza-tion must maintain and develop its relations with those socio-eco-nomic groups which precede it in the economic chain, that is, its sources of money, machines, tools, and materials, and those which follow it, that is, its customers. These strategies have to do with the economic metabolism of the organization, its intake and output. They also define the particular technological or commercial activity of the organization, what it does for a living so-to-speak. For want of a better designation, we shall refer to these strategies as the *external economic strategies* of the organization.

Other strategies concern the relations which the organization maintains with the broader community including the general public, government bodies, organized charities, schools, etc. Here we view the organization as a social entity with certain rights and privileges, duties, and obligations. These strategies we call *external social strategies*.

Finally, there are strategies which concern the way in which the organization does its job, the way in which employees are moti-vated, coordinated, and controlled, the technology and use of ma-chines and tools, the division of labor, hierarchy of authority, etc. These strategies define what constitutes effective and efficient per-formance in the Barnard sense.[2] We call these *internal organiza-tional strategies*.

Our purpose in presenting this theoretical statement has not been to develop a theory of purposeful, goal-directed organization but

[2] Chester I. Barnard, *The Functions of the Executive* (Cambridge, Mas-sachusetts: Harvard University Press, 1938).

rather to define a single concept *strategy* and show how it provides a way of thinking about industrial organization. We have tried to show that a strategy represents a structuring of a somewhat unpredictable situation where there is only fragmentary information and in which the probable behavior of others must be taken into account. Strategy also implies a particular end in view—in this case achieving and maintaining and advantageous set of relations in the socio-economic environment.[3] As such, a strategy is a conception (or "sizing up") of a situation which occurs at least simultaneously with the action taken or else precedes it. The latter is most likely if we consider that the action is purposeful and not willy-nilly and capricious.

Whether or not a strategy is a conscious conception is perhaps a more difficult question. It is possible that the structuring of a situation can occur without conscious awareness. However, even though unconscious elements are introduced, which they often are, the taking of action requires some kind of conscious plan. For example, a businessman may be unconsciously hostile to people and far more capable of observing their faults than their virtues. Under these circumstances, the strategic orientation which he has towards the general economy may be "bearish" rather than "bullish." A strategy in the terms in which we are using it is by definition a conscious plan of action influenced though it may be by unconscious factors. It is a useful concept in analyzing a business activity and industrial organization because here we find a high degree of purposeful action and an effort to control behavior in terms of conscious goals.

The problem of conscious versus unconscious also raises the question of public versus private. A public strategy may be a

[3] We have never defined precisely what we mean by an "advantageous set of relations," since it is not crucial to our statement. However, for those who wish a definition, we mean, first, a set of relations among customers, investors, sources of supply, producer, etc. which persists for whatever reason and creates an interexchange of commodities, services, and money. We mean, second, from the standpoint of those who control the business, the extraction of gain from this interexchange. Gain may take the form of profit, salary, bonus, position, prestige, etc.

rationalization for more private intentions. This is a methodological problem which must be considered in analyzing the data. It is a matter of digging, but the strategies none-the-less exist.

Still another issue is the lack of awareness of strategies which develop in multi-strategic, complex organizations where communication and control are poor and where the right hand does not know what the left hand is doing. Under these circumstances, the picture presented of the organization may be faulty, incomplete, and inaccurate. In this case, however, the strategies exist somewhere and are serving as guides for action.

There is also the problem of articulateness which must be considered. Businessmen do not ordinarily spend their time trying to develop consistent, systematic, abstract statements of the strategies on which they operate. Under these circumstances, a systematic statement of the strategies of an organization may appear as something new to the management group whose strategies it describes. But this reaction is on the level of the character in Molière's play who discovered that he had been writing and speaking prose all of his life. Again, this is a methodological rather than a theoretical problem.

The term *strategy* raises the questions also concerning its meaning and utility compared with such other terms as *decision-making* and *planning* which have been used perhaps more frequently. Actually, there is nothing wrong with these other terms if they are defined dynamically and with all the connotations implied in the concept *strategy*. A *decision,* however, in ordinary usage suggests actual choice among alternatives in a given situation. It is more specific than strategy, implying action rather than the conception preceding action. A strategy might be regarded as one of the important influences in decision-making. The term *plan* is much too static for our purposes unless qualified. There is not enough of the idea of scheming or calculation with an end in view in it to satisfy us. Plans are used to build ships. Strategies are used to achieve ends among people. You simply do not deal strategically with inanimate objects.

Chapter 5

INDUSTRIAL
HIERARCHIES: THE SOCIAL
STRUCTURE OF BUSINESS
ENTERPRISE

INTRODUCTION

The careers of all industrial leaders come to fruition in at least three important orders of rank and status in our capitalistic society. Each order and its several levels exert an incalculable influence on the industrial leader and his career and must be mastered if he is to succeed. As an infant he must start at the "beginnings" of his culture, accept its demands, learn it, and from this slavelike position move towards increasing competence and mastery. After choosing his profession each individual through time must climb up the several statuses of the business hierarchies which compose capitalistic enterprise. Finally, each must, if he and his family are to be successful and use the fruits of his enterprise rewardingly, move up the social ladder and participate at those higher levels appropriate to his increased occupational position, or if born there the young executive must marry and raise a family within the proper bounds of social class demands.

Within these statements are a series of important assumptions which are part of common knowledge but also buttressed by solid research. The enterprises of private business are social structures arranged in hierarchical statuses. These are segmental hierarchies for they do not comprise all the activities of a society or an individual; rather, their functions and purposes are sharply defined and their goals limited. The values and rules by which men climb to increased power and prestige are aristocratic and the enjoyment of higher status confined to the few.

In contrast the age levels through which they pass are more or less common to all of us. Although biologically founded, they are socially defined; infancy, childhood, adolescence, and early and late adulthood are part of all of our lives and meaningful (although impossible to categorically define) to everyone. The definitions may not be categorically discriminatory, but upper, middle, and lower classes are meaningful and referential for everyone.

Although the mobile businessman in America enters a different kind of business world from that of a colleague born to superior position and although hierarchies differ in distribution of power, prestige, and freedom, the fundamental rules of business status systems are common to all. The several selections of this chapter are concerned with the hierarchical structures of business enterprise in which businessmen must operate.

BUSINESSMEN AND THEIR ORGANIZATIONS IN EUROPE AND AMERICA: A COMPARATIVE ANALYSIS

Frederick H. Harbison and Eugene W. Burgess

When viewed comparatively and in the framework of Western capitalistic enterprise the managerial levels of American business hierarchies are demonstrably more open to mobility. The reasons for this are multiple and significant, and the consequences are socially and economically of the highest importance. These are given expert attention by the writers.

Note: See Notes on the Authors, pages 553 and 552, and item 111 in the bibliography for the full reference to this selection.

It is generally agreed that the private-enterprise system as it exists today in the United States is more "dynamic" than the capitalism which prevails in many countries of western Europe. The contrast is both strikingly illustrated and partially explained when one compares the nature of entrepreneurship on the two continents. For it is entrepreneurship or, more precisely, business management, public or private, which initiates ventures, employs workers, organizes and directs production, develops markets, and thus contributes to the building of a nation's economy.[1] Indeed, in looking closely at management we find very important clues for understanding some of the basic social, political, and economic problems of modern Europe. The nature and status of managerial systems aid in explaining the political orientation of labor organizations, the persistence of cartels and other restrictive institutions, the lower productivity of European enterprise in comparison with its American counterpart, and the current tenuous position of capitalism in many European countries.

[Here] we compare the American type of management with our conception of typical management in France, Belgium, and Italy, justifying impressionistic analysis based upon visits to both American and European firms as a temporary substitute, in the absence of objective empirical studies of entrepreneurship on the two continents. In so doing, we are aware of the dangers of constructing stereotypes of business management which may obscure significant differences not only between countries but also within them. Yet stereotypes not only serve to distinguish the differences both between and within countries but also give a reference point for measuring significant changes in progress.[2] Thus stereotypes are

[1] We use the term "management" in the same sense in which many other writers use the term "entrepreneurship." Following James H. Strauss, *the firm* rather than *the individual* is regarded as the entrepreneur, the firm being the innovator, the supplier of capital, and the manager and co-ordinator of activities through the medium of the individuals who have decision-making responsibilities. See James H. Strauss, "The Entrepreneur: The Firm," Journal of Political Economy, LII (1944), 120.

[2] The impressions set forth [here] are based upon many years of acquaintance with American business concerns and three trips by each author to western Europe. During nine weeks in France, Belgium, Holland, Luxembourg, Germany, and Italy, we made a pilot study of managerial problems

used here as a starting point for further research rather than as a faithful characterization of any enterprise system.

MANAGEMENT ON TWO CONTINENTS: A COMPARISON

The "typical" American management and its counterpart in France, Italy, and Belgium can best be compared by reference to the organizational development of the enterprise, the means of access to managerial positions, and the goals of management. This comparison is made in terms of the American system of values, which should explain what might to some seem biased statements.

In the European firm the number of persons in management is relatively small, decision-making is highly centralized, and the burden of routine administrative duties borne by individual executives is extremely heavy. The managerial force in the European firm is probably less than half that in an American firm of comparable size and technology. Whereas the American firm generally has large numbers of people engaged in activities such as market research, advertising, sales promotion, production engineering, training, industrial relations, and research, the comparable European firm customarily has only skeleton forces in most of these areas and often no specialized personnel in the others. Staff services to the line organization are rare, and even the key executives appear to have few assistants. The European executive must work harder than his American counterpart because he must personally supervise a great many of the functions of the enterprise.

For this undermanning in management there are perhaps several explanations. Many functions, such as sales and industrial relations, are performed for the firm by sales organizations, cartels, or trade associations. Others do not appear sufficiently important to

---

and management development. This study, undertaken by the University of Chicago's Industrial Relations Center under a grant from the Ford Foundation, involved interviews with approximately eighty-five persons in or serving business concerns, mostly in the ranks of top management in European enterprises. This project is part of a program of research on the utilization of human resources in selected countries, both developed and underdeveloped, throughout the world, by a team of specialists from Harvard, Massachusetts Institute of Technology, the University of California (Berkeley), and the University of Chicago.

the European businessman to require specialized managerial talent. Also, there is a shortage of capable people who can be "trusted" to fill managerial positions. Finally, some top managers in Europe take obvious pride in their ability to run a business "economically" with a small managerial force.

By American standards, the organizational structure of even the largest and most progressive European enterprises is haphazard. Organizational charts are rare, and, where they exist, they are often kept secret. Jobs in the managerial hierarchy are seldom defined, described, or aligned. The organization tends to be built around personalities, among whom the division of responsibility is not clear. As one managing director said, "the goal of most of our executives is to make themselves as indispensable as possible."

This organizational structure, which appears so nebulous to an American, is attributable in some cases to family ownership and management. In France and Italy, for example, it is often impossible to distinguish between the objectives of the family and the objectives of the firm. As David Landes points out in a penetrating study of French business enterprise,

the business is not an end in itself, nor is its purpose to be found in any such independent ideal as production or service. It exists by and for the family, and the honor, the reputation and wealth of the one are the honor, wealth, and reputation of the other."[3]

Under these circumstances, managerial organization is of necessity geared as much to personalities as to functions.

Many European enterprises are, of course, directed by professional managers rather than by family dynasties. In some cases there is a dual authority shared by a "technical" managing director and an "economic" managing director, each reporting on an equal and independent basis to a board of directors. Yet, whether the firm is run by members of the family or by a professional group, the managing directors of the typical European enterprise hold the reins in a tight grasp. Whereas the chief executive of a large American corporation is supposed to devote his major energies to build-

[3] "Business and the Businessman in France," in E. M. Earle (ed.), *Modern France* (Princeton, N.J.: Princeton University Press, 1951).

ing an organization and integrating the many functions of the enterprise, his European counterpart is more likely himself to be the boss of most of his departments. The European executive finds it difficult to delegate responsibility to subordinates. In the first place, he does not have enough people to whom he can delegate authority. Second, he feels that he cannot trust many of the subordinates he has. In France, Italy, and Belgium managing directors repeatedly explained: "We have no confidence in our subordinates"; "The people in lower management won't assume responsibility; they aren't well enough trained; they lack experience; they're too young; and some of them are even members of left-wing unions." The head of a multiplant manufacturing company would not even permit his factory managers to hire their personal secretaries until after he had himself passed upon their qualifications and potential loyalty to the organization.

Undermanning and overcentralization of management naturally discourage the growth and expansion of the enterprise. "Why should I try to expand my market," said one harassed owner of a business, "when I have to spend fourteen hours a day controlling the business I have now?" Obviously opportunities for younger executives are limited, incentives to assume responsibility are stifled, and taking initiative is not attractive. While the typical business organization may be well designed to preserve the status quo, it is peculiarly ill-adapted to dynamic growth.

Access to managerial positions is rigidly restricted. In the United States many people, including workers and union leaders, aspire to enter management, whereas in Europe only a select few ever have access to it. It is commonly understood in Europe that people get into management by virtue of being sons or heirs of existing owners, by marrying into the families of the owner dynasties, by using the leverage of a financial interest, or by acquiring a degree from a university or technical institution of higher learning. While this also happens in the United States, it is not so common a course as it is abroad. The European does not expect to work his way up into management from the ranks of the worker.

An aggressive and competent worker may become a foreman, but in Europe foremen are not members of management. Indeed, the European foreman is more comparable to the lead man or straw boss in America, a member of the working class and identified as such. He generally belongs to unions and is often active in protest movements ideologically hostile to the managerial class. Foremanship is not an avenue to upper management, as it so frequently is in the United States. It is rather the highest status to which a worker—without education or family connections—may hope to rise.

But an even more fundamental contrast lies in the educational prerequisites for entry into the managerial class. In the United States, a qualified person can get into management without "a degree"; in Europe this is much more difficult. Yet in America about five times as many people (proportionate to population) go to colleges and universities and get degrees than is the case in most European countries. Also, in the United States a very substantial proportion of persons in institutions of higher learning come from families with relatively little educational background, whereas the students in comparable institutions in Europe come predominantly from families already in the educated class. Thus in Europe business recruits its managerial personnel almost exclusively from the educated, whose numbers are already quite limited; in the United States business recruits its managers from the uneducated as well as from the educated even though the latter are proportionately much more numerous.

Thus the managerial group in France, Belgium, and Italy is a small and distinct elite. Since entry into the elite is restricted, management is decidedly class-conscious. Once admitted to the management class, either by education or through family connections, a person customarily acquires permanent tenure in the hierarchy. Moreover, once a member of management in a particular company, a man is likely to remain there throughout his entire career. It is unethical for one company to raid and woo executive personnel from another. A person who leaves the company where he has tenure as a member of management to accept a position in another firm may be branded as a disloyal and unscrupulous opportunist. For this reason vacancies are not likely to occur frequently, and members of management jealously safeguard their positions. The lack of horizontal mobility within the managerial class results in an inbreeding within business enterprises which hampers the spread of new ideas and new technology from firm to firm.

Finally, from a qualitative standpoint, the system of higher education through which one must pass to gain access to management is not well adapted to developing the kind of leaders which a more dynamic system would require. In the first place, in countries such as France and Italy the curriculums turn young people to careers in government, the armed forces, the professions, or the arts (which are looked upon as higher-status fields than business management) rather than in management leadership. In the second place, theory rather than applied practice is given predominant emphasis in university training, even of engineers. For example, in the engineering universities, there is great emphasis on higher mathematics and engineering design and relatively little on industrial engineering or on the application of engineering principles to factory operations. Courses in such subjects as management organization and administration, marketing, human relations, economics, and labor problems are rarely included. Without question, the typical graduate from the École Polytechnique in France is a brilliant and hard-working fellow who has successfully survived a system of competition which gets more and more rigorous as he advances through his training. He often turns out to be an imaginative engineer. Yet, by the same token, he may be a complete misfit in a job calling for sophistication in organization and management.

Management on both continents is interested in "greater productivity." However, American management usually thinks of greater productivity as increased output and consequent lower unit cost, whereas European management normally struggles to reduce unit cost while rigidly limiting output. The latter emphasizes such things as saving in materials, elimination of waste, and improvement of quality, whereas comparable American plants would aim at increasing production. This is a logical consequence of the European businessman's assumption that the total size and composition of the market are unchangeable. The same assumption explains in part why the European manufacturer favors high unit profits on a small volume to large volume with small unit returns.

234

Another goal of European management, apparently, is to keep free of debt and to avoid reliance on outside credit. In countries where the interest rate is two to three times that in the United States and where bankruptcy is looked upon as a catastrophe rather than a convenient means of reorganization, this is understandable. Yet this concern makes the European businessman a care-taker rather than a risk-taker. As Landes observes, the French family firm is "as solid as the rock precisely because it is almost drowned in its own liquidity."[4] In Europe the concern of the entrepreneur is to survive a recession rather than to seek opportunities which involve risks as well as chances for gain.

In Italy, France, and Belgium the successful management of an enterprise is not an end in itself. The European businessman may strive for and even enjoy leisure! His interests are apt to be broader than those of our modern tycoons. The captains of industry in Europe are certainly as brilliant as, and, if anything, more broadly cultured than, the American, and, if they are relatively poor organization-builders, it is because they lack the American compulsion to organize.

The security-conscious attitude of European management is a consequence not merely of cultural milieu, but rather of the chaotic economic environment. In the last two decades Europe has been ravaged by wars; factories and even entire industries have been demolished; fortunes have disappeared, and whole populations uprooted. Successive waves of inflation have destroyed capital investments, and unstable currencies, coupled with fluctuating foreign-exchange rates, are problems which the European businessman must face almost every day. The typical American businessman, if thrust into this sort of economic environment, might also soon lose his opportunity-mindedness and learn to play safe, and he should be cautious in criticizing European management for its lack of aggressiveness, its tendency to look back to "the old days," and its openly expressed lack of confidence in the future. However, even if currencies were stabilized, if trade barriers were eliminated, and if the ideal of the common European market were realized, the typical management in France, Italy, and Belgium would probably

[4] *Op. cit.,* p. 231.

continue to value security because of the differences in mobility and in institutional organization described above.

MANAGEMENT AND LABOR

In Europe the social distance between management personnel and workers is much greater than it is in the United States, as, to repeat, are the differences in education and income. Consequently, development of understanding between workers and management, which is a problem even in America, is far more difficult in France, Italy, and Belgium. Management-labor communication tends to be from the top down and to be dictatorial. This does not make it easy for management to enlist loyalty and interest on the part of workers in the enterprise, nor does it lead to participation among workers in lowering costs and in improving efficiency. Workers in European plants seldom "talk back" to their bosses. Upward communication is neither expected nor encouraged.

The more enlightened employers in Italy, France, and Belgium have a sense of responsibility toward their workers and express it in such things as company housing, day nurseries, medical services, clubs and recreational programs, and other services. Such employers, particularly those in small cities and towns, also recognize the necessity of providing steady employment for workers and their families. Indeed, they may be willing to sustain considerable financial loss to keep their people employed, knowing that displaced workers may be dependent ultimately upon their charity. The socially conscious employer is a benevolent industrial lord who takes care of the people in his domain partly because of humanitarian motives and partly because of fear of uprising by the masses. At the other extreme are the owners and employers who recognize no responsibility to workers, to the community, or to society as a whole—who live according to a doctrine of "sauve qui peut." They look upon labor as an economic commodity, while they live in constant fear of political agitation for basic changes in ownership and management.

In these countries, the paternalistic employer appears to develop in the working forces a feeling of gratitude and dependence mingled with resentment. Socially irresponsible management creates

236

active opposition and outright hatred. The result is an almost universal distrust of management by the working classes. The overt respect which the individual worker shows his boss in the factory in no way conceals his resentment of the authority of the employer over his life and his underlying lack of respect for the capitalistic system. It is with good reason, then, that many European businessmen are so fearful of their workers that they shudder at the thought of building any kind of genuine two-way communication with them.

Certainly we would not argue that management provides the sole explanation for the class-conscious and often revolutionary orientation of European labor movements. The laboring masses may join unions for many reasons, including protest against the government, a landed aristocracy, or simply the status quo. Yet the only logical response to the typical kind of management which exists in Europe is class-conscious unionism. In France and Italy the effective labor movements have been at various times and under various conditions reformist, syndicalist, and revolutionary. Today they happen to be Communist-dominated. The socialist and Catholic unions in Belgium, though currently more right-wing than those in the other two countries, are certainly not supporters of the existing capitalistic order. But, if the ranks of management are closed to members of the working classes and if business enterprise in collusion with government builds systems of protection to safeguard its vested interests, what could be more logical than for labor organizations to oppose the employer class politically? The character of protest movements in all societies is largely determined by the orientation, status, objectives, and practices of the elite toward which the protest is directed. If this proposition is so, then the orientation, status, and tactics of management in Europe help to explain why most labor organizations in Europe are political enemies of the employer class, whereas unions in America are for practical purposes committed to working within the framework of a private-enterprise system.

The preoccupation of management in Europe with security rather than with growth and expansion explains the dependence on cartels to share markets and on informal understandings to control competition. It accounts for the reliance of European industrialists on trade associations to come to terms with their labor unions. It explains, in part, the pressure from business for tariffs and import quotas for protection from foreign competition. In Belgium, France, and Italy management typically stands for planned protection of enterprise. Now, obviously, many American businessmen stand for some of these things. They have advocated protective tariffs, bargained with unions on an industry-wide basis, entered into collusive agreements with competitors, and sought all kinds of favors from government. However, they depend on such measures much less than the Europeans, and the proportion of rugged individualists who advocate and actually succeed in upsetting such arrangements is far greater. In America the prevailing opinion among businessmen is against most of these restrictions, whereas in Europe it is one of uncritical conformity to, if not open defense of, them.

Management, of course, is not the only class that wants protection. The laboring classes are, if anything, even more anxious for guaranties of security. In the three European countries, the social security systems are far more comprehensive and considerably more costly than those in the United States: their cost ranges from 30 to 40 per cent of payrolls, or about six to seven times that of ours. Also, the right of employers to discharge or to lay off workers is much more closely circumscribed by unions and by legislation than in the United States. So labor in Europe is less mobile, both because of restrictions and because of customs, than in this country.

The employers logically point out that these protective measures for workers result in high labor costs and unwarranted rigidity in the labor force, and act as a brake on expansion of enterprise. In short, management is prone to cite restrictions on employment and overemphasis on social security as primary reasons for Europe's failure to build more dynamic economies. Yet the lack of labor mobility has its counterpart in lack of mobility within the ranks of management. Labor's restrictions on employment tenure are matched by management's protection of the tenure of its own members, and overemphasis on social security goes hand in hand with formal and informal agreements among manufacturers to limit output and to share markets. To be sure, all these protectionist measures are manifestations of a society in which all classes want security above other things. Yet security-consciousness motivates employers as well as workers. Therefore, business management must be held responsible, at least in part, for the overriding desire of the working masses to put their immediate security ahead of economic progress.

MANAGEMENT AND PRODUCTIVITY

It is generally agreed that manufacturing firms in Europe are less productive than those in the United States. A main reason, of course, is that there is more machinery in American plants, since capital is more plentiful. Yet even in firms with comparable technology many more workers seem to be required in Europe than in America. In part, the explanation may be that labor is relatively cheap and that employers are not free to discharge surplus workers. But a possible interpretation is that the European firm has an over-developed labor force largely because of the underdevelopment of its management. Here we find a basic explanation for the fact that labor costs in Europe are high, even though wages are pitifully low.

Because of the difficulty of developing qualified and trustworthy people within the middle-management ranks, European management tends to use incentive systems of one sort or another as substitutes for effective supervision. Such a policy seldom works, even in the United States where the rapport between workers and managers is reasonably good. It is likely to be even less successful in Europe, where workers are more apathetic, more fearful of losing their jobs, and more distrustful of their employers. It is thus unrealistic to expect that the productivity of European business enterprises will automatically be increased if capital can be found to purchase equipment and engineers employed to develop new processes and new incentive systems. The typical business enterprise in the three countries studied is, from an organizational standpoint, poorly equipped to direct and manage its human resources effectively.

Many influential intellectuals as well as people at large are naturally becoming more and more critical of capitalistic systems under which the holders of economic power fail to exercise dynamic and progressive leadership. Significantly, in Europe business enterprise is neither glorified nor publicized as it is in the United States. Instead, management lives in an atmosphere of suspicious toleration rather than widespread respect. The reasons for this are not hard to find. First, management is typically security-conscious and static, and therefore it is not identified by other groups as a creative force for bringing about a higher standard of living for all. Second, the fact that management is an elite into which entry is restricted arouses the jealousy and antagonism of other classes. Third, although economically powerful, the managerial class is numerically very small, and this makes its position politically precarious in any democratic society.

DYNAMIC FORCES IN EUROPEAN ENTERPRISE

Fortunately, however, the economies of France, Belgium, and Italy are by no means static, and among their business leaders are some imaginative innovators. Indeed, there may be ground for belief that the ingrown and stagnant type of business enterprise described above is becoming obsolete under the pressure of new economic and political forces at work in western Europe.

The more progressive businessmen in France, Italy, and Belgium have correctly diagnosed the problems of undermanning and over-exclusiveness in managerial organization. They are convinced of the need for the reform of higher education as it relates to training of future leaders. They also advocate the lowering of trade barriers and the economic integration of Europe. In this respect the progressive European businessman is perhaps more honest and perceptive in criticism of himself and of his system than the American. In each country one finds a handful of very progressive business enterprises which may be the potential carriers of new techniques, new concepts, new outlooks in human relations, and new schemes of building managerial organizations.

Another straw in the wind is the concern of progressive businessmen with education for management. In all three countries "advanced management training programs" are being started on an experimental basis. In France, teams composed of businessmen, educators, labor leaders, and government representatives are studying American experience in education in industrial relations, business administration, and engineering, with a view to recommending reforms in the French system of higher education. There is widespread interest in all three countries in the establishment of business-management institutes for junior executives. The advocates of these programs appear unanimous in stressing administration, marketing, and human relations rather than the purely technical aspects of production management. This new interest appears to have been stimulated by the productivity and technical assistance programs which the United States has been developing in co-operation with the productivity centers in the European countries. To be sure, the prerequisite of long-range fundamental improvement in the system of developing people for managerial positions is a basic change in the curriculums of universities and higher technological institutes, through which practically all new entrants to the managerial class must pass. As a prominent French managing director remarked, a revolution is needed in the whole system of higher education. There are businessmen and educators in Europe who would like to lead such a revolution.

Finally, in Europe it is possible that a more dynamic type of management may be developed in publicly owned and operated industry. Here there is real opportunity for building a management profession as distinct from a class-conscious elite. Already, many of the younger and progressive members of the managerial class are being attracted to public enterprises despite the comparatively low salaries which are offered. As a French productivity expert remarked, "our goal cannot be to build a free-enterprise system which will be only 'second-best' to that in the United States. We have the opportunity to make significant innovations in the successful operation of public enterprises and in the planned integration of economic activity in Europe." In this development two questions are crucial: First, will public management be reasonably free from political control which might interfere with its effective development? Second, will it attempt to recruit some of its new blood from the ranks, or will it follow the example of private enterprise in drawing its managerial personnel almost exclusively from the educated elite?

In conclusion, there is evidence that dynamic changes may be taking place in the static enterprise systems of France, Belgium, and Italy. It is these changes, rather than the traditional stereotypes of management, which demand thoughtful consideration and future systematic study.

CONTROL AND FREEDOM IN AMERICAN CORPORATE HIERARCHIES

Ernest Dale

The placement of power and control for the proper and efficient functioning of business enterprise is an issue of practical and theoretical importance—"flat" and "vertical" structures are subjects of the present debate.

"My intention being to write something of use to those who understand, it appears to me more proper to go to the real truth of the matter than to its imagination; and many have imagined republics and principalities which have never been seen or known to exist in reality; for how we live is so far removed from how we ought to live, that he who abandons what is done for what ought to be done will rather learn to bring about his own ruin than his preservation."

—From *The Prince,* 1532

"Decentralization" like "politeness" means different things to different people, but in no case should it be taken to imply a value judgment. The term itself means the delegation of business decisions by the owners to their immediate representatives (the board of directors and the executive), and then to others further down in the management hierarchy. This is done with the aim of furthering the objectives and values of the enterprise; hence decentralization is only a means to an end.

In addition, "decentralization" is not an absolute term. There are varying degrees of decentralized authority, and the extent to which any company is decentralized must be gauged by tests.

The *locus* or *place* of the decision-making authority in the man-

Note: See Notes on the Authors, page 552, and item 61 in the bibliography for the full reference to this selection.

agement hierarchy is one criterion. The lower the rank of the executives who make given decisions, the greater the degree of decentralization. For example, decentralization is greater where larger amounts of money can be spent at lower levels for such things as capital equipment, administrative or operating purposes, or salary changes. The degree of authority for decisions that could result in a loss may also be a test. In a carpet factory, a mistake in the weave would not be serious; hence the function of quality control could be placed far down in the management hierarchy without any great degree of decentralization. In a pharmaceutical company, on the other hand, an error might cause a death, and quality decisions need to be made near the top level.

In addition, the *degree* of decision-making power at the lower levels will be a factor. This can be determined by studying the authority which can be exercised (1) without any check with higher authority at all (routinized decisions such as the billing procedure, safety enforcement, purchase of stock orders); (2) with a check or regular report after the decision is made and carried out (engagement of clerical personnel, purchases of equipment covered by budget); or (3) with a check before the decision is made or put into effect (decisions without precedent, special appropriation requests). Or there may be the simple requirement to check with a superior on all matters of policy changes, of financial appropriations, or potential and actual disagreements.

In determining the degree of decentralization, moreover, it must always be remembered that an enterprise has both *formal and informal decision-making rules*. Official policy statements may decree one type of decision-making, but actual practice may be quite different. Thus there may be a high degree of formal centralization, but if successful business conduct is not possible under such circumstances, decisions may be, in fact, made much lower down.

For instance, in one firm with about a billion dollars of sales, all purchases over $2,500 must be submitted to the president; and all changes in salaries above $4,000, all expense accounts and all public appearances of executives have to be approved by the chief. Obviously, this chief executive is unable to handle all these approvals himself. The large majority of the purchasing decisions are, in

243

fact, made by executives lower down the line, because merchandise has to be bought and sold if the business is to continue.

When objectives clash with the assignment of responsibility and authority, one or the other is likely to be disregarded. Thus, informal, centralized controls may make possible over-riding the effectiveness of formally decentralized responsibility and authority.

Again formal centralization may be offset to some extent by physical decentralization. For example, the production of certain products may be undertaken at a separate physical location; accounting records may be assembled and placed next to the immediate user. Thus in decentralization movements, headquarters are sometimes shifted away from the plant to prevent the close control that can come from propinquity.

CURRENT STATUS IN THE UNITED STATES

There is no statistical information on the extent of centralization and its reverse, the decentralization of decision-making, in U.S. industry. Business literature usually carries accounts of corporate decentralization, largely because such moves are considered "progressive" and hence newsworthy (one rarely reads today of a president boasting of centralization). However, general reasoning will show that centralization is still quite widespread. Probably "one-man control" is found in more companies and affects more employees than "control by the few" or "control by the many."

One-man control stems partly from tradition and partly from human nature. Men in commanding positions like to believe that they are indispensable—secretly hope, perhaps, that they may always be there to carry on. They fear that delegation of authority may foster the creation of "empires within the empire," and make them more dependent on others. In addition, it is hard for the one man in control to jettison all his intellectual investments. He may be committed to a belief in the virtues of benevolent dictatorship, and the power of vested ideas may well be stronger than the power of economic interests.

And this may well be a long-run trend. For there may be a difference (and sometimes an appreciable one) between the maximum profit that a company could make and the actual profit it must make to keep the stockholders from complaining too loudly. To this extent the compulsion to maximum profits no longer exists to the same degree that it did 50 years ago when owner-management was much more common. Nor is the maximization of profits as advantageous for the individual executive as it used to be, since income taxes, the decline in the value of money, and the long-run decline in the rate of interest all make large accumulations of wealth difficult and often impossible. Andrew Carnegie made many millions of dollars, but the present heads of the Carnegie-Illinois Steel Corporation have no such prospects, even though the job is probably considerably more difficult and complex than in Carnegie's time. For this reason, it may not be worthwhile to risk public opprobrium by squeezing customers or employees, and the consequent trend to "awareness of social responsibilities" may be affecting even family-owned and operated businesses to some extent.

Hence, one may be justified in studying the shift from profit to power as a major business objective and its effect on decentralization. "Power" may be sought in volume of sales or percentage of market, in professional distinction (i.e., the emphasis on "management as a profession," as an "elite," etc.). The chief executive may demonstrate his power by setting the tone in the local community or the industry, by accepting important positions in government or the foreign service. Or he may simply hold on to all major and many minor decisions in the enterprise. Even in allegedly decentralized companies the delegation of powers may go no further than from the chief executive to his vice presidents, and subordinates cannot complain because the holders of power are their immediate superiors.

Factors making for centralization in an enterprise may be many. Most important, perhaps, is the example of the chief executive. To the extent to which he retains powers, his subordinates are likely to imitate him. To the extent that he welcomes "checking," "consultation" and dependence, his subordinates are likely to do the same. Of course, the chief does not actually have to make each decision himself. He merely needs to "spot-check." For example, if he insists on passing on all increases in salaries above $400 a month and 1,000 such applications reach him every month, he needs to pass on only one or a few of them. If he raises a question (or an eyebrow) everyone will be careful to propose only such increases as can be justified under questioning by the chief.

MEASUREMENT OF RESULTS NECESSARY BUT COMPLEX

Then all the devices used to coordinate an enterprise may be used to foster centralization. Such "tools" as organization and policy manuals, methods and procedures manuals, authority limitation manuals (dealing with authority for capital expenditures, salary and personnel changes, etc.) may actually take away more authority than they confer. Sometimes they enforce systems of communication along the lines of a pyramid. Or the chief executive may set up checks and sources of information that nullify the delegation of powers. Measurement of results is, of course, necessary; the chief must know how the delegated powers are exercised. But the controls may bring about so much checking, transmission of so much information so continuously, and so much correction that the "decentralized" operators may spend a considerable part of their time explaining and defending themselves. In some companies, the saying goes: "It takes two tons of paper to make one ton of product." There is also the possibility that the chief's general staff may deliberately force executives to refer many decisions to headquarters or influence decisions without adequate consultation. Or the special staff may exercise central command powers because of actual or assumed technical knowledge, direct operation of services, "concurrent authority," superior articulation, physical proximity to the chief, or simply in default of decision-making elsewhere. There are the possible abuses of group work, the enforcement of compatibility and conformity, the use of manipulative techniques to strengthen centralization.

Finally there are the modern means of communication—telephone, telegraph, teletype, radio, and now television—which make it physically possible for the chief executive to issue direct orders to distant subordinates. And it is even possible that future technical developments may eliminate one of the main reasons for decentralization. If enough information can be brought to a central point quickly enough, there may no longer be a need to have problems settled at a point close to their source. The development of electronic devices, calculators, punch card systems, etc., together with such tools as operations research and Cybernetics, may so greatly and so quickly increase the information available to central management that the basic desire of many chiefs—to continue to make as many decisions as possible or to widen the range of their decision-making—might be gratified.

FORCES BEHIND GREATER DECENTRALIZATION

But even if these powerful factors making for "one-man control" did not exist, extensive delegation might still not be possible. For the personnel who can shoulder the additional responsibilities might not be available. Those who grew up with the chief in the business may not be able (or willing) to take more responsibility. Yet if the chief brings in outside personnel, the newcomers may be thwarted by uncooperative oldtimers.

Thus effective delegation of decision-making may be costly. Difficult personalities may be hard to replace, and both the training of new executives and their initial mistakes may be expensive. Additional functional personnel (accounting, research, industrial relations, etc.) may have to be hired in the now semi-autonomous divisions and branches and the difficult relationships to head-office worked out. Informal work groups and long-established relationships may be upset and destroyed. It is difficult and time-consuming to get executives to assume and exercise additional responsibility.

Finally, hard times and increased competition may foster centralization. When the chief executive feels that the company cannot afford mistakes, he is likely to want more power in his own hands.

So it is clear that the, tendencies toward greater centralization or at least preservation of the status quo may be strong.

HISTORY OF DECENTRALIZATION IN AMERICA

The decentralization movement in American business was probably begun by Henry V. Poor in the 1850's through his proposals for the reorganization of American railroads, when he sought to help those first large-scale organizations overcome the drawbacks of diminishing returns from management. This remarkable man coined the phrase "the science of management." Poor's suggestions were first applied by Daniel McCallum, General Superintendent on the Erie Railroad 1854 to 1857 and later one of the chief organizers of the American transport system during the Civil War.

The first successful large-scale plan of decentralization in manufacturing industry was probably that presented in 1920 to W. C. Durant, President of General Motors, by Alfred P. Sloan, Jr., then G.M. Vice President. This was a most remarkable and far-sighted document, largely formed the basis of the present General Motors organization and was put into effect by many other companies. This was adopted when General Motors was reorganized in 1921. . . .

Essentially one or more of the following characteristics mark a program of decentralization in a large corporation.

(1) *The administrative unit that usually covers the company as a whole as well as all its plants is broken into smaller administrative units—often on either a geographical or product basis.* Each is headed by a manager who may be compared to the head of a smaller enterprise. Usually he has fairly complete control over basic line functions, such as manufacturing and marketing; if he also has staff services such as accounting, engineering, research and personnel, the unit may be largely self-contained.

(2) *Provision is made for the effective utilization of a centralized staff of specialists to aid the decentralized operations to increased profitability and better relationships in order to combine the advantages of a large unit of management with those of a small one.* Central staff specialists are said to "advise and assist" the chief executive and the line operators, and perhaps handle certain centralized functions for the company as a whole, such as public relations, law and taxation. In other cases, the centralized staff specialists maintain "functional supervision" over divisional operations in their fields of expertise, such as industrial relations, finance, and possibly manufacturing and sales. Functional supervision may cover formulation of major company objectives, policies, plans and programs for line management's approval and seeing that decisions are carried out, furnishing administrative and technical advice, setting up standards, systems, procedures, controls and meas-

urement of performance, concurring in selection of key personnel and in changes in their assignment.

The essential problem in this area of decentralization is the delineation of the authority of the staff specialists. The theoretical "indirect" authority of the central staff may vary in fact from advice to command. For example, the headquarters staff specialist in personnel administration may be an adviser on personality problems, a coordinator of union negotiations, a policy-maker in job and salary evaluation, a researcher on executive development, a statistical compiler of personnel data, an operator of cafeteria services (and of his own department) or he may "concur" on urgent problems of safety (e.g., prohibiting a worker from continuing on a dangerous machine), a controller of the observance of personnel policies. Clearly there are numerous opportunities for widespread participation by "staff" in the decision-making of the enterprise, through the actual use of authority of various kinds, including the "authority" of knowledge.

(3) *A series of general staffs may be provided for the chief executive* to handle the functions which he cannot delegate and which may become increasingly burdensome as the company increases in size. For example, growth of the enterprise requires more attention to the increasing number of people affected by it. When the chief represents the company personally in these contacts, an increasing proportion of his time is spent away from his subordinates. Or it may be difficult or impossible for the chief executive to handle the growing demands of coordination and communication. Hence he may acquire staff assistance in the person of an "assistant to," who has been called "an extension of the personality of his chief," and as such acts in his name.

The use of a general staff, widely and successfully employed in the armed forces of the world, has been urged by President Eisenhower to the author as "the major application of military to business organization." It is interesting to note that a number of business leaders and pioneers of scientific management started out as "assistants to." For example, Gantt, Barth and S. E. Thompson were assistants to Taylor. Alfred P. Sloan, Jr., and Walter P. Chrysler were assistants to W. C. Durant.

Other staff variants are the "Pentagon Staff" which handles long-range planning for the company as a whole (e.g., the Bell Telephone Laboratories) and the "personal staff" whose job is to make the business life of the chief smoother and more convenient.

(4) *Centralized controls are designed to find out how well the delegated authority and responsibility are exercised.* Controls may include budgets, standards, reports, audits, visits, regular meetings and exchange of information. Instead of measuring results for the company as a whole, an attempt is made to break down profit or (controllable) cost responsibilities by operating units. This is merely a modernization of the practice of some of the great department store founders who let individual managers alone for a year or two, and then "looked at the record." Perhaps the "decentralization of measurement" partly explains the success of the Standard Oil Company of New Jersey's system of "wholly owned subsidiaries." Furthest in this direction went Orlando F. Webber, for some time the chief executive of Allied Chemical and Dye Company who ran the company on the basis of detailed monthly reports brought to him at the Waldorf Towers, his New York hotel. Not only may costs be effectively controlled by "decentralized measurement," but managerial analysis of results and remedial action are facilitated. A closer tie between effort and reward is made possible.

DECIDING THE DEGREE OF DECENTRALIZATION

Decentralization is not an ideal. It is not a series of principles or prescriptions that a businessman ought necessarily to follow. Decentralization is not necessarily good, nor is centralization necessarily bad.

Where a conscious decision to decentralize is made, ideally it should be based on economic factors. The assignment of a management decision, or any part of it, higher or lower in the management hierarchy, should depend on the additional revenue to be gained as compared to the additional cost.

The contributions of decentralization to profits must be weighed against the costs, both those that can be measured in dollars and cents and those that are more intangible. Easily measurable are the permanent extra costs that result from the larger staffs necessary, and some temporary expenses of introducing the change in management. More intangible costs are the disturbances caused by the change and their possible effects on morale. In addition, there may be "disguised unemployment" (high-priced men not fully utilized) and losses from watertight thinking or over-specialization. Finally, there are the costs (and gains) of destroying or delaying educational and promotional opportunities from some executives and creating them for others in the process of reorganization.

Basically the economic issue between centralization and decentralization is between lower total administrative costs and more effective performance.

MANAGERS, CORPORATE STRUCTURE, AND EMPLOYEE MORALE: A CASE STUDY

James C. Worthy

A great American corporation has built into its structure decentralization of authority and responsibility. The significance of this type of structure for employee morale and other aspects of corporate life were the objects of careful research and are here reported by one of the top officials of the company.

Sears, Roebuck and Co. during the past 12 years has conducted surveys covering several hundred different company units and over 100,000 employees. These units include retail stores, mail order plants, factories, warehouses, and offices; in size they range from fewer than 25 employees to more than 10,000. Geographically, the units are scattered through all sections of the United States, in communities ranging from cities of under 5,000 to the largest metropolitan centers. Types of employees covered include clerical and sales personnel, manual and professional workers, supervisory employees, and executives.

Initially, surveys were undertaken for the simple straightforward purpose of finding out how well employees liked their jobs, what

Note: See Notes on the Authors, page 557, and item 255 in the bibliography for the full reference to this selection.

their attitudes were toward supervision and management, and what factors in the employment situation might be contributing to dissatisfaction and poor working relationships. It was assumed that, once these things had been determined, it would be possible for management to take the necessary corrective action and thus exercise direct control over the quality of management-employee relationships.

This assumption has proved only partially valid. While many situations could be dealt with by specific management action, we found that some of the more difficult employee relations problems could not be properly understood (much less influenced) except in terms of the broader context of the organization in which they had developed. Gradually therefore, the scope of the studies broadened to include the functioning of the organization as a whole and the entire pattern of technical processes and formal and informal relationships which comprise the organization. (It was apparent, too, that many influences on management-employee relations are external to the organization itself. To the extent practicable, these external influences have been recognized and studied. The main emphasis of the research, however, has been on internal factors.)

This broadening of scope has been recognized by changing the name of the program from "morale surveys" to "organization surveys." Whereas originally we sought merely to determine the level of employee morale, we now seek to analyze any strains or cleavages within an operating unit which may impede its proper functioning. Determining the level of morale is useful chiefly as a means for diagnosing organization problems; it is not an end in itself.

There is clear evidence that, on the whole, Sears employees are well disposed toward the company. For instance, an analysis of the responses of some 12,000 employees to one questionnaire revealed that 72% thought Sears was either "better than average" or "one of the very best" places to work, and only 3% thought Sears "poorer than average." Some 95% said they would rather work for Sears than almost any other company of which they knew. Our interviews have yielded similar results, emphasizing the high regard most people seem to have for the company.

Nevertheless, we are keenly conscious that many problems exist and that morale varies widely among various units of the organization. For example, the lowest unit surveyed has a "morale score" (using an arbitrary scale of measurement) more than 50 points below the highest, with other units scattered between these two extremes. We have, therefore, made a real effort to gain a better understanding of the factors which account for such differences. Of course, our findings in this connection may not all be new or necessarily true for every company; their value is that they are based on a body of very real experience and that as such they should contribute to others' understanding.

The most important conclusion to which we have come is that there is no simple explanation for any given state of employee morale. Rather, our studies indicate the existence of a highly complex set of interdependent factors which combine in subtle and obscure ways to produce a particular level of employee satisfaction or dissatisfaction. Whether high or low, this level of satisfaction, in turn, seems to reinforce many of the factors producing it, thus setting in motion a kind of "circular reaction" which tends to keep good morale good and poor morale poor. It is for this reason that management, despite sincere and vigorous efforts, often finds it so difficult to bring about perceptible improvements in problem situations.

Wages, Hours, and Working Conditions. Our studies indicate that many of the factors considered of primary importance by management often play relatively minor roles. Analysis of the 12,000 responses to the questionnaire mentioned above, for instance, showed that pay ranked in eighth place among the elements related to high morale. Interestingly enough, this eighth-place item related to *pay in comparison with other jobs in the same unit;* rates of pay as such ranked in fourteenth place. Hours of work, in twenty-first place, fared still more poorly as an influence on employee attitudes.

This is not to say that hours of work, rates of pay, and proper job differentials are not important. Wherever local management is guilty of any serious shortcomings in these matters, they loom up much more importantly in employee thinking. The point is, these things in themselves are not enough; they are only the beginning. If the only basis management can conceive for employee loyalty and cooperation is the pay envelope and the short work-week, there can never be enough money or short enough hours to do the job. Management must have a firmer basis than this on which to build effective working relationships.

The Special Role of Profit Sharing. What has been said above applies with special force to the Sears profit sharing plan. This plan, in continuous operation since 1916, is open to all employees with a year or more of service. Each member of the plan deposits 5% of his earnings (up to a maximum deposit of $250 per year) in the profit sharing fund. At the end of the year the company contributes to the fund between 5% and 9% (determined according to a fixed scale) of its net profits before taxes and dividends. (The company's contribution for 1948 was $22,817,079.) These contributions are credited to the accounts of employees on a dual basis of length of service and amount of individual deposit.

Over the years the profit sharing plan has gradually assumed a role which transcends its function as tangible evidence of management's concern for the welfare of its employees. In a sense, profit sharing has become a "unifying principle" that serves as a symbol around which the entire organization revolves. Because of the magnitude of fund holdings, there is a striking community of interest between stockholders and employees. The making of profits for absentee stockholders has never been a rallying point around which the enthusiastic support of employees could be organized. However, where employees and stockholders tend more and more to become the same people, profitability of operations—with all that it implies—becomes a rallying point of greater and greater effectiveness.

The type of supervision prevailing in any organization is likely to follow closely the pattern set by those in the top levels of management. If higher executives tend to maintain friendly, easy, comfortable relations with those who report to them directly, these individuals in turn will tend to maintain similar relations with their own subordinates, down through all levels of the organization. This repetition of a pattern set by [the] top is a reflection of the tendency of executives as a group to copy, consciously or unconsciously, the traits and methods of their superiors, a fact brought out strikingly in a number of recent studies of the personality characteristics of executives.[5]

Promotion from Within. . . . Executives who rise from the ranks are likely to have a better appreciation of the employee's point of view. Promotion from within tends to increase the respect and confidence of employees for their superiors because of their knowledge that those in higher positions really know their jobs and "won their spurs" in free and open competition. Furthermore, they are "all in the same family" and "all speak the same language" because, in a sense, they "all grew up together" as part of the same organization. There thus tends to be a higher sense of the "we" feeling than is likely to be the case otherwise.

Administrative Decentralization. To an important degree, these are disadvantages inherent in large organizations. Unquestionably, they account, directly or indirectly, for much of the general deterioration of management-employee relations that has accompanied the rise of great corporations in our economic and social system. On the other hand, this situation is by no means wholly beyond management's control. In fact, our studies strongly suggest that through effective administrative decentralization it should be possible to preserve the special economic advantages of large size without losing the special human advantages of small size.

Structure of Organization. At Sears we have found it expedient to enforce decentralization not merely through policy directives but more particularly through the design of the organization itself. Top management has sought to set up an organization structure which makes it difficult for executives to operate on any other basis than that of fairly extensive delegations of authority and responsibility.

This organization structure may be characterized as "broad" or "flat" in contrast to the more "vertical" or "tall" structures in which there are many layers of supervision between top and bottom. The extent to which Sears has gone in this respect may be indicated by the fact that only four levels of supervision intervene between the president of the company and the salespeople in the stores, a diffi-

[5] William E. Henry, "The Business Executive—A Study in the Psychodynamics of a Social Role," *American Journal of Sociology,* LIV, No. 4 (January, 1949), 286.

cult achievement in an organization of approximately 110,000 employees in the retail division alone.

Degree of Specialization. Another device that Sears has employed to help enforce decentralization is that of discouraging over-specialization. In an organization as large and as diversified as Sears, a certain amount of specialization is essential, but in so far as possible it has been kept to a minimum. This policy recognizes the definite advantages of the flexible, versatile "general practitioner" (particularly at the executive level) in contrast to the narrower and less adaptive specialist. The policy also recognizes that a minimum of specialization has a salutary influence on employee morale and productive efficiency and makes possible a far less elaborate organization structure than would otherwise be necessary. . . .

Coordination of Functions. . . .

In order to achieve the necessary degree of coordination and co-operation between administratively separated functions, a management which has set up this type of organization is forced not only to create an elaborate hierarchy of many supervisory levels, but to institute a wide variety of formal controls. Unfortunately, these controls are themselves often a source of conflict, because the individual supervisor or executive is under strong compulsion to operate in such a manner as to make a good showing in terms of the particular set of controls to which he is subject, and often he can do so only at the expense of effective collaboration across departmental lines.

The administration of organizations which have been overfunctionalized to the extent characteristic of many organizations today imposes a severe burden on the top administrative group, and a specialized staff becomes necessary to help them carry the load. This growth of staff activities complicates the situation still further, because an inevitable consequence is the elaboration of formal controls of various kinds to permit the staff to perform the functions and exercise the responsibilities which have been delegated to it or which it gradually assumes in an effort to strengthen its position and extend its authority. The result is the gradual undermining of the line organization for the benefit of the staff, the impairment of flexibility and adaptability, and the weakening of the effectiveness of the entire organization.

Personal Qualities. A significant feature of the "flat" type of organization structure is the very high premium it places on the
proper selection, training, and placement of key personnel; for, if
such an organization is to function successfully, it must depend in
large measure on the quality of executive manpower at all strategic
points. While important in all types of organizations, the quality of
executive man-power is particularly vital in the "flat" structure because there are fewer levels of supervision and therefore less direction and control, thus increasing higher management's dependence
on the skill and initiative of those further down the line.

In this type of organization structure, the individual executive is
thrown largely on his own, to sink or swim on the basis of his own
individual ability. He cannot rely to more than a limited extent on
those above him; and these superiors, by the same token, cannot
too severely restrict, through detailed supervision and control, their
subordinate's growth and development.

Not all individuals can function effectively in this type of system;
it requires a very large measure of self-reliance, self-confidence,
and personal capacity. The system tends to weed out those who
lack these qualities in adequate degree. Those who are able to
adapt to this type of organization, however, are likely to be not
only better merchants and executives but also the type of people
who can build and maintain teamwork and cooperation and a high
level of employee morale, not so much because they consciously
attempt to do so as because these results are a natural by-product
of their ways of operating and a reflection of their own personalities.

On the other hand, in organizations characterized by many levels
of supervision and by elaborate systems of control, not only has the
individual little opportunity to develop the capacities of self-reliance and initiative, but the system frequently weeds out those who
do. Furthermore, our studies strongly suggest that those who survive in such an organization are often likely, by virtue of the very
qualities which enabled them to survive, to have personalities and
ways of operating which do not make for the greatest skill in building employee teamwork and cooperation.

An organization with few layers of supervision and a minimum
of formal controls places a premium on ability to stimulate and

lead. The driver type of executive, who functions through maintaining constant pressure and whose chief sanction is fear, cannot operate so effectively in such an organization. Under truly decentralized management, an executive accomplishes results and moves to higher levels of responsibility chiefly to the extent that he is able to secure the willing, enthusiastic support of his colleagues and subordinates; he does not have the "tools" (with which a more centralized system would to some extent provide him) to accomplish results in any other manner. The outcome is not only a higher level of accomplishment but, at the same time, a more satisfying type of supervision and a higher level of employee morale.

THE STATUS STRUCTURE OF MANAGEMENT

Chester I. Barnard

The functioning and malfunctioning of the managerial hierarchy are examined and the theoretical and practical significance of rank in business made explicit and meaningful.

. . . Executives are . . . conscious of the necessity of systems of status as (1) a function of the system of organization communication, the fundamental process in cooperation; (2) as an important part of the system of incentives; and (3) as an essential means of inculcating and developing a sense of responsibility and of imposing and fixing responsibility.

A system of organization communication, in order that it may operate with sufficient accuracy and rapidity, has to be so designed that it may easily and quickly be assured that particular communications are (a) authentic, (b) authoritative, and (c) intelligible.

a. Under ordinary circumstances, and especially with respect to routine matters, explicit authentication of communications is not required. Personal acquaintance with or knowledge of the communicator together with the relevance of the communication to the general context and to previous communications are sufficient. The

Note: See Notes on the Authors, page 551, and item 16 in the bibliography for the full reference to this selection.

status system is not of great importance in this connection. But in times of emergency and great danger or in respect to important matters, explicit authentication of communications often becomes necessary. Witnessed written communications or letterheads indicating the name, position, and title of the communicator and personal introductions by mutually known third parties are among the means used. There is no doubt that here the status system greatly facilitates authentication—it is one of the practical uses of insignia of office.

b. It is in respect to the authoritativeness of a communication, however, that we find the basic need for systems of status. The primary question of the recipient of a communication, assuming that it is authentic, i.e., comes from whom it purports to come, is whether the contents of the communication may be relied upon as a basis for action. This is what we mean by authoritativeness. Authoritativeness in this context is of two kinds: functional authoritativeness; and scalar or command authoritativeness.

Whether a communication reflects the facts and needs of the situation depends upon whether the individual (or body) that emits it has the general qualifications for understanding what he (or it) communicates about and whether he is *in a position* to have the essential concrete knowledge.

A report from a carpenter about the condition of a generator in a power house is initially not credible; that of the electrician in charge is credible, though not conclusive; that of an electric power engineer is more credible and *may* be accepted as final. The authoritativeness of the report depends in part upon the qualifications of those reporting, and these are presumptively established by formal status. But a report by an electrician in Des Moines about a generator in New York is not credible. He has the qualifications in general, but he is not in a position to apply them to the situation in New York.

The purpose of the report may be to secure help in the correction of some fault. The help needed may be in the form of superior technical instruction; it may be in the form of the application of some maintenance skill or of a replacement part. The electrician is not in a position to know the status of those whose services are needed. His superior does—he knows less of the concrete situation, but he has more technical knowledge or more knowledge of the relevant status system.

The functional status system is so extraordinarily convenient in providing prima-facie evidence of the authoritativeness of communications that we depend upon it almost exclusively in the conduct of daily affairs generally as well as in all organizations. It does not imply any generalized superiority or inferiority of status in this aspect. It does not exclude discrimination as between individuals having the same status, nor does it assume errors may not occur in relying upon the prima-facie evidence granted by status. The plumber, or electrician, or lawyer, or doctor may be immature or poor or even bad, as determined by experience or surmised from observation; but even so may often be presumed to be superior to those of other statuses. A poor doctor, even though inadequate, will generally be a better advisor on medical matters than an expert plumber. Systematized functional status would seem to be absolutely indispensable for the effective operation of complex divisions of labor, and it may also be indispensable even for relatively simple divisions of labor, although in the latter condition there may be some acceptable "jacks of all trade."

c. The special system of status associated with chains of command or hierarchy of authority depends upon each position being a "communication center," the inferior command being associated with restricted areas or fields, the higher command being more comprehensive. Outside the technical competence special to each field of organization, the general functions common to all hierarchies of command are: to evaluate the meaning of communications received in the form of advices and reports, largely affected by the status of the transmitter; to know to whom communications should be relayed (i.e., to know the relevant status system or "the organization"); to select that which needs to be relayed; and to translate communications, before relaying, into language appropriate to the receiver.

The system of command communication cannot effectively work except on the basis of a status system. For very small organizations communication may effectively be addressed to persons, but for larger systems status becomes primary. Contrast saying to the new office boy, "Take this order to Bill Jones in building K" (in which there are two Bill Joneses) and "Take this order to the foreman of section 12 in the Y Department in building K." Contrast the following orders: "Capt. Jones of Station Y and Capt. Smith of Station X will advise each other by telephone each morning as to their respective situations and will advise Major Allen of any unusual circumstances." "The Commandants of stations X and Y will advise each other and this office each morning of their respective situations and of any unusual circumstances." In the first case any change of personalities calls for a new order—otherwise the desired collaboration will fail.

Although both functional and scalar systems of status are essential to establishing in a practicable degree the authoritativeness of communications, authoritativeness is not sufficient. Unless communications are intelligible they cannot be acted upon correctly or effectively. Now, it is apparent that the intelligibility of a communication depends not merely upon capacity of the communicator but also upon that of the receiver. Thus communications of the same content will differ very greatly, depending upon the status of those to whom they are addressed. Whether a communication is intelligible depends upon the use of language having the same meaning to the originator and to the receiver of the communication. This requires a selection of language, depending upon from whom and to whom the communication is made. Systems of status are an indispensable guide to the selection of appropriate language. . . .

When communications are sent from a subordinate to his superior it is called a report. When it is sent from the superior to the subordinate and is in peremptory terms it is a command or order. The difference is superficial. The command implies the following report: "From my superior position I report that the situation calls for the following action on your part." Very often in fact it is in the form: The situation as known to us here is so and so; it permits you to use your own judgment, based on the local situation, i.e., issue the orders to yourself.

The executive, then, is much preoccupied with systems of status because they are important in the authentication of communications, indispensable in establishing a working presumption of the authoritativeness of their content, and essential to their intelligibility.

Systems of status are also important because maintenance of status and improvement of status are among the essential incentives to cooperation. The scarcity of effective incentives calls for use of many kinds of incentives; and their wise use requires, especially in larger organizations, their systematic use.

Status as an incentive has two aspects suggested earlier. The first is that of prestige for its own sake, as a reinforcement of the ego, as security for the integrity of the person. This is an important need of many individuals. They will work hard to satisfy it and forego much to attain it. The second aspect is that of prestige as a valuable or indispensable means to other ends. Thus some men endure publicity or accept conspicuous positions of onerous character as a means of supporting organizations or of eliciting the support of others because they like philanthropic, or scientific, or cultural work, which is their fundamental incentive.

The importance of status as an incentive is shown by the immense amount of work and sacrifice made by innumerable volunteer heads of social, philanthropic, religious, political, and scientific organizations. For some the motive is directly personal. For others it is the "good of the cause" and the personal incentive is satisfaction in the promotion of that cause.

These are perhaps the most obvious instances of the importance of status as incentive. The executive is frequently concerned with the instances where material rewards are by themselves ineffective and status proves to be the controlling or a necessary supplementary incentive. He is also concerned with the still less conspicuous cases where prestige is a negative incentive, where preferred status is regarded as too burdensome, and where it is believed to be a limitation on personal liberties.

The system of status is a strong and probably an indispensable developer of the sense of responsibility and therefore of stability and reliability. Loss of status is more than loss of its emoluments;

it is more than loss of prestige. It is a serious injury to the personality. Thus while improvement of status is important, especially to the more able, and desirable to many, loss of status is much more generally resisted. It is difficult to accept, or to be accepted in, a reduced status. Indeed, the fear of losing status is what leads some to refuse advancement of status. The desire for improvement of status and especially the desire to protect status appears to be the basis of the sense of general responsibility. Responsibility is established and enforced by specific penalties for specific failures and by limitation of status or by loss of a particular status for failure in general. Although both methods in conjunction are most effective, of the two it would appear that the second is much more effective than the first, especially as to those above low levels of status. In view of the extreme importance of dependable behavior, the function of status in creating and maintaining dependable behavior is probably indispensable. The extent of criminal behavior suggests that specific sanctions are not sufficient in general to establish adequate responsibility.

. . . [A] system of status is founded on and made necessary by the following four factors, in addition to others, relevant to the present topic: (a) differences in the abilities of individuals, (b) differences in the difficulties of various kinds of work, (c) differences in the importance of various kinds of work, and (d) the needs of the system of communication.

The first of these factors is strictly personal and individual. This does not mean, of course, that the capacities of the individual may not have been largely determined socially, but that at any given time they are the personal possession of the individual and the application or non-application of these capacities at any given time or period is taken to be a matter of personal choice or will. To the extent that status depends upon individual ability and willingness to employ it, it may be said to be individual and not social. Personal status may to this extent be said to be correlative with personal merit. Undoubtedly, evaluation from this point of view is widely conceived as just. If this were the only basis of status, it seems probable that differences of status would be accepted as proper and necessary even where material distribution could be conceived as properly made on the basis of "to each according to need."

As we ascend to the other bases of status, more and more qualification of the conception of individual merit is required. Thus the differences in the difficulties of tasks are in some degree merely matters of the nature of the physical world and of the capacities of individuals; but where acquired skills and technologies are involved, being almost entirely of social origin, relative difficulties indirectly are socially determined. Further, almost every task in a formal society involves adaptation of behavior to and utilization of the social system itself. What is rated as easy or difficult behavior is socially evaluated. Hence, individual merit in performing the difficult often lies in capacity and willingness to resign personal differences. The qualification on account of the social element in "difficult" is not important. "Difficult" reflects a social standard of measurement of abilities; the standard and the abilities together are a basis for status.

Variations in the *importance* of work as a basis for status are quite another matter. "Importance" is almost entirely determined socially in the same sense, though not necessarily in the same way, that economic value is determined by demand and supply as socially expressed, i.e., in exchange. To the extent that the individual accepts the social valuation and does that which is regarded as important, there is personal merit. Whether the status accorded is inferior or superior, however, will depend upon whether those able and willing are relatively numerous or not. Thus, low status frequently accompanies work of primary importance in the aggregate, e.g., wheat growing, in which numerous individuals are employed; high status often accompanies work which *in the aggregate* is relatively unimportant, but scarce, hence valuable, e.g., silversmithing.

The rating of the individual by the importance of his work, a social evaluation, may be necessary to effective and efficient allocation of ability in the social system, and it may therefore be essential to the adaptation of the society as a whole to its environment. However, status so determined tends, as experience shows, to be imputed to the individual *as such* rather than to a particular socially valued *role* of the individual. When inferior status is assigned on this basis, it is transferred to the individual generally, and similarly when superior status is assigned. Thus exaggeration of personal inferiority and superiority results. The effect upon the characteristics of the individual contributors to an organization is deleterious—depressing and limiting those of inferior status, stimulating and sometimes intoxicating those of superior status. Restoring or creating morale in the one, restraining the other, then becomes a major problem of organization.

The system of communication by means of which coordination is secured in cooperation is a strictly social phenomenon. Being indispensable to purposeful cooperation, the necessities of the system of communication become prime, being secondary only to the prior existence of an organization whose members are willing to cooperate. Now, undoubtedly the capacity of individuals to function in a system of communications depends upon natural abilities, general knowledge and experience, facility in general and special languages, technical and other special abilities; but though often indispensable, such general capacities and potentialities are secondary to the abilities directly associated with a particular communication position and with immediate concrete knowledge. One cannot function as or in a communication center if one is not at that center; nor, if at that center, without knowledge of the immediately precedent communication materials, i.e., what has just transpired, what further communication is called for, to whom and where further communication should be made, from whom and where communication should be elicited. Neither general nor special abilities suffice to meet the requirements if this local and concrete knowledge is not available.

Thus the primary specific abilities required in communication are those of *position*—of being at the place where communication may effectively be had and where immediate concrete knowledge may be obtained. The manning of posts of communication by those possessing the requisite abilities of position is so indispensable to cooperation that a system assuring such manning and hence of the acquirement of such abilities has precedence over all other considerations in an organization, for the breakdown of communication means immediate failure of coordination and disintegration of organization. It should not be understood from this that the general capacities and abilities of individuals are not important. If positions of communication are not manned by those of requisite general and special abilities, other than ability of position, disintegration of organization occurs slowly through failure to accomplish the aims of cooperation in ways that permit the satisfaction of the motives of the contributing individuals of an organization. The analogy is that of starvation by malnutrition as against death by trauma, such as the severing of an essential nerve. The logical as well as the instinctively acceptable choice is to avoid fatal accident even at the expense of serious and dangerous limitations; for fatal injury admits of no recovery, whereas the tendency toward dissolution even when regarded as probably certain, admits of the possibility of reversal.

It may be seen from the foregoing that schemes ensuring continuity of ordered communication are of primary importance in the adaptation of a society to its environment as well as to the attainment of ends transcending mere biological adaptation. In the past, schemes for the manning of communication posts of society have been based upon heredity (feudal systems), heredity and marriage (kinship systems), systems of property rights, systems of commission and appointment, and systems of election. All of them create differential status essential to ordered communication. The failure of any of them prior to the acceptance of a substitute system disrupts communication, and hence leads to prompt disorganization.

The indispensability of systematic communication in organization thus leads to imputing a value to the individual that relates to the role he plays and to the exaggeraton of the importance of immediate local ability in communication as against more general and more personal ability.

The dilemma involved may be brought out in terms of a practical organization problem. It will ordinarily be the experience of the general executive that there are able men available for appointment to positions occupied by men recognized to be of inferior ability, but who are immediately superior with respect to local knowledge and experience in their posts, and also superior in the sense that they are accepted in their posts by others. It may be clear that in the long run, provided immediate breakdown is not involved, it would be better to replace the inferior with the superior man. Nevertheless, to do so may involve costs in terms of immediate organizational disadvantages so substantial that the net effect even for the long run might be adverse. These disadvantages are: (a) If replacement is made, there will be ineptitude of functioning for a longer or shorter period. Insofar as this occurs because of lack of knowledge, it will correct itself in time, which in general will be shorter the greater the general ability of the replacing individual. The less difference there is in ability, the more doubtful is the utility of change. (b) Communication involves mutual relationships and habitual responsive reactions. A new man entirely aside from his intrinsic abilities in the position, is new to others in the immediate communication network. *Their* capacity to function is disturbed by change. (c) The operation of the system depends in considerable degree upon mutual confidence of the communicators. Change decreases this confidence. This is ordinarily not important as related to single changes not frequently occurring. Its importance increases at an accelerating pace as either the number or the frequency of replacements increases.

Thus, although systems of status are based upon individual abilities and propensities as related to tasks socially evaluated and upon the requirements of the system of communication in organizations, we find that the rating of the individual by the role he occupies and emphasis upon the importance to the organization of immediate local abilities of position leads to under- and overvaluation of individuals artificially, i.e., in terms of status as an end instead of as an intermediate means.

Whatever the system or principle by which posts of communication are filled, in general, errors occur, with the result that some men of inferior abilities are placed in relatively superior positions. Moreover, even if men at a given time were all placed with ideal correctness, they change so that some become inferior to their positions, and others become more than adequate for them. Further, changes in the conditions or the purposes of cooperation may make obsolete the capacities of individuals in particular positions for which they were initially well adapted. Finally, individuals will develop or mature whose abilities are superior to those of persons who have preferred status, even though the latter have not changed and at the time of selection were the best available. The effects of aging, of physical, moral, and intellectual deterioration, of changing conditions and purposes, all call for continual readjustment and replacement in the status system. The process of readjustment and replacement is well known as the "circulation of the elite." Ideally the circulation of the elite should be so free that the status of all should at any given time be in accordance with their relative capacities and the importance of their functions. It is rather obvious that failure of this circulation to the extent that generally those of inferior capacity occupy positions of superior status will so reduce the efficiency of cooperation that survival of organization is doubtful, and that the dangers of rebellion and revolution will be so great that even for the short run such a stoppage of circulation may be fatal.

Nevertheless, even a rough approach to the ideal condition of free circulation is not possible. This is due to three essential factors: (a) A considerable degree of stability of status is necessary if improvement of status is to serve as an incentive. The more uncertain the retention of achieved status is, the fewer to whom the achievement of status will appeal. (b) The resistance to loss of status is in general stronger than desire to achieve higher status, so that it is often probable that the disruptive effects of demotion made to attain a more perfect assignment of capacities more than offset the advantages. (c) Good communication depends to a great extent upon accuracy of interpretation largely associated with habitual personal relationships. These are broken down if changes are frequent.

Without a system of status, as has already been stated, injustice results to those who are the less capable, by failure to protect them against overburden. If an adequate system of status is employed, it may involve injustice when the higher emoluments of higher status are greater than warranted in the sense that they are greater than necessary. It is not intended to discuss here the problem of distributive justice generally involved in differential emoluments. We shall assume that a differential system is necessary and just. What concerns us now is the distortions of justice arising from the restrictions upon freedom of promotion and demotion. The injustices arising are of two sorts: (a) The aggregate of emoluments of higher status are excessive in the sense that they do not secure the degree of service that the capacities ideally available make possible. The "social dividend" in the broadest sense is less than it should be, and the failure is a loss to those of inferior status generally. (b) Individuals capable of filling positions of higher status better than those occupying such positions are unjustly deprived of the emoluments that they are often encouraged to seek. I am using emoluments in a most general sense, including not only remuneration, but also recognition, prestige, the satisfaction of exercising one's abilities, and, for those of philanthropic motivation, the satisfactions of the largest service of which they are capable.

These injustices inherent in the practical operations of systems of status are not hidden. Men are aware of them in general and sometimes exaggerate them; and they are also aware of them specifically as affecting them individually in many circumstances. The effect of the sense of injustice involved depends partly upon the degree to which the status system is sluggish or congealed. When status is fixed by birth or limited by race or religion the extreme of disorganization may follow. When the status of individuals corresponds well with their abilities some loss of *esprit de corps* and of cooperative efficiency only may be involved.

Nevertheless, the effects of the injustices inherent in status systems are sufficiently great to require positive balancing considerations and sentiments. The consideration of most importance is that, except as to those of the lowest status (and at least in some conditions probably also to them), conservatism is protective of individuals. Even though the retention of someone in a position of higher status may be felt to be specifically unjust to one of lower status, the situation may be duplicated with respect to the latter and someone of still lower status. In some degree recognition of a right to retain status is therefore felt to be generally just even though in particular cases the effect may be thought not so.

The sentiments supporting conservatism with respect to status are developed and maintained by rationalizations, ceremonies, and symbolism. They have for their broad purpose the inculcation of the doctrine that the primary interest of the individual is dependent upon the maintenance of the whole organization and its effective operation as a whole, and that whatever is necessary to this end, even though it adversely affects the individual, is offset even to him by the larger advantage accruing from it.

An effective system of communications requires not only the stable filling of specific positions of different status, but also habitual practices and technical procedures. Failure to follow these procedures with routine persistence in general leads to confusion, lack of coordination, and inefficiency or breakdown of the system. The lines of communication, the system of status, and the associated procedures, though by no means constituting "administration," are essential tools of administration and are the most "visible" general parts of it. Being the tangible machinery of administration and indispensable to it, the protection both of status and of procedure come to be viewed quite sincerely as the *sine qua non* of the organization.

The overvaluation of the apparatus of communication and administration is opposed to leadership and the development of leaders. It opposes leadership whose function is to promote appropriate adjustment of ends and means to new environmental conditions, because it opposes change either of status in general or of established procedures and habitual routine. This overvaluation also discourages the development of leaders by retarding the progress of the abler men and by putting an excessive premium on routine qualities.

SOCIAL STRUCTURE AND ECONOMIC INSTITUTIONS

A. R. Radcliffe-Brown

A classic statement of the place of economic life in the social structure of the larger society.

Note: See Notes on the Authors, page 556, and item 183 in the bibliography for the full reference to this selection.

Social phenomena constitute a distinct class of natural phenomena. They are all, in one way or another, connected with the existence of social structures, either being implied in or resulting from them. Social structures are just as real as are individual organisms. A complex organism is a collection of living cells and interstitial fluids arranged in a certain structure; and a living cell is similarly a structural arrangement of complex molecules. The physiological and psychological phenomena that we observe in the lives of organisms are not simply the result of the nature of the constituent molecules or atoms of which the organism is built up, but are the result of the structure in which they are united. So also the social phenomena which we observe in any human society are not the immediate result of the nature of individual human beings, but are the result of the social structure by which they are united.

. . . I regard as a part of the social structure all social relations of person to person. For example, the kinship structure of any society consists of a number of such dyadic relations, as between a father and son, or a mother's brother and his sister's son. In an Australian tribe the whole social structure is based on a network of such relations of person to person, established through genealogical connections.

Secondly, I include under social structure the differentiation of individuals and of classes by their social role. The differential social positions of men and women, of chiefs and commoners, of employers and employees, are just as much determinants of social relations as belonging to different clans or different nations.

In the study of social structure the concrete reality with which we are concerned is the set of actually existing relations, at a given moment of time, which link together certain human beings. It is on this that we can make direct observations. But it is not this that we attempt to describe in its particularity. Science (as distinguished from history or biography) is not concerned with the particular, the unique, but only with the general, with kinds, with events which recur. . . .

This important distinction, between structure as an actually existing concrete reality, to be directly observed, and structural form, as what the field-worker describes, may be made clearer perhaps by a consideration of the continuity of social structure through time, a continuity like that of the organic structure of a living body. Throughout the life of an organism its structure is being constantly renewed; and similarly the social life constantly renews the social structure. Thus the actual relations of persons and groups of persons change from year to year, or even from day to day. New members come into a community by birth or immigration; others go out of it by death or emigration. There are marriages and divorces. Friends may become enemies, or enemies may make peace and become friends. But while the actual structure changes in this way, the general structural form may remain relatively constant over a longer or shorter period of time. Thus if I visit a relatively stable community and revisit it after an interval of ten years, I shall find that many of its members have died and others have been born; the members who still survive are now ten years older and their relations to one another may have changed in many ways. Yet I may find that the kinds of relations that I can observe are very little different from those observed ten years before. The structural form has changed little.

But, on the other hand, the structural form may change, sometimes gradually, sometimes with relative suddenness, as in revolutions and military conquests. But even in the most revolutionary changes some continuity of structure is maintained.

. . . in any society there is not only an apportionment of activities, but also an apportionment of the gratifications resulting therefrom, and some sort of social machinery, relatively simple or, sometimes, highly complex, by which the system works.

It is this machinery, or certain aspects of it, that constitutes the special subject-matter studied by the economists. They concern themselves with what kinds and quantities of goods are produced, how they are distributed (i.e., their flow from person to person, or region to region), and the way in which they are disposed of. Thus what are called economic institutions are extensively studied in more or less complete abstraction from the rest of the social system. . . .

The economic machinery of a society appears in quite a new light if it is studied in relation to the social structure. The exchange

272

of goods and services is dependent upon, is the result of, and at the same time is a means of maintaining a certain structure, a network of relations between persons and collections of persons. . . .

Any full understanding of the economic institutions of human societies requires that they should be studied from two angles. From one of these the economic system is viewed as the mechanism by which goods of various kinds and in various quantities are produced, transported and transferred, and utilized. From the other the economic system is a set of relations between persons and groups which maintains, and is maintained by, this exchange or circulation of goods and services. From the latter point of view, the study of the economic life of societies takes its place as part of the general study of social structure.

Social relations are only observed, and can only be described, by reference to the reciprocal behaviour of the persons related. The form of a social structure has therefore to be described by the patterns of behaviour to which individuals and groups conform in their dealings with one another. These patterns are partially formulated in rules which, in our own society, we distinguish as rules of etiquette, of morals and of law. Rules, of course, only exist in their recognition by the members of the society; either in their verbal recognition, when they are stated as rules, or in their observance in behaviour. These two modes of recognition, as every fieldworker knows, are not the same thing and both have to be taken into account.

Chapter 6

MANAGERS, WORKERS,
AND SUPERVISORS

INTRODUCTION

In this chapter, we shall examine the several levels of management hierarchy: direct management, supervisory levels, and the workers. Particular attention will be directed toward the so-called "human-relations" approach which has come into vogue in management circles in recent years.

To the casual observer, it would at once seem apparent that the various levels of management are concerned with different problems, different perspectives, and the utilization of different capacities to handle particular assignments and responsibilities. The findings of research appear to substantiate this observation.

Within the managerial group itself, a number of differences appear. In terms of the types of decision that occur, the time perspective, the amount of structure given to the decision-maker, and the degree of social involvement tend to vary as one ascends the management hierarchy. The actual data and materials with which the executive works

274

vary all the way from highly concrete to quite abstract forms. It would appear, therefore, that on particular problems or issues, the perspectives of the various executive levels would tend to differ and that, as a result, problems of coördination would intensify. In a very real sense, then, one of the major functions of top management is that of coördinating the work of lower levels. Indeed, some would maintain that it is the primary function. The task of reconciling points of view, mediating divergent interests, and working out coöperative and effective relationships becomes, then, paramount.

To a certain extent the supervisory level must be considered as a separate entity. It is both a part of management and a part of the worker group. Tending to identify in both directions, supervisors become, as one writer has so aptly put it, "marginal men." Studies of morale have shown that in many instances the orientation of this group is of a different order from that existing at higher levels of management. Caught up in the rapid-fire activity of the production process, responsible for keeping the lines going, dealing with a sometimes recalcitrant work force, and restricted to a considerable extent by directives from management and from the union, the typical foreman usually finds little time to think through his problems and to plan ahead. Yet, in the opinion of most management people, the foreman constitutes an indispensable link for effective operation. How to constitute and motivate the foreman group in industrial organizations remains one of the most pressing of managerial problems.

The situation has been accentuated in recent years by automation. Automatic data processing, linear programming, and information systems, for example, have tended to change the job of the foreman in very significant ways. Whereas in the past he was primarily engaged in dealing with men, equipment, and raw materials, he now runs his department from a central control panel. Information is not only transmitted to him rapidly, but goes to other members of the management team so that his job is more public. The entire process of activity and communication is speeded up; his time world is of a different order.

Automation has also had its effect upon the worker. Tasks have been fragmented and made routine on the one hand, and on the other have been made more technical so that a considerable background of knowledge and experience is necessary to run and maintain the equipment. The net effect has tended to produce in the average worker a lack of interest in his job, a limited orientation, and a reluctance to contribute full effort.

275

Management in its attempt to deal with these and other problems has moved varyingly from what might be termed a "soft" to a "hard" approach. Initially it was felt that the worker's job had to be planned to the finest detail. During the 1920's and even up to the present time, the doctrine of scientific management was dominant. This philosophy applied not only to the workers but to the lower levels of management as well. Rules and procedures structured the work of foremen and superintendents so that there was little freedom or discretion. Gradually, however, it became apparent that such an approach was not, in and of itself, sufficient. The "human-relations" philosophy arose. Here was an approach characterized by an attempt to understand the nature of human behavior, a system of administration which operated in such a way that the thinking of the worker and foreman was taken into account by higher levels in decisions that were made. Participative management became an increasingly frequent form.

More recently, the human-relations approach has come under some sharp criticism. Many have felt that the swing away from the more disciplined approach of the earlier days had gone too far and that a "harder" and more direct approach was necessary. Undoubtedly a combination of both forms is the final answer, but just exactly what that blend should be has yet to be determined.

The problems of joint identification and coördination appear in various forms in different businesses and industry. For the most part, it may be said, the activities of management to find the answers to these problems can be characterized by a growing awareness and a continued endeavor to progress toward satisfactory solutions.

THE LEVELS OF MANAGEMENT AND THEIR MENTAL DEMANDS

Norman H. Martin

The types of decision encountered at the various levels of management tend to vary not only in degree but in kind. As one ascends the management hierarchy, one meets situations of more distant "temporal horizons," of a greater degree of abstractness and less structure. He

Note: See Notes on the Authors, page 555, and item 149 in the bibliography for the full reference to this selection.

becomes involved in consequences of more far-reaching social implications. It would appear, therefore, that different forms of intellectual functioning and personality are required at each of the levels of management.

Decision processes in industrial organizations may be studied from at least two points of view. The focus of inquiry may center, on the one hand, on the subjective elements of decision—on the ways in which a choice is made from among alternatives. Another approach, on the other hand, attempts to describe the more or less objective characteristics of the decision situation confronting the executive. This paper, following the latter method, reports on a case study of differential managerial decision situations in a large industrial plant.

The management group of any industrial company is typically stratified into a hierarchy of positions of differing authority and responsibility—into what in the literature is referred to as the "scalar" process. We shall show, by examination of the decisions of a specific executive group, that decision situations at lower levels of management are of a different kind from those encountered at higher levels. This is the major thesis.

A fundamental purpose of the study was to contribute both substantive and theoretical material to a growing and extensive body of literature on the nature and character of the executive process. Substantively, our aim was to present as complete and accurate a description as possible of the decision situations of a management group. Such a description should have implications for the process of executive selection and development. Theoretically, our aim was to derive sets of descriptive and explanatory generalizations relevant to theories about various aspects of the administrative activity.

THE DECISION SITUATION

A decision situation may be conceived as consisting of several major complexes of elements: (1) the antecedent phase, including the occasion for decision and the process of inquiry; (2) the actual decision or choice from among alternatives; (3) the execution and possible modification of the chosen course of action; and (4) the verification of the correctness or incorrectness of the decision. As such, it consists of a complex of subsidiary, interrelated decisions surrounding a major decision.

The initial phase of a decision situation involves the determination of whether or not the existing course of events warrants change and, if so, in what direction and when.[1] The process of inquiry is basic here. In some instances it actually initiates the occasion for decision. This is especially true when the situation is indeterminate. Through observation, analysis of past data, etc., the situation is gradually clarified, and various alternative courses of action made apparent.

The execution of the decision may be broken down into several parts: (1) the communicating of the decision and plan of action to others, (2) the taking of action or the delegation to others of the authority to act, and (3) the possible adjustment and modification of the original decision to meet changing conditions. The decision-maker must assume that the present course of events as he sees it will continue. To a certain extent, this will be the case. However, in many instances and especially if the situation is greatly extended in time, counterforces of different tendencies intrude, and the direction of events is changed. In addition, the correct assessment of situations and anticipations relative to their futurity are, at best, only approximations. As Merton had pointed out, the interplay of forces and circumstances in a given situation is so complex that "prediction of them is quite beyond reach."[2] This fact, coupled with incomplete knowledge, error, and the bias of interest, renders inevitable the occurrence of "unanticipated consequences."

[1] The situation has been described by Barnard as follows: "If we take any system, or set of conditions, or conglomeration of circumstances existing at a given time, we recognize that it consists of elements, or parts or factors, which together make up the whole system, set of conditions or circumstances. Now, if we approach this system or set of circumstances with a view to the accomplishment of a purpose (and only if we so approach it), the elements or parts become distinguished into two classes: those which if absent or changed would accomplish the desired purpose, provided the others remain unchanged; and these others. The first kind are often called limiting factors, the second, complementary factors" (Chester Barnard, *The Functions of the Executive* [Cambridge: Harvard University Press, 1938], p. 202).

[2] Robert K. Merton, "The Unanticipated Consequences of Purposive Social Action," *American Sociological Review*, I (1936), 900.

METHODOLOGY

Decision situations of four levels of management in a large industrial organization were examined. These were (1) the works manager level, (2) the division superintendent level, (3) the department foreman level, and (4) the shift foreman level.

Data for the examination of decision situations at each of these levels were obtained (1) by direct observation and recording of the activities of members of the executive group, (2) from discussions and interviews with individual executives, and (3) from examination of relevant correspondence.[3]

A major difficulty centered on the problem of defining the limits of a given decision situation. In our view, a decision situation consists of a complex of several major elements and many subsidiary decisions. It was necessary to make an arbitrary judgment and consider a decision situation as consisting of a series of actions on a given problem from the time of its inception until its final verification. We had to explore correspondence, reconstruct the past, project into the future and construct what would happen.

The management hierarchy was given. As such, it constituted an already existing set of variables. If our central theses were sound, we would expect to find decision situations differing at each of the executive levels under study.

The first step was to get the various situations classified so that they could be thought about and measured in a rough way. This meant that descriptive categories had to be formulated. Each of these general categories had to be, in turn, broken down into its detailed component elements, in order to give a wider basis upon which to form judgments.

The task of selecting the more important variables upon which to base a scheme of classification was a difficult one. A moment's reflection will convince one that a great number of factors may be associated with decision situations encountered in executive activity. In planning the study, the investigator was aware of the numerous factors that were not included, though well worth investigating.

[3] Observation and recording took place for a week at each of the executive levels studied. Wherever possible, a verbatim transcript was made of activities. In all other instances, detailed notes were kept.

We chose the following variables: (1) temporal characteristics, (2) structural characteristics, and (3) the matrix of social relationships surrounding the executive. Previous accounts have pointed to the existence of these factors as characteristics which vary from one level of management to another.[4] It seemed logical to follow these leads.

We shall present in each of the instances indicated a series of tentative generalizations derived from our research. When it was possible to gather the material, we have given quantitative support; in other cases we have had to rely on qualitative judgments.

TEMPORAL ASPECTS OF MANAGERIAL DECISION

TIME PERSPECTIVE. Extension of time perspective in decision situations tends to vary directly with movement up the management hierarchy. Significant differences exist between the various levels of management in this respect, with the lower levels tending to deal predominantly with decision situations of relatively short time perspective and higher levels with situations of long duration. A comparison of the time perspectives of the four levels of management is presented in Table 22. Differences were found to be significant at the .01 level. The greatest variation may be seen to exist between the works manager and the shift foreman levels. The shift foreman is almost completely concerned with day-to-day production decisions. In a sense he operates in the immediate present, with only slight extension into the past and future. From the time of the inception of a decision situation until its conclusion, only relatively short durations intervene. A pipe breaks, a product goes off specification, or machinery breaks down. Corrective action is taken as soon as possible. At the works manager level, in sharp contrast, 50 per cent of the decision situations observed were of over a year's duration—of a distant or remote focus.

[4] Reference here is to such works as Herbert A. Simon, *Administrative Behavior* (New York: Macmillan Co., 1947); Sune Carlson, *Executive Behavior* (Stockholm: C. A. Stromberg, Aktiebolag Pub., 1951); Barnard, *op. cit.;* Luther Gulick, "Politics, Administration, and the New Deal," *Annals,* September, 1933; Ralph Currier Davis, *The Fundamentals of Top Management* (New York: Harper & Brothers, 1951); and W. Lloyd Warner and J. O. Low, *The Social System of the Modern Factory* (New Haven: Yale University Press, 1947).

Because the true meaning of an event cannot be ascertained until it is actualized, one of the consequences of being involved in situations of distant time perspective is that the executive is in a difficult position to judge correctly the value and meaning of intervening events. To illustrate, the works manager, confronted with a problem of repeated shipping delays, decided to recommend the construction of a new warehouse. This decision was based upon a thorough analysis of the factors contributing to the shipping delays and on estimates for future demands for product. A year or so passed; the warehouse was built; shipping delays were reduced. Then demand began to fall off because of the occurrence of unforeseen events. The need for the additional warehousing space disappeared, and it stood unused. This is a case in point.

TABLE 22. Time Perspectives of Decision Situations at Four Levels of Management

Time	Works Manager (Per Cent)	Division Superintendent (Per Cent)	Department Foreman (Per Cent)	Shift Foreman (Per Cent)
Short (0–2 weeks)	3.3	54.2	68.0	97.7
Moderate (2 weeks to year)	46.1	41.4	30.4	2.1
Distant	50.0	4.3	1.5	0.0
Total	99.4	99.9	99.9	99.8

When one has to project far ahead, risks and uncertainty increase; the situation may change completely; new factors intervene. Yet the commitment has been made.

We now move into other temporal characteristics of the decisions of the various management levels. Our research indicates a difference in decision situations with respect to the temporal characteristics of continuity, duration, tempo, and the time limits for effective action.

CONTINUITY. Decision situations at the lower levels of management tend to consist of continuous units through time, whereas at higher levels they tend to display a discontinuous character, with wide intervals of time separating the various component parts of the decision situation. Here in many instances a lapse of time occurs, say, between the phase of inquiry and the actual decision —the problem is, as it were, out of sight and out of mind. The executive frequently delegates the handling of a problem to a subordinate, to return to it at a later date.

In contrast, lower levels of management are typically involved in situations in which the occasion for decision, the phase of inquiry, the choice, and its administration follow one another in unbroken sequence. The shift foreman is in close physical contact with details of the production process. Rounds of inspection make up a great part of his work. Decision as to courses of action typically take place immediately following the occurrence of an occasion for decision. He follows through almost immediately and verifies the correctness of his decision. In a sense, he follows the "flow" of events and is directly involved in them.

DURATION. The various phases of decision situations tend to be of longer duration as one moves upward from lower to higher levels. This proposition follows logically from previous generalizations, as well as being substantiated by our research. At higher levels of management, for example, the duration of the inquiry phase may last for over a year, whereas at lower levels it rarely goes beyond a day or a week. Here background and experience play a major role; long inquiry is not required.

TEMPO. Decision situations tend to increase in frequency as one moves from higher to lower levels of management. The increase, however, is not a linear one, nor is it particularly significant in terms of differences between levels. The tempo of decision is highest at the shift foreman and works manager levels, with the two intermediate strata falling in between. The data for this generalization are given in Table 23.

To a considerable extent, the rate at which decisions occur is a function of the degree to which authority and responsibility are decentralized. In a decentralized type of organization it would be predicted that the tempo of decision would be greater at the lower levels of management, inasmuch as that is where the great bulk of action would take place. We found this to be the case to a certain extent in the organization studied, as far as middle and lower levels were concerned. The high rate of decision at the works manager level could be explained by the fact that the plant under study was one of several in a multiplant organization.

TIME LIMITS OF EFFECTIVE ACTION. The time limits within which effective action can be taken tend to be more closely circumscribed at lower levels of management, whereas they are more elastic and ambiguous at higher levels.

The executive, in viewing the existing course of events and in determining whether or not they must be modified to meet a given purpose, is involved in differential time limits within which effective action can be taken. The situation may be one in which corrective action must be taken at once or in the very near future, to

TABLE 23. Decision Situations at Four Levels of Plant Management

	Works manager (N)	Division Superintendent (N)	Department Foreman (N)	Shift Foreman (N)
Average per day	33	21	27	37
Rate[a]	15	23	18	13

[a] This refers to the rate at which decisions occurred in terms of minutes, i.e., one every 15 minutes, one every 23 minutes, etc.

be effective. Thus the shift foreman must take action immediately if, for example, a pipe breaks. Should the quality of product deviate from specification, it is necessary that remedial action be instituted at once. The situation itself sets the time limits of action. They are clear-cut.

At higher levels, on the other hand, situations are frequently encountered in which the time limits are relatively immaterial or poorly defined. Here the timeliness of action is dependent upon the executive's judgment of the total situation. To illustrate, during one of our periods of observation a division superintendent conferred with the works manager with reference to a projected move of one of the division's operations to another location. The decision on this contemplated move, made ultimately by the works manager, could have taken place at that point or a week or even a month later. Time was not a factor of importance. The operation was working efficiently where it was, and the reason for moving it was primarily one of achieving a better balance in over-all operations. In such situations it is necessary for the decision-maker to judge correctly the strategic point in time at which action can best be taken.

SUMMARY. To summarize, decision situations encountered at higher levels of management tend to differ significantly from those found at lower levels with respect to certain temporal characteristics. The executive functioning at the higher levels is typically involved in making decisions which have distant time horizons; situations here are characterized by a great deal of discontinuity; the time limits within which he must take action, in order for it to be effective, are poorly defined. At lower levels the time perspective of decision is centered in the immediate; elements of the situation succeed one another in time; the time limits of effective action are clearly circumscribed.

DEGREES OF STRUCTURE

The extent to which decision situations are structured or determinate may be considered to be a function of (1) the general nature of the phenomena with which decisions are concerned, (2) the degree to which directions as to appropriate action are given, and (3) the extent to which interrelationships and meanings can be determined.

The data with which executives deal may be classified along a continuum according to their degree of abstractness. Phenomena may be classified as being concrete when they are presented directly in experience, when they can be easily verified and understood and are completely given. Conversely, they may be regarded as being abstract if they are essentially derivatives of sense experience, when they cannot be completely verified by reference to physical objects, and when they are relatively incomplete, that is, consisting only of selected or generalized aspects of sense impressions.

In some instances an executive will find before him clear-cut directions as to how and when he should act. The occasion for decision, the possible alternatives, and the methods by which he administers his choice are clearly indicated by rules and procedures. The situation is structured for him. In other cases, however, these mandates are absent. It is up to the executive himself to determine whether the situation warrants a change. He must search for and construct possible alternative courses of action; he must work out administrative procedures to implement the decision. Such situations may be termed "unstructured."

The degree to which interrelationships between events and their meanings can be determined is, at least partially, dependent upon their complexity and the extent to which they are "clearly given." For example, the operations of a piece of equipment—what it can do, how it functions, and its relation to the production process—may be considered to be "clearly given." It follows well-worked-out engineering principles, and it can be directly observed. In contrast, the possible reaction of employees to a change in work schedule or a change in wage structure is not always "clearly given" and is highly complex. Here meanings and interrelationships may be difficult to ascertain.

We turn now to an inspection of the degree of structure of decision situations typical of each of the four levels of management considered.[5]

THE DATA OF DECISION. The content of decision tends to become more abstract as one moves from lower to higher levels of administration. Higher levels of management are typically involved in situations in which the data of decision are two or three steps removed from their actual source. Reports on production, for example, consist of summaries prepared by subordinates or staff personnel; to a considerable extent, impressions of employee morale and sentiment come from subordinates, who, in turn, are interpreting from the views of their key personnel. As we have previously pointed out, executives occupying positions in upper plant

---

[5] Our method here was completely qualitative. Judgments of the relative incidence of decision situations of specific degrees of structuredness or unstructuredness at each of the four levels of management were made by the investigator and by various executives participating in the study.

management are operating, in a sense, outside and above the actual flow of events.

At the first level of supervision, on the other hand, the executive is more directly involved in the actuality of plant operations—in the world of the concrete, the realm of machines, pipes, valves, and equipment. The data of decision are basically physical, the behavior of relevant others directly observable.

DIRECTEDNESS. There is a greater probability that sets of alternatives will possess objective existence as we move from higher to lower levels of management. At higher levels, sets of alternatives tend to exist as subjective constructions of the decision-maker and hence are subject to shifts in the situation and his own psychological makeup. At lower levels, they exist as objective entities unchanged by such shifts.[6]

Comparing the four levels of management with reference to this dimension, the shift foreman was observed to function almost completely in terms of alternatives which are ready-made and enduring—given in the form of rules. In the words of one division superintendent, "Once the foremen decide that something has to be done, the rest is pretty well a matter of course—what they do and how." Action is here almost "ministerial," in that the basic question is whether or not a specific situation warrants invoking a particular rule.

At the other extreme, the works manager frequently encounters situations in which the alternatives must be constructed. To illustrate, the works manager had received instructions from his superior to reduce costs. While the general direction was clear, here was a situation in which the various possible alternatives were not given. They had to be constructed. Formulations of these alternatives were based upon cues provided by production and cost data. The "how," however, had to be developed and worked out.

In between these two extremes, the division superintendent and the department foreman levels were concerned with decision situa-

[6] For an excellent discussion of this phenomenon from a theoretical point of view see Alfred Schuetz, "Choosing among Projects of Action," *Philosophy and Phenomenological Research,* XII (1951), 161–85.

tions of a mixed form. The relative positions of each of the four levels can be placed on a continuum as follows:

Alternatives completely objective, ready-made, and enduring	Shift Foreman	Department Foreman	Division Superintendent	Works Manager	Alternatives completely subjective and constructed by the executive

INTERRELATIONSHIPS AND MEANINGS. The meaning of events and their interrelationships are more clearly given at lower than at higher administrative levels. It is extremely difficult in many instances at higher levels of management to determine what is behind a complexity of events. At lower levels, because events are more concrete and clearly given, interrelationships and meanings can usually be readily perceived.

To illustrate the ambiguity of events at the works manager level, the following case may be cited. Upon coming into the plant one morning, the works manager was met by a delegation of workers. Their spokesman stated that they would not work until specified working conditions had been changed. Now the relationship of this event to the larger system making up the entire ongoing process of the organization would be difficult to determine. Whether this represented a threat, a maneuver to commit the management to unwise action, to provoke untimely action, or what was uncertain. Yet action had to be taken—a decision reached on a situation in which the true meaning was obscure.

At lower levels of management, meanings and interrelationships are more apparent. In one instance, for example, the shift foreman had to make a decision about how to deal with an employee who had broken a rule. The situation was relatively clear-cut. The meaning of this event in terms of himself and his own authority position, the department and the company, and the man concerned clearly pointed to the necessity to take disciplinary action and to invoke a formal procedure. In such instances, where meanings and interrelationships are not clear, the foreman refers decisions to his superiors.

287

SUMMARY. Decision situations range from the highly structured environment of decision characteristic of the shift foreman level to the less highly structured form typical of the works manager. The four management levels considered group themselves along a continuum of structuredness in the following manner:

	Shift	Department	Division	Works	Unstructured
Structured situations	Foreman	Foreman	Superintendent	Manager	tured situations

The works manager and the division superintendent levels tend to be more involved in situations which lack structure, while the two lower levels operate almost exclusively in situations with a high degree of structure.

THE MATRIX OF SOCIAL RELATIONSHIPS

The executive, in considering the consequences of alternative courses of action in a decision, must anticipate the actions and reactions of relevant individuals. The reliability of these predictions is a function, in part, of the number and nature of these social relationships. To the extent that a given system of relationships around an executive have been formalized and made stable, there is a probability of accurate prediction. A number of individuals in close relationship over a period of time tend to form more or less firm expectations as to how each will act. In contrast, the administrator who must relate to a varying number of individuals, many of whom he must deal with in an impersonal manner, will tend to find the reliability of prediction rather low.

Our investigation of the characteristics of decision situations in this area pointed toward deriving descriptive propositions along the following dimensions: (1) the frequency and nature of relations with superiors, associates, and subordinates, (2) direct versus indirect contacts, and (3) in-group versus out-group relationships. After describing these social matrixes at each level of management, we were then concerned with relating them to decision situations.

SUPERORDINATE-SUBORDINATE RELATIONSHIPS. The frequency of superordinate-subordinate contacts tends to be similar at all levels of management. A significant difference exists, however, with respect to certain relationships at the shift foreman level, namely, that the shift foreman is more involved in associational relationships than are other executives. The relative frequency of these forms of relationship is given in Table 24. The nature of these

TABLE 24. Superordinate-Subordinate Associational
Contacts at Four Levels of Management

Contact	Works Manager (Per Cent)	Division Superintendent (Per Cent)	Department Foreman (Per Cent)	Shift Foreman (Per Cent)
Superordinate	29.4	21.9	28.9	20.4
Associate	1.9	6.9	4.4	18.4
Subordinate	68.6	71.2	66.7	61.2
Total	99.9	100.0	100.0	100.0

relationships is markedly different at each of the four executive levels. Each is involved in a unique social system.

The works manager's relevant social system involves multiple sets of individual-to-individual relationships—subordination to a plurality and superordination over a plurality. Here is a world of shifting social complexity. Few associational contacts were observed. It is difficult to anticipate correctly the reactions of others. Because of the absence of associational contacts, it is not easy to get cues from other works managers. The situation is conducive to a high degree of uncertainty.

The social matrix at the division superintendent level is less complex. The executive is subordinate to a single individual; he is in a superordinate position to a set number of foremen; he has many associational contacts. The social environment is, therefore, highly stable. He can, to a much greater degree, reliably anticipate the reactions of others. He can easily verify his predictions.

The system of social relationships at the department and shift foreman levels is of a still different order. The department foreman is in a highly stable set of social relations, in so far as he has only one significant superior and multiple ties with associates. However, inasmuch as his key subordinates are on shifts, he is in direct and complete contact with only one. He cannot therefore directly follow the activities of the second- and third-shift foremen.

The second- and third-shift foremen, on the other hand, do not have direct contact with their immediate superiors. Ties with subordinates are strong. In a very real sense, the shift foreman is submerged in a group—his operators. Orientation tends, therefore, to be downward. Here expectations and anticipations are highly reliable.

DIRECT VERSUS INDIRECT CONTACTS. Relationships at lower levels of management tend to be characterized by direct personal contacts with others. In contrast, a great number of social contacts at higher levels of management tend to be indirect in nature. These data are given in Table 25.

At the works manager level a great number of contacts are relatively impersonal. Considerable volume of correspondence crosses

TABLE 25. Frequency of Direct Versus Indirect and Group Contacts at Four Levels of Management

Contact	Works Manager (Per Cent)	Division Superintendent (Per Cent)	Department Foreman (Per Cent)	Shift Foreman (Per Cent)
Direct	30.76	71.18	77.61	84.31
Indirect	56.41	25.42	19.40	15.68
Group	12.82	3.38	2.98	00.00
Total	99.99	99.98	99.99	99.99

the desk of the works manager; many of his contacts are via telephone. While communication of a kind is conveyed by such means, it may be assumed that it is not so reliable as face-to-face relationships. Subtleties and nuances cannot be readily perceived. Anticipations may fail to be realized.

A sharp difference or break occurs at the next lower level of management—the division superintendent level. Approximately three-fourths of social relationships here are direct and face-to-face. A similar situation characterizes the two lower executive levels. It would appear, consequently, that, as one moves from a division superintendent position into the position of works manager, he is passing into a social world that differs not only in degree but in kind.

IN-GROUP VERSUS OUT-GROUP CONTACTS. Relationships at lower levels tend to be confined exclusively to in-group contacts. At higher levels the executive is more heavily involved in out-group relationships—those with executives from other plants and with headquarters. Data on this aspect of social relationships are presented in Table 26.

The shift and department foremen are completely immersed in the realm of the familiar and the local. People they see and talk to

TABLE 26.   In-Group Versus Out-Group Contacts at Four
Levels of Management

Contact	Works Manager (Per Cent)	Division Superin- tendent (Per Cent)	Depart- ment Foreman (Per Cent)	Shift Foreman (Per Cent)
In-group	64.13	83.05	95.52	100.00
Out-group:				
Within company	31.52	15.25	4.47	00.00
Outside company	4.33	1.68	00.00	00.00
Total	99.98	99.98	99.99	100.00

from day to day and from month to month make up their social contacts. Correct anticipation of the reactions of others in many instances becomes almost second nature. At the division superintendent level the social world expands and extends; at the works manager level, over one-fourth of relationships are with people outside the plant.

The implications for decision are quite clear. Status systems, behavior patterns, norms, etc., are well formed within the in-group. Individuals come to know what is expected of them; they can correctly anticipate one another's reactions. Uncertainty in this respect is at a minimum. As an executive moves up, uncertainty increases.

SUMMARY. It would appear from the results of our investigation that the social relationships characteristic of the four management strata considered differ not only in degree but in kind. The major break point would appear to occur between the works manager level and the division superintendent level. Executives at these levels operate in relatively different social worlds.

The social world of the works manager is one characterized by a multiplicity of superordinate and subordinate relationships, which are, to a considerable degree, indirect in nature and extending to members of out-groups. Here there is a greater probability of uncertainty in anticipations of how others will act. Decisions involve greater risk. At the divisional level and lower, executives are involved in a world of much greater stability. Anticipations can be relied upon to a much greater degree. Uncertainty is at a minimum.

IMPLICATIONS FOR EXECUTIVE SELECTION, DEVELOPMENT, AND TRAINING

Perhaps one of the most important areas of concern in present-day management is that of the selection and training of executives. Many articles and books have been written on the subject and many speeches made. Most of these deal in generalizations or objectives.

Our findings indicate that any realistic program in this area must take into account the existence of differences existing in the area of executive behavior. As we have shown, each level of management is involved in different types of decision situations. We believe, although further research is necessary in order to confirm this belief, that different orders of intellectual functioning are required at each of these levels. It would follow, therefore, that selection and training of executives must take these factors into account.

If potential executives are to be trained for given positions, it is necessary that they train at the level they are to occupy rather than in subordinate positions. Many firms, however, follow a development program for executives which involves placement of the potential individual in a position directly below that which he is to occupy. Thus a person being trained for a works manager's position is placed in a divisional superintendent's job or for a divisional superintendent's job by being placed as a department foreman.

Other firms, however, maintain corollary positions to each of their key executive's positions through "assistants," who in many cases take over the job of the executive in his absence. Our findings would indicate that this is the sounder practice of the two; for only by receiving training in the actual work he is to do, can the executive benefit by the training.

THEORETICAL IMPLICATIONS

Parsons has remarked:

It is scarcely too much to say that the most important single index of the state of maturity of a science is the state of its systematic theory. This includes the character of the generalized conceptual scheme in use in the field, the kinds and degrees of logical integration of the different elements which make it up, and the ways in which it is actually being used in empirical research.[7]

We believe that we have, to a limited extent, contributed to the formation of a part of a generalized conceptual scheme regarding managerial behavior. The function of a conceptual scheme is to provide a frame of reference—a framework of relevant categories in terms of which observations make sense and which aid the development of descriptive propositions. We have seen that our scheme is applicable to the empirical data of managerial behavior, and we have been able to derive a limited number of descriptive generalizations regarding certain aspects of behavior in a given plant.

DIRECTIVES FOR FURTHER RESEARCH

There are several directives for further research in this area: (1) the extension of research to include other types of industrial organizations; (2) the extension of research to include top levels of management, i.e., on a company or corporation level, so that comparisons between different levels of management may be broadened; and (3) research into the psychological correlates of various executive levels.

---

[7] Talcott Parsons, *Essays in Sociological Theory, Pure and Applied* (Glencoe, Ill.: Free Press, 1949), p. 17.

293

It is believed that such investigations could well center, as here, upon the decision situations existing at the various levels of management. By focusing upon this particular dimension, it is believed that insight will be gained into many phases of managerial behavior. The work of the executive is primarily that of decision-making. It would therefore follow that the locus of investigation should center upon this activity.

THE SUPERVISORY DILEMMA

Floyd C. Mann and James K. Dent

Supervisors are members of two organizational families —one composed of subordinates and associates and the other of superiors. This constitutes a problem only when conflict of interests develops between these two groups. Management must recognize this dual membership role; supervisors must be able to participate in both organizational families and integrate their goals.

Supervisors are important people. That they play a significant role in industrial organization is clear enough; management has long recognized the fact. Just what this role consists of—what these supervisors must do, how they fit into the organization, and what should be expected of them—is, however, not so clear.

Management has tried through job analysis and evaluation to define in detail the functions and responsibilities of foremen and first-line supervisors. Many job-description lists are 2 or 3 pages long and contain 50 to 75 items. Management has searched for the pattern of personal characteristics of the ideal supervisor. Such a pattern, however, has been extremely difficult to track down and almost impossible to generalize from specific situations. A consideration of the individual characteristics of the person alone is not enough. The social characteristics of the situation in which the supervisor finds himself appear to be equally important.

We all know that appointing a man as supervisor does not neces-

Note: See Notes on the Authors, pages 554 and 552, and item 145 in the bibliography for the full reference to this selection.

sarily make him one. The supervisor himself must gain the respect of those he is to lead; he must make his authority legitimate in the eyes of his subordinates. In a very real sense the supervisor's role is dependent on both superiors and subordinates.

Whether the supervisor is a member of management is an unsettled question. Sometimes he seems to be, and sometimes he seems not to be. The Taft-Hartley act has defined the supervisor as *legally* a member of management, but *psychologically* there still remains an ambiguity that disturbs management and supervisors as well.

This article will attempt to clarify the nature of the role of the supervisor by presenting research findings about this "man in the middle." A great deal has been written about the part a foreman or supervisor plays in an organization, but relatively little quantitative research has been done on the real nature of his role. There are many opinions and several ways of looking at the role, but there are few proven facts.

We shall deal first with the nature of the formal, organizational role of the supervisor; then we shall summarize research findings on the effective supervisor as he is seen by superiors, subordinates, and the supervisor himself; and finally we shall point up the implications.

THE ORGANIZATIONAL ROLE

An industrial organization contains a large number of relatively small, face-to-face work groups. At the top there is the single group made up of the president and his senior officers; at the bottom are the many groups made up of the first-line supervisors and the employees under each of them; and those at the bottom are linked to the one at the top by other similar work groups.

Each group, except the top one, is interlocked with the group above by a person who belongs to two work groups, one composed of his immediate subordinates and himself, another of his peers and their immediate superior. In one group he is leader; in the other he is subordinate. These men who belong to two groups—or to two "organizational families," as we would like to call them—are supervisors, either first-line supervisors who direct the work of employees or intermediate-level supervisors who coordinate the work of other supervisors under them.

CONFLICTS OF INTEREST. Belonging to two groups presents no special problem when there is no conflict of interest between the groups or when it is possible for the person who has dual membership to isolate his activities in one group from his activities in the other. For example, a man can isolate his activities as a member of a church and as a member of a lodge; but he may find such isolation exceedingly difficult in an organization where by design his role is to link groups having a close relationship in time and space but not necessarily in point of view. When there is a conflict of interest, the supervisor is forced to deal with it if he is to be effective in his role.

When different groups within an organization have different goals, conflicts of interest arise. Since the superior has more to say in determining the goals of a group than do his subordinates, it is possible that goals will be set which are in conflict with the needs, wants, and aspirations of subordinates. But the subordinates are at the same time dependent on their superiors for the realization of their own goals. The extent to which a supervisor is forced to try to resolve sharply conflicting interests depends in large measure on how fully top management recognizes the dual-membership character of his role.

Failure on the part of management to recognize that duality has led Fritz J. Roethlisberger to call the supervisor "master and victim of double talk," Robert Dubin to speak of the need for the supervisor to be "Janus-faced," and D. E. Wray to see foremen as "marginal men" who do not really belong to either the management or the worker group.[8]

DETROIT EDISON STUDY

We shall present here empirical evidence on how one management, in working out a scheme for evaluating and developing its

---

[8] See Fritz J. Roethlisberger, "The Foreman: Master and Victim of Double Talk," *Harvard Business Review*, Spring, 1945, p. 283; Robert Dubin, Editor, *Human Relations in Administration* (New York, Prentice-Hall, Inc., 1951), p. 139; and D. E. Wray, "Marginal Men of Industry: The Foremen," *American Journal of Sociology*, January, 1949, p. 298.

supervisory personnel, found that they were recognizing the dual-membership role of their supervisors.

NATURE OF THE STUDY. In 1949 the accounting department of The Detroit Edison Company, whose functions included meter testing, meter reading, billing, collection, property accounting, and other general accounting responsibilities, initiated a management development program. The first step was an evaluation of the effectiveness of each of the first-line supervisors.

When employee attitudes toward their supervisors and superiors' appraisals of the same supervisors were compared, there was a small but consistent agreement between them. Superiors and subordinates were most clearly in agreement about the supervisors with the highest and the lowest appraisal ratings.

The general pattern of the relationship is illustrated in Table 27,

TABLE 27. Relationship of Management Appraisal Rating of Supervisors to Employees' Evaluation of the Supervisors' Ability with People

Management Appraisal Rating	Percentage of Employees Rating Supervisors as		Percentage not Answering	Number of Employees	Number of Supervisors
	Excellent or Good	Average, Fair, or Poor			
Immediately promotable (P+)	71%	29%		28	5
Promotable (P)	47 ⎱ 53%	53		49	5
Satisfactory plus (S+)	55 ⎰	44	1%	161	19
Satisfactory (S)	45	53	2	334	30
Questionable (Q)	28 ⎱ 27%	72		92	10
Unsatisfactory (U)	24 ⎰	76		21	3

NOTE: The relationships are statistically significant at the 5% level or above.

which shows the employees' feelings about their supervisors' handling of people. For instance, 71% of the employees working under supervisors whom management appraised as "immediately promotable" feel their supervisor is excellent or good at handling people, whereas only 24% of the employees under supervisors who were rated "unsatisfactory" feel this way.

While there is agreement between the employees' and the superiors' evaluations of those supervisors with relatively high or low appraisal ratings, the relationship is not perfect for specific groups. Frequently the "promotable" supervisors were rated lower by their employees than were the "satisfactory plus" supervisors. Between the "questionable" and "unsatisfactory" supervisors, again, there is no consistent pattern. . . .

EMPLOYEES' VIEW OF SUPERVISORS. Employees were asked to indicate how well each of a number of descriptive phrases fit their supervisor. Some of the phrases connoted approval of the supervisor (e.g., "a leader of men"). Others were negative (e.g., "a driver"). . . . . More employees under "immediately promotable" supervisors than under "questionable" or "unsatisfactory" supervisors saw their supervisor as "a leader of men," "reasonable in what he expects," and "likable." More employees under the supervisors with the lowest ratings said their supervisor was "a driver," "bossy," and "quick to criticize."

These particular findings are consistent with results from two other studies in the University of Michigan Human Relations Program. In a study of clerical workers in an insurance company, the heads of high-producing sections were more frequently rated "reasonable" and less frequently rated "arbitrary" than heads of low-producing sections.[9] Among railroad workers, more men in high-producing section gangs felt that their foremen reacted in an understanding, nondisciplinary way when the men did a bad job; more men in low-producing gangs felt their foremen bawled them out or made them do it over without any explanation.[10]

Specific Behavior. The employee evaluations presented so far are general—"good at handling people," "a leader," and so on. The supervisor rated high by management generally has the approval of his employees, and the supervisor rated low generally

---

[9] D. Katz, N. Maccoby, and N. C. Morse, *Productivity, Supervision and Morale in an Office Situation* (Ann Arbor: Institute for Social Research, University of Michigan, 1950).

[10] D. Katz *et al., Productivity, Supervision and Morale Among Railroad Workers* (Ann Arbor: Institute for Social Research, University of Michigan, 1951).

does not have that approval. But these findings tell us little about the high-rated supervisor's specific behavior.[11]

. . . The majority of the subordinates of a supervisor rated high by his superiors—

1. Feel free to discuss important things about their job with him.
2. Feel free to discuss their personal problems with him.
3. Know what he thinks of their work.
4. Say he "goes to bat" for them when they have a complaint.
5. Say he uses general rather than close supervision.
6. Say he frequently or often has group meetings where they can discuss things with their supervisor.

Several of these findings are of particular interest. More employees under "immediately promotable" supervisors feel they know how they stand with their supervisor even though there is no formal rating procedure for employees in these departments. Supervisors rated high are evaluating their employees informally—letting them know where they stand as a normal part of the working relationships.

Further, a supervisor who has been singled out as most promotable by his superiors is more likely to have employees who are confident of his willingness and ability to act as their representative, to present and defend their interests. Employees were asked not only how he handled complaints, but also how much support they felt he would give them generally. Answers to both of these questions showed a direct relationship to the superiors' appraisals of the supervisors.

Another finding of particular interest is that there is easier communication between supervisors rated high and their employees. These supervisors create an atmosphere which leads their employees to feel free to discuss job and personal problems. For example, they hold more group meetings with their employees. Group discussions in which problems are shared are important because they can tap the many ideas and suggestions available in the group, they

[11] For a more detailed presentation of these findings, see Floyd Mann and James Dent, *Appraisals of Supervisors and Attitudes of Their Employees in an Electric Power Company* (Ann Arbor: Institute for Social Research, University of Michigan, 1954).

can clarify goals and give each person a feeling of responsibility for the success of the decision, and they can establish an easy relationship between members of the group and its leader.

The importance of these findings is supported by other research in the Michigan Human Relations Program. Whether or not an employee feels free to discuss problems with his supervisor is related both to his absences and to his productivity. In an electric company, white-collar men with good attendance records felt freer to discuss job problems with their supervisor than did those with poorer records; in a tractor manufacturing plant, a greater proportion of high-production workers than of low-production workers said it was easy to talk over problems with their foreman; and in an insurance company, general rather than close supervision was associated with productivity among the clerical workers.[12] It is significant that employee evaluations correlating positively with superiors' appraisals also bear a direct relationship to productivity and low absenteeism.

Extent of Recognition. Employees were asked how and to what extent their supervisor gave recognition for good work in each of 10 different ways:

1. He praises sincerely and thoroughly.
2. He makes notes of good work in his rating and reports.
3. He trains employees for better jobs.
4. He tells his superiors about good work.
5. He recommends promotions.
6. He gives more responsibility.
7. He gives privileges.
8. He recommends pay increases.
9. He gives a pat on the back.
10. He gives more interesting work.

High-rated supervisors were reported by their subordinates to use all these methods more often than supervisors rated low. The

[12] See F. Mann and H. Baumgartel, *Absences and Employee Attitudes in an Electric Power Company* (Ann Arbor: Institute for Social Research, University of Michigan, 1953); D. Katz and R. Kahn, "Leadership Practices in Relation to Productivity and Morale," *Group Dynamics,* edited by D. Cartwright and A. Zander (White Plains, New York: Row, Peterson and Company, 1953); and D. Katz, N. Maccoby, and N. C. Morse, *op. cit.*

"immediately promotable" supervisors were most clearly distinguished from their "questionable" or "unsatisfactory" colleagues in the extent to which they used the first five methods.

The one procedure on which there was the greatest difference between supervisors rated high and those rated low was training employees for better jobs. Of employees under the high-rated supervisors, 54% said their supervisor trains them for better jobs "very often" or "fairly often"; only 19% of the employees under the supervisors with the lowest evaluations said this.

Parallel to this, in the railroad study cited earlier, more railroad workers in high-producing sections than in low-producing sections reported that their supervisor trained them by teaching them supervisory duties and special techniques required in the supervisor's role.[13]

Supervisors' "Membership."   Thus far we have indicated that the supervisor rated high by department heads (and therefore due for early advancement) is seen by his employees as a member of their own work group. He creates an atmosphere of free discussion; he goes to bat for them; he lets them know what he thinks of their work; he discusses things with them as a group; he is a reasonable and likable leader; he gives them recognition for good work done, particularly by training them for better jobs. Does this mean that he is so close to his employees that he is really not a member of management?

To find the answer to this question, employees were asked: "Does your supervisor pull for the company or for the men?" They were asked to check from among the following items the one that best described his behavior:

1. He is usually pulling for the company.
2. He is usually pulling for himself.
3. He is usually pulling for the men.
4. He is usually pulling for the company and the men.

. . . The supervisor who can understand the objectives both of the company and of the men, and who is seen by employees as a

[13] D. Katz, *et al.*, *Productivity, Supervision and Morale Among Railroad Workers, op. cit.*

member and a representative of both management and his working group, is rated highest by management.

Employees' perceptions of the supervisor as pulling for himself or for the men show no consistent relationship to superiors' appraisal of the supervisor. On the other hand, supervisors classed as pulling for the company are rated low in the appraisals. Apparently this management does not want its supervisors to pull for the company alone.

Of equal importance is the over-all level of employee answers to this question. At least 50% do not feel that it is impossible to pull both for the company and for the men. At least 55% see a community of interest and absence of conflict, hence no necessity for the supervisors to take sides. It is likely that such an atmosphere was not created by first-line supervisors alone, but rather that it reflects the extent to which top management recognizes the importance of integrating the goals of individual members with those of the organization. Consciously or unconsciously this management allows for the dual character of its supervisors' role.

SUPERVISORS' VIEW OF SUPERIORS. Supervisors, like employees, filled out specially prepared questionnaires for our study (after each supervisor had had a discussion regarding his appraisal with his department head). The information obtained concerned attitudes and opinions about their jobs and their relationships with their superiors.

Superiors' Ability with People. The higher-rated supervisors felt that their superior was good at handling people. To be precise, 83% of the 29 supervisors given the top three ratings indicated that they felt their superior was excellent or good at handling people; 63% of the 30 "satisfactory" supervisors felt the same; while only 46% of the 13 given the lowest two ratings said they felt this way. . . .

Knowledge of Their Standing. Whether or not a supervisor has a high or low evaluation is related to how sure he is of how he stands with his department head. All the supervisors in the top three ratings were "very sure" they knew how they stood with their superior; 90% of the "satisfactory" supervisors were very sure; and only 54% of the supervisors evaluated "questionable" or "unsatis-factory" felt "very sure" they knew how they stood. This is in spite of the fact that these supervisors were answering the questionnaire *after* their superior had reviewed their appraisal ratings with them.

There are two possible interpretations of this finding. It is diffi-cult to tell a subordinate that he is not doing well; to tell him in such a manner that he is "very sure" how he stands is doubly dif-ficult. On the other hand, even though the supervisor knows he is not doing well, he may not be willing to admit it.

Regardless of which of these interpretations is correct, the fact remains that there are many communication difficulties for both the superior and the subordinate when the evaluation of the latter is essentially negative. In considering the implications of this find-ing it is important to remember that one of the major objectives of an evaluation procedure is to insure that subordinates, especially those who are not doing as well as expected, know how they stand with the organization.

To find out whether a supervisor determines how he stands by what his superior *tells* him or by what his superior actually *does,* we asked the question, "On what basis do you judge your standing with your immediate superior?" The following table shows the percentage of the total group of supervisors that answered *yes* to each of the listed bases:

He gives me responsibility and authority	74%
He asks my opinion frequently	58
I imply it because I work for him	58
I imply it from lack of criticism	58
I receive raises	46
He tells me where I stand	42
I receive promotions	25
I really have no basis for judging my standing	6

The above tabulation indicates that supervisors judge where they stand with their superiors more by the amount of responsibil-ity and authority they are given than by what they are told about their standing. The answer "He tells me where I stand" ranks

303

fifth among the six alternatives offered. More supervisors rated high than low check each of these items *yes,* except for the one concerning promotions (supervisors rated low check this more frequently, though the difference is not statistically significant).

Participation with Superior. On the second item in the list above, "He asks my opinion frequently," there was a large, significant difference between the supervisors rated high and those rated low. Of the supervisors given the top three ratings, 72% reported that their superior asked their opinion frequently. Only 31% of the "questionable" or "unsatisfactory" supervisors reported that their superior asked their opinion.

. . . Over twice as many of the supervisors rated high as those rated low feel they participate or are allowed to make their own decisions when changes are to be made. Twice as many of the high-rated supervisors are satisfied with the way they are brought into the decision-making process. These variations were the largest we found in the 16 questions we asked supervisors about their work situations and relationships.

Such differentiation in relationships may be due to one or both of two factors. Supervisors rated high may have greater ability and therefore may be allowed more freedom and participation by their superiors; or certain superiors may involve their supervisors in decisions about changes more frequently than others, regardless of the ability of the supervisors. There is evidence that both factors apply. But the important point here is that involvement and participation can develop subordinates and prepare them for greater responsibilities. Men are probably developed more rapidly if they are allowed to share problems and decisions than if they are simply evaluated and told where they stand.

CONCLUSION

At the outset we suggested that the structure of an industrial organization is such that a supervisor at any level is an active member of two face-to-face work groups—the group composed of his peers and his superior, and the group made up of his subordinates and himself. Membership in two overlapping organizational families is inherent in the *design* of all companies. The first-line supervisor, in particular, must be an accepted member of his own management group and an accepted member of the work group he supervises, if the total organization is to function effectively.

This dual membership poses no problem for the supervisor if the goals and the expectations of the two groups are generally compatible and if both groups recognize it.

If, on the other hand, management fails to recognize this duality and attempts to enlist a supervisor's undivided loyalty, he may lose his ability to act as a representative of his employees and eventually his effectiveness in helping management gain its objectives. At the same time, if the employees fail to recognize the duality of the supervisor's role and try to capture his complete loyalty, he may lose his ability to act as a representative of management and in the long run his effectiveness in helping employees reach their goals.

DUAL GOALS. The supervisor's role requires that he be motivated and able to integrate creatively the goals of individual subordinates and the objectives of the organization. In cases where the community of interest between employees and management is diminishing, he may find this an exceedingly trying role.

Under conditions of extreme conflict the supervisor may not be able to perform the dual representation required by his position. As a way out he may "take sides" and risk the loss of effectiveness in dealing with one or the other group. Or he may in effect renounce both groups and seek protection from their conflicting demands by joining a foreman's union. In renouncing both groups, he does become increasingly "a marginal man" as far as management and his employees are concerned.

In general, our research suggests that the proportion of supervisors who experience this feeling of being in the middle is far less than is implied by most nonquantitative studies of this role. Less than half (47%) of the supervisors in this study have feelings of standing in the middle between the workers and management. About the same proportion held for foremen in an automobile plant in another study we made (not yet published).

Regardless of whether supervisors feel that they are subject to

305

conflicting demands by those over them and those under them, it is clear that legalistic pronouncements about their status as members of management miss the mark organizationally and psychologically. By design, first-line supervisors are members of two subgroups in the organization; by design, if there are discrepancies in the expectations and objectives of the members in these two groups, the supervisor's job is to attempt to resolve them. This resolution is not aided by legal fiat; and it may even be hindered by programs designed by top officials "to ensure that the supervisor feels he belongs to management."

It is difficult, if not impossible, to remove all the differences between organizational objectives and individual subordinates' wants. Our findings indicate, however, that those supervisors whom management regarded as most ready for advancement differed from other supervisors in their ability to deal effectively with employees both on an individual and on a group basis. Their employees felt more free to discuss job and personal problems with them; these high-rated supervisors also held group meetings where problems could be discussed more frequently. In short, they were creating more opportunities for two-way communication between themselves and the employees under them. The more promotable supervisors were also distinguished from the other supervisors in that they participated with their superiors in decision making. Thus they had more opportunities for two-way communication between themselves and their superiors.

This problem sharing between superiors and supervisors, and between these same supervisors and the employees, appears to be one of the most effective ways for integrating organizational objectives and individual goals. Full participation by the supervisor in these two organizational families insures a two-way flow of relevant information and provides the maximum opportunity for coordination and synthesis of purposes. It is through this structure and process that the supervisor fulfills his integrative role in the large-scale organization. If effective supervisors are to be developed, it is up to top management to recognize the dual character of this role and to create the environment which fosters this two-way flow of communication and problem sharing.

306

HUMAN RELATIONS RECONSIDERED

William Foote Whyte

Human relations as an approach to management has
made many advances, yet much "remains to be done in
the interests of greater human satisfaction as well as
greater industrial efficiency." If progress is to continue,
it will be necessary to go beyond the human-relations
techniques of individual executives and investigate the
influences of work groups, organizational structure, and
community organizations upon work behavior.

As a field of research, teaching, and industrial training, human
relations is still relatively new. But it has grown with exceptional
rapidity, and the volume of current activity is enormous. Nevertheless, some critics still ask the disquieting question: Have we
really learned anything since we started—or, to use a significant
landmark, since 1933 when Elton Mayo's *Human Problems of an
Industrial Civilization* was published?[14]

This article is intended as a progress report on the field of human relations. As I shall point out, advances have definitely been
made; at the same time, much remains to be done in the interests
of greater human satisfaction as well as greater industrial efficiency.

OUTLINE OF PROGRESS

In oversimplified form, the progress in human relations theory
can be outlined in three stages:

1. *Staking out the claims*—This new field of study was opened up by
the research that Elton Mayo and his associates in the Department of
Industrial Research at the Harvard Business School, F. J. Roethlis-

---

[14] First published by The Macmillan Company; reprinted, Boston, Division
of Research, Harvard Business School, 1946.

Note: See Notes on the Authors, page 557, and item 250 in the bibliography for the full reference to this selection.

berger and W. J. Dickson, carried on at the Western Electric Company. Through experimentation, observation, and interviewing, they demonstrated the fallaciousness of the old established theories of human behavior in industry.

2. *Following the leads*—For some years, we all followed Mayo's leads; we accepted and elaborated on his assumptions as we worked along the lines of our particular interests. But what we had learned from Mayo was, to a large extent, clarification of what was *not* true about behavior in industry rather than information as to what *was* true. So, while sometimes we came to fruitful conclusions, more and more we found ourselves going up blind alleys.

3. *Developing a new pattern*—Realizing we did not have all the answers, we were forced to rethink the work we had been doing. This led us toward a new pattern of theory and research. The pattern is not yet clear enough to provide many practical conclusions. It is emerging, nevertheless, and that emergence promises a brighter future both for the development of research and for its application to human problems in industry.

As I see it, we have now advanced beyond Mayo in several important ways, each of which deserves independent evaluation.

- We know how to use money more effectively as an incentive.
- We have gone beyond the simple "work group" concept to discover some of the different forms of group behavior actually to be found in industry.
- We are learning how the structure of the organization can affect morale and productivity.
- We have learned some of the limitations of human relations training—a necessary step in the development of more effective action.

OLD THEORIES DISCREDITED

Mayo attacked a theory of human behavior and a theory of organization.

According to the established management theory, the working man was thought to be an individual who responded to management's actions upon a completely individualistic basis. Money was thought to be the main, if not the only, incentive to which he responded.

On the organization side, the theories that went under the name of "scientific management" dominated the scene. Two points stood out—"functionalization" and the "span of control":

(1) *Functional specialization* was equated with efficiency. The more specialization on the part of the worker or supervisor, the more effective he was supposed to be.

(2) The concept of *span of control* involved an essentially mechanical theory of organization. It placed emphasis upon the formal structure and upon building control into the organization from the top down. It assumed that one man could supervise adequately only a small number of people. The theory recognized that the number should vary with the complexity of tasks assigned and with the extent of interdependence of tasks among those supervised. However, the emphasis was upon keeping down the number of men under a single supervisor, in order to maintain adequate control.

Of course, no experienced executive believed literally in the prevailing theories of individual and organizational behavior. Nevertheless, there was a tendency to reason toward conclusions as if the theories were true.

THE CHALLENGE. It was Elton Mayo and his associates who made the first effective challenge to the prevailing theories of individual and organizational behavior. They did so by establishing the following propositions:

1. *The economic incentive is not the only motivating force to which the worker responds.* In fact, he often holds back his production to a point well below his physical capacity even when he is on piece rates and could make more money with more production. His production is importantly influenced by his relations with other workers and by his personal problems inside and outside the plant.

2. *The worker does not respond as an isolated individual.* He is a member of a work group, and the face-to-face relations he experiences have a great effect upon his behavior. Wherever men work together, they tend to build up an informal organization which may not follow the lines of the formal organization as established by management.

3. *Extreme functional specialization does not necessarily create the most efficient organization.* Mayo and his associates did not give great attention to this point, but, in their study of the bank wiring room, they noted that the wiremen and soldermen frequently exchanged jobs,

contrary to management's policy. These job exchanges had no adverse effects upon production and seemed to raise the morale of the entire work group.

LEADS AND BLIND ALLEYS. We can accept Mayo's assumption regarding functional specialization without modification. A good deal of research and experience since Mayo's day leads us to believe that extreme functional specialization results in lower productivity and lower morale. In a number of cases it has been found that both morale and productivity have been raised by job enlargement (giving the worker more tasks to perform) and by allowing the worker to change jobs from time to time.

The Western Electric study focused attention on the effects of workers' personal problems on their morale and productivity. This suggested to the researchers the desirability of establishing a personnel counseling program. The counselor had no management authority, and his conversations with workers were kept confidential. His function was to provide workers opportunity to talk out their problems to a skillful listener.

All of us who have talked out some personal problem with a sympathetic listener can recognize the value of such an experience. This then seems to be a useful personnel technique. Unfortunately, however, this technique turned out to be the main practical outcome of the research program in the Western Electric Company. It is curious that this should have happened, for it violates one of the major findings of the research program: that changes in individual behavior and attitudes are effected primarily through changing human relations in the organization. The individual worker may be helped by counseling, but he (or even his foreman) is in a very nonstrategic position for changing human relations in the organization. Thus personnel counseling has proved to be a dead end so far as research is concerned.

NEW APPROACH TO INCENTIVES

Mayo and his associates performed an important service in demonstrating that the economic incentive is not all-important. But where do we go from there?

MONEY STILL VITAL. Some researchers in the field have

gone on to assume that money—far from being all-important—is really not very important at all. This viewpoint is based on various questionnaire surveys which indicate that workers rank "good wages" seventh or eighth among the desirable conditions of work. Since items having to do with "fair treatment" by supervisors are consistently ranked higher, some people have come to think that workers are primarily concerned with human relations and do not worry very much about their take-home pay.

However, it has not been possible for us in human relations research to remove money from factory life. We have been forced to recognize that although workers may be thinking of other things too whenever they complain about wages, they are still most certainly concerned about money. Also, we have learned that the pattern of human relations in an organization can be such as to promote—or block—an enthusiastic response to an economic incentive.

It is futile to argue about the relative importance of money and human relations. We might just as well argue whether the engine or the gasoline is more important in making an automobile run. Our problem in research is to determine how the economic incentive and human relations fit together. More work has been done on this in recent years than can be summarized here, but I can point up two important areas of current research interest: the effect of incentives on intergroup relations and experimentation with new types of incentives.

DISRUPTING INFLUENCES. Industry today is full of strife growing out of intergroup problems created by incentive systems. For instance, look at the now time-honored struggle between workers on incentive pay and those on hourly rates:

Take the skilled people in the maintenance department, who usually are more skilled than any other workers in the plant. Normally, they hold relatively high status or prestige in the plant community. But since their work is not directly measurable, they are not generally included in incentive plans. Yet a piece-rate system for production workers is likely to eliminate part or all of the differential in earnings between the two groups. In some cases, the production workers actually come out ahead in pay. This narrowing or reversal of the differential inevitably generates severe pressures within the union and from the union to management.

Even within production departments, incentives often give rise to intergroup problems. For example:

Suppose the production department consists of "grinders" and "polishers." The hourly rate for grinders is $1.90, that for polishers, $2.00. The polishing job is thought to require somewhat more skill and enjoy a higher status, and the promotional ladder calls for workers to move up from grinder to polisher.

Now suppose that incentives are introduced into the department. To make it easier for management, let us assume that the rates for grinders and polishers are set up at approximately the same time—a situation that is often *not* found in practice. Ideally, the incentive system will turn out so that the polishers maintain approximately the same earnings differential as they enjoyed on day rates. However, almost as often as not—and regardless of the rate-setting methods used—the incentive earnings will turn out something like this: polishers, $2.45; grinders, $2.65.

In other words, the incentive system has turned upside down the relative positions of the two jobs. What happens now is easy to predict. The polishers put pressure on union and management in order to get a loosening of the rate and re-establish the pre-existing differential. And the grinders become very reluctant indeed to "promote" into the polisher position.

Furthermore, there is no such thing as a once-and-for-all settlement of this problem, within the framework of piece rates. Even if the rates initially established should maintain the polishers in a superior earnings position, there will be changes in machine and work methods, and these will necessitate new time studies for setting new piece rates. Somewhere along the line the grinders are bound to turn up on top of the polishers, thus setting into motion the pressures described above.

How can management meet this type of intergroup problem? Men are concerned about their pay in *relative* as well as in absolute terms; the point is obvious to anyone with industrial experience, yet all too often we fail to draw the conclusions which logically follow. This means that, in planning the introduction of an incentive system, management cannot afford to concentrate its attention on the problem of motivating one particular group of workers alone. It must, at the same time, recognize the place these workers occupy in the status and pay system of the plant.

Management must anticipate the changes that incentives are likely to produce in the relative positions of work groups in the plant status system. It must be prepared to deal with the pressures that arise in response to such changes. On the basis of what we already know, there is no excuse for management to be taken by surprise by the intergroup problems that piece rates generate.

PLANT-WIDE INCENTIVE. One way to by-pass the intergroup problems produced by piece rates is to abandon piece rates altogether. This does not necessarily mean giving up financial incentives. In recent years a few companies, following the lead of the late Joseph Scanlon, have been experimenting with incentives based on the performance of an entire plant. If the plant-wide formula does not eliminate whatever "inequities" workers may think exist, it at least has the merit of not introducing *new* inequities.

It is important to note that the plant-wide plan does not, in and of itself, produce results. Since the individual worker has so little direct effect on the payoff he receives, the success of a plant-wide formula depends on a new approach to motivation. Where the plan has been successful, it has been used as a symbol around which to reorganize human relations throughout the plant. The individual must feel that he is an important part of the organization, and he does not get this feeling simply by having management tell him how important he is. He feels appreciated only when he has an opportunity to contribute his ideas as well as his manual skills to the organization.

The plant-wide incentive program requires, therefore, a continuing program of discussion and action, whereby the individual can bring up ideas within his own department and whereby these ideas are carried for action to as high an organizational level as is necessary for decision making. This means stimulating workers to offer production ideas through the union channels. However, management people cannot just sit back and wait for union suggestions; they must also present production and cost problems to workers and union officers for discussion.

Without going into the mechanics of the system, some general comments can be made about its effectiveness. Under a successful plant-wide incentive, men will work more steadily, although it is not this harder work which accounts for most of the payoff. The successes have been achieved largely through a more effective mobilization of the knowledge and ideas of all members of the organization. In these cases, management and union have built a system in which workers gain feelings of pride and belonging through the contributions they make to the better functioning of their organization.

In the past, management has concentrated on setting up communication channels to *get the work done*. The new approach calls for setting up channels—from the bottom up as well as from the top down—through which *improvements in the organization of work* are constantly taking place. Here, the money offered by the plant-wide incentive is an important factor, but it does not motivate workers unless the social system of the plant is effectively organized.

Elton Mayo destroyed the orthodox economic theory of worker motivation. For a time we tried to develop a theory of motivation that would leave out money altogether. That too was found wanting, and we are now building a new theory that integrates economic incentives *and* human relations.[15]

ACCENT ON FACE-TO-FACE RELATIONS

Mayo and his associates showed that we cannot afford to think of an isolated individual employee. We must consider him as part of a work group. But where do we go from there?

MISLEADING CONCLUSIONS. We have elaborated upon Mayo's assumption in ways that have led toward misleading conclusions. Let us examine the steps here.

At first, we took it for granted that in *every* factory department there was a work group, and furthermore that it had a well-organ-

[15] For more on this subject, see William Foote Whyte *et al.*, *Money and Motivation* (New York: Harper & Brothers, 1955); also William Foote Whyte, "Economic Incentives and Human Relations," *Harvard Business Review*, March–April, 1952, p. 73.

ized structure that tended to have a good deal of stability. In this conclusion we were, of course, influenced by the classic Western Electric study of the bank wiring room, which did have a well-organized work group with a definite and stable structure. Neither Mayo nor any of his associates ever wrote that *all* factory departments must be organized in this pattern, but, when we had no comparable studies of other work groups, there was a natural tendency to assume that this was a universal pattern.

If there were such a work group structure, then it would follow that the foreman could supervise most effectively if he understood the structure of the group and dealt with it through the informal leadership that had arisen. We therefore focused our attention on the relations between the foreman and the *informal organization* of his workers. Without being fully aware of what we were doing, we sought to discover the factors that would make for good relations between foremen and workers—regardless of the technology involved, the distribution of job skills, the over-all structure of the organization, and so on.

From this point of view, harmonious relations between supervisor and supervised and high morale among workers seemed to depend on the human relations skill and understanding of the supervisors. As we extended our studies to union-management relations, we looked to find ways in which local union leaders could affect the degree of harmony between workers and management and the degree of satisfaction experienced by workers. We recognized that the human relations skills of union leaders could have an important impact on the resulting relationships.

The assumption underlying all this work was that the nature of human relations in the plant was primarily determined by the human relations skills of the people in leadership positions. It followed that training efforts to improve the skill and understanding of these people would result in more harmonious relations.

This line of thinking has been severely jolted by three sets of studies.

MORE POWERFUL FORCES. Clark Kerr and Abraham Siegel put to us the following embarrassing question: If cooperation in industry depends primarily on the skill and understanding of the key people involved, how do you explain the fact that there has been consistent conflict in the longshore industry in this country, and even internationally, while relations in the clothing industry have been reasonably peaceful?[16] Can it be that the key people in Industry A just happen to be skilled in human relations whereas their opposite numbers in Industry B are a bunch of bunglers?

This would be hard to believe, and as a matter of fact we do not believe it. We have had to recognize that there are certain forces operating that are more powerful than the human relations techniques of individual executives or union leaders. Along this line, Kerr and Siegel emphasize the homogeneity or heterogeneity of worker groupings on the job or in the community:

> Strike-prone industries, they argue, are those in which most workers work in close proximity on the same or similar jobs, and in which they live in close association in communities where they are cut off from intimate contact with other types of workers or with management people.

> At the other extreme, heterogeneity leads to more peaceful union-management relations: workers who do a wide variety of jobs and are scattered through the community, among other types of people, are less likely to strike.

This is an oversimplification of the Kerr-Siegel argument, but, for our purposes, it need not be presented in detail. It is enough to note that they have drawn our attention to the powerful influence of job structure and community organization upon human relations on the job.

MULTIGROUP RELATIONS. The work of Leonard Sayles and George Strauss has served to broaden our understanding of work groups.[17] A great variety of possible organizational patterns may be found among such groups. There are groups with stable organizations such as in the bank wiring room. There are also groups which may at times be so disorganized that it is hard even to speak

---

[16] "The Interindustry Propensity to Strike—An International Comparison," *Industrial Conflict,* edited by A. Kornhauser, R. Dubin, and A.M. Ross (New York: McGraw-Hill Book Company, Inc., 1954), p. 189.

[17] *The Local Union* (New York: Harper & Brothers, 1953). See also their article, "Conflicts Within the Local Union," *Harvard Business Review,* November–December, 1952, P. 84.

of them as groups. Furthermore, we cannot think simply in terms of the supervisor in relation to *the* work group. In a department of any size, the supervisor must relate himself to *several* work groups. At any given time these groups may be in competition and conflict with each other, so the supervisor must deal in intergroup relations as well as in his own relations to each group.

Sayles is now pushing ahead in an effort to discover some of the laws of work group behavior. He has tentatively identified four types of work groups, in terms of their characteristic behavior patterns:

(1) The *apathetic* group, whose members may be dissatisfied but are so divided against themselves they are unable to take concerted action.

(2) The *erratic* group, which swings from passivity to outbursts of aggressive action—and often on issues that seem to management and union leaders too small to account for the emotional heat involved.

(3) The *strategic* group, which constantly seeks to improve its position through carefully calculated, united action.

(4) The *conservative* group, whose members are capable of concerted action but who are generally satisfied enough so that they do not take the trouble to make themselves heard.[18]

Affixing a label has no value in itself, but Sayles is finding that the groups whose behavior fits a given label are reacting to very similar conditions of technology, level of skill, and arrangement of jobs. In other words, if we find groups in two different factories that fit the "erratic" behavioral description, we can expect to find them facing similar conditions in the social and technological work environment.

Study along this line is still in an early stage; within a few years we can expect to know a good deal more about work groups than we do today. Such knowledge can be invaluable in improving supervisory leadership and in increasing the effectiveness of local union leaders in their dealings with work groups. It will take us far beyond the simple work group concept.

[18] Leonard Sayles, *Technology and Work Group Behavior* (Ann Arbor: University of Michigan, Bureau of Industrial Relations, 1956).

THE ODDS ON TRAINING. The third force in upsetting our old conceptions of human relations has been provided by research evaluations of the impact of supervisory training programs.

In recent years, two solid pieces of research have been done along this line. In each case, the workers under the supervisors who were to be trained were given a questionnaire dealing with their relationship with the supervisors before the program began. The same questionnaire was administered some months after the conclusion of the program. The result? Disappointing, to say the least.

Edwin A. Fleishmann, Edwin F. Harris, and Harold E. Burtt at Ohio State found that the International Harvester Company program had effected no gain in these supervisor-worker relationships —and perhaps it had even resulted in a slight loss.[19] The University of Michigan Survey Research Center's study of a training program in two divisions of the Detroit Edison Company showed a small over-all gain.[20] However, it was found that there had been a loss of ground in one division which was more than compensated for by a gain in the other.

How can we account for these results? Were the programs in themselves no good? No doubt better training can be given, but probably these courses were a good deal better than the average in industry today.

We find the best explanation by looking at the two divisions in the Detroit Edison study. The researchers found that in the division where progress had been made, the foremen were led by a higher management which supervised them very much in line with the principles developed in the course. On the other hand, in the division which lost ground the foremen were under superiors who directed them in a manner which was entirely out of harmony with the program.

These findings suggest that the effectiveness of a training program for lower-level supervisors depends in very large measure on

[19] *Leadership and Supervision in Industry: An Evaluation of a Supervisory Training Program* (Columbus: Bureau of Educational Research, The Ohio State University, Monograph No. 33, 1955).

[20] See Norman A. Maier, *Principles of Human Relations* (New York: John Wiley & Sons, Inc., 1952), pp. 184–192.

the way that program is supported at higher levels in the organization. Nor can that support be simply verbal. Real success depends on the actions of top management in its day-to-day behavior.

What about training in human relations for the higher-ups?

Years ago management tended to make the foreman a sort of scapegoat for all human relations difficulties. It was assumed that if the foreman were only as good a leader of men as the president or vice president of the company, then there would be no problem. Today few management people are that naive. They are ready to recognize that a change in behavior at higher levels may be necessary too, if the foreman is to do the skillful job of supervision expected of him. So it makes sense to direct training at these higher levels.

Nevertheless we are becoming increasingly doubtful whether training can do the job here. We often assume that people high up in management are free agents. If they put pressure on their subordinates in a way that hinders cooperation and lowers morale, we may assume that this is because they do not have the necessary human relations skills or because they have some personality difficulties. But the truth is that the big wheels are not free to do as they please. They too are under pressure.

The plant manager is in competition for advancement with other plant managers. He is struggling to meet a budget that is deliberately set tight so as to demand his best efforts. He works with accountants and cost control people who, as Chris Argyris has explained, gain their successes through discovering and reporting the failures of production people.[21] Faced with rising material costs and wages, the manager must spur his organization to greater efficiency, so that the plant produces in greater volume and still keeps prices down and profits up. He has design engineers, industrial engineers, personnel men, and other specialists to help him and his production men do this, and yet he finds much of his time and energy devoted to untangling the snarls that arise among the people who make up the complex and sensitive organism which he directs.

[21] "Human Problems With Budgets," *Harvard Business Review,* January–February, 1953, p. 97.

319

At still higher levels, the company executive may be under less direct pressure from above, but he generates his own pressure in response to his ideal of the successful American executive. That ideal demands that he not be content with today's achievement, that he be constantly pushing to improve or expand the organization. Progress may require him to gamble millions of dollars on projects whose payoff is years away. Responsibility is a heavy weight in itself.

Our problem involves certain things that are bigger than the individual and his social skills. What are these things? We are only beginning to understand them, but one of the important factors seems to be the formal structure of the organization.

RE-ENTER FORMAL ORGANIZATION

Stimulated by research that has come out of Sears, Roebuck and Co. under the leadership of James C. Worthy (later Assistant Secretary of Commerce and now back at Sears as Director of Public Relations), we are busy taking a new look at organization structure.

We find that the way you build your organization has a great influence on its pattern of human relations. If you follow the span of control theory, you will build a long, narrow hierarchy with many levels of authority from bottom to top. Since supervisors will have few people reporting to them, they will tend to supervise those people closely. Under such conditions, the subordinate will concentrate on pleasing the boss and will have little opportunity to display initiative and assume the responsibilities necessary to developing his capacities.

The span of control theory is irrefutable if you accept the assumption about behavior on which it is based: that men perform best when they are under close supervision. The fact is that research (especially at Rensis Likert's University of Michigan Institute for Social Research) has been demonstrating the falsity of such an assumption. A number of studies have shown that both morale and productivity are higher under light, general supervision.

This means that the boss should delegate responsibility and authority to the men under him, giving them the chance to exercise their own capabilities. But can you get the boss to do this? Experience has shown that this is exceedingly difficult when the organization is based on the span of control concept and the boss has only a few people reporting to him. Despite training and management policy, he tends to keep close track (and control) of the work of his subordinates. It is easy for him to do so, and what else should he do with his time?

FLAT STRUCTURE. If we really want delegation of authority and the improved morale that seems to go with it, we might adopt the organization structure approach of giving the boss so many subordinates that he cannot possibly supervise them closely. Such a course means building a broad, flat structure with relatively few levels of authority from bottom to top. This management philosophy—the exact opposite of the span of control concept—is practiced by Sears and is becoming increasingly popular in American industry.

I am not suggesting that it is impossible to achieve a healthy degree of delegation of authority without changing the structure of the organization. And certainly not all companies would be able to model themselves after the Sears department store structure. The organizational pattern most appropriate for a particular business will depend on what it produces, its technology, the types of staff groups that must work with the line, and a number of other factors we are just beginning to investigate.

Nor am I trying to bury for all time the thinking that has gone into the span of control theory—which is still very much alive today, if we are to judge from the recent cogent statement of Lyndall Urwick.[22] My only claim is that we have come again to recognize the importance of formal structure—but now with a difference. Instead of theorizing in an *a priori* manner, we are beginning to carry on the empirical research that may some day enable us to plan the structure of the company so as to predetermine, in some degree, the nature of its human relations.

[22] "The Manager's Span of Control," *Harvard Business Review,* May–June, 1956, p. 39.

HUMAN RELATIONS IN PERSPECTIVE

In this article, I have pointed out the important influences upon human relations exercised by the pay system, the technology, the organization of work, and the formal structure. Does this mean that face-to-face relations are unimportant? Does this mean human skills and understandings do not really count for much?

The answer to both questions is *no*. However, research and experience have placed face-to-face relations in a new perspective. Both the morale and the productivity of an organization are tremendously influenced by the nature of face-to-face relations in that organization, but we have come to recognize that the relations we observe tend to be channeled within certain limits by the organization's structure, technology, and so on.

And yet these limits are not so narrow as to deprive the individual of any opportunity to influence the world around him. Man's behavior is not completely predetermined by these impersonal forces, for we have seen striking changes in human relations in some situations where there have been no substantial changes either in the form of organization or in the manner of performing the work.[23] Furthermore, organization structure and technology should not be considered as superhuman forces—they are determined by mere human decision.

In the past, management has characteristically thought only in terms of technical efficiency in planning structure and technology. Human relations entered into the picture only when disturbances arose out of technological and structural changes. Severe losses in efficiency as well as in morale have resulted from this mental separation of human relations from structure and work organization. Now that we recognize the intimate connection between the two, and as research begins to trace out the human relations patterns that go with different structural and technological arrangements, we can look for greater achievements through applying a human relations knowledge to industrial problems.

[23] William Foote Whyte, *Pattern for Industrial Peace* (New York: Harper & Brothers, 1951).

A DISSENTING VOICE ON HUMAN RELATIONS IN INDUSTRY

Malcolm P. McNair

In the chorus of praise for human relations in industry, dissenting voices are heard. No argument exists against the attempt to understand the behavior of people as workers and as members of organizations. Rather, contrary views are critical of the "sweetness and light" emphasis and the conscious attempt to practice human relations as a technique. The views of such critics can be summed up by the phrase, "So let's treat people like people but let's not make a big production out of it."

In 1956 the Inland Steel Company appointed a vice president of human relations. The Inland Steel Company, of course, is big business; but little business is not being neglected, for I note that the McGraw-Hill Book Company, Inc., is publishing a book on *Human Relations in Small Industry*. The Harvard Business School has had a chair of Human Relations since 1950; by now the number of courses in Human Relations in schools and colleges throughout the country has multiplied substantially. Even more marked is the rapid growth of executive development programs, some in schools, some in industry, but almost all of them placing emphasis on human relations.

Doctoral theses increasingly carry such titles as "A Case Study of the Human Aspects of Introducing a New Product into Production," "An Intensive Study of Supervisory Training in Human Relations and Foreman Behavior at Work," "A Case Study of the Administration of Change in the Large Modern Office," and "Emergence of Leadership in Manufacturing Work Groups." And recently the *Harvard Business Review* has reprinted a dozen arti-

Note: See Notes on the Authors, page 554, and item 142 in the bibliography for the full reference to this selection.

cles on human relations, under the title "How Successful Executives Handle People, 12 Studies on Communications and Management Skills," which include such intriguing subjects as "Making Human Relations Work," "Barriers and Gateways to Communication," and "The Fateful Process of Mr. A Talking to Mr. B."

It is obvious that human relations is very much the fashion in business thinking today. And fashions in business thinking are not a novelty; there have been many others. I can well recall that when I first joined the Harvard Business School faculty, the reigning vogue in business thinking was scientific management. Only a few years later, however, the grandiose claims of scientific management were sharply debunked. What was of solid worth remained—but a considerable amount of froth had been blown off the top.

Must we go through the same process—with all its waste and possible damage along the way—to get to what is worthwhile in human relations?

My quarrel is not with the solid substance of much that is comprehended by the phrase "human relations," but rather with the "cult" or "fad" aspects of human relations, which are assuming so much prominence.

There can be no doubt that people are of absorbing interest to other people. To verify this fact you have only to look at what makes headlines in the newspapers. There is a fascination for most of us in speculating about people and their behavior. So it is not surprising that human relations has assumed so much prominence as a fashionable mode of thinking. But, as with any kind of fashion, it can be carried to the point where people accept it without questioning—and certainly this can be dangerous when we are dealing with such an important segment of man's activity.

Therefore, just because the tide has gone so far, I must make my points in the most emphatic manner possible. Though I feel I have not distorted the picture, I do not care whether businessmen accept my interpretation in full, or even in large part, *so long as they get stirred up to do some critical thinking of their own.*

Before going any further let me try to indicate the things in this area of human relations which are really basic and with which there is no conceivable quarrel. In the first place, there can be no dispute with research in the social sciences, including the behavioral sciences. Obviously such research is highly important to business management and to business education. Business management and education must seek to understand the behavior of people as workers, the behavior of people as members of organizations, and, of course, the behavior of people as consumers. In all these areas we need more and better understanding of human behavior.

Neither is there any dispute in regard to the things that are important for a man's conduct in relation to his fellow men. The foundation is good Christian ethics, respect for the dignity of the individual human being, and integrity of character. On these we should stand fast. Personally I have always liked this paraphrase of what Theodore Roosevelt once said in a commencement address: "On the Ten Commandments and the Sermon on the Mount, uncompromising rigidity; on all else, the widest tolerance."[24] But between acceptance of high moral principles and the exigencies of day-to-day conduct of affairs there can be, with the best intentions, a very wide gap. This is the gap which by better understanding of human motivation we should try to fill.

Also there can be little dispute about the observations on the behavior of people at work which Professor Fritz J. Roethlisberger, the leader of the human relations group at Harvard, summed up half a dozen years ago:

"People at work are not so different from people in other aspects of life. They are not entirely creatures of logic. They have feelings. They like to feel important and to have their work recognized as important. Although they are interested in the size of their pay envelopes, this is not a matter of their first concern. Sometimes they are more interested in having their pay reflect accurately the relative social importance to them of the different jobs they do. Sometimes even still more important to them than maintenance of socially accepted wage differentials is the way their superiors treat them.

"They like to work in an atmosphere of approval. They like to be

[24] From the Introduction to *Theodore Roosevelt's America,* edited by Farida Wiley (New York, Devin-Adair Company, 1955), p. xxi.

praised rather than blamed. They do not like to have to admit their mistakes—at least, not publicly. They like to know what is expected of them and where they stand in relation to their boss's expectations. They like to have some warning of the changes that may affect them.

"They like to feel independent in their relations to their supervisors. They like to be able to express their feelings to them without being misunderstood. They like to be listened to and have their feelings and points of view taken into account. They like to be consulted about and participate in the actions that will personally affect them. In short, employees, like most people, want to be treated as belonging to and being an integral part of some group."[25]

In other words, "People behave like people." They have feelings. They don't always behave logically. The concept of the economic man can be a dangerous abstraction. Every individual wants to feel important, to have self-esteem, to have "face." Everybody likes to feel that he is "wanted." He likes to have a "sense of belonging." Group influences and group loyalties are important. The desire for psychological "security" is strong. People don't always reveal their feelings in words.

That all these human attitudes have important consequences for management is likewise not open to dispute. It is well accepted in management thinking today that leadership has to be earned, it cannot be conferred; that authority comes from below, not from above; that in any business unit there will be "social" groups which will cut across organization lines; that good communication involves both the willingness to listen and the ability to "get through" but not by shouting.

Dean Stanley F. Teele of the Harvard Business School recently made the statement, "As we have learned more and more about a business organization as a social unit, we have become increasingly certain that the executive's skill with people—or the lack of it—is the determining element in his long-range success or failure."[26]

---

[25] From a speech entitled "The Human Equation in Employee Productivity" before the Personnel Group of the National Retail Dry Goods Association, 1950.

[26] From a speech entitled "The Harvard Business School and the Search for Ultimate Values" at the presentation to the *Harvard Business Review* of a citation from The Laymen's Movement for a Christian World, New York, October 25, 1955.

Here we are down to the nub of the matter. What is this skill? Can it be taught? Are there dangers in the teaching of it? Is skill an appropriate concept?

Perhaps I can give a clue to the line of thought which I am developing when I say that I am essentially disturbed at the combination of *skill* with *human relations*. For me, "human relations skill" has a cold-blooded connotation of proficiency, technical expertness, calculated effect.

There is no gainsaying the fact that a need long existed in many businesses for a much greater awareness of human relations and that, in some, perhaps in a considerable number, the need still exists. The very avidity with which people prone to fashionable thinking in business have seized on the fad of human relations itself suggests the presence of a considerable guilt complex in the minds of businessmen in regard to their dealings with people. So it is not my intent to argue that there is no need for spreading greater awareness of the human relations point of view among many businessmen. Nevertheless it is my opinion that some very real dangers threaten.

The world's work has to be done, and people have to take responsibility for their own work and their own lives. Too much emphasis on human relations encourages people to feel sorry for themselves, makes it easier for them to slough off responsibility, to find excuses for failure, to act like children. When somebody falls down on a job, or does not behave in accordance with accepted codes, we look into his psychological background for factors that may be used as excuses. In these respects the cult of human relations is but part and parcel of the sloppy sentimentalism characterizing the world today.

Undue preoccupation with human relations saps individual responsibility, leads us not to think about the job any more and about getting it done but only about people and their relations. I contend that discipline has its uses in any organization for accomplishing tasks. And this is especially true of self-discipline. Will power, self-control, and personal responsibility are more than ever important in a world that is in danger of wallowing in self-pity and infantilism.

Most great advances are made by individuals. Devoting too much effort in business to trying to keep everybody happy results in conformity, in failure to build individuals. It has become the fashion to decry friction, but friction has its uses; without friction there are no sparks, without friction it is possible to go too far in the direction of sweetness and light, harmony, and the avoidance of all irritation. The present-day emphasis on "bringing everybody along" can easily lead to a deadly level of mediocrity.

We can accept the first part of a statement by Peter Drucker: "The success and ultimately the survival of every business, large or small, depends in the last analysis on its ability to develop people. . . . This ability . . . is not measured by any of our conventional yardsticks of economic success; yet it is the final measurement." Drucker, however, goes on to add a further thought, which opens more opportunity for debate. He says, "Increasingly from here on this ability to develop people will have to be systematized by management as a major conscious activity and responsibility." In this concept there is the familiar danger of turning over to a program or a course or an educational director a responsibility that is a peculiarly personal one.

The responsibility for developing people belongs to every executive as an individual. No man is a good executive who is not a good teacher; and if Drucker's recommendation that executive development be "systematized by management as a major conscious activity" is interpreted as meaning that someone trained in the new mode of thinking should be appointed as director of executive development, then the probable outcome will be simply another company program in human relations. While this may be good for some of the executives, no long-run contribution to the development of good people will be made unless the good individuals personally take the responsibility for developing other individuals.

Please do not misunderstand me. I am not talking about old-fashioned rugged individualism or the law of the jungle, and I am not holding up as ideals the robber barons of the nineteenth century, or even some of the vigorous industrialists of the early twentieth century. But I ask you to consider whether some of today's business leaders, well known to all of us—Clarence Randall,

Gardiner Symonds, Neil McElroy, Tex Colbert, Earl Puckett, Fred Lazarus, and so on—are not primarily products of a school of friction and competitive striving. We need more men like them, not fewer. It may be appropriate here to cite the recent observations of Dean Teele on "inner serenity" and "divine discontent":

"Any realistic approach to the nature of top business management, and therefore to the problems of selection and development for top business management, makes abundantly clear that the balance between these two [attributes] is perhaps the most important determinant of success in top business management. Let me elaborate.

"Psychiatrists, psychologists, and religious advisers join with ordinary lay observers in noting how often human efficiency is greatly reduced by sharp inner conflicts—conflicts which usually center around value judgments. That is to say, conflicts as to basic personal purposes and objectives, as to the values to be sought in life, are far more often the barriers to effective performance than intellectual incapacity or lack of necessary knowledge. The goal then from this point of view is the development of that inner serenity which comes from having struggled with and then resolved the basic questions of purpose and values.

"On the other hand, in business as in the world generally, discontent is an element of the greatest importance. Dissatisfaction with oneself, with one's performance, is an essential for improvement. So important to the progress of the world is discontent on the part of the relatively few who feel it, that we have come to characterize it as divine discontent. Here . . . the need is for both inner serenity and divine discontent—a need for both in a balance between the two appropriate for the particular individuals."[27]

To keep that important balance of inner serenity and divine discontent in our future business leaders, we need to focus educational and training programs more sharply on the development of individuals than is the fashion today. What is important for the development of the individual? Obviously, many things; but one prime essential is the ability to think, and the nurturing of this ability must be a principal objective of all our educational effort.

In the field of business education this ability to think, to deal

[27] "The Fourth Dimension in Management," an address to the American Management Association, New York, May 25, 1956.

with situations, to go to the heart of things, to formulate problems
and issues, is not an innate quality. It has to be cultivated, and it
requires long and rigorous and often tedious practice in digging out
significant facts, in weighing evidence, foreseeing contingencies,
developing alternatives, finding the right questions to ask. In all
business education, whether at the college or graduate level or at
the stage of so-called executive development, we must not omit
the insistence on close analysis, on careful reasoning and deduc-
tion, on cultivation of the power to differentiate and discriminate.

There is a very real danger that undue preoccupation with human relations can easily give a wrong slant to the whole process of
education for business leadership. For one thing, it tends to give a
false concept of the executive job. Dealing with people is emi-
nently important in the day's work of the business executive, but
so are the processes of analysis, judgment, and decision making. It
takes skill and persistence to dig out facts; it takes judgment
and understanding to get at the real issues; it takes perspective and
imagination to see the feasible alternatives; it takes logic and intuition to arrive at conclusions; it takes the habit of decision and a
sense of timing to develop a plan of action.

On the letterhead of the general policy letters that are sent peri-
odically to the managing directors of all 80-odd stores in the Allied
Stores Corporation there is this slogan:

> To LOOK is one thing.
> To SEE what you look at is another.
> To UNDERSTAND what you see is a third.
> To LEARN from what you understand is still something else.
> But to ACT on what you learn is all that really matters, isn't it?

An executive's ability to see, to understand, to learn, and to act
comprises much more than skill in human relations.

Awareness of human relations as one aspect of the executive's
job is of course essential. But, in my view, *awareness of human
relations* and the *conscious effort to practice human relations on
other people* are two different things, and I think this is crucial.

As soon as a man consciously undertakes to practice human

relations, one of several bad consequences is almost inevitable. Consciously trying to practice human relations is like consciously trying to be a gentleman. If you have to think about it, insincerity creeps in and personal integrity moves out. With some this leads by a short step to the somewhat cynical point of view which students in Administrative Practices courses have described by coining the verb "ad prac," meaning "to manipulate people for one's own ends."

A less deliberate but perhaps even more dangerous consequence may be the development of a yen for managing other people's lives, always, of course, with the most excellent intentions. In the same direction the conscious practice of human relations leads to amateur psychiatry and to the unwarranted invasions of the privacy of individuals.

Hence I am disturbed about the consequences to business management of human relations blown up into pseudoscience—with a special vocabulary and with special practitioners and experts. In fact, to my mind there is something almost sinister about the very term "human relations practitioner," though I am sure that all sincere devotees of human relations would vigorously disclaim any such imputation.

For me much of the freshness and the insight which characterized a great deal of the earlier work in this field—exemplified by the quotation from Professor Roethlisberger which I cited in my introductory statement—has been lost as the effort has progressed to blow human relations up into a science—something to be explored and practiced for its own sake.

I realize that many people in the human relations field—Professor Roethlisberger in particular—are also disturbed about this trend, and about its unintended repercussions. But it was almost inevitable that other people would run away with such a fruitful concept, and set it up as an idol with appropriate rituals of worship (usually called "techniques"). Once you throw yourself into trying to "listen," to "gain intuitive familiarity," to "think in terms of mutually independent relationship," and so on, you can easily for-

331

get that there is more to business—and life—than running around plying human relations "skill" to plumb the hidden thoughts of everybody with whom you come in contact, including yourself.

This is the same mistake that some consumer motivation researchers make, as Alfred Politz has pointed out—trying to find out the attitudes, opinions, and preferences in the consumer's mind *without regard* to whether these factors are what determine how he will act in a given buying situation.[28] In his words, the "truth" that such researchers seek—and he always puts the word in quotes—is not only of a lower order than the scientifically established facts of how consumers react in real life, but it is also of less use to managers in making marketing decisions.

The whole thing gets a little ridiculous when, as pointed out in another article in this issue, foremen are assumed to have progressed when they have gained in "consideration" at the expense of something called "initiating structure"—yet such was the apparent objective of one company's training program.[29]

From the standpoint of developing really good human relations in a business context, to say nothing of the job of getting the world's work done, the kind of training just described seems to me in grave danger of bogging down in semantics and trivialities and dubious introspection. I am totally unable to associate the *conscious practice of human relations skill* (in the sense of making people happy in spite of themselves or getting them to do something they don't think they want to do) with the *dignity of an individual person created in God's image.*

Apparently this "skill" of the "human relations practitioner" consists to a considerable degree of what is called "listening." The basic importance of the ability to listen is not to be gainsaid; neither is it to be denied that people do not always reveal their inward feelings in words. But in the effort to blow human relations up into a science and develop a technique of communication, some of

[28] "Science and Truth in Marketing Research," *Harvard Business Review,* January–February, 1957, p. 117.
[29] Kenneth R. Andrews, "Is Management Training Effective? II. Measurement, Objectives, and Policy," *Harvard Business Review,* March–April, 1957, p. 63.

the enthusiasts have worked up such standard conversational gambits as "This is what I think I hear you saying," or "As I listen, this is what I think you mean."

No doubt there are times when a silent reaction of this kind is appropriate, but if the human relations practitioner makes such phrases part of his conversational repertoire, there are times when these cute remarks may gain him a punch in the nose. Sometimes people damn well mean what they are saying and will rightly regard anything less than a man-to-man recognition of that fact as derogatory to their dignity.

That a group of foremen who were given a course emphasizing human relations and thereafter turned out to be distinctly poorer practitioners than they had been before taking the course, as in the above case, would not, to my mind, be simply an accident. I think it a result that might well be expected nine times out of ten. In other words, the overemphasis on human relations, with all its apparatus of courses, special vocabulary, and so on, tends to create the very problems that human relations deals with. It is a vicious circle. You encourage people to pick at the scabs of their psychic wounds.

In evaluating the place of human relations in business, a recent incident is in point:

At a luncheon gathering Miss Else Herzberg, the highly successful educational director of a large chain of stores in Great Britain, Marks and Spencer, Ltd., described at some length the personnel management policies of that concern and the high state of employee morale that existed. Throughout her description I was listening for some reference to human relations. I did not hear it, and when she had finished I said, "But, Miss Herzberg, you haven't said anything about human relations." Immediately she flashed back, "We live it; we don't have to talk about it."

In point also is a recent remark of Earl Puckett, chairman of the board of Allied Stores Corporation, when in discussing a particular management problem he said, "Of course you treat people like people."

And so, although I concede that there is still too little awareness of human relations problems in many business organizations, I think that the present vogue for human relations and for executive development programs which strongly emphasize human relations holds some real dangers because it weakens the sense of responsibility, because it promotes conformity, because it too greatly subordinates the development of individuals, and because it conveys a one-sided concept of the executive job.

I turn now more specifically to the dangers to business education at the college level which seem to me inherent in the present overemphasis upon human relations. Business executives should have as much concern with this part of the subject as teachers—perhaps more, because they must use the young men we turn out; furthermore, they represent the demand of the market and so can have a real influence on what the educators do.

The dangers to the education of young men, in my opinion, are even more serious than the dangers to business executive development programs for mature men. After all, we are well aware that businessmen follow fads, and so fairly soon the human relations cult in business will begin to wane and operations research or something else will become the fashion. Also, as remarked earlier, there is still a substantial need in business for greater awareness of human relations, and more businessmen are sufficiently adult to separate the wheat from the chaff. Thus in advanced management training programs for experienced executives there is no doubt greater justification for courses in Human Relations than there is in collegiate and immediate graduate programs.

From the general educational standpoint perhaps the first question is whether human relations can be taught at all. I do not deny that something can be learned about human relations, but I do maintain that direct emphasis on human relations as subject matter defeats the purpose. When things must come from the heart, the Emily Post approach won't do; and if behavior does not come from the heart, it is phony. Clarence Budington Kelland, that popular writer of light fiction, in a recent *Saturday Evening Post* serial entitled "Counterfeit Cavalier," makes one of his characters say:

"A very nice person has to start by being nice inside and have an aptitude for it. . . . They don't have to learn. It comes natural. No

334

trimmings, but spontaneous. . . . If you have to think about it, it is no good."

Good human relations do not lend themselves to anatomical dissection with a scalpel. How do people normally acquire good human relations? Some of course never do. In the case of those who do enjoy success in human relations and at the same time retain their sincerity, the result, I am convinced, is a composite product of breeding, home, church, education, and experience generally, not of formal Human Relations courses.

Hence in my view it is a mistake in formal education to seek to do more than develop an awareness of human relations, preferably as an integral part of other problems. This does not mean, of course, that the results of research in human behavior should not be utilized in the teaching of business administration. Certainly such results should be utilized (with due circumspection to avoid going overboard on theories that are still mostly in the realm of speculation). To take account of human relations in marketing problems and in personnel management problems and in labor relations problems and industrial management problems, and so on, of course makes sense. What I am decrying is the effort to teach human relations as such. Thus, I applaud the training of personnel managers, but I am exceedingly skeptical of training human relations practitioners.

I should like also to venture the personal opinion that human relations in its fairly heavy dependence on Freudian psychology is headed the wrong way. In the long history of mankind, the few centuries, dating perhaps from the Sumerian civilization, during which we have sought to apply an intellectual and moral veneer to man the animal are a very short period indeed as compared with the time that has elapsed since our ancestors first began to walk erect; and it seems to me that a large part of the job of education still must be to toughen and thicken this veneer, not to encourage people to crack it and peel it off, as seems to have been the fashion for much of the last half century. I suspect that modern psychiatry is in a vicious circle, that some of the principal causes of increased mental disease lie in morbid introspection, lack of strong moral convictions, and leisure that we have not yet learned how to use.

I believe that one of these days a newer school of thought in these matters will re-emphasize the importance of will power, self-control, and personal responsibility. I can well recall hearing Charles William Eliot, on the occasion of his ninetieth birthday, repeat his famous prescription for a happy life: "Look up, and not down, look forward and not backward, look out and not in."

Our present preoccupation with the emotional and nonlogical aspects of life seems to me in many ways responsible for the prevalent wishful thinking of the American people. As a higher and higher proportion of American youth goes to college, it might be supposed that intelligently realistic ways of looking at things would be on the increase, but the contrary seems to be true. As people we are more prone than ever to let our desires color our thinking. More and more the few people who have the courage to present realistic viewpoints on national and world affairs find that the public will not listen to what it does not wish to hear. Why isn't education bringing us a more intelligent outlook on life?

Can it be that one of the reasons is that education itself has surrendered so far to the ideas that are concerned primarily with the current fashionable interest in the emotional and nonlogical aspects of living? In reviewing Joan Dunn's book, *Why Teachers Can't Teach—A Case History,* E. Victor Milione remarks, "Our educational system has substituted training in life adjustment for education."[30] Obviously there are many analogies between the doctrines of the progressives in education and the overemphasis on human relations. Personally I prefer a more rigorous educational philosophy. I can well recall a remark of A. Lawrence Lowell that "the business of education is making people uncomfortable."

In any event, I think it is the job of education to push for more and not less emphasis on logics and morals in dealing with social problems. The following quotation from C. C. Furnas, chancellor of the University of Buffalo, makes much sense to me:

"We must recognize, of course, that it takes much more than pure intellect to answer social questions. Great problems involving many

---

[30] *The Freeman,* March, 1956, p. 59.

people are usually handled in an atmosphere of high emotion and the participants often show but little evidence of being rational human beings. But, even though it acts slowly, it is certainly true that intelligence can and does have some influence in shaping mass emotions. It is in this slow modification of mass emotional patterns that the average intelligent person can and should play a continuing role within his own sphere of influence."[31]

How can we do this if we encourage immature minds to regard the nonlogical aspects as the most important? Not that teachers necessarily intend it this way—though I am sure some have been carried so far—but simply that putting so much explicit emphasis on the emotional and irrational makes the student feel it is all-important. No protestation to the contrary can undo that impression—that perhaps *nonlogical* impression—which is exactly what an understanding of human behavior ought to lead us to expect in the first place.

But perhaps my principal quarrel with the teaching of human relations has to do with timing. Discussion of such problems as what men should learn, and how they should learn it, is probably as old as education itself, but much less attention has been given to the question, "When should men learn?"

The whole modern development of adult education has brought into disrepute the old adage that you can't teach an old dog new tricks. In fact, in the area of business administration it is quite plausible that teaching of certain managerial skills is best accomplished in later years, after men have gained considerable experience in business activities. William H. Whyte, Jr., the author of *Is Anybody Listening?* and *The Organization Man,* in discussing the Alfred P. Sloan Fellowship Program at the Massachusetts Institute of Technology, has this to say:

"But on one point there is considerable agreement: to be valuable, such a course should be taken only when a man has had at least five years' business experience. The broad view can be a very illusory thing. Until a man has known the necessity—the zest—of mastering a specific skill, he may fall prey to the idea that the manager is a sort of neutralist expediter who concerns himself only with abstractions such as human relations and motivation. Those who study these subjects after ten

[31] *Ibid.,* p. 24.

years or so of job experience have already learned the basic importance of doing a piece of work; in the undergraduate business schools, however, the abstractions are instilled in impressionable minds before they are ready to read between the lines and to spot the vast amount of hot air and wishful thinking that is contained in the average business curriculum."[32]

Among those managerial skills the specific teaching of which had better be left to later years is the handling of human relations. Thus I should not only rewrite the old adage in the form, "There are some tricks you can teach only to an old dog," but I should go on to the important corollary, "There are some tricks that you had better not try to teach to young dogs." The dangers in trying to teach human relations as such at the collegiate or immediate graduate level are substantial. Indeed, by developing courses in human relations for college graduates in their early twenties without previous business experience we are essentially opening Pandora's box.

Such courses lead to a false concept of the executive's job. There is a de-emphasis of analysis, judgment, and decision making. Someone has said that the job of the modern executive is to be intelligently superficial. This statement is true in the sense that when a man reaches an important executive post, he does not have time to go to the bottom of every problem that is presented to him, and he certainly should not undertake himself to do the work of his subordinates. If he does these things, he is a poor executive. But if an executive has not learned at some stage to go to the bottom of problems in one or more particular areas, he will not in the long run be a successful manager.

Human relations expertise is not a substitute for administrative leadership, and there is danger in getting young men to think that business administration consists primarily of a battery of experts in operations research, mathematics, theory of games, and so on, equipped with a Univac and presided over by a smart human relations man. Undoubtedly many of the new techniques are substantial aids to *judgment,* but they do not fully replace that vital

[32] *Fortune,* June, 1956, p. 248.

quality. One of the great dangers in teaching human relations as such at the collegiate or immediate graduate level is that the student is led to think that he can short-cut the process of becoming an executive.

The study of human relations as such also opens up a wonderful "escape" for the student in many of his other courses. Let's admit it: none of us is too much enamored of hard thinking, and when a student in class is asked to present an analysis of some such problem as buying a piece of equipment, or making a needed part instead of buying it, he frequently is prone to dodge hard thinking about facts in favor of speculation on the probable attitudes of workers toward the introduction of a new machine or new process.

For some students, as for some businessmen, the discussion of human relations aspects of business management problems can even lead to the development of the cynical "ad prac" point of view, which assumes that the chief end of studying human relations is to develop skill in manipulating people; this perhaps is the present-day version of high-pressure selling.

A different but equally dangerous result occurs in the case of the student who becomes so much interested in human relations that he turns himself into an amateur psychiatrist, appraises every problem he encounters in terms of human relations, and either reaches an unhealthy state of introspection or else develops a zeal for making converts to human relations and winds up with a passion for running other people's lives.

The sum of the matter is this. It is not that the human relations concept is wrong; it is simply that we have blown it up too big and have placed too much emphasis on teaching human relations as such at the collegiate and early graduate level. A sound program in business education, in my opinion, will of course envisage research in human behavior; it may, with some possible good results, venture on offering specific courses in Human Relations for mature executives; but for students in their twenties who have not yet become seasoned in practical business activities we should keep away from specific courses in Administrative Practices and Human Relations, while at the same time inculcating an awareness of human relations problems wherever they appropriately appear in other management courses. In other words, let us look closely enough at what we are doing so we can be sure that the gains we make in this area turn out to be *net* gains.

Finally, to express a personal conviction on a somewhat deeper note, I should like to refer again to Dean Teele's comments, cited earlier, on "inner serenity." The attainment of that all-important goal, in my opinion, is not to be sought through the present vogue of interest in human relations. Inner serenity is an individual matter, not a group product. As Cameron Hawley puts it, "A man finds happiness only by walking his own path across the earth."

Let's treat people like people, but let's not make a big production of it.

Chapter 7

CONFLICT AND COÖPERATION: UNIONS AND MANAGEMENT

INTRODUCTION

The purpose of this chapter is to examine the dimensions of the problem of industrial conflict in American society, to bring the field more sharply into focus and provide insights into the determining influences and conditions that give rise to conflict. Finally, it aims at presenting points of view for its resolution.

Problems of labor and management have occurred throughout the history of capitalism. Owners and managers and the wage earners which they hire could be expected to develop different perspectives and to pursue divergent actions in line with their own interests. Undoubtedly industrial conflict is inevitable and despite heavy emphasis in recent years on common goals and the virtues of harmony, the pursuit of opposed aims continues to cause strife. Witness the recent and prolonged strike at the Kohler plant in Wisconsin.

Conflict arises out of situations of contrast—from the conscious seeking of individual and group values to the exclusion of others. Its form, ranging from direct and violent opposition to apathy and withdrawal, is directly conditioned by the social conditions out of which it arises. It is most intense in periods of rapid social change.

In the opinion of many, some degree of conflict is inevitable in any organized group. Unequal distribution of power and of influence create division. The "have-nots" strive to attain power; the "haves" to prevent this and to maintain position. Rarely, however, are the issues ever fully resolved. Compromise usually occurs. The situation becomes redefined, new alignments emerge, and fresh problems result. The dialectic continues.

Organized labor has grown tremendously in recent years both in numbers and in power. Some 13 million workers, it is estimated, belonged to unions as of 1950. Without doubt, labor now exercises a major economic and political influence, and with the recent merger of the two major federations its potential is even greater. While initially the union primarily concerned itself with wages and working conditions, there has been a strong tendency in recent years to move into the field of so-called "management prerogative." Not only has the union been the agent of the working man but it has also moved strongly toward organizing the "white-collar" worker and by so doing extending its area of operations.

On the other hand, management has stoutly defended its position and its prerogatives. Large corporations have come to dominate the scene. As owners of the means of production, they have been able to capitalize on the play of supply and demand in strengthening their own power position. In effect, then, we now have two major powers in American society—labor and management.

Strikes and violence are the most spectacular forms of industrial conflict and certainly the most disturbing. However, they represent only one form of opposition. Others are conflict in contract negotiations, grievances, complaints, slowdowns, and negativism. On the part of management conflict is manifested in overstrict discipline, speed-ups, layoffs, and demotions. Such conflict has resulted in lost production and wages; it has brought about a high degree of turnover and untold hardships to the families of workers and to the community.

Nor is conflict confined to the organization itself. In terms of the larger society, massive campaigns have been conducted by both sides in order to gain the support of public opinion. Lobbying and public-relations activities have attempted to influence both legislation and executive decisions.

Industrial conflict is by no means, however, completely in the negative. It serves to make explicit the grounds which separate the groups who are in opposition. Each comes to know the other. Group action is facilitated and progress frequently results.

As a result of conflict, issues are brought out in the open subject to public opinion and control through the application of legal and administrative action. From the standpoint of the larger society, conflict serves to stabilize the social structure by clarifying the identity of the power-holding groups.

THE PURPOSES AND RESOLUTION OF
INDUSTRIAL CONFLICT

Clark Kerr

Within the field of union-management relations, conflict serves many positive functions: it assists in the solution of controversies, reduces intergroup tensions, and balances management power against union power. Mediation, which may be either tactical or strategic in nature, serves to reduce irrationality, aids in the exploration of solutions, and assists in obtaining the integration of workers and employers.

Industrial society, quite generally, is highly disposed in favor of law and order. Aggressive conflicts between capital and labor are considered both undesirable and largely unnecessary. It is often suggested that carefully devised mediation machinery administered by skilled practitioners can be effective in greatly reducing such conflict. [We are here] concerned with this series of attitudes and beliefs.[1] [We] advance the contrary theses that aggressive in-

[1] Paper presented to the Second Congress of the International Sociological Association, Liege, Belgium, August, 1953. This discussion assumes the cultural context of an "open society"—a democratic, capitalistic, industrialized society within which the state, the employers, and the unions are separate and largely independent entitites; a society not marked by rigid class stratification and one in which the strike is an economic rather than a political weapon; societies such as those of the United States, England and the Scandinavian nations. This discussion does not relate to industrialized so-

Note: See Notes on the Authors, page 554, and item 123 in the bibliography for the full reference to this selection.

dustrial conflict,[2] in one form or another, cannot be eliminated and can be only temporarily suppressed; that such conflict, provided that it takes place within certain broad rules of the game, can serve important social functions; and that tactical mediation, which will be defined a little later, has limited value in reducing aggressive conflict and, under certain conditions, may even increase it. Strategical mediation will be presented as being more effective but also more difficult.

THE NATURE OF INDUSTRIAL CONFLICT

Organized groups, like individuals, may develop four general types of relationship toward one another. They may isolate themselves; they may co-operate, voluntarily or involuntarily; they may compete; or they may enter into conflict. Each type has, of course, its subtypes and its degrees; and any single relationship may be a combination of two or more of the generalized types. Competition and conflict are distinct types of relationship, although they do bear some similarity to each other. In competition, two or more parties seek to gain reward from a third party

---

cieties in which labor-management relations take the form of warfare between social movements, the political strike is common, and conflict is not of the "limited-purpose" type; nor does it relate to those in which aggressive conflict between managers and managed is suppressed.

[2] "Industrial conflict" is used loosely to mean at least three things. Sometimes it includes the sources of discontent, the bases of hostility, the grievances, the oppositions of interest. Thus labor and management are said to be in conflict over wage payments or managerial prerogatives in the sense that they have different desires. Sometimes it covers all forms of opposed action, both nonviolent, such as collective bargaining, and violent, such as the strike. In this sense conflict means not the incompatible views of the parties but the battle between them which finds its source in these views. Sometimes conflict is opposed to peace. Thus a strike is said to constitute industrial conflict, while bargaining is peaceful.

In this paper the following terminology is employed: (1) "sources of conflict" covers the various dissatisfactions and discontents of the parties with each other; (2) "conflict" will designate all opposed action which emanates from these or other (external) sources; (3) "diplomatic conflict" will mean opposed actions which rely primarily upon verbal persuasion, such as contract negotiation and grievance handling; and (4) "aggressive conflict" will identify those actions which are of a forceful nature and are intended to harm the other party so that he will be compelled to respond in a desired manner, for example, by strikes and lockouts.

or parties. Thus two automobile manufacturers may compete for the consumer's dollar. In conflict, two or more parties seek to gain from each other. (If there are few competitors and particularly in bilateral monopoly, competition and conflict become much alike, for then what one gains is taken away from the other in a quite personal way.) Thus a union may seek to transfer prerogatives from management to itself. Conflict, by its very nature, is likely to be more personal, more intense, and more destructive than competition.

Labor-management relations are a classic form of conflict. Except possibly where joint collusive arrangements against consumers are entered into (and even here there is likely to be conflict over the division of the spoils), organized labor and management are primarily engaged in sharing between themselves what is, at any one moment of time, a largely given amount of income and power.[3] The more the one gets or keeps, the less the other has.

INEVITABILITY. Conflict between organized labor and management is more than an expression of irrationality or ill will. Given a rational reaction of each party to the other and mutual good will (and the two are not necessarily always compatible), conflict is still inherent in the situation for at least four reasons.

1. The desires of the parties are more or less unlimited, while the means of satisfaction are limited. Wages can never be as high as workers desire or profits or salaries as high as owners or managers might wish; yet the money available for distribution between the contending claimants is always limited in the short run. The power to make those decisions lying within the orbit of an economic enterprise is also finite. Given the survival of both parties, they must share it in some fashion, and neither can ever be entirely happy with the distribution, for, so long as the other has any power at all, it can make unsatisfactory decisions.

2. Someone manages and someone is managed, and this is an

[3] The "pie" to be divided is not, of course, always fully given. Particularly under conditions of industry-wide bargaining in periods of prosperity when the employers can pass on added costs to the consumers fully and immediately, the expansibility of the "pie" is quite significant. The size of the "pie" is enlarged to accommodate labor's gains without injuring industry. The power "pie," however, is always fixed in dimensions. The more fixed the size of the "pie," of course, the more intense the conflict is likely to be.

345

eternal opposition of interest, which may be made bearable but can never be eliminated in a complex, industrial society. The larger the basic productive unit, the greater this opposition of interest is likely to be.

3. Industrial societies are dynamic. Even if a certain distribution of income and power could be devised which, in a given situation, was not subject to controversy (though this seems unlikely), the situation itself would change—because of new regulations by the state, changed expenditure patterns of consumers, higher costs of raw materials, a reduced value of the monetary unit, increased real income for a comparable group elsewhere—and the parties would need to seek a new allocation of income and power.

4. If management and labor are to retain their institutional identities, they must disagree and must act on the disagreement. Conflict is essential to survival. The union which is in constant and complete agreement with management has ceased to be a union. It has destroyed itself; and the same is true for management. Institutional, like individual, independence is asserted by acts of criticism, of contradiction, of conflict, of competition.

Thus labor-management conflict flows inevitably from the unsatiated desires of men, the relationship of managers and managed, the need to adapt to changed conditions in one fashion or another, and the drive for institutional separateness. In the cultural context which we have assumed, there are sources of conflict, and organized groups can make decisions which translate their discontents into action against another party.

VARIETY. Industrial conflict has more than one aspect, for the manifestation of hostility is confined to no single outlet. Its means of expression are as unlimited as the ingenuity of man. The strike is the most common and most visible expression. But conflict with the employer may also take the form of peaceful bargaining and grievance handling, of boycotts, of political action, of restriction of output, of sabotage, of absenteeism, or of personnel turnover. Several of these forms, such as sabotage, restriction of output, absenteeism, and turnover, may take place on an individual as well as on an organized basis and constitute alternatives to collective action. Even the strike itself is of many varieties. It may involve all the workers or only key men. It may take the form of refusal to work overtime or to perform a certain process. It may even involve such rigid adherence to the rules that output is stifled.

These various kinds of actions are alternatives to one another. Knowles has shown recently[4] that in England absenteeism and strikes seem to be substitutes for each other, as are also trade-union expenditures on strikes and on political action. In Sweden, where strikes during a contract are illegal, the "masked strike" takes the place of the open strike. The forms of contention may be broadly classified as the "diplomatic," such as bargaining and grievance handling, and the "aggressive," such as the strike, the boycott, and restriction of output. (Conflict, additionally, may take the form of political action against the interests of the opposed party.) In a democratic nation, where the coercive power of the state against individuals and groups is limited, some forms of aggressive conflict cannot be effectively stopped, except for very short periods. Even in time of war, strikes cannot be entirely prohibited, and it is even more difficult to arrest restriction of output or the planned absenteeism or quitting of key men.

ACCEPTABILITY OF CERTAIN AGGRESSIVE CONFLICT. Aggressive industrial conflict is not wholly evil. It does lead at times, it is true, to grievous injury to the parties themselves or to third parties; but the costs are frequently greatly exaggerated. Man-days lost owing to industrial disputes are far fewer than losses due to unemployment or illness. In the industrialized and democratic nations, they currently average about one-half man-day per year for all nonagricultural employees. Against these costs (and they are not the only ones) must be reckoned the gains, for aggressive industrial conflict, like conflict generally, as Simmel argued so forcefully,[5] has a positive role. First, out of aggressive conflict or its latent possibility comes the resolution of many disputes. The strike and the lockout and the threat of these actions

---

[4] K. G. J. C. Knowles, *Strikes—a Study in Industrial Conflict* (Oxford: Basil Blackwell, 1952), pp. 210–211 and Appendix A, pp. 225–226.

[5] See Georg Simmel, *Sociology,* chap. 1, "The Sociological Nature of Conflict" (trans. Kurt Wolff [unpublished manuscript]).

are means for inducing agreement—out of war or the threat of war comes the settlement of controversies.[6] It is through such aggressive conflict or its potentiality that the parties find the bases for continued association and acceptance of each other. Collective bargaining and grievance handling are the more effective because of the more violent alternatives at hand. In the absence of aggressive conflict, controversies would be much longer drawn out, since there would be no decisive terminal point, and the absence of a settlement can be costly, too, in increased irritability and tension between the parties. Fortunately, unlike war between nations, aggressive conflict between labor and management cannot last too long or harm the parties too much, since they have limited staying power and can only survive individually as they survive jointly.

Second, conflict, and particularly open conflict, reduces tensions.[7] In modern industrial society the sources of unrest and hostility are enormous. The strike provides an outlet for them when they are so severe as to require forceful expression. As in the ancient Greek tragedies, reconciliation follows more easily if retribution has preceded. In a sense, thus, strikes are constructive when they result in the greater appreciation of the job by the worker and of the worker by management. It is a not uncom-

---

[6] "A strike in the ordinary industrial relationship is, as you know, a part and a very useful part of the machinery of collective bargaining . . . In the last fifteen minutes of big controversies it is the right to strike or the threat of a strike, the possibility of a strike, that is the instrument with which the controversy is settled. It is always present at the conference table. It is the thing that puts a limit on unreason, and it is the thing that holds the parties in the last fifteen minutes to the full responsibility of making their own decisions. And without that responsibility you do not have collective bargaining" (William H. Davis, "Collective Bargaining and Economic Progress," in *Industrial Disputes and the Public Interest* [Berkeley and Los Angeles: Institute of Industrial Relations, University of California, 1947], pp. 12–13).

[7] "Smouldering discontent may exist for a long time without coming to a head. Such discontent is reflected in decreased efficiency and an increased cost of production. Even strikes may be preferable, clearing a surcharged atmosphere and affording a basis for a fresh start. Many an industry which has had no strikes for years nevertheless has anything but satisfactory industrial relations.

"Labor disputes are not necessarily an evil" (Edwin E. Witte, *The Government in Labor Disputes* [New York: McGraw-Hill Book Co., Inc., 1932], pp. 3–4).

mon occurrence for productivity to rise after a strike. The chance to rebel against the other party on occasion establishes the independence of the group and of the individual, makes acceptance of the surrounding social system easier, and, therefore, can make a net addition to satisfaction and to production. The "five-and-dime" revolution can be readily absorbed into a flexible social system.

Third, out of the conflict of management and union—and this on occasion may involve aggressive action—the worker is better served. As the two parties compete for his loyalty, his interests are advanced. Further, this conflict protects him from domination. In its absence, one or the other organization might become too powerful for him to retain a minimum of personal liberty. Management and union check and balance each other.

This is not to advance the notion of violence for violence' sake or to say that unlimited antagonism is desirable. Rather, it is to argue for the golden mean, for some reasonable combination of conflict—even aggressive conflict—and co-operation between the extremes of anarchy and complete collaboration, and to argue against the view that there should be a unitary solution to the worker-management relationship, that a monistic organization including both is desirable, and that conflict should be entirely suppressed. Limited antagonism serves a social purpose.

OBSERVATIONS. If industrial conflict is natural, if it may take several forms, including aggressive ones, and if, in reasonable amounts and restricted expressions, it serves the welfare of society, then certain conclusions follow.

1. There are no utopian solutions which will bring universal industrial peace through better understanding and more effective systems of communication, through the application of the science of semantics to clarify the meaning of words, even through better mediation machinery or more skilled mediators, or through any other special device.[8]

---

[8] In fact, misunderstanding and the misuse of words have probably made a substantial contribution to industrial peace. If the parties had more often fully appreciated each other's motives, there would undoubtedly have been more conflict than has been the fact, and a barrier of imprecise language has often kept the parties from lunging at each other's throats.

2. If industrial dissatisfaction cannot be entirely suppressed in the long run, then a realistic choice should be made as to the forms of its expression. In the industrial field, collective bargaining and its natural companion, the normal strike, are probably the most satisfactory forms. They take place in the open and can be handled effectively and in a disciplined fashion between the two parties. A conflict of this sort is more subject to compromise than one on a larger scale in the political arena—more subject to a definitive solution than organized absenteeism or restriction of output or sabotage. Industrial conflict should be accepted as a natural concomitant of an industrial society and should be channeled along constructive lines.

In summary, there are real sources of conflict in an industrial society of managers and managed; these sources of conflict can find an expression in actions of semi-independent interest groups in a democratic nation; some of these expressions are aggressive in nature in the sense that they are intended to coerce the opposite party; such aggressive expressions and their availability make nonaggressive forms of conflict more effective in settling disputes, and, additionally, the fact of aggressive conflict and its accessibility eases social tensions. But conflict may be destructive, as well as constructive, and thus it needs to be guided if the social fabric is to be protected and serious injury to individuals and groups avoided.

In industrial relations, where they must live together indefinitely in some degree of conflict, the parties almost universally establish, formally or informally, some rules of the game to limit the conflict, or they accept establishment of such rules by the state. These rules normally protect the survival of both parties, reduce the potential injury to each, introduce some predictability into their actions, and protect third parties from undue harm. The employer, for example, may forego the use of strikebreakers, the discharge of strikers, or the blacklist. The union may forego sabotage, the boycott of products, or violence against officials of the company. Together they may limit the initiation of conflict to stated intervals or to stated subjects, and they may specify the successive steps it will follow. The state may intervene to forbid violence or to enforce contracts during their term of life. The development of these rules is of the greatest importance, and in time they tend to grow more complex and rigid, until conflict may become quite stylized and perhaps even ceremonial. Such fully developed rules remove much of the cost to the parties and much of the impact on the public at large. Warfare is neither constant nor unrestricted.

These responses to conflict affect mediation in at least two ways. First, mediation appears always to be successful. Given the necessity, and usually the urgent necessity, of agreement, since aggressive conflict is so costly to both sides, all disputes end at some point, and all strikes are concluded. Perhaps no agency of government can post such a record of constant success as its mediation service, and few mediators even fail. Contrariwise, mediation might be said to make little or no contribution in the sense that all disputes would be settled sometime without outside intervention. In fact, there is no accurate quantifiable test of its efficiency.[9] Second, much mediation, where relations are well established, is quite ceremonial. The mediator enters the case as a matter of established practice or as proof proffered by the leaders to their constituencies on both sides that they carried on a bona fide dispute and did not yield too soon or too much. In either event, the participation of the mediator may be quite perfunctory. Mediation is part of the game but not an essential part.

TACTICAL MEDIATION

Guidance by a third party to an acceptable accommodation is the essence of mediation, which thus stands midway between conciliation, that is, adjustment of a dispute by the parties themselves, and arbitration, that is, decision by a third party. Mediation, in its traditional sense, involves the intervention of a third party into a particular dispute, and this participation of a third party in a situation which is already given will be called "tactical" medi-

[9] For attempts to measure the effectiveness of mediation see Arnold M. Rose, "Needed Research on the Mediation of Labor Disputes," *Personnel Psychology*, Autumn, 1952. See also J. W. Steiber, *Ten Years of the Minnesota Labor Relations Act* (Industrial Relations Center Bull. 9 [Minneapolis: University of Minnesota Press, 1949]).

ation. "Strategical" mediation consists, instead, of the structuring of the situation itself, of the creation of a favorable environment within which the parties interact. The purpose of tactical mediation is to bring existing nonviolent conflict between the parties to a mutually acceptable result so that there will be no need for it to become violent or to end violent conflict by agreement or by transfer to nonviolent means. Strategical mediation aims instead at reducing the incidence of conflict and channeling it along nondestructive lines of development.

Tactical mediation is a particularly appealing method of reducing industrial conflict. It is simple to apply. It relies on persuasion rather than on force. It is almost universally supported, at least at the verbal level. But what contribution, in fact, can a tactical mediator make to the resolution of a conflict which the parties cannot provide for themselves? The parties will usually be more familiar with the situation and will have the greater incentive. Viewed analytically, the following are the major potential contributions.[10]

1. REDUCTION OF IRRATIONALITY. The mediator can bring the parties toward a more rational mood by giving the individuals involved an opportunity to vent their feelings to him, by keeping personal recriminations out of joint discussions, and by drawing the attention of the parties to the objective issues in dispute and to the consequences of aggressive conflict.[11]

---

[10] This discussion will deal with an analysis of the mediation process. It will not describe legal mechanisms or actual techniques. A particularly helpful recent discussion of mechanisms and techniques is found in Elmore Jackson, *The Meeting of Minds* (New York: Harper & Brothers, 1952). For a discussion of techniques see also Rose, *op. cit.;* E. L. Warren and I. Bernstein, "The Mediation Process," *Southern Economic Journal,* XV, No. 4 (April, 1949), 441–57; F. H. Bullen, "The Mediation Process," *Proceedings of the New York University Annual Conference on Labor,* 1948, pp. 105–43; and John T. Dunlop and James J. Healy, *Collective Bargaining* (rev. ed., Homewood, Ill.: Richard D. Irwin, 1953), chap. iv.

For a study relating the mediator's personality and background to the mediation process see Irving R. Weschler, "The Personal Factor in Labor Mediation," *Personnel Psychology,* Summer, 1950.

[11] Sometimes, however, the mediator may encourage settlement by inducing an irrational desire on the part of the representatives for agreement through the use of all-night sessions or of liquor, for example.

2. REMOVAL OF NONRATIONALITY. The mediator can aid the parties in reaching a full appreciation of reality by clarifying the intentions of the parties toward each other, the issues in controversy, and the pertinent facts and by leading each party to accurate calculations of the cost of aggressive conflict and of the prospective results of such conflict. Quite commonly, each party, particularly when collective bargaining is new to it, underestimates these costs and overestimates the potential gain. The mediator can often bring a truer estimate of the strength of the opposite party and a truer expectation of the outcome than is available initially.[12] While it is not normally too difficult to assist the leaders in these realizations, the task of reaching the constituencies on both sides is often an impossible one. The constituencies may come to recognize reality only through the fire of combat, for the endurance of a strike often serves an educational purpose. It is one of the functions of a strike to raise the calculation of cost and reduce the prospect of gain. The intervention of a mediator is sometimes timed to correspond with the growing recognition of true costs and realistic prospects.

3. EXPLORATION OF SOLUTIONS. Not only can a skilled mediator help the parties explore solutions which have occurred to them independently, but he can create new solutions around which positions have not yet become fixed.[13] In collective bargaining, as elsewhere, there are several means to the same end, and some of these means will be less abhorrent than others to the op-

[12] The mediator, however, is unlikely to be interested in removing nonrationality in those cases in which one or both parties has overestimated the strength of the opponent or has underestimated the potential result. Furthermore, he normally wishes to encourage an exaggerated estimate of costs and a minimal estimate of gains. In other words, his goal is a peaceful settlement, not the removal of a non-rationality in the parties, although the latter, in the standard situation, conduces to the former.

[13] George W. Taylor has emphasized the "art of proposing the alternate solution" as the crucial part of the mediation process. The skilful application of this art also involves assistance in the "graceful retreat" (see below), which Taylor has termed bringing about a "consent to lose." (See "The Role of Mediation in Labor-Management Relations" [address at a conference of regional directors of the Federal Mediation and Conciliation Service, Washington, D.C., June 23, 1952], pp. 15 ff., and "Instead of Strike-bargaining," *New York Times Magazine,* July 6, 1947, p. 27.)

posite party. The mediator can assist in finding those solutions in which, for a given cost to one party, the advantage of the other is maximized, or, phrased reversely, in which a certain gain for one party can be secured at the minimum cost to the other. The exploration of solutions is generally most effective before the positions of the parties have become strongly solidified. It is particularly difficult to mediate disputes when the parties have rationalized or theorized their positions or have tied them in with a general ideological orientation. They are then not practical problems but matters of principle.

4. ASSISTANCE IN THE GRACEFUL RETREAT. All, or almost all, collective bargaining involves some retreat by both parties from their original positions. The union normally asks for more than it expects ultimately to receive, and the employer offers less than he expects ultimately to concede. There are at least two major reasons for this. First, neither party is likely to know exactly what the best offer of the other party will be. Thus it is only prudent to make one's own original demand well below or well above the most likely level of concession of the opponent to avoid any chance of having foregone a possible gain. Second, to insist to the end on the original proposal is almost an unfair labor practice, under the rules of the game, for it denies the other party the opportunity of forcing some concession and thus claiming a victory of sorts.

Normally both parties must retreat from their original positions, and much of the fascination of collective bargaining is in the tactics of retreat. Each party seeks to discover and profit from the best offer of the other without disclosing and having to concede his own. The mediator can assist the retreat in at least three ways. First, he can call the parties together. Particularly when a strike is in process, neither side may wish to request negotiations for fear it will betray a sense of weakness. The mediator can help avoid such embarrassment by issuing the call.

Second, the mediator can act as a go-between on the making of offers. Not only is it unwise to retreat a step without getting the other party to retreat a step also, but any open retreat at all may be unwise if it appears that no agreement may be reached, for then the parties may wish to resume their original positions unencumbered by face-to-face concessions. The mediator can help control the pace of retreat, for, if one party initially retreats too rapidly, the other may miscalculate the ultimate stopping point, and, in trying to push too far, cause aggressive conflict. Moreover, the mediator can speed up the retreat for both sides by making it more revocable, since he, rather than the parties themselves, seems to be making the suggestions. The more revocable a concession, the easier it is to make. The mediator makes it possible for the parties to yield without seeming to yield and thus to disclose their true positions to each other without being eternally committed to them. Each offer, after all, is presented as the "last offer," not as the "next to last" offer, and there is no point in prematurely becoming committed to the truly last offer unless it is necessary and will settle the controversy.

Third, he can help "save face." The mere entrance of a mediator is a face-saving device. In collective bargaining there are no really objective tests of the performance of the representatives of each side, yet their constituencies seek to test them, and they seek to justify their stewardship. Appearances thus are important. One proof of capable stewardship in negotiations is that the results are as good as or better than those achieved in similar situations elsewhere; another is that concessions were wrung from the opposite party; another is that an elected negotiating committee participated in the negotiations; and another is that the controversy was so hard fought that a mediator had to be brought in.

But a mediator may do more than put in an appearance: he may make recommendations, perhaps even public recommendations (as in the case of a so-called "fact-finding board").[14] A party can sometimes accept such recommendations, particularly if they come from a person of prestige, when it could not make a similar offer itself or accept such an offer from the other party.[15] The mediator shoulders some responsibility for the result, and the responsibility

[14] Advanced forms of mediation approximate arbitration, just as arbitration of disputes over new contractual arrangements (as contrasted with grievance disputes) often takes on many of the aspects of mediation.

[15] "Agreement" requires that both parties reach the same point in their concessions to each other. "Acceptability" only means that they are close enough to a point set by a third party so that they will not revolt against it. The range of "acceptability" may, of course, be wide or narrow.

of the representatives is consequently lightened. The bargaining positions and arguments of the parties are preserved more intact for the next conflict. The public normally lends its support to third-party recommendations, and this makes their acceptance also more accountable. Such recommendations may even be privately handed to the mediator by one or both parties, with the comment that they will be acceptable if the mediator will take public responsibility for their suggestion. Defeat or partial defeat at the hands of a third party is more palatable than a similar surrender to the second party.

5. RAISING THE COST OF CONFLICT. A mediator may also raise the cost of conflict to one or both parties as an inducement to settle by bringing or threatening to bring public wrath down on their heads, by persuading their allies to withdraw their support, by threatening retribution (or reward) from government or customers or some other source, by going behind the backs of the representatives to reach and influence the principals in favor of a settlement. But these tactics are not normally pursued and are usually reserved for only the most crucial cases of great public concern. The mediator masquerades as a friend of the parties, and particularly of their representatives, with whom he has face-to-face dealings, and these are the acts of an enemy. Moreover, no mediator who employs such tactics is long acceptable as a mediator.

Some disputes are not subject to a mediation settlement short of aggressive conflict, regardless of the skill of the mediator. There are situations where aggressive conflict has positive values in itself—where there is some institutional gain from such conflict, such as a larger or more devoted membership; where the leaders need an external war to improve their internal positions; where one or both parties want to "burnish the sword"; where, as Pigou notes,[16] an employer may wish to use a strike to get rid of excess stocks or may encourage a strike during a slack period so that one during a peak period will be less likely; where an employer uses a strike as an excuse for raising prices or for withholding produc-

[16] A. C. Pigou, *The Economics of Welfare* (4th ed.; New York: The Macmillan Company, 1950), p. 454.

tion until a more favorable tax period arrives; where one or the other party seeks to further some end external to the relationship —it might be political, or it might be the union leader's need for an occasional strike to encourage the sale of "strike insurance"; or where a strike is desired as a relief from tension. A strike for strike's sake must run its course.

A particularly difficult controversy to mediate, strangely enough, is one in which the costs of aggressive conflict to each party are enormous.[17] Then any one of many solutions is better than a strike, and the process of narrowing these possible solutions to a single one is an arduous task.

While several important types of dispute are not susceptible to effective mediation at all, short of aggressive conflict, mediation does undoubtedly settle some controversies peacefully.

THE CONTRIBUTION OF TACTICAL MEDIATION

Mediation, undoubtedly, does make a substantial net contribution to the reduction of aggressive industrial conflict, but this does not mean that it does so in every case: indeed, it may even increase the propensity to strike. It may encourage a strike, of course, where an unskilled mediator serves only to turn the parties more against each other or to obscure solutions; but it may do so also when the mediator is skilled, for he may aid the parties to fight, as well as to retreat, gracefully. (The sophisticated negotiator is more likely to need help to fight gracefully under certain circumstances than to retreat gracefully under the same circumstances.) If the public is opposed to strikes and may take action against them, the participation of a mediator in a dispute may convince it of the good faith of the parties' attempts to reach a settlement, making the public more tolerant of a strike and thus making it easier for the parties to strike; or, if a strike is in process, the entrance of a mediator may forestall more drastic public intervention and thus make it possible to strike for a longer period.

Likewise, if a strike serves a leadership but not a membership

[17] *Ibid.,* p. 354.

purpose,[18] the use of a mediator may help convince the membership that the leaders made a determined effort to reach a settlement, when in fact they did not, and thus ease membership acceptance of strike costs. This ruse will not be successful if the membership is sufficiently sophisticated, but this is very seldom the case.

The mediator has been employed in both situations as a device to make the situation appear different from what it really is, to camouflage true intentions, to mislead the public or the members. This is "for-the-record" mediation. . . .

The mediator may be an unwitting party, in the hands of skilled practitioners, to this deception, but he may also participate willingly, for basically he works for the representatives of both sides, not for the principals or for the public. It is the representatives with whom he associates and from whom he expects acceptance. But in some cases, particularly those of vital public concern, the mediator may go behind the backs of the representatives to reach the principals (or, in the case of the union, also to higher levels of the union organization) and encourage them to press their representatives for a peaceful settlement; or he may go over their heads to the public to exert pressure for settlement, by, for example, attacking the stubbornness of the representatives of one or both parties. . . . The former is particularly difficult, however, for it involves a partial or complete repudiation of the representatives. The latter is especially effective in a culture, such as that of Germany, which places great stress on law and order and great reliance on public authority, and, conversely, it is less effective in the United States.[19] Where the public is unconcerned about a strike or is concerned but is unable to take effective action or where the

[18] This assumes, of course, that there is a "membership purpose," but the membership may be and sometimes is so divided in its desires or interests that no single membership purpose can be said to exist.

[19] Mediation occurs at four levels of intensity: (1) where the mediator convenes the parties and transmits their offers back and forth (often called "conciliation"); (2) where the mediator makes suggestions and raises considerations on his own; (3) where the mediator makes public recommendations; and (4) where the mediator tries to manipulate the situation against the wishes of the representatives.

membership has no control over its representatives, the mediator, of course, has no recourse beyond the representatives themselves. . . .

More common are the situations in which the mediator can aid the leaders or members or both toward a more rational position or can bring skill beyond that available to the parties in making proposals or in aiding the retreat. . . .

When a member joins an organization, he does so, in part, to purchase rationality and skill not otherwise available to him. If this purchase were always a successful one, mediation would be largely unnecessary. It finds its justification basically in the failings in this act of purchase—leaders are not skilled or are not rational or are not representative, or the members do not believe them if they are.[20]

There is no convincing evidence that tactical mediation has had much of an effect in reducing the totality of aggressive industrial conflict. Strikes seem to go their own way, responsive to other, more persuasive forces. To understand the role of tactical mediation, we must thus examine not only the internal characteristics of situations but also the external environments within which they arise.[21]

[20] This leadership-membership relationship is a difficult one, at best, for, if the members are not themselves rational, they can hardly know whether they did, in fact, purchase rationality, and, if they are rational, the purchase may be unnecessary. The former is the more common case and helps explain the usual skepticism and cynicism of the members vis-a-vis their representatives.

[21] Proposals for strengthening the effectiveness of the mediation process have generally been concerned with recommendations which are confined within the tactical-mediation orbit. Establishing orderly organized-procedure arrangements or fixing a definite time period as appropriate for mediation ("after collective bargaining has ended in disagreements and before a work stoppage has begun"), as Leiserson, for example, has suggested, could at best reflect in the efficacy of tactical mediation but could not circumvent the inherent limitation of tactical mediatory practice per se. (See William M. Leiserson, "The Role of Government in Industrial Relations," in *Industrial Disputes and the Public Interest* [Berkeley and Los Angeles: Institute of Industrial Relations, University of California, 1947], and his presidential address before the Industrial Relations Research Association, "The Function of Mediation in Labor Relations" in L. Reed Trip [ed.] Proceedings of the Fourth Annual Meeting of the Industrial Relations Research Association, 1951).

359

STRATEGICAL MEDIATION

A strike is not an isolated event, a solitary episode. It occurs within a given social context, a surrounding economic and political environment. The major variations in the incidence of such conflict relate not to the efficacy of the direct ministrations to the conflict, such as tactical mediation, but to the total milieu within which it arises. Fewer strikes are experienced in Sweden than in the United States, and fewer in the garment industry than in coal-mining, not because tactical mediation is more skilled in Sweden than it is in the United States or is more skilled in one industry than in another, but rather because of the differing surrounding environments. Aggressive industrial conflict varies greatly from nation to nation, industry to industry, firm to firm, and time to time. Which situations are most conducive to nonviolent, and which to violent, conflict?

Strategical mediation is concerned with the manipulation of these situations and thus with factors quite external to the parties themselves.[22] From one point of view, society is a huge mediation mechanism, a means for settling disagreements between rival claimants—taxpayers and recipients of benefits, buyers and sellers, proponents of opposing political ideologies—so that people may live together in some state of mutual tolerance. Some societies mediate their disagreements, through their markets, their courts, their political processes, more effectively than do others. Society in the large is the mediation machinery for industrial as well as other forms of conflict.

Two recent studies demonstrate the crucial relationship of the

[22] Intermediate between tactical mediation and strategical mediation lies "preventative tactical mediation." It takes for its province more than the individual dispute but less than the total relevant environment. It deals with the relationships of the parties in general. It may be concerned with a long-run change in the attitudes of the parties toward each other or toward their mutual problems, with the nature of the leadership on one side or another, with the pressures to which the parties may be subject, with the timing of contract expiration dates, or with the alliances of the parties. It seeks to manipulate the parties and their relationships in advance in favor of nonviolent conflict.

environment to industrial conflict. The first[23] investigated the strike proneness of industries in eleven nations and found that some industries (like mining and longshoring) universally evidenced a high propensity to strike and others (like clothing and trade) a low propensity. The second study[24] summarized the environmental characteristics of a series of industrial plants in the United States noted for their industrial peace and concluded that these plants all fell within a definable environmental setting. Drawing on these two studies and, among others, on recent ones by Ross and Irwin[25] and by Knowles,[26] the social arrangements which seem in the long run generally most favorable to nonviolent industrial conflict, within the cultural context with which we are here concerned, may be set forth as follows:

1. INTEGRATION OF WORKERS AND EMPLOYERS INTO SOCIETY. To the extent that workers and employers consider themselves primarily citizens with roughly equal status, privileges, and opportunity, the sting is taken out of their relationship. The greater the social mobility, the more mixed in membership the various social associations, the more heterogeneous the community's occupational composition, the more accepted the institutions of workers and the greater their participation in general community life, the

[23] Clark Kerr and Abraham Siegel, "The Inter-industry Propensity to Strike—an International Comparison" (to be published by the Society for the Psychological Study of Social Issues, in a volume on Industrial Conflict, edited by Robert Dubin, Arthur Kornhauser, and Arthur Ross).

[24] Clark Kerr, "Industrial Peace and the Collective Bargaining Environment," published by the National Planning Association as part of its final report in its series on "Causes of Industrial Peace."

[25] Arthur M. Ross and Donald Irwin, "Strike Experience in Five Countries 1927–1947: An Interpretation," *Industrial and Labor Relations Review*, April, 1951, pp. 323–42. See also comment by Adolf Sturmthal (pp. 391–94) and rejoinder by Ross (pp. 395–98) in the April, 1953, issue of the same journal.

[26] *Op. cit.* See also his paper presented to the Second Congress of the International Sociological Association, Liege, Belgium, August, 1953, "Strike-Proneness and Its Determinants" [which appears in this issue.—Journal Eds.]. Another paper presented to the same congress by Harold L. Sheppard, "Approaches to Conflict in American Industrial Sociology," suggests that only those studies of industrial conflict which take account of the broad environmental milieu can be productive of fruitful generalization.

more secure the worker in his job and the higher his skill—the less violent will be the industrial conflict in the long run.

2. STABILITY OF THE SOCIETY. The incidence of strikes is directly related to major changes in the operation of the society—particularly to the business cycle and to wars.[27] Each major economic or political change creates a new situation for the parties, and they must adjust their relationship to it, often in a trial of strength. Similarly, unusually rapid growth or decline of an industry or technological change in it is likely to raise problems in a form which invites a violent solution. The parties normally can adjust more peacefully to gradual than to precipitous change.[28]

3. IDEOLOGICAL COMPATIBILITY. The attitudes of people and groups toward each other and their over-all orientation toward society affect industrial relationships. Where people believe in brotherly love or the equality of man, for example, their disagreements will be fewer, less sharp, and more amenable to easy compromise. Where, however, they believe in the inevitable opposition of classes, in the rapacity of other men, then violent industrial conflict is more likely. The perspectives of men, it should be noted, are not unrelated to their actual experiences in their social environments. The close co-operation of leaders of industry and labor in the Netherlands during the German occupation in World War II, for example, has been a source of their intimate relations since then.

4. SECURE AND RESPONSIVE RELATIONSHIP OF LEADERS TO MEMBERS. For the minimization of violent industrial conflict, it is desirable that leaders be (a) relatively secure in their positions and (b) responsive to their constituencies. Security of position, on the

[27] See Sheila V. Hopkins, "Industrial Stoppages and Their Economic Significance," *Oxford Economic Papers* (new ser.), June, 1953, pp. 209–220, for one of the more recent of the many studies which note the tendency of fluctuations in business activity to affect the frequency and duration of industrial unrest.

[28] See Robin M. Williams, Jr., *The Reduction of Intergroup Tensions* (Social Science Research Council Bulletin No. 57), pp. 56–58, where the propositions that "intergroup conflict is the more likely the more rapid and far-reaching the social changes to which individuals have to adjust" and that "conflict is especially likely in periods of rapid change in levels of living" are singled out as significant factors in the incidence of hostility and conflict.

union side, for example, means lack of intense rivalry for leadership and solidarity of the organization against defection of its members or attack by a rival group. When the leaders are under pressure directly or indirectly, they may respond by encouraging an external war. Vested interests in conflict may be particularly damaging when the leaders make the decisions but the members pay the costs. Under these conditions the leaders will seek to assure the irrationality or nonrationality of the members.

At the same time, leaders should be responsive to their constituencies; otherwise, they may make aggressive use of the organization as a means to an end external to the life of the organization, or by their neglect they may encourage internal revolt with its repercussions. It is relatively easy in many mass organizations for the leadership to exploit the membership in one fashion or another. The proper combination of security and responsiveness of leadership is not always readily attainable, for these two requirements point in somewhat contrary directions.

5. THE DISPERSION OF GRIEVANCES. The mass grievance, one which is held by many people in the same place at the same time against the same antagonist, grows and feeds on itself. Society can more readily accommodate and adjust the small grievance.[29] Thus it is helpful if discontent can find several outlets—individual quitting of jobs and political expression, for example, as well as organized economic action; if it is directed against several individuals and groups—the merchant, the landlord, the state, for example—rather than against an employer who also provides housing, retail facilities, and law enforcement; if it coagulates into small lumps by craft, by firm, by industry, rather than over the

---

[29] "A society riven by many minor cleavages is in less danger of open mass conflict than a society with only one or a few cleavages. . . . In the most extreme case of mass violence: An essential step in the development of revolution is the gradual concentration of public dissatisfaction upon some one institution and the persons representing it" (quoted from L. P. Edwards, *The Natural History of Revolution* [Chicago: University of Chicago Press, 1927], p. 46, in Robin M. Williams, Jr., *op. cit.*, p. 59). Williams points out further that "the reduction of intergroup conflict depends upon . . . proper canalization of existing hostilities, through sanctions, diversions, redefinition of situations, etc." (p. 62).

whole society; if it finds expression a little at a time, rather than in a single explosion; if it can be blunted by the imposition of relatively impersonal laws and rules standing between the parties on the basis of which decisions can be made which flow not alone from the parties in controversy but from less volatile sources; if it finds expression in several stages through appeal or through periodic reopening of questions and if it seldom encounters a final barrier to its voicing; if freedom to act and react is constantly preserved. At the opposite extreme is the mass grievance against a single source of power, subject to a single personal decision.

6. STRUCTURING THE GAME. As we have seen above, rules which reduce the risks of the parties and limit the means they may employ, without unduly stifling the conflict, can make a substantial contribution to nonviolent resolution of controversy or can mitigate the destructive consequences of violent conflict. Rules which guarantee the independent sovereignty of each party, which raise the cost of fighting (as does multiemployer bargaining),[30] which set some fairly precise norms for the settlement (as does the "pattern bargain"), which prohibit use of certain provocative means of combat, which limit conflict to intermittent periods, which confine the subjects for disagreement to some reasonable area at any one time —all aid the nonviolent settlement of industrial disputes. The rules of the game aid rationality—knowledge of costs and consequences—and thus diplomatic resolution of controversies. Fortunately, in industrial relations, contrary to international relations, these rules are enforcible by society if not accepted by the parties voluntarily.

These are not easy prescriptions, although all of them are potentially subject to some utilization—not, however, in totality by any single "third party" or even by a single institution. Strategical mediation relates to an over-all community approach to its organization and to the handling of its problems, and to a general philosophical orientation toward the management of the affairs of men.

---

[30] A high degree of horizontal and vertical integration of worker and employer interests does not, however, prevent strikes. Witness, for example, the largest strike in Swedish history—the metal-workers' strike of 1945.

CONCLUSION

Industrial conflict, then, may be affected in three crucial ways: (1) by reducing the sources of mutual discontent; (2) by affecting the process by which decisions to act are made, either (a) by reducing the power to make such decisions (through control of one party by the other or both by the state) or (b) by facilitating the making and implementing of decisions to act nonviolently; and (3) by channeling the conflict along the least destructive lines. Tactical mediation is concerned with 2b; strategical mediation, with 1 and 3. It is suggested that the latter, by the advance creation of favorable situations, can make the greater contribution to the minimization of aggressive industrial conflict and particularly of its most socially harmful aspects.

THE PROBLEM OF DUAL ALLEGIANCE

T. V. Purcell

The worker is involved in a system of dual allegiance. He is both an employee of the company and a member of the union. He must identify with both. His work attitudes are influenced in various ways by both. On a broader level, industry must face the task of integrating the plant community (the local union and the local plant) with the company and union power centers above it.

. . . The purpose of this research was "to see how the dual presence of company and union affects the work attitudes and motivations of the worker as member of both, of his immediate superiors in each, and thus to find what basis the worker offers for harmonious opposition." Of the three basic questions that we formulated, the first two were the most important:

I. Will the average worker actually have dual allegiance to, or satisfaction from, both company and union?

Note: See Notes on the Authors, page 556, and item 182 in the bibliography for the full reference to this selection.

II. Will the worker have allegiance which is necessarily dual, in that he says his wants can be satisfied only by both organizations?

These questions inquire whether the worker at the plant level will be favorable to both his company and his union as institutions. The second goes beyond the first to ask whether or not the worker is convinced that both organizations are necessary to satisfy his needs in the industrial plant community. We saw the answers to these questions gradually evolve as we listened to the men and women of the plant community, and we found that most of the workers say they want both company and union. We saw who has dual allegiance and who has not.

The third question helps us focus more sharply on the nature of dual allegiance and the possible threats to its existence in the plant community:

III. Will the worker's allegiance to one of the two organizations in the plant community pull him away from the other organization, thus straining his dual allegiance, or will the allegiance he gives to one organization not noticeably affect the allegiance he gives to the other?

The purpose of this question, as we said, is to help us find out whether one or the other of the two organizations competing for the favor of the worker may be pulling him away from the opposite one, even though the over-all fact is the existence of dual allegiance. We want to know whether or not dual allegiance in the Swift-UPWA plant community is under stress and strain and whether or not the two parties are pulling it apart to any degree.

The facts do not support completely either alternative presented in this question. In other words, dual allegiance is not under a strain for many workers, but it is for some. We have seen that the two groups of people in the plant community officially identified with the two organizations, the foremen on the one hand, and the stewards and union leaders on the other, are among the least favorable people in the community to the opposite organization. These men have strong allegiance to the organization they represent and this, along with the official role they play, tends to draw them away from the opposite organization. For them we can say: Their allegiance to company (or union) tends to diminish their allegiance to union (or company). For them, their "mother" organization tends to alienate their favor to the other. I say "tends," because most of them do have allegiance to both organizations.

For example, the comments of some of the foremen with unequal allegiance are like this: "It's been my experience that we were treated fair and square without a union." "If you have good supervision, a union is not necessary. When I worked in the gang I was well treated." "Swift is a good company; they would give those benefits anyway." These men have strong confidence in the company and its good intentions, but their company allegiance is no greater than the average of the work force. Why is their union allegiance less than this average? Not because of their greater favorableness to the company but because of the official role they must play as foremen, a role that occasionally brings them in conflict with union officials.

The stewards and union leaders, though they have company allegiance, are the most union-minded and the least company-minded of anybody in the plant community. Their strong union identification undoubtedly holds in check their favor toward the company. For example, steward Richard Rex, a staunch advocate and antagonistic to the company, makes much of the fact that "Our foreman has fought the union in every way possible. . . . It's company policy to fight the union because the company backs up the foreman.". . . If Rex were not such a union man, he would not resent so much the alleged action of the company. His strong union allegiance leads him to lesser company allegiance. He does not want challenged the organization that is dear to him.

As to whether the rank-and-file work force is affected by the competition of company and union for their allegiance, the answer is that the pull of the company seems to attract a few workers, but not most, from full allegiance to the union. Likewise, the pull of the union affects the company allegiance of some.

We must therefore conclude that dual allegiance is under some strain for the foremen and local union leaders and stewards, but for the work force in general, we find that certain clusters of workers give evidence that their allegiance to one organization tends to pull them away somewhat from the other—more away from the union than from the company. These clusters are especially the long-service women and the short-service men (therefore of opposite sex and length of service). They represent about one-third of the work force. There may be others so affected. We estimate that at least one-third, but not more than one-half of the Swift-UPWA people are affected by the opposing pulls of company and union.

IMPLICATIONS FOR SOCIAL AND INDUSTRIAL PSYCHOLOGY

It is time to make explicit the meaning of our findings for the psychology of industrial relations. As a science concerned with people in their social relationships, social psychology asks two key questions: "What do people think about each other and why?" "Why do they act the way they do?" Social psychology is principally concerned with peoples' attitudes and their formation, and their motivation. We shall apply our findings to these two theoretical categories, principally to check the validity of accepted theory against the concrete detail of people in everyday work situations not always reached by psychological test, experiment or clinic.

The Complexity of Attitudes. We saw that the worker's attitudes toward an institution, a race, a job, a fellow-worker, or a foreman may be at times quite definite and simple, yet often they are highly complex. Sometimes they are contradictory, like those of the man who said: "I like the union and I don't." Sometimes they include real loyalty, or emotion or ego-involvement; sometimes they are simply dry approval. Sometimes they affect behavior greatly, depending on their volitional and emotional content; sometimes they affect it very slightly; but always they have some effect upon it, and always they are important.

Influences on Attitudes. We are as interested to know why a man thinks the way he does, as what he thinks. The influences affecting the work attitudes of Swift-UPWA people are intriguing and limitless. We have isolated a few of the most important ones. We have seen how the worker's company allegiance affects his union allegiance, and vice versa, in the data referring to our third question. We have seen how the past history of social relations in the plant community, and how the neighborhoods, wages, contract, production methods, and so on, affect attitudes.

We have seen other attitudes influence allegiance to the company, such as one's attitude to his foreman, his job, pay, gang, working conditions, but just as important, we have seen that the worker's attitude toward the company as an institution is a distinct attitude which the worker himself distinguishes, for instance, from his attitude toward his foreman: "It's not the company, it's the people." We saw a similar pattern for the union.

The influences of sex, race, and service over the attitudes of working people we have studied in detail. We are not surprised that these variables, differentiating a man's personality and social environment, should also influence his attitudes. We were especially interested to see how these variables actually work, and how they are inevitably related to other variables. Do Negroes want a union that protects their racial status? Of course. But not all Negro workers are union-minded. We have seen that other factors influence their attitudes. The long-service colored women, for instance, are quite indifferent to the union as an institution. Indeed, if we do no more here than bring out the fact that not all the people of any group think alike, that neither union, management, men, women, colored nor white are monolithic in their attitudes, we have helped a bit to dispel the stereotyping that the lazy human race likes to stamp upon itself.

Attitudes and Motivation. The relationship between attitudes and motivation or the needs, wants, fears, and ambitions of the worker comes strong in our findings. Because of the ebb and flow of work, the worker needs the security of steady employment in order to support his family and live decently without fear of creditors. A primary reason for his favorable attitude toward Swift & Company is that the company provides him with a secure and steady job. And because the American worker is a human being and needs recognition, status, a say in things, and dignity, like anybody else, he has a favorable attitude toward the union primarily because it gives him the protection, status and, more fundamentally, the dignity he wants.

Attitudes and Behavior. We saw especially the influence of work attitudes on behavior toward the union, toward joining the union and toward participating in it. We found that the union allegiance attitude of the Swift-UPWA people has a definite influence on their union behavior. But we also found that their union allegiance and behavior toward the union are not the same thing. We found a variety of attitudes from very favorable to very unfavorable among people who participate slightly in the union. And among those who have union allegiance we found many degrees of actual participation-behavior in union affairs. Yet we also found some definite association between union allegiance and union participation.

Finally we might ask: How does the dual allegiance that we found affect "dual behavior" toward company and union, when leaders of each are in sharp opposition? If that opposition arises because one organization challenges the existence or basic objectives of the other, then the workers will either strike or scab. For dual allegiance does not necessarily mean exact obedience to the commands of either organization but rather approval of the existence, basic objectives, and over-all policies of both. The workers do not want to see their dual government threatened. They will strike if the company tries to put the union out of business. They will scab if the union tries to put the company out of business.

Strikes or scabbings over "immediate" collective bargaining issues (not involving the existence or objectives of either institution) may arise from time to time. Dual allegiance will not entirely prevent nor perfectly predict them. The workers of the Swift-UPWA plant community very probably had dual allegiance when they struck in 1946 over issues they believed in. They certainly had dual allegiance in 1948 when many of them scabbed over issues they did not believe in. Today in 1953 they are generally satisfied with conditions and would oppose a strike. What might happen in 1963 is anybody's guess. Of course the relative amounts of company and union allegiance possessed by the workers would influence them to strike or to scab, though factors quite apart from allegiance would have a more important influence: the workers' opinion of these "immediate" issues, their fear of picket lines, reprisals or scorn of fellow-workers, or their fear of losing their seniority or jobs.

But to repeat, the main behaviorial fact flowing from the dual allegiance which we found is that the workers want their two-in-one government intact and will act accordingly! They want management to give their union its right to equal voice in determining working conditions. "Without a union, there's not anyone to speak for your rights. . . . If you got union, you got leader. He go to see Big Mens in office." They want the union to give their management its right to manage. "The union should be fifty-fifty for company and union . . . the foremen should have a say too!" They will oppose either one in its attempt to undermine the other. They strongly resent a struggle for existence between the two organizations they support. It would be well for both management and labor leaders to recognize this dual allegiance if industrial peace is to be advanced.

Attitudes and Rationality. In our listening to the people of the Swift-UPWA plant community we remarked at frequent intervals how reasonable, fair-minded, dispassionate, and objective the workers could be in their perceptions, judgments, and reasoning. We also noted that emotional, nonlogical motivation at times does influence and distort their attitudes and judgments. But the point is—and it needs to be said—the workers are often very rational indeed in their attitudes. By "rational" we mean simply that emotion, bias, prejudice, motivational need do not greatly distort or twist the worker's perception, judgment, or attitude from a close connection with objective fact and objective evidence.

Some psychologists and sociologists have exaggerated the very real influence of "drives," "urges," and "unconscious motives" to the denigration of man's capacity and desire to reason logically. But men like Bartlett have well brought out man's striving after meaning. And Pareto puts as one of his strongest "residues" the residue to make "derivations," that is, to make sense. Our findings agree.

For example, when a man joins Local 28 not because he has something against the company, but because he wants protection against being "kicked around by the foreman," because he wants some say in the governance of the community in which he works, because basically he wants to express the dignity he believes he has—then the words nonlogical, emotional, are inadequate to describe his behavior, though some emotion may enter into it. Quite possibly in his mind the worker even makes a syllogism about his decision to join the union, as he did implicitly in more than one interview: "I want job protection, the help of someone to look out for my interests, and some voice around here. The union is a help in that. Therefore, I want the union."

Even if the worker joins the union from fear of scorn or violence, as a minority do, he is doing something not only emotional, but also rational. He wants to live with the people of his department in peace. If he has to pay union dues to get that peace, he will pay.

The Manifest and Latent Content of Attitudes. The distinction between what appears on the surface of a worker's attitudes and what may sometimes lie beneath, was well brought out by Roethlisberger and Dickson. It is a basic part of psychological theory and we came across it from time to time in the plant community. Many complaints about the operation of the Standards wage-incentive system, as we developed them at length, rest basically on the worker's dissatisfaction with being a machine tool of mass production. This distinction between the manifest and latent content of attitudes must be made cautiously. Analysis of the total interview helps to make it.

Implications of Our Findings for the Theory of Motivation. As we listened to the people . . . we asked as we went along: What are their basic work needs, fears, wants, ambitions? The answer should help us to clarify psychological motivation theory, and also to understand better the nature of harmonious opposition in the American plant community. Here is what we found:

SOME WANTS *of some or many workers:*	SOME FEARS AND AVERSIONS *of some or many workers:*
Steady work, without layoffs or reduction of hours.	Being out of a job with almost no savings and constant expenses.
A foreman "who leaves you	Arbitrary discipline by foreman,

| SOME WANTS | SOME FEARS AND AVERSIONS |
| (*Cont.*) | (*Cont.*) |

alone," "who doesn't stand over you," "who listens."	"getting pushed around."
A clean job, not too wet, nor too cold, nor too hot, nor too dusty.	"Arthritis" or ill health allegedly caused by working conditions.
More pay.	A cut in the wage rate, or more commonly a cut in hours worked.
A chance to be a skilled butcher or a craftsman.	The frustration of doing a routine unskilled job all their lives.
A chance to be a foreman.	
Their children to go elsewhere and get a "better" job.	Advancement ceilings due to race.
Recognition for work well done.	Constant rising prices, especially food and rent.
Answers to their requests for a raise.	The subtle "superiority attitude" of some whites.
Advancement for the Negro race through themselves or even through another.	The "aggressiveness" of some colored.
Better understanding of wage-incentives.	"Not the company, but the people."
A union.	Radical union leadership that will "kill the goose that lays the golden egg."
A chance to go to the "Big Boss" through the grievance procedure.	Scorn of fellow-workers if they do not join the union.
A steward who is "intelligent."	That company is not primarily concerned with their interests —so they belong to union.
Union leaders to "work along" with company.	
Company to "work along" with union.	That dual allegiance will be split.
Dual allegiance to be had in the plant community.	That they'll "work themselves out of a job."
The company really to accept the union.	That the union is getting too strong [Supervision].

These wants and fears are more or less reciprocal. Our lists are neither complete nor logically arranged. They are simply a brief suggestion of the basic forces exerting a directive and dynamic influence upon the people of the Swift-UPWA plant community. These are real wants and not fictitious ones. And the worker will strive to gratify them, by one means or another. The industrial relations and institutions of the community must take account of these wants and build upon them. In turn, the worker's fears and aversions are highly real to him. Sound industrial relations and union policy will try to reduce such fears as far as possible.

. . . We have seen how peoples' wants differ from each other. We have watched the influence of race, sex, and service, the influence of the foreman and steward roles. We saw the high morale of Swift top management so conscious of the Swift family spirit and Swift leadership. We saw the desire of the assembly-line worker for a steady job, some security and dignity. Occasionally we saw conflict in motivations: "As a foreman I'm not so favorable to the union, but as a man I am." We saw the worker who wants to be a loyal union man cross the picket line because the 1948 strike is long and his family in need. We have seen how these motivations are affected by attitudes, and affect them in return, how they influence behavior—behavior that sometimes seems incomprehensible to the man with different needs. Finally, we have seen how reasonable many of these wants and fears really are. Of course it is not easy to put one's self in another fellow's shoes and take on his wants and fears. No one can do it perfectly. But understanding those wants and fears is the first step. Understanding plus a measure of empathy will go a long way toward a betterment of social relations of the plant community.

Finally, while we have analyzed the people of the plant community into their attitudes, motivations, allegiances, for the sake of scientific understanding, we realize that no analysis gives a perfect picture. That is why we have always tried to show the interrelationship of these psychological abstractions.

AREAS FOR FUTURE CONSIDERATION

Our investigation of the past and present industrial relations in the Chicago Swift-UPWA plant community leads us toward certain observations which may promote greater dual allegiance, loyalty, and harmony in the plant community. These are made with full awareness that it is the people of the plant community who would

374

have the practical task of working them out. They may be tabulated as follows:

FOR THE COMPANY	FOR THE UNION
(1) Basic Attitude. With trust and good faith, let all management grow in full internal acceptance of the union as a good and even as a necessary institution in the plant community.	(1) Basic Attitude. Let the union rid itself of its minority of Marxist, left-wing leaders [Local 28, at least, did this in the 1953 elections], and with trust and good faith, view the company as a partner and not an enemy or a threat.
(2) Accept the union as a legitimate partner in the plant community, and give its affairs normal place in company publications.	(2) Periodically stress the members' obligation toward the company to do a fair day's work, etc.
(3) Consider giving additional union security (perhaps of the compromise type in the GM-UAW contract), as a practical demonstration of the company's acceptance of the union.	(3) Encourage steady, responsible leadership by reducing factionalism.
(4) Consider joint labor-management committees with the union for study of wage-incentives, work-simplification, etc., giving full access to the facts and agreeing to protect the worker's position by contract guarantees.	(4) Agree to form with the company joint educational committees for time study, work simplification, etc., with the contract guarantees [building on the safety committees already set up].
(5) Provide a company meeting-room, or time off, or pay to the union stewards for their own program of steward training.	(5) Accept the company hall and/or time for union-steward training programs, without charging company paternalism, thanks in part to union security.
(6) Consider advancement of qualified Negroes into Chicago plant supervision and office.	(6) Encourage white participation in the local by maintaining balance of white officers [attained in 1953 elections], and by less frequent and more persuasive talk about Negro rights.

375

For the Company (*Cont.*)	For the Union (*Cont.*)
(7) Revise Standards payments so that the employee is paid on 100 per cent of the work units he produces over 60, instead of on 75 per cent. [Beginning with the 1952 contract this was done.] Continue the present foreman-training in the Standards System and extend it as far as possible to hourly-paid.	(7) Consider moving the UPWA District One Hall back near stockyards in a neighborhood equally acceptable to whites and colored.

The mutual dependence of these observations is nowhere more complete than in the first basic attitude necessary for both union and company, an attitude of trust and good faith. Without this, none of the other practical ideas are likely to be made operative.

On management's part, the growth of this attitude will mean acceptance of the union as a legitimate and even a necessary partner, and not merely a *de facto* power group. On the union's part, this growth will certainly mean ousting its Communist minority for whom good faith in the company is a denial of dogma. Moreover, it will mean for the unionists no more suspicion and fear that the company is trying to undermine the union allegiance of their fellows when it takes an interest in its employees and even in the union. The plant community is much influenced by the International UPWA, and unfortunately the UPWA in recent years has been beset by factionalism, communism, and distrust. Until the International UPWA can rectify and stabilize itself, the rest of the suggestions are simply ephemeral.

Without a doubt observation (3) on additional union security is controversial. There are many forms of such security. Perhaps the compromise form adopted by General Motors and the United Auto Workers might be considered here. Under this arrangement, present members of the union must continue in the union, as a condition of employment. Nonmembers shall not be required to join, though anyone who does join must remain in. New employees must join the union for one year. After this time, they may withdraw from the union, during a two-week period. If they do not withdraw, they must remain in the union from then on.

Many conditions of employment are now set unilaterally by management: a man may not work in the Swift-UPWA plant community unless he has a certain degree of health, unless he wears a white coat if his job requires it, and so on. The various forms of union security may be considered as other conditions of employment. If the union is a legitimate bargaining agent for the workers, possesses good leadership for the most part, does not discriminate against its members, and if the majority of its members want the union shop, there can be, on principle, no valid argument against it. The argument against it in practice might become valid, if one of the above conditions were not verified.

The need for a reasonable degree of union security in the Swift-UPWA plant community emerges out of [our] findings . . . , for again and again our data point to it. The union leaders complain frequently of the "free riders," employees who are glad to get the benefits of collective bargaining, raises, fringe benefits, but who are unwilling to pay dues to and support the union which is in part responsible for their benefits. To the union man, this disloyalty is a constant irritation. He will never be at peace with it. In addition, the considerable turnover in the plant community and in the packing industry also leads to free riders. The steady influx of new employees means that Local 28 must constantly sell itself and the union movement to these people. Therefore it will stay in the somewhat insecure state of perpetual organization with much of the aggressiveness of its old organizing days of the late thirties, when the local was struggling for its existence. Can we expect a high degree of industrial harmony under these circumstances? Some people complain that union leaders are not mature, that they behave like aggressive organizers instead of administrators. The answer is that employee turnover forces them to remain organizers.

Our data have shown us the clear and pronounced union allegiance of the Swift-UPWA workers. We have seen that this allegiance grows out of the needs of the worker and is not just imposed by demagogues. If some women and old-timers fail to have this allegiance, the GM-UAW compromise formula exempts them from joining the union. The union allegiance of the great majority of the workers indicates that a union has a definite place in the plant community.

What about our finding of low worker-participation in Local 28's affairs? Would the GM-UAW formula increase participation? Generally when people pay dues to an organization they are more likely to take part in it. The nonparticipant free riders lead the way toward encouraging general nonparticipation.

Some of the insecurity of Local 28 and UPWA leaders may well arise because they wonder whether Swift has really accepted their union. Union-management coöperation in the fields of steward training and time-study may be facilitated under some more tangible form of union security.

When we asked a certain UPWA leader about steward training on company time, we recall his answer: "No. It would be too close to the company. It would be company-dominated. The union would be called a company-union by the rest of the unions. I can't help feeling that a man is controlled by where his money is coming from." This brings out the interdependence of the above observations. Steward training (5) depends on union security (3), and this in turn depends on trust and good faith (1), especially with respect to the left-wing element of the UPWA.

Observation (4) recommending joint union-management committees of time study and work simplification is also merely utopian without additional union security. We recall that Swift made this offer, and the offer was rejected by the UPWA. We heard another UPWA leader say that he would not accept Swift's offer to study the Bedaux System because: "I might have to tell someone to work faster. And that's no good!" And we recall the wise comments of Golden and Ruttenberg of ten years ago regarding wage rates, and applicable just as well to incentive payments: "Certainly a union is not free to adjust a member's rate downward when, as a consequence, he can immediately quit the union and agitate for other members to follow his example."

Above all, additional union security might help the UPWA to realize that it has "arrived," and that it is wanted. Such union security might well win real labor-management coöperation from the UPWA. We realize that such security is a matter for national bargaining as it affects the entire Swift chain and not simply the Chicago plant community, and that it is subject to various state laws. Only the two parties involved will know best the time and manner of its implementation.

Labor-management committees (4), merits special comment. The possibilities for fruitful coöperation by joint UPWA-Swift committees for work simplification and time study are tremendous. The mere fact that in many industries during the second World War such committees did not work is not proof that they cannot work. The fact that Swift and the UPWA have just established joint safety committees in their 1952–1954 Agreement is a hopeful sign for the future.

. . . One of our findings is that the mass-production revolution is a covert cause of discontent and frustration in the plant community. An important step toward the solution of this twentieth-century American problem can be taken through labor-management committees, in which the worker has a chance to participate, to contribute his finger-tip knowledge of the job toward plans for incentive payments, for job simplifications and method of improvements. It is possible that the worker will develop a creative interest in his work and in his department through these committees, that will offset the repetitive machine-tool work now being demanded of so many Swift-UPWA men and women.

Furthermore, the chance for increased productivity through these committees is great. As we saw, nobody knows the job better than the man doing it, not even the foreman. The workman can see short cuts, time-saving and work-saving methods undreamed of by the engineer. Let us put it bluntly: Swift has not even begun to tap the talent of its workers, including its unskilled common labor. But with an insecure union and an insecure worker, such coöperation must remain forever untapped. That is why, in addition to growth in trust and good faith, guarantees will need to be written into the Swift-UPWA contract. A man who makes a labor-saving suggestion needs to be guaranteed that he will not suffer through downgrading and less hourly pay as a result. Possibly the guarantee would be that his successor in the job would receive the lower rate, but that his rate would be preserved. Admittedly, there are many practical problems involved in the spelling out of such guarantees. But mutual good-will should solve them.

Finally, we shall discuss only three other observations, those involving racial relations, (6) for the company, and (6) and (7) for the union. . . . For Swift management, surely a more aggressive and far-sighted program of trying to improve interracial relations would be wise. An important part of this program will be the full incorporation of qualified Negroes into the ranks of supervision, and into foreman-training programs. The *Swift News* from time to time could explicitly treat interracial questions in the effort to educate both white and colored people to live and work together as the UPWA *Packinghouse Worker* has done. The *News* for years has been trying to educate Swift workers against socialism, so this would not be something entirely new.

For Local 28, observations (6) and (7) are simply two of many possible explicit measures that might increase white participation in union affairs. Since the field work was done . . . , the new right-wing officers of Local 28 already have a better balance of white and colored. While it is not desirable, by any means, that the union give up its talk about Negro rights and interracial relations, if this talk is less constant than it was under the Communist aegis in 1950, and persuasive rather than aggressive, it will probably have greater success. Both colored and white union leaders should be aware that there are two sides to the race question, with faults on both sides, though the predominant unfairness must be laid at the door of the whites. Racial relations in Local 28 and the plant community are greatly affected by the general race and housing picture in Chicago. Local 28 and the UPWA cannot be expected to solve all the problems in Chicago. There are other organizations for that. But if the union can go on improving the interracial work relations of its members, it will be doing a good service.

Finally, we can hardly overstress the mutual interdependence of these suggestions. They are like a circle. They can become a vicious circle unless both company and union are daring enough to apply several of the ideas at the same time. Fearfulness will not conquer the throttle grip of a vicious circle; only courage on both sides can transform these conflicts into the state of harmonious opposition which is at present the highest aim of the industrial plant community.

MUTUAL SURVIVAL

E. Wight Bakke

Basic issues in labor management relations arise from the fact that each group is concerned primarily with its own individual welfare and interprets the actions of the other as a threat to its own survival. Under such conditions, coöperation is difficult. Therefore, industrial warfare will plague America until leaders of both labor and management understand and respect the survival needs of each. The goal must be mutual survival.

Industrial warfare will plague America until leaders of labor and management understand and respect the survival needs of each other. Management has deep convictions, born of experience, about the "principles of sound management." Labor leaders have deep convictions, born of experience, about the "principles of effective unionism." Each is convinced that if he compromises his principles he encourages a threat to his own survival. Many labor leaders believe that if unions become the kind management labels "sound," they will cease to be "real" unions. Many employers believe that if management yields much more to union pressure, it will cease to be "real" management. That belief keeps both in a fighting mood basically. Each group sees in the attitudes, actions, and policy of the other a threat to its own survival.

I am not talking about physical survival. That alone isn't what men are willing to fight for in a civilized community. They

Note: See Notes on the Authors, page 551, and item 13 in the bibliography for the full reference to this selection.

will fight to preserve the familiar opportunities for reaching their goals: the respect of their fellows, economic security, control and independence, understanding, and integrity. They will fight to preserve in traditional form the kinds of organizations and institutions which provide them with those opportunities. They will fight for the privilege of continuing to act as they always have acted, in ways which their group considers effective and proper. They will fight to preserve the ideas, the symbols, the ritual which re-enforce such behaviour and make it "right" in their eyes. The survival of this whole structure of living is what men mean by survival.

When that structure is threatened, they do not want peace until the threat is removed. That is the basic problem. Why? Because men will not cooperate with those whose actions, they believe, threaten their survival. They may have the skills and the brains to cooperate, but they will not use them for that purpose. Because arrangements for reducing conflicts through collective bargaining haven't a chance to succeed unless they are consistent with the jobs both management and labor leaders have to perform. Because agencies such as mediation and arbitration boards will not be used willingly and with confidence unless their activity is compatible with doing those jobs well. Because codes and laws will be resented at best and short-circuited and disobeyed at worst if they do not meet the fundamental survival needs of those whose actions are governed.

The basic issue in labor-management relations at the moment then, arises from the fact that each party is concerned primarily with its *individual* survival. Its attention is focused on the means to that end. The leaders of each group are trying in every industrial negotiation and every political maneuver not merely to solve a specific problem. They are trying to solve it in a way that preserves their own structure of living intact. They are expecting peace on terms consistent with the maintenance of their own sovereignty. Preoccupied with that expectation and the effort to implement it, they have forgotten a very fundamental truth: that sovereignty in a democracy must be shared, not exclusively possessed by a particular group. Many have neglected the fact that partnership is essential to a democratic relationship in industrial as in political and family life; and that if one would be a partner, the other partner's interest must become one's own, at least to that degree which permits cooperative effort toward a common goal.

This does not mean that the individual interests of the parties must be identical or even that there must be no conflict between them. The achievement of peace and workable arrangements in labor-management relations is not premised upon the immediate disappearance of conflict. It is not unreasonable to suggest, however, that the conflict can be conducted in an atmosphere of mutual respect without resort to the methods of open and violent warfare.

The difference in interests among workers, union leaders, and management is rooted deeply in the objectives, responsibilities, functions, and traditions of each; it arises from a difference in economic and social status to preserve or improve which the parties have developed different ways of life, supported by different philosophies, folklore, symbols, slogans, and codes. Even when they use the same words, the meaning for each differs, for the meaning is built from the facts of life which each experiences. When management, owners, union leaders, and workers use the words "wages," "production," "profits," "justice," and others, they fill the words with content that bears the mark of their own way of living. The conflict over wages, for instance, is not merely a battle over a particular rate, but a competition among three patterns of life in one of which wages are items on the cost sheet, in another are the foundation of living, and in the third are one focus of a service rendered. But such differences and conflicts need not lead inevitably to open warfare.

Peace in industrial relations is best defined, in Sumner's phrase, as a state of antagonistic cooperation. Although pursuing each his own interest, the parties recognize their mutual dependence upon each other, agree to respect the survival needs of the other, and to adjust their differences by methods which will not destroy but rather improve the opportunities of the other.

The conditions required to accomplish such a result are many and complex. . . . I have discussed only one. But I think it is basic. It is this: that each party shall understand thoroughly the

383

kind of a job the other has to do, his convictions about what is necessary if he is to do that job well, the way in which the nature of the job and those convictions impel him to act as he does; that each shall see to it that his action, based on that understanding, does not threaten the survival of the job or the organization with which the other identifies himself.

Understanding the behaviour of the other party does not imply the necessity for approval. One need not, and probably cannot, approve all he understands. But to know why the other behaves as he does is to be armed with useful knowledge upon which intelligent action can be based. In the day-to-day development of workable relations between management and labor it is far more important for each to know *why* the other behaves as he does than to have convictions about how he *ought* to behave. The *why* in terms of the compulsions placed upon him by the nature of his job and his structure of living represents facts which are as realistic as a payroll or a power line. Knowing such facts as they are, not as one would like them to be, is the first step toward achieving industrial peace.

It is only the first step; but until it is taken, the nature and direction of further progress cannot be determined intelligently. The adjustment itself which must be made in thousands of individual circumstances is the ultimate necessity. It will test the realism of the knowledge each party has of the facts which determine the action of the other. It will demonstrate whether both really want peace consistent with those facts. It will challenge the best skills and wisdom that practical men have. It will prove whether civilized men in labor and management can supplant the techniques required for *self-survival* through domination with the skills and wisdom required for *mutual survival* through cooperation.

The task is hard, but not impossible. The chances for success are reflected in the satisfactory relations of thousands of managements and unions over the country. Whether or not they develop the will to succeed is not a matter of choice for union leaders who desire the survival of free unions and for management leaders who desire the survival of free management. For the result of failure to work out the means of *mutual survival* will not be the elimination of one by the other, but the elimination of both as free institutions by public regimentation. Never were the words of the sage more applicable than to all leaders of labor and management in twentieth-century America, "No man liveth unto himself."

THE FUTURE OF INDUSTRIAL CONFLICT

Arthur Kornhauser

It appears that in a free society there is no end to industrial conflict. Two opposing views seem to exist with reference to the future: one view stresses a trend toward a more stable, orderly dealing with conflicts; the other emphasizes the dynamic aspect of industrial conflict. Both views are important. The future is not settled; rather it is still in the making. Therefore, we must be open-minded in the weighing of alternative futures for industrial conflict.

These . . . comments may well begin with the reminder that industrial conflict has its psychological roots in the beliefs people hold regarding their own interests and the ways in which their goals can best be achieved. Many industrial workers in our society are not fully satisfied with the rewards and the conditions of their employment and with their lives as wage earners. Even among those who are not actively dissatisfied, large numbers believe that they can better their position through organized pressures as well as by individual efforts. Correspondingly, many owners and managers feel that they cannot live and work as they should, that they cannot satisfactorily perform their functions of operating profitable and enduring enterprises, if they submit to the pressures and acquiesce in the expanding demands of working people. In this basic sense, it appears that, in a free society, there is no end to industrial conflict.

The extent and nature of the conflict, its intensity, and the ways

Note: See Notes on the Authors, page 554, and item 130 in the bibliography for the full reference to this selection.

it is manifested and resolved depend upon the influences that shape people's desires and expectations, the gratifications and deprivations they experience, the social sanctions for particular kinds of conflict behavior, the disapproval of other types, and the social machinery evolved for dealing with conflicts. The future course of industrial conflict must be estimated with due reference to all these complex social determinants. Students of labor affairs inevitably differ in the weight they attach to the several influences and in their reading of expected change or absence of change in these influences.

Two principal orientations can be distinguished among the diverse views: One stresses the trend toward progressively more stable, regularized, institutionalized industrial relations, in which conflict is dealt with in a steadily more orderly manner. The other view emphasizes the dynamic factors that constantly produce new strains in modern society, new turns to group power relations; it points to the changing, emergent quality of personal motivations and of institutions and accordingly sees industrial conflict itself undergoing irregular changes and unruly phases—encountering lulls and accelerations and shifts of direction rather than proceeding along an established course. Obviously there are many degrees and variations of these two views and many intermediate positions, but the simplified contrast will serve to bring into focus some important unsettled questions about the future of labor-management relations.

The first view seems to be growing in popularity, that is, the belief that union-management relations have now entered a period of maturity and stability, under businesslike collective bargaining arrangements, and that this relationship is destined to undergo smooth progressive improvement. Some social scientists go farther and see a drift toward unification of management's and labor's efforts, leading to greater and greater cooperation, teamwork, and harmony. Under both these conceptions, government is assigned a relatively minor role. Unions are perceived as fitting into the industrial system as it now is, with no essential change in the organization of industry or the power positions of the parties. There is much to support these views. The extension of stabilized collective bargaining to ever larger sections of American industry has certainly represented a major trend in labor-management relations. It is reasonable to suppose that continued institutionalization along present lines may, indeed, prove to be the main course of the future. . . . It is wise, nevertheless, to recognize that this emphasis may be overdone, to the neglect of other quite different developments affecting industrial conflict.

A contrasting interpretation holds that forces are at work in our society which may disrupt current patterns of labor-management relations and produce conflict over an expanded range of political as well as economic issues. Not that the growth of collective bargaining will cease or diminish in importance, but it needs to be seen in a larger sociopolitical setting. According to this view, there are no fixed goals or "proper" areas of concern for labor; working people's organizations will adapt to the wants and expectations of their members and to the dominant internal and external pressures affecting the group and the leaders at the time. Similarly, management, if conditions are favorable, will employ a dynamic strategy and endeavor to improve its position by changing some of the rules of the game which are currently in effect. The labor-management conflict relationship, it is suggested, is such that it will tend to break through any fixed, neatly circumscribed limits. Both the forces within industry and those in the larger society tend constantly to create new strains and set up new tensions. Moreover, the day-to-day conduct of union-management affairs increasingly extends into the community—in the form of educational, propaganda, public-relations, and political efforts by both parties. To confine discussion of industrial conflict to the direct dealings between managements and unions *in industry,* according to this conception, is bound to produce a false and misleading picture of the processes at work. Industrial conflict is still *industrial* conflict even when the battle is waged on the political and communications front.

The central aim here is to call attention to the challenge presented by this second interpretation, since the considerations that it stresses tend too often to be neglected. The questions asked in this section are intended particularly to suggest that the future in respect to industrial conflict may not be so settled as much present-day thinking pictures it.

In many labor as well as management circles, it is unpopular to point to divergent group interests, problems of changing power relations, and the importance of political action in industrial affairs. Such emphasis smacks of class consciousness and foreign labor movements. Within this climate of values, there is a disinclination to weigh possible alternative conceptions of organized labor's role in reference to industrial conflict. To raise questions like those that follow . . . is often viewed as equivalent to *advocating* the unpopular position. What is less clearly seen is that failure to raise the questions is equally to be an advocate—but of the accepted "going" views. It is not my purpose to plead a case for any particular interpretation or any particular path to be taken by union-management relations. It *is* my intention to advocate open-minded weighing of alternative futures for industrial conflict, the influences making for one or another trend, and the considerations that may lead people to choose one course or another.

That one's own value premises affect the points he elects to stress is undeniable. But this is a universal phenomenon. A principal purpose of this section, in fact, is to point up the value issues that all must face in pursuing studies of labor-management relations and in arriving at answers in regard to industrial conflict. To ignore the issues is to adopt a restrictive frame of reference that itself goes far to predetermine the conclusions.

It should be clearly stated that the aim here is not to predict what *will* happen any more than it is to prescribe what *should* be. No implication is intended that only one answer can be given to the questions asked below. The questions are rather to suggest that the future of industrial conflict is in significant measure undetermined and that we must be wary of social-science predictions that assume a fatalistic continuation of whatever trends are now exhibited. More analytical studies of psychological and social determinants are required. The following questions simply indicate some of the factors to be taken into account in such further studies.

1. Will the economic demands of workers and their organizations remain within "reasonable" boundaries, and will unions ac-

cept a role of "mature," "responsible," businesslike negotiating, with power relations and rules of the game remaining essentially as they are; or is it to be anticipated that labor groups from time to time will try to break through the fences and seek to change the rules and relative power positions by resort to tests of strength? The question is really whether an essential function of unions is to push for gains that reach beyond those that can be achieved without coercive influence; whether, by its nature, a union is impelled to press for "more" when in a strategic position to do so; and, hence, whether strong unions are likely indefinitely to fit into a relationship of prolonged stability.

The question is not whether new points of dispute will occur between unions and companies; this is assumed to be true. It is also certain that many of the new issues and demands will be amicably settled through bargaining, with or without an occasional well-controlled and not too damaging strike. But the all-important additional question is whether "fighting" issues will continue to arise which may *not* be handled so smoothly. Will unions and managements try to reach for gains that cannot readily be accommodated within the existing collective-bargaining system? Will battles occur to change old norms and assumptions governing the relations of the parties? Will there be struggles over reforms that transcend businesslike bargaining in particular companies? A philosophy of settled and stabilized relationships implies a continuation or, at most, a gradual evolution of laws, regulations, and assumptions concerning collective bargaining; but such a philosophy might not survive efforts to change the old norms drastically.

2. Are working people and their organizations likely to confine their demands to the familiar economic gains, or will their aims expand and produce increased conflict over non-economic demands that management will perceive as threatening its prerogatives and freedom of action? If further economic gains from the individual firm should grow less obtainable and if changing conditions accent intangible social and personal deprivations, the latter could assume new saliency and emerge as new sources of contention. What we know of human motivation—the variety and complexity of wants, their constant redefinitions and shifts of intensity under

changing social influences, and the manifold interferences they en-counter—strongly suggests a continued tendency for demands to spread and give rise to new conflicts. In a society which attaches central importance to its democratic values and which insistently stresses ideals of personal worth and human dignity, individual development and self-expression, and rights of equal treatment and participation, it appears probable that unsatisfied aspirations will continuingly be aroused that may be channeled into pressures for industrial change—change beyond that dictated by economic considerations and beyond that willingly tolerated by management except under compelling pressures.

Most important, perhaps, is the question of whether demands will grow for effective participation in decisions and sharing of responsibility at the work-group level. Will there be demands for increasing independence and democratic rights in industry to par-allel those enjoyed as citizens in the community? And beyond the confines of the shop, will the future witness expanding expectations in regard to social-security measures, medical care, and improved opportunities for education, housing, recreation, and whatever else the common man may come to feel is his due? Will such expanding demands or the prospect of their occurrence bring counter-moves by business to restrict and "contain" unions—moves that in turn may precipitate new conflicts?

3. A further set of questions may be asked in regard to influ-ences affecting unions as institutions: Will the public and political pressures of the years ahead tend to make for continued "limited-function," job-centered unionism or for a broadened range of aims and activities? Traditional business unions, working directly in the self-interests of their members, run athwart the interests of various other groups. The problem becomes more serious as unions grow larger and more powerful. The union is feared and damned for its militancy and social irresponsibility; it is viewed by many as a self-ish interest group that threatens the general welfare. As such it be-comes a political target and is likely to be subjected to stricter political control in the "public interest."

The question then arises whether the union, under such pres-sures from public opinion and government, must either retreat from vigorous pursuit of its aims or advance by expanding its activities to make them better accord with what the unorganized public conceives to be the common welfare. This latter course might mean a type of unionism that would continue to work for direct economic benefits for its members but would strive at the same time to help members meet their personal and social needs, in and out of industry, and would join with other groups to secure governmental and community action in the interests of all working people. The possibility is suggested that labor organizations may increasingly come to believe that, by extending the unions' horizons and functions, they can escape the politically vulnerable position created by the pursuit of narrow self-interested objectives under the conditions of their new size and strength. Conditions in the larger society may induce major labor groups to adopt the view that the wise course for them is to battle not merely each for its own special group but for the welfare of working people and the society as a whole. There are many signs that this changed outlook has already impressed itself on the thinking of important labor leaders.

4. A final question, which I believe deserves vastly greater attention than is usually accorded it, has to do with public opinion and the social values that are held in respect to labor-management relations. The questions may be stated in this way: To what extent will organized labor increase its efforts to balance and offset what many labor leaders believe to be a predominantly business-oriented control of the news, ideas, and interpretations that are circulated? Will influence exerted by business in shaping public opinion through control of mass media and through pressures on schools, clergymen, writers, and other opinion leaders be felt as a serious threat to labor unions, their continued growth, and their bargaining effectiveness? If so, will this aroused concern lead labor organizations to attempts to combat the one-sided influences, as they see it, and to provide the public with other information and alternative views more favorable to union efforts and to social changes in the interests of working people? In a word, may we expect to see intensified industrial conflict on the level of political action and psychological warfare? Will sophisticated labor and

business leadership increasingly perceive their long-run relations as largely determined by public opinion (including workers' opinions) and its political expression, and will their conflicting goals, accordingly, be sought largely through contending efforts to win moral approval and support in the public mind?

These questions of how greatly labor-management relations are affected by the prevailing value structure, thought patterns, and social outlook of the times and of how these orientations are influenced and changed may turn out to be the most crucial considerations determining the course of labor relations. Yet it is these very matters that are ignored or assumed to remain constant in many over-all prognoses concerning labor-management affairs. From the standpoint of organized labor, the issue is whether emphasis on the collective-bargaining function alone, without attention to public opinion and political influence, might mean that bargaining would tend more and more to be conducted within an atmosphere and a legal framework thoroughly in accord with management views and devoted to preserving management rights unmodified. If unions should become the predominant power in public influence, the shoe would, of course, be on the other foot—but the essential fact would remain that basic elements of industrial conflict would be carried on outside the industrial sphere. The question, then, is whether organized labor and employers will feel that collective bargaining is not enough and that it is only as dependable as the state of opinion, law, and politics permits it to be.

For labor leaders, these same issues may take this form: Will labor leaders predominantly strive to gain prestige and power by winning *public* support—frequently in opposition to corporations —or by winning acceptance and backing of the companies with which they deal? Will working people and the public see the latter type of relationship as effective, realistic labor leadership, supportive of the American way of life, or will it be stigmatized as "sellout," weakness, and "collaboration?" Either *could* happen. It will presumably depend on future economic and political conditions— and especially on the social interpretations that become current. The latter brings us back once more to the importance of the ideas that are communicated in the society, the values that are inculcated, and the alternative views that are circulated.

Not only labor-management relations but the course of our sociopolitical life in general may be determined in great measure by the answers to these questions having to do with public opinion. From a broad social standpoint, the question is whether large-scale corporate business and organized labor will, each in its own interests, exert influence curtailing and balancing any disproportionate concentration of social power in the hands of the other. The exercise of such offsetting group influence may well be indispensable if freedom of inquiry and discussion is to flourish, if our society is to search freely for new and better answers to our social and economic problems, and if non-conformist thinking is to be encouraged or even tolerated when it takes directions distasteful to an established elite.

The foregoing questions point to some of the social and psychological factors that may prominently influence the course of industrial conflict. Analysis of the influences, rather than leading to fixed predictions, emphasizes that the future is still in the making. Industrial-relations trends will depend upon the shifting forces at work and on the emergent aims, convictions, and action programs they evoke. The task of inquiry and reflection is to help delineate the alternative roads open, the influences favoring one or another alternative, and the probable consequences of moving in each direction. In the light of such knowledge, it is for the groups concerned (potentially this includes everyone) to choose the road they prefer to follow and, within the limits of their democratically exercised power, to try to shape social policy accordingly.

In addition to underscoring the indeterminateness of the road ahead, our analysis again calls attention to the fact that conflict of aims is deeply rooted and enduring and that it is an essential feature of the employer-employee relationship, viewing industry as a whole. The opposition stems from the firm determination of those at the top of the economic pyramid to protect their interests (and the general welfare as they see it) against the threatening gains of working people striving for a larger share of the good things of life—including a greater measure of participation and influence through labor organizations and through government.

To suggest, however, that industrial conflict may continue to wax and wane, to break out of each newly achieved period of equilibrium, to spread to fresh areas of contention—to mention these possibilities is by no means to deny that industrial conflict has been undergoing significant constructive changes. A great deal of evidence reported . . . testifies that orderly procedures for dealing with conflict have been on the increase and that resort to violence has sharply declined. It is reasonable to anticipate a continuation of this long-run tendency for union-management conflict to grow more institutionalized, more fully subject to formal and informal social controls. But this is not to forecast harmony in the more general relationships of organized labor in the society. The trend toward more strictly controlled conflict may indeed enlarge the areas of controversy, since it acutely raises the wider questions of who controls the social controls and whether industrial relations are being institutionalized in a pattern less congenial to one side than to the other. In short, conflict relations may tend to subside on the industrial front while becoming more intense in regard to political issues and efforts to win public support and favorable governmental action.

A main thesis here is that industrial-conflict trends cannot be properly appraised if they are viewed only in the perspective of direct union-management dealings and disputes over economic and job-centered gains. While it seems reasonable to believe that the future may witness gradual extension of union activities into the government of industry, with an accompanying development of constructive collaboration between unions and management (though with continuing conflict as well), at the same time, struggles over social policies and political power intimately affecting union-management relations may become the new storm centers.

It has been suggested that pressures are operating that may impel unions to pursue their goals on the broad sociopolitical scene as well as in industry itself. The future role of unions and, hence, the outlook for labor-management relations are likely to depend on how citizens as a whole come to answer the basic question: Are strong labor unions, independent and able to exert economic and political influence opposed to that of big business, essential for the nation's democratic progress? Are expanded union activities needed as a check on business power in the decisions of industry and government, or does a satisfactory balance now exist? If such questions are answered in a manner that implies a continuation of group conflict, then that condition may have to be accepted as part of a vigorous democratic process. The goal must then be conceived not as labor-management harmony but as progressive improvement in which all people's interests are fully represented.

Since so much of [what has been said] concerns itself with the organized and formal expressions of conflict between unions and employers, it should again be emphasized that there is need for giving full recognition to the many other manifestations of conflict between working people and the owners and managers of industry. In weighing alternative interpretations of trends, there is scant justification for looking only at organized union and management activities. A wide range of informal, unorganized, and individual conflict behavior remains. . . . Even if formal union-management relations were to be thoroughly regularized and handled in the most peaceful and coöperative manner, industrial conflict would persist in other of its myriad forms. Directly or indirectly, individuals will find expression for their frustrations and hostilities and their unfulfilled aspirations—both those engendered by their industrial situations and those displaced upon industry. Unless our institutions undergo revolutionary changes, much of the dissatisfaction and effort for group improvement will continue to be directed against the owners and managers of industry. The basic problem will exist as long as there are felt oppositions of interests and goals arising from people's differing economic roles in the industrial society.

Finally, I believe that we must recognize the heavy responsibility upon social scientists who deal with a problem such as that of industrial conflict. The fact cannot be side-stepped that social scientists not only describe, analyze, and interpret; they inevitably also influence the processes which they report. Wittingly or unwittingly, those who write . . . have some impact on the interpretations that are accepted in the larger society and on the social behavior that ensues. Scholarly writings become part of the context that helps sanction or condemn conflict and that leads the public to believe in harmony and cooperation or to look further and ask what price harmony; to feel that a satisfactory balance has been reached and that industrial rights and power relations should be maintained essentially as they are or that processes of change should go forward to more satisfying accommodations of divergent interests. It is reflections like these that have dictated efforts . . . to look at industrial conflict from different standpoints and with frequent warnings against too hasty or too firm commitment to particular answers. The search for better answers is a never-ending one. Acceptable conclusions will be those hammered out by the whole society.

Chapter 8

INDUSTRY, SOCIETY,
AND THE BUSINESS
EXECUTIVE

INTRODUCTION

The role of the big business leader is too often conceived *in vacuo* or at best confined to the economic limits of his company or his industry. This oversimplification of the problem occurred partly because the economists by their early start preëmpted the scientific field and because the novelists and early muckrakers wrote "biographies" about the titans of industry in terms of individual morality. The economic determinism of the Marxists, classical economists, and liberal intellectuals helped create a climate for these conceptions when other and more comprehensive theories were available.

The businessman and his enterprises, it should go without saying, live in, and are influenced by, the larger society of which they are no more than important parts. What the executive role is and how he rises to power may more often be determined in the private conversations of kinsmen and clique-mates. Moreover, the definition and control of the role of the business leader varies according to time and region. Business enterprise and business leaders may be something quite different within the business traditions and social systems of the South from what they are in New York or Boston.

The advantages of examining the role within several contexts—the community, the United States, and Western civilization—as well as the sophistication and insight gained by the use of several disciplines are clearly demonstrated in Mr. Lamb's selection. The effect of the powerful traditions of a region on business enterprise and its leaders is of great importance. The relations of the development of the managerial role to the increasing complexity of the division of labor and its significance to the community and nation should also be underscored. Some of the theoretical implications of these several parts for our understanding of managers are indicated in Elton Mayo's "rabble hypothesis." The selections previous to his in this chapter are theoretically founded on the assumptions of society and culture being present and dominant. Mayo demonstrates the fearful consequences of conceiving man only in the image of the separate economic individual in an economic aggregate without the sustaining forces of society to guide him and the overriding beliefs and values of culture to contain and nurture him. Such men, in Mayo's belief, are "the rabble" who without meaning and form can become the simple digits, the meaningless items of the all-powerful totalitarian state.

THE LOWELLS AND THE EMERGENCE OF AN AMERICAN MANAGERIAL ELITE

Robert K. Lamb

Robert Lamb brilliantly traces the history of a great business family in America and demonstrates the need for the use of several disciplines, including economics, social history, and anthropology, to understand the meanings of executive life. (May we add a personal note: Lamb's early death is a cause of personal sorrow and professional loss to all of us.)

Note: See Notes on the Authors, page 554, and item 133 in the bibliography for the full reference to this selection.

Entrepreneurial studies need to advance simultaneously from two ends, taking the development of the whole community—in its time and space dimensions—as the largest unit, and an individual decision as the smallest unit. From these two starting points we can surround our problem.

Within this framework I suggest these two statements as hypotheses: first, the detailed workings of entrepreneurship are best studied in the setting of a single (local or regional) community, and among its entrepreneurial group or groups; and, second, the assumptions within which entrepreneurs in such groups operate need to be understood in the setting of a national economy.

Using these statements as hypotheses, I propose to discuss the role of entrepreneurship in a particular nation and period, the United States between 1787 and 1816. By three related examples of communities, national, regional, and local, taken from American economic history, I shall show some of the evidence on which I base these hypotheses.[1]

Entrepreneurship is that form of social decision-making performed by economic innovators. Social decision-makers draw their sanction from the political, legal, economic, and social assumptions around which the people of the community organize their lives. It is the entrepreneur's reciprocal function as an economic innovator to help change these assumptions. He does so by the effect of his decision-making upon the structure and functions of the community (especially its economic structure and functions).[2]

---

[1] By permission of its editors, I have used here in considerably altered form certain material published under the title "Entrepreneurship in the Community," appearing in *Explorations in Entrepreneurical History*, vol. II, No. 3, pp. 114–127, a publication of the Research Center in Entrepreneurial History, Harvard University, Cambridge, Massachusetts. See also my essay on "Entrepreneurship and Community Development," in *Explorations in Economics* (Notes and Essays Contributed in Honor of F. W. Taussig, New York: McGraw-Hill, 1936); and my unpublished doctoral dissertation at Harvard's Widener Library on "The Development of Entrepreneurship in Fall River, Massachusetts: 1813–1859," submitted to Harvard University in 1935.

[2] The reader will find in the following biological analogies a first approximation of what I mean by social structure, function, and change:

Structure: those social institutions whose operations at a moment of time

The questions we shall undertake to answer are: How were the organizers of the structures and functions of our national economic system related to the entrepreneurs of the textile industry? How did certain communities, mercantile centers before the Revolution, become regional textile-industry capitals after the ratification of the Constitution? What entrepreneurs were responsible for these developments, and how much did they depend on other groups in their local or regional communities, or in the national community?

To answer these questions we must consider the emergence of the American national economy in its historical setting, and this requires a reëxamination of the events leading up to our independence. The American Revolution, seen as one of a series of related movements occurring within western culture, appears as an eco-

---

may be compared with the skeleton, the nerves, and the tissues of the human body: for example, the family as an economic group, the corporate organization of economic life (or its individual enterprises, including the firm, the association, etc.); the banking system; the public agencies of the national economy, including the Treasury, the First and Second Banks of the United States, etc.

Function: something analogous to the circulation of the blood in the human body, as described by Harvey and his successors, or the operation of the nervous system, as described by Rosenbluth and others (out of which cybernetics has developed). The social analogies include: in a primitive economy, the use of barter; in advanced societies, the circulation of money, the day-to-day operations of markets, the transfer of paper claims, the flow of goods through the factory system and the sale of its products, or indeed the whole system of economic circulation and intercommunication.

Change: both quantitative and qualitative change over time. To indicate the characteristics of qualitative changes consider the biological analogy of the hormones or endocrine glands; they are strategically located in the body so as to stimulate it at periods of transition from infancy to childhood, to adolescence, to maturity, to senescence. The bodily changes they helped to regulate are analogous to the changes from a society rooted in the soil (organizing its economic, social, and political life around the family as its principal social institution, its basic building block) into a city-state community; and the federation of a number of city-states into a nation. When a major economic and political decision-maker appears at a strategic point in the history of a community, his decisions change its structure and function fundamentally: Alexander Hamilton enabled Philadelphia—and later New York —to unify the city and state economies of our original colonies into a national economy. The process of change is most readily observed as it unfolds within a community; for example, from city-state to nation-state to world-metropolitan economy.

nomic, political, and social rebellion against the effort to consolidate a world-wide London metropolitan economy and a British Empire, following the global victory of Britain over France in the Seven Years' War.

By stating in a few words how the economist, the political scientist, and the social anthropologist would each approach this period of consolidation of the London economy within the British Empire, we can see why a model is needed to describe comprehensively the structure and function of a national and international community. For the economist these developments may be summarized in the phrase "growth of a market economy," if we include the growth of a *world-wide* money market based upon London, and the expansion of world-wide commodity markets similarly focused upon London and Liverpool. For the political scientist the phrase "rise of constitutional government" parallels that of the market economy. For the social anthropologist this historical movement may be summed up in such phrases as the shift from "status" to "contract"; within this we see "increasing social mobility" as illustrated by the marriage of self-made men into local, regional, or national family groups of social leaders.

To bring these several approaches together into one systematic whole, we need models descriptive of the structures and functions of national and international communities at moments of time, and of their changes through time. These models should be made by students of entrepreneurship, working with political, social, and economic historians. To build such models we need, for example, to trace the pattern of a given social structure, such as an extended-kinship family at a moment of time, study its connections with the surrounding community, and follow its changes over time.

By relating the major groupings from which the structure of a given community is formed to the functions performed at strategic points within its structure, we shall have a general description of those interrelationships which organize the economic, social, and political life of that community. For instance, if the chief political institution is a parliament or a congress, membership in that congress is a key to the political structure of the community. If we find a correlation between its membership and the social leadership of the communities politically represented in the national assembly, we are on the way to a broader understanding of the social structure and functioning of the community. If we are then able to trace a further connection between these points of social and political decision-making and the strategic points where economic decisions are made, we begin to see how leadership is provided for the individual communities, and for the regional and national communities of which they are parts. By watching these structures and functions as they change over time, we shall begin to be able to describe the processes by which certain decision-makers at strategic points in the social structure contribute to economic, political, and social change.

Turn, now, to the London metropolitan economy as the matrix within which Britain and America developed in the eighteenth and nineteenth centuries. While the final establishment of London as metropolitan center of a world-wide economy developed after Britain's removal of France as a major opponent after 1750, London emerged as the potential hub of such a world-wide economy after the Revolution of 1689; it became the economic center of a consolidated British Empire by formation of the Bank of England in 1694, by reform of the British currency in 1695, reëstablishment of the Board of Trade and Plantations in 1696, and reorganization of the East India Company in 1702.

Sixty years later, the little American metropolitan centers of Boston, Providence, New York, Philadelphia, and Charleston were growing stronger and more self-conscious at just that moment when the problems of empire seemed to their British rulers to call for tightening up the system governing colonial trade. Prior to 1760 these various provincial city-states tended to conduct their affairs with little intercommunication among themselves, and with direct reliance on London as the economic and political capital city. Only for Indian affairs and speculation in frontier lands did they look to a focal point on the American continent: Albany; hence, the Albany Congress of 1754 which brought together American land speculators from colonies north of Virginia, and ratified Franklin's Plan of Union.

When the new restrictive policies began to bear heavily on colonial shipowners and land speculators after 1763, merchants and mechanics joined the gentry in resisting Britain. Their first great intercolonial protest resulted in the Stamp Act Congress at New York in 1765; they next succeeded in calling the first Continental Congress in 1774, where a new nation came into being, an American national economy centering upon the political and economic metropolis of Philadelphia.

We need to remind ourselves that the events of this formation of our new national economy have few parallels in history. They provide in foreshortened form a process requiring decades and centuries to unfold elsewhere: creation of the objective conditions wherein a group of able men can organize a continental economic system within a new nation-state.

A group of leaders of provincial city-states within the orbit of a world metropolitan community broke with their mother country by a revolution, waged as a civil war in the colonies, and overthrew that group of American families whose members continued to serve the King and his royal governors. Between the removal of the French in 1763 and the outbreak of the Revolution in 1775, forces at work in the colonies since their foundation came to a head. By combining political and military attack against the Crown and Parliament with a social upheaval against the local ruling class, the indigenous Patriot aristocracy cleared the way for their own social, political, and economic control of each colony. The assembling of a continental congress in 1774 composed of spokesmen for the leading groups in each colony carried them the next step towards a continental merger of their provincial vested-interests, and speeded up social change. When these representatives formed congressional committees to defend their interests against Britain they recognized their mutual interdependence: their need to stand together at home, and to seek alliances abroad. War contracts and authority to privateer multiplied chances for entrepreneurial activity.

The entrepreneurs of the new national economy used their membership on (or family connections with members of) congressional committees to lay the foundations of a nation-state. Successful war economies are of necessity centralized and closely integrated

403

in their operation: the American Revolutionary war economy proved hard to integrate, but not for lack of effort by many of these men. They had great obstacles to overcome: the absence of a continental system prior to the war, due to economic and political gravitation of the separate colonies around London; the poor communications of the times; the heavy emphasis upon the family system as the means for achieving economic security in the absence of well-developed business organizations.

When the Confederation was established in 1781, the balance of power shifted to the conservative bloc centered in New York and Pennsylvania, who had congressional allies in Boston, Providence, Charleston, and other towns. This group, acting as the chief war contractors and privateers, had learned to work together within a continental pattern. With the defeat of Britain, they sought a stronger political union and, even before the negotiation of a peace treaty, began projecting new economic ventures: banks, land companies, and the funding of foreign debts. These undertakings called for new and more impersonal, more widespread, corporate institutions.

The deep-seated contest between centralizers and decentralizers continued to divide Americans down to the Civil War, and beyond. It was rooted in differences between them as to whether the individual state seemed to provide a sufficient base (legal, political, and economic) to protect the social system favored by each of these two groups. The continentalists (as Hamilton called them) wanted the benefits of a funded national debt, a national money market, the protection of a national navy for their merchant marine, and of a national army to defend their expanding land-speculations against Indian attacks. They were very confident that they could secure and maintain control of such a national government. The states-rights group, many of them landlords, thought they could retain control of state legislatures, but would find it harder to dominate the Federal executive, legislative, and judicial departments.

The continentalists became Federalists; the states-rights supporters became anti-Federalists, after the signing of the Constitution. Through the contract clause and other parts of the new Constitution, the Federalists were able to give national legal protection and executive and legislative encouragement to their new corporate institutions. For a generation after the Constitution was ratified, the leading Federalist families dominated the new corporate structure.

These Federalist families and their anti-Federalist opponents united in attacks on Parliament and the Crown on the eve of the Revolution, whereas they split during and after the Revolution over questions of centralization *versus* decentralization of the economic and political systems of the states and nation. To relate the growth of these families and their development of colonial metropolitan centers before the Revolution to the postwar rise of the textile industry, we focus on the life of Boston and Providence, and their satellite towns. Both centers were active in smuggling, defying the Sugar Act; both depended heavily on contraband trade with foreign ports in violation of the Navigation Acts; both resisted imperial restraints.

In Providence, the leading family on the eve of the Revolution was that of the Browns, whose ancestors had been among its first settlers. By the 1760's four Brown brothers, Nicholas, Joseph, John, and Moses, were trading in rum, slaves, and other West India goods through the firm their father James Brown and his brother Obadiah had formed thirty years earlier.[3] By 1763 the four brothers were at the center of a "trust," the Spermaceti Candle Manufacturers, operating in Providence, Newport, Boston, and Philadelphia. Moses' three brothers became active Patriots, and his brother John was widely believed to have been the ringleader in the Gaspee affair. But in 1773, after his wife (Obadiah's daughter) died, Moses Brown withdrew from the family firm and turned Quaker, objecting to slave trading and war profiteering.

When war broke out, and the Secret Committee of the Continental Congress gave out Rhode Island war contracts through his brother Nicholas, Moses did not share in them. Instead he turned

[3] On the Browns of Providence, I am indebted to the work of Professor James B. Hedges of Brown University; and on the relations of Moses Brown and Samuel Slater, I have referred to G. S. White, *Memoir of Samuel Slater* (Philadelphia: 1836).

his attention to manufacturing experiments. The Browns were ready, when the federated American states achieved a national union, to make Providence a center for commercial activity at home and abroad comparable to its rival Newport before the Revolution. Among the four Brothers, Moses was prepared to go even further, and to lay foundations for Providence as a manufacturing center.

The Lowells of Boston[4] show a family system like that of the Browns in Providence, their founding entrepreneur being John Lowell, son of the Reverend John Lowell of Newburyport. After graduating from Harvard in 1760, and studying law in Boston, young John Lowell returned to Newburyport to practice and quickly became attorney for the town's leading merchants, Patrick Tracy and Tristram Dalton. In January 1767, he married Sarah Higginson, daughter of Stephen Higginson and Elizabeth Cabot of Salem. Sarah Higginson Lowell died in 1772, and John Lowell married her cousin Susan Cabot. In 1775, John and Susan had a son, Francis Cabot Lowell, whose mother died within two years; in 1778 John Lowell took Mrs. Rebecca Russell Tyng, a widow, as his third wife.

By his father's three marriages to a Higginson, a Cabot, and a Russell, Francis Cabot Lowell grew up in an extended-kinship group second to none in Boston and its satellite towns on the North Shore, a family connection based upon several generations of merchant-shipowning. The marriages of Francis and the other sons and daughters of the Judge were to enlarge that family circle. Families like the Higginsons of Salem, the Cabots of Beverly, the Russells of Charlestown, were active in the same trade on which the Browns of Providence founded their fortunes. They were not all among the earliest to defy the Crown, but were handsomely rewarded for their American patriotism through war contracts and privateering.

During the war Judge Lowell served as attorney for various Loy-

---

[4] On the Lowells of Boston, I rely especially on Ferris Greenslet, *The Lowells and their Seven Worlds* (Boston: Houghton Mifflin, 1946).

alist estates, including that of former Governor Hutchinson—chief target of the rebels Sam Adams and James Otis. Lowell also found time to act as counsel for his privateering relatives by marriage, the Higginsons, Cabots, and Russells, and personally filed seven hundred of the eleven hundred libels against prize vessels in the Boston court, being concerned as assistant counsel in nearly half the rest. We can understand why he was one of the first to move up from the North Shore to Boston when the Tories sailed away to Halifax; they left opportunities in the legal and mercantile life of Boston for able men with financial backing.

Lowell served in the Continental Congress in 1782, where he became familiar with John Brown of Providence, Alexander Hamilton and other New Yorkers, and the Philadelphia group around Robert Morris and his partner Thomas Willing, who a year earlier founded the Bank of North America hoping to make it a national central bank patterned after the Bank of England. Late in 1782 Lowell was given a congressional appointment as judge of appeals in admiralty cases; on returning to Boston he joined with his family connection in organizing the Massachusetts Bank, the first bank in Boston. It was opened in 1784. His cousin, also named John Lowell, was made its teller, and the "judge" served for a while as cashier.

Judge Lowell, according to his son and partner John Lowell, accumulated during the war upwards of $200,000, but held much of it in continental paper money. He and his relatives by marriage became, after peace was signed, leaders of the group seeking a constitutional convention and a new national union to replace the Confederation. His relatives, and especially his brother-in-law George Cabot, were spokesmen for the Essex Junto which elected James Bowdoin as the first Federalist Governor of Massachusetts in 1785, and went on to put down Shays' rebellion the next year.

The Judge died on May 6, 1802. Four years earlier his son Francis had married Hannah Jackson, daughter of the Judge's old friend and neighbor Jonathan Jackson, and granddaughter of Lowell's wealthy client, Patrick Tracy. Francis had already assumed responsibility for investing the Judge's fortune, chiefly in "Adventures at Sea," and was established as a Boston merchant-shipowner operating eight vessels; his brother-in-law Patrick Tracy Jackson was his partner.[5]

Beginning with the first Continental Congress in 1774, a national economy was formed by the efforts of provinical leaders like the Browns in Providence and John Lowell and his family connection in Boston. After these local entrepreneurs became active in the national war effort, by a series of gradual changes they created a new economy to fill the vacuum left by separation of the American colonies from London's metropolitan economy. During the war this new economy enabled Americans to trade with France and other continental nations, and their island possessions; once war ended, the problem became: how to compete in trade abroad in the face of the growing industrial revolution in Great Britain, and how to restore the disrupted peacetime economies of the individual American states.

By 1789, when President Washington was inaugurated, the aristocratic family groups consolidated by the American Revolution had tacitly agreed on one chief economic spokesman: young Alexander Hamilton who in 1780 had married General Philip Schuyler's daughter Betsey. From 1772, when Hamilton arrived in New Jersey as a boy, he was the protégé of the Livingston-Schuyler-Van Rensselaer connection, chief manorial families of New York and New Jersey. During the war he served as Washington's military secretary, forming a more extensive acquaintance among leading Americans than did any other young man of his generation.

Building on these connections, Hamilton became at a remarkably early age one of three or four chief exponents of a constitutional convention, and one of its youngest delegates. He had been proposed for the Superintendency of Finance in 1781 at the age of

[5] As a boy, Francis Cabot Lowell visited his uncle George Cabot's horse-driven cotton factory at Beverly, and may have gained there his continuing interest in the possibilities of American manufacture of cotton textiles. That Beverly mill was in operation a year before Moses Brown hired Samuel Slater to work with Ozias Wilkinson at Pawtucket, and Brown knew about the Beverly experiment. George Cabot was one of the three appraisers of John Lowell's estate (the old Judge, drawer of wills, died intestate).

twenty-four, when Robert Morris was chosen. Once the new nation was formed, Hamilton was a logical candidate for the Secretary-ship of the Treasury in the first Washington Administration, as head of an alliance between the leading mercantile and landed families in other cities; for example, the Browns of Providence and the Lowell family connection in Boston.

Hamilton was now in a position to become the great entrepreneur of the new American national economy. With the aid of William Duer (the first Assistant Secretary of the Treasury), Tench Coxe (Duer's successor, a protégé of Morris, Willing, and Benjamin Franklin), and other representatives of his alliance, Hamilton established the original financial patterns for the new nation, and in a series of famous reports laid down its original economic programs and principles. Working together they defined the structure and function of the Federal Treasury, the first Bank of the United States, the New York and Philadelphia money markets, a national currency, and the outlines for a protective tariff. Within this national structure, the regional groups centered in the chief towns could organize their own new patterns of entrepreneurial activity. We exaggerate if we argue that this was a singlehanded performance of one financial genius. What Hamilton and his friends were able to do was to complete by their initiative the work of a generation.

The foundation of Lowell in 1822 marked a turning point for Boston: a general movement began, spreading the manufacturing interests of Boston to the larger water powers of New England. Later in 1822 some of the stockholders of the Merrimack Company started a similar development at Chicopee, with some capitalists from the Connecticut River Valley. Both at Lowell and at Chicopee new mills rose in rapid succession, as the Boston associates saw markets expand in pace with their output. Within the next fifteen years the Boston group developed other water powers at Taunton, Massachusetts; Manchester and Somersworth, New Hampshire; Saco and Biddeford, Maine; and elsewhere. As steam-boating on the Mississippi, grain traffic on the Great Lakes, and the building of the Erie Canal boomed western lands, the population of the country grew rapidly and the textile industry boomed also. This boom collapsed in 1837, but was soon revived by the railway expansion of the two decades before the Civil War.

The group of entrepreneurs who create a new community provide the most spectacular example of the role of the entrepreneur in relation to the community. Once the site was chosen and the town launched, these entrepreneurs among the Boston associates carried through their age-old entrepreneurial functions of organizing new institutions such as local banks, savings banks, real estate companies, manufacturing corporations, branch railroads, and the like. Meanwhile, these economic and social institutions within the local communities were being duplicated in Boston to tie the new industrial towns to their regional metropolitan capital. The growth of the region, stimulated by the "plantation" of these new towns, was accelerated after the development of the railroad and the importation of new working populations from abroad. New England differed from areas further west, however, by reason of close-knit relationships between these long-established mercantile families and the newcomers whom they associated with their group. Town-building assumed one pattern in the more settled regions of the east and another along the lines of railway expansion in the west; the resulting communities show to this day important differences in their patterns of entrepreneurship.

Let us turn now from this review of economic history to a discussion of its implications for studies of entrepreneurship.[6] When the economic history of communities like those of Fall River and Boston is dissected so as to lay bare their differentiation of function, their subdivision of labor, their channeling of growth, studies of individual entrepreneurs will reveal more than a limited, and distorted picture of entrepreneurial activity. By the same token, questions directed at students of entrepreneurship by economists can secure more adequate answers from a rounded picture of the

[6] Throughout this discussion of entrepreneurship I have neglected the problems inherent in the bureaucratic operations within the institutions over which entrepeneurs preside, or from which they depart when their jobs are done. We need parallel studies of entrepeneurship and of bureaucracy, of routine decision-makers within private and public social institutions. One of the problems of entrepeneurs is to create bureaucracies, to deal with them, and where necessary to by-pass them.

context in which decisions are made within the community and its individual firms. One of the great shortcomings of the economists has been their failure to show clearly how community-building contributes to the incomes of this central group of decision-makers, and enables them to continue to channel the economic life of the community into the institutions they control.

Economists will urge, and rightly so, that the units in which entrepreneurs operate, whether family firms, banks, industrial corporations, or of whatever form, are dependent upon the economic rules of that society. As a corollary, economists will say that, insofar as we are studying that group of decision-makers we call *entrepreneurs,* we are or should be primarily concerned with economic decisions. The economists must remember, however, that these decisions are most meaningful, and often *only* meaningful, within their social context.

If students of entrepreneurship have erred by overemphasizing biographies of individual entrepreneurs, as their critics charge, economists have erred by depersonalizing the functions of decision-making. More recently, economists emphasizing price fluctuations as the chief data of economic theory have sought to give these fleeting facts about economic life an appearance of substantial reality, and to build systematic models around them. While abstractions are necessary to theory, both groups prefer the data of biography or price theory to the substance of social institutions set up by flesh-and-blood decision-makers who shape or respond to events, build new economic, political, and social structures among interrelated human beings, and organize them to perform new functions. We are a long way from creating a science of society, and many students of society doubt that such a general social science can be attained, but certainly the orderly methods of the physical sciences can help students of society. For students of the economic aspects of society, social institutions are the basic data.

Here "model-building" is relevant, provided that model-builders are as aware as are the physical scientists of how abstractions can generate errors in reasoning. The family or other small groups, the association, the corporate or institutional entity, and communities of various sizes and kinds provide the basic models for students of

411

society, who need to remember the risks of building models on insufficient evidence. They need constantly to realize, also, that participants in a given situation are the best (although by no means the only reliable) witnesses as to the structure and function of such groups, associations, corporate and institutional entities.

With these precepts in mind, we can say that Fall River and Boston provide "models" of the middle group of communities: the local industrial city, and the metropolitan city at the center of a sizable region. The United States in 1789 provides a model of the new national economy, within the new nation-state. Our "models" as described above give a chronological account of certain contributions made by a few of their economic decision-makers towards the development of these communities, and show whence these men derived much of their strength. These models indicate only part of the structure and functions of social and economic institutions in the communities we are studying. They emphasize the processes involved in the creation and extension of such institutions: they show their dependence on family connections during this period of community development; and the social, economic, and political relationships of individuals and groups within the communities in which these entrepreneurs operate.

By studying the processes of decison-making as they developed in their time and space dimensions within the local "model" of Fall River, the regional "model" of Boston, and the "model" of the American nation-state in 1789, we can understand the changing character of the problems confronting their decision-makers. We see their decisions as dependent upon the point in time when each arrived upon the scene, and upon whether he was located in a local, regional, or national community setting. For example, interlocking models of such communities show the pattern of decision-making as it is woven between local and regional, or regional and national, centers: new structure is formed when state incorporation laws initiated in Boston permit the transformation of family firms in Fall River into corporations; new function is developed when the national protective tariff after 1816 encourages the Boston overseas merchant to become an industrial entrepreneur; change is achieved when Hamilton and his friends tie local and regional

412

business groups together around the United States Treasury and the first Bank of the United States.

We can now, I think, venture some hypotheses as to what studies of entrepreneurship may gain by reëxamining the economic decision-maker within his community setting: the entrepreneur, active in economic life at points of strategic importance for decision-making, influences changes in the organization of society so as to increase economic efficiency, to raise profits, to create new economic and social institutions, and to transform and connect old ones by his innovations. Our examples drawn from Fall River, Providence-Pawtucket, and Boston show a direct relationship between the social setting of individual entrepreneurs like Holder Borden, Moses Brown, and Samuel Slater, or Francis Cabot Lowell (and, on the national scene, Alexander Hamilton and Tench Coxe), and the degree and kind of economic and social success they achieved within it, hardly attainable outside that setting.

For students of entrepreneurship, the individual *must* be considered as the basic unit around which each social system revolves. As we have seen, however, the individual entrepreneur (or any other decision-maker taken out of a given social setting) is a mere figment of the theorist's imagination; he becomes a reality only when he is studied as a member of his society. The social groupings or institutions of that social system wherein he operates prove, on investigation, to have their own value systems and goals of activity, within the larger set of assumptions which organize that society. . . . Entrepreneurs, like other decision-makers, depend for their success on the measure of acceptance their values and goals of activity command from that society. As we have seen, they tend to act in small groups, and to work out their value systems in such groups as family or clique. Studies of these smaller groupings lead in turn to a series of more comprehensive social studies of communities in their time and space dimensions.

Our examination of certain communities and our study of some of their outstanding economic decision-makers indicates that, whereas decision-making is necessary in all societies regardless of their form of economic organization, ours has been the era and the civilization of economic men. The dominance of *economic* decision-makers achieved its maximum spread during the nineteenth century. The entrepreneur is the economic man in his outstanding role: as guide of economic change. It is necessary but not sufficient to say that individual entrepreneurs made great contributions to the building of individual firms, and the formation of economic institutions such as stock exchanges, commodity markets, and the like. All such accomplishments must be viewed as part of the larger process of building local, regional, national, and international communities.

Studies of economic innovation require a comprehensive understanding of the relationship of all forms of decision-making, from the individual entrepreneurial decision to the development of entire communities. A reëxamination of entrepreneurship within this context will show the critics of entrepreneurial studies how necessary it is for these studies to cast their net wide. In analyzing economic decision-making as one aspect of social decision-making, students are bound to consider the structure, functions, and processes of change of the societies in which entrepreneurs operated, to see in what ways the entrepreneur effects political and social as well as economic changes.

CULTURE, SOCIETY, AND INDUSTRIAL DEVELOPMENT

Glenn Gilman

The relations of management and labor are something more than the economic counters passed back and forth at the bargaining table. The full, rich traditions of the southeastern United States, their consequences in the definitions of the roles of managers and workers, and the events of industrialization in that region are analyzed and their significance for understanding management and labor presented.

The society to which the industrial worker under the massways must turn for relief when he needs it is an intangible. It is not

Note: See Notes on the Authors, page 553, and item 95 in the bibliography for the full reference to this selection.

something the worker can realize, from which he can draw a real sense of belonging. It is a code of laws, a system of jurisprudence, a matter of rules and regulations. It is far away, impersonal, insensitive. The feeble cry of a single man protesting an injustice only serves to emphasize its aloofness. And if the combined cries of many men finally prod it into activity, its ponderous processes grind with maddening deliberation. The resulting law, or decision, or whatever may come out must be "general" in order to apply to the many; it may have little application to the situation of any one of the many, even if the decision is rendered with sufficient celerity to be of some practical good. The latter is unlikely to be true. The mass society operates to effectuate justice, but in the long run; and the industrial worker cannot wait out the long run. . . . The worker cannot wait out the inexorable grinding of the massways. He wants his rights now, today, next week.

Because he is a human being, it is inevitable that he will do something to short-circuit the round-about processes of the mass society. As a human being, he is still capable of voluntary co-operation; and he is not alone in his need, his anxiety, and his frustration. Others in the enterprise share his plight. Almost as an emotional response, hardly realizing the logic of his action, he and the others go on strike. . . .

The presence of the union demonstrates the conclusion of a work force that it dare not, in the future, place its faith either in management or in the society. It represents the judgment of the industrial worker that for practical purposes the plant is a closed social system, that there is no point in his looking elsewhere for relief or assistance. The rights which he regards as his he must guarantee himself, by means of the ever-present threat of his collective power as represented by his union. The union is his answer to a situation where he sees himself at the mercy of an impersonal management and forgotten by society.

The basic plight of the industrial worker is no different in the folk society than in the mass society. Just as his opposite number does in the great industrial cities of the Northeast and the Midwest, the industrial worker in the Piedmont cotton textile industry lacks essential command over that portion of his daily life upon which all the rest hinges. He neither owns the tools with which he works nor is he, by and large, called upon to employ skills that make him irreplaceable in an economic sense. Within the context of the firm itself, he is potentially subject to all the anxieties and frustrations that plague the industrial worker anywhere.

The potentiality is theoretical, however. Practically, he is somewhat less subject to them even within the context of the firm itself. Unlike the typical work force under the massways, his is not mere physical aggregation of individuals ordered by the massways but with no real social bonding between its individual members except in the extreme case of common despair. The industrial worker in the folk regions of the United States seldom lacks organization whether he possesses a union or not. His organization is informal and implicit, but none the less powerful. It is that organization which proceeds out of possession of a common background of custom and tradition, mores and folkways; it is the kind of organization that is based on possession of mutual understanding, ability to foretell in advance the line of action of the other simply by putting one's self in his place; it is the kind of organization that is based upon possession of a common ground against which events are judged, a common point of view from which they are seen against that ground. It is above all the kind of organization that is shot through and through with sympathetic rapport, so that what happens to one happens to a degree to all.

Under such conditions, management *cannot* deal with the work force on an individual basis. It speaks of individual bargaining *versus* collective bargaining; but as a practical matter of fact, its every activity must be rehearsed as it will be viewed by the group rather than merely by the particular individual immediately involved. "You've got to watch your step with these folks," an overseer told the writer. "You forget yourself and get short-tempered with one of them, and you just haven't got him sore at you. There's his brothers, his sisters, perhaps his father and mother, his uncles and his aunts, his cousins, all his in-laws and his friends. You may have half the mill stirred up before you know it."

The informal organization not only facilitates communication, but it enforces it, in a manner of speaking. Because management is so well aware that group action is quite likely to follow upon what seems an action directed only at an individual, it is under the necessity of constantly revising and enriching its imagery of the work force. It cannot be content with mere factual information about people who work for it; the nature of their feelings and attitudes must be ascertained in order that their roles may be effectively taken both individually and collectively. Management is immediately reminded of the unhappy consequences of neglecting any of the dimensions of human nature; it finds it unwise ever to settle back and relax in its certainty that it now knows all there is to know about the people. It finds it necessary constantly to pay attention to them. It is not permitted, even should it attempt to do so, to "take them for granted."

Concepts of what is right and wrong under the folkways make it difficult for a management to remain unaware of the attitudes of its people, even when it makes no deliberate attempt at communication. "It's your duty to tell the boss when you think he's wrong," a long-service employee told the writer. "Maybe he isn't doing the wrong thing on purpose—maybe his mind was on something else, or somebody told him the wrong thing, or something. If you tell him he's wrong, and he still goes on doing whatever it is the way he was doing it in the first place, why that's for him to decide. You figure maybe he's got a reason you don't know about. But it ain't right to stand by and let a man do something wrong, and not tell him about it."

We have previously noted that the spontaneous walkout has long been a weapon of southern work forces when they have felt themselves to be ignored. The strike, under such conditions, has a different aspect than in the mass society. Basically, it is a communicative device, an emphatic demand for attention in a situation where the people feel themselves to be in possession of information that ought to be brought to the attention of management and that has obviously been overlooked in a managerial decision. It is this characteristic of the southern strike that explains its generally quick and satisfactory settlement as long as the union is not injected as an issue. Very often it has occurred in cases where for some reason the people are prevented from easy communication with top management. One plant experienced a series of such work stoppages during the early 1930's, often confined to single departments. A worker who had taken part in some of them explained the situation to the writer. "Mr. _____ (the president) and Mr. _____ (the general manager) were pretty decent people. You could get a square deal from them. The trouble was, you just couldn't ever get to them—there were a whole bunch of 'little bosses' that blocked the way. We finally found out that the thing to do, when we had trouble, was just to walk out. Then we got to see the people we wanted to see, and things got straightened out. They finally caught on around the plant, and let us go up to see them in the first place when we wanted to, and there wasn't any more trouble."

Nor can policies be permitted to become rigid under circumstances of this sort. The work force under the folkways insists that every problem be settled in accordance with principles of what is right and wrong; and this can be accomplished only by policies that have sufficient flexibility to permit allowances to be made for differing circumstances. The relatively simple policy structure of the typical Piedmont cotton textile mill, in combination with its short and effective formal lines of communication and numerous personal contacts between top management and hourly-rated people, means that the latter are well aware of managerial attitudes and intentions and the probable nature of their modification under particular circumstances. There is high validity of prediction in both directions, a rather important requirement for effective co-operation. Much emphasis in present-day discussion of personnel relations is placed upon the necessity for a management to understand its work force; but it is equally or even more important that the work force understand management through knowledge of its policies as well as of its persons.

This high level of accuracy of prediction as to the probable intentions, objectives, attitudes, and value judgments of the other results in a variety of unconscious accomodation of interest behind every managerial decision involving the work force and every worker response to that decision. Any particular decision announced by management may appear to be completely unilateral in nature. Actually, a rehearsal of its probable consequences in terms of its assessment by the work force will either have consciously or unconsciously preceded its adoption. It will have been modified, revised, and reshapen in terms of the probable interpretation and response of the people. In its final form it represents a compromise between what management would like to do and what it feels the people would like to see done and there will have been a considerable amount of informal checking to assess the accuracy of this latter estimation. The decision, when it is announced, is likely to meet with general approval; the people who have ordinarily been aware of the circumstances that have called for the decision have themselves, in attempting to predict what it will be, been balancing what they would like against what they think the company will be able to do. The announced decision is not likely to be much different from the predicted decision because of the informal and almost intuitive accommodation of interests that enters into its formulation and its acceptance.

This high degree of informal organization of work forces under the folkways has actually worked to facilitate union organization in the Piedmont textile industry. In those cases in which a breach has been permitted to develop between management and the people and in which the informal leaders of the work force run into serious difficulties in their attempts to restore communication and rapport, the union can move in with amazing swiftness. It does not have to "organize" the plant. All it has to do is convince the leadership of an already informally organized group that it can be of some assistance. This characteristic has on occasion given the union a false impression of its persuasive powers. After some kind of a settlement has been worked out, the union is dismayed to find that it cannot hold its membership. It never had them; it was merely used on an *ad hoc* basis as a convenient way of getting a job done by an organization already in existence.

It was very unlikely, as a matter of fact, that the work force thought seriously one way or the other about a permanent and continuing alliance with the union. It just did not see it in those terms. The textile worker has not supported institutionalized collective bargaining simply because it has not fitted into the pattern of his day-to-day behavior. It has possessed only one feature of interest to him, its ability to run a strike in a professional manner. And even here, as we have noted, the purpose behind the strike is different.

Under more usual conditions, when the union is attempting to organize a plant where no labor dispute is in progress, it finds itself opposed by the informal organization. It discovers that before it can proceed with its own pattern of organization it must disorganize what is already in existence. It must attempt to create a breach between the work force and management to begin with; and then it must attempt to break up the informal organization itself, discredit its leadership and swing the people to the new leadership offered by the union. It is seldom successful in doing so. The folk group is too powerful. In case after case, the union is able to enroll in its ranks only those elements in the work force that are not in the folk organization to begin with. The remnants of the floating textile work force figure largely in this fringe group, as do local people whose behavior patterns are for some reason unacceptable to the solid core of the work force. The net result is that the union starts out in the plant without the support of the main body of the people, and draws its local officers from that group least likely to be able to win such support in the future.

The society to which the southeastern textile worker turns for protection is not, under the folkways, something vague, ephemeral, and theoretical, an abstract concept of social justice, for instance. It is as living and real as the people who walk the streets of the textile town and collectively form it. Even during this time of trouble, this society was a real entity to the textile worker. He continued to enjoy the attention of a portion of it though, for a while, it was neither the right kind of attention nor paid by the right group. As he made his displeasure with the state of affairs that existed unmistakably evident, the entire community once more became interested in him and remained so. It is made up of flesh-and-blood people whom the worker recognizes, people whose status he is aware of, the weight of whose judgments are grounded in the same ethical code as his own; when they are in possession of

420

the same facts as he, they are likely to hold the same opinions as he as to what is right and wrong.

Except for brief periods in what was a minority of the mills, and these largely concentrated in the decade between 1925 and 1935, the implicitly enforced set of community expectations with regard to the conduct of industrial relations in the Piedmont textile plants has been the worker's protection against the possibility of an arbitrary and unsympathetic management, and has done much to protect him from the impersonal vagaries of the market.

The worker has depended upon the power of community opinion to bring into line, in the subtle fashion of the folk, those managements that would deviate from the "right" pattern of conduct.[7] Community opinion as to what constitutes "right" treatment is that it will in more cases than not seem reasonable to the textile worker. He has in general been reasoning from the same premises, is in possession of the same facts, and comes to the same conclusions. It is because the "policies" that order his industrial life are, in their most essential aspects, folkways that have their roots in the community and strike back into the very region itself that the textile worker has faith in their eventual ability to make things right. A single management may evade them for a while, but not for long. Eventually they will swing him into line with a power that makes federal and state legislation and formal collective bargaining appear infantile by comparison.

The power of these folkways over management lies in the fact that they are for the most part unrealized as compulsive forces. Piedmont managements are themselves of the folk. They are members of their communities as well as managers of mills. They have internalized community expectations and attitudes and made them a part of their selves, a powerful censoring device that enters into their every decision. Without consciously realizing why they do it, they follow practices that have been developed under the folkways

[7] See Liston Pope, *Millhands and Preachers* (New Haven: Yale University Press, 1942) for an account of the attitude of the Gastonia community and its manifestations during the early days of the Gastonia strike before it was complicated by the issue of communism.

as the most effective and efficient means of meeting fundamental human needs under given conditions. Yet these guides for action do not become static and rigid, despite their compulsive nature at any one time. Because they have never been formalized, they are constantly under a process of revision. One does not call a meeting of the Board of Aldermen to revise the folkways. The folk do it themselves.

THE MANAGER IN SIMPLE AND COMPLEX SOCIETIES

W. Lloyd Warner and J. O. Low

> The emergence of the roles of manager and worker and their changing functions in the community and nation are traced; the change from a simple to a complex society with a high division of labor is related to the role definitions of managers and workers.

When we explore the social and industrial history of Yankee City, moving back through the years marked by the beginning of industrial capitalism and through the brilliant years of the Clipper Ship era to the simple folk economy of the earliest community—noticing how an earlier phase of the constantly changing society limits and molds the succeeding ones—it becomes certain that some of the knowledge necessary for explaining the strike can be, and must be, obtained by this scientific process. Furthermore, we see very clearly the times when certain necessary factors which explain the strike appear in the life of the town and how, in conjunction with other causes, their gradual evolution made the strike inevitable. It also becomes abundantly clear that the Yankee City strike was not a unique event but must be treated as representative of a type and that this type is almost certainly worldwide in its importance and significance.[8]

The town began in 1635. The colonial settlers of Yankee City,

[8] This chapter was written under the influence of Emile Durkheim, *The Division of Labor in Society* (New York, The Macmillan Company, 1933),

Note: See Notes on the Authors, pages 557 and 554, and item 242 in the bibliography for the full reference to this selection.

having been tenant farmers in England, founded an agricultural community. For several generations thereafter the colonists continued to perpetuate social and economic patterns essentially similar to those in which they had participated in the motherland; their rural agricultural life centered around the political institution of the town and the religious institution of the church. As in the case of all societies recently transplanted, the community was beset with threats to its existence, both internal and external, and met them by close adherence to traditional modes of life.

From a simple and undifferentiated society, there developed in Yankee City the type of economic life with which standard histories of New England have made us familiar. During the era of shipbuilding, shipping, and fishing, a great number of handicrafts also developed. These included such primary industries as woodcarving, cordage-making, carpentering, black-smithing, and sail-making. During the winter months the fishermen of Yankee City, as of other New England towns, made shoes. The women manufactured wool and cotton garments within the household. During the nineteenth century, numerous other independent crafts appeared, such as silversmithing, comb-making, leather-tanning, and carriage-building. The most important industry in view of its later development, however, was the manufacture of shoes.

---

and L. T. Hobhouse, G. C. Wheeler, and M. Ginsberg, *The Material Culture and Social Institutions of the Simpler Peoples* (London, Chapman & Hall, 1915). Its orientation is ethnological. The first draft was constructed from original materials gathered within Yankee City, including interviews, only those histories of the town written by local historians, and original documents. When we wrote it we followed a rule laid down at the beginning of the research . . . : "To be sure that we were not ethnocentrically biased in our judgment, we decided to use no previous summaries of data collected by anyone else (maps, handbooks, histories, etc.) until we had formed our own opinion of the city. In part this was a mistake since it greatly lengthened our field work; in compensation, once we had arrived at our conclusions, we were certain of the facts and operations on which our opinions were founded.

Later we consulted the writings of professional historians and social economists, in particular Samuel Eliot Morrison's excellent works on New England histories and John R. Commons' brilliant study of the shoe industry in the United States. We are deeply indebted to both of these writers, and, in particular, Dr. Commons . . . Much of what we say here will be an old story to social economists and economic historians.

During the first years of the settlement of Yankee City and New England and in the earliest phase of shoemaking, families made their own shoes. The second phase of the first stage was characterized by the itinerant shoemaker who, owning his own tools, made shoes in the kitchen of his customer, using materials supplied by the customer. In this process, the shoemaker was assisted by his customer's family and received his compensation largely in the form of board and lodging. Many families in Yankee City and in the outlying communities, particularly those dwelling on the north bank of the river, became proficient in the art of shoemaking at this stage. They made their own shoes during the winter months, passing down the art in the home from generation to generation. This section of New England has, therefore, a strong tradition of shoemaking.

The next stage began (*circa* 1760) when the shoemaker set up a small shop and made shoes to order for his local customers. These shops were known as "the ten-foot shops," and the customer's order was known as "bespoke." During the first part of this period, the shoemaker still made the complete shoe, but his relation with the market became indirect. The entrepreneur appeared. He was a capitalist shoemaker, hiring workers in their homes to make boots and shoes for him to sell at retail or wholesale. In the second phase of the period the central shop developed where materials were sorted. The parts were cut in the shop, distributed and served in the homes, then collected and the soles joined to the uppers in the shop. Machines were used scarcely at all. The processes of shoemaking were divided, and workmen specialized in one or more operations. Jobs were thus defined within the industry; for the most part, the worker no longer faced his customers.

During this period the market remained local, and the interests of the merchant-master and the journeyman were the same. When improved land and water transportation brought about an expansion of the market, the merchant became an increasingly dominant figure. The bargain became one of price as well as quality, and the interest of the merchant to produce cheaply in order to undersell competitors began to conflict with the maker's desire to earn as much as he could from his labor.

Professor John R. Commons, in an article entitled "American

Shoemakers 1648–1895,"[9] traced the evolution of the industry in this country from court records of cases involving conflicting interests both within and without the industry. He reports that the first guild of shoemakers, known as the "Shoomakers of Boston," was granted a charter of incorporation in October 1648. Since the days of the "Shoomakers of Boston" other formal organizations have come into existence and left concrete evidence of the various conflicts of interests within the industry.

Before 1852, the menaces to the industry and to the groups within it resulted mainly from the expansion of markets. Until this time all shoes were made by hand, and each craftsman owned his own set of tools. But to meet the increasingly exacting demands of an expanding market, as to both price and quality, it was inevitable that the growing technological knowledge would be utilized to mechanize some phases of shoe manufacture. In 1852 a sewing machine for stitching uppers was invented, and the following decade saw the mechanization of many other processes. This development intensified the split in interests between the owner-control group and the operatives; it also established the subordinate position of the latter which they have occupied ever since. Accelerated mechanization of the industry in the decades after the Civil War occasioned changes in the social structure of the shoe factory.

One of the most important results of the introduction of machinery into shoemaking was the enormous decrease in labor costs. The cost per one hundred pairs was reduced by the machine to well under one-tenth of the costs of 1850, and the average labor cost in 1932, we were told, had dropped to forty cents per pair. Another result was the great potential increase in production. For example, an expert hand-laster produced fifty pairs a day; a lasting machine, from three hundred to seven hundred per day. A welt machine is fifty-four times as fast as welt sewing by awl and needle. The introduction of machines into shoemaking converted it from a strictly hand trade to one of the most specialized of machine industries. The position of labor was greatly modified by the technical revolution. The product has changed only in detail, but the process of manufacture has changed from a single skilled trade,

[9] John R. Commons, "American Shoemakers, 1648–1895," *Quarterly Journal of Economics,* XXIV, No. 1 (November, 1909), 39–84.

carried on by a craftsman from start to finish, to one of two to three thousand operations in greater part done by machine.

The security of the workers as craftsmen was threatened by the new developments. The shoe workers did not make the machines they were suddenly forced to operate, and they had no way of predicting what jobs would next be mechanized. The owning group had in the machines an effective weapon to lessen the value of the worker's craftsmanship.

Out of this situation arose the Knights of St. Crispin, active from 1868–1872, the most powerful labor organization known up to that time and probably the most important one previous to the modern labor unions. The Knights were organized to protest against the substitution of many "green hands" for the old-time craftsmen, which was made possible by the new use of machines. It was a violent protest, but its life was short.

Since the collapse of the Knights of St. Crispin there have been few effective labor organizations among New England shoe operatives and none in Yankee City until the strike of 1933. Mechanization, however, did not cease, and with it went the subjugation of the workers. Several complete processes of shoemaking were standardized in the course of time. One of them was the "turn" process, particularly adapted to the manufacture of high-quality women's shoes. This process, one of the oldest of modern shoe-building techniques, was standard in Yankee City at the time this study was made in 1931–35.

The turn process has given way, in Yankee City as elsewhere, before the inroads of price competition. Cheaper shoes for women are replacing those made by more complicated and costly processes such as the welt, McKay, and turn methods. Cement and lockstitch processes were evolved to produce shoes that could be sold at a lower retail price. These changes also permit great factory flexibility in adjusting to style variations, an important consideration to the modern manufacturer of women's shoes. The rapidity with which styles change has created rush work demands, necessitating speed in manufacturing processes and a quick and ready adaptability to change. When an order is received, the factory must push production so that the order may be completed before the style changes. With the changing styles, there is a decreasing demand for standardized types of shoes. The result is alternation between rush work and lay-offs. This trend in the manufacture of women's shoes induces a greater than average fluctuation in employment.[10] These factors have contributed to the instability of employment in Yankee City shoe factories.

Another factor in the instability of the shoe factories is the practice of leasing machines. The leasing system was first introduced by Gordon McKay in 1861 and was continued by the larger shoe-machinery companies. The machine manufacturers adopted a royalty system in which the rates per unit of output were the same to both large and small manufacturers. This worked to the disadvantage of the former, who preferred a sliding scale. The small entrepreneur who had been attracted by this feature of shoe manufacture seldom had sufficient capital investment to insure success. The relatively small initial cost of establishing shoe factories resulted in a high mortality among these enterprises.

With the development of a large market in the West and South, the shoe industry has moved many of its production units away from the New England states and closer to the markets. One entire NRA hearing in January 1935 was devoted to a study of the migration of the boot and shoe industry from Massachusetts,[11] and showed that state's share in the national production of shoes to have declined from 47.13 per cent in 1899 to 20.05 per cent in 1934, while its volume of production had diminished—in spite of the increase in national production—from 102 million pairs in 1899 to 71 million in 1934. Some of the important factors contributing to the migration of the shoe industry[12] were the following:

(1) labor disturbances;

(2) the necessity to reduce manufacturing expenses and obtain lower labor cost, in order to meet severe price competition;

(3) the location of manufacturing plants in or near the principal markets;

[10] Factories making shoes for men experience smaller seasonal fluctuations and fewer changes in consumer demand.

[11] National Recovery Administration, Division of Review, *Report of Survey Committee on the Operation of the Code for the Boot and Shoe Manufacturing Industry* (Washington, D.C., Government Printing Office, July 16, 1935).

[12] *Ibid.*, pp. 81 ff.

(4) inducements offered to Massachusetts manufacturers by cities and towns located in other states to move to their localities. Such inducements take the form of freedom from taxes, free rent, donations of factory sites and/or property, and, frequently, cash subsidies.

The conditions which we have described (national, state, and local) have placed the Yankee City shoe worker in a precarious position. Changing methods of production and the vicissitudes of the trade itself have led to instability among shoe-manufacturing enterprises. Yankee City is in no position to absorb the output of its factories, and the latter have become more and more dependent on the large chain stores for retail distribution. The number of shoe companies operating in Yankee City and the number of employees have varied from year to year. In 1929, sixteen shoe factories were operating in Yankee City—the largest number operating at one time. The peak in actual employment was reached in 1926 when 2,060 individuals were employed in the shoe factories in the city.

The shoe industry, not only in Yankee City but throughout the country, was one of the first to suffer before the general depression of 1929, showing a decline from a 1923 peak in value of product. During the period of high production, the shoe workers were in a position to dictate their own wages, but during the period of decreasing employment the manufacturers held the dominant position in the internal factory organization and gradually forced down the price of labor.

This pressure, deriving ultimately from retail-price competition, stimulated a concentrated effort on the part of the workers to organize in order that they might resist the manufacturers' desire to reduce costs by reducing wages.

THE STRIKE AND THE EVOLVING SOCIAL AND ECONOMIC SYSTEMS

Before we ask ourselves what this economic history has told us about the causes of the strike, let us re-assess our findings. We have spoken of an economic history. However, we do not have one history but several—at least six histories can be traced. We can conveniently divide the technological history of Yankee City's shoe industry into five phases (see Chart III). At least two important stories are to be found here; the tools change from a few basic ones entirely hand-used to machines in an assembly line, and the product from a single pair of shoes to tens of thousands in mass production.

The changes in the form of division of labor (see Chart III) are another story of the utmost importance.[13] In the beginning, the family made its own shoes, or a high-skilled artisan, the cobbler, made shoes for the family. In time, several families divided the high-skilled jobs among themselves, and later one man assigned the skilled jobs to a few men and their families. Ultimately, a central factory developed and the jobs were divided into a large number of systematized low-skilled jobs. The history of ownership and control is correlated with the changes in the division of labor. In early days, tools, skills, and materials were possessed by the family; eventually, the materials were supplied by the owner-manager, and soon he also owned the tools and machines. The sequence of development of producer-consumer relations tells a similar story. The family produced and consumed its shoes all within the circle of its simple unit. Then, the local community was the consumer-producer unit, and ultimately the market became national and even worldwide. Worker relations (see Chart III) changed from those of kinship and family ties to those of occupation where apprenticeship and craftsmanship relations were superseded and the individual unit became dominant in organizing the affairs of the workers. The structure of economic relations changed from the immediate family into a local hierarchy and the locally owned factory into a vast, complex system owned, managed, and dominated by New York City.

With these several histories in mind (and with the help of Chart III), let us ask ourselves what would have happened if the strike had taken place in each of the several periods. In period one, with a family-producing and consuming economy, it is obvious that such

---

[13] The sequences in the vertical columns of the chart are exactly ordered; the horizontal interrelations are approximations and indicate basic trends.

	Technology	Form of Division of Labor	Form of Ownership and Control	Producer-Consumer Relations	Worker Relations	Structure of Economic Relations
IV The Present (1920–1945)	*Machine Tools* mass production, assembly line methods	Nearly all jobs low skilled; a very large number of routinized jobs	*Outside* ownership and control of the factory (tools leased)	Very few retail outlets; factory merely one source of supply for a chain of shoe stores	Rise of industrial unions, state supervised . . . no (or weak) unions	Center of dominance New York. Very complex financial producer and retail structure. Local factory not important in it
III Late Intermediate Period (Approximately to World War I)	*Machine Tools* machines predominate; beginning of mass production through use of the machine (McKay)	A central factory with machines; still high degree of skill in many jobs	First small, and later, large *local* men of wealth own or lease the tools and machines	National market and local capitalist; many outlets	Craft and apprenticeship (St. Crispin's Union)	Center of dominance local factory; complex hierarchy in local factory system
II Early Intermediate Period (Approximately to the Civil War)	*Machine Tools* few machines first application (Elias Howe, etc.)	One man assigns highly skilled jobs to few men; highly skilled craftsmen ("letting-out" system)	Small, locally controlled manufacturers; tools still owned by workers, materials by capitalist, market controlled by owner	Owner and salesmen to the consumer regional market	Informal, apprenticeship and craft relations	Simple economic no longer kinship; worker subordinate to manager
	Hand Tools increasing specialization and accumulation of hand tools	Specialization among several families; a few highly skilled jobs	*Local Control* not all shoemakers need own all tools; beginning of specialization	Local buyer from several producer families sells products (no central factory)	Kinship and neighbors among workers	Semi-economic but also kinship and neighborliness
I The Beginning (Early 1600's)	*Hand Tools* few, basic, and simple	All productive skills in the family, including making of shoes; a few cobblers for the local market	*Local Control* skills, tools, and materials owned and controlled by each family; or by the local cobbler	The family produces and consumes shoes and most other products	Largely kinship and family relations among workers	Very simple non-economic; the immediate family

CHART III. The History of the Differentiation of the Yankee City Shoe Industry a conflict would have been impossible. The social system had not evolved to sufficient complexity; the forces had not been born which were to oppose each other in civil strife. In the second phase, several families in a neighborhood might have quarreled, but it is only in one's imagination that one could conceive of civil strife among the shoemakers.

In the third phase, however, there appears a new social personality, and an older one begins to take on a new form and assume a new place in the community. The capitalist is born and during the several periods which follow he develops into full maturity. Meanwhile the worker loses control and management of his time and skills and becomes a subordinate in a hierarchy. There are, thus, distinct and opposing forces set up in the shoemaking system. What is good for one is not necessarily good for the other, but the interdependence of the two opposing groups is still very intimate, powerful, and highly necessary. The tools, the skills, and the places of manufacture belong to the worker; but the materials, the place of assembly, and the market are now possessed by the manager. Striking is possible but extremely difficult and unlikely.

In the fourth period, full capitalism has been achieved; the manufacturer is now the owner of the tools, the machines, and the industrial plant; he controls the market. The workers have become sufficiently self-conscious and antagonistic to machines to organize into craft unions. Industrial warfare still might prove difficult to start, although it did occur, because in a small city where most people know each other the owner or manager more often than not knows "his help" and they know him. The close relation between the two often implies greater compatibility and understanding, which cut down the likelihood of conflict. But when strikes do occur the resulting civil strife is likely to be bitter because it is in the confines of the community.

In the last period, the capitalist has become the super-capitalist; the workers have forgotten their pride in their separate jobs, dismissed the small differences among themselves, and united in one industrial union with tens and hundreds of thousands of workers throughout the country combining their strength to assert their interests against management. . . .

431

THE RABBLE HYPOTHESIS VERSUS
STRUCTURAL ANALYSIS

Elton Mayo

A theoretical analysis of the political and moral consequences of reducing men and their motives to individual economic units. They become a "dust of ashes"
and a "rabble," the willing prey of a totalitarian state.

For nearly two centuries economic study has been supposed to
provide the social skills requisite for the effective handling of civilized human activities. And in some areas its more concrete studies
have unquestionably fulfilled this demand. For example, questions
of cost accounting, marketing, and the large-scale organization of
industry in its formal aspect have been handled with considerable
and growing skill. But in these affairs there has developed economic practice of a valuable kind far removed from classical economic theory. E. H. Carr has said that in recent years the "chronic
divorce" between economic theory and practice has become more
marked than ever.[14] And he pictures economic theory "limping be-
wildered and protesting" in the train of economic practice. Chester
Barnard, himself an executive of great experience, finds that effective leadership in industry, that is, successful administration,
"has to be based on intuitions that are correct, notwithstanding
doctrines that deny their correctness."[15]

This divorce suggests a question as to the original clinical or
practical adequacy of economic theory to the facts it studied.
Science begins in the clinic and is effectively developed in the
laboratory. In the clinic one uses relatively simple logics to examine
complicated fact; in the laboratory clinically developed skill has
suggested the isolation of certain aspects of the complex fact for

[14] Edward Hallett Carr, *Conditions of Peace* (New York, The Macmillan
Company, 1942), p. 79.
[15] Chester I. Barnard, *The Functions of the Executive,* Preface, p. xi.

Note: See Notes on the Authors, page 555, and item 154 in the bibliography for the full reference to this selection.

separate study and, when successful, this may result in the development of highly complicated logic. The one method informs and develops the other—simple logic and complex fact, simplified fact and complex logic. But, even when the laboratory has come to aid the clinician with highly developed techniques of examination, it is nevertheless the clinician who has finally to piece together the various scraps of detailed information thus obtained and, guided both by scientific training and by experience, to determine the diagnosis and treatment in the *particular instance*—i.e., the patient. Economics, like other human studies, would seem to have been over-eager to arrive at laboratory methods and to have ignored the need for continuous detailed study of all the various aspects of actual industrial situations. Yet this clinic-laboratory relationship is the essential of scientific method.

One has to realize, with respect to common economic practice and its relation to social and political urgencies, that the actual industrial situation has changed immensely since the early part of the nineteenth century. Carr, in the book I have already quoted, asserts that in the days of the classical economists the industrial system was made up chiefly of small industries and businesses. His implication is that the whole theory of competition and the value of competition was based upon such an actual society. A former colleague, the late Philip Cabot, was accustomed to talk of his early life in New England as having been lived in such a society. He used to declare that the mills and industries of New England fifty or sixty years ago were essentially small organizations. They employed perhaps a few hundred people, and the life of any such business was rarely more than two generations of proprietorship or at most three. Cabot attributed this to the fact that the organizing ability of a father did not usually survive two generations of success. He pointed out, however, that the cessation of such a business did not create a problem for the community in which it was situated. By the time that a particular organization ceased to operate, some local rival had developed and was prepared to employ the skilled workmen, if indeed it had not already done so. Consequently there was no local community problem of widespread unemployment following a shutdown. In these days, the general situation is altogether different. During the economic depression of the early thirties, many manufacturing organizations accustomed to employ thirty or forty thousand people found themselves faced with a much diminished demand for products. Instances can be quoted where the roster of employees fell to ten thousand or even less. And this did not mean a stony disregard of human welfare: in many cases a company struggled for years to retain as many of its employees as it could without facing economic disaster itself. But in the then existing situation such attempts were doomed to failure; and in certain industrialized areas, with a period of months, many thousands of workers were inevitably "released." A situation such as this cannot compare with the characteristic nineteenth-century situation of which Carr and Cabot speak.[16] The so-called release of twenty or thirty thousand persons in two or three suburbs of a large city inevitably becomes a community problem of the first magnitude. And a problem of this kind cannot be left to "individualism" or "enlightened self-interest"; that nineteenth-century track is closed. Cabot was accustomed to say that, instead of expecting the life of a particular business to come to an end in two or three generations, we have, by improving industrial organization, conferred upon such businesses a "species of immortal life" which must be maintained by the community at its peril.

All this indicates that a primary assumption of nineteenth-century economic theory is no longer tenable. Even one hundred years ago, it was probably easy to believe in the essential relevance and propriety of the principle that the pursuit of individual interest is the basis of economic organization. But, although this assumption is still voiced by economic and political theorists, it is perfectly clear that business and political practice are based nowadays upon a vitally different conception of human society. This divergence between theory and practice is perhaps the source of at least part of the confusion that prevails in politico-economic dis-

[16] Detailed consideration of the depressions of 1837, 1873, and 1893 is not relevant to this discussion. But, no doubt, a competent historian could show that the widespread unemployment in these periods was not unrelated to the already increasing pace of technical advance.

cussions of the present. Whereas the economic theorist of the university still assumes individual interest as a sufficient basis for theory and the development of economic insight, the administrator with actual experience of handling human affairs bases his action upon a contrary, but empirically derived, assumption. This leads to endless confusion, not only in the public mind, but also in the writings of economists themselves. The practical economist stands on firmer ground but is troubled by a lack of clinical experience and by an uneasy allegiance to economic theory.

Economic theory as at present understood may be said to have begun originally with the physiocrats, especially with the publication by Francois Quesnay, physician to Louis XV, in 1758, of his *Tableau Economique*. . . . The ideas of the physiocrats were strongly developed by the so-called liberal school of economists, sometimes known as the Manchester School, in England. For a long time the physiocratic phrase, *laisser faire, laisser passer,* served as its motto. Gide gives the principles of this liberal school as three:

(1) Human societies are governed by natural laws *which we could not alter, even if we wished,* since they are not of our own making. Moreover, *we have not the least interest in modifying them, even if we could;* for they are good, or, at any rate, the best possible. The part of the economist is confined to discovering the action of these natural laws, while the duty of individuals and of governments is to strive to regulate their conduct by them.

(2) These laws are in no wise opposed to human liberty; on the contrary, they are the expression of relations which arise *spontaneously* among men living in society, wherever these men are left to themselves and are free to act *according to their own interests.* When this is the case, a *harmony* is established among these individual interests which are apparently antagonistic; this harmony is precisely the natural order of things, and is far superior to any artificial arrangement that could be devised.

(3) The part of the legislator, if he wishes to insure social order and progress, must therefore be limited to developing individual initiative as fully as possible, to removing whatever might interfere with such development, and to prevent individuals from meddling with one another. Therefore the *intervention of governments*

435

ought to be reduced to that minimum which is indispensable to the security of each and of all,—in a word, to the policy of "let alone."[17]

These principles give us in a few words the essential theoretic background of the economic and political thinking of the nineteenth century. There is much in this conception of human cooperative activity which is still important and still to be commended. A chief source of difficulty for the writers who expounded *laisser faire* lay in the restricted manner in which they developed to explicit statement the second of these principles, namely, "the relations which arise spontaneously among men living in society, wherever these men are left to themselves and are free to act according to their own interests."

The origin of the misapprehension upon which the whole of economic theory is based must be traced to David Ricardo. . . .

Under what conditions, then, are the postulates of economics satisfied? . . . I think it may be said that [Ricardo] bases his studies and his logic upon three limiting concepts. These are:

1. Natural society consists of a horde of unorganized individuals.
2. Every individual acts in a manner calculated to secure his self-preservation or self-interest.
3. Every individual thinks logically, to the best of his ability, in the service of this aim.

For many centuries the rabble hypothesis, in one or other form, has bedeviled all our thinking on matters involving law, government, or economics. From this theory is evolved the conviction of need for a Leviathan, a powerful State, which by the exercise of a unique authority shall impose order on the rabble. So that in these days many of our liberals and our lawyers have come to enunciating doctrines that are only with difficulty distinguished from the pronouncements of a Hitler or a Mussolini. Indeed, the major difference seems not to be logical, but rather of the nature of a humane assurance that the liberal concept of state administration will

[17] Charles Gide, *The Principles of Political Economy* (London, D. C. Heath and Company, 1909), English translation by C. W. A. Veditz, p. 24–25. (The italics are Gide's.)

permit greater freedom of speech and action than the National Socialism of Germany.

. . . For in truth the notion of isolated individuality is the shadow of a dream. . . . In the real world, the isolated individual does not exist; he begins always as a member of something and . . . his personality can develop only in society, and in some way or other he always embodies some social institution. I do not mean to deny the distinctness of individual life, but this distinction can function only inside a society.[18]

A contrary claim must be made for exponents of the rabble hypothesis. They seem to be, almost exclusively, persons remote from the active world of affairs—academics, writers, lawyers. This is still true; those who support most keenly the Ricardian view, who mistake its postulates for facts of observation, are students of law, government, philosophy. Very few, if any, have taken responsibility for the life, work, and welfare of their brother humans. They have small knowledge-of-acquaintance of various social situations, a negligible equipment of social skill, and are consequently able to ignore the facts of human organization, and the extreme importance of these facts for him who would direct the work and thought of others. There is a recent book which is not in this category, probably the most important work on government and administration published in several generations. It is not surprising that this difficult but interesting study has been ignored by political science schools.

Mr. Chester Barnard is president of the New Jersey Bell Telephone Company: since he has worked his way upwards in the company, he has proved, not only his knowledge-of-acquaintance of the facts of human cooperative systems, but also his skill in handling the many and diverse problems of human organization. . . .

Next to the question of authority as source of learned confusion, Barnard places "the exaggeration of the economic phases of human behavior which the early formulation of economic theory made far too convenient." Adam Smith and his successors have, by their theories, greatly diminished the "interest in the specific social

---

[18] John Neville Figgis, *Churches in the Modern State.* . . .

processes within which economic factors are merely one phase"; these writers, he claims, have "greatly overemphasized" economic interests.[19] This is conjoined with a false emphasis upon the importance of "intellectual, as compared with emotional and physiological, processes" in the determination of behavior. Consequently in the current thought of many, man is still an " 'economic' man carrying a few non-economic appendages." His own experience in an organization, Barnard points out, has been quite otherwise:

> . . . though I early found out how to behave effectively in organizations, not until I had much later relegated economic theory and economic interests to a secondary—though indispensable—place did I begin to understand organizations or human behavior in them. . . .[20]

Once again it is evident that knowledge-of-acquaintance and the intuitions that result from intimate and sustained familiarity are more trustworthy than elaborate logics uncontrolled by developed skill and responsibility.

Nowhere is the difference between knowledge of the facts and inference from words more apparent than in Barnard's discussion of authority as it is actually exercised in an organization. Gone are the thunders and lightnings on the secret top of Oreb or of Sinai, gone also philosophical discussions of unity and indivisibility. Authority is a convenient fiction which "is used because from the standpoint of logical construction it merely explains overt acts."[21] The person who exercises so-called authority is placed at an important point in the line of communication—from below upwards, from above down, if one thinks in terms of an organization chart. It is his business to facilitate a balanced relation between various parts of the organization—so that the avowed purpose for which the whole exists may be conveniently and continuously fulfilled. If he is unsuccessful in this, he will have no actual authority in the organization—however important may be his title. An "approximate definition" of authority is that it "is the character of a communication (order) in a formal organization by virtue of which it

---

[19] Chester I. Barnard, *op. cit.*, preface, p. x.
[20] *Ibid.*, preface, p. xi.
[21] *Ibid.*, p. 170.

is accepted by a contributor or 'member' of the organization as governing the action he contributes . . . under this definition the decision as to whether an order has authority or not lies with the persons to whom it is addressed, and does not reside in 'persons of authority' or those who issue these orders."[22] Barnard is careful to specify a "zone of indifference": not all the communications of a day are critical for the sustenance of authority. But this apart, it remains true that "the efficiency of organization" depends upon "the degree to which individuals assent to orders."[23] "Thus authority depends upon a cooperative personal attitude of individuals on the one hand; and the system of communication in the organization on the other."[24] Authority therefore in actual exercise demands a capacity for vision and wise guidance that must be re-achieved daily: since the cooperation of others is a vital element in it, social understanding and social skill are involved equally with technical knowledge and capacity. Under the influence of economic theory, we have a system of education that trains young men in technical understanding and technical skills; we do nothing whatever to develop social insight or to impart social skill. Indeed we provide an education that operates to hinder the development of such skills.

When Barnard says of any particular organization that it must be *effective* (accomplish the "objective of the system") and also *efficient* (satisfy individual motives),[25] he is enunciating a principle that may be applied widely to any society as a whole. The social organization of any group must secure for its members, first, the satisfaction of their material needs, and second, the active cooperation of others in the fulfillment of many and diverse social functions. These are not ranked here as first and second in order of importance; both are important and must be simultaneously effected. But an inspection of primitive cultures might lead one to suppose that, of the two, the latter—the need to cooperate continuously—is more vital to the communal life. For the rituals of

[22] *Ibid.,* p. 163.
[23] *Ibid.,* p. 169.
[24] *Ibid.,* p. 175.
[25] *Ibid.,* p. 56.

any primitive tribe are almost wholly devoted to the promotion of cooperative harmony, to discipline that enhances the certainty of unity in work; the tribe apparently assumes implicitly that, if cooperation be assured, the material needs of the group will inevitably be satisfied.

Now there cannot be cooperation without organization. Any industrial organization is at once a way of working—which must be technically expert and effective—and also a way of living for many people—a cooperative system which must be efficient, satisfactory as a way of living. Our civilization has been immensely successful in respect of material and technical accomplishment, an utter failure as a cooperative system. Not only have we failed to secure continuous cooperation within the nation or as between nations; we have also committed ourselves to doubtful theories, at best of limited application, that seem to regard this failure as a civilized achievement. We have an economics that postulates a disorganized rabble of individuals competing for scarce goods: and a politics that postulates a "community of individuals" ruled by a sovereign State. Both these theories foreclose on and discourage any investigation of the facts of social organization. Both commit us to the competitive and destructive anarchy that has so far characterized the twentieth century. Now it is certain that economic studies have had many uses, and it may be that the time given to political science in universities has not been wholly wasted; but, for so long as these topics are allowed to substitute for direct investigation of the facts, the total effect will be crippling for society.

"Now the State did not create the family, nor did it create the Churches; nor even in any real sense can it be said to have created the club or the trade union; nor in the Middle Ages the guild or the religious order, hardly even the universities or the colleges within the universities: they have all arisen out of the natural associative instincts of mankind. . . ."[26] Figgis continues: "What I have tried . . . to make clear is this: that we are divided from our adversaries by questions of principle, not of detail; that the principle is concerned . . . with the very nature of the corporate life of men and therefore with the true nature of the State. . . ."[27]

[26] John Neville Figgis, *Churches in the Modern State*, p. 47.
[27] *Ibid.*, pp. 49–50.

He goes on to claim that, for so long as "the doctrine of State omnipotence remains unconquered," free institutions cannot develop freely. For the true function of State organization is to provide a framework "under which the perennial social instincts of men can develop."[28] And he repudiates as a "scientific monstrosity" the idea of an "omnipotent State facing an equally unreal aggregate of unrelated individuals."

This conception of an all-powerful State and a rabble of unrelated individuals is implied by economic theory, expressly stated by law and political science. It has given us a Mussolini and a Hitler, and has confused the whole course of democratic politics.

The Axis powers have pressed these theories of law and politics beyond their ultimate logical conclusion to actual application. Perhaps this will give pause to academic expositions of the sovereign State and induce reflection, perhaps even some investigation of the actual human facts. The democracies have succeeded in developing toward a cooperative commonweal—if, indeed, they have succeeded—because of the unexpressed but actual resistance of democratic peoples to tyrants, divine right, and the State Absolute. Time and again in history our ancestors have refused to give allegiance to authority imposed from above and have cast their vote for free expression from below as the sole source of genuine leadership. This has maintained the possibility of progressive development and has kept democracy upon the pilgrims' way undisturbed by the lures or byways of political theory. Parliamentary representation and periodic elections are a partial safeguard of this development—but only partial. Not yet, even in the democracies, are we rid of the danger of political tyranny. Mr. Harold Butler reports a mountain guide's sage observation, 'We have overthrown the power of the aristocracy and the power of the Church. Now we shall have to overthrow the power of the politicians, and that will be a hard fight."[29] The forms of democracy are not enough; the active development of social skill and insight must make these dry bones live. . . .

[28] *Ibid.,* p. 51.
[29] Harold Butler, *The Lost Peace* (New York, Harcourt, Brace and Company, 1942), p. 89.

Chapter 9

MANAGEMENT IDEOLOGIES

INTRODUCTION

Earlier we discussed the attack on big business and its executives (the opening to Chapter 1) and promised to return to the polemics of attack, defense, and counter defense following our examination of some of the important knowledge we now have about the basic characteristics of the business executive. It was hoped that our study of the role of the executive, an examination of the industrial hierarchies in which he functions, and knowledge of his career, would help us to evaluate some of the basic issues about businessmen that are a necessary part of a free society.

Most criticism, well-informed as it may be, is the expression of an ideological position. It is rare that criticisms, for or against, are derived from careful scrutiny and evaluation of the relevant evidence. Popular tribunals are built on values, sometimes intelligently thought through and curbed by sound judgment, but more often violently emotional and partisan.

The ideologies about managers and executives and the world of big business in which they play major roles are important factors too in determining the issues and dilemmas of capitalistic society and its industrial empires. The evidence about these ideologies is pressed upon us by

442

too many people. Much of it is worthless, yet that which matters is of critical importance and comes from the more significant critics of our time and from excellent research.

THE CREED OF AMERICAN BUSINESS ENTERPRISE

Francis X. Sutton, Seymour E. Harris, Carl Kaysen, and James Tobin

The moral beliefs and values of business enterprise as they are presented by business itself are analyzed.

Praise for the achievements of American capitalism is one of the dominant themes in the literature of the Business Creed. Material achievements—especially the high and rising standard of living—take first place; discussion of non-material achievements is subordinate in frequency of repetition throughout the body of ideology and in prominence of place in systematic expositions of it. Both the material and the non-material achievements are explained by a rigid cause-and-effect link with the System: the achievements flow from and validate the System, and the two are inseparably bound together. . . .

MATERIAL ACHIEVEMENTS OF AMERICAN CAPITALISM

The central achievement of the system has been the great rise in standard of living to its present level, high in comparison with the past and in comparison with other countries today. All elements of this rise are praised: the great increase in total output, the introduction of new goods, the conversion of the luxuries of yesterday's rich to the necessities of today's masses, and the great reduction of working time. But the first three are praised more frequently than the last. A typical expression of the claims of progress is provided by the Advertising Council's pamphlet, *The Miracle of America:*

Today the American way of life provides the highest standard of living ever enjoyed by any people in the world.

Note: See Notes on the Authors, pages 553, 556, and 557, and item 225 in the bibliography for the full reference to this selection.

This is no mere boast. It is a statement of thrilling fact—that men can raise their level of living by greater productivity if they are free to do it.

Electricity, running water, central heating, one house or apartment per family, are quite general in America. To the Russian or Chinese worker, whose whole family is often crowded in one room, with no private kitchen or bath and no central heating, our homes would represent dreams of luxury.

With only one-fifteenth of the world's population and about the same proportion of the world's area and natural resources, the United States —has more than half the world's telephone, telegraph and radio networks—more than three-quarters of the world's automobiles—almost half the world's radios—and consumes more than half the world's copper and rubber, two-thirds of the silk, a quarter of the coal and nearly two-thirds of the crude oil.[1]

An hour's work in 1914 and 1948 would buy the following:[2]

	1914	1948
Men's Work Shoes	9 hours	3 hours
Baby Carriage	21 hours	15½ hours
Electric Light Bulbs	102 minutes	12 minutes
Electric Fan	49 hours	4 hours

Another example, emphasizing the comparison between the United States and the U.S.S.R., which is now common in the context of the world political struggle, appears in an advertisement of the Columbia Steel and Shafting Company:

It may seem a small thing to you that an average worker in the U.S. earns more than enough in two 8-hour shifts, even at this year's prices, to put a Thanksgiving dinner fit for a king on the family table—plump-breasted gobbler and all the other fixin's, down to pumpkin pie and whipped cream and a cherry on top.

But it isn't a small thing at all. It's one more instance of the direct results of a productive system that has brought more health and happiness to more people, more things and better things at less cost, than any other system ever has or ever will.

---

[1] *The Miracle of America, as discovered by one American family,* Advertising Council, Inc. (New York, n.d.), pp. 11–12.

[2] *Ibid.,* p. 12.

The average Russian worker, now—he'd have to work four full 40-hour weeks, plus a couple of hours of over-time to set the same dinner in front of his wife and kids. It's lucky for him that Russia doesn't have a Thanksgiving Day. Very appropriate, too. After all, under the Communistic system of slave labor, with no freedom of action, speech, religion or anything else, what would he be thankful for?[3]

Benson Ford, of the Ford Motor Company, in a speech before the Los Angeles Chamber of Commerce emphasizes the great rate of material progress:

In the year 1900, there was one automobile for every 9,500 people in this country. Today there is one automobile for every 4½ to 5 people in the United States.

In the year 1925, 2,700,000 families had radios. Today 37,000,000 families—or 95 per cent of all American families—have radios.

In 1935, 16 per cent of families or spending units in this country had an income of over $2000. Last year 64 per cent had incomes over $2000 a year, . . . Progress is always an unfinished business in America.[4]

Both time and space comparisons which portray the success of the American System are often put into dramatic form. Thus McGraw-Hill shows how much of the world's production the United States accounts for, despite its relatively small size:

The United States contains only about 6 per cent of the world's population. But our national income, before the war, amounted to almost 25 per cent of the world's income. Our industrial output as a whole approximates 45 per cent of world totals. We are now producing a like percentage of the world's railroad mileage; 25 per cent of merchant fleet tonnage; 50 per cent of the world's telephones; 45 per cent of steel production; 40 per cent of aluminum production; 33 per cent of coal output. We are refining (though part of the production comes from imports) 55 per cent of the world's copper, and 70 per cent of its petroleum. We are now producing 50 per cent of the world's rubber (though

[3] Columbia Steel & Shafting Company advertisement, *Business Week,* Nov. 20, 1948.

[4] Benson Ford (Vice President of Ford Motor Company), *Five Jobs for Young Men,* address before the Los Angeles Chamber of Commerce, Los Angeles, Calif., Feb. 28, 1949, p. 7.

post-war resumption of natural rubber production will sharply reduce
this balance). Our shares of agricultural production are, of course, much
smaller, but just before the war we accounted for 35 per cent of world
cotton production, 15 per cent of wheat, and 10 per cent of wool.[5]

Paul Hoffman makes a similar point:

. . . Ours may not be a perfect system but under it 7 per cent of the
people of the world do produce nearly 50 per cent of the world's manufactured goods. . . .[6]

And the Advertising Council tells us:

*Compared to the record of all civilization, this free world of yours is
ten minutes old.*
Yet in ten short minutes it's done more *good for more people* than
anything that ever happened on earth.[7]

The last examples serve to illustrate another important aspect
of progress which is emphasized in the creed—sheer productivity
and efficiency in itself. There is, of course, a logical connection between a rise in the standard of living and an increase in productivity. But frequently, increases in efficiency are celebrated as
achievements in themselves without reference to their fruits in
terms of increased living standards. A General Electric Company
advertisement tells how G.E. products have become increasingly
efficient.

Fluorescent lamps, introduced by General Electric Scientists, give
about 2½ times as much light as filament lamps of the same voltage
. . . often last from three to six times longer . . . G.E. research and

[5] "What Does America Want?," McGraw-Hill advertisement, *Washington Post,* December 1944.
[6] Address by the Honorable Paul G. Hoffman before the National Board
of Fire Underwriters, May 25, 1950, p. 8.
[7] "A Tremendous Thing Has Happened in the Last 10 Minutes," an advertisement approved by the Public Policy Committee of the Advertising
Council. This is a favorite metaphor; see for example. S. Wells Utley, *The
American System, Shall We Destroy It?* (Detroit, 1936), p. 74, where
United States history is compressed into the last twenty-five seconds of
twelve hours of human history.

engineering have improved the household refrigerator so that today's model runs on less than half the current used 20 years ago . . .[8]

The Advertising Council, in the *Miracle of America,* tells us:

. . . the average worker can produce about five times as much per hour as in 1850 without expending any more energy than he did then. That's why net output of goods and services increased 29 times from 1850 to 1944, though working hours were much shorter and the population only six times greater. *If we were still producing at the 1850 rate per hour, we would need over 300 million workers, each putting in 43 hours a week to produce as much as we did in 1944![9]*

This same pamphlet illustrates another, and somewhat curious, form of the emphasis on production for its own sake; in summarizing the progress of the American system, it cites the rise in the proportion of the population gainfully employed from 320 per thousand in 1850 to 420 per thousand today.

The business creed is not exaggerating when it emphasizes the high standard of living in the United States compared with the rest of the world, the great speed with which output and consumption have grown in the last 100 years, and the introduction of countless new goods; any historian would see these facts in much the same perspective. In the material sense, industrialization has changed the world with unbelievable rapidity and has done so more rapidly in the United States than elsewhere.

NONMATERIAL ACHIEVEMENTS

Among the nonmaterial achievements of the system, three are given particular importance in the business creed: the creation by and in business of the spirit of service; the opportunity for personal achievement and social recognition which the business world presents to all who have the talents to use it; and, broadest of all, the achievement of Freedom—political, religious, and personal— which the system and the system alone makes possible.

According to the creed, business creates a spirit of service and its objectives go far beyond meeting the needs of the cash custom-

---

[8] General Electric advertisement, *Boston Globe,* June 13, 1948.
[9] *Miracle of America,* p. 13.

ers, or even creating new needs for new cash customers. Thus the authors of *USA, The Permanent Revolution,* picture the heavy social responsibilities of a business executive and their importance to society at large:

"There are times, as I sit behind a desk piled high with the day's unread correspondence, when I stare darkly out of the window," Walter H. Wheeler, Jr., President of Pitney-Bowes, Inc., of Stamford, Connecticut, was speaking on the *Social Responsibility of Business.* "Trying to see me are three conscientious executives, who would like to remind me, if they dared, that we're in business to make a profit and that I must spend *some* time on the problem of sales, manufacturing, and development. There is a Community Chest meeting in five minutes, and a directors' meeting tomorrow morning, neither of which I am prepared for . . . It seems to me that none of us can look forward with hope over the years unless all of us can find solutions to problems bigger than our immediate material progress."

Every American man-of-affairs will recognize Mr. Wheeler's complaint . . . The truth is that Americans are just about as busy with their non-official, unremunerated, voluntary activities as they are with their official duties; and these unpaid, unofficial, off-duty activities have a deeper and more lasting effect upon American life, and even American policies, than do the official ones.[10]

Another variation on the service theme is provided by the picture of Henry Ford drawn in a life insurance company advertisement:

Young Henry Ford saw something quite different in the shadows of the shop that night.

He saw his little automobile speeding a doctor to a remote farmhouse to save a life.

He saw a million miles of roads opening up for all Americans the glories of their big country . . . making the man from Maine a neighbor of the man from California.

He saw people riding to work, to market, to school, to church freed at last from the old tyranny of distance.

And he saw new jobs, better incomes, more free time for everybody . . .

Such was the vision of young Henry Ford in the little shop on Bagley

---

[10] *USA, The Permanent Revolution,* by the Editors of *Fortune* with the collaboration of Russell Davenport (New York, 1951), pp. 128–129.

Avenue . . . Like every enterprise we look upon as basic . . . the auto industry has earned its success by contributing something deep and lasting to the welfare of all Americans.[11]

The emphasis on disinterested and non-materialistic motivations in this quotation provides a counterpoint to the more usual materialistic themes; it might be called a spiritualization of material progress.

The picture of business as the provider of the sinews of war and national defense is also part of the service theme. This picture, with its appeal to patriotic sentiments and national solidarities, first became important in the Second World War, and for a time became the staple ingredient of advertising. The theme is frequently repeated today in the context of the cold war, often in terms of "first in war, first in peace." But the implied obligation, that business should be first in the hearts of its countrymen, is not always honored as business feels it should be. Thus the President of the United States Steel Company pictures the achievements of business in winning the war in a somewhat plaintively defensive context:

It was only a few years ago—in the war years—that the government gloried in the size of its industrial giants and honored them for doing successfully the giant tasks—the almost impossible production tasks—that our national security demanded. It called upon United States Steel to outproduce, single handed, all the Axis nations put together. We did it. It called upon our great research laboratories and our skilled technicians to design and to create such storybook miracles as a "portable" landing field for aircraft. We did so. It called upon our management to use all of its experience, ingenuity, efficiency, and know-how, to build, to man and to operate vast new steel-making plants for the government. We did so. And the government sang our praises.

. . . After World War I those who had produced the weapons that defeated our enemies were denounced as "merchants of death." Today, after World War II, they are branded as "oligopolists."[12]

[11] John Hancock Life Insurance Company advertisement, *Newsweek,* Jan. 24, 1949.
[12] B. J. Fairless, *Business—Big and Small—Built America,* U.S. Steel Corporation, 1950, pp. 5–6. Statement in *Study of Monopoly Powers, Hearings* before the subcommittee of the House Committee of the Judiciary (Celler Subcommittee), Eighty-first Congress, 2nd session, February–July 1950.

A second non-material benefit claimed in the creed is that the business system creates equality of opportunity and rewards those who take advantage of it. The Bell Telephone advertisement which tells us:

> Year by year the next half century will be increasingly theirs [those starting out]. New leaders will appear from among them. Step by step, rung by rung, they will mount the ladder to the top. For telephone management is employee management and comes up from the ranks.
> There will be more good jobs in the telephone business in 1958 and 1998 than now. It just can't help being this way . . .[13]

is typical. Similarly, the paper of the Eastern Railroad Presidents' Conference has a column entitled "Career Open to Merit," which tells us, for example, that the new Chairman of the Board of the Pennsylvania Railroad started as a rodman on a track engineering corps in 1901 and that the new President of the Erie Railroad began as a yard clerk in 1908.[14]

Opportunity is often linked with freedom and together they are portrayed as the crowning achievement of the system. Freedom as an achievement is usually given a place of honor in comparisons with the slavery and low living standards of the Communist world. Thus a Warner and Swasey advertisement states:

> If every Communist knew what every sane person in a capitalist country knows—the high standard of living which capitalism makes possible, the pride of individual accomplishment, the satisfaction of knowing you can go as far as your own abilities and ambition will take you, the security of justice, the joy of knowing your son can go even farther than you have gone . . . if every Communist knew the facts about capitalism, there wouldn't be any Communists.[15]

Freedom also appears in contrast with government control in a broad sense, rather than specifically with the lack of freedom in a totalitarian Communist state. This is especially the case in discussions of the proper role of government: the Chamber of Commerce

---

[13] Bell Telephone System advertisement, *Harper's,* March 1948.
[14] *Railroad Data,* June 1949, September 1949.
[15] Warner & Swasey advertisement, *Newsweek,* Aug. 9, 1948.

argues that without the freedoms embodied in the right "to keep his living where he can find it, and to venture his means where profit seems likely, it is pure delusion to imagine that political freedom, even if it exists, can long endure."[16] And, in a somewhat different context, the then Chairman of the Board of the United States Steel Corporation celebrated another aspect of freedom:

. . . No other nation possesses so many private universities as we do; and no nation, I suppose, enjoys the same full measure of individual liberty that we have known. That can hardly be a coincidence.

. . . But I am suggesting that Freedom of Education and Freedom of Enterprise are part and parcel of the same thing—and they are inseparable—and that neither can survive without the other.[17]

These nonmaterial benefits claimed in the creed cannot be measured as can output, consumption per head, and productivity.[18] One cannot define precisely, far less quantify, how much freedom there is in one society compared with another; much the same thing is true of opportunity, although the problems here are not quite so great. Yet it can fairly be said that the creed is rather selective in claiming nonmaterial achievements for the System. This is not to say that its claims are false; the major claims of freedom and free opportunity are certainly justified on any fair view of American society. But they are one-sided. No rounded account of the matter would push so far the claims of the uniqueness of American freedom, and of its necessary association with a particular set of economic arrangements. With respect to equality of opportunity, there is an even clearer process of selection at work. Individual success stories abound, but no attempt is made to examine the overall statistical situation. Such an examination might well

[16] *Measuring Monopoly: A New Approach,* A statement of the U.S. Chamber of Commerce (Washington, 1949), p. 23.

[17] I. S. Olds, *Our Mutual Ends,* address at a dinner celebrating the 250th Anniversary of Yale University (19 October 1951), published by the U.S. Steel Corporation, pp. 1, 8.

[18] Of course, a sufficiently sophisticated economist will reject the notion that any of these magnitudes can be measured with any precision for the purposes of intemporal or international comparisons, but such refinement is hardly in order in the context of this discussion.

lead to more tempered conclusions about American freedom of opportunity.[19]

EXPLAINING THE ACHIEVEMENTS—THE AMERICAN SYSTEM

These great achievements are, according to the business creed, mainly due to the American System of free enterprise and limited government. James B. Walker, "an active participant in the business system,"[20] concludes his history of business on this continent with a careful consideration of the factors responsible for the spectacular success of America. He gives credit to the environment: climate, geography, natural resources. The people, he finds, had spiritual as well as physical strength. But the climactic position in his list goes to the Constitution, "a Bill of Rights for a free enterprise economy," which fostered inventiveness, business acumen, and thrift.[21] Similarly, the authors of the National Association of Manufacturers' two-volume study give credit to a variety of factors but place of honor to the system:

No one factor has been responsible for this progress. The character of our people, our abundant supply of natural resources, our form of government, the type of business system we have developed, the international environment in which we have operated—all these and many other factors have played their part.

Nevertheless, two of these things have been of outstanding and dominating importance in our development: our system of representative democracy and our system of individual enterprise.

. . . inevitably and irrevocably the two go hand in hand.[22]

[19] See, for example, the studies of William Miller in the social origins of American business leaders: "American Historians and the Business Elite," *Journal of Economic History,* November, 1949; "The Recruitment of the Business Elite," *Quarterly Journal of Economics,* May, 1950; and "American Lawyers in Business and Politics," *Yale Law Journal,* January, 1951; F. W. Taussig and C. Jocelyn, *American Business Leaders;* and Upsell and Bendix, in the *American Journal of Sociology,* January and March, 1952.

[20] James B. Walker, *The Epic of American Industry* (New York, 1949), p. xi.

[21] *Ibid.,* pp. 476–479.

[22] National Association of Manufacturers, Economic Principles Commission, *The American Individual Enterprise System, Its Nature and Future,* 2 vols., (New York: McGraw-Hill, 1946), p. 873. This treatise will be cited NAM, I or II. This book is the single most important systematic exposition of the business creed in the current literature.

Other ideologists are even more emphatic. They see nothing distinctive in America's endowment of natural resources or in the quality of the population. The System is the unique element, and to it must be credited the unique achievements.

It is true that our land is richly endowed with fertile fields and raw materials, but this can be said with equal truth of Mexico, Central America, and South America. Our people have been thrifty, diligent, and intelligent, but there is no sound basis for the assumption that they overstep the rest of the world in these qualities by any such margin as is shown by their material progress.[23]

To say that it's because of our natural resources is hardly the answer. The same rich resources were here back when the mound builders held forth. Americans have had no monopoly on iron, coal, copper, aluminum, zinc, lead, or other materials. Such things have always been available to human beings. China, India, Russia, Africa, all have great natural resources.

Is it because we work harder? Again the answer is "NO" because in most countries the people work much harder on the average than we do.

Can it be that we are a people of inherent superiority? . . . Down through the centuries our ancestors, including the Anglo-Saxons, have starved right along with everyone else.[24]

Both of these authors, after rejecting other explanations, find the answer in the discovery, in this country in the late eighteenth century, of the way to release human energy.

There is no mystery as to the causes . . . The reasons . . . are clear and definite forces which have been exerted in the lives of human beings, forces as eternal in their action as the laws of physics or gravitation. We, as a people, can continue to be guided by them and keep on to still greater heights, or we can cast them aside and return to the same stagnation which enveloped the race in former times.

During the last quarter of the eighteenth century, man evolved a new basis for human relationships.[25]

[23] Utley, *The American System,* p. 79.

[24] Henry Grady Weaver, *Mainspring, the Story of Human Progress and How NOT to Prevent It* (Irvington-on-Hudson, N.Y., 1947), p. 4 (italics as in original).

[25] Utley, *The American System,* p. 79.

. . . The United States is conceived as a nation uniquely blessed by a remarkable economic system, which is the central part of the larger American System. Like any ideology, the creed is chiefly concerned with the immediate historical situation in which it arises; it may reach out to view Socialist Britain, or the lessons of the fall of Rome, but most of the writings and speeches by which it is conveyed deal with concrete problems in contemporary America. Through the material of the creed there runs a persistent effort to define the essential features of the United States as a whole. The result is the definition and characterization of an American System, grounded in a particular economic organization, which, as Senator Robertson argued, was inherent in the System from its start.

THE NATURE OF THE SYSTEM—ECONOMY AND SOCIETY

As seen in the business creed, the economy is the central core of the American System, around which the rest of the society is built. Like Marxism, the creed views modern society as a single, consistent, highly integrated pattern. Both ideologies see the economic engine as the prime mover of the social vehicle, though Marxism is much more explicit in this respect than the business creed. In any broad comparative perspective, this is remarkable; rarely has the economic structure of a society been given so central a place in the society's total view of itself as in the modern West. In most societies, fairly stable patterns of economic activity become so traditionalized, so interwoven with kinship, community, and political systems that the economy and its workings occupy a relatively minor place in prevailing ideology.[26]

The idea of the tight interdependence of economy and society is central to the business ideology. The comprehensive statement of the creed prepared by the National Association of Manufacturers opens with this expansive treatment of the "economic system":

The term "economic system" means not merely business as this word is commonly used. It includes all those activities and relations which

---

[26] See the account of the Kula in B. Malinowski, *Argonauts of the Western Pacific* (London, 1932), for a striking case in which social and ritualistic aspects have obscured the functioning of the economy.

have an influence upon, or affect, our making a living. It is concerned just as much with the organization of government as with the organization of business, with social problems as with production problems, and with training workers. All these elements are a part of the whole which is the "American way of life". . . and anything that affects one part will alter the whole.[27]

A little later, the authors in an even more embracing statement appear to make the "economic and political system" coextensive with the whole of American society:

Our political and economic system is simply you and I and the millions like us. It is you as you argue with your neighbors over politics, religion, working conditions, foreign policy, and the weather. It is you as you work at your jobs alongside a lathe, behind a plow, or in front of a kitchen stove. It is you as you sit at night and help your boys and girls with their lessons, and as you fret and worry and plan for their future. It is you as you sit and read the evening paper, or listen to the radio, or go for a ride in the country, or gossip over the back fence. It is you as you say "the blessing" when you sit down to eat and as you go to worship.

These—the thousand and one things which make "our day, our daily bread"—are the American political and economic system.[28]

The tendency of the ideology to intertwine "economy" and other aspects of society reflects, in part, the realistic problems of making distinctions of this sort in a complex society; in part it reflects a more general ideological tendency to emphasize the integrated wholeness of society.

In contexts where the lines between economic and other institutions are more clearly drawn, the business creed again parallels that of its Marxist critics: the one finds American society good, and the source of its virtues lies in its "economic system"; the other finds America wicked, and the same "economic system" is the source of its vices. A favorite linkage between the economic system and the rest of society in the business creed is the edifice of American freedoms. Thus a former president of the NAM told that society on its fiftieth anniversary:

[27] NAM, I:1.
[28] NAM, I:17–18.

. . . [more Americans must be made to] realize that competitive enterprise, civil and religious freedom, and political freedom are inseparably bound up together and that when one of the three is undermined, all the liberty they now so smugly enjoy will soon be devoured in the maw of dictatorship.[29]

The indivisibility of freedom demands that the economic system be both "free" and free from competition from another system in the same society. No departures from the creed's model of a competitive economy are admitted; the business creed denies the viability of a "mixed" economy in which government economic activity plays a significant and legitimate role.

BIG BUSINESS: THE IDEOLOGY OF ATTACK

John D. Glover

> The major attacks on big business by those who oppose
> it or would correct its faults are studied and their sig
> nificance pointed out to businessmen and others.

One might suppose that "big business" is something that could be defined precisely and concretely, even if arbitrarily. Conceivably, for instance, it might be defined as companies having, say, assets stated at more than $1,000,000, $10,000,000, $100,000,-000, or $1,000,000,000, as the case might be. Given any such definition, one could then list by name all the companies included in the group.

A scattering of critics have attempted to set up exact definitions of this sort. Some have even listed the particular corporations which, for them, comprise "big business." But no such definition commands a preponderant following.

Actually, the matter of defining "big business" isn't nearly so simple as that anyway.

---

[29] H. W. Prentis, Jr., President of Armstrong Cork Co., *Competitive Enterprise versus Planned Economy,* address issued as a pamphlet by the NAM, August 1945, p. 9.

Note: See Notes on the Authors, page 553, and item 97 in the bibliography for the full reference to this selection.

When you take a look at the nouns, the terms, the figures of speech which critics use to describe what it is they are opposed to, it becomes quite clear that it is something more than just an uncertain list of particular corporations. And when you take a look at the nouns, the terms, the concepts which are used to describe what they approve and favor *instead* of "big business," it becomes clearer still.

Here is a sample list of the expressions used by *economic* critics when they are talking about what it is *they* are critical of:

"big business," "Big Business," "bigness," "The Big";
"Trusts";
"Industrial Combinations," "great combinations";
"giant consolidations," "consolidations," "mergers";
"mammoth corporations," "giant corporations," "corporate empires";
"great establishments," "massed capital";
"monopoly," *"prima facie* monopoly," "monopolistic competition," "oligopoly";
"monopoly power," "economic power," "substantial control of the market";
"large business," "large-size in American business";
"large business units";
"large-scale production," "large-scale operations";
"large enterprise";
"large companies," "modern business";
"corporations";
"anyone important enough to affect the prices of the things that he sells and buys . . . almost every businessman . . . the ordinary businessman . . ."

And here, in contrast, is a sample list of the terms used by critics on the economic plane when they are talking about what it is they are *not* attacking, or about that which they favor instead:

"separate concerns," "independent concerns," "independent companies," "small companies";
"other companies" (as distinguished from "big companies");
"competing corporations," "the competitor," "competition," "pure competition";
"representative firms";

"the small enterpriser," "the small businessman," "smaller units," "smaller firms";
"little workshops," "little establishments";
"the millions of farmers."

When we pass to the critics who attack "big business" on the social and political plane, . . . the collection of terms used changes somewhat. Some of the expressions encountered on the economic plane are carried over, but many new ones are added. Some carry an emotional charge of considerable force close to the surface. And we encounter concepts at even higher levels of abstraction than before.

For example, these are some of the expressions met with on this next plane of criticism:

"big business," "Big Business," "big companies," "bigness";
"trusts," "combinations";
"great corporations," "huge corporations," "giant corporations";
"mammoth financial complexes," "colossi";
"the 200 largest nonfinancial corporations";
"the 250 largest corporations";
"the largest corporations";
"the larger companies";
"industrial concentration," "economic concentration," "big economic power";
"concentration of economic power," "concentration of private power";
"massive concentration of corporate wealth," "unlimited financial power";
"power that controls the economy," "organized economic power";
"the money power";
"short-sighted and muscle-bound private control over the economy";
"the free-wheeling bandwagon of big business";
"political and financial privilege," "the privileged," "privilege";
"the entrenched economic group";
"the special interests," "the vested interests," "business interests";
"the controlling influences" "captains of industry," "the plutocratic circle";
"industrial aristocracy," "industrial oligarchy," "plutocracy";
"the corporate community," "the corporate system";
"large-scale enterprise," "modern machinery," "modern industry";

"giant technology," "functional rationalization";
"the large corporation," "the modern corporation";
"modern business," "modern business organization";
"Industrial Capitalism," "the business system";
"the corporation";
"organized business enterprise";
"businessmen," "the businessman";
"business."

And here is a sample list of the terms put up in contradistinction to "big business" and such like when political and social critics are talking about that which they hold up as something of an "ideal":

"the individual workman . . . the small merchant . . . the petty employer";
"the individual businessman," "individual industry," "independent entrepreneurs";
"small enterprises," "smaller companies," "the small entrepreneur";
"little business, local business";
"small competitive businessmen," "small and independent business";
"the typical business corporation of the last century";
"widely distributed property," "tiny individual economic units";
"resident proprietors beholden to no one";
"classless individualism," "middle-class capitalism";
"the naturally harmonious world of the small entrepreneur";
"economic democracy";
"organization of industry in small units";
"the competitive model," "competition";
"a cultural system drenched with the artisan spirit of small enterprise";
"private enterprise," "free enterprise";
"individualism," "liberalism," "laissez-faire," "democratic society," "democracy";
"private business";
"the plain people," "the common people," "the many," "the people";
"the little man," "the common man."

The criticism on the *ethical and moral* plane uses terms which take over where these lists leave off. There, the expressions become even more abstract. . . .

The target of the criticism is clearly something more than just a particular, if uncertain, group of corporations, be it more or less

459

extensive. Essentially, it seems to me, the common bond among the critics is their opposition to departure from some sort of an "ideal" way of things in which economic life, political life, and social life is based upon independent, unorganized, unrelated, and even isolated individuals. This ideal is embodied in the individual as the economic unit, the political unit, and the social unit. "Colossi," "mammoth corporations," and even "larger companies" are merely the more obvious, outstanding manifestations of deviation. For some critics, all "modern business" and even the "ordinary businessman" represent a deviation from this "ideal." They are an embodiment of this deviation. They are among the principal prime movers of this deviation.

It is the deviation from the "ideal," and everything associated with this deviation—in reality or in fancy—which is the ultimate object of the criticism directed against "big business." This criticism expresses *reaction* against the modern industrial revolution.

Lest any "ordinary businessman" who reads this be in doubt, when it comes right down to it, the critics are not just talking exclusively about "corporate empires," or even "large companies." They are talking about *you*.

. . . I shall henceforth use the term big business, without initial capitals and without quote marks, to stand for the whole welter of things which critics have in mind.

And now to the first of the three levels of attack, the economic.

The economic attack on big business boils down to two arguments: that it is inefficient; that it is monopolistic. These two propositions run as continuous strands down through the history of the criticism which has been levelled at big business on economic grounds. They are its essence.

The development of the economic attack over the past fifty years or more represents the maturing and the refinement of these two ideas. This is no happenstance. It was a matter of logical, if not of ideological, necessity that these two arguments should have become the crux of the criticism on this plane.

The whole matter goes back to the basic theory and justification of laissez-faire capitalism. This was the doctrine, and still is, in its classical form, that the free unhampered activity of individuals seeking their own private material gain will lead, of automatic necessity, to the best of all possible worlds. This organizational structure of society—or, perhaps, this nonorganization—will lead to results that could be equalled, if at all, only by an infallible, all-wise, all-powerful central control. It leads to the greatest possible national product. To a national product composed ideally of what the people as a whole want most. It leads to a completely fair, objectively determined parcelling out of shares of that product among all individuals. It leads to an ideal use of all resources, natural and human. Since this system leads to results which are ideal in every particular, it obviously cannot be improved upon. Any other arrangement must necessarily be inferior. This was, and is still, the classical rationalization of laissez-faire capitalism.

One of the basic, one of the cardinal, premises of that classical doctrine is that economic activity will be carried on by a *large number* of necessarily *small* units. These units are so small that the activity of any one of them, or even of several of them acting together has no perceptible effect on the sum total of what happens. It has only been within the past twenty years, interestingly enough, that this essential premise has been fully developed in detail. But even the critics of fifty years ago who could not think and express themselves in the elaborated concepts of modern economics seemed to have known intuitively that it was one of the basic premises of this classical theory.

Business units which are *big,* and necessarily *few,* stand opposed to that fundamental premise. Obviously a *big* business is not *minute.* It is self-evident that the number of big corporations necessarily must be *few* as compared to the number of small enterprises. Big corporations do not correspond to the basic unit which the whole classical theory presupposes and is founded upon: the *minute,* absolutely competitive, and—it should be added—the completely irresponsible, economic atom. Among other things—according to this theoretical scheme—it follows, therefore, that they will not, automatically and of necessity, be freely and unreservedly competitive. They will be monopolistic.

From the first days of the Trusts, certainly by 1900, it was generally felt—even if only vaguely and uneasily—by their friends and foes alike, that big corporations did not look very much like the ideal atom of the ideal system. They were bigger than that. Quite apart from whether *big* atoms would be monopolistic or not, or even whether they might be conspiratorial, many of the critics clearly and vigorously opposed these new large companies on the ground that they were a far cry from the free, unassociated, and unbeholden individual. It could not be by such large, new entities as these that the best of all possible worlds was to be brought about.

The defenders of the Trusts, including economists of great prestige in their time, also were aware, if only intuitively, of the disparity between the classical individual atom and these new large units which had so rapidly come upon the scene. Since the classical system led to the *best* of all possible worlds, how could a system made up of such new, contrasting entities lead to anything else than something inferior? The burden of proof that they were not an undesirable deviation from the ideal automatically fell upon them. In hearings before the Industrial Commission of Congress in 1899–1900, it is perfectly clear that witness after witness felt this burden. They had to offer a justification for the departure from the classical rationalization. They did. They argued that, while, to be sure, big corporations—in those days they were commonly equated with "trusts" and "combinations"—did represent a departure, it was a justified departure. They would be more efficient. Greater efficiency, with greater abundance for everyone, was held out as an end which fully justified the departure from the principle.

This vindication on the basis of an expediency, more than anything else, was persuasive. At least, so it would seem, to very many.

Moreover, the defenders of the Trusts, combinations, and big businesses generally, held that, despite their great size, they were not really monopolies. They were not alone in their respective fields. They had competitors. And in any case, there were always *potential* competitors. The readiness of these potential competitors to swarm in if the Trusts exacted too high a toll would always hold them in check. Officers of trusts said so. Eminent economists agreed.

Big business carried the day.

462

But the attack, beaten off, lived to fight another day.

Voices, increasingly influential voices, began to say, and then to proclaim, that the highly touted efficiency of the Trusts was pure humbug. They were not more efficient. They were *less* efficient. These were persuasive voices.

But the facts didn't seem to bear them out. Trusts—supposedly inefficient—actually prospered. Not only that. Big business generated a growing flood of low-cost, mass-produced goods. Not only old familiar staples, but *new* things, things unknown a generation earlier—like automobiles and electrical appliances. The theory was hard to reconcile with the facts. The explanation offered by critics was that they were only *seemingly* more efficient. Their *real* inefficiency was said to be concealed by the gains they were able to exact by virtue of their monopoly powers. But this argument couldn't be made to stick.

The new big corporations actually *weren't* monopolies in the traditional sense of the word. The traditional sense of a "monopoly" was a literal one: a single seller. But these big companies all had competitors, if only much smaller ones. Also, these large enterprises held no royal or legislative charter which gave them the sole right to engage in their particular line of business. It was a free country. Anyone could go into any business he wanted to. Competitors would swarm in—so it was said—if the big companies exacted too high a profit, or didn't give the best product for the lowest cost. So they weren't monopolistic. And if they weren't monopolistic, *ergo* they must be competitive.

Economic critics had no completely convincing answer to that.

At least, not until the Depression of the Thirties. Then, in the Depression, the pent-up hostility toward big business was unleashed in a torrent. In the Depression, many big corporations looked pretty feeble. Some, especially among the railroads and utilities, had gotten mixed up in pretty curious, not to say odorous, kinds of deals. In the minds of many, these situations reflected discredit on all big business. They didn't look like vigorous, more efficient building blocks of an order of things which was superior even to the classical mechanism. Giving big business a backhanded sort of credit for being a key instrumentality in the American economy, critics said it was responsible for the Depression. The operation of the economy, all too obviously, was far from ideal. That was one thing.

Another, perhaps even more important so far as the criticism was concerned, was the appearance of a new development of economic theory which seemed to show that big corporations *were* like monopolies after all. They weren't "monopolies" in the old sense, to be sure. But they weren't competitive either. They were "monopolistic." And they led to results which looked more like the results of monopoly than the results of competition.

The whole issue was fully re-opened on a grand scale. Big businesses *were* a deviation from the ideal atom after all. An economic mechanism made up of such units *was* inferior to the ideal mechanism of old. And, as for their supposed greater efficiency, it didn't exist. Big business was a deviation from principle which could no longer—critics said—be justified as an expedient leading to more for everyone.

Beginning in 1938 there was a great governmental economic inquiry, the Temporary National Economic Committee. More than anything else, it was preoccupied with bigness in business.[30] Just about at the height of its activity, war in Europe broke out. The Committee ended its work and filed a final report on a note of

[30] "Among us today a concentration of private power without equal in history is growing.

"This concentration is seriously impairing the economic effectiveness of private enterprise as a way of providing employment for labor and capital and as a way of assuring a more equitable distribution of income and earnings among the people of the Nation as a whole. . . ."

"Private enterprise is ceasing to be free enterprise and is becoming a cluster of private collectivisms; masking itself as a system of free enterprise after the American model, it is in fact becoming a concealed cartel system, after the European model. . . ."

". . . Men will dare to compete against men but not against giants."—*Message from the President of the United States Transmitting Recommendations Relative to the Strengthening and Enforcement of Antitrust Laws,* 75th Cong., 3d Sess. (April 29, 1938). (This letter of President Franklin D. Roosevelt resulted in the setting up of the Temporary National Economic Committee.) Reprinted in T.N.E.C., *Investigation of Concentration of Economic Power,* Part I, *Economic Prologue,* 75th Cong., 3d Sess. (Washington: Government Printing Office, 1940), pp. 185–187.

uncertainty. Maybe big business was saved by the bell. Maybe that particular attack had spent itself. In any case, within a few months, the United States was in the thick of a multifront war. The war gave everyone something else to do besides attack or defend big business. The attack went on, to be sure, but on a far-reduced scale. Such as it was, it was pretty well drowned out by the din of a real battle against foreign enemies.

Since the war, the attack on big business has been twice renewed in full measure. In 1949 by the "Celler Committee" of the House of Representatives. In 1952 by the Subcommittee of the Senate Select Committee on Small Business.

The attack has continued. . . . The end is not in sight.

In recent years, big business has looked efficient again. It played a notably, and often spectacularly efficient, role in enabling America to join in the defense of the free world. Along with small business, and with everyone joining in, it produced untold quantities of unheard of weapons with a speed that confounded the enemy. Since the war big business has been profitable. In postwar years, more often than not, big businesses have acted with more restraint than small in the effort to hold prices down. But there are many who still question its social efficacy. They still say that it is monopolistic.

And the fact is—and this is a very important fact, even if it is a fact in the realm of philosophy—the only fully and systematically articulated doctrine of economics, indeed, one which is widely accepted—holds that big business *is* monopolistic. In the realms of theory and ideology, the big corporation is still a deviant from the ideal minute atom of classical doctrine. One of the ironies of our time—and this may come as a shock to many administrators of big business—is that still, at this late date, there does not exist a fully developed logic which reconciles and integrates the big corporation with the very basic, traditional justification of laissez-faire capitalism. Nor, has there been developed a *new* philosophy of laissez-faire capitalism that does provide positively for big business. Men who are practical men of affairs should not underestimate the importance of that fact of the realm of ideas.

Advocates of big business often still try hard to reconcile the

465

large corporation with the traditional, classical doctrine of how and why it is that laissez-faire capitalism leads to the best of all possible worlds. Surveying the world of reality, it looks as though the facts might well justify such a notion. At least as compared to other systems. But those who believe there is a real and important place for big business still don't have the great strength that comes from being supported by a nicely integrated, elegantly elaborated ideology.

This lack shows up in Congressional hearings. It shows up in litigation under the antitrust acts and the Federal Trade Commission Act. It shows up in the public statements of administrators of big business. It shows up in the doubt that many of our friends abroad have concerning America.[31]

So there, in the broadest of strokes, is the history of the economic criticism of big business since the turn of the century. . . .

Criticisms of the basic ethical and moral character of our industrial, big business civilization have been made by men who come from most dissimilar backgrounds and who look upon the world from vastly differing standpoints. The particular expressions of these criticisms are as varied as the individuals making them. But despite the particular differences of viewpoint and the variety of emphasis, and the differing amounts of charity, pessimism, and vehemence with which these criticisms are made, there is a basic uniformity which runs through them: Our society is *rich* enough—or so at least many of the critics concede. Some of them, indeed, say it is too well off. And our society may be *democratic* enough. But we are not a *good* society. In terms of human and spiritual values—not economic and political values—our society, *these* critics say, is destitute. Some of them say we suffer from "weariness." Some say we are barbarous. Some say "Satanic."

If one could cast up a consensus of these views—a sort of a "sense of the meeting"—it might run something like this: Our civilization, at best, is beset by spiritual and moral doubts. It is an

---

[31] "After all, we agree on some issues with either side: with the Russians, we reject what seems to us the jungle philosophy of big business capitalism. . . ."—Tom Driberg (British Labour M.P. and "an influential Christian socialist"); "A British View of U.S. Policy," *Time,* October 12, 1953, p. 23.

"Age of Anxiety." Or, it is empty of those ethical and spiritual values which are necessary to the good society—to "Peace of Mind," or "Peace of Soul." Some critics speak of a Lost Generation, a Disillusioned Generation, or a Beat Generation. We are told that we live in "an age starved for spiritual values."[32] At worst, our civilization is a literal hell on earth in which mankind can live only an animal life, not a human life.

The present Pope, Pius XII, asks, "What age has been, for all its technical and purely civic progress, more tormented than ours by spiritual emptiness and deep-felt interior poverty?" And His Holiness speaks of ". . . the spiritual and moral bankruptcy of the present day. . . ."[33] Albert Schweitzer, in 1923, spoke of the "decay of civilization."[34] In 1949, in one of the most powerful and moving fables ever written, C. Virgil Gheorghiu (a Roumanian novelist, now a refugee in France) likened present-day industrial civilization to a submarine, hopelessly sunken and with enough oxygen to sustain life for only a few more hours:

"The atmosphere in which contemporary society lives. Man cannot endure it much longer. Bureaucracy, the army, the government, central and local administration, everything is conspiring to suffocate man. Contemporary society is suitable for none but machines and mechanical slaves. It was created for their benefit. But for human beings it is asphyxiating. As yet they are unconscious of it. They believe that they are living normally as they did before. They are like those sailors in the submarine who go on working in the poisonous atmosphere for another six hours. But I know we are nearing the end."[35]

This is the kind of ethical and moral questioning which is encountered beyond the economic, political, and social criticism of big business.

One of the interesting things about this underlying criticism of modern industrial civilization is that it is not, for the most part, di-

[32] Francis Henry Taylor, Director, Metropolitan Museum. (As in *Time,* December 29, 1952, p. 50.)
[33] Encyclical, *Summi Pontificatus* (October, 1939).
[34] *The Decay and Restoration of Civilization* (London: A. & C. Black, Ltd., and New York: The Macmillan Company, 1923).
[35] *The Twenty-fifth Hour* (New York: Alfred A. Knopf, 1950), p. 122.

rected explicitly at "big business" as such. . . . The word "business" doesn't crop up as often as in the material we have sampled up to now. Essayists, playwrights, poets, and theologians simply express themselves in terms and frames of reference which are different from those of, say, economists, business administrators, social theorists, or presidential candidates. For this reason, it is possible to let the point occasionally slip away that this criticism applies every whit as much to big business as anything we have seen so far.

I'll try to nail this point down.

First of all, let's consider the terminology and concepts of the ethical and moral critics. They often express themselves in highly abstract terms. They speak with dismay or vehemence about "life in the twentieth century," "industrial civilization," "the Machine." These high-level abstractions and most broadly generalized ideas and concepts simply represent the far end of a series which begins at about where the terminology of the political and social critics leaves off. Retracing back down to the lower levels of abstraction and to the less generalized concepts of the ethical and moral critics, the terms encountered become again those of the more familiar order: "the modern trust," "the corporation," "businessmen," "the businessman."

Basically, and especially *concretely,* the target of the ethical and moral critics is the same as that of the economic and the political and social critics.

Here, for instance, in roughly ascending order of abstraction and generality, is a sample of the terms that ethical and moral critics use to label what it is *they* are attacking:

"the modern trust . . . the consolidated corporate monopoly . . . (which) are the practical realization of the commercial spirit in its most despotic form";
"corporations for private profit," "the corporation";
"the prevailing forms of business enterprise";
"men of business," "businessmen";
"the expansion of investment," "the commercial community";
"private interests";
"private enterprise," "private capitalism";

"capital," "capitalistic enterprise," "the capitalist system," "capital-ism";

"the modern economic order";

"the spirit of capitalism," "the ethos of capitalism";

"capitalist morality," "business morality";

"the profit motive";

"decent godless people";

"men who turn from GOD . . . Engaged in devising the perfect me-chanical refrigerator";

"power . . . wielded by the irresponsible private owners of the sources of production, or their agents";

"accumulation of power";

"immense power and economic domination . . . concentrated in the hands of the few";

"industrialism," "mass-production industrialism," "modern industry";

"modern technics," "our present industrial set-up," "the new industrial structure";

"our world of commerce and finance and mass production";

"our sensual and materialistic generation";

"industrial enterprise," "industrial capitalism";

"uniformity and standardization," "the factory system";

"the Factory," "the Machine," "the assembly line";

"industrial civilization," "capitalist civilization," "business civilization";

"the neotechnic phase of civilization," "our civilization," "civilization";

"a world . . . ruled by men of business";

"industrial culture," "asphalt culture";

"modern society," "a mechanistic society," "the acquisitive society";

"the City," "soulless giant cities," "city existence";

"this age of industrialism," "the present age," "the Age of Anxiety";

"modern times," "the world today";

"life in the twentieth century."

To the extent that such high-level abstractions as "life in the twentieth century," "capitalistic enterprise," "the modern eco-nomic order," and "this age of industrialism" can be related back down to things which are concrete, it is to the techniques, the work-ings, the products, and the consequences of "big business"—of the very same thing the economic and the political and social critics are after: "the corporation," "the trust," and "men of business."

Truly, it stands to reason that this should be so. For "industrial civilization," and "life in the twentieth century" *are* very largely distinguished, for better or worse—I believe for better—from the civilizations of other times and places by the workings, the products, and the consequences of large-scale private enterprise. Of big business.

And by "big business" I mean here just about what most of the critics mean. Not merely such large corporations as the Union Pacific Railroad Company, American Telephone and Telegraph Company, General Motors Corporation, General Electric Corporation, United States Steel Corporation, and Standard Oil Company (New Jersey)—all of whose influences on American civilization are so very obvious. But also all businesses employing as many as 1000 or even 500 people. For, relative to the individual "atoms" of economic and political theories, and as compared to the run of productive units of other times and in most of the rest of the world today, even companies employing a mere 500 are *big*. And it is precisely the methods, the processes, the products—the total impact—of business concerns of this size and up, which have done so much to bring about the revolutionary changes which now distinguish this civilization from others of the past and present.

As much as anything else, modern American civilization *is* the civilization of "big" business. Whatever may have been their contributions to our welfare and our progress—and these contributions in the aggregate surely have been enormous—it is not "little workshops," "small merchants," "petty employers," and "tiny individual economic units" which have generated those characteristics which now palpably *distinguish* America from other civilizations.

Simply consider the modern development and exploitation of natural resources; our transportation and communication methods and systems; consider how our food is farmed and processed; how our clothing is made; consider the materials of which our buildings are constructed. Consider how we treat and cure ourselves when we are sick. Consider how all these things contrast to their counterparts, say, of the Europe of the seventeenth Century, or of the countries of Asia and the Middle East even in this century. The ways and the means of life in our industrial civilization are obviously and profoundly different. Consider that modern industrial civilization is the only civilization in which large-scale private enterprise has evolved as a *general* and *commonplace* method of organizing cooperative productive effort. The point need not be labored. Industrial civilization and big business have evolved hand in hand in a close, reciprocally influencing relationship. Industrial civilization *is* the civilization of big business.

All civilizations have had their critics. Massachusetts Bay had the Mathers. Florence was scourged by Savonarola. Athens had its Socrates. Judah and Jerusalem had Isaiah and Jeremiah. Humanity still not having achieved perfection, we must in our age as well expect our own due measure of ethical and moral criticism. But in our day such criticism very often takes a turn which is not to be found in earlier critics—say, in the prophets of the Old Testament. And it is this turn, with its implicit message, which brings so much of the ethical and moral criticism of *our* civilization to bear so heavily on big business.[36]

Isaiah and Jeremiah cried dreadful warnings aloud to the sons and daughters of Zion. As I read their words, they were decrying the willful waywardness of fully and individually responsible human beings of free will. These great critics, I think, did not attribute the spiritual and moral shortcomings of their audience to the facts that they were an essentially rural people, with a tribal politi-

---

[36] A homely, if heart-rending, example of this way of thinking:

America's Plenty Blamed

"Israel Lichtenstein, thirty-seven, stabbed his attractive wife, Analise, twenty-eight, while she was asleep in their seventh-floor room at 601 W. 160th St. at 7:30 A.M. and then dashed up three floors to the roof and plunged to his death. She died shortly after she was brought to Mother Cabrini Hospital.

" 'He did it,' according to a physician who had been treating Mr. Lichtenstein for nervousness, 'because his wife had a domineering attitude about everything and considered herself physically, mentally, and spiritually superior to her husband. Had they stayed in Europe where there are not as many beauty parlors, nylon stockings and other such things, they would have been happy and this never would have happened.' . . ." *New York Herald Tribune,* January 27, 1954, p. 17.

cal and social order, employing the productive techniques of the late Bronze or early Iron Age. To these still stirring prophets, the evils which they deplored and their correction were—it would seem—matters of individual human will and responsibility.

In contrast, throughout much of the criticism of modern times there is an unmistakable implication that the spiritual and moral shortcomings in industrial civilization are due to economic, political, and social institutions and organization structures; to the predominately urban way of life; and to the use of the products, techniques, and equipment of large-scale production. A goodly amount of modern criticism seems to hold that the sins of contemporary society arise because it is possessed of demons—in the form of private entrepreneurs, businessmen.

It is upon the external circumstances, conditions, and arrangements of modern life that many critics now seem to lay the burden of blame for human error and sin, not upon the individual—and on a small demonic "class." There is an unmistakable tendency in many of the critics . . . *not* to attribute the evils *they* decry to an everlasting capacity for error and sin on the part of individually responsible beings with free will.

In a sense, this is something of a counterpart of political theories which hold that power is not inherent in individuals, but in their relationships to property, to things. Virtue and vice seem to be seen by many of the ethical and moral critics not to be internal matters of the spirit—of individual will—within people themselves. Rather, the spiritual nature and content of life seem to be seen as determined by the relationship of individuals to things of the external world—to property; to the physical circumstances of life; to the techniques of the productive activity they are engaged in—and by the prevailing political and social institutions.

That is to say, many of the economic, political, and social critics see human attitudes and behavior as shaped by material environment and by organization mechanisms and structures. And so do many of the ethical and spiritual critics of our day. In this, they are unlike the prophets of the Old Testament from Isaiah to Malachi.

472

BIG BUSINESS: AN IDEOLOGY OF DEFENSE

David E. Lilienthal

The necessity of bigness in business for the great society
is cogently argued by an outstanding liberal.

The people of the United States of America now produce as
much as all the rest of the people of the world put together, with a
mere 6 per cent of the world's population and about the same per
cent of its land area and natural resources. This production will
probably be increased greatly in the next ten to twenty-five years.
It is only at the beginning.

At this moment this is the most important fact in the world, for it
is America's mastery of productivity that stands between freedom
and the tidal wave of Communist militarism threatening the world
with a new era of darkness.

This technique of production—and with it the equally important
art of an ethical distribution of production—is a *creative* thing, a
combination of poetry and sweat. It calls for imagination, vitality,
faith, as well as the skills of science, management, human relations and modern governmental techniques. This unfolding of
American productive and social genius is the most exciting spectacle in the history of modern times.

Man has been working at wealth creation since the beginning of
time in order to fight off hunger, exposure, degradation. He has
been trying to push back his enemy, poverty, trying for enough
breathing space so his whole day and night would not be needed
just to get enough food and warmth and shelter to survive. He has
been trying to get a margin so he could be a man, not merely an
animal fighting to stay alive.

In America of the mid-fifties of this century, we have done this
wealth-creation job better by all odds than any generation ever

Note: See Notes on the Authors, page 554, and item 139 in the bibliography for the full reference to this selection.

did. Our over-all productivity keeps climbing year after year. Since 1939 we have doubled our total industrial production; and we go right on adding to it year after year.

More important still, we are learning, through an imaginative synthesis of private and governmental action, how to get the benefits of this vast flood of goods and services distributed in a democratic and an ethical way. The result is fewer very poor and fewer very rich than in any large community since the dawn of history.

What accounts for this almost-miracle? It is very important indeed that we try to understand why this great and creative art came to fruition now, in mid-twentieth century U.S.A., and what it is we can do to stimulate and nourish this distinctive talent of ours. I have thought about this a great deal, as have ever so many other people.

Here is a summary of my thinking:

First: Our productive and distributive superiority, our economic fruitfulness, rest upon Bigness. Size is our greatest single functional asset.

Second: Against the dangers of Bigness—concentration of economic power and overcentralization—we either already have adequate public safeguards, or know how to fashion new ones as required.

Third: We need to sense what an asset we have in Bigness. We need to examine it critically, but affirmatively, without old and outworn prejudices.

Fourth: The time has come when it is in the interest of the whole country that we promote and encourage and nourish those principles and practices of Bigness that can bring us, in increasing measure, vast social and individual benefits. We can deliberately and consciously fashion public safeguards and private incentives whereby through Bigness we can bring closer to reality the American dream: individual freedom, social justice, material well-being, world moral leadership.

Our present legal policy concerning Bigness is embodied in a latter-day interpretation of the Sherman and Clayton antitrust laws. Those laws were enacted many years ago as the creative Magna Carta of economic freedom for an America emerging from

474

an agricultural economy. There are few greater legislative achievments than these laws that struck at the monopoly practices of the trusts of the nineties and the early years of this century, with their price agreements, pools, rebates and the ruthless slaughter of industrial newcomers. It is clear that business-policing activities to ferret out and punish specific crimes against competition need to be maintained and even increased in vigor. . . .

But the doctrine that Bigness is an evil, in and of itself, and against the Sherman Act even though there are no specific acts against competition, is a thoroughly unsound development of our governmental policy toward Bigness; it is a policy that cripples our country.

Such an interpretation of the fundamental business laws of the country, and our antagonistic, suspicious emotions toward Bigness are out of tune with the realities of the twentieth-century industrial and urban country we are today. This confusion and conflict prevent the full flowering of the advantages of Bigness so valuable to us, and so greatly needed for our national security. We are dependent upon big-scale undertakings, and not alone of private business, but also co-operatives, nonprofit mutual organizations and governmental institutions. Our urgent need, then, is to recognize the great social asset we have in Bigness.

America is a country with a special talent for Bigness; but by this I do not mean to imply that it is *only* the United States that has shown such talent. The United Kingdom and Canada both contain outstanding examples of Big Business, of course, and so do several European industrial nations. But it is the United States that is most characteristically a country of large-scale undertakings.

I am aware that in advocating better understanding and a more affirmative climate of opinion toward big-scale undertakings I move in a highly controversial field. It is an area where equally sensible and public-spirited men disagree, and where the memory of past corporate wrongs and abuses makes difficult a calm and objective analysis of today's circumstances. But these matters, controversial as they are, need to be discussed in the open air of reason. They need to be discussed widely, on their present merits, with a minimum of emotion, except the dominant emotion of furthering the strength and health of a country hard pressed with the increasing burdens of world leadership.

Some of the issues concerned with Bigness are necessarily discussed by legal and economic experts with such detail and complexity as to be beyond the understanding of most of us. This I have tried to avoid, and in doing so may have laid myself open to the charge that I have oversimplified.

I have not attempted to set up a precise definition of what is "big" in business. When I write of Bigness in industry, however, I do *not* by any means refer only to the relatively few corporations at the very top in size: Du Pont, General Electric, Union Carbide, U.S. Steel, etc. In 1937, the Twentieth Century Fund, in a study entitled "Big Business," described as the "giants" those "with total assets in 1933 of at least $50,000,000 or total net income of at least $5,000,000 each." Today (only twenty years later) we would not, of course, classify corporations no larger than this minimum as the "giants." They would of course qualify as "big" today; yet units half this size or even less in some industries are examples of Big Business. Even what is sometimes called "medium-sized" business is huge by almost any standard. This is a country of Bigness.

The argument about what is big enough and what is too big, I regard, generally, as not the central issue. My concern here is with the establishing to the fullest of a *climate of opportunity for growth and attainment of size,* as a means of greater productivity, better distribution of goods and income, and greater well-being for the country.

I have tried to avoid reopening what I regard as a sterile quarrel between "little business" and "Big Business," as if we were faced with a choice of one or the other. That we need "little business" is too clear to require argument, and that smaller business has not been extinguished by Bigness is manifest. There are—outside of agriculture—more than 4,000,000 firms in this country, and 40 per cent of total private national income is produced by unincorporated business proprietors. More than one-third of the country's output (aside from farming) is produced by what the census classifies as "small business"; and more than half the corporate assets of the country are owned by 500,000 small or medium-sized corporations.

What is more important than such figures is to comprehend that it is of the essence of Bigness that it *creates diversity* in size of business, big *and* little—and nourishes diversity: diversity of size and of function, so that what is small becomes bigger, so that what is big in turn creates many little businesses, which in turn compete with and stimulate and discipline what is big. Of this mutually invigorating relation between big and small business I shall have more to say. . . .

Nor am I here concerned with economic prejudice, inflamed by dated oratorical flourishes and trumpetings that our fate is controlled by a "handful of rich and all-powerful men." This is a picture faded, unreal, a quaint daguerreotype of a world that is no more.

"As I belong to a class of poeple who have great faith in this country," wrote Henry Adams to his friend Charles Milnes Gaskell in 1877, "and who believe that in another century it will be saying, in its turn, the last word of civilization, I enjoy the expectation of the coming day. . . ."[37]

I, too, "enjoy the expectation of the coming day." But whether such faith is sustained by the event depends upon the answer to this question: As a people, will we be *big* enough? We have indeed climbed to new heights in human history, we Americans of the mid-twentieth century. Now what? Will we lose our great chance because we do not ourselves understand and therefore cannot fully use one of the vital secrets of our own strength?

An individual cannot do his best if he is confused about basic things. Neither can a nation. This nation *is* confused, for we say one thing about size in business, and we do another and almost opposite thing. We distrust and inhibit and even threaten with criminal proceedings the very economic talent which is one of our sources of strength and freedom, our capacity for large-scale undertakings.

[37] *The Selected Letters of Henry Adams,* ed. by Newton Arvin. Farrar, Strauss and Young, Inc., 1951, xxvi.

Our basic economic law, the Sherman Antitrust Act, as it is more recently construed, symbolizes our distrust, giving concrete expression to a temperamental aversion to Bigness and to our belief in competition. How sometimes confused and contradictory this idea is I shall demonstrate . . . by indicating that today Bigness in industry is itself one of the most effective ways—sometimes the only effective way—to maintain genuine competition.

The belief that Bigness is, in itself, something evil is a theme that runs through the political thinking of this country. The same theme, with only minor variations, has been repeated in the political campaigns of both Republicans and Democrats. Usually described as "concentration of economic power," the ever-mounting size of corporate undertakings has been, and continues to this day to be, the subject of unremitting criticism, suspicion, warning, attack and governmental action.

At the time the Federal Trade Commission was established in 1914, a Joint Committee told Congress: "The concentration of wealth, money, and property in the United States under the control and in the hands of a few individuals or great corporations has grown to such an enormous extent that unless checked it will ultimately threaten the perpetuity of our institutions."

Nearly forty years later, in 1951, the Federal Trade Commission used almost the same words: "If nothing is done to check the growth in concentration, either the giant corporations will ultimately take over the country, or the government will be impelled to step in and impose some form of direct regulation."

We Americans are individualists. This is one of our great and distinctive qualities. Our whole philosophy and outlook are built around the individual, the smallest unit of all. This individualism runs through everything we do. We reject the idea of being cogs in a big machine.

So, being individualists, it is not unnatural that initially we should distrust Bigness. Most of us, brought up on trust busting and the fear of monopoly, have imbedded in our memory the history of abuses, arrogance and disregard of public and individual welfare by large-scale business in past decades.

478

We do not as yet fully comprehend what profound changes have taken place in the past three decades, or that our dependence is today upon Bigness for the very security of the country.

It is big enterprise that provides the American people with many of the things we want. The things we want are not only physical things—goods and services, the "highest standard of living in the world." Size accounts in a measure for those things we want which are *not* physical and material, but without which we could not enjoy such physical things as shelter, food, clothing, recreation.

So that when I speak of Bigness I am not thinking simply of "efficiency" of large-scale production and distribution. I am thinking of people, about my friends and neighbors and their aspirations and hopes and needs as individuals. To a large degree our human needs, our nonmaterial needs, are determined by the physical setting of our lives, by how we as a people earn our living, produce and distribute goods and services, how we build and manage our communities. The prospect of maintaining those human values we hold dear, our standards of what is good and what is shoddy or evil, depends largely upon this physical setting we usually call our economic system. I am not myself so much interested in the system as such, as in its purposes and its consequences for individual values and standards.

I conceive the purpose of American economic society not as the production and consumption of so many billions of units of steel, copper, automobiles, refrigerators. The purpose of our economic society and system is to promote freedom for the individual, as one prime essential of happiness and human fulfillment. By freedom I mean essentially *freedom to choose* to the maximum degree possible. Freedom is by no means merely a freedom to vote without coercion. "Did you suppose," asked Walt Whitman, "democracy was only for elections, for politics?"

Freedom of choice in economic matters means freedom to choose between competing ideas or services or goods. It means the maximum freedom to choose one job or one profession or one line of business as against some other. It means a maximum range of choice for the consumer when he spends his dollar. It means a maximum possible area of choice for the man who has saved up capital to invest.

These are economic choices. They are, however, more than economic or business acts. They are the mark of men who are free, as free as in society it is possible or workable for men to be. We call our economic system, quite appropriately, free enterprise. To maintain and nourish the essentials of free enterprise for all our people we must maintain and nourish the freedom of choice that makes the system come into being and flourish.

It is the vital role of Big Business in furthering just this freedom of choice that I emphasize. . . . And yet we still carry around our inherited conviction that Bigness means monopoly, which implies the absence of free choice.

It is natural enough that we should so generally regard *Bigness* and *monopoly* as synonymous. During the first years of this century, when many of us acquired our economic and political ideas, it was so often the case that Bigness and monopoly tended to be the same.

There were periodic curbs put on Big Business through these years. Woodrow Wilson created the Federal Trade Commission. Charles Evans Hughes, writing a great chapter of devoted public service, exposed the evils of big utilities and insurance companies. Louis D. Brandeis, with the power of his great spirit and mind, exposed the "curse of bigness," and it was anything but a pretty picture.

The depression of the thirties brought a resurgence of public condemnation and distrust of size: the Pecora investigation of Wall Street, the Temporary Economic Committee, the constructive and overdue reforms of the abuses of finance and large business during the first seven years of the administrations of Franklin Roosevelt.

The apparent contradictions of my own experience are illustrative of those of almost everyone else. I was brought up, like most men and women of my generation, to be suspicious and distrustful of things that are big. My father and his friends, who were small businessmen, spoke with deep apprehension of the trusts and cheered Teddy Roosevelt in his Bull Moose campaign; they thought the world was in a bad way when the first five-and-ten bought out an old individual family business and began the "chain-store" influx in our Indiana town. At home and at school, my generation heard the same refrain of fear and antagonism and distrust of Bigness—though at the same time we bragged about things because they were big. And yet by the time I was forty, I found myself directing the biggest integrated power system in the world, the TVA, which was itself the creation of an old-time trust buster, George Norris, and an outstanding critic of Bigness, Franklin D. Roosevelt. For over thirteen years I helped develop, as a unit, a region larger geographically than Great Britain, that embraced parts of seven Southern states. And, in 1946, I was made head of the largest industrial monopoly of history, the Atomic Energy Commission of the United States.

Despite our antagonism, despite handicaps of law and public opinion, Bigness of units has nevertheless developed rapidly until today size is a chief and outstanding characteristic of the way we do business, the way we live. And we like the material fruits of size at the very same time that we continue to view it with distrust. There is an apparent contradiction between our deep fears of Bigness and our need of it, that for a good many years has confused and troubled me. Can these two be reconciled? More narrowly, can Bigness and competition be reconciled?

The Sherman Antitrust Act has had a profound effect upon the course of American economic and social development. It was a great feat of statesmanship, an exhibition of remarkable insight.

But to the extent that it has recently been so construed as to condemn Bigness *per se,* the Sherman Act does not live up to the present needs of the United States. For basic reasons going to the very dynamics of modern industry, it is Bigness that helps keep competition a flourishing reality today. . . .

It is not, however, with the provisions and interpretations of the Sherman Act that we laymen should be deeply concerned today, but with the underlying assumptions, "the picture in the mind," the philosophy for which that act stands as it is applied to large-scale undertakings. It is the economic and political philosophy and emotion, affecting its present interpretation, that badly needs re-examination. It is by the new facts of the fifties in contrast to the essential facts about our country as it was a generation or two ago, that we need to judge whether Bigness should today be penalized or encouraged, feared or promoted.

Such a fundamental re-examination is appropriate, is indeed essential and vital, at a time like the present. In such a period of crisis and strain, of heart-searching and anxiety about basic things, we need to examine such an all-pervasive issue as this. If, by that inexplicable process of general public consensus by which Americans determine fundamental issues, we decide that Bigness is our ally, that its risk and dangers are now manageable and with wisdom can be surmounted, if we conclude to end this contradiction between our enjoyment of the fruits of Bigness and the suspicions we visit on it, then we can accelerate our progress toward the goals of America in a way that takes one's breath away to contemplate.

THE AMERICAN IMAGE OF BIG BUSINESS

Burleigh B. Gardner and Lee Rainwater

The thoughts and feelings of the common man in America about big business are carefully gathered and analyzed with great insight. The meanings of bigness to him do not necessarily correspond to the highly rationalized meanings of bigness to intellectuals or some of the leaders of the ordinary man.

"The body of firm factual knowledge as to what the American public at large thinks and feels about big business is limited," writes J. D. Glover.[38] "Almost nonexistent" would be a more accurate description. For the men in management and public relations who must formulate ways of communicating effectively with the

[38] J. D. Glover, *The Attack on Big Business* (Boston: Division of Research, Harvard Business School, 1954), p. 107.

Note: See Notes on the Authors, pages 552 and 556, and item 93 in the bibliography for the full reference to this selection.

public, this is an unfortunate state of affairs, since they necessarily depend on their own insight into limited facts and figures to form conclusions on which to base their efforts.

USING THE TOOLS

Our studies of big business deal with the views of the "middle majority" or mass market group, which comprises 65% of the population and consists of families of clerical and white-collar workers, salesmen, craftsmen, small business proprietors, semiskilled workers, and service employees. . . .

Three psychological characteristics seem to play a leading role in the life of middle majority people:

(1) They have a strong need for security.
(2) They have to rely heavily on others for gratification of this need.
(3) They tend to judge and evaluate reality in terms of what they see in their immediate, concrete experiences.

Big business enters into the interplay of these three characteristics in subtle ways.

Middle majority people are often persistently uneasy about their ability to achieve their life goals. They are apprehensive, too, about the possibilities of guarding against the vicissitudes of what they often see as an unsympathetic world. Maintaining their integrity is complicated by an unpredictable future. With respect to industry, this striving for security is expressed in the hope that business is run morally and benevolently. Business leaders, the middle majority hopes, will be respectable and will be equitable in their relations with the "little man."

It is from their personal experiences that members of the middle majority form their attitudes toward big business. They are not ideologists who evaluate business from the viewpoint of a coherent socioeconomic theory. They are relatively concrete in their thinking, and their positive and negative judgments reflect tangible circumstances or the concrete "myths" of their own group.

Most of these people have prospered for almost two decades. They feel reasonably well-satisfied with their accomplishments. Big business, they feel, has done well by them, has seen to their basic needs and desires for a more prosperous life. They feel gratified by the material abundance that is all around them. While uncertain how this abundance evolved, the middle majority seems ready to credit big business for much of the accomplishment. And it expects—or hopes—that big business will create even more opportunities.

As a result of all this, these people have developed definite attitudes, not only about the blessings of bigness but about the dangers of bigness and the limitations that should be put on bigness.

BLESSINGS OF BIGNESS. 1. *Big business is seen as the pace setter of the American economy.* The middle majority sees bigness as the dominant feature of business and industry, and therefore expects large firms to lead and give tone to all the others.

Under these circumstances, bigness in business gives the middle majority a feeling of reassurance. To conceive of big business as dominant, to see a few large corporations as the essential leaders and pace setters for all firms has a certain appeal. This conception replaces the mood of insecurity that for these people accompanies the traditional picture of many smaller firms competing without any authoritative guidance. It includes, also, a prominent element of hierarchy, *much like the familiar social and occupational hierarchies of American society.* The middle majority people accept differences in power—not happily, however, unless they feel assured that the more powerful exercise their power constructively and morally. They tend to believe, too, that smaller firms can succeed by working with, rather than against, big business.

2. *Only big business can handle the job of production.* The middle majority person is overwhelmed by trying to think about the seemingly colossal task of organizing the circuit of raw materials to finished product. He finds it difficult to conceive how small companies could handle the job. Thus, in a matter-of-fact way he regards big business as the appropriate mode of organizing large-scale production. The automobile industry is to him perhaps the most vivid symbol of both the necessity and the value of colossal size.

3. *Big business is good because mass production techniques provide goods of uniform quality and at low cost.* Because a

business is big, it needs to turn out a popular and good product which will be sold at low prices in order to broaden the market further. Companies that use mass production techniques are more efficient; they are assumed to be making use of the best technical knowledge in order to turn out so many units of good quality.

4. *Big business is good because it invests heavily in research and development activities.* "You can't have these expensive research programs without having big industries," sums up the general feeling. Most of the material advances of recent years are attributed to big business. These people believe that they and the nation as a whole benefit from the ability of large firms to engage in research (even though their knowledge of research and what it involves is not sophisticated).

5. *Big business provides many jobs and greater opportunity to work.* Nowhere does the pragmatism of the middle majority show itself so clearly as in the reasons cited for the favorable evaluation of big business. The "plus" on jobs follows the simple logic that if the largest plant in town employs 6,000 people while the average neighborhood firm employs 20 or 30 people, big business is the more bountiful employer. Also expressed is the idea that big business is stable and thus better able to provide steady employment.

We see that judgments made about big business are usually based on concrete factors: Do big companies make good products? Do the prices seem reasonable? Does the company deal fairly with its employees? Does it give the little fellow a chance? Much less important are the remote questions relating to restraint of trade, monopoly of natural resources, patent abuses, and the like. Given affirmative beliefs to the first set of questions, only the strongest evidence moves middle majority people to a negative evaluation of big business.

DANGERS OF BIGNESS. The middle majority's need for security and for reliance on others shows up as respect for power, which leads it to respect big business. *But* the same factors also account for attitudes quite unfavorable to big business.

Against the threat of unscrupulous men of power, the life circumstances of the middle majority people give them small protection. American folklore abounds with tales of the unscrupulous enterpriser who swindles his customers. Although middle majority people believe that the day of the ruthless businessman is largely past, their apprehension still lurks close to the surface. It is quickly activated by fact or fiction casting doubt on the moral uprightness of the businessman, be he grocer, druggist, or corporation president.

The middle majority person's respect for power is readily fused with anxiety once he feels the power is incompatible with him. Consequently, his own uneasiness is magnified by doubts of the beneficence of big business, which is conceived as largely beyond his control. Even more dangerous, he fears, is the possibility of this power being used against him.

The butcher can tip the scale with his thumb and the grocer can misrepresent a product; these shortcomings are of no great consequence to the middle majority man. But if he feels that the largest firms are unscrupulous too, then he loses hope for all people like himself. The primary fear is that big business may separate its interests from those of the public and pursue a policy of "the public be damned." The middle majority person is anxious for evidence that big business leaders take the public interest into account and that they take their responsibility seriously.

LIMITS ON BIGNESS. Since the middle majority is quite uncertain of its ability to fend off possible attacks from potentially unscrupulous big business, it looks to other powerful institutions for protection, especially the national government and labor unions. These are expected to protect the public interest, insofar as each limits the excesses to which big business may go. Although an individual might be anxious and fearful of these institutions too, he is at the same time reassured by their power.

In our society, gripes against the government are easily verbalized —we talk about scandals in high places, corruption, overcentralization in Washington, and so on. (Of course the research used here studied attitudes toward government only in its relation to business, and covers only a small aspect of public attitudes toward government.) Thus, attacks on government control and guidance are frequent. Yet when the chips are down and the danger is great, people turn to government. Alien as the government may be to an individual, he feels that it is *his* government, something which he does not feel about big business.

Middle majority people gripe about how national government is handled and often distrust the sincerity of "the politicians"—Democrats or Republicans. Nevertheless, they see the government as a strong power that can oppose the power of big business and thereby protect them against any excesses of big business.

Labor unions as a limitation on big business are most meaningful, of course, to union members and their families. Our studies and others indicate that union members believe big business is fine—as long as they know the union is there to check the power of management.[39] Clearly, union members as workers can easily grasp the employment advantages of big business. In some cases, at least, union members among the middle majority felt less threatened by big business than did nonunion members. Nonmembers were comparatively uneasy and isolated, perhaps because they saw no powerful institution to protect them against possible excesses on the part of big business.

Not big business, nor national government, nor the labor union, escapes either criticism or praise. By and large, the latter two are more openly criticized than is big business. Apparent mistrust, however, should not mislead the observer to believe that the government and the labor union are regarded negatively. Among the middle majority, the following represents a fairly typical evaluation: "I think the labor unions have done one hell of a lot for the people in America; I just hope *they* don't start abusing *their* power."

[39] Cf. unpublished research of Edith M. Lentz, *Steelville: A Study of Voting Behavior in One Industrial Community,* 1950 (University of Chicago Library).

Chapter 10

ISSUES AND DILEMMAS

INTRODUCTION

It is probably true that every generation regards its particular era as fraught with conflict and change. Undoubtedly industrial man of fifty years ago regarded his situation with some bewilderment and doubt; without question he wondered where the rapidly increasing pace of life might take him. Change is basic, but whether it is any more rapid today than it was yesterday is open to question.

Be that as it may, there is little doubt about the rapid pace of change in modern American society. We are in a period of transition—transition not only from a technological standpoint but from a social, economic, and political point of view as well. With such rapid and far-reaching change, it is inevitable that a considerable number of issues and dilemmas should present themselves and that writers in all fields should concern themselves increasingly with the modern predicament.

There is, however, a considerable problem in identifying a real issue from a spurious one. One issue is so closely related to another that it is, as it were, only the other side of the coin. The first task is, therefore, to identify clearly the various issues that confront us.

Once this is done it will be possible for us to deal with them in a more

488

realistic manner; otherwise we tend to "tilt at windmills" or set up straw men to knock down. Following this, we must ask: given a problem confronting American business society, what are the various factors which are contributing to its creation? What are its ramifications in terms of the larger society? What alternatives are there whereby its effect might be diminished or even eliminated if that is desired? How can possible solutions be placed in effect and by whom?

Thinking about and acting on these problems cannot be left to the professional—to the business executive, to the government, or to the student. It must become the concern of every individual. Each should think through the various issues and dilemmas as they affect him; each should bring to bear his thinking upon those who are in a position to do something about it. Problems are not purely the province of a privileged few in our society; they are part of everyone's responsibility.

Issues in modern-day American business society appear to be taking form along several major lines:

1. The relationship of the industrial organization to the individual. In the past, the worker possessed relatively little power in relation to the organization in which he worked. The thesis of scientific management was strongly adhered to; the worker was told specifically what to do and he did it. Today, however, it appears that he has become more militant; he is organized into unions. The question of the right balance between organizational and individual concerns occupies a position of high priority in business society.

2. The relationship of the individual to himself. Increasingly writers have become concerned with this relationship. Fromm, Riesman, Whyte, and others have taken the position that the individual has become too "other-directed," that he is afraid to be himself, and that as a result he is not coming up to his full potential. Afraid to fail and anxious to please, he is cast in the role of an individual with no direction except from without.

3. The relationship of the organization to other organizations. With the changing form of American industry—with its trend toward bigness and with the tendency for organizations in the same field to band together to present a united front on the many issues they have to deal with, the question must be raised as to the particular relationship which should exist between industrial organizations. What should be the character of the relationship between industries participating in the same field of concentration? To what extent should they pool resources and to what extent should they operate independently and competitively?

489

4. The relationship of the industrial organization to labor unions. In theory, the collective bargaining process should operate to produce a resolution of the various problems arising between management and labor. While gigantic strides have been made toward producing industrial harmony, conflict still exists. The situation can be described in many instances as a type of "cold war"—a condition in which both sides mutually distrust the other and wait only for an opportunity to gain an advantage when the guard of the other is down.

5. The relationship of the industrial organization to the larger society. Undoubtedly, this is one of the most difficult of problems. We are dealing with abstractions. When we talk about defining the relationship of a given industrial organization to the community and to the larger society, just what do we mean? What society? Responsibility to whom? On a larger scale, what are the ethical responsibilities of business? What do we mean by "ethical" in this context? To what extent, for example, does the so-called "golden rule" apply to practical business conduct?

There are, no doubt, other areas where issues and dilemmas might well exist. We have not exhausted the spectrum but only indicated several dimensions. As we have pointed out, the initial task is to identify exactly what and where the issues are. This has yet to be done. In this, our concluding chapter, we will present a number of selections which deal with several of the issues and dilemmas which we have pointed out.

THE SOCIAL ETHIC

William H. Whyte, Jr.

Modern industrial man has tended to become an organization man. In an age of conformity, the guiding ideology of yesterday, the Protestant Ethic, has been replaced by the Social Ethic in which the major aim of individuals is to be accepted by their fellows and to become members of the group. Equipped to lead an organization life, they are "more acted upon than acting" —and their future, therefore, determined as much by the system as by themselves. Here is the conflict between the individual and the group.

Note: See Notes on the Authors, page 557, and item 253 in the bibliography for the full reference to this selection.

Officially, we are a people who hold to the Protestant Ethic. Because of the denominational implications of the term many would deny its relevance to them, but let them eulogize the American Dream, however, and they virtually define the Protestant Ethic. Whatever the embroidery, there is almost always the thought that pursuit of individual salvation through hard work, thrift, and competitive struggle is the heart of the American achievement.

But the harsh facts of organization life simply do not jibe with these precepts. This conflict is certainly not a peculiarly American development. In their own countries such Europeans as Max Weber and Durkheim many years ago foretold the change, and though Europeans now like to see their troubles as an American export, the problems they speak of stem from a bureaucratization of society that has affected every Western country.

It is in America, however, that the contrast between the old ethic and current reality has been most apparent—and most poignant. Of all peoples it is we who have led in the public worship of individualism. One hundred years ago De Tocqueville was noting that though our special genius—and failing—lay in co-operative action, we talked more than others of personal independence and freedom. We kept on, and as late as the twenties, when big organization was long since a fact, affirmed the old faith as if nothing had really changed at all.

Today many still try, and it is the members of the kind of organization most responsible for the change, the corporation, who try the hardest. It is the corporation man whose institutional ads protest so much that Americans speak up in town meeting, that Americans are the best inventors because Americans don't care that other people scoff, that Americans are the best soldiers because they have so much initiative and native ingenuity, that the boy selling papers on the street corner is the prototype of our business society. Collectivism? He abhors it, and when he makes his ritualistic attack on Welfare Statism, it is in terms of a Protestant Ethic undefiled by change—the sacredness of property, the enervating effect of security, the virtues of thrift, of hard work and independence. Thanks be, he says, that there are some people left —e.g., businessmen—to defend the American Dream.

He is not being hypocritical, only compulsive. He honestly wants to believe he follows the tenets he extols, and if he extols them frequently it is, perhaps, to shut out a nagging suspicion that he, too, the last defender of the faith, is no longer pure. Only by using the language of individualism to describe the collective can he stave off the thought that he himself is in a collective as pervading as any ever dreamed of by the reformers, the intellectuals, and the utopian visionaries he so regularly warns against.

The older generation may still convince themselves; the younger generation does not. When a young man says that to make a living these days you must do what somebody else wants you to do, he states it not only as a fact of life that must be accepted but as an inherently good proposition. If the American Dream deprecates this for him it is the American Dream that is going to have to give, whatever its more elderly guardians may think. People grow restive with a mythology that is too distant from the way things actually are, and as more and more lives have been encompassed by the organization way of life, the pressures for an accompanying ideological shift have been mounting. The pressures of the group, the frustrations of individual creativity, the anonymity of achievement: are these defects to struggle against—or are they virtues in disguise? The organization man seeks a redefinition of his place on earth—a faith that will satisfy him that what he must endure has a deeper meaning than appears on the surface. He needs, in short, something that will do for him what the Protestant Ethic did once. And slowly, almost imperceptibly, a body of thought has been coalescing that does that.

I am going to call it a Social Ethic. With reason it could be called an organization ethic, or a bureaucratic ethic; more than anything else it rationalizes the organization's demands for fealty and gives those who offer it wholeheartedly a sense of dedication in doing so—*in extremis,* you might say, it converts what would seem in other times a bill of no rights into a restatement of individualism.

But there is a real moral imperative behind it, and whether one inclines to its beliefs or not he must acknowledge that this moral basis, not mere expediency, is the source of its power. Nor is it simply an opiate for those who must work in big organizations. The search for a secular faith that it represents can be found throughout our society—and among those who swear they would never set foot in a corporation or a government bureau. Though it has its greatest applicability to the organization man, its ideological underpinnings have been provided not by the organization man but by intellectuals he knows little of and toward whom, indeed, he tends to be rather suspicious.

Any groove of abstraction, Whitehead once remarked, is bound to be an inadequate way of describing reality, and so with the concept of the Social Ethic. It is an attempt to illustrate an underlying consistency in what in actuality is by no means an orderly system of thought. No one says, "I believe in the social ethic," and though many would subscribe wholeheartedly to the separate ideas that make it up, these ideas have yet to be put together in the final, harmonious synthesis. But the unity is there.

In looking at what might seem dissimilar aspects of organization society, it is this unity I wish to underscore. The "professionalization" of the manager, for example, and the drive for a more practical education are parts of the same phenomenon; just as the student now feels technique more vital than content, so the trainee believes managing an end in itself, an *expertise* relatively independent of the content of what is being managed. And the reasons are the same. So too in other sectors of our society; for all the differences in particulars, dominant is a growing accommodation to the needs of society—and a growing urge to justify it.

Let me now define my terms. By Social Ethic I mean that contemporary body of thought which makes morally legitimate the pressures of society against the individual. Its major propositions are three: a belief in the group as the source of creativity; a belief in "belongingness" as the ultimate need of the individual; and a belief in the application of science to achieve the belongingness.

. . . Man exists as a unit of society. Of himself, he is isolated, meaningless; only as he collaborates with others does he become worth while, for by sublimating himself in the group, he helps produce a whole that is greater than the sum of its parts. There should be, then, no conflict between man and society. What we think are conflicts are misunderstandings, breakdowns in communication. By applying the methods of science to human relations we can eliminate these obstacles to consensus and create an equilibrium in which society's needs and the needs of the individual are one and the same.

Essentially, it is a utopian faith. Superficially, it seems dedicated to the practical problems of organization life, and its proponents often use the word *hard* (versus *soft*) to describe their approach. But it is the long-range promise that animates its followers, for it relates techniques to the vision of a finite, achievable harmony. It is quite reminiscent of the beliefs of utopian communities of the 1840's. As in the Owen communities, there is the same idea that man's character is decided, almost irretrievably, by his environment. As in the Fourier communities, there is the same faith that there need be no conflict between the individual's aspirations and the community's wishes, because it is the natural order of things that the two be synonymous.

Like the utopian communities, it interprets society in a fairly narrow immediate sense. One can believe man has a social obligation and that the individual must ultimately contribute to the community without believing that group harmony is the test of it. In the Social Ethic I am describing, however, man's obligation is in the here and now; his duty is not so much to the community in a broad sense but to the actual, physical one about him, and the idea that in isolation from it—or active rebellion against it—he might eventually discharge the greater service is little considered. In practice, those who most eagerly subscribe to the Social Ethic worry very little over the long-range problems of society. It is not that they don't care but rather that they tend to assume that the ends of organization and morality coincide, and on such matters as social welfare they give their proxy to the organization.

It is possible that I am attaching too much weight to what, after all, is something of a mythology. Those more sanguine than I have argued that this faith is betrayed by reality in some key respects and that because it cannot long hide from organization man that life is still essentially competitive the faith must fall of its own weight. They also maintain that the Social Ethic is only one trend

494

in a society which is a prolific breeder of counter-trends. The farther the pendulum swings, they believe, the more it must eventually swing back.

I am not persuaded. We are indeed a flexible people, but society is not a clock and to stake so much on counter-trends is to put a rather heavy burden on providence. Let me get ahead of my story a bit with two examples of trend vs. counter-trend. One is the long-term swing to the highly vocational business-administration courses. Each year for seven years I have collected all the speeches by businessmen, educators, and others on the subject, and invariably each year the gist of them is that this particular pendulum has swung much too far and that there will shortly be a reversal. Similarly sanguine, many academic people have been announcing that they discern the beginnings of a popular swing back to the humanities. Another index is the growth of personality testing. Regularly year after year many social scientists have assured me that this bowdlerization of psychology is a contemporary aberration soon to be laughed out of court.

Meanwhile, the organization world grinds on. Each year the number of business-administration majors has increased over the last year—until, in 1954, they together made up the largest single field of undergraduate instruction outside of the field of education itself. Personality testing? Again, each year the number of people subjected to it has grown, and the criticism has served mainly to make organizations more adept in sugar-coating their purpose. No one can say whether these trends will continue to outpace the counter-trends, but neither can we trust that equilibrium-minded providence will see to it that excesses will cancel each other out. Counter-trends there are. There always have been, and in the sweep of ideas ineffectual many have proved to be.

It is also true that the Social Ethic is something of a mythology, and there is a great difference between mythology and practice. An individualism as stringent, as selfish as that often preached in the name of the Protestant Ethic would never have been tolerated, and in reality our predecessors co-operated with one another far more skillfully than nineteenth-century oratory would suggest. Something of the obverse is true of the Social Ethic; so complete a denial of individual will won't work either, and even the most willing believers in the group harbor some secret misgivings, some latent antagonism toward the pressures they seek to deify.

But the Social Ethic is no less powerful for that, and though it can never produce the peace of mind it seems to offer, it will help shape the nature of the quest in the years to come. The old dogma of individualism betrayed reality too, yet few would argue, I dare say, that it was not an immensely powerful influence in the time of its dominance. So I argue of the Social Ethic; call it mythology, if you will, but it is becoming the dominant one.

This . . . is not a plea for nonconformity. Such pleas have an occasional therapeutic value, but as an abstraction, nonconformity is an empty goal, and rebellion against prevailing opinion merely because it is prevailing should no more be praised than acquiescence to it. Indeed, it is often a mask for cowardice, and few are more pathetic than those who flaunt outer differences to expiate their inner surrender.

I am not, accordingly, addressing myself to the surface uniformities of U.S. life. There will be no strictures in this book against "Mass Man"—a person the author has never met—nor will there be any strictures against ranch wagons, or television sets, or gray flannel suits. They are irrelevant to the main problem, and furthermore, there's no harm in them. I would not wish to go to the other extreme and suggest that these uniformities per se are good, but the spectacle of people following current custom for lack of will or imagination to do anything else is hardly a new failing, and I am not convinced that there has been any significant change in this respect except in the nature of the things we conform to. Unless one believes poverty ennobling, it is difficult to see the three-button suit as more of a strait jacket than overalls, or the ranch-type house than old law tenements.

And how important, really, are these uniformities to the central issue of individualism? We must not let the outward forms deceive us. If individualism involves following one's destiny as one's own conscience directs, it must for most of us be a realizable destiny, and a sensible awareness of the rules of the game can be a condition of individualism as well as a constraint upon it. The man who drives a Buick Special and lives in a ranch-type house just like hundreds of other ranch-type houses can assert himself as effectively and courageously against his particular society as the bohemian against his particular society. He usually does not, it is true, but if he does, the surface uniformities can serve quite well as protective coloration. The organization people who are best able to control their environment rather than be controlled by it are well aware that they are not too easily distinguishable from the others in the outward obeisances paid to the good opinions of others. And this is one of the reasons they do control. They disarm society.

I do not equate the Social Ethic with conformity, nor do I believe those who urge it wish it to be, for most of them believe deeply that their work will help, rather than harm, the individual. I think their ideas are out of joint with the needs of the times they invoke, but it is their ideas, and not their good will, I wish to question. As for the lackeys of organization and the charlatans, they are not worth talking about.

Neither do I intend . . . a censure of the fact of organization society. We have quite enough problems today without muddying the issue with misplaced nostalgia, and in contrasting the old ideology with the new I mean no contrast of paradise with paradise lost, an idyllic eighteenth century with a dehumanized twentieth. Whether or not our own era is worse than former ones in the climate of freedom is a matter that can be left to later historians, . . . I write with the optimistic premise that individualism is as possible in our times as in others.

I speak of individualism *within* organization life. This is not the only kind, and someday it may be that the mystics and philosophers more distant from it may prove the crucial figures. But they are affected too by the center of society, and they can be of no help unless they grasp the nature of the main stream. Intellectual scoldings based on an impossibly lofty ideal may be of some service in upbraiding organization man with his failures, but they can give him no guidance. The organization man may agree that industrialism has destroyed the moral fabric of society and that we need to return to the agrarian virtues, or that business needs to be broken up into a series of smaller organizations, or that it is govern-

497

ment that needs to be broken up, and so on. But he will go his way with his own dilemmas left untouched.

I am going to argue that he should fight the organization. But not self-destructively. He may tell the boss to go to hell, but he is going to have another boss, and, unlike the heroes of popular fiction, he cannot find surcease by leaving the arena to be a husbandman. If he chafes at the pressures of his particular organization, either he must succumb, resist them, try to change them, or move to yet another organization.

Every decision he faces on the problem of the individual versus authority is something of a dilemma. It is not a case of whether he should fight against black tyranny or blaze a new trail against patent stupidity. That would be easy—intellectually, at least. The real issue is far more subtle. For it is not the evils of organization life that puzzle him, *but its very beneficence.* He is imprisoned in brotherhood. Because his area of maneuver seems so small and because the trapping so mundane, his fight lacks the heroic cast, but it is for all this as tough a fight as ever his predecessors had to fight.

Thus to my thesis. I believe the emphasis of the Social Ethic is wrong for him. People do have to work with others, yes; the well-functioning team is a whole greater than the sum of its parts, yes— all this is indeed true. But is it the truth that now needs belaboring? Precisely because it *is* an age of organization, it is the other side of the coin that needs emphasis. We do need to know how to co-operate with The Organization but, more than ever, so do we need to know how to resist it. Out of context this would be an irresponsible statement. Time and place are critical, and history has taught us that a philosophical individualism can venerate conflict too much and co-operation too little. But what is the context today? The tide has swung far enough the other way, I submit, that we need not worry that a counteremphasis will stimulate people to an excess of individualism.

The energies Americans have devoted to the co-operative, to the social, are not to be demeaned; we would not, after all, have such a problem to discuss unless we had learned to adapt ourselves to an increasingly collective society as well as we have. An ideal of individualism which denies the obligations of man to others is manifestly impossible in a society such as ours, and it is a credit to our wisdom that while we preached it, we never fully practiced it.

But in searching for that elusive middle of the road, we have gone very far afield, and in our attention to making organization work we have come close to deifying it. We are describing its defects as virtues and denying that there is—or should be—a conflict between the individual and organization. This denial is bad for the organization. It is worse for the individual. What it does, in soothing him, is to rob him of the intellectual armor he so badly needs. For the more power organization has over him, the more he needs to recognize the area where he must assert himself against it. And this, almost because we have made organization life so equable, has become excruciatingly difficult.

To say that we must recognize the dilemmas of organization society is not to be inconsistent with the hopeful premise that organization society can be as compatible for the individual as any previous society. We are not hapless beings caught in the grip of forces we can do little about, and wholesale damnations of our society only lend a further mystique to organization. Organization has been made by man; it can be changed by man. It has not been the immutable course of history that has produced such constrictions on the individual as personality tests. It is organization man who has brought them to pass and it is he who can stop them.

The fault is not in organization, in short; it is in our worship of it. It is in our vain quest for a utopian equilibrium, which would be horrible if it ever did come to pass; it is in the soft-minded denial that there is a conflict between the individual and society. There must always be, and it is the price of being an individual that he must face these conflicts. He cannot evade them, and in seeking an ethic that offers a spurious peace of mind, thus does he tyrannize himself.

There are only a few times in organization life when he can wrench his destiny into his own hands—and if he does not fight then, he will make a surrender that will later mock him. But when is that time? Will he know the time when he sees it? By what standards is he to judge? He does feel an obligation to the group; he does sense moral constraints on his free will. If he goes against the group, is he being courageous—or just stubborn? Helpful—or selfish? Is he, as he so often wonders, right after all? It is in the resolution of a multititude of such dilemmas, I submit, that the real issue of individualism lies today.

THE PROBLEM OF FREEDOM

Bennett E. Kline and Norman H. Martin

Undoubtedly one of the major ideological cornerstones of the American system is the ideal of freedom. Yet most of our industrial organizations are run on the basis of authority and have a tendency to become bureaucracies in which the individual possesses relatively little freedom. Is freedom possible? How can our industrial organizations develop freedom for their personnel? How can freedom be administered? These questions should be answered if our economy is to be consistent with our social ideals.

It is probably inevitable that in any organized effort a division of labor, a hierarchy of authority, and a complex network of superior-subordinate relationships will develop. In some societies this has presented no problem. But in our society it is a major task to make this authoritarian structure compatible with American ideals of freedom and equality.

The management of a corporation has the responsibility of attaining efficiency and discipline and at the same time of allowing individuals freedom to display initiative, to create, and to express themselves. Otherwise it cannot keep faith with our economic ideals of progress or with our Christian ideals of the dignity of the individual. Granted that not all people in a company will use their freedom, however hard management tries to maintain it. But if there is to be freedom for the few who *will* take advantage of it,

Note: See Notes on the Authors, pages 554 and 555, and item 128 in the bibliography for the full reference to this selection.

freedom must be offered to the many. If any lesson is clear from history, it is this.

LOST HORIZONS

To cope with the problem of maintaining discipline and freedom at the same time, we must resolve a conflict between the stereotype of our economic system which is believed in by businessmen (and taught to their employees) and life as it is actually experienced by the employees in their daily work.

FREEDOM FOR WHOM? The free market system, as the business executive sees it, has as its chief beneficiaries the consumers; but employees gain better and more interesting jobs as a result of the system's built-in motion toward progress. Employees (the employer argues) also profit from the free market for labor, one of a chain of markets which makes up the system.

Together these markets constitute the disciplinary system within which authoritarian enterprises are tolerable in a democracy. They are tolerable because all members of the free-enterprise community—the employee, the customer, the investor—are afforded a way out, and escape from any authority that becomes undesirable. The investor who dislikes the arbitrary behavior of an enterprise can sell his stock and invest elsewhere. The customer who dislikes the arbitrary behavior of an enterprise can buy elsewhere in the competitive market. And the employee who dislikes the arbitrary behavior of an enterprise can always quit and shop for a more suitable job—more suitable in terms of pay, working conditions, security, benefits, personal treatment, or whatever he may choose.

This is the way the top executive sees it, but others are not so certain. It appears to many millions of Americans that, while they live in a free society, earning and using their incomes in a free economic system, they spend most of their working hours in authoritarian institutions playing the role of the managed. The employing institutions do not match the system in their use of freedom. Being managed, it seems, is not the same as exercising freedom.

INSTITUTIONALIZED IGNORANCE? There is still another conflict in viewpoint. Executives and management consultants gen-

501

erally assume that human groups organize themselves, or are organized, in order to become more efficient. The more competent, it is thought, rise to positions of greater responsibility and take over the direction and control of those below. The few make most of the decisions which will be carried out by the many. The problem of management then becomes the problem of seeing that these decisions are actually carried out in the manner and at the time desired. We say we are organizing for the most effective use of our knowledge, skill, and wisdom.

This concept seems logical enough, but it ignores the probability that the chief characteristic of the command hierarchy, or any group in our society, is not knowledge but ignorance. Consider that any one person can know only a fraction of what is going on around him. Much of what that person knows or believes will be false rather than true. And many of the directions he gives to those under him will be misunderstood. At any given time, vastly more is not known than is known, either by one person in a command chain or by all the organization.

It seems possible, then, that in organizing ourselves into a hierarchy of authority for the purpose of increasing efficiency, we may really be institutionalizing ignorance. While making better use of what the few know, we are making sure that the great majority are prevented from exploring the dark areas beyond our knowledge. And while we progress, our increasing knowledge is more than matched by the emergence of new areas of ignorance, and the trappings of status are substituted for the dignity which naturally crowns achievement. At least, that is how it seems to millions down the line.

DOUBLE DILEMMA. It follows, then, that we may have a double dilemma. Our system stresses freedom; but our employing institutions stress authority, direction, and control. Our progress depends on expanding knowledge and increasing the "accidents" of discovery and invention; but our institutions foster the maximum use of existing knowledge, deliberately organizing to inhibit creativity and innovation. This conflict is clear to some businessmen; witness this statement by General Robert E. Wood, former chairman of the board of Sears, Roebuck and Company:

"We complain about government in business, we stress the advantages of the free enterprise system, we complain about the totalitarian state, but in our industrial organization, in our striving for efficiency we have created more or less of a totalitarian system in industry, particularly in large industry. The problem of retaining our efficiency and discipline in these large organizations and yet allowing our people to express themselves, to exercise initiative and to have some voice in the affairs of the organization is the greatest problem for large industrial organizations to solve."[1]

It has long been known that within the hierarchy of command it is through the delegation of authority that management can make use of the individual's drive and skill. The form of organization which is most conducive to widespread delegation from the highest levels of management to the lowest is decentralized administration. When the process of decentralization reaches the lowest level of organization, it is called "job enlargement," "putting planning back into the job," or something else which indicates the delegation of more authority. (Of course, usually some system of centralized control is maintained to achieve efficiency.)

Decentralization has come to be rather widely accepted as an ideal form of organization, and in the past decade or so many companies have either put such a form of organization into effect, or have at least developed it on paper. In many instances, however, it has not worked out too well. Controlled efficiency has not been attained, and not enough personnel have been judged to be ready to assume the responsibilities of decision making. As a result, many companies which decentralized at one time have gone back to a modified system of centralization.

FRESH DIRECTION

At this stage in the development of organizational theory and practice, therefore, it may be well to re-examine the concept of delegation and the process of decentralization. Perhaps we need

---

[1] Quoted in Boris Emmet and John E. Jeuck, *Catalogues and Counters: A History of Sears, Roebuck and Company* (Chicago, University of Chicago Press, 1950), p. 371.

to shift to some fresh direction in our approach if we are to have efficiency and discipline as well as freedom and creativity.

The trouble with conventional thinking is this: delegation of authority as the formal power to influence others inevitably creates a relationship of dependency between the superior and the subordinate. The subordinate is dependent on his superior for continued favor and for support to back him up if he runs into trouble in carrying out his actions. His conduct tends to be determined by the personal ties and sentiments he forms toward his superior. In effect, his behavior over the course of time becomes similar to that of his boss. Differences are not encouraged, often not tolerated.

As a result, the formation of cliques and power blocks occurs with high frequency. When such a process is widespread, problems of coordination increase; decisions tend to become the result of compromise. Individuals and departments maneuver to maintain and enhance their power, adopting tactics of the Machiavellian variety. In the final analysis, long-run coordination is achieved through the development of a common likeness of all.

In these circumstances individual potentials for large numbers of people are gradually reduced to a low level. No positive links attach one person to another, and the barriers which separate one group from another are marked. The moral order comes to rest on power alone. If one has the authority, his actions come to be thought of as right. Where creativity and innovation would be useful to both superior and subordinate, defensiveness and resistance are all too often the pattern of subordinate reaction. To meet resistance, superior authority brings more power to bear, which in turn causes more resistance—a well-known pattern. And so we have the cult of authority and control.

GRANTING OF FREEDOM. To break out of this vicious circle, let us take a new look at the decentralization concept. In considering how we can bring the freedom inherent in our political and economic systems into our industrial organizations, let us talk not about delegating authority to act, but about granting *freedom* to act. The difference is an important one. Different perspectives, relationships, and forms of administration are involved.

A manager who has authority to act may have power, but it is often implied that he must act in an approved manner. A manager with freedom to act, by contrast, may have a clearly defined area to move around in—but within his bailiwick he can do the job in his own way. It is much the same difference as between the American municipality, which can choose between the New England town meeting, the city manager plan, or some other form of government, and the local political unit in a totalitarian state, which is expected to follow a certain pattern of operations.

The granting of freedom to act by the superior is evidence of confidence in the subordinate. The response to this trust and confidence is a constructive sense of responsibility which grows naturally out of the mutual recognition of the subordinate's individuality. The subordinate becomes aware that he is an end in himself, and not simply a means toward the ends of his superior. This acceptance of responsibility by the subordinate means changed responsibilities for the superior, and each finds himself playing a new role. The superior-subordinate situation is now looked at from a new point of view, and, as the semanticists have long since demonstrated, the new point of view means a new situation. People's feelings about freedom are different from their feelings about authority.

Freedom cannot be defined as the absence of superior authority. Nor is it relative, so that one person can be said to have "freedom" simply because he has more leeway than someone else. The superior either grants freedom to the subordinate, or he does not. The extent to which the subordinate can be free of interference is the same as the extent to which the superior can be free; the boss cannot give something that he does not have himself. The real test as to whether freedom prevails is this: *Will the superior support the subordinate in carrying out the task in a manner different from that which he himself would have used?*

Freedom is the acceptance of the individuality of the subordinate. It means that he can be different without fear of reproach. Where there is freedom, there is individual growth; creativity and innovation are natural, perhaps inevitable.

JOINT RESPONSIBILITIES. The superior must be willing to create and to maintain a realistic environment of freedom from interference around the subordinate. This means that he must adopt an attitude of "hands off" once the grant of freedom is made. Also, he must create such an administrative structure that the freedoms of different individuals do not clash, and that orderly relationships will evolve. This means that he must provide an adequate system of information and communication so that subordinates will have all the knowledge necessary for the making of decisions. He becomes literally a resource to those below.

From the standpoint of the subordinate, freedom means that he must assume a good deal of responsibility for self-development. He must make his own way. Moreover, his involvement in the administration of his unit is greater, for he must keep his superior informed of his actions. The responsibility for follow-up belongs to him just as much as to the person above him.

MAKING FREEDOM WORK

What do we have to do to make freedom work within the organization the way it works in the economic system? How can we assure that company people will not think of it simply as a different label for the organizational philosophy—the same old wine in new bottles?

The administration of freedom requires at least five things: (1) a particular attitude on the part of the superior toward a subordinate; (2) the development of a comprehensive system of rules; (3) the maintenance of an adequate system of communication and information; (4) a thorough and unique pattern of follow-up; and (5) an atmosphere sympathetic to freedom. Let us examine each of these requirements.

The superior, when he grants a subordinate the freedom to decide and act, does not—or, at least, should not—abdicate any of his responsibility for getting results. He can be as demanding in his standards of ultimate performance as ever; in fact, he would do well to plan to become gradually *more* demanding over a period of time as the advantages of the new policy take hold. To be sure, the primary motive for granting freedom is to apply a philosophy that we believe in as Americans, not just to increase divisional or corporate profits. But certainly better managerial performance should be a result. If it is not, the company might well question whether it really *did* increase its employees' freedom.

At the same time, the boss *does* relinquish a good deal of day-to-day control over his men. The subordinate is free to question. He is free to break from tradition and pursue new lines of inquiry. He is free to look beyond the horizon previously drawn by the superior, to dream, to experiment. He is free to seek new knowledge, even to find it by accident.

Of course, he is not free to withhold, distort, or fabricate information. He is not free to misapply or misrepresent the work of another. He is not free to commit fraud or malfeasance, or to interfere with the legitimate freedom of someone else in the organization. And he is not free to overlook departmental objectives; he is committed to work toward company goals.

What a "free" subordinate needs is confidence, understanding, stimulation, and help in self-development. If he responds with a constructive sense of responsibility (and he will if he has been well selected for the job), then there will be little need for "control," "direction," "discipline," and the like. The latter are provided by the goals to be met and the circumstances to be dealt with, as they are in the free market system. In the words of S. Reid Warren, Jr.:

"A basic justification for the freedom of the individual in the United States today is the idea that each man has the privilege to develop his own mind and spirit, and the obligation to contribute to his own progress and that of his contemporaries. Therefore, each individual needs to be stimulated to develop himself. This is perhaps nothing more than involved translation of the word 'educate' which, of course, means 'to lead' or 'to bring out.' "[2]

So the superior must see his role as that of the teacher rather than as the ultimate authority and taker of action manipulating subordinates who have only enough information to carry out parts of the grand plan. Without this insight on the part of the superior there can be no freedom for the subordinate.

SYSTEM OF RULES. The general function of a system of rules

[2] "The Motivation of Engineering Students in the Study of English," *Journal of Engineering Education,* November 3, 1956, p. 234.

in an organization is to guide and direct the routine conduct of individual members. As such, it provides a nonpersonal and objective method of supervision and coordination. Rules relate the individual to the environment in the light of the experience of others.

No really adequate method of classifying rules has been set forth in the literature. We will, therefore, suggest a provisional typology in order to illustrate more clearly the place and form of rules in the administration of freedom.

Rules may be classified in terms of whether they are (a) aimed toward structuring the objective situation surrounding the individual members of the organization or (b) addressed directly to the behavior of personnel. The former may be referred to as situational rules, the latter as behavioral rules. To amplify the differences between them:

Situational rules only indirectly influence behavior. They commonly state objectives, define responsibilities and organizational relationships, establish standards and procedures, and so forth. They are usually stated in the indicative mood and in the present (or sometimes the future) tense.

Behavioral rules, on the other hand, demand certain more or less specific actions of an individual or group. They commonly state that if such and such happens, then such and such ought to, should, must, or shall be done. (Note the contrast between "shall" and the simple future "will.") Their degree of imperativeness is indicated by the verb form. Thus, the "must" or "shall" variety, which may be referred to as *rules of duty,* carry a strong mandatory connotation. They have all the force and effect of a command. Disobeying the rule places the individual in a position of being liable to punishment or penalty.

Rules which are stated in the "should" or "ought" form, however, carry a different connotation. They are *rules of reason.* The implication is that any rational person would come up with the same course of action as set forth in the rule. Noncompliance does not invalidate the action taken, nor does it leave the subordinate in a position of exposure to penalty if he has good reason to act in a way counter to that indicated by the rule. The responsibility for action is with him rather than with higher authority.

The administration of freedom requires the existence of a comprehensive system of rules in order to insure a maximum of "elbowroom" for each individual and at the same time a maximum of co-ordinated and efficient action. It would appear, on the basis of what we know about organizational behavior thus far, that such a system should consist primarily of situational rules together with a strong admixture of behavioral rules of the "ought" or "should" form.

The justification of such a rules system, in which individuals are subject to impersonal discipline rather than to arbitrary authority, is well known to the American industrialist because it is the basis of his eloquent defense of the free-enterprise system against spreading bureaucratic government power. Such expressions as "free enterprise is not a hunting license" (made by Clarence Randall, former chairman of the board of directors, Inland Steel Company) carry strong implications of the moral rightness of an economy in which a firm must be responsible or be disciplined in the market place. So it would be, also, with a free individual in an administrative hierarchy. He has a good deal of discretion, but he must accept the consequences of his behavior.

FULL INFORMATION. If managers are to take advantage of freedom and discharge adequately the heavy responsibilities which it imposes, they have to be furnished with sufficient information at the right time. Indeed, this is crucial, because one of the chief ways in which power-oriented superiors control and thwart strong subordinates is to deny them the full knowledge they need to take action. Such superiors see the denial of information as a control.

How much does a subordinate need to know? The information provided him should be sufficiently broad in scope so that his horizons can be extended beyond the limits of his particular organizational boundaries. He must know something of the strategy of the organization and its broad goals. He must have an understanding of the purposes and actions of other departments and branches. Above all, he must be advised of the expectations and actions of his associates.

Hence, the superior's insight into his role as a teacher is critical. A teacher is aware of his responsibility for providing information and for making his expectations clear. Unquestionably, there is a place for staff departments in this matter of communication, and few would deny that much needs to be done in the direction of clarifying that place. The present failures in the flow of information downward in many organizations could not be tolerated if those below were free to act on the information they are now getting.

IMPERSONAL FOLLOW-UP. If the granting of freedom is to result in creativity and innovation, there must be a thorough revision of some of our present notions of follow-up.

It has been common practice to put the burden of follow-up on the boss. There has been no alternative. If he has a monopoly on decision-making information, and if he considers himself responsible for a subordinate's day-to-day operations, who else can keep checking up on the job being done? But *if* we give the subordinate all the decision-making data he needs, and *if* we say that he—not the boss—is responsible for the way he does a job, then the traditional system is no longer the only practical one. As a matter of fact, it may even become impractical. Can the boss follow up efficiently on a job that is not being done as he would do it—in a way that may even make little sense to him?

Our proposal is that the main responsibility for follow-up be given to the subordinate to whom the freedom is granted. This may sound like having him judge his own acts; but it is not, because he has clearly defined goals to accomplish. He has sat down with the boss and learned what his boss expects of him. As he reports on his progress from time to time, both he and the boss are looking at this "control data" in the light of the same goals.

In one sense, what we are arguing for here is the impersonal atmosphere of the market place. Of course, wherever human relations are concerned, there will be emotions and prejudices. But we can put management relationships on a more factual basis—factual in terms of assignments, objectives, and results. A judgment as to whether a job has been (or is being) accomplished well can then be made in much the same impersonal, unemotional way as a judgment as to whether a product has sold well.

This being so, the subordinate can *predict* what the evaluation of his work will be. He can read the progress reports he makes up in the same way that the boss will read them. Nobody is looking over his shoulder, but he has some targets and target dates looking up at him from his desk. He can truly carry the main burden of follow-up and control himself, going to his superior whenever necessary to discuss problems that are slowing him down and to revise his original objectives and target dates.

REALISTIC ATMOSPHERE. In most instances an executive will agree in principle that subordinates should have freedom to act. However, as soon as it comes down to actually granting such freedom, many tend to shy away from taking such a step. Why?

There are undoubtedly many factors which contribute to behavior of this kind. It seems likely, however, that one of the leading causes is an environment of uncertainty and insecurity. Caught in the grip of anxiety, "authoritarian personalities" tend to center decision-making powers in themselves; reluctant to strengthen those below, they hold on to what they have. One psychologist has concluded:

". . . the high authoritarian, when faced with an anxiety-producing conflict . . . rejects ambiguity in order to allay his anxiety; due to this mode of dealing with cognitions, especially of people, he becomes ingroup-outgroup conscious; this structuring of the world into ingroups (superior) and outgroups (inferior) makes him increasingly status aware and status anxious; in order to reduce his status anxiety, he is convinced (by distorted perception if necessary) that there are real, important and recognizable differences between the ingroup and the outgroup; all of this leads to identification-compulsion which requires extensive stereotyping."[3]

The anxieties of such a person, while sometimes inherent in his personality structure, are often traceable to the atmosphere he breathes. All too frequently, some levels of management are interested in having other levels practice decentralization while they themselves centralize.

If a realistic atmosphere of freedom is to be built, it must permeate the entire organization—not just the top, the middle, or the lower levels. The requisites for the administration of freedom which

[3] Sidney Siegel, "Certain Determinants and Correlates of Authoritarianism," *Genetic Psychology Monographs*, May 1954, p. 224.

we have outlined cannot be confined to one or another level; they must become part of the total philosophy and practice of all in management. If this is not done, the good men go down in the political battles, the bad ones win, and the many at the bottom of the hierarchy, losing faith in freedom, seek some exterior protection from authority which they feel to be irrational.

CREATIVE COMPETITION

We all know that when there is freedom in the market place, competition is keen. And the more a superior power intervenes in the market through restrictions, controls, edicts, and the like, the more subordinate is the consumer and the more competition is reduced or eliminated. In business administration it will be the same. There will be more competition among managers who have freedom of action than among managers closely supervised by their superiors. The competitive instinct is strong among executives, but it is necessarily curbed whenever there is a strong top-down pressure to conform.

The question is whether, given an atmosphere of freedom and competition, competition will degenerate into conflict. Much depends on the moral climate in the company:

If the superior encourages subordinates to succeed by working toward challenging and up-to-date goals, stated in the impersonal terms of the work to be done, then cooperation and teamwork will be the order of the day.

But if he listens to and engages in connivance and intrigue and allows an individual's success to be achieved at the expense of his competitors', then an excess of conflict will result.

The difference is largely a matter of whether or not the superior understands that, where freedom is concerned, the means is more important than the end. The philosophy of working toward individual goals is more important *at any one time* than the goals themselves—although over a period of time it is the accomplishment, of course, which justifies the philosophy.

Perhaps this understanding could light the way toward an ideal set forth by H. W. Johnson, vice president in charge of steel manufacturing, Inland Steel Company: "dedicated people who will learn how to produce without destroying."[4] Is this not the real issue underlying the previously mentioned conflict between the employer's view of a free system and the employee's view of an authoritarian daily life? To produce material things by wearing out the land and crushing the spirit of man—this is for slaves, robots, and organization men. But to produce without destroying, to create, innovate, and elevate—this is for free men. If we are to approach this idea, we must give careful thought to four significant questions:

1. *The Role of Leadership.* The relationship of leadership to freedom, while frequently discussed, still remains something of a paradox. In any organized effort, someone comes to the fore in the vital role of leader. Emotions, both positive and negative, tend to center on certain individuals. Inevitably, power becomes focused. What is to be the role of leaders with power in an environment of freedom? Should we, for example, distinguish between power to plan objectives and power to regulate administrators' behavior?

2. *Preparing for Freedom.* Many individuals are reluctant to assume responsibility. While it is certain that a management *group* will grow under freedom, the process of individual growth cannot be left to chance. What, then, is the best way to develop managers? How can they best be prepared for freedom?

3. *Handling of Incompetency.* Mistakes in recruiting, developing, and promoting personnel are inevitable in any organization. How is incompetency to be dealt with under the concept of freedom? Individuals must be free to make mistakes; at the same time, organizations cannot long permit inefficiency due to incompetency. How can inefficiency be controlled without destroying freedom?

4. *Selling the Idea.* Any superior in a chain of command can, by changing his role, grant freedom to his subordinates. But how can he be sure that *they* will do likewise? It has been demonstrated over and over that decentralization at one level may be followed by strong centralization at the next lower level. How can this be prevented? Above all, what measures of the degree of freedom at the lower levels can be designed?

[4] H. W. Johnson, commencement speech delivered at Michigan College of Mining and Technology, Houghton, Michigan, June 9, 1957.

The main reason for taking a fresh point of view toward the delegation of authority is to open the door to developments in administration which cannot now be imagined because they will be innovations. This step should be taken not as a result of logical demonstration but because of faith—faith in the Christian attitude toward the individual, the faith in the free market system. With all of our lack of knowledge, there is one certainty: we can assure freedom to the few who will discover great things only by giving it to the many. Unfortunately, we cannot tell in advance who the great discoverers will be or when and where they will appear.

THE PROBLEM OF POWER

Norman H. Martin and John Howard Sims

"Beneath the general principles, attitudes, and ideals of 'human relations' lie the actual tactics and day-to-day techniques by which executives achieve, maintain, and exercise power. In the current enthusiasm for 'democratizing' business procedures, these hard, practical devices tend to be overlooked. Yet they exist just the same —and, in many ways, do not depart substantially from the scorned advice of Niccolo Machiavelli, whose name has become a symbol of cynicism, ruthlessness, and deception. It is time we began to think through and discuss them as being important in their own right, whether good or bad."

Executives—whether in business, government, education, or the church—have power and use it. They maneuver and manipulate in order to get a job done and, in many cases, to strengthen and enhance their own position. Although they would hate the thought and deny the allegation, the fact is that they are politicians. "Politics," according to one of the leading authorities in this complex and fascinating field, "is . . . concerned with relationships of control or of influence. To phrase the idea differently, politics deals

Note: See Notes on the Authors, pages 555 and 556, and item 151 in the bibliography for the full reference to this selection.

with human relationships of superordination and subordination, of dominance and submission, of the governors and the governed."[5] In this sense, everyone who exercises power must be a politician.

It is true, as many others have pointed out in different connections that we in this country have an instinctive revulsion against the term "power." It carries immoral connotations for us, despite the definitions of men like R. H. Tawney, the economic historian, who divorces it from any ethical attributes by calling it simply "the capacity of an individual or group of individuals to modify the conduct of other individuals or groups in the manner which he desires, and to prevent his own conduct from being modified in the manner which he does not."[6]

Furthermore, though we glorify ambition in the abstract, we frown on its practice and are distressed at the steps which must be taken if ambition is to be translated into actual advancement. Thus when power is coupled with ambition, we shy away and try to pretend that neither really exists.

But the fact is that we use power and exercise our ambitions just the same—troubled though we may be by the proverbial New England conscience which "doesn't prevent you from doing anything—it just keeps you from enjoying it!"

The complexity of the problem is increased when we recall that the real source of power is not the superior but the subordinate. Men can only exercise that power which they are allowed by other men—albeit their positions are buttressed by economic, legal, and other props. The ultimate source of power is the group; and a group, in turn, is made up of people with consciousness and will, with emotion and irrationality, with intense personal interests and tenaciously held values.

The human being resists being treated as a constant. Knowledge, reason, and technical know-how will not suffice as methods of control, but give way to the arts of persuasion and inducement, of tactics and maneuver, of all that is involved in interpersonal rela-

[5] V. O. Key, Jr., *Politics, Parties & Pressure Groups* (New York, Thomas Y. Crowell Company, 2nd edition, 1948), p. 3.

[6] R. H. Tawney, *Equality* (London, George Allen and Unwin, Ltd., 4th edition, 1952), p. 175.

tionships. Power cannot be given; it must be won. And the techniques and skills of winning it are at the same time the methods of employing it as a medium of control. This represents the political function of the power-holder.

In such a light, we see why the successful functioning and advancement of the executive is dependent, not only on those aspects of an enterprise which are physical and logical, but on morale, teamwork, authority, and obedience—in a word, on the vast intricacy of human relationships which make up the political universe of the executive.

The real question then becomes: How can power be used most effectively? What are some of the political stratagems which the administrator must employ if he is to carry out his responsibilities and further his career? This is an area that has carefully been avoided by both students and practitioners of business—as if there were something shady about it. But facts are facts, and closing our eyes to them will not change them. Besides, if they are important facts, they should be brought into the open for examination.

Accordingly, we present here some of the findings of the first stage of a fairly extensive investigation of just how the executive functions in his political-power environment. We have searched the biographies of well-known leaders of history, from Alexander to Roosevelt; we have explored the lives of successful industrialists like Rockefeller and Ford; and we have interviewed a number of contemporary executives.

There follows an account of certain tactics which we have found to be practiced by most men whose success rests on ability to control and direct the actions of others—no doubt, raw and oversimplified when reduced to a few black-and-white words, but for this very reason more likely to be provocative. With further refinement, these generalizations will serve as hypotheses in the succeeding stages of our research, but in the meantime we present them to businessmen to look at openly and objectively—to ask, "Do we not use just such techniques frequently?" and, if so, to ponder, "How can we best operate in this particular area, for our own interest as managers and for the good of people under us?"

Taking Counsel. The able executive is cautious about how he seeks and receives advice. He takes counsel only when he himself desires it. His decisions must be made in terms of his own grasp of the situation, taking into account the views of others when he thinks it necessary. To act otherwise is to be subject, not to advice, but to pressure; to act otherwise too often produces vacillation and inconsistency.

Throwing a question to a group of subordinates is all too often interpreted as a delegation of power, and the executive may find himself answered with a decision instead of counsel. He must remember that he, not the group under him, is the responsible party. If an executive allows his subordinates to provide advice when he does not specifically call for it, he may find himself subject, not only to pressure, but to conflicting alignments of forces within his own ranks. A vague sort of policy which states, "I am always ready to hear your advice and ideas on anything," will waste time, confuse issues, dilute leadership, and erode power.

Alliances. In many respects, the executive system in a firm is composed of complexes of sponsor-protégé relationships.[7] For the protégé, these relationships provide channels for advancement; for the sponsor, they build a loyal group of followers. A wise administrator will make it a point to establish such associations with those above and below him. In the struggles for power and influence that go on in many organizations, every executive needs a devoted following and close alliances with other executives both on his own level and above him if he is to protect and to enhance his status and sphere of influence.

Alliances should not be looked upon, however, merely as a protective device. In addition, they provide ready-made systems of communication, through which the executive can learn at first-hand how his decisions are being carried out, what unforeseen obstacles are being encountered, and what the level of morale in the organization is at any moment.

Maneuverability. The wise executive maintains his flexibility, and he never completely commits himself to any one position or

[7] See Norman H. Martin and Anselm S. Strauss, "Patterns of Mobility Within Industrial Organizations," *Journal of Business,* April, 1956, p. 101.

program. If forces beyond his control compel a major change in company policy, he can gracefully bend with the wind and co-operate with the inevitable, thus maintaining his status.

An executive should preserve maneuverability in career planning as well. He ought never to get in a situation that does not have plenty of escape hatches. He must be careful, for instance, that his career is not directly dependent on the superior position of a sponsor. He should provide himself with transferable talents, and interfirm alliances, so that he will be able to move elsewhere if the conditions in his current organization become untenable.

Communication. During recent years emphasis has been placed on the necessity for well-dredged channels of communication which run upward, downward, and sideways. Top management should supply its subordinates with maximum information, according to this theory; subordinates in turn must report fully to their chiefs.

It is possible, however, that executives have been oversold on maximizing the flow of information. It simply is not good strategy to communicate everything one knows. Rather, it may often be advantageous to withhold information, or to time its release. This is especially true with reference to future plans—plans which may or may not materialize; it is also valid in the case of information that may create schism or conflict within the organization; and it is prudent when another executive is a threat to one's own position. Furthermore, information is an important tactical weapon, and should be considered as such.

It would appear, then, that executives should be concerned with determining "who gets to know what and when," rather than with simply increasing the flow. Completely open communication deprives the executive of the exclusive power of directing information which should be his.

Compromising. The executive should accept compromise as a means of settling differences with his tongue in his cheek. While appearing to alter his view, he should continue to press forward toward a clear-cut set of goals. It is frequently necessary to give ground on small matters, to delay, to move off on tangents, even to suffer reverses in order to retain power for future forward movement. Concessions, then, should be more apparent than real.

Negative Timing. The executive is often urged to take action with which he is not in agreement. Sometimes pressure for such action arises from the expectations of subordinates, the influence of his associates with his superiors, the demands of custom and tradition, or other sources he would be unwise to ignore.

To give in to such demands would be to deny the executive's prerogative; to refuse might precipitate a dangerous crisis, and threaten his power. In such situations the executive may find it wise to use what might be called the technique of "negative timing." He initiates action, but the process of expedition is retarded. He is considering, studying, and planning for the problem; there are difficulties to be overcome and possible ramifications which must be considered. He is always *in the process* of doing something but never quite does it, or finally he takes action when it is actually too late. In this way the executive escapes the charge of dereliction, and at the same time the inadvisable program "dies on the vine."

Self-Dramatization. Most vocal communication in which an executive engages—whether with his superiors, his colleagues, or his subordinates—is unpremeditated, sincere, spontaneous. His nonvocal communication—the impression projected by his posture, gestures, dress, or facial expressions—is commonly just as natural.

But executives would do well to re-examine this instinctive behavior, for many of them are overlooking an important political stratagem. The skill of the actor—whose communication is "artistic" as opposed to "natural"—represents a potential asset to an administrator. Dramatic art is a process by which selections from reality are chosen and arranged by the artists for the particular purpose of arousing the emotions, of convincing, of persuading, of altering the behavior of the audience in a *planned direction*.

The actor's purpose is no different from that of the manager who wants to activate his subordinates in certain specific directions—to secure a certain response from those with whom he communicates. The actor's peculiar gift is in deliberately shaping his own speech and behavior to accomplish his purpose. The element of chance, the variable of the unknown, is diminished, if not removed; and rehearsal with some foreknowledge of what is to occur takes its place. The *how* of communicating is considered as well as the *what*.

Of course, this is no easy task. The effectiveness of the actor's performance depends on his ability to estimate what will stimulate the audience to respond. And once he makes his choices, he must be able to use them skillfully. His voice and body must be so well disciplined, so well trained, that the images he chooses may be given life. The question is, how can an executive acquire the skill of artistic communication; how can he learn to dramatize himself?

The development of sharper powers of observation is the first step. Having witnessed effective communication—whether a TV drama or an actual meeting of the board of directors—the executive should try to determine what made it effective. He should pay attention to *how* a successful man handled himself, not what he said or did. Formal classes can provide the executive with control over his voice—its pitch, tone, color, speed, diction; training can do the same for his body—gesture, posture, and mime. Most important, the executive should seize any opportunity to gain actual experience in putting such skills to work, in amateur theatricals or "role-playing" sessions.

It would be foolish to deny that such skills cannot be entirely learned; to some extent they depend on the unknowns of flair, talent, and genius. But such an acknowledgment does not excuse the executive from making an effort, for the range of possible improvement is very great.

Confidence. Related to, but not identical with, self-dramatization is the outward appearance of confidence. Once an executive has made a decision, he must look and act decided. In some instances genuine inner conviction may be lacking, or the manager may find it difficult to generate the needed dynamics. The skillful executive who finds himself in such a situation will either produce the effect of certainty or postpone any contact with his associates in order to avoid appearing in an unfavorable light.

Thus the man who constantly gives the impression of knowing what he is doing—even if he does not—is using his power and increasing it at the same time.

Always the Boss. Warm personal relations with subordinates have sometimes been considered the mark of a good executive. But in practice an atmosphere of social friendship interferes with the efficiency of an operation and acts to limit the power of the manager. Personal feelings should not be a basis for action—either negative or positive. The executive should never permit himself to be so committed to a subordinate as a friend that he is unable to withdraw from this personal involvement and regard the man objectively as an element in a given situation.

Thus a thin line of separation between executive and subordinate must always be maintained. The situation should be one of isolation and contact—of the near and far—of marginality. No matter how cordial he may be, the executive must sustain a line of privacy which cannot be transgressed; in the final analysis, he must always be the boss. If we assume, then, that the traditional "open-door" policy of the modern executive is good strategy, we must always ask the question: "How far open?"

The foregoing discussion will undoubtedly raise questions, and even indignation, in the minds of some readers. In the last two decades, the finger of censure has often been pointed at the interpersonal relations in the management of industrial organizations, questioning whether they are harmonious with a democratic society and ideology.[8] Executives have been urged to adopt practices and programs aimed at "democratizing" their businesses. Perhaps they have even developed a sense of guilt from the realization of their own position of authority, and the fact that they cannot be completely frank, sincere, honest, and above-board in their interpersonal relations. We live in an era of "groupness"; we are bombarded with admonitions which insist that everyone who is participating in an enterprise should have a part in the management of it.

In the light of such a trend even the terminology used in this article—"power," "maneuver," "tactics," "techniques"—appears disturbing when set down in black and white. But in fact it is neither immoral nor cynical to recognize and describe the actual daily practices of power. After all, sweeping them under the rug—making believe that they are not actually part of the executive's activity—does not cause them to vanish. Open and honest dis-

[8] See Thomas C. Cochran, "Business and the Democratic Tradition," *Harvard Business Review*, March–April, 1956, p. 39.

cussion of the political aspects in the administrator's job exposes these stratagems to the constructive spotlight of knowledge. They exist; therefore we had better take a look at them and see what they are really like.

As we delve deeper into the study of political tactics in business management, the contrast with modern human relations theory and practice will stand out in ever sharper relief. Mutual confidence, open communication, continuing consultation and participation by subordinates, friendship, an atmosphere of democracy seem hard to reconcile with much of the maneuvering and power plays that go on in the nation's offices and factories every day.

Yet businessmen must develop some rationale of executive behavior which can encompass the idealism of democracy and the practicality of politics—and, at the same time, be justified in terms of ultimate values. If they do not, they will feel like hypocrites as the day-to-day operation of their offices clashes with their speeches before women's clubs. The old cliché that "business is business" is no longer satisfying to the general public, nor to the executive himself.

One way to try to fit human relations theory and political tactics together is to state that the means or ways of exercising power are neutral. In and of themselves, they have no moral value. They take on moral qualities only in connection with the ends for which they are used. Power can be used for good or ill according to this theory, and we should have the courage and knowledge to use it wisely. Conscious, deliberate, and skilled use of executive power means responsible use of power. If men in the past have employed power for evil ends, that is unfortunate; it is just as true that other men, if they had made use of business politics in an effective fashion, might have been a greater force for good.

The difficulty with this line of thought lies in the well-known pitfalls inherent in the timeless means-ends controversy. In real life, what are means and what are ends? Can you achieve good ends by bad means? If the way one man conducts his relationship with another has no moral implications, what human activity does have moral significance?

Others may take the position that "so long as my general philosophy is sound and moral, the specific actions I have to take in the course of my job don't matter." But one may question the validity of a philosophy of life that breaks down every time it comes into contact with reality.

Still another formula could be found in the statement, "The good of the company comes before that of an individual. If I have to violate moral codes and democratic principles in dealing with one man, that is too bad for him. But I cannot allow any single person to overshadow the interests of all our other employees, stockholders, and customers." The skeptical listener might then raise the issue of collectivism versus individualism, and ask whether the general welfare really overrides the worth and dignity of the individual. Can we build a society on the idea of the individual's importance if we violate the principle whenever it interferes with what we consider to be the good of the group?

There are, of course, other approaches, but they too are fraught with internal contradictions. The riddle, then, remains unsolved; the conflict between the use of power and the principles of democracy and enlightened management is unrelieved. Businessmen, who face this paradox every day in countless situations, cannot avoid the responsibility of explaining or resolving it. If a viable philosophy of management is to be developed, they must contribute their ideas—for the sake of their own peace of mind, if nothing else.

If this article succeeds in getting more businessmen to do some thinking along this line, then it will have served its purpose.

THE RESPONSIBILITIES OF MANAGEMENT

Peter F. Drucker

The task of relating the welfare of the enterprise to the public good constitutes the ultimate responsibility of management. With the advent of the modern corporate enterprise and its growing social character, the discharge of this responsibility becomes an absolute imperative.

Note: See Notes on the Authors, page 552, and item 68 in the bibliography for the full reference to this selection.

"The responsibility of management is decisive not only for the enterprise itself but for management's public standing, its success and its status, for the very future of our economic and social system and the survival of the enterprise as an autonomous institution."

Our discussion has so far treated the business enterprise as primarily existing by and for itself. True, we have stressed the relationship to the outside—to customers and market, to the labor union, to the social, economic and technological forces at work in our society. But these relations have been viewed somewhat like the relationship between a ship and the sea which engirds it and carries it, which threatens it with storm and shipwreck, which has to be crossed, but which is yet alien and distinct, the environment rather than the home of the ship.

But society is not just the environment of the enterprise. Even the most private of private enterprises is an organ of society and serves a social function.

Indeed the very nature of the modern business enterprise imposes responsibilities on the manager which are different in kind and scope from those of yesterday's businessman.

Modern industry requires an organization of basic resources which is radically different from anything we have known before. In the first place, the time span of modern production and of business decisions is so long that it goes way beyond the life span of one man as an active factor in the economic process. Secondly, the resources have to be brought together into an organization—both of material objects and of human beings—which has to have a high degree of permanence to be productive at all. Next, resources, human and material, have to be concentrated in large aggregations—though there is of course a question how large they have to be for best economic performance and how large they should be for best social performance. This in turn implies that the people who are entrusted with the direction of this permanent concentration of resources—the managers—have power over people, that their decisions have great impact upon society, and that they have to make decisions that shape the economy, the society and the lives of individuals within it for a long time to come. In other words, modern industry requires the business enterprise, which is something quite different and quite new.

Historically, society has always refused to allow such permanent concentrations of power, at least in private hands, and certainly for economic purposes. However, without this concentration of power which is modern enterprise, an industrial society cannot possibly exist. Hence society has been forced to grant to the enterprise what it has always been most reluctant to grant, that is, first a charter of perpetuity, if not of theoretical immortality to the "legal person," and second a degree of authority to the managers which corresponds to the needs of the enterprise.

This, however, imposes upon the business and its managers a responsibility which not only goes far beyond any traditional responsibility of private property but is altogether different. It can no longer be based on the assumption that the self-interest of the owner of property will lead to the public good, or that self-interest and public good can be kept apart and considered to have nothing to do with each other. On the contrary, it requires of the manager that he assume responsibility for the public good, that he subordinate his actions to an ethical standard of conduct, and that he restrain his self-interest and his authority wherever their exercise would infringe upon the commonweal and upon the freedom of the individual.

And then there is the fact that the modern business enterprise for its survival needs to be able to recruit the ablest, best educated and most dedicated of young men into its service. To attract and to hold such men a promise of a career, of a living, or of economic success is not enough. The enterprise must be able to give such men a vision and a sense of mission. It must be able to satisfy their desire for a meaningful contribution to their community and society. It must in other words embrace public responsibility of a high order to live up to the demands the manager of tomorrow must make on himself.

No discussion of the practice of management could therefore leave out those functions and responsibilities of management that arise out of the social character and the public existence of even the most private of enterprises. In addition the enterprise itself must demand that management think through its public responsibilities. For public policy and public law set the range for the actions and activities of the enterprise. They decide what forms of organization are open to it. They prescribe marketing, pricing, patent and labor policies. They control the ability of the enterprise to obtain capital and its price. They decide altogether whether private enterprise is to remain private and autonomous and to be governed by managements of its own choosing.

The responsibility of management in our society is decisive not only for the enterprise itself but for management's public standing, its success and status, for the very future of our economic and social system and the survival of the enterprise as an autonomous institution. The public responsibility of management must therefore underlie all its behavior. Basically it furnishes the ethics of management.

The discussion of management's public responsibility tends today, at least in this country, to begin with the consideration of management as a leading group in society. But properly it should begin with management's responsibility to the enterprise of which it is an organ. This responsibility cannot be compromised or side-stepped. For the enterprise is management's specific trust; everything else arises out of this trust.

The first responsibility which management owes to the enterprise in respect to public opinion, policy and law is to consider such demands made by society on the enterprise (or likely to be made within the near future) as may affect attainment of its business objectives. It is management's job to find a way to convert these demands from threats to, or restrictions on, the enterprise's freedom of action into opportunities for sound growth, or at least to satisfy them with the least damage to the enterprise.

Even the staunchest friend of management would not claim that the job done so far could not be improved upon.

One illustration should suffice. It should have been clear ten years ago that the changing age structure of the American population, coupled with the steady drop in the purchasing power of the dollar, would produce an irresistible demand on business to do something for old employees. Some managements faced the problem years ago; we have good pension plans going back to 1900. But many more refused to see the inevitable. As a result they were forced to accept demands for employee pensions which tend to impose the greatest rather than the least burden on the enterprise though they do not actually meet the issue. For it is becoming increasingly obvious that pensions will not solve the problem of the old employee. If one fifth of the work force is of pensionable age, as it soon will be in our society, compulsory pensioning of the older people puts an all but unbearable burden on the production of the younger men. At the same time the great bulk of the people who reach what used to be considered old age are both able physically to continue work and eager to do so. What management should have done was to work out plans for keeping employed those older people who want to work and are able to do so, with pensions as something to fall back on for those who are unable or unwilling to keep on working. At the same time these plans would have to make sure that the older employees who are retained do not bottle up the promotional opportunities for younger men or endanger their employment security. Having failed to think through the problem, managements will almost certainly find themselves faced with compulsory employment programs for older people—imposed by unions or by government—which will mean additional cost and new restrictions.

American managements are on the verge of making the same mistake in respect to the stability of income and employment. That this demand will have to be met can hardly be disputed any more. It expresses not only the need of the worker for income security, but the need of our society to symbolize the worker's middle-class status. Also the demand has behind it the force of the deep "depression psychosis" that we inherited from the thirties.

I have tried to show earlier that this demand could be satisfied in such a way as to improve and strengthen the enterprise, increase its productivity and raises its over-all profits. If managements, however, refuse to face the responsibility to make the inevitable productive for the enterprise, they will only saddle their businesses with the guaranteed annual wage—both the most expensive and the least effective way to take care of a real social need.

Management is also responsible for making sure that the present actions and decisions of the business enterprise will not create future public opinion, demands and policies that threaten the enterprise, its freedom and its economic success.

During the last years many companies have dispersed their plants geographically. In doing so many of them have simply built, in a new location, a replica of the original plant, turning out the same product for the same market. In many cases both the old and the duplicate plants are the main source of employment in their respective communities. Examples are a rubber company with old plants in Akron and a new plant in a small southern town; a ball-bearing company with an old plant in a small New England town and a new plant in a small town in Ohio; a shirt maker with old plants in upstate New York and a new plant in rural Tennessee.

In a depression this can only lead to serious public reaction. For management will then be forced to decide which of these plants to close down and which to keep open—the new plants, which represent a high capital investment, have by and large a high break-even point and thus require capacity operations to be profitable, or the old plants around which a whole community may have grown up. But will any community, no matter how eager it was to obtain the new industry, take quietly a decision to deprive it of its main source of income so as to keep up employment in some other place? If the market and the forces of the business cycle bring about unemployment, that is one thing. But if management, by unilateral action, does so, it is quite another. It may therefore be a vital management responsibility to organize new plants so that they have their own market and their own product rather than only be separated geographically. Otherwise expansion will lead to a clash between management and the community, between the requirements of the business and of public policy.

Other practices which may tend to breed public opinion and policies hostile to the enterprise, are the exclusive hiring of college graduates for management positions, thus cutting off chances for men inside the company; the narrowing of promotional opportunities for foremen, thus cutting off the most important rungs on the traditional American ladder of success; or the policy of not hiring older workers or disabled people. To discharge its responsibility to the enterprise management must carefully think through these practices and their impact upon the public welfare.

In brief, management, in every one of its policies and decisions, should ask: What would be the public reaction if everyone in industry did the same? What would be the public impact if this behavior were general business behavior? And this is not just a question for the large corporations. In their totality, small businesses and their managements have fully as much of an impact on public opinion and policy. And all, large and small, should remember that if they take the easy way out and leave these problems to "the other fellow," they only assure that their solution will eventually be imposed by government.

THE SOCIAL IMPACT OF BUSINESS DECISIONS

This discussion should have made it clear that the impact of management's decisions on society is not just "public" responsibility but is inextricably interwoven with management's responsibility to the enterprise. Still, there is a responsibility of management to the public interest as such. This is based on the fact that the enterprise is an organ of society, and that its actions have a decisive impact on the social scene.

The first responsibility to society is to operate at a profit, and only slightly less important is the necessity for growth. The business is the wealth-creating and wealth-producing organ of our society. Management must maintain its wealth-producing resources intact by making adequate profits to offset the risk of economic activity. And it must besides increase the wealth-creating and wealth-producing capacity of these resources and with them the wealth of society.

It may seem paradoxical that this responsibility of management is most clearly recognized in the Soviet Union. Profitability is the first and absolute law for Soviet management and the essence of what the Russians proudly proclaim to be their great economic discovery: "management by the ruble." But a source which the Kremlin would hardly admit as authority has said as much; I refer, of course, to Our Lord's Parable of the Talents.

This responsibility is absolute and cannot be abdicated. No management can be relieved of it. Managements are in the habit of saying that they have a responsibility to the shareholder for profits. But the shareholder, at least in a publicly owned company, can always sell his stock. Society, however, is stuck with the enterprise. It has to take the loss if the enterprise does not produce adequate profits, has to take the impoverishment if the enterprise does not succeed in innovation and growth.

For the same reason management has a public responsibility to make sure of tomorrow's management without which the resources would be mismanaged, would lose their wealth-producing capacity and would finally be destroyed.

Management is responsible for conducting the enterprise so as not to undermine our social beliefs and cohesion. This implies a negative responsibility: not to usurp illegitimate authority over citizens by demanding their absolute and total allegiance.

In a free society the citizen is a loyal member of many institutions; and none can claim him entirely or alone. In this pluralism lies its strength and freedom. If the enterprise ever forgets this, society will retaliate by making its own supreme institution, the state, omnipotent.

The tendency today of so many, especially of our larger, enterprises to assume paternal authority over their management people and to demand of them a special allegiance, is socially irresponsible usurpation, indefensible on the grounds alike of public policy and the enterprise's self-interest. The company is not and must never claim to be home, family, religion, life or fate for the individual. It must never interfere in his private life or his citizenship. He is tied to the company through a voluntary and cancellable employment contract, not through some mystical and indissoluble bond.

But responsibility for our social beliefs and cohesion also has a positive component. At least in this country it imposes on management the duty to keep open the opportunity to rise from the bottom according to ability and performance. If this responsibility is not discharged, the production of wealth will, in the long run, weaken rather than strengthen our society by creating social classes, class hatred and class warfare.

There are other areas in which responsibilities can be asserted.

I would, for instance, consider it a responsibility of the management of the large company to develop a capital-expenditure policy which tends to counteract the extremes of the business cycle (with Automation such a policy becomes a business necessity). I believe that management has a responsibility to develop policies that will overcome the deep-seated hostility to profits, for the simple reason that this is a threat to our economic and social system. I finally believe that any business, in the present world situation, has the responsibility to make its best contribution to the defensive strength of its country.

But what is most important is that management realize that it must consider the impact of every business policy and business action upon society. It has to consider whether the action is likely to promote the public good, to advance the basic beliefs of our society, to contribute to its stability, strength and harmony.

MANAGEMENT AS A LEADING GROUP

Only now can we raise the question of the responsibility that management should assume by virtue of being one of the leading groups in society—responsibilities over and above those grounded in the business itself.

Hardly a day goes by when a spokesman of management does not assert a new public responsibility of this kind. We have been told that management should hold itself responsible for the survival of the liberal arts colleges, for the economic education of workers, for religious tolerance or for a free press, for strengthening the United Nations or for abolishing it, for "culture" in its broadest form and for every one of the arts in particular.

There is no doubt that being a leading group entails heavy responsibility; and there is nothing more destructive than to shirk these responsibilities. There is also, however, nothing more destructive than to assert responsibilities for a group which it does not have, nothing more dangerous than to usurp responsibilities. The present management approach tends to do both: it shirks responsibilities that exist and usurps others that do not and must not exist.

For whoever says "responsibility" also implies "authority." One does not exist without the other. To assert management's responsibility in any area is therefore to assign it authority in the area in question. Is there any reason to believe that management in a free society should have any authority over the colleges, over culture and the arts, over the freedom of the press or over our foreign policy? To raise the question is to answer it: such authority would be intolerable. Even the impassioned twaddle permitted, by hoary custom, to the commencement speaker or the boss at the annual employees' picnic should avoid such a claim.

Management's public responsibility as one of the leading groups should therefore be restricted to areas in which management can legitimately claim authority.

As a "rule of thumb" I recommend that management religiously avoid asserting or assuming responsibility for any activities it does not want to see controlled either by the union leader or the government. These are the activities which should be free, that is, organized by spontaneous, local, pluralist action of the citizens, not by any one group or any governing organ. If management does not want the union leader to control an activity, it is a fair assumption that the union leader (and his sizeable following) would not want management to control the activity either. And it would be reasonable to assume that society would find sole control of such an activity by either management or union leader intolerable. It would demand the obvious and easy substitute for non-control of these areas: control by the organized government as the representative of the entire people.

And if the business enterprise becomes a source of financial support for important causes and institutions—as our tax laws force it increasingly to be—management must take scrupulous care not to let financial support become "responsibility," not to let itself be misled into usurping authority where it has and should have none.

But from the fact that responsibility and authority go together, it follows also that management owes to society responsibility wherever its special competence gives it authority.

One major area here is that of fiscal policy. Because we have not modernized our tax structure even though it was built when the maximum income tax was 4 per cent (and that rate applied to millionaires only), we have today an illogical, unmanageable, indeed an immoral system of taxation that encourages and rewards irresponsible actions and decisions of businesses and private individuals alike. Here management can make a major contribution—and it has therefore a major responsibility. But it has responsibility for positive action.

It is not enough to scream that taxes are too high as some people in management have been doing. What we need is a policy that reconciles the necessity of continuing high government expenditures, in the world we live in, with the requirements of society and economy. As long as management confines itself to shouting "down with taxes" it will not have discharged its responsibility for fiscal policy. In fact, it will have been totally ineffectual and will only have made itself look irresponsible.

Wherever management's competence gives it authority, wherever therefore management has a responsibility, this responsibility must be discharged on the basis of the public interest. It is not good enough to start out with the premise that "what is good for the business is good for the country," even though the assertion may be substantially correct for the very large company which is in effect a cross section of the American economy. For while its competence is the basis for management's authority, the only basis on which this authority can be used is the public interest. What is good for the business—or even for all businesses—is irrelevant.

But the final conclusion from the consideration of management's public responsibility as one of the leading groups is the most important one: It is management's public responsibility to make whatever is genuinely in the public good *become* the enterprise's own self-interest.

To be disinterested is not enough for a leading group in society. It is not even enough that the group subordinate its own interests to the common good. It must succeed in harmonizing public and private interest by making what is the common good coincide with its own self-interest. "This company must be so managed as to make everything likely to strengthen our country, or to advance its prosperity, add strength to the company and advance its prosperity"; thus the management of one of our most successful companies, Sears, Roebuck. In economic fact, "what is good for the country must be made to be good for Sears" may not be so different from "what is good for the business is good for the country." In spirit, in essence, in assertion of responsibility, however, it is completely different.

The Sears statement does not imply pre-established harmony between the private self-interests of a group and the commonweal. On the contrary; to make what is good for the country good for the enterprise requires hard work, great management skill, high standards of responsibility and broad vision. It is a counsel of perfection. To carry it out completely would require the philosopher's stone that can transmute the basest element into pure gold. But if management is to remain a leading group—indeed, if it is to remain autonomous management running free enterprises—it must make this rule the lodestar of its conduct, must consciously strive to live up to it, and must actually do so with a fair degree of success.

Two hundred and fifty years ago an English pamphleteer, de Mandeville, summed up the spirit of the new commercial age in the famous epigram: "private vices become public benefits"—selfishness unwittingly and automatically turns into the common good. He may have been right; economists since Adam Smith have been arguing the point without reaching agreement.

But whether he was right or wrong is irrelevant; no society can lastingly be built on such belief. For in a good, a moral, a lasting society the public good must always rest on private virtue. No leading group can be accepted on de Mandeville's foundation. Every leading group must, on the contrary, be able to claim that the public good determines its own interest. This assertion is the only legitimate basis for leadership; to make it reality is the first duty of the leaders.

That "capitalism," as the nineteenth century understood the term (and as Europe still too prevalently understands it), was based on de Mandeville's principle may explain its material success. It certainly explains the revulsion against capitalism and capitalists that has swept the Western world during the last hundred years. The economic doctrines of the enemies of capitalism have been untenable and often childish. Their political doctrines have carried the threat of tyranny. But these answers have not been sufficient to quiet the critics of capitalism. Indeed they have usually appeared quite irrelevant to the critics, as well as to the people at large. For the hostility to captialism and capitalists is moral and ethical. Capitalism is being attacked not because it is inefficient and misgoverned but because it is cynical. And indeed a society based on the assertion that private vices become public benefits cannot endure, no matter how impeccable its logic, no matter how great its benefits.

Fifty years ago de Mandeville's principle was as fully accepted here as it still is in Europe. But today it has become possible if not commonplace in this country to assert the opposite principle that the business enterprise must be so managed as to make the public good become the private good of the enterprise. In this lies the real meaning of the "American Revolution" of the twentieth century. That more and more of our managements claim it to be their responsibility to realize this new principle in their daily actions is our best hope for the future of our country and society, and perhaps for the future of Western society altogether.

To make certain that this assertion does not remain lip service but becomes hard fact is the most important, the ultimate responsibility of management: to itself, to the enterprise, to our heritage, to our society and to our way of life.

THE PROBLEM OF BIGNESS

Kenneth Boulding

Much of our basic economic thinking assumes an economic system not dominated by large organizations. As such, it is geared to earlier systems. Today, however, bigness dominates the industrial scene, presenting problems both for economic policy on the part of government and standards of economic morality on the part of individuals.

THE IMPACT UPON ECONOMIC LIFE

In regard to economic life, the main impact of the development of large economic organizations has been to make prices and money

Note: See Notes on the Authors, page 552, and item 27 in the bibliography for the full reference to this selection.

wages more "sticky" and less flexible than they would otherwise have been. It is commonly believed that labor and farm organizations, for instance, have had an important effect on the relative prosperity of these groups. It is supposed, for instance, that labor organizations have raised real wages at the expense of profits, and that farm organizations have raised farm income at the expense of nonfarm income. Some small effects in this direction there may have been . . . however, . . . the distribution of income in the U.S.A. from 1929, suggests that these effects on distribution are small, and are quite overshadowed by the general effects of inflation and deflation. Special studies all point to the same conclusion.[9] This conclusion contradicts the "mythology" of many of these groups; nevertheless the evidence seems irrefutable.

Even if the organized economic groups do not succeed very well in bettering themselves at the expense of others, this does not mean that they have no impact on economic life. Their development means in general the replacement of simple person-to-person transactions and price setting by collective bargaining or by businesses with some degree of monopoly power. This means that the price-setting process becomes "public" rather than "private"; it achieves much greater social visibility. Contrast, for instance, the way in which agricultural wages are set, by man-to-man agreement over the fence among millions of farmers and hired men without any fuss or feathers or publicity, with the determination of steel or automobile wages in months of bargaining between giant organizations and a great fanfare of excitement. Yet, during the war inflation, the wages of the unorganized agricultural workers rose much faster than trade-union wages. Similarly during depressions the wages of unorganized workers fall much faster than the wages of the organized workers. Before the days of agricultural organization agricultural prices were much more flexible than industrial prices; they fell in depression and rose in prosperity.

The development of inflexible prices and wages has important effects upon the economic system and economic policy. Still more

[9] See especially Harold M. Levinson, *Unionism, Wage Trends, and Income Distribution, 1914–1917* (Ann Arbor, Michigan: University of Michigan Press, 1951).

significant perhaps is the fact that the inflexibility of prices is not universal. It applies only to part of the price system, so that in effect the price system is broken in two, one set of prices being rather inflexible and the other set being flexible. If there were no changes in the general level of prices or of money incomes, price inflexibility would not create serious problems, though it might prevent certain desirable shifts of resources between occupations, and it might result in certain injustices and exploitation of the unprotected and unorganized people by those protected by organized groups. When, however, various basic economic changes, such as changes in the quantity of money, in its velocity of circulation, in population, or in productivity, necessitate changes in the general price level or in the national money income, the presence in the system of "sticky" prices that are resistant to pressures for change may cause serious trouble.

The difficulty may be illustrated by supposing (what is approximately true in short periods) that, when the national income changes, the *value* of the output of various industries changes in approximately the same proportion. Now the value in dollars-worth of the output of any industry is equal to the physical quantity of commodity which it produces, multiplied by the price of that commodity. Thus if the wheat industry produces 100 million bushels of wheat and the price of wheat is $2 per bushel, the total dollar value of the wheat output, which is the same thing as the gross contribution of the wheat industry to the national income, is $200 million. Now let us suppose that for various reasons the national money income is halved. The total dollar value of the wheat output is likely to be about halved too—say, to $100 million. If the price is flexible, it will fall to about $1 per bushel, and the output will remain the same at 100 million bushels. If, however, the price were inflexible, and stayed up at $2 per bushel, the only way in which the total value of the output could be reduced would be by reducing the physical quantity of output—say, to 50 million bushels.

What this means is that if the national money income is permitted to decline in a system with inflexible prices, the decline will be taken out in the form of reductions in output and employment in these industries and occupations where prices are inflexible, as it cannot be taken out in the form of a decline in money prices and money wages. Where prices are flexible, however, a decline in the national money income can be achieved without any reduction in output and without the development of unemployment, if the price and money-wage level falls in rough proportion to the decline in the national money income.

Statistical evidence strongly supports these propositions. In the course of the great depression, for instance, agricultural output and employment were approximately constant, but agricultural prices fell sufficiently to reduce the money value of agricultural output to about half what it had been before. We may have been acutely uncomfortable in many ways during the depression, but at least we had as much to eat—on the average—as before. Industrial prices and wages, however, fell less in proportion to the national income, and hence severe unemployment and reduction of industrial output took place. The above picture is complicated, of course, by the fact that the decline in investment (which was the main factor in the depression) shifted demand away from industrial goods, but in outline it is substantially true.

This does not mean, however, that we must advocate a policy of price flexibility at all costs—the cost being a ruthless policy of suppression of organizations of all kinds, trusts, labor unions, and farm organizations alike. Organization-busting is neither practicable nor desirable; and, unless organization of the market can be reconciled with price flexibility (a choice which does not seem to be open to us), the only alternative is to design over-all economic policy on the assumption that many prices will not be flexible. What this means in practice is that we cannot afford to have a monetary deflation; any substantial *reduction* of the price or money-wage level is simply out of the question. The national money income must be kept constantly rising, or at least must be kept from falling. If there are substantial areas of inflexible prices in the economy, we cannot afford even to keep money incomes per head constant and allow real incomes to rise through a fall in prices. The prices will simply not fall adequately, and incomes will adjust through a decline in output and in real income per head.

If population is increasing and if rising productivity brings rising real output per head, money income per capita must increase as fast as productivity, and total money income as fast as population, if a declining price level is to be avoided. There must be a continual increase in the quantity of money unless there is a constant increase in velocity of circulation, which, short of constantly increasing inflation, is unlikely. This increase in the quantity of money can most conveniently come in our society from deficits in the federal cash budget; if government pays out more money than it takes in, the result is an increase in the quantity of money in the hands of the public. The banking system also is a potential source of increased money holdings in the form of bank deposits, and has functioned as such over the decades. Its tendency to cumulative contraction or expansion, however, makes the banking system unreliable as an automatic governor of the money supply.

It is clear, then, that the development of strong economic organizations does not *necessarily* mean that we must have depressions and unemployment. The budgetary and monetary policies of government can be adjusted to prevent this kind of deflationary situation in which the price inflexibility attendant upon economic organization produces unemployment. Nevertheless the question remains whether in a highly organized society it is possible to prevent an almost constant rate of inflation. If deflation is impossible, inflation cannot be corrected. Even if the problem were not complicated by war, therefore, a full employment policy in a highly organized society would almost inevitably lead to a slow but steady increase in the general level of prices. It should be recalled that even an increase at 5 per cent per annum is a 32-fold increase during a lifetime; at 10 per cent per annum the price level will increase a thousand times during a lifetime!

With war becoming the normal relationship of states, much larger rates of inflation may be looked for, as it is virtually impossible to finance even a small war, starting from full employment, without inflation, as the Korean instance indicates. It must be confessed also, since the growth of economic organizations has made price and wage determination so much more publicly visible than it used to be, that a highly organized society is much easier to run in an inflationary period. The organizations can "bring home" to their members "bacon" which they would have got anyway, and hence can retain the support of their membership even in the absence of any real services performed. Thus unions get credit for higher money wages, but get no credit for higher real wages when these are due to falling prices. It is no accident that the lot of the union leader is much easier in inflation than in deflation.

It is not impossible, of course, for a society to adjust to a constant inflation, but we have certainly not faced the many problems involved. A great many of our economic institutions are based on the assumption that the price level may be expected to be reasonably constant in the long run—an assumption which over the past 150 years has been justified. The accounting system, the financial system, including the whole structure of borrowing and lending, provision for old age in the form of pensions, insurance, and money or bond savings, are all based on the assumption of a constant value of money. If the value of money is constantly going to decline, most of our pension and insurance plans will be worthless, and unless nominal rates of interest rise markedly the real rate of interest will become permanently negative, with consequent disorganization of the whole system of finance. If prices are rising at 5 per cent per annum, the nominal rate of interest would have to be 8 per cent in order to make the real rate of interest 3 per cent.

Another important aspect of the rise of organizations is the increase in conflict which may result. This is a problem which goes beyond the limits of economics, though it has important economic aspects. The improvement in organizing techniques has removed, or rather pushed back, some of the internal limitations on the growth of organizations. As organizations grow, however, we find the external limitations becoming of more and more importance. Firms run into imperfect markets; an expansion of sales requires either a price cut or further selling cost. All organizations run into increasing difficulties in attracting new members as they grow in size beyond the point where the most easily organized come in. This principle is so universal that we have named it the Principle of Increasingly Unfavorable External Environment.

The external environment, moreover, involves direct conflict with other organizations, and the fewer the number of organizations in contact with each other, the more acute this conflict becomes. One organization among many can expand without affecting any single one of its rivals enough to provoke notice or retaliation. One organization among few, however, can expand only at the obvious expense of its rivals, and such expansion is likely to provoke counterattacks. Thus we have price wars and advertising wars in business, jurisdictional disputes among labor organizations, and an immense intensification of the burden of international warfare. The very success of an organization may spell its doom. It grows to the point where it cannot live with its neighbors, and yet it cannot grow to the point where it absorbs its neighbors. This dilemma is particularly acute in international relations, and is threatening our whole civilization with destruction.

THE ETHICAL PROBLEMS

Ethics—at least "practical" ethics—is concerned mainly with the standards or criteria by which conduct is judged, both the conduct of individuals in purely personal relationships and of individuals in their roles as responsible directors of organizations. By implication, therefore, it includes the standards by which the behavior of organizations is judged. There is not universal agreement as to what these standards should be. Nevertheless, ethical ideas are not arbitrary; a pattern of both form and development can be traced through their diversities. The difficulties of ethical thought arise mainly because we are faced with a number of different "goods" or ends which may compete. A thing which is good in itself may have to be sacrificed to obtain a greater good. The greatest ethical confusions have arisen because people have assumed that if something is good it should be pursued indefinitely, or that some particular good is to be identified with good-in-general or with bad-in-general. Thus statements such as "trade unions are bad (or good); cooperatives are good (or bad); cartels are bad (or good)" are almost meaningless. The truth is that *some* unions, co-ops, cartels, etc. are good and some are bad, or that some *aspects* of unions, co-ops, cartels, etc. are good and some are bad.

All conduct conforms to *some* kinds of standards. When, however, we are distinguishing between "ethical" and "unethical" conduct, we are thinking largely of the *objectivity* of the standards concerned. "Disapproved" conduct is that which conforms only to the standards of the individual concerned, and does not conform to the accepted standards of the society in which he lives. Not all conduct, however, which is disapproved is unethical. Indeed conduct may be disapproved for two reasons: either because it falls short of the standards of society or because it rises above them (the saints and prophets have nearly always got themselves into serious trouble!). From the side of motivation, therefore, it seems not unreasonable to regard ethical conduct as that which is motivated by the larger and more objective interest as against the smaller and more personal interest. This is one meaning of the injunction to love our neighbor as ourselves: that we should not act as if we were the center of interest of the universe, but that we should see ourselves as we really are, and should act in the interest of the "whole." Action in the general interest is the heart of ethical conduct.

Perhaps the two most difficult groups of ethical problems which arise out of the development of economic organization are, first, those connected with the conflict between the private and the general interest, and, second, those connected with the use of coercion.

CONFLICTING INTERESTS. Difficulties arise, however, where general and particular interests conflict. The ability of men to act in the general interest depends first on the extent to which they identify themselves with the general interest (i.e., on where they draw the line between what concerns "them" and what does not). It depends secondly on the extent to which action in the general interest actually involves their personal survival. If action in the general interest leads to self-destruction, it demands a sense of identity with the whole greater than most people seem to possess. It is indeed the main object of social institutions of all kinds to create artificially a situation in which the conflict between the personal and the general interest is not so acute as to cause a breakdown of ethical conduct, so that within reason the individual in acting in his own interest is also acting in the general interest.

There are two broad devices through which individual interest is brought closer to the general interest. One is the economic device of competition and specialization; i.e., the "market," which creates a situation in which the welfare of an individual depends on his ability to satisfy the market demands of others more satisfactorily than his competitors. The other is the political device of *representation*, whereby an individual is made responsible for his action "to" others because of their power to elect other representatives to fill the role he is playing. This too is a form of competition. A representative if he is to stay in office has to "sell" himself to his constituents much as a manufacturer has to sell his products to his customers.

The development of economic groups has made the "market" somewhat less effective as a protector of the general interest, and has increased the importance of "representation"; it represents, that is to say, a shift from more strictly "economic" to more "political" institutions. In some directions this involves gain, and in other directions loss.

From the point of view of ethical *motivation* there is sometimes a real gain in this broadening of the individual's interest. Insofar as people are motivated by loyalty to a group and are prepared to make personal sacrifices for the group, their motives must be rated ethically superior to those of persons who are motivated only by personal interest. The danger, however, is that the motivation, by the very intensity of its association with a group which is less than the whole, comes to stop all the more sharply at the boundaries of the group; that there is no carryover beyond the organized group into society at large. The "good union man" identifies himself so completely with his fellow workers and makes such personal sacrifices for their cause that he becomes blind to the larger interests of society—or assumes unquestioningly that the interests of his group are identical with those of society at large. Similarly, the patriot identifies himself so completely with the national interest that he becomes blind to the interests of mankind at large; or he habitually identifies the good with the welfare of his own country. It must be emphasized that the national state is one economic group among many and that there is no ethical superiority of the national interest over, say, class interest.

The principal disadvantage of control by representation over control by the market is that representatives are usually responsible *to,* and are elected by, a much smaller group of people than their actions affect. Consequently the representative who acts deliberately in the widest possible public interest is all too liable to find himself out of a job—whether he is a director of a corporation elected by stockholders, a director of a co-operative or of a trade union elected by the members, or an executive or legislator of a nation elected by popular vote. There is a profound tendency for leaders of any group to "grow away" from the followers, and even to become "reasonable" to the point where their followers no longer support them. Representation cannot, it seems, in the present state of political skill and organization, be regarded as a complete substitute for the market as a check on arbitrary power, though it may be used to correct some of the defects and abuses of an unregulated market mechanism.

THE USE OF COERCION. Coercive power is the ability of an organization to defend and maintain itself by influencing the behavior of those within its sphere of influence by *fear* of possible injury which the organization has power to inflict. The opposite of coercive power is "attractive" power, i.e., the ability of organizations to attract voluntary allegiance and support. Virtually all organizations rely on a mixture of attraction and coercion to insure their continued existence. The national state, of course, relies principally on the coercive power, though there are great variations between the tyrannies which have so little attractive power that they must rely almost wholly on the coercive power and the democracies which can inspire the voluntary allegiance of most of their own citizens. Economic organizations on the whole have to rely mainly on attractive power for their defense. A business, for instance, survives mainly by being sufficiently productive of things for which there is a demand, so that it can attract workers and managers to it voluntarily.

There is a tendency, however, for economic organizations to attempt to capture the coercive power of the state for their own defense. Legal monopolies (e.g., in Elizabethan times) are a striking example. In our day the labor movement has also come to rely more and more on legal sanction to get and keep its membership rather than on "selling itself," as in an earlier day employers relied on legal sanctions such as the injunction to prevent unions from "selling themselves" to their potential members. The tariff is another good example of a successful attempt by minority economic groups (frequently in this case rather loosely organized and bound together by a community of interest rather than of organization) to channel the coercive power of the state in directions which they believe (often falsely) are in their own benefit. Agricultural policy is, by and large, another example.

The ethical evaluation of coerciveness is not easy. Unless one is a complete anarchist one must admit the historical necessity of certain coercive elements in social life. Nevertheless it should be possible to agree that coerciveness *in itself* is an evil, and that any development in society toward less coercive forms of social organization that have survival value is desirable. The problem is one of substituting competition in "love" for competition in "fear"; that is, of creating a moral and organizational environment in which those organizations which are not meeting the needs of man, and which are not serving to right wrongs, will not survive in competition with those organizations which are meeting the needs of man. This is the problem of ethical dynamics; that is, of how things in fact get better instead of worse. Organization of some kind is essential to this process, for only by an organization—that is, an information-communication-executive-effector chain—can knowledge be transformed into action. If things go from bad to worse, instead of from bad to better, the reason must be looked for in a failure of the organizational system. One of the principal reasons for such failure is the existence of coercion, for it is this which permits the survival of those organizations which are *not* making things better. The reduction of coercion, however, is itself a problem in organization, and many institutions—for example, schools, churches, clubs, families at the local level, and representative government and international organizations on the larger scale—have this end in view. We need to organize still more consciously, and more imaginatively, toward the great objective of a noncoercive society.

On the score of its contribution to ethical dynamics—that is, to the "rate of betterment"—the organizational revolution has, like

545

most movements, a mixed record. There is a general presumption that improved techniques of organization will have a favorable impact on the rate of betterment, simply because betterment always comes about through organization of some kind, even if it is through the mental and physical bodily organization of a single individual. Nevertheless, the rise of *large* organizations has created certain important special problems. The rise in the technical proficiency of organizations has made the power of coercive organizations greater, and thereby increased the danger that coercion will undermine the forces of betterment. On the other hand the improved ability to organize has resulted in some cases in the substitution of conflict for coercion, where a coerced group has been able to organize and apply countercoercion to the coercer. Thus the labor movement has arisen largely in response to the feeling which the individual, unorganized worker has—in the absence of an active labor market—of being coerced by his employer. Its object up to a point has been to neutralize the coercive power of the employer by developing coercive power of its own.

The rise of nationalism has similar roots, as the essence of nationalism is the use of the coercive power against potential or actual foreign coercers of the national group. Zionism is an interesting example of this phenomenon: the Jew is hoping to get rid of his age-old oppression by organizing a military power in Israel. Unfortunately it seems to be almost impossible to get rid of oppression in this way without becoming an oppressor. There is still something to be said for Isaiah, and the Jew as the suffering servant may be remembered when the state of Israel is a forgotten footnote on the page of history. Two opposite coercions do not necessarily cancel out, and, indeed, frequently result in extremely destructive forms of competition, both economic and political. The appalling breakdown of national defense in our day is a sad tribute to the dead end into which the short cut of countercoercion leads.

THE CONTINUING DILEMMA. The only answer to the problem of coercion which does not seem to end in frustration and conflict is that of the *integration* of the coercer and the coerced through the spread of the ideal of responsibility and organs of control. What this means is that *the interaction of organizations must itself*

be organized; otherwise this interaction is capable of producing intolerable ethical strains. Unorganized and ungoverned interaction
produces too great a conflict between the individual and the general
interest for the individual to bear.

An interesting example of this proposition is found in the ethical
conflicts which are raised by inflation and deflation. Any individual
who expects, with some degree of certainty, that there is going to
be either an inflation or a deflation will, if he acts in his own interests, intensify the very thing which he anticipates. Thus a businessman who wants his business to survive an impending deflation
may try to become "liquid" by turning as much of his assets as
possible into cash or safe bonds, even at the cost of closing down
much of his operations and creating unemployment. Such a course
of action applied generally will accelerate the deflation, and if
prices and money wages do not fall as fast as money incomes, unemployment and depression will result. Each individual in attempting to save himself only pushes the economy farther down. Similarly, in a time of inflation, the individual seeking to protect himself
will get rid of as much of his cash and bonds as possible and rush
to buy the things that he expects will rise in price or become short.
This action will raise prices faster and make supplies still shorter.

The search for national security lands us in a rather similar dilemma. Every nation tries to make itself secure by increasing its
armaments. The armaments of one nation, however, make other
nations feel less secure. Hence the attempt on the part of each nation to establish its security by its own efforts results in greater insecurity for all.

Unfortunately exhortation has proved to be an ineffective instrument for resolving the conflict of the particular and the general
interest. This is especially true where the conflict is one not of individuals but of organizations. The "ethical breaking point" at
which the individual finds the conflict between the private and the
general interest too great for him, and acts to defend himself rather
than his society, comes at a low enough level for most individuals
acting on their own account. But it is apt to come at much lower
levels for individuals acting as representatives of a group. Individuals can sometimes be found who will sacrifice themselves for the

group, especially for a small group. Indeed, the pehnomenon is not at all rare—"Greater love hath no man than this."

I know of no instance in history, however, where a group or an organization has voluntarily laid down its life in the interest of humanity. In the defense of their nation, their church, their union, their business, their family, men have been known to lie, cheat, steal, and even murder with a single-mindedness of intent that an individual as such rarely achieves. A divergence of private and social interest is all the more serious, therefore, when the private interest concerns a group within society, even where that group is as large as a nation. It is a divergence of interest against which moral exhortation is singularly ineffective, because the fact that the individual is serving *some* group which is greater than himself binds him to the fact that his group is only a part of the whole. There is no substitute, therefore, for government, in the literal sense of a governing mechanism, universally operative, which will act counterwise to the kind of movement which creates dangerous divergences of private from general interest.

The case of inflation and deflation is again a good example of the above principle. There is clearly need for a monetary governing mechanism—an agency which can act in an inflationary manner when the rest of the economy is being deflationary, and in a deflationary manner when the rest of the economy is being inflationary. Such machinery would not be too difficult to construct if people could be convinced that it can be done. In the case of national security the problem is more difficult. The more complex the variables, the less mechanical the apparatus for controlling them, the more difficult becomes the question of what to control and how to control the controller. The perfect world state would no doubt be able to prevent war. It might also degenerate into a world tyranny from which there would be no escape, a "brave new world" of technical skill and clever manipulation. It is a slightly nightmarish thought that social science may be even more damning to mankind than physical science. Physical science merely culminates in the pain and death of the body under the bomb; social science may culminate in the damnation of the soul in the manipulative society.

548

The final conclusion, therefore, is that though organizations are here to stay and though the only solution to many of the problems which they raise seems to be ever more and larger organizations, yet there is also no substitute for the Word of God—the sharp sword of truth in the prophetic individual, the penetrating moral insight that cuts through the shams and excuses of even the best-organized society. However clever we become and however far we move toward betterment through cleverness and skill, there is always a place for wonder, for humility, for reverence, for sensitivity to the still small voice of the Creator of all men and all morals.

NOTES ON THE AUTHORS

   1. *Abegglen, James C.*, was formerly Research Associate with the Committee on Human Development at the University of Chicago and Visiting Professor at the Center for International Relations at Massachusetts Institute of Technology. At present, he is in the Far East with International Telephone and Telegraph. A social psychologist, he is co-author (with W. Lloyd Warner) of *Big Business Leaders in America* and *Occupational Mobility in American Business and Industry."*

   2. *Bakke, E. Wight*, is Sterling Professor at Yale University and Director of its Labor and Management Center. He has long been a consultant on industrial relations and one of the foremost writers in the field of management and organization. Perhaps his best-known works are his *Mutual Survival; the Goal of Unions and Management, Bonds of Organization*, and *The Fusion Process.*

   3. *Barnard, Chester I*, former President of New Jersey Bell Telephone, is one of the foremost writers in the field of management and executive behavior. His work, *The Functions of the Executive*, has achieved the status of a classic in the field and has become a major source of influence on contemporary writers and scholars. His other works, and especially his *Organization and Management*, have greatly contributed to our knowledge of business operations.

4. *Boulding, Kenneth E.,* is Professor of Economics at the University of Michigan. Perhaps his best-known works are *The Organizational Revolution* and *Economic Analysis.* He has, in addition, written widely in the fields of economic theory, economics and ethics, and general systems theory.

5. *Burgess, Eugene W.,* is coauthor (with Frederick H. Harbison) of the article "Modern Management in Western Europe." Formerly a counselor to management, Mr. Burgess is at present Assistant Dean of the Graduate School of Business Administration and Lecturer in Business Administration, Graduate School of Business Administration at the University of California at Berkeley.

6. *Cyert, Richard M.,* is Associate Professor in the Department of Industrial Management at the Graduate School of Industrial Administration at Carnegie Institute of Technology. An economist working in the field of decision processes and the theory of the firm, Mr. Cyert has contributed "Observation of a Business Decision" written in collaboration with Herbert Simon and Donald B. Trow.

7. *Dale, Ernest,* is an Associate Professor of Business Administration and Economics of the Graduate School of Business Administration at Cornell University. Specializing in the theory of administration and managerial economics, Mr. Dale is perhaps best known for his work, *Planning and Developing the Company Organization Structure.* His article "Centralization Versus Decentralization" is a clear and lucid account of the characteristics of these two patterns of organization.

8. *Dent, James K.,* is Study Director of the Human Relations Research Program at the Survey Research Center of the University of Michigan. He was formerly engaged in economic research for General Motors Corporation. In coauthorship with Floyd Mann, Mr. Dent has written the article "The Supervisor: Member of Two Organizational Families."

9. *Drucker, Peter F.,* is Professor of Management at the Graduate School of Business Administration at New York University. Mr. Drucker, one of America's leading consultants on business management, has written *The Concept of the Corporation* and *The Practice of Management,* both of which have become landmarks among management publications.

10. *Gardner, Burleigh B.,* is Executive Director of Social Research Incorporated, one of the leading firms engaged in motivational research. Formerly with the Committee on Human Relations in Industry at the University of Chicago, Mr. Gardner is coauthor with Professor

David G. Moore of the well-known *Human Relations in Industry,* and with Dr. Lee Rainwater of "The Mass Image of Big Business."

11. *Gilman, Glenn W.,* is Professor of Industrial Management at Georgia Institute of Technology. His *Human Relations in the Industrial Southeast* is a noteworthy contribution to our knowledge of the interrelationship of industry and the community. He has done extensive consulting work with industrial organizations, and is at present serving as employee relations advisor to the Georgia Division of the Lockheed Aircraft Corporation.

12. *Glover, John D.,* is Professor at the Graduate School of Business Administration at Harvard University. Mr. Glover, one of the most distinguished writers in the field of business management, has made a significant contribution to our knowledge of the business enterprise with his *The Attack on Big Business.*

13. *Harbison, Frederick H.,* is Professor of Economics and Director of the Industrial Relations Section of Princeton University. Long known for his work in the field of industrial relations, Mr. Harbison is coauthor (with John R. Coleman) of the book, *Goals and Strategy in Collective Bargaining,* and (with Robert Dubin) of *Patterns of Union Management Relations.* His article, "Modern Management in Western Europe," is one of the foremost studies of comparative management.

14. *Harris, Seymour E.,* is Professor and Chairman of the Department of Economics at Harvard University. He has written extensively within the fields of money and finance, international and regional economics, and education. He is a coauthor of the book *The American Business Creed.*

15. *Henry, William E.,* is Associate Professor of Psychology at the University of Chicago. A clinical psychologist, Mr. Henry has contributed major insights into the personality of executives with his "The Business Executive: The Psychodynamics of a Social Role."

16. *Katona, George,* is Program Director, Survey Research Center of the University of Michigan and Professor of Psychology and Economics. His brilliant *Psychological Analysis of Economic Behavior* stems from extensive explorations of price-setting decisions. It represents one of the most creative and significant works in our understanding of economic behavior.

17. *Kaysen, Carl,* is Associate Professor of Economics at Harvard University and a consultant with Rand Corporation. His primary areas of interest are price theory, industrial organization, and antitrust legislation. He is coauthor of *The American Business Creed.*

18. *Kerr, Clark,* Professor of Industrial Relations and formerly Director of the Institute of Industrial Relations of the University of California. Mr. Kerr is now President of the University of California. His works include *Unions and Union Leaders of Their Own Choosing, Labor, Management and the Public* (with E. Wight Bakke), and the article, "Industrial Conflict and Its Mediation."

19. *Kline, Bennett E.,* was formerly Director of Management Development and Training, Indiana Harbor Works, Inland Steel Company. Prior to this, he was Associate Professor of Industrial Management at Purdue University. At present he is vice president of Wabash College where he is pursuing further research into the problem of freedom in industrial organizations, a subject which is discussed in his article (with Norman H. Martin) "Freedom, Authority and Decentralization."

20. *Kornhauser, Arthur,* is Professor of Psychology at Wayne State University. Focusing upon the psychology of industrial relations and worker attitudes and motivations, Mr. Kornhauser is coeditor of the book *Industrial Conflict.* Other significant works include *When Labor Votes; a Study of Auto Workers* and *Problems of Power in American Democracy.*

21. *Lamb, Robert K.,* of the Massachusetts Institute of Technology, Department of English and History, was one of the pioneers in the field of entrepreneurial history. His "The Entrepreneur and the Community" is a brilliant and penetrating analysis of the relationship between the entrepreneur and his sociocultural environment.

22. *Lilienthal, David E.,* is undoubtedly best known for his work as Chairman of the Tennessee Valley Authority. He is, at present, Chairman and Chief Executive Officer of the Development and Resources Corporation. His *Big Business: A New Era* is a brilliant account of the development of the large-scale enterprise in America.

23. *Low, J. O.,* Senior Partner of a Wall Street firm and research associate at the University of Chicago. Mr. Low was coauthor with W. Lloyd Warner of the book, *The Social System of the Modern Factory,* a work characterizing the interrelationships of factory and community.

24. *McNair, Malcolm P.,* is Lincoln Filene Professor of Retailing at the Harvard Business School. A director of Indian Head Mills, Inc., Allied Stores, and other firms, Mr. McNair is primarily known for his work in the field of marketing. Among his works is his crisply incisive "What Price Human Relations?"

25. *Mann, Floyd C.,* Assistant Program Director of the Human Re-

lations Research Program at the Survey Research Center, University of Michigan, has had extensive experience as an economist and statistician. He is coauthor (with James K. Dent) of "The Supervisor: Member of Two Organizational Families."

26. *Marquand, John P.*, one of America's most distinguished authors, has contributed remarkable insights into American life and manners and into the character of the community social structure. His best known works include *H. M. Pulham, Esq., Point of No Return,* and *The Late George Apley.*

27. *Martin, Norman H.*, is a Professor of Business Administration at Michigan State University. Formerly he was Associate Professor of Industrial Relations, School of Business and Research Director of the Industrial Relations Center of the University of Chicago. Writing from a background of consulting experience, Mr. Martin's articles include "Patterns of Mobility Within Industrial Organizations" and "Differential Decisions in the Management of an Industrial Plant.

28. *Mayo, Elton,* was Professor of Industrial Research, Graduate School of Business Administration, Harvard University. His work represents one of the pioneering efforts in the application of the social sciences to our understanding of industrial operations. His most significant books include *The Social Problems of an Industrial Civilization* and *The Human Problems of an Industrial Civilization.*

29. *Merton, Robert K.*, is Professor of Sociology at Columbia University. In addition to his well-known work, *Social Theory and Social Structure,* he is author of the article, "Bureaucratic Structure and Personality."

30. *Miller, William,* one of the early members of the Harvard University Research Center in Entrepreneurial History, is one of the foremost representatives of this complex and difficult field of understanding. He is editor of the classic work *Men in Business.*

31. *Moore, David G.*, is Professor and Head of the Department of Management in the School of Business and Public Service at Michigan State University. Writing in the field of industrial and human relations, Mr. Moore has had extensive industrial and consulting experience. He is coauthor (with Burleigh B. Gardner) of *Human Relations in Industry* and author of the unpublished work *Managerial Strategies and Organization Dynamics in Sears Retailing.*

32. *Newcomer, Mabel,* is Professor of Economics and Sociology at Vassar College. Her excellent study, *The Big Business Executive,* has contributed greatly to our knowledge of businessmen and their origins.

33. *Purcell, (Rev.) T. V.*, is Associate Professor of Psychology and Industrial Relations at Loyola University. Combining psychological insights and experience in union affairs, Father Purcell has written the work, which is rapidly assuming the proportions of a classic, entitled *The Worker Speaks His Mind on Company and Union*.

34. *Radcliffe-Brown, A. R.*, was one of the world's foremost social anthropologists. Professor of Anthropology at Oxford University, he has had a profound and extensive influence on the direction of research in the social sciences. Among his best-known works are *The Andaman Islanders* and *Structure and Function in Primitive Society*.

35. *Rainwater, Lee*, is Director of Special Studies at Social Research, Inc. He has participated in studies of political attitudes of industrial workers and the relationship of social class and personality characterization at the University of Chicago. He is coauthor (with Burleigh B. Gardner) of "The Mass Image of Big Business."

36. *Randle, C. Wilson*, is author of "How to Identify Promotable Executives." He is a partner and Director of Management Research in Booz, Allen and Hamilton, one of the largest of the management consulting firms. Prior to this, he was Dean of the School of Business at Western Reserve University.

37. *Simon, Herbert A.*, is Professor of Administration and Associate Dean, Graduate School of Industrial Administration at Carnegie Institute of Technology. One of the foremost scholars in the field of administration and organization, Mr. Simon's work, *Administrative Behavior: A Study of Decision-Making Processes in Administration*, has become the standard work in the field. His "Observation of a Business Decision" (with Richard M. Cyert and Donald B. Trow) is an initial report on extensive research into the decision-making process.

38. *Sims, John Howard*, is Research Assistant with the Committee on Human Development at the University of Chicago. Coauthor (with Norman H. Martin) of the article "Power Tactics," he is currently working on *The Study of Federal Executives* (with W. Lloyd Warner, Paul van Riper and Norman H. Martin).

39. *Strauss, Anselm L.*, is a social psychologist working in the field of the sociology of occupations and urban life. He was formerly Assistant Professor of Sociology at the University of Chicago and is presently engaged in research in hospital administration. He is coauthor (with Norman H. Martin) of "Patterns of Mobility Within Industrial Organizations."

40. *Sutton, Francis X.*, is Program Associate of the Ford Founda-

tion. A sociologist, he has done extensive work in the field of ideology, social structure, and economic sociology. Formerly an Assistant Professor of sociology and general education at Harvard University, he is coauthor of *The American Business Creed.*

41. *Tobin, James,* is Professor of Economics and Director of the Cowles Foundation for Research in Economics at Yale University. Specializing in econometrics, economic theory, and consumer behavior, he is coauthor of *The American Business Creed.*

42. *Trow, Donald B.,* is Assistant Professor of Sociology at Yale University. While at Carnegie Institute of Technology he participated in their research on the decision-making process in business. A social psychologist, he is coauthor (with Richard M. Cyert and Herbert Simon) of the article "Observation of a Business Decision."

43. *Warner, W. Lloyd,* is University Professor of Social Research at Michigan State University. Formerly he was Professor of Anthropology and Sociology at the University of Chicago. He has devoted many years to the study of businessmen and their organizations. Some of his books on this subject are *Big Business Leaders in America* (with James Abegglen) and *The Social System of the Modern Factory* (with J. O. Low).

44. *Whyte, William Foote,* is Professor, New York State School of Industrial and Labor Relations at Cornell University. A consultant and sociologist, he has done extensive work in the field of human and industrial relations. Among his many works are *Pattern for Industrial Peace, Money and Motivation* and "Human Relations Theory: A Progress Report."

45. *Whyte, William H., Jr.,* is the author of the widely known work, *The Organization Man.* An editor of Fortune magazine and an able commentator upon American business and social life, Mr. Whyte is also author of the insightful book *Is Anybody Listening?*

46. *Worthy, James C.,* is a vice-president of Sears, Roebuck and Company. Formerly an Assistant Secretary of Commerce, Mr. Worthy has had a continuing and strong interest in employee relations and management theory. He is author of the articles, "Factors Influencing Employee Morale" and "Organizational Structure and Employee Morale."

SELECTED BIBLIOGRAPHY

1. Action Society Trust, *Management Succession* (London: The Action Society Trust, 1956).
2. Adams, Leonard P., and Aronson, Robert L., *Workers and Industrial Change: A Case Study of Labor Mobility* (Cornell University, Cornell Studies in Industrial and Labor Relations, Vol. 8, 1957).
3. Adams, Stuart, "Trends in Occupational Origins of Business Leaders," *American Sociological Review*, Vol. 19, No. 5, October 1954, pp. 541–548.
4. Anshen, Ruth Nanda (ed.), *Freedom, Its Meaning* (London: George Allen and Unwin, 1942).
5. Appley, Lawrence A., *Management in Action* (New York: American Management Association, 1956).
6. Arensberg, Conrad M., "Industry and the Community," *American Journal of Sociology,* Vol. 48, 1942, pp. 1–12.
7. Arensberg, Conrad M., *et al.* (eds.), *Research in Industrial Human Relations: A Critical Appraisal* (New York: Harper & Brothers, 1957).
8. Argyris, Chris, *Executive Leadership, an Appraisal of a Manager in Action* (New York: Harper & Brothers, 1953).

9. Argyris, Chris, "Organizational Leadership and Participative Management," *Journal of Business,* Vol. 28, No. 1, January 1955, pp. 1–7.

10. Argyris, Chris, "The Individual and Organization: Some Problems of Mutual Adjustment," *Administrative Science Quarterly,* Vol. 2, No. 1, June 1957, pp. 1–24.

11. Argyris, Chris, *Personality and Organization* (New York: Harper & Brothers, 1957).

12. Bakke, E. Wight, *Bonds of Organization* (New York: Harper & Brothers, 1950).

13. Bakke, E. Wight, *Mutual Survival; The Goal of Unions and Management* (New Haven: Yale University Labor and Management Center, 1946), pp. 79–82.

14. Barbash, Jack, *The Practice of Unionism: an Inside Picture of Labor Unions Today* (New York: Harper & Brothers, 1956).

15. Barkin, Solomon, "A Pattern for the Study of Human Relations in Industry," *Industrial and Labor Relations Review,* Vol. 9, No. 1, October 1955, pp. 95–99.

16. Barnard, Chester, "Functions and Pathology of Status Systems in Formal Organizations," in William F. Whyte (ed.), *Industry and Society* (New York: McGraw-Hill Book Company, Inc., 1946), pp. 46–83.

17. Barnard, Chester, *The Functions of the Executive* (Cambridge: Harvard University Press, 1947).

18. Barnard, Chester, *Organization and Management* (Cambridge: Harvard University Press, 1948).

19. Becker, Howard S., and Strauss, Anselm L., "Careers, Personality, and Adult Socialization," *The American Journal of Sociology,* Vol. 62, No. 3, November 1956, pp. 253–263.

20. Bendix, Reinhard, *Work and Authority in Industry: Ideologies of Management in the Course of Industrialization* (New York: John Wiley and Sons, 1956).

21. Benewitz, Maurice C., "Social Cost and Collective Bargaining," *American Journal of Economics and Sociology,* Vol. 15, No. 2, January 1956, pp. 189–193.

22. Berger, Morroe, *et al.* (eds.), *Freedom and Control in Modern Society* (New York: D. Van Nostrand and Company, 1954).

23. Bernard, Jessie, "The Theory of Games of Strategy as a Modern Sociology of Conflict," *The American Journal of Sociology,* Vol. 59, No. 5, March 1954, pp. 411–425.

24. Blau, Peter M., *The Dynamics of Bureaucracy: A Study of Inter-personal Relations in Two Government Agencies* (Chicago: The University of Chicago Press, 1955).

25. Blau, Peter M., *et al.,* "Occupational Choice: A Conceptual Framework," *Industrial and Labor Relations Review,* Vol. 9, No. 4, July 1956, pp. 531–543.

26. Bloomberg, Warner, Jr., "The State of the American Proletariat, 1955," *Commentary,* Vol. 19, No. 3, pp. 207–216.

27. Boulding, Kenneth E., *The Organizational Revolution* (New York: Harper & Brothers, 1953), pp. 208–221.

28. Bowen, Howard R., *Social Responsibilities of the Businessman* (New York: Harper & Brothers, 1953).

29. Bowen, Howard R., "Business Management: A Profession?" *The Annals,* Vol. 297, January 1955, pp. 112–117.

30. Broehl, Wayne G., "Ethics and the Executive: The Small Decisions that Count," *Dun's Review and Modern Industry,* Vol. 69, No. 7, May 1957, pp. 45 ff.

31. Brown, Courtney C., and Smith, E. Everett (eds.), *The Director Looks at His Job* (New York: Columbia University Press, 1957).

32. Burns, Tom, "Management in Action," *Operational Research Quarterly,* Vol. 8, No. 2, June 1957, pp. 45–60.

33. Bursk, Edward C. (ed.), *The Management Team* (Cambridge: Harvard University Press, 1954).

34. Bursk, Edward C. (ed.), *Human Relations for Management* (New York: Harper & Brothers, 1956).

35. Bursk, Edward C., and Fenn, Dan H., Jr. (eds.), *Planning the Future Strategy of Your Business* (New York: McGraw-Hill Book Company, Inc., 1956).

36. Caplow, Theodore, "Organizational Size," *Administrative Science Quarterly,* Vol. 1, No. 4, March 1957, pp. 484–505.

37. Carlson, Sune, *Executive Behavior: A Study of the Work Load and the Working Methods of Managing Directors* (Stockholm: C. A. Stromberg, 1951).

38. Carnegie Institute of Technology, Pittsburgh Graduate School of Industrial Administration, *Fundamental Research in Administration: Horizons and Problems* (Pittsburgh: Carnegie Press, 1953).

39. Chamberlain, Edward H., *et al., Labor Unions and Public Policy* (Washington: American Enterprise Association, 1958).

40. Chamberlain, Neil W., *The Union Challenge to Management Control* (New York: Harper & Brothers, 1948).

41. Chamberlain, Neil W., *Social Responsibility and Strikes* (New York: Harper & Brothers, 1953).
42. Chamberlain, Neil W., *A General Theory of Economic Process* (New York: Harper & Brothers, 1955).
43. Chamberlain, Neil W., "The Structure of Bargaining Units in the United States," *Industrial and Labor Relations Review,* Vol. 10, No. 1, October 1956, pp. 3–25.
44. Childs, Marquis W., and Cater, Douglass, *Ethics in a Business Society* (New York: Harper & Brothers, 1954).
45. Chinoy, Ely, *Automobile Workers and the American Dream* (Garden City: Doubleday and Company, Inc., 1955).
46. Christensen, C. Roland, *Management Succession in Small and Growing Enterprises* (Boston: Graduate School of Business Administration, Harvard University, 1953).
47. Coates, Charles H., and Pellegrin, Roland J., "Executives and Supervisors: Informal Factors in Differential Bureaucratic Promotion," *Administrative Science Quarterly,* Vol. 2, No. 2, September 1957, pp. 200–215.
48. Cochran, Thomas C., "Business and the Democratic Tradition," *Harvard Business Review,* Vol. 34, No. 2, March–April 1956, pp. 39–48.
49. Collier, Abram T., "Dilemma in Human Relations," *Harvard Business Review,* Vol. 33, No. 5, September–October 1955, pp. 59–67.
50. Commons, John R., *Economics of Collective Action* (New York: The Macmillan Company, 1950).
51. Constas, Helen, "Max Weber's Two Conceptions of Bureaucracy," *The American Journal of Sociology,* Vol. 43, No. 4, January 1958, pp. 400–407.
52. Copeland, Frederick W., "The Illusion of Owning a Business," *The Atlantic,* Vol. 198, No. 3, September 1956, pp. 66–68.
53. Copeland, Melvin T., *The Executive at Work* (Cambridge: Harvard University Press, 1951).
54. Cordiner, Ralph J., *New Frontiers For Professional Managers* (New York: McGraw-Hill Book Co., Inc., 1956).
55. Coser, Lewis A., "The Functions of Small-Group Research," *Social Problems,* Vol. 3, No. 1, July 1955, pp. 1–6.
56. Cussler, Margaret, *The Woman Executive* (New York: Harcourt, Brace and Company, 1958).
57. Cyert, Richard M., and March, James G., "Organizational Fac-

tors in the Theory of Oligopoly," *Quarterly Journal of Economics,* Vol. 70, No. 1, February 1956, pp. 44–64.

58. Cyert, Richard M., Simon, Herbert A., and Trow, Donald B., "Observation of a Business Decision," *Journal of Business,* Vol. 29, No. 4, October 1956, pp. 237–248 (Copyright 1956, University of Chicago).

59. Dahl, Robert A., and Lindblom, Charles E., *Politics, Economics and Welfare* (New York: Harper & Brothers, 1953).

60. Dale, Ernest, "New Perspectives on Managerial Decision-Making," *Journal of Business,* Vol. 26, No. 1, January 1953, pp. 1–8.

61. Dale, Ernest, "Centralization Versus Decentralization," *Advanced Management,* Vol. 20, No. 6, June 1955, pp. 11–16.

62. Dankert, Clyde E., *Sharing the Gains of Technological Change* (Hanover: Amos Tuck School of Business Administration, Dartmouth College, 1955).

63. Davies, Daniel R., and Livingston, Robert T., *You and Management* (New York: Harper & Brothers, 1958).

64. Davis, Keith, *Human Relations in Business* (New York: McGraw-Hill Book Co., Inc., 1957).

65. Diamond, Sigmund, *The Reputation of the American Businessman* (Cambridge: Harvard University Press, 1955).

66. Dill, William R., "Environment as an Influence on Managerial Autonomy," *Administrative Science Quarterly,* Vol. 2, No. 4, March 1958, pp. 409–442.

67. Dimock, Marshall E., *A Philosophy of Administration Toward Creative Growth* (New York: Harper & Brothers, 1958).

68. Drucker, Peter F., *The Practice of Management* (New York: Harper & Brothers, 1954), pp. 6–17, 381–392.

69. Drucker, Peter F., "America's Next Twenty Years, I: The Coming Labor Shortage," *Harper's Magazine,* Vol. 210, No. 1258, March 1955, pp. 27–32.

70. Drucker, Peter F., "Integration of People and Planning," *Harvard Business Review,* Vol. 33, No. 6, November–December 1955, pp. 35–40.

71. Drucker, Peter F., *America's Next Twenty Years* (New York: Harper & Brothers, 1957).

72. Drucker, Peter F., "Business Objectives and Survival Needs: Notes on a Discipline of Business Enterprise," *Journal of Business,* Vol. 31, No. 2, April 1958, pp. 81–90.

73. Dubin, Robert (ed.), *Human Relations in Administration* (New York: Prentice-Hall, Inc., 1951).

74. Dubin, Robert, "Industrial Workers' Worlds: A Study of the 'Central Life Interests' of Industrial Workers," *Social Problems,* Vol. 3, No. 3, January 1956, pp. 131–142.

75. Dubin, Robert, "Power and Union-Management Relations," *Administrative Science Quarterly,* Vol. 2, No. 1, June 1957, pp. 60–81.

76. Dubin, Robert, *The World of Work; Industrial Society and Human Relations* (New York: Prentice-Hall, Inc., 1958).

77. Eby, Kermit, "Organized Labor and American Ethics," *The Annals,* Vol. 297, January 1955, pp. 83–89.

78. Eby, Kermit, "The Moral Dilemma of Democratic Man: The Social Ethic and the Working Man," *American Journal of Economics and Sociology,* Vol. 15, No. 2, January 1956, pp. 149–160.

79. Ellsworth, John S., *Factory Folkways? A Study of Institutional Structure and Change* (New Haven: Yale University Press, 1952).

80. Emmet, Boris, and Jeuck, John E., *Catalogues and Counters: A History of Sears, Roebuck and Company* (Chicago: The University of Chicago Press, 1950).

81. Fiedler, Fred E., *Leader Attitudes and Group Effectiveness* (Urbana: University of Illinois Press, 1958).

82. Fitch, John A., *Social Responsibilities of Organized Labor* (New York: Harper & Brothers, 1957).

83. Fortune, Editors of, *The Art of Success* (New York: J. B. Lippincott Company, 1956).

84. Fortune, Editors of, *The Executive Life* (Garden City: Doubleday and Company, 1956).

85. Friedmann, Georges, "Outline for a Psycho-sociology of Assembly Line Work," *Human Organization,* Vol. 12, No. 4, Winter 1954, pp. 15–20.

86. Friedmann, Georges, "What is Happening to Man's Work?" *Human Organization,* Vol. 13, No. 4, Winter 1955, pp. 29–33.

87. Friedmann, Georges, *Industrial Society: The Emergence of the Human Problems of Automation* (ed. Harold L. Sheppard) (Glencoe: The Free Press, 1955).

88. Fromm, Erich, *Escape From Freedom* (New York: Farrar and Rinehart, Inc., 1941).

89. Fromm, Erich, *Man For Himself: an Inquiry Into the Psychology of Ethics* (New York: Rinehart, 1947).

90. Galbraith, John Kenneth, *American Capitalism: The Concept of Countervailing Power* (Boston: Houghton Mifflin Company, 1952).
91. Galbraith, John Kenneth, *Economics and the Art of Controversy* (New Brunswick: Rutgers University Press, 1955).
92. Gardner, Burleigh B., and Moore, David G., *Human Relations in Industry* (Homewood: Richard D. Irwin, Inc., 1955).
93. Gardner, Burleigh B. and Rainwater, Lee, "The Mass Image of Big Business," *Harvard Business Review,* Vol. 33, No. 6, November–December 1955, pp. 61–66.
94. Gaudet, Frederick J., and Carli, Ralph, "Why Executives Fail," *Personnel Psychology,* Vol. 10, No. 1, Spring 1957, pp. 7–21.
95. Gilman, Glenn, *Human Relations in the Industrial Southeast* (Chapel Hill: University of North Carolina Press, 1956), pp. 295–310.
96. Ginzberg, Eli, *What Makes an Executive* (New York: Columbia University Press, 1955).
97. Glover, J. D., *The Attack on Big Business* (Boston: Division of Research, Graduate School of Business Administration, Harvard University, 1954), pp. 3–14, 201–206, 208–209.
98. Goble, George W., "An Alternative to the Strike," *Labor Law Journal,* Vol. 6, No. 2, February 1955, pp. 83–86 ff.
99. Goldberg, Arthur, "The Rights and Responsibilities of Union Members," *Labor Law Journal,* Vol. 9, No. 4, April 1958, pp. 290–303.
100. Gomberg, William, "The Use of Psychology in Industry: A Trade Union Point of View," *Management Science,* Vol. 3, No. 4, July 1957, pp. 348–370.
101. Gordon, Robert A., *Business Leadership in the Large Corporation* (Washington: Brookings Institution, 1945).
102. Gordon, Thomas, *Group-Centered Leadership* (Boston: Houghton Mifflin Company, 1955).
103. Grabbe, Eugene M., *Automation in Business and Industry* (New York: John Wiley and Sons, Inc., 1957).
104. Guetzkow, Harold (ed.), *Groups, Leadership and Men: Research in Human Relations* (Pittsburgh: Carnegie Press, 1951).
105. Guetzkow, Harold, and Simon, Herbert, "The Impact of Certain Communication Nets in Task Oriented Groups," *Management Science,* Vol. 1, Nos. 3 and 4, April–July 1955, pp. 233–250.
106. Guetzkow, Harold, and Bowes, Anne, "The Development of Or-

ganizations in a Laboratory," *Management Science,* Vol. 3, No. 4, July 1957, pp. 380–402.

107. Gulick, Luther, *et al.* (eds.), *Papers on the Science of Administration* (New York: Institute of Public Administration, Columbia University, 1937).

108. Haire, Mason, "Size, Shape and Function in Industrial Organizations," *Human Organization,* Vol. 14, No. 1, Spring 1955, pp. 17–22.

109. Handlin, Oscar, "A Note on Social Mobility and the Recruitment of Entrepreneurs in the United States," *Explorations in Entrepreneurial History,* Vol. 8, Winter Supplement, 1956, pp. 1–5.

110. Hare, A. Paul, Borgatta, Edgar F., and Bales, Robert F. (eds.), *Small Groups: Studies in Social Interaction* (New York: Alfred A. Knopf, 1955).

111. Harbison, Frederick H., and Burgess, Eugene W., "Modern Management in Western Europe," *The American Journal of Sociology,* Vol. 60, No. 1, July 1954, pp. 15–23.

112. Henry, William E., "The Business Executive: The Psychodynamics of a Social Role," *The American Journal of Sociology,* Vol. 54, No. 4, January 1949, pp. 286–291.

113. Hertz, David B., and Livingston, Robert T., "Contemporary Organizational Theory; A Review of Current Concepts and Methods," *Human Relations,* Vol. 3, No. 4, November 1950, pp. 373–394.

114. Hoslett, Schuyler D. (ed.), *Human Factors in Management* (Parkville, Mo.: Park College Press, 1946).

115. Jaques, Elliott, *Measurement of Responsibility: A Study of Work, Payment and Individual Capacity* (London: Tavistock Publications, 1956).

116. Johnson, Harold L., "Can the Businessman Apply Christianity?" *Harvard Business Review,* Vol. 35, No. 5, September–October 1957, pp. 68–76.

117. Jones, Manley Howe, *Executive Decision Making* (Homewood: Richard D. Irwin, Inc., 1957).

118. Kahn, Robert L. (ed.), "Research on Human Relations in Industry," *Adult Leadership,* Vol. 3, No. 8, February 1955, pp. 13–27.

119. Katona, George, *Psychological Analysis of Economic Behavior* (New York: McGraw-Hill Book Company, Inc., 1951), pp. 193–210.

120. Katz, Robert L., "Skills of an Effective Administrator," *Harvard Business Review*, Vol. 33, No. 1, January–February 1955, pp. 33–42.

121. Katzell, Raymond A., "Looking Around: Is Individualism Disappearing?" *Harvard Business Review*, Vol. 36, No. 1, January–February 1958, pp. 139 ff.

122. Kavesh, Robert A., *Businessmen in Fiction: The Capitalist and Executive in American Novels* (Dartmouth College: Amos Tuck School of Business Administration, 1955).

123. Kerr, Clark, "Industrial Conflict and Its Mediation," *The American Journal of Sociology*, Vol. 60, No. 3, November 1954, pp. 230–245.

124. Kerr, Clark, *Unions and Union Leaders of Their Own Choosing* (New York: Fund For the Republic, 1957).

125. Kirk, Russell, "The Inhumane Businessman," *Fortune*, Vol. 55, No. 5, May 1957, pp. 160–161 ff.

126. Kircher, Paul, "Management Planning and Control—What Next?" *Management Science*, Vol. 3, No. 1, October 1956, pp. 1–8.

127. Klaw, Spencer, "The Entrepreneurial Ego," *Fortune*, Vol. 54, No. 2, August 1956, pp. 100–103 ff.

128. Kline, Bennett E., and Martin, Norman H., "Freedom, Authority and Decentralization," *Harvard Business Review*, Vol. 36, No. 3, May–June 1958, pp. 69–75.

129. Kolko, Gabriel, "Economic Mobility and Social Stratification," *The American Journal of Sociology*, Vol. 63, No. 1, July 1957, pp. 30–39.

130. Kornhauser, Arthur, "The Undetermined Future of Industrial Conflict," in Arthur Kornhauser, Robert Dubin, and Arthur M. Ross (eds.), *Industrial Conflict* (New York: McGraw-Hill Book Company, Inc., 1954), pp. 519–526.

131. Kruisinga, H. J. (ed.), *The Balance Between Centralization and Decentralization in Managerial Control* (Leiden: H. E. Stenfert Kroese, 1954).

132. Lahne, Herbert J., and Kovner, Joseph, "Local Union Structure: Formality and Reality," *Industrial and Labor Relations Review*, Vol. 9, No. 1, October 1955, pp. 24–31.

133. Lamb, Robert K., "The Entrepreneur and the Community," in William Miller (ed.), *Men in Business* (Cambridge: Harvard University Press, 1952), pp. 91–117.

134. Lauterbach, Albert, *Men, Motives and Money: Psychological Frontiers of Economics* (Ithaca: Cornell University Press, 1954).

135. Leavitt, Harold J., "Small Groups in Large Organizations," *Journal of Business,* Vol. 28, No. 1, January 1955, pp. 8–17.

136. Leavitt, Harold J., *Managerial Psychology* (Chicago: University of Chicago Press, 1958).

137. Levitt, Theodore, "The Lonely Crowd and the Economic Man," *Quarterly Journal of Economics,* Vol. 70, No. 1, February 1956, pp. 95–116.

138. Lieberman, Seymour, "The Effects of Changes in Roles on the Attitudes of Role Occupants," *Human Relations,* Vol. 9, No. 4, 1956, pp. 385–402.

139. Lilienthal, David E., *Big Business: A New Era* (New York: Harper & Brothers, 1953), pp. 31–43.

140. Lipset, Seymour M., Trow, Martin A., and Coleman, James S., *"Union Democracy: the Internal Politics of the International Typographical Union* (Glencoe: The Free Press, 1956).

141. McMurry, Robert N., "The Case for Benevolent Autocracy," *Harvard Business Review,* Vol. 36, No. 1, January–February 1958, pp. 82–90.

142. McNair, Malcolm P., "Thinking Ahead: What Price Human Relations?" *Harvard Business Review,* Vol. 35, No. 2, March–April 1957, pp. 15–16 ff.

143. Magistretti, Franca, "Sociological Factors in the Structuring of Industrial Workers' Teams," *The American Journal of Sociology,* Vol. 60, No. 6, May 1955, pp. 536–541.

144. Mandell, Milton M., "How to Gage Executive Potential," *Dun's Review and Modern Industry,* Vol. 69, No. 5, March 1957, pp. 43–45 ff.

145. Mann, Floyd C., and Dent, James K., "The Supervisor: Member of Two Organizational Families," *Harvard Business Review,* Vol. 32, No. 6, November–December 1954, pp. 103–112.

146. Marquand, John P., *Point of No Return* (Boston: Little, Brown and Company, 1949), pp. 542–559.

147. Marquart, Frank, "The Auto Worker," *Dissent,* Vol. 4, No. 3, Summer 1957, pp. 219–233.

148. Marschak, J., "Elements for a Theory of Teams," *Management Science,* Vol. 1, No. 2, January 1955, pp. 127–137.

149. Martin, Norman H., "Differential Decisions in the Management of an Industrial Plant," *Journal of Business,* Vol. 29, No. 4,

October 1956, pp. 249–260 (Copyright 1956, University of Chicago).

150. Martin, Norman H., "Practical Politics in Administration," *Personnel Administration*, Vol. 20, No. 4, July–August 1957, pp. 7–11.

151. Martin, Norman H., and Sims, John Howard, "Thinking Ahead: Power Tactics," *Harvard Business Review*, Vol. 34, No. 6, November–December, 1956, pp. 25–36 ff.

152. Martin, Norman H., and Strauss, Anselm L., "Patterns of Mobility Within Industrial Organizations," *Journal of Business*, Vol. 29, No. 2, April 1956, pp. 101–110 (Copyright 1956, University of Chicago).

153. Maurer, Herrymon, *Great Enterprise: Growth and Behavior of the Big Corporation* (New York: The MacMillan Company, 1955).

154. Mayo, Elton, *The Social Problems of an Industrial Civilization* (Boston: Division of Research, Graduate School of Business Administration, Harvard University, 1945), pp. 34–56.

155. Menninger, William C., and Levinson, Harry, "Psychiatry in Industry: Some Trends and Perspectives," *Personnel*, Vol. 32, No. 2, September 1955, pp. 90–99.

156. Merton, Robert K., "Bureaucratic Structure and Personality," *Social Forces*, xvii (1940), 560–568.

157. Merton, Robert K., *Social Theory and Social Structure* (Glencoe: The Free Press, 1957).

158. Metz, Harold W., and Thomson, Charles A. H., *Authoritarianism and the Individual* (Washington: The Brookings Institution, 1950).

159. Miernyk, William H., *Depressed Industrial Areas—a National Problem*, Planning Pamplet No. 98, National Planning Association, 1957.

160. Miller, Delbert C., and Form, William H., *Industrial Sociology* (New York: Harper & Brothers, 1951).

161. Miller, S. M., "The Concept of Mobility," *Social Problems*, Vol. 3, No. 2, October 1955, pp. 65–73.

162. Miller, William, "The Business Elite in Business Bureaucracies," in William Miller (ed.), *Men in Business* (Cambridge: Harvard University Press, 1952), pp. 286–305.

163. Mills, C. Wright, *The Power Elite* (New York: Oxford University Press, 1956).

164. Mills, C. Wright, *White Collar: The American Middle Classes* (New York: Oxford University Press, 1956), pp. 100–111.

165. Milward, G. E. (ed.), *Large-Scale Organization* (London: MacDonald and Evans, 1950).

166. Moore, David G., *Managerial Strategies and Organization Dynamics in Sears Retailing,* unpublished Ph.D. dissertation, Department of Sociology, University of Chicago, 1954, pp. 4–14.

167. Moore, David G., and Renck, Richard, "The Professional Employee in Industry," *Journal of Business,* Vol. 28, No. 1, January 1955, pp. 58–66.

168. Moore, Wilbert E., *Industrial Relations and the Social Order* (New York: The Macmillan Company, 1951).

169. Mueller, John H., "Perspective on the Organization Man," *Business Horizons,* Vol. 1, No. 2, Spring 1958, pp. 83–91.

170. Neumann, John von, and Morgenstern, Oskar, *Theory of Games and Economic Behavior* (Princeton: Princeton University Press, 1947).

171. Newcomer, Mabel, *The Big Business Executive: The Factors That Made Him,* 1900–1950 (New York: Columbia University Press, 1955).

172. Newman, William H., *Administrative Action: The Techniques of Organization and Management* (New York: Prentice-Hall, Inc., 1953).

173. Norton-Taylor, Duncan, "How Top Executives Live; The New Management," *Fortune,* Vol. 52, No. 1, July 1955, pp. 78–83.

174. Ohmann, O. A., "Search for a Managerial Philosophy," *Harvard Business Review,* Vol. 35, No. 5, September–October 1957, pp. 41–51.

175. Palmer, Gladys L., "Attitudes Toward Work in an Industrial Community," *The American Journal of Sociology,* Vol. 63, No. 1, July 1957, pp. 17–26.

176. Parsons, Talcott, "Sociological Approach to the Theory of Organization, I & II," *Administrative Science Quarterly,* Vol. 1, Nos. 1 and 2, June 1956, pp. 63–85, and September 1956, pp. 225–239.

177. Pederson-Krag, G., *Personality Factors in Work and Employment* (New York: Funk and Wagnalls, 1955).

178. Pellegrin, Roland J., and Coates, Charles H., "Absentee-Owned Corporations and Community Power Structure," *The American Journal of Sociology,* Vol. 61, No. 5, March 1956, pp. 413–419.

179. Pellegrin, Roland J., and Coates, Charles H., "Executives and Supervisors: Contrasting Definitions of Career Success," *Administrative Science Quarterly*, Vol. 1, No. 4, March 1957, pp. 506–517.

180. Perlman, Mark, *Labor Union Theories in America: Background and Development* (Evanston: Row, Peterson & Company, 1958).

181. Petro, Sylvester, *The Labor Policy of the Free Society* (New York: The Ronald Press, 1957).

182. Purcell, Theodore V., *The Worker Speaks His Mind on Company and Union* (Cambridge: Harvard University Press, 1953), pp. 266–280.

183. Radcliffe-Brown, A. R., *Structure and Function in Primitive Society* (London: Cohen & West, 1952), pp. 190–198.

184. Randle, C. Wilson, "How to Identify Promotable Executives," *Harvard Business Review*, Vol. 34, No. 3, May–June 1956, pp. 122–134.

185. Riegel, John W., *Employee Interest in Company Success* (Ann Arbor: University of Michigan, Bureau of Industrial Relations, 1956).

186. Riesman, David, Denney, Reuel and Glazer, Nathan, *The Lonely Crowd: A Study of the Changing American Character* (New Haven: Yale University Press, 1950).

187. Riesman, David, *Individualism Reconsidered* (Glencoe: The Free Press, 1954).

188. Riesman, David, and Benney, Mark, "Asking and Answering," *Journal of Business*, Vol. 29, No. 4, October 1956, pp. 225–236.

189. Roberts, B. C., "Employers and Industrial Relations in Britain and America," *The Political Quarterly*, Vol. 27, No. 3, July–September 1956, pp. 324–339.

190. Roethlisberger, Fritz, and Dickson, William J., *Management and the Worker* (Cambridge: Harvard University Press, 1941).

191. Roethlisberger, Fritz, *Management and Morale* (Cambridge: Harvard University Press, 1943).

192. Rogoff, Natalie, *Recent Trends in Occupational Mobility* (Glencoe: The Free Press, 1953).

193. Rosen, Hjalmar, and Rosen, R. A. Hudson, *The Union Member Speaks* (New York: Prentice-Hall, Inc., 1955).

194. Ross, Murray, and Hendry, Charles E., *New Understandings of Leadership* (New York: Association Press, 1957).

195. Roy, Donald, "Efficiency and 'The Fix': Informal Intergroup Re-

lations in a Piecework Machine Shop," *The American Journal of Sociology,* Vol. 60, No. 3, November 1954, pp. 255–267.

196. Salveson, M. E., "An Analysis of Decisions," *Management Science,* Vol. 4, No. 3, April 1958, pp. 203–217.

197. Sampson, Robert C., *The Staff Role in Management: Its Creative Uses* (New York: Harper & Brothers, 1955).

198. Schoen, Donald R., "Human Relations: Boon or Bogle?" *Harvard Business Review,* Vol. 35, No. 6, November–December 1957, pp. 41–47.

199. Seidman, Joel, *et al., The Worker Views His Union* (Chicago: The University of Chicago Press, 1958).

200. Seidman, Joel, "Some Requirements for Union Democracy," *American Economic Review,* Vol. 48, No. 2, May 1958, pp. 35–43.

201. Selekman, Benjamin M., "Is Management Creating a Class Society?" *Harvard Business Review,* Vol. 36, No. 1, January–February 1958, pp. 37–46.

202. Selekman, Benjamin, "Trade Unions—Romance and Reality," *Harvard Business Review,* Vol. 36, No. 3, May–June 1958, pp. 76–90.

203. Selekman, Sylvia, and Selekman, Benjamin, *Power and Morality in a Business Society* (New York: McGraw-Hill Book Co., Inc., 1956).

204. Selznick, Philip, *TVA and the Grass Roots* (Berkeley and Los Angeles: University of California Press, 1949).

205. Selznick, Philip, *Leadership in Administration: A Sociological Interpretation* (Evanston: Row, Peterson and Company, 1957).

206. Shartle, Carroll L., *Executive Performance and Leadership* (New York: Prentice-Hall, Inc., 1956).

207. Sheppard, Harold L., "Approaches to Conflict in American Industrial Sociology," *The British Journal of Sociology,* Vol. 5, No. 4, December 1954, pp. 324–341.

208. Shister, Joseph, *Economics and the Labor Market* (New York: J. B. Lippincott Co., 1956).

209. Shultz, George P., and Baldwin, George B., *Automation: A New Dimension to Old Problems* (Washington: Annals of American Economics, Public Affairs Press, 1955).

210. Simmel, Georg, *Conflict. The Web of Group Affiliations* (trans. Kurt H. Wolff and Reinhard Bendix) (Glencoe: The Free Press, 1955).

211. Simmel, Georg, "The Sociology of Conflict," *The American Journal of Sociology,* 1903–1904, pp. 490–525, 672–689, 798–811.

212. Simmel, Georg, *The Sociology of Georg Simmel,* Kurt H. Wolff (trans.) (Glencoe: The Free Press, 1950).

213. Simon, Herbert A., *Administrative Behavior: A Study of Decision-Making Processes in Administrative Organization* (New York: The Macmillan Company, 1957).

214. Sloan, Alfred P., *Adventures of a White Collar Man* (New York: Doubleday, Doran, 1941).

215. Solomon, Benjamin, "Dimensions of Union Growth: 1900–1950," *Industrial and Labor Relations Review,* Vol. 9, No. 4, July 1956, pp. 544–561.

216. Spencer, Lyle M., "Ten Problems That Worry Presidents," *Harvard Business Review,* Vol. 33, No. 6, November–December 1955, pp. 75–83.

217. Stagner, Ross, *The Psychology of Industrial Conflict* (New York: John Wiley and Sons, 1956).

218. Stanley, Marjorie Thines, "The Amalgamation of Collective Bargaining and Political Activity by the UAW," *Industrial and Labor Relations Review,* Vol. 10, No. 1, October 1956, pp. 40–47.

219. Stevenson, Adlai E., "My Faith in Democratic Capitalism," *Fortune,* Vol. 52, No. 4, October 1955, pp. 126–127 ff.

220. Strauss, George, "The Changing Role of the Working Supervisor," *Journal of Business,* Vol. 30, No. 3, July 1957, pp. 202–211.

221. Strauss, George, and Sayles, Leonard R., "The Scanlon Plan: Some Organizational Problems," *Human Organization,* Vol. 16, No. 3, Fall 1957, pp. 15–22.

222. Strong, Lydia, "Every Day is Doomsday: The Ordeal of Executive Decision," *Management Review,* Vol. 44, No. 11, November 1955, pp. 746–755.

223. Stryker, Perrin, "Who is an Executive? The New Management—XII," *Fortune,* Vol. 52, No. 6, December 1955, pp. 107–109 ff.

224. Stryker, Perrin, "On the Meaning of Executive Qualities," *Fortune,* Vol. 57, No. 6, June 1958, pp. 116–119 ff.

225. Sutton, Francis X., Harris, Seymour E., Kaysen, Carl, and Tobin, James, *The American Business Creed* (Cambridge: Harvard University Press, 1956), pp. 19–31.

226. Tannenbaum, Robert, and Massarik, Fred, "Leadership: A Frame

of Reference," *Management Science,* Vol. 4, No. 1, October 1957, pp. 1–19.

227. Thole, Henry C., "Looking Around: Review of Literature on Organizational Control," *Harvard Business Review,* Vol. 32, No. 6, November–December 1954, pp. 141–150.

228. Thole, Henry C., and Gibbons, Charles C. (eds.), *Business Action in a Changing World* (Chicago: Public Administration Service, 1956).

229. Thomas, Lawrence G., *The Occupational Structure and Education* (Englewood Cliffs: Prentice-Hall, Inc., 1956).

230. Thompson, James D., and McEwen, William J., "Organizational Goals and Environment," *American Sociological Review,* Vol. 23, No. 1, February 1958, pp. 23–31.

231. Thompson, James D., "Authority and Power in 'Identical' Organizations," *The American Journal of Sociology,* Vol. 62, No. 3, November 1956, pp. 290–301.

232. Tumin, Melvin M., and Feldman, Arnold S., "Theory and Measurement of Occupational Mobility," *American Sociological Review,* Vol. 22, No. 3, June 1957, pp. 281–288.

233. Turner, Arthur N., "Interaction and Sentiment in the Foreman-Worker Relationship," *Human Organization,* Vol. 14, No. 1, Spring 1955, pp. 10–16.

234. Turner, Arthur N., "Management and the Assembly Line," *Harvard Business Review,* Vol. 33, No. 5, September–October 1955, pp. 40–48.

235. Urwick, Lyndall F., *The Pattern of Management* (Minneapolis: The University of Minnesota Press, 1956).

236. Urwick, Lyndall F., "How the Organization Affects the Man," *Management Review,* Vol. 46, No. 7, July 1957, pp. 54–61.

237. Villers, Raymond, "Control and Freedom in a Decentralized Company," *Harvard Business Review,* Vol. 32, No. 2, March–April 1954, pp. 89–96.

238. Wald, Robert M., and Doty, Roy A., "The Top Executive—a Firsthand Profile," *Harvard Business Review,* Vol. 32, No. 4, July–August 1954, pp. 45–54.

239. Walker, Charles R., Guest, Robert H., and Turner, Arthur N., *The Foreman on the Assembly Line* (Cambridge: Harvard University Press, 1956).

240. Walker, Charles, "Life in the Automatic Factory," *Harvard*

Business Review, Vol. 36, No. 1, January–February 1958, pp. 111 119.

241. Ward, Alfred Dudley, *The American Economy—Attitudes and Opinions* (New York: Harper & Brothers, 1955).

242. Warner, W. Lloyd, and Low, J. O., *The Social System of the Modern Factory* (New Haven: Yale University Press, 1947), pp. 54–65.

243. Warner, W. Lloyd, and Abegglen, James, *Big Business Leaders in America* (New York: Harper & Brothers, 1955), pp. 63–75, 84–105.

244. Warner, W. Lloyd, and Abegglen, James C., *Occupational Mobility in American Business and Industry, 1928–1952* (Minneapolis: Minnesota University Press, 1955), pp. 4–9, 24–36.

245. Wendzel, Julius T., *The Dynamics of Capitalism: Correctives Toward Continuous Growth* (New York: Harper & Brothers, 1956).

246. Whisler, Thomas L., "The Assistant-to: The Man in Motley," *Journal of Business,* Vol. 29, No. 4, October 1956, pp. 274–279.

247. Whisler, Thomas L., "Performance Appraisal and the Organization Man," *Journal of Business,* Vol. 31, No. 1, January 1958, pp. 19–27.

248. Whyte, William F., *Pattern For Industrial Peace* (New York: Harper & Brothers, 1951).

249. Whyte, William F., *et al., Money and Motivation: An Analysis of Incentives in Industry* (New York: Harper & Brothers, 1955).

250. Whyte, William F., "Human Relations Theory: A Progress Report," *Harvard Business Review,* Vol. 34, No. 5, September–October 1956, pp. 125–132.

251. Whyte, William F., "Problems in Industrial Sociology," *Social Problems,* Vol. 4, No. 2, October 1956, pp. 148–160.

252. Whyte, William H., Jr., *Is Anybody Listening?* (New York: Simon and Schuster, Inc., 1952).

253. Whyte, William H., Jr., *The Organization Man* (New York: Simon and Schuster, Inc., 1956), pp. 4–14.

254. Witte, Edwin E., *The Evolution of Managerial Ideas in Industrial Relations,* Bulletin 27, New York State School of Industrial and Labor Relations, November 1954, Cornell University, Ithaca, New York.

255. Worthy, James C., "Factors Influencing Employee Morale," *Harvard Business Review,* Vol. 28, No. 1, January 1950, pp. 61–73.

Also in *Human Relations: Rare, Medium, or Well-Done? 12 Studies on Communication and Management Skills,* Compilation from the *Harvard Business Review* (Boston: 1955).

256. Worthy, James C., "Organizational Structure and Employee Morale," *American Sociological Review,* Vol. 15, No. 2, April 1950, pp. 169–179.

257. Wright, David McCord, "Adventure or Routine," *Harvard Business Review,* Vol. 33, No. 5, September–October 1955, pp. 33–39.

258. Zaleznik, A., *Worker Satisfaction and Development: A Case Study of Work and Social Behavior in a Factory Group* (Cambridge: Harvard University, Division of Research, Graduate School of Business Administration, 1956).

ACKNOWLEDGMENTS

We wish to thank the distinguished men who wrote the selections in this book for permitting us to use parts of their published works. We both know it a great honor to be associated with them. We also feel a debt of gratitude to their publishers.

We are indebted to the Louis W. and Maud Hill Family Foundation whose generous financial assistance has made this, as well as many other works, possible.

Valuable editorial assistance has been furnished by Mildred Warner, Caroline Warner, and Sarah Wilson. Alice Chandler and Katherine Martin gave immeasurable aid.

W. LLOYD WARNER
NORMAN H. MARTIN

INDEX OF AUTHORS AND TITLES